OSSIPEE
NEW HAMPSHIRE
VITAL RECORDS
1887-2001

Richard P. Roberts

HERITAGE BOOKS
2003

HERITAGE BOOKS
AN IMPRINT OF HERITAGE BOOKS, INC.

Books, CDs, and more – Worldwide

For our listing of thousands of titles see our website
at
www.HeritageBooks.com

Published 2003 by
HERITAGE BOOKS, INC.
Publishing Division
1540 Pointer Ridge Place #E
Bowie, Maryland 20716

COPYRIGHT © 2002 RICHARD P. ROBERTS

OTHER HERITAGE BOOKS BY THE AUTHOR:

New Hampshire Name Changes 1768-1923
Alton, New Hampshire Vital Records 1890-1997
Barnstead, New Hampshire Vital Records, 1887-2000
Barrington, New Hampshire Vital Records
Dover, New Hampshire Death Records, 1887-1937
Farmington, New Hampshire Vital Records, 1887-1938
Gilmanton, New Hampshire Vital Records, 1887-2001
Milton, New Hampshire Vital Records 1888-1999
Moultonborough, New Hampshire Vital Records
New Castle, New Hampshire Vital Records 1891-1997
Vital Records of New Durham and Middleton, New Hampshire 1887-1998
Vital Records of Wakefield, New Hampshire 1887-1998
Wolfeboro, New Hampshire Vital Records 1887-1999

All rights reserved. No part of this book may be reproduced or transmitted in any form or by any means, electronic or mechanical, including photocopying, recording or by any information storage and retrieval system without written permission from the author, except for the inclusion of brief quotations in a review.

International Standard Book Number: 0-7884-2242-1

TABLE OF CONTENTS

Introduction 1

Births 4

Marriages 156

Deaths 421

INTRODUCTION

Early vital records of many New Hampshire towns can be located either through the State's Vital Records Department or on microfilms made available through LDS Family History Centers. Some, however, have been lost or are inaccessible for various reasons. A valuable, but time-consuming, source of information for events occurring after 1886 is the vital statistics which are provided in a section of the Annual Town Reports of many New Hampshire towns. Many of these town reports have been collected at the New Hampshire State Library in Concord, as well as more local repositories.

The amount of information published in these Annual Town Reports varies tremendously over time. Early records are far more detailed and comprehensive. Recent records are rather cursory, but issues of confidentiality and sensitivity to the privacy of those residents still living offsets the lack of information of genealogical value.

While the information provided is often very helpful, one must remember that it is not fool-proof or universally accurate, nor is it the primary source or the actual vital record itself. The fact that much of the data is self-reported suggests that it is reliable. However, errors in transcription, spelling (particularly with respect to French-Canadian and European families), and printing often are obvious. In addition, there may be, for example, two children listed as the third child of a particular couple, or the mother's maiden name, age or place of birth differs or is inconsistent from one entry to another. It is also important to note that a birth, marriage or death may have been reported in another town although the subject resided in Ossipee, or the entry may not have been made in the first place.

Despite these shortcomings, the information contained in the Annual Town Reports can be a valuable tool for the genealogist. Marriage and death records from the late 1800's often identify parents who were married nearly a century before. In addition, as the county seat and location of both the county "home" and "farm" at various times, individuals who had formerly resided in other towns may be found here. Finally, those families that have remained in Ossipee or adjacent towns for several generations can be traced and connected to the present.

Births - To the extent the information is available, the entries in the list of births are given as follows: child's name; date of birth; place of birth; the number of children in the family; father's name, place of birth, age and occupation; and the mother's maiden name, age and place of birth. The residence of the parents is sometimes given when it is shown as other than Ossipee. As noted above, the amount of information in earlier records is substantially greater than in more recent years.

At times, the given names of many children are missing from the early reports. In this case, the sex of the child is given and they are listed chronologically at the beginning of the surname heading. On occasion, the child's name can be determined from marriage or death records, as well as secondary sources. These names are shown in brackets where available.

Marriages - To the extent the information is available, the entries in the list of marriages follow this format: groom's name; groom's residence; bride's name; brides residence; date of marriage; place of marriage; H, signifying husband's information, and W, signifying wife's information, each in the following order - age, occupation, number of the marriage (if other than first), father's name, father's place of birth, father's occupation, mother's name, mother's place of birth, and mother's occupation. The name of the official conducting the marriage has been omitted but is generally provided in the original document. A separate listing of brides in alphabetical order follows this section in order to allow for cross-referencing.

Deaths - To the extent available, the entries in the list of deaths contain the following information: name of decedent; place of death; date of death; age at death; cause of death; marital status; birthplace; father's name; father's place of birth; mother's name; and mother's place of birth. Most of the entries listing a cause of death are self-explanatory.

Additional genealogical information specific to Ossipee may be found in several books, two of which merit special mention. Edward M. Cook, Jr.'s Ossipee, New Hampshire, 1785-1985 is a good general source. Eva Blake Loud's Early Cemetery Records: Ossipee, New Hampshire, which was published in conjunction with the national bicentennial in 1976 contains thousands of inscriptions and is a valuable source of information for the years preceding those covered by this book.

In most recent years, the age at death was not provided in the report. That information is often available from the Social Security Death Benefits database or from obituaries published in local or regional newspapers and has not been provided.

BIRTHS

ABBOTT,
son, b. 7/7/1888; second; Lyford Abbott (farmer, Ossipee) and Etta M. Abbott (Freedom)
stillborn son, b. 8/19/1888; first; Harrison R. Abbott (farmer, Tuftonboro) and Emma F. Abbott (Effingham)
daughter, b. 3/6/1890 in Ossipee; first; Almond Abbott (pressman, Ossipee) and Mary Dowe (Ossipee)
daughter, b. 9/16/1893 in Ossipee; second; George H. Abbott (mechanic, Ossipee) and Jennie Champion (Effingham)
son, b. 7/23/1895 in Ossipee; fifth; Lyford Abbott (mechanic, Ossipee) and Etta M. Ward (Ossipee)
daughter, b. 12/16/1895 in Ossipee; first; Joseph C. Abbott (farmer, Ossipee) and Maud Abbott (Ossipee)
son, b. 12/10/1897 in Ossipee; second; Joseph Abbott (laborer, 34, Ossipee) and Maude Abbott (23, Ossipee)
son, b. 12/13/1897 in Ossipee; sixth; Lyford Abbott (mill man, 37, Ossipee) and Etta M. Ward (31, Ossipee)
daughter, b. 10/2/1900 in Ossipee; first; Wilber Abbott (laborer, 21, Ossipee) and Florence Cook (19, Ossipee)
daughter [Geraldine], b. 8/7/1902 in Ossipee; seventh; Lyford Abbott (millman, 41, Ossipee) and Etta M. Ward (35, Ossipee)
daughter [Louise A.], b. 12/25/1904 in Ossipee; eighth; Lyford A. Abbott (millman, 43, Ossipee) and Etta M. Ward (37, Ossipee)
son, b. 5/5/1905 in Ossipee; second; Wilbur Abbott (farmer, Ossipee) and Florence Cook (Ossipee)
son [Carroll Guy], b. 8/1/1907 in Ossipee; first; Guy L. Abbott (laborer, Ossipee) and Fannie Templeton (Ossipee)
stillborn son, b. 4/3/1909 in Ossipee; first; Jacob Abbott (farmer, Ossipee) and Bessie Ainsworth
daughter, b. 4/3/1909 in Ossipee; second; Jacob Abbott (farmer, Ossipee) and Bessie Ainsworth
son, b. 9/5/1915; third; Ernest Abbott (laborer, Ossipee) and Etta Colby (Ossipee)
child, b. 9/27/1926; third; Ernest Abbott (Ossipee) and Ruth Elliott (Exeter)
daughter, b. 3/30/1940; fourth; Carroll G. Abbott (Ctr. Ossipee) and Bertha Mary Page (Tamworth)
Eva Jane, b. 4/3/1936; second; Carroll Guy Abbott (Moultonville) and Bertha M. Page (Somersworth)
Fred, b. 5/2/1913; fourth; Jacob N. Abbott (farmer, Ossipee) and Bessie Ainsworth (Montpelier, VT)
George E., b. 5/3/1930; third; Ernest Abbott (Ossipee) and Ruth M. Elliott (Exeter)
Gloria Frances, b. 5/9/1944; first; Frances May Abbott (Ctr. Ossipee)
Irving A., b. 2/17/1921; first; Wade Abbott (mill hand, Ossipee) and Josephine A. Eldridge (Ossipee)

Jean Frances, b. 2/9/1939; third; Carroll Guy Abbott (Ctr. Ossipee) and
    Bertha Mary Page (Tamworth)
Jedidiah David, b. 2/24/1992; David Wayne Abbott and Wendy Lynn White
May Lizzie, b. 11/5/1926; first; Herman F. Abbott (Wolfeboro) and Edith
    Brown (W. Campton)
Megan Naomi, b. 9/5/1985; Richard John Abbott and Laurie Naomi Wykes
Myrtle C., b. 7/13/1891; first; G. H. Abbott (mechanic, Ossipee) and -----
    (Effingham)
Richard P., b. 2/20/1912; first; Almon W. Abbott (merchant, Effingham)
    and Harriet Tighe (Rollinsford)
Roland W., b. 8/3/1923; second; Wade Abbott (Ossipee) and Josephine
    Eldridge (Ossipee)
Ruth E., b. 3/1/1920; first; Harry V. Abbott (teamster, Ossipee) and G.
    Shortridge (Wakefield)
Ruth May, b. 11/7/1957; first; George E. Abbott (NH) and June L. Hodge
    (NH)
Sarah Jean, b. 2/26/1983; David Wayne Abbott and Renee Jean Hamel
Tiffany Dawn, b. 10/26/1987; Donald W. Abbott and Robyn Jackson
Wallace H., b. 5/1/1911 in Ossipee; third; Jacob M. Abbott (laborer,
    Ossipee) and Bessie Ainsworth (Montpelier, VT)

ADAMS,
Amber, b. 11/5/1986; Gary Adams, Jr. and Leona Irene Gauthier
Christopher Ronald, b. 5/6/1981; Ronald Nathaniel Adams and Karen
    Elizabeth Karl
Elizabeth England, b. 7/30/1979; Ronald Nathaniel Adams and Karen
    Elizabeth Karl
Gary, III, b. 8/29/1988; Gary Adams, Jr. and Leona I. Gauthier
Robert Donald, b. 10/14/1974; Gilbert Crocker Adams, Jr. and Barbara
    Ruth Carter

ADJUTANT,
Alice E., b. 8/1/1926; fifth; Harry Adjutant (Wolfeboro) and Jennie M. Dore
    (Wolfeboro)
Carol L., b. 6/18/1960; fifth; Chester W. Adjutant and Marjorie A. Harmon
Catherine Pearl, b. 1/25/1949; fifth; Ervin F. Adjutant (Wolfeboro) and
    Catherine Pearl (Brownfield, ME)
David A., b. 10/24/1968; Dennis W. Adjutant and Alice H. Grau
Dorothy E., b. 8/13/1955; fourth; Chester Adjutant (NH) and Marjorie
    Harmon (ME)
Gregory Alexander, b. 8/8/1991; Matthew Anthony Adjutant and Deana
    Mae Wiggin
Harold M., b. 8/13/1916; fourth; Martin B. Adjutant (farmer, Wolfeboro)
    and Hattie M. Hooper (Wakefield); residence - Wolfeboro

Irene Mae, b. 3/20/1951; third; Chester Adjutant (NH) and Marjorie
    Harmon (ME)
Jennifer Hazel, b. 8/31/1981; Randy Martin Adjutant and Ann Marie Wiggin
Kenneth R., b. 7/10/1941; fourth; Ervin Adjutant (Wolfeboro) and
    Catherine Quimby (Brownfield, ME)
Kimberly Nicole, b. 9/21/1994 in Wolfeboro; Norman M. Adjutant and Alta
    M. Beam
Lester Ervin, b. 4/4/1938; first; Ervin F. Adjutant (Ossipee) and Catherine
    P. Quimby (Brownfield, ME)
Lindsey Lee, b. 9/24/1989; Randy Martin Adjutant and Ann Marie Wiggin
Michael Anthony, b. 9/21/1988; Matthew Anthony Adjutant and Deana Mae
    Wiggin
Shirley Louise, b. 10/14/1939; second; Ervin F. Adjutant (Wolfeboro) and
    Catherine P. Quimby (Brownfield)
Timothy Matthew, b. 11/3/1990; Christopher Allen Adjutant and Laura
    Elaine Moore

AIKENS,
Mary E., b. 2/21/1947; first; James Aikens (Philadelphia, PA) and Margaret
    Honeybone (King's Cleare, England)

AINSWORTH,
daughter, b. 8/17/1910 in Ossipee; William Ainsworth (teamster, VT) and
    Nellie Alexander
stillborn son, b. 9/4/1913; first; Wallace Ainsworth (teamster, Stow, VT)
    and Alice Harmon
Elvin, b. 1/10/1907 in Ossipee; ninth; William Ainsworth (lumberman,
    Calais, ME) and Nellie ----- (Contacook, Canada)

ALBERTI,
Dorothy Louise, b. 4/25/1926; fourth; Arcady Alberti (Russia) and Ruby
    Chesley (Freedom)

ALBRECHT,
child, b. 1/5/1927; second; Arthur Albrecht (Dorchester, MA) and Louise
    Reissfelder (Roslindale, MA)

ALLAN,
son, b. 9/30/1901 in Ossipee; fifth; Walter S. Allan (optician, Chelsea, MA)
    and Lena M. Boynton (Lowell, MA)

ALLSOP,
Eleanor Marie, b. 8/26/1981; Robert William Allsop and Linda Diane
    Folsom

ALTHOFF,
Rebecca S., b. 4/26/1965; first; John S. Althoff and Patience K. Peale
Sarah L., b. 10/30/1967; second; John S. Althoff and Patience K. Peale

ALWARD,
David A., b. 4/7/1958; fourth; Robert Alward (Framingham, MA) and
 Georgiena Sawyer (Lexington, MA)

AMES,
daughter, b. 10/16/1893 in Ossipee; first; Daniel W. Ames (farmer,
 Ossipee) and Mattie A. Dore (Ossipee)
Alan Adalbert, b. 10/3/1950; first; James Ames (Tamworth) and Joanne
 Stoddard (Melrose, MA)
Ashley Lynn, b. 9/23/1989; Derek John Ames and Karen Marie LaRochelle
Eric Paul, b. 7/5/1978; Roger Stanley Ames and Sandra Lee Ryder
Paul T., b. 11/7/1954; third; Roy M. Ames (NH) and Lois A. Conner (NH)
Robin M., b. 9/23/1959; fourth; Roy Ames (S. Tamworth) and Lois Conner
 (Ctr. Ossipee)
Roger Stanley, b. 10/17/1956; third; Roy M. Ames (NH) and Lois A.
 Conner (NH)
Roy M., Jr., b. 5/23/1953; second; Roy Ames (NH) and Lois Conner (NH)
Shirley May, b. 11/23/1951; first; Roy Ames (NH) and Lois Conner (NH)
Tracy, b. 3/13/1972; Alan Adalbert Ames and Jo-ann Thompson

AMIDON,
Dana Robert, b. 10/25/1977; Robert Howard Amidon and Martha Agnes
 Doyle

ANCTIL,
Daniel David, b. 7/23/1983; David Michael Anctil and Rebecca Anne Allen

ANDERSON,
Madison Jade, b. 10/11/1998 in Wolfeboro; David C. Anderson and
 Margaret Irene Owens

ANDREA,
Chelsey Rose, b. 5/3/1989; Robert Anthony Andrea and Janice Marie
 Bourgault
Geri Beth, b. 5/28/2001 in N. Conway; Robert Andrea and Janice Andrea

ANDREWS,
stillborn daughter, b. 6/5/1911 in Ossipee; first; Austin D. Andrews
 (farmer, NB) and Alice P. Young (Ossipee)

daughter, b. 8/17/1915; third; A. D. Andrews (farmer, Boston, MA) and
    Alice Andrews (Ossipee)
Arthur, b. 7/31/1917; fourth; Austin D. Andrews (merchant, Hampton, NB)
    and Alice Young (Ossipee)
Edward C., b. 5/26/1892 in Ossipee; first; Ezekiel B. Andrews (physician,
    Freedom) and Emma A. Burke (Somerville, MA)
Helen O., b. 9/9/1901 in Ossipee; fourth; E. B. Andrews (physician, 40,
    Freedom) and Emma Burke (37, Somerville, MA)
Hugh March, b. 3/8/1898 in Ossipee; second; E. B. Andrews (physician,
    36, Freedom) and Emma Burke (33, Somerville, MA)
Ruth Winifred, b. 7/28/1899 in Ossipee; third; E. B. Andrews (physician,
    37, Freedom) and Emma Burke (34, Somerville, MA)
Vea E., b. 9/25/1913; second; Austin Andrews (farmer, Hampton, NB) and
    Alice Young (Ossipee)

ANTHONY,
Gregory Alan, II, b. 3/5/1973; Gregory Alan Anthony and Linda Lee
    Fulcher
Richard Louis, b. 9/19/1950; second; Rupert Anthony (Brownfield, ME)
    and Elizabeth Warren (Denmark, ME)
Wendy Elizabeth, b. 11/1/1974; Bruce Gordon Anthony and Barbara Ruth
    Carter

ARCHAMBAULT,
Madlynn Ann, b. 4/6/2000 in Wolfeboro; Jeremy Archambault and Carie
    Archambault

ARMSTRONG,
Thereasa L., b. 7/9/1968; James L. Armstrong and Louise M. Underhill

ARNOLD,
daughter, b. 6/11/1910 in Ossipee; George L. Arnold (laborer, Nashua)
    and Maud L. Hartford (Deerfield)
Donald C., Jr., b. 7/31/1932; first; Donald C. Arnold (Atlanta, GA) and
    Doris Bennett (Ossipee)

ARSENAULT,
stillborn daughter, b. 7/31/1910 in Ossipee; second; Leon Arsenault
    (laborer, PEI) and Sadie Templeton (Ossipee)
Chelsea Elizabeth, b. 6/26/1998 in Wolfeboro; Paul Arsenault and Sheila
    Arsenault
Jilian Brie, b. 8/22/1984; Richard John Arsenault and Bonnie Joyce Cole
Keenan John, b. 9/24/1987; John E. Arsenault and Susan W. Kittle

ASHBY,
Zeth Adon-Kai,, b. 11/26/2000 in N. Conway; Lemuel Ashby and Karson Ashby

ASPINALL,
Joni Lynn, b. 2/20/1956; first; George W. Aspinall (NH) and Gloria V. Boucher (NH)

ATKINS,
John Thomas, b. 8/25/1988; John L. Atkins and Denise R. Dumont

AUFUCHONT,
Louis, b. 6/25/1948; sixth; Homer Aufuchont (Worcester, MA) and Mildred C. Voutour (Pepperell, MA)

AVERY,
Clynton Dore, b. 5/27/1982; Lewis T. Avery and Ruth Dore
Colt Jacob William, b. 10/28/1998 in Laconia; Lewis Avery and Kathleen Avery

AXELSON,
Judith, b. 5/22/1949; second; William Axelson (Providence, RI) and Shirley Wilkins (Providence, RI)

AYERS,
son, b. 4/14/1889; John M. Ayers (farmer, Ossipee) and Carrie S. Ayers (Boston, MA)

BACIGALUPO,
Walter L., b. 4/7/1935; third; Fred Bacigalupo (Boston, MA) and ----- (VT)

BAMFORD,
Allen Hale, b. 11/4/1946; second; Clayton F. Bamford (Caribou, ME) and Lee B. Howard (Chaton, AL)
Melody Carolie, b. 11/6/1952; fourth; Clayton Bamford (ME) and Lee Howard (AL)
Pamela Lee, b. 5/22/1950; third; Clayton Bamford, Jr. (Caribou, ME) and Lee Howard (AL)

BANFILL,
Beatrice A., b. 9/17/1922 in Sanford, ME; second; Fred R. Banfill (teamster, Franklin) and Meleda Besharnais (Canada)
Harry G., b. 6/30/1929; first; Charles W. Banfill and Evelyn A. (Tamworth)

Joan Elizabeth, b. 12/8/1949; first; Fred G. Banfill (Wolfeboro) and Lillian Bisbee (Tuftonboro)

BARRETT,
Cassidy Elizabeth, b. 5/3/2000 in Wolfeboro; John Barrett and Jennifer Barrett
Derik Andrew, b. 12/19/1989; Ronald Andrew Barrett, Jr. and Vicki Lynn Towle
Joshua Andrew, b. 2/6/1999 in Wolfeboro; Alan Fayne Barrett, Sr. and Christine Marie Hargrove Barrett
Savannah Pearl, b. 7/6/2000 in Wolfeboro; Alan Barrett and Christine Barrett

BARRON,
Ruth Agnes, b. 11/14/2000 in Lebanon; Roy Barron and Karen Barron

BARROWS,
Kenneth Moore, Jr., b. 7/31/1973; Kenneth Moore Barrows and Gloria Katherine Clark
Scott Thomas, b. 11/6/1974; Kenneth Moore Barrows and Gloria Catherine Clark

BARTER,
Dennis Herbert, b. 6/15/1952; first; Herbert Barter (Whitefield) and Nancy Hilton (Madison)
Elizabeth Marion, b. 5/7/1956; first; Leiton D. Barter (NH) and Pauline Taylor (NH)
Virginia S., b. 4/9/1957; second; Leiton Barter (NH) and Pauline Taylor (NH)

BARTON,
Kelly A., b. 8/31/1968; Frederick H. Barton and Mary E. Varney
Scott Frederick, b. 1/11/1970; Frederick Harry Barton and Mary Elizabeth Varney
Steven E., b. 9/1/1967; first; Frederick H. Barton and Mary E. Varney

BATES,
Joseph Robert, b. 12/12/1970; Robert Arthur Bates and Cecile Mary Plourde

BEACHAM,
daughter, b. 6/22/1892 in Ossipee; first; George A. Beacham (farmer, Ossipee) and Lillian Gilman (Ossipee)

BEAN,
son, b. 4/22/1893 in Ossipee; first; Herbert Bean (farmer, Ossipee) and I. E. Knowles (Moultonboro)
daughter, b. 8/16/1894 in Ossipee; second; Charles S. Bean (farmer, Ossipee) and Clara Abbott (Ossipee)
child [Maud], b. 11/11/1895 in Ossipee; second; Fred Bean (laborer, Ossipee) and ----- Nichols (Ossipee)
son, b. 11/25/1896 in Ossipee; third; Charles S. Bean (39, Tuftonboro) and Clara B. Abbott (26)
daughter, b. 5/18/1902 in Ossipee; sixth; Fred Bean (fisherman, 30, Eaton) and Anna Nichols (26, Ossipee)
son, b. 6/14/1904 in Ossipee; seventh; Fred Bean (fisherman, 32, Eaton) and Anna Nichols (28, Ossipee)
son, b. 2/1/1908 in Ossipee; seventh; Fred Bean (fisherman, Ossipee) and Anna Nichols (Ossipee)
daughter, b. 8/22/1908 in Ossipee; second; Etta Bean (Ossipee)
daughter, b. 4/11/1910 in Ossipee; ninth; Fred E. Bean (fisherman, Madison) and Georgiana Nichols (Ossipee)
child, b. 4/5/1932; first; Ernest D. Bean (Ossipee) and Marion M. Welch (Ossipee)
child, b. 12/5/1937; fourth; Ernest Bean (Ossipee) and Marion Welch (Ossipee)
Alex Frank, b. 12/12/1992; Clyde Leroy Bean, III and Angel Margaret Dixon
Annette K., b. 12/15/1936; second; Harris Bean (Wolfeboro) and Lavinia Crockett (Hallowell, ME)
Cheryl L., b. 11/6/1959; second; Clyde Bean (Ossipee) and Joyce Reed (Wolfeboro)
Clyde, b. 12/25/1912; tenth; Fred Bean (hunter, Madison) and Georgianna Nichols (Ossipee)
Clyde L., 3rd, b. 11/10/1969; Clyde L. Bean, Jr. and Joyce L. Reed
Doris, b. 1/6/1924; first; Harold Bean (Ossipee) and Cora York (Barrington)
Edith, b. 10/17/1915; eleventh; Fred Bean (laborer, Eaton) and Anna Nichols (Ossipee)
Ernest Clifford, b. 3/21/1940; fourth; Harris Bean (Wolfeboro) and Lavinia Crockett (Augusta, ME)
Ernest D., Jr., b. 4/5/1932; second; Ernest D. Bean (Ossipee) and Marion M. Welch (Ossipee)
Henry, b. 5/10/1900 in Ossipee; fifth; Fred E. Bean (D. B. fisherman & hunter, 29, Eaton) and Georgana Nichols (25, Ossipee)
Laura Elizabeth, b. 10/21/1990; Jeffrey Allen Bean and Susan Elaine Phelps
Lillian May, b. 7/13/1938; fourth; Clyde LeRoy Bean (Ctr. Ossipee) and Hazel L. Downing (Milton)

Loraine, b. 6/11/1933; first; Clyde Bean (Ossipee) and Hazel Downie (Ossipee)
Margaret Idella, b. 6/11/1941; third; Ernest Dore Bean (Ossipee) and Marion Mabel Welch (Ossipee)
Mary-Jane, b. 6/28/1966; second; Clyde L. Bean, Jr. and Joyce L. Reed
Nancy Jane, b. 10/9/1935; third; Ernest Dore Bean (Ctr. Ossipee) and Marion M. Welch (Ctr. Ossipee)
Patricia Irene, b. 7/15/1941; sixth; Ernest Harris Bean (Wolfeboro) and Lavinia Zita Crockett (Hallowell, ME)
Robert Edward, b. 12/18/1936; third; Clyde LeRoy Bean (Ctr. Ossipee) and Hazel L. Downing (Milton)
Rosemary, b. 1/22/1958; first; Clyde L. Bean (Ossipee) and Joyce Reed (Wolfeboro)
Sara Mildred, b. 8/23/1995 in Wolfeboro; Clyde Leroy Bean III and Angel Margaret Dixon

BEATS,
Paige Elizabeth, b. 4/22/1987; John-Mark Beats and Stora Lee Montgomery

BEAUDET,
Christopher Michael, b. 7/29/1974; Michael Ray Beaudet and Shirley Jean Johnson

BECKWITH,
child, b. 7/24/1929; first; Mabel Beckwith (Providence, RI)
Barbara A., b. 2/23/1947; first; Burt W. Beckwith (Providence, RI) and Dorothy B. Tibbetts (Hathorne, MA)

BEDLEY,
Benjamin Michael, b. 3/2/1997 in Wolfeboro; Michael Dean Bedley and Brandi Ann Piper
Michael Dean, b. 10/31/1973; John Freeman Bedley and Deborah Jane Libby

BELL,
Richard Allen Libby, b. 6/25/1980; Robert Lee Bell, Jr. and Lucinda Elizabeth White
Robert Charles, b. 6/27/1972; Robert Lee Bell and Lucinda E. White

BENES,
Ashley Erwin, b. 5/18/1980; Robert Chester Benes, Jr. and Susan Jean Gaudet

Justin Nathan, b. 12/17/1978; Robert Chester Benes, Jr. and Susan Jean Gaudet

BENNETT,
son, b. 10/21/1908 in Ossipee; first; A. Bennett (woodman) and Lilla ----- son [Russell E.], b. 8/14/1909 in Ossipee; second; Sumner Bennett (farmer, Sandwich) and Rose Wood (Freedom)
Bruce Earl, b. 9/26/1941; second; Russell Elden Bennett (Ossipee) and Gretchen Goldsmith (Ossipee)
Gordon Russell, b. 5/16/1939; first; Russell Bennett (Ossipee) and Gretchen Goldsmith (Ossipee)

BENSON,
Brandon James, b. 9/23/1995 in Wolfeboro; James Mark Benson, Jr. and Bambi Marie Dixon
Lisa Marion, b. 7/15/1989; Howard Colson Benson and Brenda Lee Evans
Ross Mykel, b. 11/6/1991; Howard Colson Benson and Brenda Lee Evans

BERGERON,
Courtney Alice, b. 7/11/1990; Gerard Roland Bergeron and Gayle Contois
Hannah Marie, b. 8/1/1994 in Wolfeboro; Gerard R. Bergeron and Gayle Contois

BERKOWITZ,
Mathew Loud, b. 9/3/1980; Brian F. Berkowitz and Karen Thurber Loud

BERNARDO,
Hayley Helen, b. 3/5/1993 in Wolfeboro; Sonny Bernardo and Kerry Anne DeGloria

BERRY,
daughter, b. 5/22/1901 in Ossipee; first; Herman D. Berry (laborer, 24, Portsmouth) and Margaret Holley (26, Ireland)
daughter [Irene Agnes], b. 2/7/1906 in Ossipee; third; Herman Berry (laborer, Tamworth) and Margaret Holly (Ireland)
son [Ernest N.], b. 8/1/1908 in Ossipee; fourth; Herman D. Berry (millman, Tamworth) and Margaret A. Holly (Ireland)
daughter [Teresa E.], b. 1/11/1911 in Ossipee; fifth; Herman Berry (sawyer, Ossipee) and Margaret Holly (Ireland)
Barbara J., b. 8/6/1953; ninth; Ernest Berry (NH) and Phyllis Merrow (NH)
Brandon Asa, b. 11/17/1997 in Wolfeboro; John Adrian Berry and Jennifer Lee Nichols
David Arnold, b. 7/30/1938; third; Ernest Maurice Berry (Ctr. Ossipee) and Phyllis L. Merrow (Ossipee)

Dean Phillip, b. 8/29/1972; Duane Herman Berry and Donna Elaine Alden
Duane Ernest, b. 8/6/1970; Duane Herman Berry and Donna Elaine Alden
Duane Herman, b. 1/14/1952; eighth; Ernest Berry (NH) and Phyllis
  Merrow (NH)
Dwight Wayne, b. 10/30/1944; fifth; Ernest M. Berry (Ctr. Ossipee) and
  Phyllis I. Merrow (Ctr. Ossipee)
Ernest Morris, b. 8/5/1936; second; Ernest M. Berry (Ctr. Ossipee) and
  Phillis I. Merrow (Ossipee)
Gordon D., b. 2/15/1942; third; Ernest M. Berry (Ctr. Ossipee) and Phyllis
  I. Merrow (Ctr. Ossipee)
Henry E., b. 9/14/1903 in Ossipee; second; Herman Berry (millman, 27,
  Tamworth) and Margaret A. Holly (29, Ireland)
Holly Jane, b. 12/24/1956; first; Ernest M. Berry, Jr. (NH) and Eva J.
  Abbott (NH)
Jacqueline R., b. 8/8/1958; tenth; Ernest Berry (Ctr. Ossipee) and Phyllis
  Merrow (Ctr. Ossipee)
Jill Morgan, b. 9/20/1999 in N. Conway; John Berry and Jennifer Berry
Joan D., b. 1/22/1957; tenth; Ernest M. Berry (NH) and Phyllis I. Merrow
  (NH)
John Adrian, b. 9/16/1972; John Merrow Berry and Gaye Ellen Robie
John Merrow, b. 10/21/1946; sixth; Ernest M. Berry (Ossipee) and Phyllis
  E. Merrow (Ossipee)
Lenora M., b. 5/9/1932; first; Theresa Berry (Ossipee)
Martha Jean, b. 11/15/1948; seventh; Ernest M. Berry (Ossipee) and
  Phyllis I. Merrow (Ossipee)
Mary Ann, b. 3/27/1956; second; Raymond A. Berry (NH) and Charlotte E.
  Palmer (NH)
Patricia J., b. 3/15/1960; eleventh; Ernest M. Berry and Phyllis I. Merrow
Raymond A., Jr., b. 5/29/1930; first; Raymond A. Berry (Tamworth) and
  Gladys Eldridge (Ossipee)
Scott Allen, b. 2/8/1970; Gordon Daniel Berry and Gloria Frances Gagne

BICKFORD,
daughter, b. 12/30/1896 in Ossipee; first; Lilla Bickford (20, Ossipee)
son [Lucy G.], b. 2/8/1897 in Ossipee; first; George Bickford and Edith M.
  Cook (18)
son, b. 5/25/1898 in Ossipee; first; Belmont Bickford (farmer, Ossipee)
  and Dora Bickford
son, b. 5/3/1899 in Ossipee; second; Belmont Bickford (farmer, 39,
  Ossipee) and Dora Bickford (19, Bartlett)
Dwight Roy, b. 5/14/1938; first; Pearl Bickford (Wolfeboro)
Jennah Nichole, b. 10/14/2001 in Lebanon; Jeffrey Bickford and Kimberly
  Bickford
Terrence Ralph, b. 12/31/1956; first; Irving B. Bickford (NH) and Joyce E.
  Templeton (NH)

BIERWEILER,
Marion Agnes, b. 10/30/1949; first; Donald Bierweler (Somerville, MA) and Annie Clark (Kennebunk, ME)

BILADEAU,
son [John], b. 6/12/1889; John Biladeau (laborer, Canada) and Mary Biladeau (Canada)

BILLINGS,
Clarissa Marian, b. 7/10/1995 in Laconia; Condict Moore Billings and Debra Ann Plummer
Elizabeth Marie, b. 10/30/1980; Peter D. Billings and Joanne M. E. P. Billings
Ethan Brian, b. 4/29/1990; Condict Moore Billings and Debra Ann Plummer
Henry Smathers, b. 9/14/1972; Peter Don Billings and Ellen McLain Smathers
Katlynn Moore, b. 8/25/1992; Condict Moore Billings and Debra Ann Plummer
Savannah Rose, b. 10/15/1998 in Laconia; Condict Moore Billings and Debra Ann Plummer
Sheldon Ryan, b. 10/15/1998 in Laconia; Condict Moore Billings and Debra Ann Plummer

BISBEE,
Barbara Jeanne, b. 7/7/1937; second; Chester A. Bisbee (Parsonsfield, ME) and Mildred Beckman (Newburyport, MA)

BLAISDELL,
daughter [Gertie], b. 10/9/1894 in Ossipee; first; Irving A. Blaisdell (laborer, 22, Boston) and Jennie Linscott (18, Porter, ME)

BLAKE,
Daniel Richard, b. 5/20/1970; Richard Malcolm Blake and Marilyn Janet White
Eva F., b. 7/30/1893 in Ossipee; first; Simeon Blake (farmer, Ossipee) and Mabel E. Fall (Ossipee)
Rick A., b. 2/25/1947; first; Robert A. Blake (Lynn, MA) and Barbara P. Moffitt (Southwest Harbor, ME)

BLY,
Carrie Lynn, b. 8/16/1978; Rufus Willis Bly, Jr. and Carol Ann Kelley

BOATMAN,
Carole J., b. 1/23/1961; first; Lawrence R. Boatman and Margaret A. Dore
Keith C., b. 3/19/1962; second; Lawrence Boatman and Margaret Dore

BODGE,
daughter, b. 6/25/1909 in Ossipee; first; Walter C. Bodge (farmer, Tuftonboro) and Maud F. Hanson (Ossipee); residence - Tuftonboro
Ruth, b. 7/18/1917; fourth; Walter C. Bodge (farmer, Tuftonboro) and Maude Hanson (Ossipee)

BODWELL,
Mark Allen, b. 3/26/1975; Debra Lynne Bodwell

BOEHM,
Breyon Dawn, b. 12/25/1989; Donald William Boehm and Marianne Helen Patrie

BOEWE,
Daniel Edward, b. 12/6/1983; Ward Anthony Boewe and Gail Ann Farrell

BOGGS,
Cole Edgerly, b. 6/10/1992; Christopher Edwin Boggs and Lisa Ann Edgerly

BOHMILLER,
Justin Donald, b. 2/11/1994 in Wolfeboro; Stephen A. Bohmiller and Lori J. Watson

BOISVERT,
Paula Ann, b. 5/2/1993 in Wolfeboro; Paul Joseph Boisvert and Deborah Jean Black

BOLTON,
Colleen M. , b. 7/9/1969; John P. Bolton, Jr. and Corinne A. Correiro

BONEYMAN,
William H., b. 4/9/1911 in Ossipee; first; Fred K. C. Boneyman (salesman, Boston) and Marie F. Cady (Boston)

BORG,
Robert James, b. 1/27/1946; third; Robert M. Borg (Smithfield, PA) and Lillian P. Hewitt (Pillington, MA)

BOUCHER,
Michael J., b. 11/18/1954; first; Ernest J. Boucher, Jr. (NH) and Constance M. LeBlanc (MA)

BOURGAULT,
Alex Daniel, b. 10/17/1987; Daniel R. Bourgault and Lynn Shannon
Ashley Lynn, b. 11/2/1988; Daniel R. Bourgault and Lynn Marie Shannon

BOUTIN,
Andrew James, b. 11/9/1983; Raymond Paul Boutin and Robin Anita Pohl
Raymond Paul, II, b. 11/29/1980; Raymond Paul Boutin and Robin Anita Pohl
Stacy Elizabeth, b. 12/27/1990; Ray Paul Boutin and Robin Anita Pohl

BOWERS,
Marcia H., b. 3/9/1918; first; Howard Bowers (laborer, NS) and Beatrice Davis (Effingham)

BRACK,
Albert F., III, b. 11/4/1961; second; Albert Brack, Jr. and Ruthanne Letteney
Carol L., b. 3/6/1959; first; Albert Brack, Jr. (Winchester, MA) and Ruthanne Letteney (Foxboro, MA)

BRAUN,
Jeffrey Kenneth, b. 12/27/1991; Kenneth Randolph Braun and Caryn Dorothea Robiller

BRESNAHAN,
Shannon Lynne, b. 11/10/1982; Brian D. Bresnahan and Karie L. Shannon

BRISTOWE,
Dwight A., b. 7/2/1961; first; Robert Bristowe and Pauline Forand

BROCHU,
Darlene A., b. 7/11/1955; eighth; Leopold Brochu (ME) and June Durgin (ME)
Leopold, Jr., b. 4/12/1954; seventh; Leopold Brochu (ME) and June D. Durgin (ME)
Russell N., b. 10/28/1961; thirteenth; Leo P. Brochu and June D. Durgin

BROOKE,
Michael Raymond, b. 11/25/1949; third; Ambrose Brooke (Conway) and Alice Smith (Brooklyn, NY)

Paul Joseph, b. 11/25/1949; fourth; Ambrose Brooke (Conway) and Alice Smith (Brooklyn, NY)

BROOKS,
Dianne, b. 8/21/1958; fourth; Raymond Brooks (Leominster, MA) and Marjorie M. Cowee (Natick, MA)
Kathleen Mary, b. 6/22/1956; third; Raymond B. Brooks (MA) and Marjorie M. Cowes (MA)
Paula Rae, b. 1/9/1949; second; Raymond B. Brooks (Leominster, MA) and Marjorie M. Cowee (Natick, MA)
Spencer Lee, b. 12/4/1946; first; Raymond B. Brooks (Leominster, MA) and Marjorie M. Cowee (Natick, MA)
Vanessa Faye, b. 9/13/1987; Harold V. Brooks, Jr. and Francine M. Frankino

BROTHERS,
Christopher Allen, b. 7/4/1982; Stanley Neal Brothers and Dianne Lynn Aleska
Corey Dean, b. 12/31/1979; Stanley Neal Brothers and Diane Lynne Aleska
Elmer Wayne, b. 1/28/1928; first; Laurence Brothers (N. Adams, MA) and Beatrice E. Palmer (Washington, ME)
Jeffrey A., b. 10/16/1952; fourth; Elmer Brothers (NH) and Esther Ames (NH)
Jeremy Paul, b. 1/30/1992; Michael Brian Brothers and Vicki Ann Hayford
Michael Brian, b. 7/1/1949; first; Elmer Brothers (NH) and Esther Ames (NH)

BROWN,
daughter, b. 5/19/1898 in Ossipee; first; Thomas H. Brown (painter, Ossipee) and Betsey Pease (Freedom)
daughter [Muriel G.], b. 7/4/1901 in Ossipee; third; Thomas H. Brown (painter, 26, Ossipee) and Bessie Pease (24, Freedom)
Carol L., b. 12/9/1931; second; Roy Leon Brown (N. Conway) and Nulida Paquette (Stonstead, PQ)
Clyde Herbert, b. 6/24/1900 in Ossipee; second; Thomas Brown (painter, 24, Ossipee) and Bessie Pease (24, Freedom)
Gabrielle Maria, b. 10/10/1992; Scott Michael Brown and Sandra May Stockbridge
Ida M., b. 2/16/1920; sixth; William Brown (teamster, Madison) and Mabel Schultz (Boston, MA)
Jacquelyn Marie, b. 5/19/1997 in Laconia; Scott Michael Brown and Sandra May Stockbridge
Jared Dana, b. 5/17/1981; Douglas Martin Brown and Helena Belle Anderson

Kevin J., b. 10/25/1964; third; Franklin Brown and Phyllis Daris
Kristen Marie, b. 5/6/1982; James E. Brown and Robin M. Kilmer
Robert Clyde, b. 3/19/1935; second; Clyde Brown (Ossipee) and Lucinda Nason (Brookfield)

BROWNELL,
daughter, b. 10/2/1894 in Ossipee; third; Benjamin F. Brownell (farmer, 38, Ossipee) and Ida Thurley (35, Ossipee)
son, b. 3/24/1897 in Ossipee; fourth; Benjamin F. Brownell (farmer, 40, New Bedford) and Ida M. Thurley (37, Ossipee)
son, b. 7/8/1902 in Ossipee; fifth; Benjamin Brownell (farmer, 45, New Bedford, MA) and Ida M. Thurley (42, Ossipee)
Bryan Keith, b. 7/21/1977; Keith Warren Brownell and Barbara Pike
Debbie, b. 11/24/1956; third; Lawrence Brownell (NH) and Frances L. Williams (NH)
Edwin P., b. 2/20/1933; first; Clifford Brownell (Effingham) and Barbara Merrow (Ossipee)
Fred Robert, b. 5/3/1970; Ralph Wayne Brownell and Jane Ruth Stanton
Harold Lincoln, b. 10/4/1939; first; Harold P. Brownell (Effingham) and Evelyn Rose Banfill (S. Berwick, ME)
Karole W., b. 7/3/1968; Keith W. Brownell and Barbara G. Pike
Kathleen E., b. 11/30/1936; second; Clifford R. Brownell (Effingham Falls) and Barbara Merrow (Ctr. Ossipee)
Keith W., b. 5/12/1947; fifth; Harold P. Brownell (Effingham) and Evelyn R. Banfill (S. Berwick, ME)
Kem Marina, b. 6/26/1956; second; Edwin P. Brownell (NH) and Ingrid M. Henz (Germany)
Lynn Marie, b. 8/1/1974; Ralph Wayne Brownell and Jane Ruth Stanton
Melanie, b. 2/3/1954; first; Lawrence M. Brownell (NH) and Francis L. Williams (NH)
Michael D., b. 1/9/1959; fourth; Lawrence Brownell (Effingham) and Frances Williams (Tamworth)
Stephen C., b. 6/14/1955; second; Laurence Brownell (NH) and Frances Williams (NH)

BRULE,
Michael Jayson, b. 9/27/1985; Kathleen Margaret Brule

BRYANT,
Lester A., b. 2/25/1904 in Ossipee; first; Elmer O. Bryant (farming, 29, Effingham) and Daisy B. Bisbee (27, Effingham)
Linda Ann, b. 11/19/1940; first; Loren R. Bryant (Holland, VT) and Beulah Merryfield (Ctr. Sandwich)
Patricia Elaine, b. 4/5/1939; third; Lawrence A. Bryant (Rockland, ME) and Geraldine S. Bennett (S. Paris, ME)

BUCHANAN,
Carolee N., b. 11/30/1957; sixth; Ralph Buchanan (Boston, MA) and Vera Wiggin (NH)
Christine A., b. 7/31/1955; fifth; Ralph Buchanan (MA) and Vera Wiggin

BUCHIKOS,
Justin Allen, b. 6/29/1992; William Allen Buchikos, Jr. and Wanda Lee Nichols
Samantha Lee, b. 9/18/1994 in Wolfeboro; William A. Buchikos and Wanda L. Nichols
William Allen, III, b. 10/14/1995 in Wolfeboro; William Allen Buchikos, Jr. and Wanda Lee Nichols

BUCKNAM,
Gladys W., b. 9/27/1919; fourth; William Bucknam (farmer, Lynn, MA) and Mabel O. Fisher (Cambridge, MA)

BUDROE,
daughter, b. 6/20/1910 in Ossipee; first; Joe Budroe (laborer, Conway) and Bertha Welch (Ossipee)
Edward H., Jr., b. 10/27/1948; first; Edward H. Budroe, Sr. (Wolfeboro) and Barbara J. Eldridge (Ossipee)

BUNKER,
son, b. 7/20/1946; second; Frank R. Bunker (Tamworth) and Charlotte Lewis (N. Conway)

BURGON,
Abigail Dawn, b. 1/14/1993 in Portsmouth; Eric Trott Burgon and Karen Dawn Corporon

BURKETT,
Brandon Dean, b. 6/10/1999 in Rochester; Jack Burkett and Jaime Burkett

BURLEIGH,
son [Arthur S.], b. 9/28/1894 in Ossipee; first; Jewett Burleigh (farmer, 35, Ossipee) and Julia Roberts (40, Madison)

BURNS,
William Anthony, b. 6/1/1926; second; Harold Burns (Milford, MA) and Agnes Dore (Ossipee)

BUSCH,
Bernadette M., b. 6/30/1960; second; Roger H. Busch and Priscilla L. Jack

BUSHEY,
Jacob Alan, b. 5/5/1993 in Plymouth; Jeffrey Alan Bushey and Christine Lea Boyd

BUSHMAN,
Hannah Isabelle, b. 5/24/2000 in Wolfeboro; Robert Bushman and Kelley Bushman

BUSWELL,
son [Aphia B.], b. 7/6/1889; Isaac Buswell (stone cutter, Ossipee) and Jennie Gilman (Ossipee)
daughter [Bernice L.], b. 5/12/1901 in Ossipee; second; Walter Buswell (farmer, Ossipee) and Lela Locke
son [Ellis W.], b. 4/3/1910 in Ossipee; third; Walter Buswell (carpenter, Ossipee) and Lela Locke
son [Lloyd F.], b. 1/20/1912; fourth; Walter Buswell (farming, Ossipee) and Lelia Locke
Dorothy, b. 8/31/1930; third; Shirl E. Buswell (Ossipee) and Laura Nickerson (NS)
Gordon C., b. 12/30/1931; fourth; Ellis Buswell (Ossipee) and Pauline Werner (Wolfeboro)
Isaac Lloyd, b. 10/11/1936; first; Isaac Lloyd Buswell (Ossipee) and Catherine Clancy (Ossipee)
James M., b. 3/27/1960; third; Isaac L. Buswell, Jr. and Mary E. Neergaard
John L., b. 10/17/1957; first; Isaac L. Buswell, Jr. (NH) and Mary E. Nurgaard (MA)
Richard R., b. 4/19/1968; Robert R. Buswell and Charlotte A. McColloch
Ricky R. b. 12/3/1969; Robert R. Buswell and Charlotte A. McColloch
Robert R., Jr., b. 10/29/1947; first; Robert R. Buswell (Madison) and Louise C. Hobbs (Tamworth)
Roland R., b. 10/22/1954; fourth; Robert R. Buswell (NH) and Louise C. Hobbs (NH)
Sandra Jean, b. 9/6/1950; second; Robert Buswell (Albany) and Cora Hobbs (Tamworth)
Sharon Lee, b. 7/21/1952; third; Robert Buswell (Albany) and Louise Hobbs (Tamworth)
Shirl E., b. 5/6/1900; Walter Buswell (NH) and Lelia B. Locke (NH) (1957)
Shirley Ann, b. 10/26/1956; fifth; Robert R. Buswell (NH) and Louise C. Hobbs (NH)
Stephen, b. 1/24/1959; second; Isaac Buswell (Wolfeboro) and Mary Neergaard (Woburn, MA)

CALLAHAN,
Taylor Lorinda, b. 12/14/1990; John Dyer Callahan and Tawna Marie Poirier

CAMPBELL,
Forest E., b. 3/9/1931; second; Forest Campbell (Brookfield) and Winifred Eldridge (Ossipee)
John C., b. 9/30/1965; second; Charles M. Campbell and Marion Koffinas
Richard D., b. 10/28/1929; first; Forrest Campbell (Strafford) and Winifred Eldridge (Ossipee)

CAMPION,
Jessica Jean, b. 7/20/1992; Edwin James Campion and Patricia Anne Chevalier

CANNEY,
daughter, b. 3/31/1893 in Ossipee; first; Fred M. Canney (farmer, Ossipee) and Emma F. Hilton (Ossipee)
son [Fred F.], b. 7/19/1894 in Ossipee; second; Fred N. Canney (farmer, 27, Ossipee) and Emma F. Hilton (21, Ossipee)
child, b. 12/24/1896 in Ossipee; third; Fred M. Canney (farmer, 30, Ossipee) and Emma F. Hilton (23, Ossipee)
son, b. 3/22/1898 in Ossipee; fourth; Fred N. Canney (farmer, 32, Ossipee) and Emma F. Hilton (25, Ossipee)
daughter [Bernice L.], b. 4/28/1903 in Ossipee; fifth; Fred M. Canney (37, Ossipee) and Emma F. Hilton (30, Ossipee)
daughter [Beatrice M.], b. 1/24/1906 in Ossipee; sixth; Fred M. Canney (farmer, Ossipee) and Fannie Hilton (Ossipee)
son, b. 4/27/1910 in Ossipee; seventh; Fred M. Canney (farmer, Ossipee) and Emma Hilton (Ossipee)
Haven E., b. 12/17/1933; third; Fred Forrest Canney (Ossipee) and Roxy Philbrick (Limerick)

CAPLES,
Kristen Marie, b. 2/26/1989; Richard Francis Caples and Karen Marie Nault

CARLETON,
Virginia M., b. 12/25/1912; third; B. A. Carleton (physician, Richmond, VA) and Cora B. St. John (Plainfield, VT)

CAROVNIA,
William, b. 3/12/1927; second; Paul Carovnia and Silvia Fifield

CARPENTER,
Kenneth L., Jr., b. 11/20/1958; first; Kenneth Carpenter (Berwick, ME) and Frances A. Evans (N. Conway)

CARR,
Matthew James, b. 3/25/1987; James Joseph Carr and Carolyn Rose Bender

CARRO,
Albert F., b. 8/5/1911 in Ossipee; second; Paul Carro (laborer) and Maud Currier

CARRUTHERS,
Jefferson Earl, b. 11/18/1985; Richard Wade Carruthers and Kathleen Marie Rines

CARVER,
Andrea Meka, b. 8/17/1981; Dennis Emmitt Carver and Karen Noreen Capach
Rebecca Lynne, b. 7/20/1978; Dennis Emmett Carver and Karen Noreen Capach
Ryan Joseph, b. 2/11/1980; Dennis Emmit Carver and Karen Noreen Capach

CASE,
Rosonna Noelle, b. 2/24/2000 in N. Conway; James Case and Jessica Case

CATE,
daughter, b. 10/29/1888; second; George L. Cate (t. operator, Wolfeboro) and Etta A. Cate (Ossipee)

CATLETT,
Dillion Patrick, b. 6/15/1989; Terry Wayne Catlett and Laura Lyn Norder

CAULKINS,
Alyson Dale, b. 2/2/1999 in Dover; Dale Caulkins and Cynthia Caulkins

CHADBOURNE,
child, b. 11/28/1896 in Ossipee; second; Herbert Chadburne (sic) (mill man, 29, Ossipee) and Carrie Nason (21, Parsonsfield, ME)
Clarence, b. 4/20/1895; Herbert Chadbourne (NH) and Carrie Chadbourne (NH) (1958)

CHAMBERL[A]IN,
Brien J., b. 7/1/1964; first; James Chamberlain and Charlotte Glidden
Christiana Eliza, b. 6/3/1974; Francis J. Chamberlain and Corlis Joan Kimball
Howard Arthur, b. 12/7/1985; Charles Allen Chamberlin and Zita Marie Clough
Jerome David, b. 9/10/1989; Charles Allen Chamberlin and Zita Marie Clough
Joseph Andrew, b. 1/19/1991; Charles Allen Chamberlin and Zita Marie Clough
Kevin, b. 1/26/1966; second; James E. Chamberlain and Charlotte E. Glidden

CHAMBERS,
Celinda Geneve, b. 1/14/1979; Richard John Chambers and Colby LeBaron

CHANDLER,
daughter, b. 5/22/1894 in Ossipee; Manley Chandler (farmer, Ossipee) and Ida Cook (Fryeburg)

CHAPMAN,
Ralph Cleveland, b. 5/19/1985; Ralph Warren Chapman and Dorrene Ann Waldron

CHASE,
David Lee, b. 8/26/1985; James Lee Chase and Dianne Dorothy MacLeod
Harold Gordon, b. 4/12/1935; first; ----- (Conway) and Annie Chase (Tamworth)
Susan M., b. 6/7/1961; second; Richard Chase and Roberta LeClair

CHENEY,
Albert Edwin, b. 2/22/1940; first; Albert M. Cheney (Moultonboro) and Elinor Louise Lord (Limerick, ME)
Wayne E., b. 7/14/1942; John G. Cheney (Ellensburg Depot, NY) and Edna S. Young (Watertown, MA)

CHICK,
James F., b. 6/20/1892 in Ossipee; second; Samuel B. Chick (farmer, ME) and Mary Clough (Ossipee)

CIABATTONI,
Dawn A., b. 8/5/1967; third; Robert W. Ciabattoni and Linda R. Dellolio

CLANCY,
Edward J., b. 9/23/1921; first; Edward J. Clancy (laborer, Lynn, MA) and Verna Merrow (Lynn, MA); residence - Lynn, MA

CLARK,
daughter, b. 3/29/1894 in Ossipee; third; John Clark (farmer, Ossipee)
daughter, b. 7/29/1896 in Ossipee; first; Fred Clark
Craig Stanley, b. 1/1/1974; Frank Herbert Clark and Dorothy Ellan Adjutant
Edward F. B., b. 4/4/1895 in Ossipee; fourth; John Clark (laborer, NY) and Nellie M. Smith (Durham, England)
Frederick Ralph, b. 4/28/1950; first; James Clark (Washburn, ME) and Glennie Stevens (Parkman, ME)
George A., b. 10/31/1896 in Ossipee; fifth; John H. Clark (laborer, 33, NY) and Nellie M. Smith (England)
Rachel B., b. 1/19/1901 in Ossipee; second; Belmont Clark (farmer, Kennebunk, ME) and Annie A. Walker (Newfield)
Roy, b. 11/11/1897 in Ossipee; sixth; John Clark (laborer, 33, NY) and Nelle Clark (31, England)

CLAVETTE,
Michael Benjamin, b. 11/9/1996 in N. Conway; Michael Joseph Clavette and Bridget Louise Grogan

CLOUGH,
Garth Everett, b. 3/16/1937; second; Everett Clough (Kennebunkport, ME) and Helen Donovan (Lawrence, MA)
Troy Delano, b. 3/10/1986; Gregory Allen Clough and Jennifer Balluet Chardon

CLOW,
Elizabeth, b. 6/19/1915; second; Henry L. Clow (physician, Wolfeboro) and Annie E. Shipley (Baltimore, MD)

COAN,
Frances, b. 1/10/1918; second; Pierce H. Coan (grocer, Swampscott) and Edna R. Lewis (Patterson, NJ); residence - Swampscott

COBURN,
Althea, b. 12/3/1907 in Ossipee; first; Charles H. Coburn (laborer, Walkins, NY) and Eva C. White (Ossipee)
Dorothy M., b. 10/21/1912; second; Charles H. Coburn (auto garage, Watkins, NY) and Eva C. White (Ossipee); residence - Tilton

COCHRANE,
Benjamin Joseph, b. 11/13/2001 in Wolfeboro; Bruce Cochrane and Marianne Cochrane
Samuel Edward, b. 4/3/2000 in Wolfeboro; Bruce Cochrane and Marianne Cochrane

COLBATH,
Stacey Lee, b. 4/23/1980; Dale R. Colbath and Deborah Murphy

COLBY,
stillborn son, b. 10/22/1899 in Ossipee; first; Ralph Colby (laborer, 20, Ossipee) and Minnie P. Fall (16, Ossipee)
son [Perley], b. 2/8/1903 in Ossipee; second; Ralph Colby (millman, 24, Moultonboro) and Pearl Fall (19, Ossipee)
daughter [Beatrice E.], b. 9/11/1908 in Ossipee; third; Daniel Colby (laborer, Ossipee) and Josie Evans (Ossipee)
stillborn son, b. 6/2/1911 in Ossipee; third; Plummer Colby (laborer, Moultonboro) and Etta Bean (Ossipee)
daughter, b. 4/28/1919; sixth; Plummer Colby (laborer, Tuftonboro) and Etta Bean (Ossipee)
Arthur, b. 10/6/1915; fifth; Plummer Colby (laborer, Ossipee) and Etta Bean (Ossipee)
Arthur R., b. 3/17/1942; third; Royal P. Colby (Ossipee) and Florence L. Littlefield (Oakland)
Etta M., b. 2/17/1895; Daniel Colby and Mary J. Evans (1960)
Marie Carroll, b. 12/18/1936; first; Royal P. Colby (Ossipee) and Florence Littlefield (Oakline, ME)
May Electa, b. 6/25/1938; second; Royal Plummer Colby (Ctr. Ossipee) and Louise F. Littlefield (Oakland)
Norma D., b. 7/14/1932; seventh; Plummer Colby (Ossipee) and Etta Bean (Ossipee)
Plummer, b. 1/22/1914; fourth; Plummer Colby (laborer, Ossipee) and Etta Bean (Ossipee)
Robert Stephen, b. 1/10/1941; third; Royal Plummer Colby (Ossipee) and Florence L. Littlefield (Oakland)
Stephen Rice, b. 8/29/1950; second; George Colby (MA) and Betsy Foxcroft (ME)

COLE,
John, b. 6/21/1897 in Ossipee; eighth; Joseph B. Cole (farmer, 59, Cornish, ME) and Emma Nason (44, Wakefield)

COMO,
Andrea Barbara, b. 9/1/1976; Ronald Joseph Como and Linda Sue DeRochemont

Jennifer Lee, b. 12/26/1989; William John Como and Catherine Mary Maker

CONNER [see Connor],
son [Harlan E.], b. 12/28/1910 in Ossipee; fifth; Edwin C. Conner (teacher, Ossipee) and Mary E. ----- (Stanstead, PI)
stillborn son, b. 1/3/1920; first; Arthur Conner (laborer, Ossipee) and Manie Pascoe (Freedom)
Arthur N., b. 3/1/1890; William Conner (NH) and Annie Hodgdon (Quebec) (1955)
Donald Albert, b. 5/15/1936; first; Albert H. D. Conner (Exeter) and Carolyn L. Langley (David City, NE)
Julian, b. 5/28/1925; first; Charles E. Conner (Exeter) and Freda Eldridge (Ossipee)
Lois A., b. 7/23/1932; third; John Conner (Ossipee) and Evelyn Sargent (Ossipee)
Richard E., b. 5/3/1928; second; Charles E. Conner (Exeter) and Elfreda Eldridge (Ossipee)
William N., b. 7/4/1922; second; Arthur N. Conner (chauffeur, Ossipee) and Mamie Pascoe (Freedom)

CONNOR [see Conner],
Daniel Charles, b. 1/11/1984; Mark Alan Connor, Sr. and Anita Diane Benoit
Jennifer Aileen, b. 10/19/1982; Raymond Francis Connor and Lisa Jane Potter
John E., b. 4/30/1931; second; John B. Connor (Exeter) and Evelyn Sargent (Ossipee)
Raymond, b. 5/29/1897 in Ossipee; first; Fred E. Connor (printer, 26, Ossipee) and Maud Hodges (21, Ossipee)
Roland Edwin, b. 4/1/1944; second; Albert H. Connor (Exeter) and Carolyn L. Langley (David City, NE)
William Marshall, b. 12/26/1984; Mark Alan Connor, Sr. and Anita Diane Benoit

COOK,
son [Clayton], b. 4/4/1904 in Ossipee; third; William Cook (laborer, 33, Porter) and Rosa Lewis (24, Wolfeboro)
son [Howard E.], b. 7/19/1905 in Ossipee; second; Walter Cook (farming, 29, Ossipee) and Hattie Philbrick (22, Tuftonboro)
son, b. 11/23/1906 in Ossipee; third; Walter Cook (laborer, Ossipee) and ----- Philbrick (Ossipee)
son, b. 6/13/1911 in Ossipee; fourth; Walter R. Cook (laborer, Ossipee) and Hattie A. Philbrick (Wolfeboro)

child, b. 2/21/1930; third; Clayton Cook (Ossipee) and Beatrice Canney (Ossipee)
Amber Virginia, b. 10/11/1980; Malcolm W. Cook and Judith Marion Mason
Arthur C., b. 7/17/1954; second; Arthur E. Cook (NH) and Carolyn A. Nichols (NH)
Arthur E., b. 6/24/1927; second; Clayton R. Cook and Beatrice M. Canney (Ossipee)
Glen Richard, b. 2/22/1935; fourth; Clayton Cook (Ossipee) and Beatrice Canney (Ossipee)
Malcolm Wayne, b. 5/6/1952; first; Arthur Cook (NH) and Carolyn Nichols (NH)
Meredith Joan, b. 4/12/1938; fourth; Ralph Clayton Cook (Ctr. Ossipee) and Beatrice May Canney (Ossipee)
Mickey Alan, b. 4/15/1975; Arthur Clayton Cook and Kimberley Alan Rowell
Ricky Elwin, b. 8/2/1956; third; Arthur E. Cook (NH) and Carolyn A. Nichols (NH)
Virginia Arlene, b. 1/17/1926; first; Clayton Cook (Ossipee) and Beatrice Canney (Ossipee)

COOMBS,
Linda J., b. 6/10/1954; second; Victor R. Coombs (MA) and Barbara M. Pare (MA)

COOPER,
Alisha Paige, b. 3/15/1985; David Wellington Cooper and Susan Marjorie Dickinson
Kathryn Ashley, b. 5/23/1989; David Wellington Cooper, Jr. and Susan Dickinson

COPP,
son [Ralph E.], b. 11/14/1909 in Ossipee; first; Leroy Copp (teamster) and Lizzie Wood (Ossipee)
daughter [Ruth E.], b. 5/13/1911 in Ossipee; second; Arthur L. Copp (laborer, Bangor, ME) and Elizabeth Wood (Ossipee)
daughter, b. 4/19/1916; fourth; Arthur L. Copp (teamster, Bangor, ME) and Rena Bean (Ossipee)
Ann Priscilla, b. 10/2/1937; fourth; Ralph Copp (Ossipee) and Louise Nichols (Ossipee)
Barbara M., b. 3/4/1933; second; Ralph Copp (Ossipee) and Louise Nichols (Ossipee)
Corey R., b. 3/22/1969; Ralph E. Copp, Jr. and Barbara A. Joyce
Dana Simon, b. 10/30/1927; fifth; Maynard Copp (Orrington, ME) and Nora F. Eldridge (Ossipee)

Donald E., b. 9/1/1931; first; Ralph Copp (Ossipee) and Louise Nichols (Ossipee)
Francis, b. 8/17/1921; second; Maynard Copp (laborer, Bangor, ME) and Nora Eldridge (Ossipee)
Harlam W., b. 9/23/1918; first; Owen C. Copp (teamster, Orrington, ME) and Rose I. Welch (Ossipee)
Mildred E., b. 4/20/1924; third; Maynard Copp (Bangor, ME) and Nora Eldridge (Ossipee)
Ralph Elton, Jr., b. 6/13/1939; fourth; Ralph Elton Copp (Ossipee) and Louise Nichols (Ctr. Ossipee)
Richard O., b. 2/14/1922; second; Owen Copp (laborer, Orrington, ME) and Rose Welch (Ossipee)
Robert Nichols, b. 9/1/1936; third; Ralph Copp (Ossipee) and Louise Nichols (Ossipee)
Thomas B., b. 9/6/1920; first; Maynard Copp (teamster, Bangor, ME) and Nora Eldridge (Ossipee)
Timothy J., b. 2/27/1964; first; Ralph Copp, Jr. and Barbara Joyce
William M., b. 11/1/1926; fourth; Maynard Copp (Orrington, ME) and Nora Eldridge (Ossipee)

COPPLESTONE,
Anna Miriam, b. 11/9/1984; Robert Jeffrey Copplestone and Sarah Leigh Branin

CORCORAN,
McKleary Dane, b. 5/22/1998 in Wolfeboro; Robert Holmes Corcoran, Jr. and Debra Elizabeth Esposito

CORROW,
Jeremy Lee, b. 1/18/1980; Wendell F. Corrow and Sharon L. Ripley
Karen B., b. 7/1/1968; Wendell F. Corrow and Brenda E. Bodwell

COSLETT,
Brandi Lee, b. 2/24/1979; John Scott Coslett and Leeann Louise Colbath

COUGHLIN,
child, b. 5/2/1927; Edward G. Coughlin (Springvale, ME) and Alice L. Doe (Ossipee)
Edward G., Jr., b. 7/25/1924; first; Edward G. Coughlin (Portsmouth) and Alice L. Doe (Ossipee)

COUSINS,
Jason Richard, b. 11/27/1983; Richard Brian Cousins and Noreen Mary Piche

Jessica Rose, b. 11/21/1981; Richard Brian Cousins and Noreen Mary Piche

COX,
Ann, b. 8/15/1969; Frederic L. Cox and Ellen Bowe
Jane, b. 4/23/1965; first; Frederic L. Cox and Ellen Bowe
Martha, b. 4/14/1967; second; Frederic L. Cox and Ellen Bowe

CRAM,
Annie Lamie, b. 2/26/1936; Raymond Perry (Canada) and Mary Cram (Moultonboro)
Kirk Bernard, b. 1/6/1984; Marshall Grant Cram and Leona Jan Samuelson

CRESSEY,
Corey Stephen, b. 4/2/1991; Wayne Llewellyn Cressey and Terry Lynn Verrill
Elizabeth Ann, b. 3/9/1984; Albert Ebin Cressey and Kim Yvonne Bellini
Eric Andrew, b. 4/26/1989; Wayne Llewellyn Cressey and Terry Lynn Verrill
Nicole Lynn, b. 5/4/1987; Wayne L. Cressey and Terry Lynn Verrill
Philip Wayne, b. 6/6/1979; Wayne Llewellyn Cressey and Betsy Carol Drew
Stephanie Frances, b. 3/18/1982; Wayne L. Cressey and Betsy Carol Drew

CROWELL,
Jennifer Marie, b. 9/29/1981; Thomas Michael Crowell and Laura Theo Calkins

CROWLEY,
Romona Lee, b. 1/22/1956; first; Wilfred F. Crowley (NH) and Marion L. Sawyer (ME)

CULLEN,
Dana Bruce, Jr., b. 1/28/1987; Dana Bruce Cullen and Belinda Williams

CUMMINGS,
Lois Ann, b. 2/7/1943; fourth; Merle L. Cummings (Harrison, ME) and Helen A. Lewis (Westbrook, ME)
Wayne Allen, b. 8/18/1941; third; Merle L. Cummings (Harrison, ME) and Helen Arline Lewis (Westbrook, ME)

CURRIER,
son, b. 7/12/1898 in Ossipee; third; Joseph Currier (laborer, 25, Canada) and Adelia Mattress (18, Moultonboro)
Ann R., b. 12/10/1947; second; John M. Currier (Ossipee) and Janet Downs (Pine Bluff, AR)
David L. A., b. 12/18/1937; sixth; Frank Currier (Newburyport, MA) and Ruth Morse (Laconia)
John M., Jr., b. 8/1/1953; third; John Currier (NH) and Janet Dewrs (AR)
Jon Robin, b. 5/30/1960; first; Jesse A. Currier, Jr. and June M. Lee

CUSTEAU,
daughter, b. 11/13/1999 in N. Conway; Frank Custeau and Anna Custeau
Frank Eli, Jr., b. 11/30/1998 in Wolfeboro; Frank Eli Custeau and Anna Marie Baldwin
Juliette Rose, b. 10/23/1997 in Wolfeboro; Frank Eli Custeau and Anna Marie Baldwin

CUTTING,
daughter, b. 1/1/1897 in Ossipee; second; Sherman Cutting (farmer, 31, Weld, ME) and Ida Sanborn (19, Parsonsfield, ME)

DAIGLE,
Sara Jean, b. 7/3/1992; Paul Michael Daigle and Mary Josephine Horgan

DALE,
Cynthia Lynn, b. 7/24/1951; first; Arthur Dale (England) and Gertrude Richards (Atlanta, GA)
Marcia A., b. 3/7/1953; second; Arthur Dale (England) and Gertrude Richards (GA)
Maria A., b. 3/7/1953; third; Arthur Dale (England) and Gertrude Richards (GA)
Susan, b. 7/18/1957; fourth; Arthur J. Dale (Sheffield, England) and Gertrude E. Richards (Atlanta, GA)

DAMON,
Christina Lee, b. 12/18/1980; Christopher Stephen Damon and Dorcas Ann Margeson

DARLING,
Chester A., b. 9/10/1916; first; Henry Darling (laborer, Ossipee) and Ethel I. Davis (Dorchester, MA); residence - Bangor, ME

DAVIDSON,
Kimberly Ann, b. 2/14/1989; William Henry Davidson and Vicki Sue Parkhurst

DAVIES,
John Anthony, b. 10/5/1990; John Anthony Davies and Wendy Jo Savin

DAVIS,
son [Ralph T.], b. 5/22/1889; Albion L. Davis (laborer, Effingham) and Ella F. Davis (Ossipee)
son, b. 9/30/1889; John C. Davis (teamster, Tamworth) and Minnie A. Mason (Ossipee)
son, b. 12/16/1896 in Ossipee; third; Albion Davis (laborer, 51, Effingham) and Ella A. Thurley (34, Ossipee)
daughter, b. 3/4/1905 in Ossipee; third; Alvah Davis (farmer, 28, Ossipee) and Florence Wiggin (26, Ossipee)
son, b. 6/17/1906 in Ossipee; fourth; Alvah Davis (farmer, Ossipee) and Lizzie Wiggin (Ossipee)
son, b. 7/3/1911 in Ossipee; seventh; Albion Davis (farmer, Ossipee) and Florence B. Wiggin (Ossipee)
child, b. 4/9/1925; first; Walter M. Davis (Malden, MA) and Margaret P. Gale (Parsonsfield, ME)
Alan G., b. 1/23/1959; third; Merland Davis (Ossipee) and Lucille Davis (S. Hiram, ME)
Andrea Lynne, b. 8/25/1984; Walter Merland Davis and Deborah Lee Dearborn
Clifford K., b. 2/13/1892; John C. Davis (NH) and Minnie A. Nason (NH) (1957)
Cynthia, b. 4/27/1962; fourth; Merland Davis and Lucille Holland
Danna Kay, b. 4/9/1938; third; Walter M. Davis (Malden) and Margaret Pearl Gale (Parsonsfield)
Errol Heath, b. 7/14/1986; Alan G. Davis and Saima J. Breed
Gloria A., b. 12/1/1957; second; Merland Davis (NH) and Lucille F. Holland (S. Hiram, ME)
Joanne Margaret, b. 2/7/1956; first; John E. Davis (NH) and Constance Honeybone (England)
Joshua Michael, b. 9/17/1989; Rickey Allen Davis and Michele Ann Forte
Katie Michelle, b. 7/19/1987; Walter M. Davis and Deborah L. Dearborn
Lisa A., b. 6/20/1962; third; Johny Davis and Ramona Bunker
Merland F., b. 9/22/1928; second; Walter M. Davis (Malden, MA) and Margaret Gale (Parsonsfield, ME)
Paul Edward, b. 12/22/1985; Walter Merland Davis and Deborah Lee Dearborn
Walter Merland, b. 1/24/1956; first; Merland F. Davis (NH) and Lucille F. Holland (ME)

Willard P., b. 11/13/1928; second; Willard R. Davis (Malden, MA) and
Doris Parker (Whitefield)

DAVISON,
Dianna J., b. 6/10/1961; third; Robert Davison and Irene F. Welch
Harry J., b. 3/2/1955; second; Robert Davison (NS) and Irene Welch (NH)
Robert L., Jr., b. 6/26/1953; first; Robert Davison (NS) and Irene Welch (NH)

DAY,
Abigail White, b. 6/5/1980; Douglas George Day and Helen May White
Patricia Lou, b. 2/13/1948; fourth; Roland E. Day (Kezar Falls, ME) and Arlene E. Day (Brownfield, ME)
Scott E., b. 12/27/1968; Earle C. Day and Nancy L. Adams
Tammy Louise, b. 10/3/1968; Erwin F. Day and Carlyne W. Eldridge
Verne E., b. 9/28/1948; first; Forrest E. Day (Kezar Falls, ME) and Carlyne W. Eldridge (Milton)

DEBLOIS,
Charles E., b. 11/9/1943; first; Remi A. DeBlois (Laconia) and Gertrude F. Garneau (Berlin)

DEBOW,
Currie Hunter, b. 10/14/1992; Currie Newton Jones DeBow and Gretchen Irene DeBow Jones

DEBUTTS,
Golden Elaine, b. 1/21/1941; second; Daniel Brynard DeButts (Dorchester, MA) and Velma Pearl Emack (Ossipee)
Merland C., b. 11/30/1942; second; Daniel B. DeButts (Dorchester, MA) and Velma P. Emack (Ctr. Ossipee)

DECATUR,
Matthew Michael, b. 11/7/1990; Stephen Ernest Decatur and Teresa Lynn Van Straten

DEDEUS,
Hilbert, Jr., b. 2/26/1986; Hilbert DeDeus and Elana Anne Roscillo

DEGAGNE,
Joshua Abel, b. 8/26/1979; Phillip Girard DeGagne and Suzanne Mary Low

DEIGHAN,
Joseph Henry, b. 2/27/2001 in Rochester; Joseph Deighan and Karen Deighan

DELANO,
Joshua Earl, b. 1/7/1980; Ralph Clark Delano and Christina Ann N. Gagnon

DELK,
Jeremy Paul, b. 5/12/1970; David Maurice Delk and Devon Elizabeth Eckhoff

DELP,
Startlett Marie, b. 3/13/1989; David Barry Delp and Diane Mariam Scripture

DEMAINE,
Autumn Lee, b. 1/14/1982; Douglas James Demaine and Debra Anna Dubois
Melissa, b. 12/15/1978; Douglas James Demaine and Debra Anna Dubois

DEMERITT,
daughter, b. 10/2/1888; fifth; Calvin S. Demeritt (merchant, Ossipee) and Anna Metcalf (Auburn, ME)

DENNIS,
Leslie Allen, b. 10/14/1939; first; Leslie D. Stewart and Mildred A. Dennis (Wilmington, DE)

DENSE,
James Alfred, b. 6/13/1941; third; Harold George Dense (Swartwood, NY) and Dorothy Evelyn Morse (Franklin)

DEUSO,
Erin Marie, b. 6/28/1989; Brian Wayne Deuso and Bridgetta Louise Kempf

DEVORK,
Constance P., b. 8/5/1946; first; Harold Devork (Steubensville, OH) and Grace M. Dale (Sheffield, England)

DEWITT,
son, b. 7/4/1913; fifth; Arthur DeWitt (laborer, Eaton) and Myrtle Jones (Conway)

Heidi Elin, b. 4/18/1996 in N. Conway; Michael Everett Dewitt and Ingrid Dorothea Carlson
Kristina Ingrid, b. 5/14/1994 in N. Conway; Michale E. DeWitt and Ingrid D. Carlson

DIAMOND,
Connor James, b. 12/11/1995 in Wolfeboro; Eric James Diamond and Diane Marie Johnson
Sean Michael, b. 2/15/1994 in Wolfeboro; Eric J. Diamond and Diane M. Johnson

DICAPUA,
Ashley Marie, b. 6/12/1994 in Dover; Edmond C. DiCapua and Linda A. Titus
Stephanie Monique, b. 10/13/1990; Edmund Charles DiCapua and Linda Ann Titus

DILLER,
Peter Welles, b. 8/26/1941; first; Kendrick Welles Diller (Montclair, NJ) and Gretchen Davis (Dorchester, MA)

DINSMORE,
son, b. 8/15/1896 in Ossipee; first; Fred M. Dinsmore (21, Jackson) and Josie Mansfield (20, Fryeburg, ME)

DOE,
son [Frank B., Jr.], b. 10/21/1899 in Ossipee; first; Benjamin F. Doe (sectionhand, 28, Ossipee) and Clarinda Davis (18, Effingham)
daughter [Alice L.], b. 4/22/1901 in Ossipee; second; Benjamin F. Doe (sectionman, 29, Ossipee) and Clarinda Davis (19, Effingham)
daughter, b. 11/18/1903 in Ossipee; third; Frank B. Doe (section man, 31, Ossipee) and Clarinda Davis (21, Effingham)
son, b. 11/11/1905 in Ossipee; fourth; Frank B. Doe (section hand, 33, Ossipee) and Clara Davis (23, Effingham)
son [Walter E.], b. 10/10/1906 in Ossipee; fifth; Frank B. Doe (section hand, Ossipee) and Clara Davis (Effingham)
daughter, b. 10/29/1909 in Ossipee; sixth; Frank B. Doe (section hand, Ossipee) and Clara Davis (Effingham)
Edward David, b. 4/4/1956; fifth; Walter E. Doe (NH) and Evelyn M. Wasson (NH)
Edwin A., b. 2/1/1931; second; Frank Doe, Jr. (Ossipee) and Lena L. Eaton (Freedom)
Gordon E., b. 6/2/1933; third; Frank B. Doe (Ossipee) and Lena L. Eaton (Freedom)

Helen Elaine, b. 3/14/1940; second; Walter E. Doe (Ossipee) and Evelyn
M. Doe (Ossipee)
Jennifer Marie, b. 12/9/1981; Russell James Doe and Dawn Marie Eldridge
Sallie A., b. 8/1/1947; fourth; Walter E. Doe (W. Ossipee) and Evelyn M.
Wasson (Ossipee)
Sandra Jean, b. 12/12/1945; third; Walter E. Doe (Ossipee) and Evelyn
Wasson (Ossipee)
Walter Everett, b. 8/11/1935; first; Walter E. Doe (W. Ossipee) and Evelyn
Wasson (Ctr. Ossipee)

DOHERTY,
John Howard, b. 7/26/1972; Paul David Doherty and Pamelia Jane Fox

DOLIBER,
Maria Carole, b. 2/24/1989; Benjamin Godfrey Doliber and Carolann
Shannon

DOMBEK,
Anne Lillian, b. 2/4/1988; Joseph S. Dombek and Jacqueline P. Canuel
Elizabeth Naomi, b. 12/26/1986; Joseph S. Dombek and Jacqueline P.
Canuel

DONNELLY,
Erin Jill, b. 3/5/1982; Peter Richard Donnelly and Maryann Lynch

DORAN,
Ashley Elizabeth, b. 12/31/1989; Craig Evan Doran and Christina Lynn
LaBrie

DORE,
son, b. 7/7/1888; fourth; Everett Dore (farmer, Middleton, MA) and Rose E.
Dore (Limington, ME)
son, b. 10/26/1894 in Ossipee; sixth; Everett Dore (farmer, 44, Ossipee)
and Rosa Smith (40, Limington, ME)
Agnes, b. 10/6/1908 in Ossipee; first; Leroy H. Dore (laborer, Ossipee)
and Blanche E. Davis (Effingham)
Edna Rose, b. 11/27/1937; first; Walter Dore (Ossipee) and Rose Stanley
(Farmington)
Eldora M., b. 9/14/1962; second; Ernest Dore and Irene Huntress
Ernest G., Jr., b. 8/11/1961; first; Ernest G. Dore and Irene Huntress
Kodi Alexander, b. 1/31/1995 in Wolfeboro; Roger Allen Dore and Kathryn
Viola Avery
Linda L., b. 5/19/1947; third; Lewis A. Dore (Wolfeboro) and Evelyn L.
Eldridge (Ossipee)

Luke R., b. 9/9/1963; third; Ernest G. Dore and Irene Huntress
Margaret A., b. 7/10/1942; first; Lewis A. Dore (Wolfeboro) and Evelyn L. Eldridge (Ossipee)
Randy W., b. 6/11/1957; first; George W. Dore (NH) and Linda L. Britton (NH)
Roxanne, b. 3/9/1960; second; George W. Dore and Linda L. Britton
Ruth M., b. 3/9/1965; fourth; George W. Dore and Linda L. Britton
Samantha K., b. 10/18/1986; Roger A. Dore and Kathryn V. Avery
Skyla Morgan, b. 9/17/1998 in N. Conway; George Lawrence Dore and Jennifer Anne Deal

DORR,
Pamela M., b. 3/25/1962; fourth; Horace Dorr, Jr. and Dorothy M. Towle

DOUVILLE,
Deanna May, b. 3/10/1941; second; Romeo Leo Douville (Willimansett, MA) and Dorothy E. Welch (Ossipee)

DOW,
Aubri Lisa, b. 2/3/1977; Wayne Arnold Dow and Marilyn Louise McGloin
Chad Matthew, b. 4/7/1982; Curtis Marvin Dow and Deborah Lynne Garland
Clay Mathew, b. 4/8/1987; Curtis Marvin Dow and Deborah Lynn Garland
Curtis M., b. 6/6/1963; third; Ellis M. Dow and Janet Taylor
Don LeRoy, b. 4/14/1950; fourth; Roland Dow (NH) and Greta May (VT)
Ellis Milton, b. 6/6/1935; seventh; Ellis M. Dow (Moultonboro) and Agnes M. Phinney (Rumford Falls, ME)
Frances A., b. 2/10/1925; second; Ellis M. Dow (Moultonboro) and Agnes Phinney (Rumford Falls, ME)
Jessica Marie, b. 4/27/1985; Rodney Ernest Dow and Sandra Lee Yanov
Johnathan Stephen, b. 6/8/1973; Stephen Roland Dow and Lynda Lee Johnson
Karen M., b. 3/10/1958; second; Ellis M. Dow (Wolfeboro) and Janet Taylor (Parsonsfield, ME)
Marena Ann, b. 9/15/1990; Ellis Milton Dow and Carol Suzanne Lessard
Mathew Ellis, b. 9/29/1995 in Wolfeboro; Ellis Milton Dow III and Carol Suzanne Lessard
Matthew Eric, b. 9/23/1991; Rodney Ernest Dow and Julie Louise Wheeler
Meredith J., b. 3/7/1933; sixth; Ellis M. Dow (Moultonboro) and Agnes Phinney (Rumford Falls, ME)
Michael Thomas, b. 7/2/1986; Rodney Ernest Dow and Sandra Lee Yanov
Rodney Christian, b. 11/21/1975; Stephen R. Dow and Lynda Lee Johnson
Virginia A., b. 7/1/1926; third; Ellis Dow (Moultonboro) and Agnes Phinney (Rumford Falls)

Wayne A., b. 11/18/1947; second; Roland D. Dow (Ossipee) and Greta E. May (Canaan, VT)
Winona Marion, b. 6/13/1937; eighth; Ellis Dow (Moultonboro) and Agnes Phinney (Rumford, ME)

DOWNING,
Abigail Suzanne, b. 2/8/1986; Joel Paul Downing and Debra Jean Anderson
Carolyn S., b. 4/15/1962; fifth; Donald Downing and Caroline Wise
Geoffrey A., b. 7/3/1959; third; Donald Downing (Wolfeboro) and Carolyn Wise (Bath, NY)
Jackson, b. 1/17/1993 in Wolfeboro; Joel Downing and Fern Marie Muise
Jared Paul, b. 2/8/1986; Joel Paul Downing and Debra Jean Anderson
Jessica Elaine, b. 4/3/1981; Geoffrey Alan Downing and Ellen Marie Wallace
Joel P., b. 1/11/1961; fourth; Donald Downing and Caroline Wise
Lawrence E., b. 2/4/1936; Stephen E. Downing (Milton) and Madeline ----- (N. Conway)
Leola Janice, b. 8/5/1934; first; Steve E. Downing (Milton) and Madeline Brown (N. Conway)
Saylee J., b. 4/17/1964; fifth; Donald Downing and Caroline Wise

DOWNS,
child, b. 10/23/1927; Frank Downs (Milton) and Edna H. Johnson (Rochester)
Elias E., b. 12/20/1923; second; Elmer E. Downs (Tamworth) and Ada A. Blodgett (Brookline, MA)

DRAKE,
daughter, b. 4/23/1893 in Ossipee; first; B. M. Drake (laborer, Ossipee) and L. L. Farnham (Ossipee)

DRAKELY,
Clayton Walter, b. 10/3/1996 in Wolfeboro; Michael Drakely and Jessica Mae Kolb

DREW,
Ashley Marie, b. 10/18/1991; Richard Wendell Drew and Jacqueline Rae Berry
Betsy Carol, b. 4/9/1952; third; Philip Drew (NH) and Frances Eldridge (NH)
Beverley Ann, b. 9/17/1943; second; Philip D. Drew (Sandwich) and Frances J. Eldridge (Tamworth)
Courtney Frances, b. 10/21/1998 in Wolfeboro; Daniel Steven Drew and Terri Lee Brooks

Danella Evelyn, b. 7/2/1970; Charles Lawrence Drew and Virginia H. Adjutant
David P., b. 11/3/1963; second; Wendell R. Drew and Arlene LaFreniere
Dennis E., b. 6/14/1954; second; Selden E. Drew (NH) and Dorothy P. Buswell (NH)
James, b. 2/5/1966; first; Charles L. Drew and Virginia H. Adjutant
Judith L., b. 1/22/1968; Wendell R. Drew and Arlene P. LaFreniere
Kathleen Joy, b. 6/4/1974; Tony Paul Drew and Helen Elizabeth Loring
Kyle Michael, b. 8/4/1988; Richard W. Drew and Jacqueline R. Berry
Lori L., b. 3/27/1967; second; Charles L. Drew and Virginia H. Adjutant
Matthew Steven, b. 9/10/2001 in Wolfeboro; Daniel Drew and Terri Drew
Richard W., b. 8/8/1962; first; Wendell Drew and Arlene LaFreniere
Sandra Jeanne, b. 10/29/1979; Wendell Richard Drew and Arlene Patricia Lafreniere
Wendall Richard, b. 8/12/1941; third; Phillip William Drew (Sandwich) and Frances Josie Eldridge (Tamworth)

DROWN,
daughter [Evelyn D.], b. 4/25/1912; fourth; Joel Drown (laborer, Ossipee) and Maud Gilman (Denmark, ME)
Edgar I., b. 12/21/1892; first; Steven D. Drown (Eaton) and Carrie C. Peavey (Farmington) (1942)
Eleanor, b. 1/21/1911 in Ossipee; first; Howard Drown (laborer, Ossipee) and Eliza Towle (Madison)
Mabel, b. 2/10/1884; Elijah A. Drown (Eaton) and Victoria Harriman (Eaton) (1942)
Margie V., b. 8/7/1895; Steven D. Drown (Eaton) and Carrie C. Peavey (Farmington) (1942)
William F., b. 5/13/1933; tenth; Edgar Drown (Ossipee) and Irene Newcombe (Westley, RI)

DROWNS,
son, b. 9/16/1889; Elijah Drowns (laborer, Eaton) and Victoria Drowns (Eaton)
Charles L., Jr., b. 9/5/1945; first; Charles S. Drowns (Newfield, ME) and Sadie M. Tappan (Moultonboro)

DRUMEA,
Agnes Iris, b. 2/21/2001 in Portland, ME; Flavius Drumea and Irina Gogu

DUCHARME,
Armand Ernest, b. 5/6/1956; third; Joseph P. Ducharme (ME) and Norma N. McDowell (PA)

DUCHESNE,
Carol Elizabeth, b. 10/25/1970; Joseph Henry Duchesne and Jacqueline Seeckts
Joseph Adam, b. 1/22/1976; Joseph Henry Duchesne and Jacqueline N. Seeckts

DUFFANY [see Duffoney],
Eloise Nancy, b. 3/16/1936; fifth; Leo Duffany (Fall River, MA) and Elsie Lockwood (Lynn, MA)

DUFFONEY [see Duffany],
Mary R., b. 7/27/1931; third; Leo F. Duffoney (Fall River, MA) and Elsie M. Lockwood (Lynn, MA)

DUNFIELD,
son, b. 11/19/1896 in Ossipee; first; Charles W. Dunfield (farmer, 34, Bradford) and Emily W. Sinclair (25, Ossipee)
daughter, b. 4/28/1899 in Ossipee; third; Charles W. Dunfield (farmer) and Emily Sinclair (Ossipee)
Charles Harry, b. 4/14/1898 in Ossipee; second; Charles W. Dunfield (farmer, 36, Bradford) and Emily W. Sinclair (27, Ossipee)

DUPUIS,
Bruce M., b. 9/4/1963; second; Alan J. Dupuis and Catherine Moulton
James, b. 11/27/1965; third; Alan J. Dupuis and Catherine J. Moulton

EASTMAN,
David W., b. 9/10/1964; first; David Eastman and Mildred Buchanan
Felene M., b. 8/12/1921; first; Anna O. Eastman (Milan)
Kathryn Anna-Marie, b. 11/15/1991; Jeffrey Gene Eastman and Tara K. L. Burdette

EBEL,
Julie A., b. 9/1/1960; third; Maximmillian Ebel and Doris R. Eckert
Karen E., b. 10/14/1954; first; Max. F. J. Ebel, Jr. (Germany) and Doris I. R. Eckert (Germany)
Linda M., b. 9/13/1958; second; Maximilian F. Ebel, Jr. (Germany) and Doris R. Eckert (Germany)

ECKHOFF,
Peter B., b. 12/8/1959; fourth; John Eckhoff, Jr. (Bronx, NY) and Ruth Bowlend (Stanton Is., NY)
Sarah Frances, b. 7/29/1984; Peter Bowlend Eckhoff and Elaine Marie Jones

Steven J., b. 12/2/1957; third; John Eckhoff, Jr. (NY) and Ruth C. Bowlend (NY)

EDGERLY,
Patricia A., b. 3/27/1935; second; Herman D. Edgerly (Chocorua) and Natalie White (W. Ossipee)
Sandra N., b. 10/9/1933; first; Herman D. Edgerly (Chocorua) and Natalie White (Ossipee)

EDWARDS,
Adam Roy, b. 4/29/1980; Keith Elwin Edwards and Sonia Marie Maxfield
Wanda L., b. 7/6/1954; first; Lewis E. Edwards (NH) and Leola J. Downing (NH)

EGAN,
Shannon Elizabeth, b. 8/18/1988; Susan A. Egan

EISCHEN,
Benjamin M., b. 2/14/1987; Joseph E. Eischen and Patricia J. Fuller

ELDRIDGE,
son, b. 4/26/1889; Harrison Eldridge (laborer, Ossipee) and Laura E. Eldredge (Ossipee)
son, b. 11/23/1889; Ivory Eldridge (laborer, Ossipee) and Emma P. Welch (Ossipee)
son, b. 3/7/1890 in Ossipee; fourth; William Eldridge (farmer, Ossipee) and Rosena Eldredge (Ossipee)
son, b. 4/10/1897 in Ossipee; first; George Eldridge (laborer, 33, Ossipee) and Ida Welch (22, Ossipee)
daughter [Verna], b. 1/22/1898 in Ossipee; first; Everett Eldridge (teamster, 24, Ossipee) and Nettie Pike (18, Ossipee)
son, b. 6/29/1898 in Ossipee; third; Orrin Eldridge (laborer, 35, Freedom) and Sarah Goodwin (23, Eaton)
daughter, b. 1/20/1899 in Ossipee; first; Woodbury Eldridge (laborer, 31, Ossipee) and Dora B. White (15, Ossipee)
daughter, b. 4/25/1899 in Ossipee; third; Eliza Eldridge (22, Ossipee)
daughter, b. 4/25/1899 in Ossipee; fourth; Eliza Eldridge (22, Ossipee)
daughter, b. 8/5/1900 in Ossipee; second; George Eldridge (laborer, 36, Ossipee) and Ida Welch (23, Ossipee)
son, b. 8/11/1900 in Ossipee; first; Herbert Eldridge (laborer, 23, Ossipee) and Lillie Welch (20, Ossipee)
daughter, b. 10/24/1901 in Ossipee; first; Dana Eldridge (laborer, 19, Ossipee) and Susie A. Wiggin (19, Tuftonboro)
son, b. 4/1/1902 in Ossipee; fourth; Orrin Eldridge (laborer, 32, Freedom) and Sarah E. Goodwin (28, Eaton)

son, b. 5/22/1902 in Ossipee; fifth; Orodon Eldridge (laborer, 40, Ossipee) and Lucy Welch (25, Ossipee)

son, b. 5/2/1903 in Ossipee; sixth; John P. Eldridge (laborer, 30, Ossipee) and Emma Welch (25, Ossipee)

daughter [Hazel E.], b. 5/21/1904 in Ossipee; first; Edward Eldridge (laborer, 28, Ossipee) and ----- Wilkins (21, Ossipee); parent's color - "B"

daughter, b. 10/1/1905 in Ossipee; fourth; Woodbury Eldridge (sawyer, 38, Ossipee) and Dora White (22, Ossipee)

daughter [Gladys Mabel], b. 6/15/1906 in Ossipee; seventh; John P. Eldridge (laborer, Ossipee) and Emma Welch (Ossipee)

stillborn son, b. 9/28/1906 in Ossipee; first; Myrtle Eldridge (Ossipee)

son [Louis R.], b. 12/6/1906 in Ossipee; third; Harrison Eldridge (laborer, Ossipee) and Georgia Williams (Ossipee)

son, b. 4/1/1907 in Ossipee; fifth; Everett Eldridge (laborer, Ossipee) and Nettie Pike (Ossipee)

son, b. 4/15/1907 in Ossipee; fourth; George Eldridge (laborer, Ossipee) and ----- Welch (Ossipee)

daughter, b. 9/30/1907 in Ossipee; third; Herbert Eldridge (laborer, Ossipee) and Lilla Welch (Ossipee)

son, b. 4/26/1908 in Ossipee; second; Lafayette Eldridge (laborer, Ossipee) and Myrtle Eldridge (Ossipee)

daughter [Lida B.], b. 8/4/1908 in Ossipee; first; Charles M. Eldridge (laborer, Ossipee) and Nettie Nichols (Ossipee)

son [Chauncey J.], b. 1/12/1910 in Ossipee; sixth; Everett Eldridge (laborer, Ossipee) and Nettie Pike (Ossipee)

daughter [Sylvia G.], b. 6/24/1910 in Ossipee; second; Charles M. Eldridge (laborer, Ossipee) and Nellie Nichols (Ossipee)

son [Clyde A.], b. 4/3/1911 in Ossipee; seventh; George H. Eldridge (laborer, Ossipee) and Idella Welch (Ossipee)

daughter, b. 1/7/1912; first; Wilbur Eldridge (laborer, Ossipee) and Myrtle Templeton (Ossipee)

daughter [Reta M.], b. 4/17/1912; seventh; Everett Eldridge (laborer, Ossipee) and Nettie Pike (Ossipee)

daughter, b. 5/3/1912; first; Perley Eldridge (laborer, Ossipee) and Maggie Templeton (Ossipee)

daughter, b. 2/12/1913; first; Maud Eldridge (Ossipee)

daughter, b. 2/12/1913; third; Herbert Eldridge (laborer, Ossipee) and Clara Wiggin (Ossipee)

daughter, b. 11/26/1913; second; Wilbur Eldridge (laborer, Ossipee) and Myrtle Templeton (Ossipee)

son [Harold], b. 12/24/1914; eighth; Everett Eldridge (laborer, Ossipee) and Nettie Pike (Ossipee)

daughter, b. 1/7/1915; third; Lafe Eldridge (laborer, Ossipee) and Myrtle Eldridge (Ossipee)

stillborn daughter, b. 7/25/1915; fifth; Herbert Eldridge (laborer, Ossipee) and Clara Wiggin (Ossipee)
son, b. 1/25/1916; third; Perley Eldridge (laborer, Ossipee) and Maggie Templeton (Ossipee)
son, b. 8/6/1916; second; Fred Eldridge (laborer, Ossipee) and Dora Sargent (Ossipee)
daughter, b. 8/21/1916; fourth; Lafe Eldridge (laborer, Ossipee) and Myrtle Eldridge (Ossipee)
son [Ralph C.], b. 12/22/1916; fourth; Charles M. Eldridge (farmer, Ossipee) and Nettie L. Nichols (Ossipee)
son [Andrew W.], b. 1/8/1917; first; Willie Eldridge (laborer, Ossipee) and Cora Williams (Ossipee)
daughter, b. 2/19/1920; fourth; Wilbur Eldridge (laborer, Ossipee) and Myrtle Templeton (Ossipee)
child, b. 12/21/1924; fifth; Wilbur Eldridge (Ossipee) and Myrtle Templeton (Ossipee)
child, b. 2/24/1925; fourth; Raymond Eldridge (Ossipee) and Etta Eldridge (Ossipee)
child, b. 3/4/1925; eleventh; Everett Eldridge (Ossipee) and Nettie Pike (Ossipee)
child, b. 12/1/1926; second; Carleton Eldridge (Ossipee) and Esther Haley (Tuftonboro)
child, b. 5/8/1927; seventh; Fred Eldridge (Ossipee) and Dora Sargent (Ossipee)
child, b. 12/25/1928; fourth; Chester Eldridge (Bartlett) and Hazel Eldridge (Ossipee)
child, b. 1/6/1928; fifth; Harry Eldridge (Ossipee) and Vivian Hobbs (Ossipee)
child, b. 1/30/1929; sixth; Raymond Eldridge (Ossipee) and Etta Eldridge (Ossipee)
child, b. 2/11/1930; twelfth; Wilbur Eldridge (Ossipee) and Myrtle Templeton (Ossipee)
child, b. 1/14/1931; seventh; Raymond Eldridge (Ossipee) and Etta Eldridge (Ossipee)
child, b. 1/11/1933; first; Lester H. Eldridge (Ossipee) and Florence Varney (Berwick, ME)
child, b. 1/11/1933; second; Lester H. Eldridge (Ossipee) and Florence Varney (Berwick, ME)
child, b. 7/28/1940; first; Clyde A. Eldridge (Ossipee) and Eleanor L. Gilman (Tamworth)
child, b. 4/28/1943; second; Clyde A. Eldridge (Ossipee) and Eleanor L. Gilman (Tamworth)
Agnes, b. 4/20/1918; third; Wilbur Eldridge (laborer, Ossipee) and Myrtle Templeton (Ossipee)

Ahial, b. 10/12/1921; fifth; Wilbur Eldridge (laborer, Ossipee) and Myrtle Templeton (Ossipee)

Alan C., b. 10/1/1948; seventh; Chester C. Eldridge (Bartlett) and Hazel E. Eldridge (Ossipee)

Alfred, b. 12/31/1901 in Ossipee; first; Herbert Eldridge (laborer, 21, Ossipee) and Melinda Littlefield (20, Conway)

Alfred P., b. 10/12/1947; sixth; Lawrence J. Eldridge (Ctr. Ossipee) and Rita E. Lane (Tamworth)

Alfred S., b. 5/13/1900; Fred W. Eldridge (NH) and Cora Eldridge (NH) (1957)

Angela May, b. 1/7/1975; Dennis Wayne Eldridge and Martha Jean Berry

Ashley Elizabeth, b. 7/15/1994 in Laconia; Carl R. Eldridge, Jr. and Carolee E. Erickson

Austin Melvin, b. 6/21/1922; Charles Eldridge (Ossipee) and Nettie Nichols (Ossipee) (1949)

Barbara, b. 8/26/1929; sixth; Harry Eldridge (Ossipee) and Vivian Hobbs (Ossipee)

Bernard H., b. 9/5/1928; sixth; Perley Eldridge (Ossipee) and Maggie Templeton (Ossipee)

Betsy Carol, b. 8/13/1949; third; John Eldridge (Ossipee) and Charlotte Weed (Waterville, ME)

Betty Ann, b. 3/4/1948; third; Clyde A. Eldridge (Ossipee) and Eleanor L. Gilman (Tamworth)

Beverley A., b. 10/26/1945; third; Charles P. Eldridge (Tamworth) and Reba Annette Vittum (Tamworth)

Bradley W., b. 10/15/1960; third; Donald W. Eldridge and Beverly A. Blake

Brenda E., b. 4/4/1945; first; Austin M. Eldridge (Ctr. Ossipee) and Barbara Drinkwater (Taunton, MA)

Brenda Joyce, b. 1/10/1952; first; Bernard Eldridge (NH) and Joyce Berry (NH)

Bruce E., b. 10/26/1933; sixth; Perley E. Eldridge (Ossipee) and Margaret Templeton (Ossipee)

Bruce Edward, b. 3/21/1946; first; H. P. Eldridge, Jr. (Ossipee) and Cristabel Stacy (Tamworth)

C. Brayton, b. 9/24/1954; second; Austin M. Eldridge (NH) and Barbara Drinkwater (NH)

Carl R., b. 2/22/1953; second; Robert Eldridge (NH) and Eva Judkins (NH)

Carl Robert, Jr., b. 3/29/1971; Carl Robert Eldridge and Kathleen Grace White

Celia, b. 1/15/1911 in Ossipee; sixth; Orodon Eldridge (laborer, Ossipee) and Lucy Welch (Ossipee)

Chandler Carl, b. 10/11/2000 in Laconia; Carl Eldridge and Carolee Eldridge

Charles P., b. 6/29/1942; Charles P. Eldridge (Ossipee) and Reba A. Vittum (Tamworth)

Cherie Lynn, b. 2/7/1981; Douglas Edward Eldridge and Mary Susan Dubois
Chester Clinton, b. 7/24/1950; fourth; Roy Eldridge (Ossipee) and Jean Campbell (Freedom)
Chris A., b. 2/27/1957; fourth; Harry Eldridge, Jr. (NH) and Christobell I. Stacey (NH)
Chris Ann, b. 4/12/1956; seventh; Roy Eldridge (NH) and Jean M. Campbell (MA)
Christopher Charles, b. 5/17/1991; Mark Allen Eldridge and Cynthia Ann Allen
Cindi L., b. 9/8/1961; first; Lawrence Eldridge, Jr. and Sandra R. Hamel
Cindy L., b. 9/1/1957; second; William Eldridge (NH) and Elizabeth M. Moulton (MA)
Clifford, b. 1/23/1898; Fred Eldridge (NH) and Cora Welch (NH) (1958)
Darlene A., b. 4/11/1958; second; Norman Eldridge (Ctr. Ossipee) and Marie E. Hodge (Wolfeboro)
Darlene A., b. 1/12/1962; fourth; Donald Eldridge and Beverly Blake
Darlene A., b. 3/28/1965; second; Richard C. Eldridge and Sandra L. Charles
Darrin M., b. 10/23/1968; Harry P. Eldridge, Jr. and Beverly F. Hillsgrove
Dawn M., b. 9/19/1959; second; Donald Eldridge (W. Ossipee) and Beverly Blake (Portland, ME)
Dawson Cole, b. 1/23/2000 in Wolfeboro; Michael Eldridge and Sarah Eldridge
Debra L., b. 8/23/1954; first; William H. Eldridge (NH) and Elizabeth M. Moore (MA)
Denise Elaine, b. 12/28/1972; Dennis Wayne Eldridge and Martha Jean Berry
Dennis Wayne, b. 9/3/1949; eighth; Raymond Eldridge (Ossipee) and Etta Eldridge (Ossipee)
Donald, b. 6/10/1930; sixth; Chester Eldridge (Bartlett) and Hazel Eldridge (Ossipee)
Donald L., b. 7/3/1931; third; Lester Eldridge (Ossipee) and Florence Varney (Berwick, ME)
Donald Winthrop, b. 12/13/1934; ninth; Harry P. Eldridge (Ossipee) and Vivian Hobbs (Ossipee)
Dorothy Clara, b. 1/29/1939; second; Lawrence Eldridge (Ossipee) and Rita Lane (Tamworth)
Dorothy Janet, b. 7/3/1937; first; Lawrence Eldridge (Ossipee) and Rita Lane (Tamworth)
Douglas Clifford, b. 6/20/1949; fourth; Clyde Eldridge (Ossipee) and Eleanor Gilman (Tamworth)
Douglas E., b. 12/17/1961; third; Harry Eldridge, Jr. and Beverly Hillsgrove
Edgar Arthur, b. 3/9/1926; second; Arthur Eldridge (Ossipee) and Olive Holborne (E. Hartland, CT)

Edith Dorothy, b. 11/16/1940; first; Guy H. Eldridge (Tamworth) and Dottie Edith Moulton (Wolfeboro)
Elaine C., b. 2/3/1954; sixth; Roy Eldridge (NH) and Jean M. Campbell (MA)
Eleanor J., b. 3/9/1932; first; Chauncey Eldridge (Ossipee) and Esther Adjutant (Ossipee)
Eleanor M., b. 2/8/1931; second; Lester Eldridge (Ossipee) and Ida Judkins (Ossipee)
Erdine, b. 4/5/1914; first; Fred H. Eldridge (laborer, Ossipee) and Dora O. Sargent (Ossipee)
Ernest Clyde, b. 4/26/1979; Langdon John Eldridge and Alecia Mae Daigneau
Eva, b. 5/30/1925; sixth; Fred Eldridge (Ossipee) and Dora Sargent (Ossipee)
Eva Marie, b. 3/4/1944; fifth; Lester Eldridge (Ossipee) and Ida Judkins (Effingham)
Frances Loetta, b. 3/12/1924; first; Arthur Eldridge (Ossipee) and Olive Holborne (E. Hartland, CT)
George Michael, b. 10/11/1950; fourth; Charles Eldridge (Tamworth) and Reba Vittum (Tamworth)
Gertrude, b. 5/16/1892; Orren Eldridge (Carroll) and Elizabeth Williams (Carroll) (1958)
Gladys M., b. 5/1/1892; James F. Eldridge (NH) and Abbie J. Hodsdon (NH) (1954)
Gloria Jean, b. 6/14/1949; third; Roy Eldridge (Ossipee) and Jean Eldridge (Winchester, MA)
Gordon A., b. 9/17/1955; fifth; Charles Eldridge (NH) and Reba Vittum (NH)
Gordon Larrie, b. 7/20/1940; first; Carroll H. Eldridge (Ossipee) and Dorothy Ethel Prokey (Ossipee)
Gregory A., b. 10/20/1959; first; Harry Eldridge, Jr. (W. Ossipee) and Beverly Hillsgrove (Concord)
Guy H., Jr., b. 4/2/1948; fourth; Guy H. Eldridge, Sr. (Tamworth) and Lottie E. Moulton (Wolfeboro)
Harry, b. 12/11/1920; tenth; Everett Eldridge (laborer, Ossipee) and Nettie Pike (Ossipee)
Hazen, b. 1/9/1920; second; Willie Eldridge (farmer, Ossipee) and Cora Williams (Ossipee)
Heidi Elizabeth, b. 3/23/1972; James Raymond Eldridge and Beverly Ann Budroe
Helen R., b. 11/29/1927; second; Lester Eldridge (Ossipee) and Florence Varney (Berwick, ME)
Helen Sadie, b. 8/9/1926; sixth; Wilbur Eldridge (Ossipee) and Myrtle Eldridge (Ossipee)

Hillary Marguerite, b. 6/15/1997 in N. Conway; Rodney Herbert Eldridge, Jr. and Caroline Jennifer Bickford
Hope Danielle, b. 12/27/1998 in Wolfeboro; Jeremy Eldridge and Dorothy Eldridge
Inez Emma, b. 7/9/1907; John Eldridge (NH) and Emma Welch (NH) (1951)
Ira Templeton, b. 12/17/1950; second; Ahiel Eldridge (NH) and Lena Greisshammer (Czechoslovakia) (1951)
Irma M., b. 1/27/1903; Woodbury Eldridge and Dora B. Eldridge (1960)
Isabelle Diane, b. 3/26/2000 in Portland, ME; Bradley Eldridge and Deborah Eldridge
Jacqueline L., b. 6/16/1949; first; Ahiel Eldridge (Ossipee) and Lina Griesshammer (Czechoslovakia)
Jannette, b. 3/16/1931; third; Harry Eldridge (Ossipee) and Vivian I. Hobbs (Ossipee)
Jason Carroll, b. 9/18/1979; John Carroll Eldridge and Peggy Edith Adjutant
Jeanette L., b. 4/12/1935; eighth; Raymond Eldridge (Ossipee) and Etta Eldridge (Ossipee)
Jennifer Lynn, b. 3/12/1974; George Michael Eldridge and Charmein Twombly
Jeremiah Clyde, b. 3/30/1996 in Wolfeboro; Jeremy Clyde Eldridge and Dorothy Cora Brewer
John, b. 5/27/1914; third; Charles M. Eldridge (farmer, Ossipee) and Nettie Nichols (Ossipee)
John, b. 5/28/1928; tenth; Wilbur Eldridge (Ossipee) and Myrtle Templeton (Ossipee)
John L., b. 6/5/1942; third; John L. Eldridge (Ossipee) and Rita E. Lane (Tamworth)
John Philip, b. 5/28/1972; Alfred Philip Eldridge and Myrtle Lou Johnson
John R., b. 5/28/1958; sixth; Charles P. Eldridge (NH) and Reba A. Vittum (NH)
John Wayne, b. 9/8/1945; second; Ralph F. Eldridge (Ossipee) and Arlene Virginia Frost (Madison)
Joyce Beverly, b. 5/12/1930; second; Howard J. Eldridge (Ossipee) and Cora E. Kirkwood (Ossipee)
Kris E., b. 12/30/1965; fifth; Carlton O. Eldridge and Martha M. Hayes
Kristine, b. 1/12/1971; Douglas Clifford Eldridge and Rebecca Elaine Deatte
Krystal Leigh, b. 2/23/1983; Gordon A. Eldridge and Joan Berry
Langdon J., b. 1/21/1959; seventh; Clyde Eldridge (Ossipee) and Eleanor Gilman (S. Hiram, ME)
Larry E., b. 10/4/1949; second; Bernard Eldridge (Ossipee) and Joyce Berry (Ossipee)

Lawrence, b. 7/7/1915; eighth; George Eldridge (laborer, Ossipee) and Ida Welch (Ossipee)
Lawrence J., III, b. 7/19/1962; second; Lawrence Eldridge and Sandra Hamel
Lee Sherman, b. 5/31/1934; eighth; Lester H. Eldridge (Ossipee) and Florence Varney (Berwick, ME)
Linda Mae, b. 7/28/1944; second; Guy Henry Eldridge (Tamworth) and Lottie Edith Moulton (Wolfeboro)
Linda Mae, b. 2/20/1949; first; Robert W. Eldridge (Ossipee) and Eva M. Junkins (S. Effingham)
Lucille M., b. 10/10/1954; third; Robert Eldridge (NH) and Eva M. Judkins (NH)
Lucy A., b. 2/25/1957; fourth; Carlton O. Eldridge (NH) and Martha M. Hayes (MA)
Margaret Elaine, b. 7/12/1956; sixth; Clyde A. Eldridge (NH) and Eleanor L. Gilman (NH)
Marilyn, b. 5/19/1931; first; Ernest Eldridge (Ossipee) and Ruth Hodge (Milton)
Marion, b. 1/5/1899 in Ossipee; third; Wilbur A. Eldridge (laborer, 25, Ossipee) and Nettie M. Eastman (25, Bartlett)
Matthew William, b. 8/12/1971; Rodney Herbert Eldridge and Sharon Anne Charles
Maurice, b. 7/31/1917; eighth; Everett Eldridge (laborer, Ossipee) and Nettie Eldridge (Ossipee)
Melvin, b. 3/26/1905 in Ossipee; second; Herbert W. Eldridge (laborer, 29, Ossipee) and Lillian D. Welch (25, Ossipee)
Michael Norman, b. 12/9/1974; Norman Francis Eldridge, Jr. and Kira Magit Brownell
Michael Roy, b. 7/15/1952; fifth; Roy Eldridge (Ossipee) and Jean Campbell (Winchester, MA)
Michelle Linda, b. 2/27/1973; Carl Robert Eldridge and Kathleen Grace White
Moses O., b. 9/12/1899; Oradon Eldridge (NH) and Lucy Eldridge (NH) (1951)
Natasha Rose, b. 7/25/1990; William Israel Eldridge and Deanna Lee Drake
Neil Gordon, b. 9/14/1975; Gordon Allen Eldridge and Joan Darlene Berry
Norman F., b. 8/18/1932; ninth; Fred W. Eldridge (Ossipee) and Dora T. Sargent (Ossipee)
Norman F., Jr., b. 1/19/1956; first; Norman F. Eldridge (NH) and Marie E. Hodge (NH)
Patricia L., b. 5/20/1947; third; Ralph F. Eldridge (Ossipee) and Arlene V. Frost (Madison)
Paul Edward, b. 2/27/1973; Larry Edward Eldridge and Reita Lee Willey
Perley E., b. 5/22/1891; Ivory Eldridge and Emma Welch (1962)

Permelia, b. 9/17/1943; first; Ralph C. Eldridge (Ctr. Ossipee) and Margaret R. Winkley (Ctr. Ossipee)
Peter M., b. 6/20/1948; second; John K. Eldridge (Ctr. Ossipee) and Charlotte A. Weed (Waterville, ME)
Philip Clyde, b. 9/8/1973; Philip Wayne Eldridge and Diane Ballou
Philip Wayne, b. 5/23/1954; fifth; Clyde A. Eldridge (NH) and Eleanor L. Gilman (NH)
Rachel May, b. 10/31/1975; John Carroll Eldridge and Peggy Edith Adjutant
Raymond, b. 12/9/1923; second; Chester C. Eldridge (Ossipee) and Hazel E. Eldridge (Ossipee)
Raymond Wayne, b. 7/1/1989; Timothy Wayne Eldridge and Karen Beth Savage
Rebecca M., b. 9/1/1947; second; Harry P. Eldridge, Jr. (W. Ossipee) and Christobell I. Stacy (Tamworth)
Richard Junior, b. 4/9/1926; first; Lester Eldridge (Ossipee) and Florence Varney (Berwick, ME)
Robin L., b. 9/29/1963; third; Lawrence J. Eldridge, Jr. and Sandra Hamel
Rodney H., b. 8/13/1943; second; Charles Eldridge (Tamworth) and Reba Vittum (Tamworth)
Rodney H., Jr., b. 12/30/1963; second; Rodney H. Eldridge and Sharon A. Charles
Roland, b. 12/10/1928; second; Lester Eldridge (Ossipee) and Ida Sprague (Freedom)
Roxanne C., b. 4/16/1960; third; Norman F. Eldridge and Marie E. Hodge
Roy, b. 8/21/1926; fourth; Chester C. Eldridge (Bartlett) and Hazel E. Eldridge (Ossipee)
Ruth, b. 5/10/1925; third; Chester C. Eldridge (Bartlett) and Hazel Eldridge (Ossipee)
Scotty A., b. 1/16/1967; first; Scott C. Eldridge and Sandra Emerson
Scotty Clifton, b. 5/24/1939; fourth; Lester A. Eldridge (Ossipee) and Ida M. Judkins (Effingham)
Shane Allen, b. 7/11/1994 in Wolfeboro; Timothy W. Eldridge and Karen B. Savage
Stephen L., b. 4/22/1962; eighth; Roy Eldridge and Jean Campbell
Susan Jane, b. 7/28/1944; third; Guy Henry Eldridge (Tamworth) and Lottie Edith Moulton (Wolfeboro)
Sylvia M., b. 1/10/1913; John P. Eldridge (Ossipee) and Emma P. Welch (Tuftonboro) (1948)
Tammy L., b. 10/2/1963; first; Richard C. Eldridge and Sandra Charles
Tedd Oscar, b. 4/24/1944; fourth; Lawrence J. Eldridge (Ossipee) and Rita Elizabeth Lane (Tamworth)
Timothy Edwin, b. 7/6/1977; Norman Francis Eldridge, Jr. and Kira Margit Brownell
Timothy W., b. 4/11/1969; Dennis W. Eldridge and Martha J. Berry

Tina Marie, b. 6/9/1978; Philip Wayne Eldridge and Diane Ballou
Tony Curtis, b. 11/7/1974; Stanley Wayne Eldridge and Mary Ann Hebert
Tracy E., b. 12/23/1967; first; Chester C. Eldridge and Janet E. Gerry
Walter C., b. 4/2/1962; eighth; Clyde Eldridge and Eleanor Gilman
Wayne, b. 1/17/1966; first; Stanley W. Eldridge and Mary A. Hebert
Wayne D., b. 12/26/1969; Douglas C. Eldridge and Rebecca E. Deatte
Wayne E., b. 12/4/1968; Bernard H. Eldridge and Joyce A. Berry
Wendell Richard, b. 2/22/1939; seventh; Raymond C. Eldridge (Ossipee) and Etta May Eldridge (Ossipee)
Wesley Eugene, b. 8/27/1926; first; Howard Eldridge (Ossipee) and Cora Kirkwood (Ossipee)
William H., b. 11/9/1928; eighth; Fred Eldridge (Ossipee) and Dora Sargent (Ossipee)
Winnifred, b. 5/25/1911 in Ossipee; tenth; Plummer Eldridge (laborer, Ossipee) and Emily Welch (Ossipee)
Wynetta E., b. 8/26/1948; third; Harry P. Eldridge, Jr. (W. Ossipee) and Christobel Stacey (S. Tamworth)
Zachary Lawrence, b. 9/9/1993 in N. Conway; Wayne Allen Eldridge and Jessika Jean Moulton

ELLIOTT,
Elaine Betty, b. 3/10/1937; first; Leon Elliott (Alton) and Erdine Eldridge (Ossipee)
Jasond Elsworth, b. 7/29/1982; Michael Almon Elliott, Sr. and Jo-Ann Heighe
Jean S., b. 11/24/1943; second; Harry A. Elliott (Lakeport) and Kilda Castonguay (Rochester)
Thomas E., b. 8/23/1947; second; Leon F. Elliott (Alton) and Erdine C. Eldridge (Ossipee)
Wyllow Lee Louise, b. 8/22/1997 in Wolfeboro; Vincent Elwin Elliott, Jr. and Michelle Louise Morrill

ELLIS,
Jonathin Little, b. 7/14/2001 in Rochester; Jon Ellis and Peggy Ellis
Mickayla Bea, b. 4/22/1996 in Wolfeboro; Edward Earl Ellis, II and Donna Marie Grow

EMACK,
daughter, b. 12/31/1921; third; William Emack (laborer, Parsonsfield, ME) and Eva Perkins (Ossipee)
Alexander D., b. 9/28/1909 in Ossipee; first; Benjamin Emack (laborer, NS) and Florence Welch (Ossipee)

EMERSON,
son, b. 2/3/1916; sixth; Amos N. Emerson (teamster, Effingham) and Nettie M. Clough (Effingham)
daughter, b. 5/8/1919; first; Levi Emerson (laborer, Effingham) and Bernice Hamm (Ossipee)
David A., b. 1/28/1962; first; Alan D. Emerson and Brenda Eldridge
Deborah A., b. 1/31/1957; first; Harvey Emerson (MA) and Nellie O. Millis (NC)
Gary C., b. 9/12/1963; second; Alan D. Emerson and Brenda Eldridge
Jack Nelson, b. 12/12/1946; fourth; Ralph W. Emerson (Ossipee) and Pearl A. Nelson (Ctr. Effingham)
Lorey L., b. 2/22/1959; second; Harvey Emerson (Lynn, MA) and Nellie Mills (Sneads Falls, NC)
Robert, b. 7/12/1947; fifth; Levi W. Emerson (Effingham) and Margaret L. Pennell (Milton)
Robert D., b. 8/5/1936; first; Ralph W. Emerson (Ossipee) and Gertrude Sturtevant (Dorchester, MA)
Theodore W., b. 11/14/1941; second; Levi W. Emerson (Effingham) and Margaret L. Pennell (Milton)
Valerie M., b. 8/27/1967; second; Theodore W. Emerson and Eva M. Eldridge
Wayne Winfield, b. 3/29/1938; Hazel R. Emerson (East Burke, VT)

EMERY,
son, b. 4/11/1904 in Ossipee; first; H. Dana Emery (laborer, 35, Bartlett) and Ina M. Drew (21, Ossipee)
Sophia Helen, b. 10/30/2000 in Portland, ME; Dallas Emery and Charon Emery

ENGLISH,
Eric A., b. 8/26/1968; Urbain H. English and Maureen Heath
Vaughn U., b. 2/8/1965; second; Urban H. English, Jr. and Maureen Heath

ENGLUND,
Brian Carl, b. 5/9/1977; Carl Robert Englund, III and Frances Marion Lyle

ENMAN,
Judith Sherrill, b. 7/16/1952; fourth; Arthur Enman (Chichester) and Marjorie Backer (Manchester)

ENRIGHT,
Rebecca Marie, b. 3/21/1989; Stephen Dominic Enright and Marie Cecile Smith

ERICKSON,
Carolee, b. 2/5/1973; Leigh F. Erickson and Debbie Lee Fisher

ESCHENBACH,
Marci Rochelle, b. 6/29/1988; Michael A. Eschenbach and Sandra L. Yanov

ESTEY,
Marion L., b. 4/5/1945; first; Gilbert A. Estey (Hudson) and Beatrice L. Critchett (Manchester)

EVANS,
daughter, b. 5/26/1933; third; Frank Evans (Erie, PA) and Evelyn Dow (Tuftonboro)
John Wayne, b. 5/15/1946; second; Elmer E. Evans, Jr. (Manchester) and Jeannette B. Orfield (Raymond)
Melissa Rose, b. 1/22/1989; Arthur Warren Evans, III and Carol Ann Stonge

EVITTS,
Alice, b. 2/13/1914; second; Arthur Evitts (farmer) and Cora Jenks (Brookline, MA)
Arthur P., b. 12/21/1909 in Ossipee; first; Arthur J. Evitts (farmer, Richmond, VA) and Cora N. Jenks (Brookline, MA)

FAIRTILE,
Lindsay Tage, b. 6/19/1983; William Allen Lund and Stephanie Jane Fairtile

FALL,
son, b. 6/15/1888; fourth; George A. Fall (farmer, Ossipee) and Susie Fall
son, b. 4/21/1892 in Ossipee; seventh; George Fall (farmer) and Louise Nutter
son, b. 11/30/1922; second; Clinton H. Fall (painter, Ossipee) and Mildred Price (Woodstock, NB)
Alan G., b. 11/12/1954; first; Gordon R. Fall (NH) and Velma C. Watson (NH)
Ausbrey C., b. 4/22/1885; Plummer Fall (NH) and Nellie Fall (NH) (1953)
Beverly L., b. 5/24/1960; third; Gordon R. Fall and Velma C. Watson
Gorden R., b. 8/9/1924; second; Raymond Fall (Ossipee) and Hazel Keith (Conway)
Melvin R., b. 5/20/1957; second; Gordon R. Fall (NH) and Velma C. Watson (NH)

Richard G., b. 6/10/1916; first; Clinton H. Fall (painter, Ossipee) and Mildred Price (Woodstock, NB)
Virginia P., b. 3/11/1922; first; Raymond E. Fall (laborer, Ossipee) and Hazel Keith

FAUCETTE,
Justin Parker, b. 3/21/1991; John Henry Faucette and Rose Marie Emerson

FAULKNER,
Samantha Marie, b. 11/17/1995 in Laconia; Robert Joseph Faulkner and Katherine Ann Rollins

FEHRMANN,
Richard Walter, b. 9/17/1970; James Richard Fehrmann and Karen May Osgood

FERGUSON,
Daniel, b. 9/30/1960; fifth; Edward R. Ferguson and Dorothy M. O'Toole
Scott, b. 9/30/1960; sixth; Edward R. Ferguson and Dorothy M. O'Toole

FERNALD,
daughter [Grace Mildred], b. 9/10/1901 in Ossipee; first; Frank Fernald (farmer, 28, Ossipee) and Achsa Hilton (22, Ossipee)
son [Leon F.], b. 11/18/1903 in Ossipee; second; Frank A. Fernald (farmer, 30, Ossipee) and Achse E. Hilton (24, Ossipee)

FICKETT,
daughter [Ruth H.], b. 10/23/1918; second; Daniel A. Fickett (farmer, Standish, ME) and Georgia Goldsmith (Tuftonboro)

FINNISS,
Kaitlin Elizabeth, b. 3/21/1996 in Wolfeboro; Erik Clifford Finniss and Melanie Marie Lennox

FISCHBEIN,
Charles Ashley, b. 2/8/1981; Daniel Walter Fischbein and Deborah May Busch
Joshua David, b. 7/18/1975; Daniel Walter Fischbein and Deborah May Busch

FISHER,
Sydney Elizabeth Lynn, b. 4/4/1978; John F. Fisher and Mary Linda Welch

FITZGERALD,
child, b. 6/8/1925; sixth; Daniel C. Fitzgerald (Chester, VT) and Maud S. LaFost (Brandon, VT)
Frank A., b. 6/3/1918; Daniel Fitzgerald (Chester, VT) and Maude LaCost (Brandon, VT) (1952)

FITZSIMMONS,
Rebecca, b. 4/21/1959; second; James Fitzsimmons (Guilford, ME) and Charlotte Knox (Worcester, MA)

FLANAGAN,
Charles Sherman, b. 12/19/1938; second; Paul A. Flanagan (Lowell) and Hilda J. Colby (Ctr. Ossipee)
Donna M., b. 6/22/1947; fourth; Paul Flanagan (Lowell, MA) and Hilda J. Colby (Moultonville)
Eleanor A., b. 12/3/1942; first; Paul A. Flanagan (Lowell, MA) and Hilda J. Colby (Ctr. Ossipee)
Francis E., b. 7/14/1954; second; Paul A. Flanagan (MA) and Irene B. Gagne (NH)
Margaret, b. 7/20/1946; fifth; Paul Flanagan (Lowell, MA) and Hilda J. Colby (Ossipee)

FLANDERS,
Amethyst Rose, b. 10/1/1998 in Wolfeboro; Donald Warren Flanders, Jr. and Tressa Jean Custeau

FLANEGAN,
Helen Mary, b. 9/7/1936; first; Paul Flanegan (Lowell, MA) and Hilda J. Colby (Moultonville)

FLETCHER,
Derek James, b. 11/26/1982; James Ernest Fletcher and Jill Elizabeth Nystedt

FLORIA,
Amy Christine, b. 6/16/1975; Ralph Douglas Floria and Marcia Ann Dale
Beth Ellen, b. 1/17/1977; Ralph Douglas Floria and Marcia Ann Dale
Travis Richmond, b. 7/24/1973; Ralph Douglas Floria and Marcia Ann Dale

FOGG,
daughter, b. 11/15/1887; second; Daniel Fogg (farmer, 31, Ossipee) and Julia (21, Worcester, MA)

daughter, b. 3/1/1890 in Ossipee; third; Daniel Fogg (farmer, Ossipee) and Julia M. H. Collins (Worcester, MA)
child, b. 10/22/1892 in Ossipee; fourth; Daniel Fogg (farmer, Ossipee) and Julia Collins (Worcester, MA)
son, b. 2/13/1895 in Ossipee; fifth; Daniel Fogg (farmer, Ossipee) and Julia Collins (Worcester, MA)
daughter, b. 9/1/1897 in Ossipee; fifth; Daniel Fogg (40) and Julia Collins (29, Worcester, MA)
daughter, b. 9/17/1899 in Ossipee; seventh; Daniel Fogg (farmer, Ossipee) and Julia Collins (Worcester, MA)
daughter, b. 12/4/1901 in Ossipee; eighth; Daniel Fogg (farmer, Ossipee) and Julia Collins (Worcester, MA)
son, b. 11/21/1903 in Ossipee; ninth; Daniel Fogg (farmer, Ossipee) and Julia ----- (Worcester, MA)
daughter, b. 9/21/1908 in Ossipee; first; George W. Fogg (farmer, Ossipee) and Carrie B. Garland (Ossipee)
Alana Corrinne, b. 5/4/1946; first; Frank A. Fogg (Bar Harbor, ME) and Shirley J. Bamford (Caribou, ME)
Almon H., b. 12/4/1948; second; Frank A. Fogg (Bar Harbor, ME) and Shirley J. Bamford (Caribou, ME)
Amy Megan, b. 3/18/1987; Relf Gregory Fogg and Annette Rae Propp
Harold, b. 3/25/1929; first; Harold Fogg (Deerfield) and Rose Bedell (Great Neck, NY)
Richard A., b. 9/16/1932; fourth; Harold H. Fogg (Deerfield) and Rose Rundell (Great Neck, L.I.)
Tenley A., b. 1/14/1954; first; Frank A. Fogg (Bar Harbor, ME) and Shirley J. Bamford (Caribou, ME)

FOLEY,
Kristin Lloyd, b. 2/7/1980; James Patrick Foley and Sheila Anne Redmond

FORD,
Eric Paul, b. 11/8/1984; Paul Robert Ford and Kelly Jean Bickford

FORTIER,
son, b. 7/24/1893 in Ossipee; tenth; Charles Fortier (laborer, Canada) and Divian Beledeux (Chicago, IL)
Lillian Helen, b. 5/19/1913; first; Horace J. Fortier (laborer, Ossipee) and Mary E. Sands (Roxbury, MA)

FOSS,
son, b. 1/11/1894 in Ossipee; first; Charles H. Foss (painter, 24, Dover) and Stella Davis (19, Ossipee)
son, b. 10/5/1909 in Ossipee; first; Clarence Foss (Cornish, ME) and Minnie Stuart (Cornish, ME); residence - Cornish, ME

Annabelle Theresa, b. 5/10/1938; first; Charles Gilbert Foss (Temple) and
    Anastasia E. Crockett (Hallowell)

FRANZ,
Jack R., b. 11/9/1997 in Wolfeboro; Robert John Franz and Amy Beth
    Lundstrom

FREDRICKSON,
Erica, b. 12/5/1968; Scott G. Fredrickson and Judy A. Landman

FRENCH,
Arline L., b. 2/7/1920; fifth; Benjamin French (teamster, Conway) and
    Lillian M. Ray (Tallapoosa, GA)
Dorothy L., b. 4/2/1918; fourth; Benjamin French (truck man, Conway) and
    Lillian M. Roy (Talapoosia, GA)
Gordon, b. 4/21/1935; fifth; Benjamin French and Marjory Frost (Madison)
Jeanette Grace, b. 1/30/1928; first; Lewis L. French (Conway) and
    Gertrude Merrow (Ossipee)
Joyce Rae, b. 9/6/1937; third; Edwin S. French (Minneapolis) and Ruth A.
    Garnett (Conway)
Lewis L., b. 10/7/1929; second; Lewis L. French (Conway) and Gertrude
    Merrow (Ossipee)

FROST,
Amy Jean, b. 7/1/1977; Edwin Carl Frost and Rosalie May Stanley
April Marie, b. 11/4/1980; Edwin Carl Frost, Jr. and Rosalie May Stanley
Colleen Joyce, b. 2/9/1941; seventh; Randolph Frost (Silver Lake) and
    Sadie Hallett (Ossipee)
Randolph, Jr., b. 10/11/1939; fifth; Randolph Frost (Madison) and Sadie
    Hallett Frost (Ossipee)
Wilfred F., b. 10/5/1962; fourth; Wilbur Frost and Arlene Winslow

FRYE,
Paul Ernest, b. 5/18/1940; fourth; John Harvey Frye (Milton) and Hilda
    Dean Bowers (Brownsville, VT)
Richard Henry, b. 12/24/1938; third; John Harvey Frye (Wilton) and Hilda
    D. Bowers (Brownville)

FULLERTON,
Amanda Lynne, b. 6/15/1985; Peter Earl Fullerton and Susan Dale
Jennifer Ann, b. 4/2/1982; Peter Earl Fullerton and Susan Dale
Jeremy Dale, b. 10/27/1978; Peter Earl Fullerton and Susan Dale
Mark, b. 10/15/1966; fourth; Earl R. Fullerton and Mary P. Cawthron

Michelle Lorraine, b. 3/18/1972; Wayne Ryder Fullerton and Theresa
Lorraine Cotton

FURTADO,
Christopher, b. 7/10/1964; first; Arthur Furtado and Laurinda Kirkwood

GAGNE,
Betty Jane, b. 5/13/1948; third; Alfred J. Gagne (Wolfeboro) and Frances
Abbott (Ossipee)
Ernest Alfred, b. 4/23/1951; third; Alfred Gagne (Wolfeboro) and Frances
Abbott (Ossipee)
Lindsay Rene, b. 4/18/1986; David Paul Gagne and Susan Margaret
Bachelder
Peter Allen, b. 9/29/1946; second; Alfred Joseph Gagne (Wolfeboro) and
Frances M. Abbott (Ossipee)
Terry D., b. 5/12/1953; fourth; Alfred Gagne (NH) and Frances Abbott (NH)

GAGNON,
David Morgan, b. 7/13/1981; Gary Allen Gagnon and Terry Ann Caulkins
Kristopher Doyle, b. 3/4/1989; David Russell Gagnon and Patty Michelle
Espling
Nikolaus Charles, b. 6/11/1992; David Russell Gagnon and Patty Michele
Espling

GALE,
Hazen Frederick, b. 2/10/1934; first; Parkman Gale (Chitervale) and Lucille
Gray (Columbia)
Mary Ellen, b. 2/24/1938; third; Hartland D. Gale (Bartlett) and Lucille
Mary Gray (Columbia)
Philip Evan, b. 1/18/1937; second; Parkman D. Gale (Bartlett) and Lucille
Gray (Columbia)
Robert Eugene, b. 2/2/1940; third; Parkman D. Gale (Bartlett) and Lucille
Mary Gray (Columbia)
Sierraland Luna Nita, b. 6/19/2000 in West Ossipee; Robert Jay Gale and
Beth Ellen Floria Gale

GALLAGHER,
Judith Dee, b. 9/29/1941; first; Keith William Gallagher (Limestone, ME)
and Theresa S. Goldsmith (Wolfeboro)

GALLANT,
Joshua Alex, b. 10/21/1993 in Rochester; Jeffrey Alan Gallant and
Deborah Grace Goupil

GAMMONS,
Liza, b. 5/19/1976; Carl Randolph Gammons and Linda Blais

GARDNER,
Andy L., b. 9/16/1957; fifth; Francis R. Gardner (Cambridge, MA) and Muriel A. Campbell (Roxbury, MA)
Fred C., b. 4/10/1942; Charles F. Gardner (Georges Mills) and Madeline D. Hersey (Westfield, ME)
Oliver J., b. 3/13/1948; third; Charles F. Gardner (Georgia Mills) and Madeline D. Hersey (Westfield, ME)
Sharon Ann, b. 6/2/1943; second; Charles F. Gardner (Georges Mills) and Madeline D. Hersey (Easton, ME)
Timothy, b. 9/27/1954; fourth; Rev. Francis R. Gordon (sic) (MA) and Muriel A. Campbell (MA)

GARLAND,
Karen E., b. 12/20/1942; Howard A. Garland (Sanbornville) and Ruth F. Hutchinson (Athol, MA)
Matthew, b. 9/23/1959; second; Richard Garland (S. Tamworth) and Barbara Whearty (Ctr. Ossipee)

GAROD,
Brandon Harris, b. 6/5/1987; Harvey Jay Garod and Marla Lynn Teitler
Eric Spenser, b. 5/7/1990; Harvey Jay Garod and Marta Lynn Teitler

GARRITY,
son, b. 10/10/1913; second; William Garrity (teamster, England) and Lilla Smith (Canada)
son, b. 10/10/1913; third; William Garrity (teamster, England) and Lilla Smith (Canada)

GASPER,
daughter, b. 6/16/1909 in Ossipee; second; Charles W. Gasper (farmer, Ossipee) and Ethel Hartford (Manchester)

GAUDET,
Christopher Leo, b. 4/18/1989; Scott Wayne Gaudet and Susan Elizabeth McDonald

GAUDETTE,
son, b. 6/1/1920; first; George Gaudette (laborer, Somersworth) and Millie Cummings (Northwood)

GAUTHIER,
Paul William, b. 2/18/2001 in N. Conway; Stephen Gauthier and Susan Gauthier

GEORGE,
son, b. 10/17/1909 in Ossipee; first; Michael George (store keeper, Syria) and Marza Hbio (Syria)

GERO,
stillborn son, b. 3/28/1890 in Ossipee; third; Robert Gero (farmer, Canada) and Hulda Bemmer (Island Pond, ME)

GERRISH,
James, b. 3/5/1966; first; Vernor T. Gerrish and Carole Rand

GETCHELL,
David Wilfred, b. 3/22/1939; second; Robert B. Getchell (Salem, MA) and Edith Mary Martin (Melrose, MA)

GETSON,
Hillary Joyce, b. 7/29/1990; Donald Alan Getson and Penny Lynn White

GILL,
Angus Simon, b. 12/20/1996 in N. Conway; Thomas Alexander Gill and Christina Marie Buben
Byron Christopher, b. 3/29/1993 in N. Conway; Thomas Alexander Gill and Christina Marie Buben
Harrison Thomas, b. 5/26/1990; Thomas Alexander Gill and Christina Marie Buben
Lydia Elizabeth Gill, b. 10/17/1991; Thomas Alexander Gill and Christina Marie Gill

GILMAN,
Ellinore Joan, b. 8/9/1934; fourth; Cecil E. Gilman (Madison) and Florence M. Hodge (Bartlett)
Keith Alan, b. 1/5/1951; fifth; Orestes Gilman (Denmark, ME) and Irene Pike (Effingham)

GILPATRIC,
Aaron David, b. 8/5/1982; David Lester Gilpatric and Judy Ruth Mason

GLICK,
Ephraim Nathaniel, b. 12/30/1981; Michael J. Glick and Victoria Carlotta Nass

Henry Bernard, b. 11/29/1984; Michael Jay Glick and Victoria Carlotta Nass

GLIDDEN,
Gracie Marie, b. 6/18/1998 in Wolfeboro; Robert James Glidden and Jessica Marie Short
Kaleb Robert, b. 1/4/2000 in Wolfeboro; Robert Glidden and Jessica Glidden

GOBELLE,
Norman Roger, b. 1/20/1938; first; Arthur Gobelle (Whitman) and Evelyn Wiggin (Union)

GODFREY,
Katelyn Jane, b. 12/23/1987; Brian F. Godfrey and Karen A. Mulcahy

GOLDSMITH,
Kenneth, b. 6/7/1933; third; Chester Goldsmith and Stella Evans

GOLDTHWAITE,
Chelsi Elizabeth, b. 4/23/1990; Keith Charles Goldthwaite and Rachelle Alice Hamel

GOODWIN,
son, b. 6/9/1914; third; John Goodwin (merchant, Ossipee) and Eva Rattie
Dianna Parkman, b. 8/17/1940; first; Edwin R. Goodwin (Amesbury, MA) and Florence P. Parkman (Montague, PEI)
Elizabeth Anne, b. 12/30/1940; first; Payson H. Goodwin (Ossipee) and Antoinette M. Duguay (Haverhill, MA)
Jessica Ann, b. 7/28/1989; Harold Thomas Goodwin and Gina Hebert
Nicole Marie, b. 8/30/1999 in Wolfeboro; Harold Goodwin and Gina Goodwin

GOOGOO,
Garry A., b. 5/3/1957; fifth; William Googoo (NS) and Muriel A. Nichols (NH)
Pamela J., b. 1/29/1954; second; William J. Googoo (Canada) and Muriel A. Nichols (NH)
Steven Allen, b. 4/25/1956; fourth; William J. Googoo (Canada) and Muriel A. Nichols (NH)
William J., Jr., b. 5/6/1955; William Googoo (Canada) and Muriel Nichols (NH)

GOSS,
Jaime Lynn, b. 1/27/1982; Joseph Wallace Goss and Ellen Frances Nason

GOUIN,
child, b. 8/19/1929; first; Thornton Gouin (Wolfeboro) and Leona Libby (Ossipee)

GOULD,
Joshua Ryan, b. 7/6/1995 in Peterborough; Jason Ryan Gould and Cynthia Jean Gernat

GRAF,
Jonathan William, b. 8/31/1982; John William Graf and Margaret Elizabeth Fazzino
Kelly Lynn, b. 4/20/1977; John William Graf and Margaret Elizabeth Fazzino

GRAHAM,
Hannah Day, b. 7/21/1989; Richard Alton Graham III and Amanda Jean Chase
Rachel Alton, b. 11/17/1993 in N. Conway; Richard Alton Graham III and Amanda Jean Chase

GRAMES,
daughter, b. 5/18/1892 in Ossipee; third; Charles Grames (laborer, Halifax, NS) and Josephine Grames (Bartlett); residence - Bartlett

GRANT,
Ada C., b. 10/27/1928; sixth; Robert B. Grant (Jackson) and Helen ----- (Boston, MA)
Betty Joan, b. 8/9/1934; second; Henry F. Grant (Granite) and Ruth H. Hitchcock (Granite)
Clayton Wilbur, b. 6/15/1936; third; Henry F. Grant (Jackson) and Ruth H. Hitchcock (Ossipee)
Donald B., b. 1/9/1931; eighth; Robert B. Grant (Jackson) and Helen Grant (Charlestown)
Edna J., b. 12/21/1931; ninth; Robert Grant (Jackson) and Helen Grant (Charlestown, MA)
Elinor G., b. 1/29/1930; seventh; Robert Grant (Jackson) and Helen Grant (Charlestown, MA)
Eugene Frank, b. 10/18/1934; tenth; Robert B. Grant (Jackson) and Helen M. Grant (Charlestown, MA)
Herbert S., b. 11/4/1936; eleventh; Robert B. Grant (Jackson) and Helen M. Grant (Charlestown, MA)

Priscilla Elizabeth, b. 8/10/1940; first; John Francis Grant (Holyoke, MA) and Priscilla R. Axtell (Blair, NE)

GRASSO,
Michael Robert, b. 6/1/1979; Leonard Albert Grasso and Laurie Ann Melanson Grasso

GRAY,
daughter, b. 3/13/1898 in Ossipee; fifth; William H. Gray (mechanic, 37, Brownfield, ME) and Elizabeth A. McNeal (30, PEI); residence - Madison
son [Harold], b. 8/31/1904 in Ossipee; second; Walter A. Gray (sawyer, 28, Lunenburg, VT) and Hattie B. Mason (17, Albany)
Albert E., b. 4/11/1933; first; Roland Stickney (Lancaster) and Mary M. Gray (Madison)
Amanda Lee, b. 9/10/1980; Donald Paul Gray and Debora Ann Connor
John Ross, b. 6/18/1984; Donald Paul Gray and Debora Ann Connor

GREEN,
Angelique Nicole, b. 9/24/1995 in Wolfeboro; Douglas Mark Green and Lauri Sue Eldridge
Kyle Davis, b. 2/17/1993 in Rochester; Douglas Mark Green and Lauri Sue Eldridge

GREENWALD,
Jacob Louis, b. 12/21/2001 in Wolfeboro; Thomas Greenwald and Amy Greenwald

GRENQUIST,
Mark, b. 3/10/1948; second; Vernon L. Grenquist (Roslindale, MA) and Barbara C. Harney (Chelsea, MA)

GRIDLEY,
Brian Lee, b. 1/12/1971; Lee Edward Gridley and Ruth Jane Bennett
Heather R., b. 1/24/1969; Lee Gridley and Ruth J. Bennett
Tracey Jane, b. 6/14/1978; Lee E. Gridley and Ruth J. Bennett

GRIFFIN,
daughter, b. 3/13/1913; sixth; Leroy Griffin (laborer, NB) and Minnie Brownell (Ossipee)
Catherine Arvilla, b. 5/19/1939; first; Francis J. Griffin (Ctr. Effingham) and Louise May Nelson (Somerville, MA)

GROVER,
Kiersten Kylee, b. 9/18/1997 in N. Conway; William Paul Grover and Kerry Kathleen Spencer

GROW,
Debra Michelle, b. 1/5/1982; Donald Francis Grow and Donna Marie Champagne

GUAY,
Sandra L., b. 9/28/1969; Leo A. Guay and Jacqueline H. Richard

GUIDI,
Kristi Lee, b. 6/13/1987; Richard S. Guidi and Kerry L. Lang

GUSTAFSON,
Max Whittier, b. 1/26/1993 in Wolfeboro; Scott Merle Gustafson and Christine Linda Whittier
Ryan Lynn, b. 10/18/1990; Scott Merle Gustafson and Christine Linda Whittier

HADDOCK,
daughter [Georgia], b. 6/11/1895 in Ossipee; fifth; George Haddock (laborer) and Lucinda Cole (Cornish, ME)
daughter, b. 4/15/1897 in Ossipee; George Haddock (laborer, 30) and ----- Cole (28, Ossipee)
daughter, b. 9/22/1899 in Ossipee; fourth; George Haddock (laborer) and ----- Cole (Ossipee)
daughter, b. 2/13/1905 in Ossipee; thirteenth; George Haddock (laborer, 39, Center Harbor) and Lucinda Cole (38, Cornish, ME)
son, b. 5/2/1910 in Ossipee; sixth; George Haddock (laborer) and Lucinda Cole (Ossipee)
Tiffany Mahriah, b. 2/25/1997 in Wolfeboro; Andrew Robert Haddock and Lisa M. Elliott

HAFFORD,
Billy Jo, b. 1/19/1988; Richard L. Hafford and Linda A. Hartford
Ernest Arthur, b. 10/6/1982; Richard Leigh Hafford and Linda Alice Hartford
Ronald Cyrus, b. 10/18/1992; Richard Leigh Hafford and Linda Alice Hartford

HAGGART,
Ann Gertrude, b. 11/19/1949; third; Lorin Haggart (Berlin) and Barbara Pattee (Pueblo, Mexico)

Elizabeth C., b. 8/24/1946; second; Lorin F. Haggart (Berlin) and Barbara E. Pattee (Puebla, Mexico)

HALEPIS,
James Michael, b. 12/13/1977; Andrew Manuel Halepis and Cheryl Adeline Riley

HALL,
Dana H., b. 8/28/1957; first; Herbert E. Hall (NH) and Natalie A. Vittum (NH)
David C., b. 9/3/1958; second; Herbert Hall (Rochester) and Natalie Vittum (Wolfeboro)
Debra A., b. 3/26/1968; Herbert E. Hall and Natalie A. Vittum
Diana J., b. 12/13/1961; third; Herbert Hall and Natalie Vittum
Raymond Allen, b. 7/6/1941; second; Warren Burton Hall (Appleton, ME) and Margaret J. Pickard (Newburg, ME)
Zachary Laurence, b. 3/1/1988; Dana H. Hall and Julie A. Stacey

HALLOWAY,
Mary E., b. 2/23/1932; third; Cedric Halloway (Roxbury, MA) and Norma Young (Lincolnville, ME)

HAMM,
son, b. 7/24/1890 in Ossipee; first; A. J. Hamm (farmer, Ossipee) and Mary E. Wentworth (Wakefield)
child, b. 7/3/1895 in Ossipee; third; Judson Hamm (farmer, Ossipee) and Etta Wentworth (Wakefield)
Bernice, b. 8/13/1896; Alpheus Hamm (NH) and Mary Wentworth (NH) (1959)
Charles, b. 3/6/1899 in Ossipee; sixth; A. Judson Hamm (farmer, Ossipee) and Etta Wentworth (Ossipee)
Edna, b. 4/18/1892 in Ossipee; third; A. Judson Hamm (farmer, Ossipee) and Etta Wentworth
Florence, b. 5/8/1907 in Ossipee; seventh; A. J. Hamm (farmer, Ossipee) and Etta M. Wentworth (Wakefield)

HAMMOND,
son, b. 10/27/1900 in Ossipee; second; William Hammond (farmer, Ossipee) and Dora Sawyer
daughter, b. 8/12/1906 in Ossipee; first; Flora Hammond (Ossipee)
son, b. 1/13/1909 in Ossipee; first; Howard Hammond (laborer, Ossipee) and Urdine Eldridge (Ossipee)
Olin L., b. 5/21/1898 in Ossipee; ninth; Daniel Hammond (farmer, Ossipee) and Ella Bunker

HANEY,
Glenn A., b. 2/20/1933; second; Ralph A. Haney (Sanbornville) and Hazel Brown (Malden, MA)

HANSCOM,
Hailey Jordan, b. 7/28/1999 in Wolfeboro; Michael Hanscom and Naomi Hanscom

HANSON,
son, b. 12/5/1889 in Ossipee; fourth; James W. Hanson (farmer, Ossipee) and Anna A. Dore (Ossipee)
child, b. 1/4/1924; second; Lewis M. Hanson (Ossipee) and Karew Canney (Ossipee)
Alice M., b. 2/4/1919; first; Lewis M. Hanson (farmer, Ossipee) and Karen Canney (Ossipee)
Brian M., b. 2/3/1955; first; Kenneth Hanson (NH) and Irene Wilkins (NH)
Kenneth Roland, b. 4/4/1926; third; Lewis Hanson (Ossipee) and Karen Canney (Ossipee)
Mitchell L., b. 7/20/1959; second; Kenneth Hanson (Ossipee) and Irene Wilkins (Ctr. Ossipee)

HARBISON,
James Alan, b. 6/27/1981; Cameron Craig Harbison and Nancy Lee Bruning

HARDING,
daughter, b. 5/16/1902 in Ossipee; first; Howard Harding (teacher, Cornish, ME) and Cora Sanders (Ossipee)

HARDY,
Robert Alden, b. 5/6/1935; first; John Hardy (Pepperell, MA) and Alice Mattern (Mansfield, CT)

HARKINS,
Bevin Kathleen, b. 11/26/1978; James Malcom Harkins and Barbara Joyce Horowitz

HARMON,
son, b. 5/11/1889; Charles M. Harmon and Lizzie O. Harmon (Conway)
daughter, b. 8/29/1889; Daniel Harmon (farmer, Ossipee) and Abbie E. Harmon (Effingham)
daughter, b. 6/12/1890 in Ossipee; second; Melvin A. Harmon (physician, Freedom) and Nellie Towle (Freedom)

daughter, b. 6/15/1891; second; M. A. Harmon (physician, Freedom) and ----
---- (Freedom)
son, b. 10/31/1891; Daniel Harmon (farmer, Ossipee) and ----- (Ossipee)
daughter [Ethel F.], b. 4/8/1915; second; John H. Harmon (dray man, Brookfield) and Georgie Frost (Madison)
daughter [Bertha], b. 8/26/1918; third; John H. Harmon (section hand, Brookfield) and Georgia Frost (Madison)
child, b. 4/30/1920; fourth; John H. Harmon (teamster, Brookfield) and Georgia I. Frost (Madison)
child, b. 2/15/1923; fifth; John Harmon (Brookfield) and Georgia Frost (Madison)
child, b. 11/3/1926; sixth; John Harmon (Brookfield) and Georgia Frost (Madison)
Brenda J., b. 7/4/1947; first; John F. Harmon (Ossipee) and Thelma E. Meserve (Rochester)
Cheryl Jean, b. 4/5/1949; second; John F. Harmon (Ossipee) and Thelma Meserve (Rochester)
Deborah Jane, b. 5/29/1950; third; John Harmon (Ossipee) and Thelma Meserve (Rochester)
Elizabeth Georgie, b. 7/22/1913; first; John Harmon (teamster, Brookfield) and Georgie Pierson (Madison)
Shirley Eloise, b. 1/5/1931; first; Elizabeth Harmon (Ossipee)
Sonya Trisha, b. 7/22/1975; Thomas John Harmon and Margaret Grace Jones

HARRINGTON,
Kelly Ann, b. 7/5/1979; Warren Thomas Harrington and Kathleen Suzanne Boyd
Kevin Warren, b. 4/29/1985; Warren Thomas Harrington and Kathleen Suzanne Boyd

HARRIS,
Alison, b. 1/30/1987; George S. Harris and Brenda Warner
Mason James, b. 2/18/1995 in Wolfeboro; Andrew Harris and Kimberly Anne Jack

HARRISON,
Jennifer Nicole, b. 1/14/1973; James Joseph Harrison and Elizabeth Louise White
Jillian Rae, b. 9/23/1987; Paul D. Harrison and Deborah L. Varrell
Paul Dennis, Jr. b. 4/26/1980; Paul Dennis Harrison and Deborah Lynne Varrell
Shana Lyn, b. 10/7/1985; Paul Dennis Harrison and Deborah Lynne Varrell

HART,
Marine Anne, b. 8/18/1994 in Portsmouth; Michael B. Hart and Maria G. Schintu

HARTFORD,
son, b. 12/24/1909 in Ossipee; seventh; Perley Hartford (shoemaker)
Angie G., b. 8/28/1924; third; Daniel Hartford (Rochester) and Nora F. Knox (Ossipee)
Arthur Dana, b. 9/23/1982; Paul Edmund Hartford, Sr. and Betty Ann Page
Beryl Knox, b. 8/20/1929; fourth; Daniel Hartford (Rochester) and Nora F. Knox (Ossipee)
David O., b. 6/25/1945; first; Everett R. Hatch (Dover) and Gertrude A. Hartford (W. Ossipee)
Eleanore M., b. 11/23/1921; second; Daniel Hartford (laborer, Rochester) and Nora F. Knox (Ossipee)
Jimmie Leigh, b. 1/27/1984; Paul Edmund Hartford, Sr. and Betty Ann Page
Myrtle F., b. 9/3/1918; first; Daniel Hartford (shoe shop, Rochester) and Nora F. Knox (Ossipee); residence - Rochester

HARVEY,
Melissa Laraine, b. 6/18/1997 in Wolfeboro; Mark John Harvey and Angela Marie Nichol

HASER,
Timothy Allen, Jr., b. 6/2/1985; Timothy Allen Haser and Linda Ann Hatch

HATCH,
Laura Rose, b. 9/18/1984; Charles Stanley Hatch and Mary Marie Bielowski
Paul Rollins, b. 6/5/1937; third; Charles A. Hatch (St. Albans, VT) and Marjorie Hatch (Wolfeboro)

HAYDEN,
John DeWolf, b. 12/13/1943; second; Dean A. Hayden (Concord) and Helen L. Gamons (Mattapoisett, MA)

HAYES,
daughter, b. 6/18/1946; second; Kenneth M. Hayes (E. Ryegate, VT) and Helen K. Ashe (Bloomfield, VT)
Susan Kathryn, b. 5/15/1950; third; Kenneth Hayes (E. Ryegate, VT) and Helen Ashe (Bloomfield, VT)

HAYFORD,
Eric Joseph, b. 5/17/1981; James Edward Hayford and Judith Marie Varney
Harlan Boyd, b. 3/14/1939; sixth; Arthur L. Hayford (N. Conway) and Leona Herrick (Bryant Pond, ME)
Heidi Patricia, b. 3/17/1970; Randall Everette Hayford and Susan Mae Weare
Jeffrey G., b. 6/20/1964; third; Daniel Hayford and Patricia Jack
Jill Lynn, b. 6/30/1975; Timothy Ernest Hayford and Holly Jane Berry
Joel Ernest, b. 5/12/1973; Timothy Ernest Hayford and Holly Jane Berry
John A., b. 10/12/1922; second; John E. Hayford (mechanic, Tamworth) and Elva I. Nason (Wakefield)
Paulette G., b. 4/27/1952; second; Paul Hayford (NH) and Caroline Demeritt (NH)
Randall Everett, b. 8/1/1951; first; Daniel Hayford (Laconia) and Patricia Jack (Laconia)
Timothy Joseph, b. 4/21/1989; Timothy Ernest Hayford and Julie Lynn Boisvert

HAYNES,
daughter, b. 10/3/1887; fifth; William H. Haynes (farmer, 39, England) and Laura E. Abbott (28, Ossipee)

HEALD,
James, b. 7/7/1932; first; Alfred Gagnon (Wakefield) and Helen Heald (Hallowell, ME)

HEATH,
Heather Anne, b. 3/20/1976; Richard Henry Heath and Nancy Jane Moulton
Patricia, b. 7/14/1942; Harold G. Heath (Washington, MA) and Marjorie E. Bodurthe (Blandford, MA)

HEBERT,
Amanda Ellen, b. 5/27/1977; Philip Leon Hebert and Constance Virginia West
Billy Joe, b. 11/23/1970; Philip L. Hebert and Barbara A. Varney
Dory, b. 9/18/1966; first; Philip L. Hebert and Barbara A. Varney
Joseph Alan, b. 4/14/1984; Timothy Lewis Hebert and Deborah Lyn Scripture
Justin James, b. 1/29/1984; Daniel Peter Hebert and Julie Silcox
Melissa Sue, b. 9/5/1985; Timothy Lewis Hebert and Deborah Lynn Scripture
Michelle Lynn, b. 5/5/1978; Philip Leon Hebert and Constance Virginia West

Sherry Lynn, b. 3/26/1981; Timothy Lewis Hebert and Deborah Lyn Scripture
Sue Ann, b. 10/30/1971; Philip Leon Hebert and Barbara Ann Varney
Tracy A., b. 3/16/1969; Philip L. Hebert and Barbara A. Varney

HECKEL,
Frederick William, V, b. 9/7/1983; Frederick William Heckel, IV and Katherine Louise Fowler
Sadie Elizabeth, b. 10/4/1987; Frederick William Heckel and Kate Louise Fowler

HEHL,
Jacqueline E., b. 8/1/1960; first; Jacob L. Hehl and Barbara J. White
Margaret M., b. 4/28/1964; third; Jacob Hehl and Barbara White
Winifred M., b. 9/30/1961; second; Jacob L. Hehl and Barbara J. Hill

HELME,
son, b. 4/25/1900 in Ossipee; tenth; Charles Helme (farmer, 45, Hingham, MA) and Emma J. Ames (33, Guilford)
son, b. 5/1/1904 in Ossipee; twelfth; Charles W. Helme (farmer, 49, Hingham, MA) and Emma J. Helme (38, Gilford)
son, b. 6/4/1910 in Ossipee; thirteenth; Charles W. Helme (farmer) and Emma Ames (Gilford)
Aidan Snow, b. 12/22/1974; David Alvin Helme and Wenda Snow Thompson
Christopher A., b. 10/9/1945; third; Alvin Fuller Helme (Ossipee) and Elizabeth Chamberlain (Tamworth)
David Alvin, b. 1/16/1940; second; Alvin Fuller Helme (Ossipee) and Elizabeth Chamberlain (Tamworth)
David Chadbourn, b. 12/2/1976; David Alvin Helme and Wenda Snow Thompson
Phyllis E., b. 3/24/1931; first; Alvin F. Helm (sic) (Ossipee) and Elizabeth Chamberlin (Tamworth)

HEMANN,
Christopher Ian, b. 11/10/1980; John William Hemann and Marie Elizabeth Hawn

HENDERSON,
Megan Cate, b. 4/6/1990; Allan Henry Henderson and Linda Edith Pyburn

HERBERT,
daughter, b. 3/2/1932; sixth; Ralph Herbert (Wolfeboro) and Leah Wiggin (Ossipee)

HERLIHY,
Elaine Marcia, b. 1/4/1940; second; James A. Herlihy (Newfields) and Bernice P. Johnson (Lawrence, MA)
Hunter Thomas, b. 5/5/2001 in N. Conway; Thomas Herlihy and Alexandra Herlihy
Jack Keegan, b. 5/5/2001 in N. Conway; Thomas Herlihy and Alexandra Herlihy

HERRIMAN,
son, b. 9/12/1889; Frank L. Herriman (laborer, Boston, MA) and Sadie A. Harmon (Kittery, ME)

HERSEY,
child, b. 8/22/1939; first; Ernest H. Hersey (Wolfeboro) and Florence H. Harmon (Ossipee)
Barbara J., b. 8/7/1943; third; Howard E. Hersey (Wolfeboro) and Florence H. Harmon (Ossipee)
Kiaunah Katherine, b. 3/5/2001 in N. Conway; David Hersey and Kaysee Hersey
Patricia Elouise, b. 4/8/1941; second; Ernest Howard Hersey (Ossipee) and Florence H. Harmon (Ossipee)

HICKEY,
James Daniel, b. 2/23/1974; Stephen Eugene Hickey and Bonita Marie Swan
John Paul, b. 7/21/1972; Stephen Eugene Hickey and Bonita Marie Swan

HILL,
Brycen Taite, b. 1/18/1998 in N. Conway; Richard Wayne Hill and Starr Leita Seamans
Cheryl Ann, b. 3/29/1979; Wayne Edward Hill and Annie Marie Blomstrom
Logan Trask, b. 3/28/1992; Richard Wayne Hill and Donna Lou Smith

HILTON,
son, b. 8/15/1889; Freeman Hilton (farmer, Ossipee) and ----- (Ossipee)
son, b. 6/20/1906 in Ossipee; first; Newell C. Hilton (farmer, Ossipee) and Lizzie Webster (Tamworth)
Barbara F., b. 6/16/1948; sixth; Maynard Hilton (Ossipee) and Nora F. Drew (Madison)
Jennifer J., b. 12/9/1965; first; Leonard R. Hilton and Barbara J. Grace
Leonard R., b. 4/13/1945; fifth; Maynard W. Hilton (Ctr. Ossipee) and Nora Florence Drew (Madison)
Stuart N., b. 1/6/1942; third; Maynard W. Hilton (Ossipee) and Nora F. Drew (Madison)

HITCHCOCK,
son [Austin C.], b. 5/2/1903 in Ossipee; third; Wilbur Hitchcock (farmer, Ossipee) and Addie Templeton (Ossipee)
daughter, b. 6/2/1905 in Ossipee; fifth; Wilbur Hitchcock (laborer, 35, Ossipee) and Addie Templeton (24, Ossipee)
daughter, b. 5/21/1921; tenth; Wilbur T. Hitchcock (farmer, Ossipee) and Ada Templeton (Ossipee)
Mildred L., b. 8/25/1908; Wilbur T. Hitchcock and Addie T. Hitchcock (1960)
Newell W., Jr., b. 11/23/1952; first; Newell Hitchcock (NH) and Alice Abbott (NH)
Ruth, b. 4/30/1913; seventh; Wilbur T. Hitchcock (farmer, Ossipee) and Addie Templeton (Ossipee)
Sharon A., b. 10/15/1955; second; Newell Hitchcock (NH) and Alice Abbott (NH)
Stanley R., b. 11/9/1918; W. Hitchcock (farmer, Ossipee) and Addie Templeton (Ossipee)

HMIELESKI,
Christopher Michael, b. 7/6/1993 in Wolfeboro; Robert Edward Hmieleski and Christine Jennifer Ayer

HOAGLAND,
Megan Louise, b. 8/15/1992; Gary Wayne Hoagland and Mary Louise Cook

HOBBS,
daughter, b. 9/16/1899 in Ossipee; first; W. B. Hobbs (merchant, 58, Ossipee) and Myra Knox (38, Ossipee)
Burlo A., b. 12/9/1894; Samuel Hobbs (NH) and Annie B. Tibbetts (ME) (1959)
Don P., b. 4/21/1880; Orodon P. D. Hobbs (NH) and Winnifred M. Atwood (NH) (1954)
Elvnor, b. 9/5/1921; first; Herbert Hobbs (auto mechanic, Tamworth) and Ethel L. Moody (Tamworth)
Inez Lizette, b. 12/13/1885; Orodon Hobbs (NH) and Winnifred Hobbs (ME) (1950)
Leon F., b. 11/27/1963; first; Frank W. Hobbs and Sandra Watson
Nola Elizabeth, b. 2/26/1897; Samuel Hobbs (Ossipee) and Annie Tibbetts (Augusta, ME) (1949)
Nora May, b. 2/26/1897; Samuel Hobbs (Ossipee) and Annie Tibbetts (Augusta, ME) (1949)

HODGDON,
Jessika Haley, b. 12/3/1991; Jeffrey G. Hodgdon and Tina MacDonald

HODGE,
son, b. 12/8/1899 in Ossipee; second; Fred Hodge (laborer, 24, Ossipee) and Bertha Nichols (20, Effingham)
son [John L.], b. 8/22/1908 in Ossipee; third; Bert N. Hodge (painter, Ossipee) and Nettie F. Loring (Ossipee)
son [Eugene William], b. 12/20/1912; fourth; Bert N. Hodge (mail carrier, Ossipee) and Nettie F. Loring (Ossipee)
child, b. 12/21/1926; first; Elwood Hodge (Ossipee) and Rachel Merrow (Ossipee)
Allyn N., b. 8/12/1943; third; Eugene W. Hodge (Ctr. Ossipee) and Myrtle Langley (Parsonsfield, ME)
Bert Wayne, b. 10/1/1938; first; Eugene W. Hodge (Ctr. Ossipee) and Myrtle S. Langley (W. Parsonsfield)
Bruce Allan, b. 7/10/1941; second; Carleton LeRoy Hodge (Ossipee) and Alice Maria Jordan (Ellsworth Falls, ME)
Burton J., b. 10/20/1947; second; John L. Hodge (Ctr. Ossipee) and Beatrice R. Milliken (Parsonsfield, ME)
Charles Francis, b. 8/17/1945; third; Carleton L. Hodge (Ossipee) and Alice Maria Jordan (Ellsworth, ME)
Constance Louise, b. 7/19/1938; sixth; Elwood N. Hodge (Ossipee) and Edith Bickford (Dover)
Debra Faye, b. 12/26/1956; second; Fenton A. Hodge (NH) and Jennette R. Eldridge (ME)
Donna F., b. 12/30/1961; third; Fenton A. Hodge and Jennette Eldridge
Fern Florence, b. 10/2/1934; fourth; Elwood N. Hodge (Ossipee) and Edith Bickford (Dover)
Gary Eugene, b. 12/4/1941; second; Eugene William Hodge (Ossipee) and Myrtle Sylvia Langley (Parsonsfield, ME)
John, b. 4/24/1907 in Ossipee; second; Bert Hodge (carpenter, Ossipee) and Nettie Loring (Ossipee)
June L., b. 7/5/1929; first; Elwood N. Hodge (Ossipee) and Edith Bickford (Dover)
Laura H., b. 4/7/1932; third; Elwood N. Hodge (Ossipee) and Edith Bickford (Dover)
Lloyd B., b. 11/17/1928; second; Bernard Hodge (Ossipee) and Doris Welch (Ossipee)
Marie E., b. 7/28/1936; fifth; Elwood Hodge (Ossipee) and Edith Bickford (Dover)
Muriel E., b. 3/11/1927; first; Bernard Hodge (Ossipee) and Doris Welch (Ossipee)
Philip Lee, b. 8/18/1938; third; Bernard L. Hodge (Ctr. Ossipee) and Doris Marion Welch (Moultonville)
Richard Jordan, b. 12/8/1936; first; Carleton Hodge (Ctr. Ossipee) and Alice Jordan (Ellsworth, ME)

Robert M., b. 5/13/1928; second; Elwood N. Hodge (Ossipee) and Rachel Merrow (Ossipee)
Sarah Beth, b. 7/4/1981; Dennis Fenton Hodge and Ronda Lee Caulkins
Virginia Lee, b. 6/13/1941; third; Bernard Loring Hodge (Ossipee) and Doris Marion Welch (Ossipee)

HODGES,
Deborah G., b. 5/8/1947; first; Peter M. Hodges (Norfolk, MA) and Sarah M. Arnold (Springfield, KY)
Jennifer Jean, b. 10/2/1948; second; Peter M. Hodges (Attleboro, MA) and Sarah M. Arnold (Washington Cty., KY)

HODSDON,
child, b. 1/1/1926; Helen Conner (Exeter)

HOLBROOK,
Irene I., b. 11/21/1922; second; Clement H. Holbrook (baggage master, Mendon, MA) and Mary Berry (Ossipee)
Janice, b. 12/23/1920; first; Clement Holbrook (laborer, Ossipee) and Mary F. Berry (Mendon, MA)
June E., b. 11/2/1926; third; Clement Holbrook (Mendon, MA) and Mary Berry (Ossipee)

HOLLADAY,
Alex Matthew, b. 10/29/1997 in N. Conway; Eric James Holladay and Rachel Ailene Emond

HOLMER,
Charlie C., b. 7/19/1898 in Ossipee; first; Charlie C. Holmer (hostler, 21, Rochester) and Jennie Kimball (19, Ossipee); residence - Rochester

HOLT,
son, b. 4/5/1919; second; Charles W. Holt (laborer, Milford) and Georgia M. Ames (Ossipee)

HOOPER,
daughter, b. 10/–/1895 in Ossipee; third; Frank Hooper (clergyman, Trowbridge, England) and Delener Taylor (Woodstock, NB)

HORN,
David C., b. 11/13/1965; first; Raymond H. Horn and Irene E. Libby

HORNE,
stillborn son, b. 12/5/1913; second; Harry E. Horne (fireman, S. Berwick, ME) and Elizabeth Snow (Milton, MA)
daughter, b. 10/5/1917; third; Harry Horne (fireman, Berwick, ME) and Elizabeth Snow (Milton, MA)
Megan Lynn, b. 12/30/1993 in Wolfeboro; Robert Glen Horne, Jr. and Sarah Lynne Althoff
Melanie A., b. 4/18/1968; Robert G. Horne and Thurley-Ann Perry
Robert, Jr., b. 9/4/1966; first; Robert G. Horne and Thurley-Ann Perry

HOUGH,
Nicholas Thomas, b. 7/3/1997 in Wolfeboro; John Kelly Hough and Theodora Constantaris

HOWARD,
Matthew A., b. 5/11/1988; Gregory W. Howard and Gail E. Austin
Patrick Casey, b. 1/19/1990; Gregory Webster Howard and Gail Elizabeth Austin
Sydney Kaelin, b. 1/24/1996 in Wolfeboro; David Paul Howard and Rachelle Alice Hamel

HOWE,
Linda Katelynn, b. 5/14/1993 in Wolfeboro; Paul Edward Howe and Deborah Elizabeth Walker

HOWLAND,
son, b. 1/13/1917; third; Fred Howland (laborer, Lisbon) and Nellie Martin (Wolfeboro); residence - Wakefield

HUCKINS,
daughter, b. 7/17/1906 in Ossipee; first; Ernest C. Huckins (merchant, Freedom) and Jane T. Merrow (Freedom)
stillborn daughter, b. 2/22/1915; first; Albert O. Huckins (lumber dealer, Freedom) and Katherine McNally (Providence, RI)

HUNT,
Carol D., b. 7/24/1947; second; Edgar F. Hunt (Lebanon) and Carol Johnson (Warner)
Sierra Elizabeth, b. 8/24/1995 in Portsmouth; Roger Leslie Hunt and Patricia Ann Converse

HUNTLEY,
Marshall Goodblood, b. 4/1/1986; William Gates Huntley and Judith Goodblood

HURD,
daughter, b. 8/28/1911 in Ossipee; third; Homer H. Hurd (blacksmith, Sanford, ME) and Grace Staples (Parsonsfield, ME)
son, b. 10/5/1913; fourth; Homer H. Hurd (blacksmith, Sanford, ME) and Grace Staples (Parsonsfield, ME)
Homer E., b. 6/27/1910 in Ossipee; second; Homer H. Hurd (blacksmith, Sanford, ME) and Grace Staples (Parsonsfield, ME)
Newell, b. 11/8/1916; fourth; Homer H. Hurd (blacksmith, Ossipee) and Grace Staples (Parsonsfield, ME)

HUTCHINS,
son, b. 11/9/1933; sixth; John C. Davis (Tamworth) and Isabel Hutchins (Tamworth)
Emma Leah, b. 5/21/1904 in Ossipee; first; Morris B. Hutchins (veterinary, 43, New York City) and Alice Walker (27, Wakefield)

HVEDLISIAN,
child, b. 5/31/1927; first; Isabel Hvedlisian (Medford, MA)

JACK,
Priscilla, b. 2/19/1935; third; Guy Jack (PA) and Gladys Shortridge (Ossipee)

JACKSON,
Hayley Josephine, b. 7/19/1996 in N. Conway; Peter Jackson and Julie Taliento

JACOBS,
Calysta Tamara, b. 2/14/1997 in Wolfeboro; Mark Leroy Jacobs and Juliann Cloutier
Mikayla Breanna, b. 7/14/1993 in Wolfeboro; Mark LeRoy Jacobs and Juliann Cloutier

JACOBSEN,
Karen Turid, b. 7/28/1950; first; Thomas Jacobsen (Kvalvig-Faro Islands) and Annie Libby (Ossipee)
Laurie A., b. 3/11/1959; fourth; Thomas Jacobsen (Denmark) and Annie Libby (Ossipee)
Martin Dean, b. 8/18/1952; third; Thomas Jacobsen (Reykvigfaro Island) and Annie Libby (Ossipee)
Thomas S., II, b. 8/19/1963; fifth; Thomas S. Jacobsen and Annie Libby

JANNESSE,
Harvey Lloyd, b. 3/13/1934; first; John I. Jannesse (Wolfeboro) and Florence E. Dyer (W. Baldwin, ME)

JAY,
Laura Rose, b. 8/30/1992; Paul David Jay and Paula Dean Oliver

JENNESS,
daughter, b. 6/17/1887; second; Frank Jenness (laborer, 25, Wakefield, MA) and Abbie (21, Ossipee)
Crystal Gayle, b. 8/17/1987; Wayne H. Jenness and Margaret E. Eldridge
Harvey, Jr., b. 7/12/1959; first; Harvey Jenness (Cornish, ME) and Marie Wiggin (Wolfeboro)
Wayne H., b. 5/2/1961; second; Harvey Jenness and Marie Wiggin

JEROME,
daughter, b. 10/15/1892 in Ossipee; third; Edward Jerome (farmer, Island Pond, VT) and Josephine Clough (Newfield, ME)

JEWETT,
Craig Martin, b. 4/6/1951; third; Edgar Jewett (Washington, DC) and Mary Martinneau (Walden, VT)
Lu A., b. 7/28/1955; third; Edgar Jewett (Washington, DC) and Mary Martineau (VT)

JOHNSON,
stillborn child, b. 2/11/1909 in Ossipee; first; Fanny Johnson
Barbara Ann, b. 9/3/1950; first; David Johnson (MA) and Patricia Dickinson (NH)
Darrell W., b. 2/1/1967; first; Dennis W. Johnson and Rose M. Hobbs
Forrest Roger, b. 9/27/1951; sixth; Forrest Johnson (NH) and Effie Bean (NH)
Jessica Jane, b. 7/18/1977; Chester Forrest Johnson, Jr. and Ann Louise Lunt
Jessica Sylvia, b. 7/21/1988; Kirk E. Johnson and Gail A. Nelson
Kelley J., b. 10/18/1960; third; Arthur J. Johnson and Janice E. Kelley
Kerry Dori, b. 7/26/1973; Donald Harry Johnson and Marsha Ellen Murphy
Kirk E., b. 12/13/1960; fourth; Donald E. Johnson and Sylvia L. York
Larry A., b. 8/31/1947; second; Marshall B. Johnson (Tamworth) and Alice E. Williamson (E. Machias, ME)
Nickolas Ross, b. 12/17/1996 in N. Conway; Darrell W. Johnson and Rebecca L. Ross
Reita Lee, b. 9/7/1949; second; Donald Johnson (Medford, MA) and Sylvia York (Wolfeboro)

Susan Carol, b. 10/9/1951; second; David Johnson (MA) and Patricia
    Dickinson (NH)
Tammy Lyn, b. 5/6/1971; Glenn Edward Johnson and Karren Elaine Mann

JOHNSTON,
Alexandra Jean, b. 12/30/1984; Richard Alexander Johnston and Patricia
    Ann Hamel

JONES,
Chester David, b. 4/28/1975; David Henry Jones and Debra Plummer
Meredith Donovan, b. 4/22/2000 in Manchester; Andrew Jones and Claire
    Donovan
Robert Edward, b. 9/26/1982; Robert George Jones and Cynthia Ann
    Berry
Scott Dnaiel, b. 1/1/1981; Daniel Paul Jones and Renee Sandra Elliott
Staci Lyn, b. 5/4/1985; Carl Duane Jones and Cynthia Jean Anthony
Thomas Robert, b. 7/2/1981; Robert George Jones and Cynthia Ann Berry

JONSSON,
Erica Lee, b. 4/24/1982; Harry Erick Jonsson and Patricia Helen Ann
    Cotton
Krista Lin, b. 10/30/1979; Harry Erik Jonsson and Patricia Helen Ann
    Cotton
Tara Erin, b. 1/19/1978; Harry Eric Jonsson and Patricia Helen Ann Cotton

JORDAN,
child, b. 10/3/1923; second; Arthur F. Jordan (Ellsworth, ME) and Mildred
    H. Safford (Bath, ME)
Edward Russell, b. 3/17/1949; third; Ralph Jordan (Ossipee) and Phyllis
    Cacicia (Quincy, MA)
Harold B., b. 7/13/1925; third; Arthur F. Jordan (Ellsworth, ME) and
    Mildred Safford (Bath, ME)
Harry Newton, b. 7/7/1930; fifth; Arthur F. Jordan (Ellsworth, ME) and
    Mildred Safford (Bath, ME)
Janice Carol, b. 12/4/1946; first; Ralph Jordan (Ossipee) and Phyllis Ann
    Garicia (Quincy, MA)
Kenneth H., b. 9/1/1927; fourth; Arthur Jordan (Ellsworth, ME) and Mildred
    Safford (Bath, ME)
Sumner Danae, b. 5/19/1977; Peter Allen Jordan and Diane Marie Hebert

JUDKINS,
Charlotte, b. 3/26/1958; second; Thomas Judkins (Effingham) and Dorothy
    Eldridge (Ossipee)
Janet M., b. 6/9/1964; sixth; Thomas Judkins and Dorothy Eldridge
Roberta, b. 9/21/1966; seventh; Thomas Judkins and Dorothy Eldridge

Susanne L., b. 10/17/1962; fifth; Thomas Judkins and Dorothy Eldridge
Thomas, Jr., b. 3/13/1956; first; Thomas Judkins (NH) and Dorothy C.
Eldridge (NH)

KARCHER,
Waneta V., b. 12/28/1918; sixth; William Karcher (laborer, Charlestown,
MA) and Martha Wilfort (Roxbury, MA)

KEEFE,
son, b. 12/2/1896 in Ossipee; first; William Keefe (farmer, 23, Boston) and
Grace A. Chute (23, Effingham)
Luella Winnifred, b. 9/22/1900 in Ossipee; second; William Keefe (farmer)
and Grace Shute (Ossipee)

KEHOE,
Elysia Donna, b. 3/20/1993 in N. Conway; Anthony James Kehoe and
Kathy Ann Goss

KELLEHER,
Stacy Lynne, b. 11/14/1997 in Rochester; Paul Joseph Kelleher and Susan
Lynne Davis

KELLEY,
Carla Ann, b. 5/15/1970; Ralph Merrow Kelley and Judith Ann Wasson
Gail Elaine, b. 9/14/1944; fifth; Philip H. Kelley (Northboro, MA) and
Marion M. Merrow (Ctr. Ossipee)
Jeffrey Wingate, b. 12/14/1976; Ralph Merrow Kelley and Judith Ann
Wasson

KENISON,
Arthur E., b. 4/12/1912; third; Arthur Kenison (lawyer, Conway) and
Isadore Rowe (ME)
Wesley Alan, b. 10/1/1978; Alan Arthur Kenison and Angela Leon

KENISTON,
Brenda Lee, b. 9/16/1983; Scott David Keniston and Lorena Lee Corrow
Carroll H., b. 3/31/1962; fifth; Robert Keniston and Elizabeth Gagne
David Scott, b. 9/12/1986; Scott David Keniston and Lorena Lee Corrow

KENNARD,
Jeffrey S., b. 5/12/1952; fifth; Raymond Kennard (NH) and Ruth Pearson
(NH)
Jill Elizabeth, b. 6/17/1956; sixth; Raymond S. Kennard (NH) and Ruth E.
Pearson (MA)

Kathryn L., b. 10/21/1948; second; Raymond S. Kennard (E. Barrington) and Ruth E. Pearson (Malden, MA)
Laura Mae, b. 4/16/1952; first; Benjamin Kennard (Nottingham) and Edna Lord (NH)
Martin S., b. 2/11/1954; fifth; Raymond S. Kennard (NH) and Ruth E. Pearson (MA)
Raymond S., Jr., b. 6/2/1947; first; Raymond S. Kennard (E. Barrington) and Ruth E. Pearson (Malden, MA)
Thomas Stephen, b. 1/28/1950; third; Raymond Kennard (Nottingham) and Ruth E. Pearson (Malden, MA)

KENNETT,
child, b. 12/29/1932; first; Clarence R. Kennett (Silver Lake) and Edith M. Hamilton (Somerville, MA)
Frederick W., Jr., b. 9/12/1954; first; Frederick W. Kennett (NH) and Nora L. Chambers (TX)

KENNY,
Cameron Joseph, b. 7/10/1999 in Wolfeboro; Thomas Kenny and Michelle Kenny

KEYES,
Susan M., b. 11/24/1965; second; William C. Keyes and Cynthia Ellison
William A., b. 8/13/1969; William C. Keyes and Cynthia Ellison

KEYS,
daughter, b. 5/28/1888; fourth; Charles E. Keys (merchant, Ossipee) and Lizzie S. Chamberlin (Ossipee)
daughter [Iola], b. 12/20/1890 in Ossipee; Charles Keys (merchant, Ossipee) and Sarah E. Keys (Wolfeboro)

KILBRETH,
Jeremiah, b. 2/27/1971; Walter Paul Kilbreth and Jane Evelyn Hann

KIMBALL,
daughter, b. 9/23/1889; Charles P. Kimball (farmer, Ossipee) and Vilenor Kimball (Moultonboro)
Adam Michael, b. 7/28/1992; Clayton Dennis Kimball and Kimberly Susan Wilks
Adelaide, b. 5/21/1897 in Ossipee; Horace Kimball (farmer, Ossipee) and Viola Fogg (Ossipee)
Colton Douglas, b. 3/17/2000 in Portland, ME; Douglas Kimball and Joanne Kimball

Robert H., b. 10/23/1936; first; Albert E. Kimball (Everett, MA) and
Beatrice Huckins (Ossipee)

KIMBLE,
Judson Brian, b. 7/24/1984; Brian Raymond Kimble and Judith Roberta
Haag

KINCAID,
daughter, b. 8/12/1888; third; W. E. Kincaid (m. cutter, Cornish, ME) and
Anna Kincaid (Rutland, VT)

KING,
son, b. 11/3/1908 in Ossipee; second; H. H. King (laborer, Springfield, ME)
and Mabel Willey (Springfield, ME)
Christina Marie, b. 5/28/1991; Johnathan Wayne King and Marianne
Abbott
Debra Eileen, b. 10/7/1987; Charles A. King and Helen M. Walker
Kimberly Ann, b. 7/25/1987; Johnathan W. King and Marianne Abbott
Victoria Anne, b. 10/3/1989; Johnathan Wayne King and Marianne Abbott

KINMOND,
Heather L., b. 6/21/1968; David W. Kinmond and Brenda J. Frisbee
Kayla Audrie, b. 3/1/1994 in Wolfeboro; Scott D. Kinmond and Anne M.
Fogarty
Meghan Anne, b. 3/17/1996 in Wolfeboro; Scott David Kinmond and Anne
Marie Fogarty

KIRCH,
Sarah Elizabeth, b. 8/8/1990; Wayne Henry Kirch and Vicky Lynn Williams

KIRKWOOD,
Bonnie Mae, b. 7/12/1941; first; Lawrence D. Kirkwood (Ossipee) and
Mary Knight Lord (Ossipee)
Cora E., b. 11/21/1902; George Kirkwood (NH) and Clara Eldridge (NH)
(1955)
Cynthia L., b. 3/24/1959; seventh; Lawrence Kirkwood (Ossipee) and Mary
Lord (W. Ossipee)
Dane C., b. 1/9/1957; sixth; Laurence Kirkwood (NH) and Mary K. Lord
(NH)
Deborah J., b. 10/6/1947; third; Lawrence Kirkwood (Ctr. Ossipee) and
Mary K. Lord (W. Ossipee)
George L., b. 3/6/1954; fifth; Lawrence D. Kirkwood (NH) and Mary K. Lord
(NH)

Jean P., b. 11/27/1923; second; Dana J. Kirkwood (Ossipee) and Bessie Phillips (Scotland)
Laurinda D., b. 8/6/1944; second; Lawrence Kirkwood (Ctr. Ossipee) and Mary Knight Lord (W. Ossipee)
Lawrence D., b. 2/9/1922; first; Dana G. Kirkwood (laborer, Ossipee) and Bessie Phillips (Scotland)
Victoria M., b. 4/25/1952; fourth; Lawrence Kirkwood (NH) and Mary Lord (NH)

KNAPP,
Korin Gabrielle, b. 3/16/1979; Thomas Francis Knapp and Dianne Frances Shannon
Michelle Lynn, b. 6/19/1983; Robert Allen Knapp and Kathryn Anderson
Rebecca Lynn, b. 8/3/1956; first; Richard A. Knapp (NH) and Carmen R. Davis (NH)
Richard A., b. 4/18/1932; first; George B. Knapp (KS) and Leda B. Eldridge (Ossipee)
Robert A., b. 9/19/1959; second; Richard Knapp (Wolfeboro) and Carmen Davis (N. Conway)
Scott Allen, b. 2/19/1981; Robert Allen Knapp and Kathryn Anderson
Shirley Ann, b. 7/13/1937; second; George B. Knapp (Norton, KS) and Leda B. Eldridge (Ossipee)
Steven Thomas, b. 8/12/1984; Clinton Dale Knapp and Tammy Jean Tozier

KNIGHT,
Michael Charles, b. 5/4/1990; Linda May Pattangall

KNOWLES,
Edna Martha, b. 10/5/1940; third; Winslow Knowles (Everett, MA) and Anna L. Gambell (Dorchester, MA)

KNOX,
daughter [Fay Ora], b. 9/1/1894 in Ossipee; fifth; Charles E. Knox (mechanic, 43, Berwick, ME) and Mary Chesley (28, Ossipee)
son [Edward C.], b. 7/28/1900 in Ossipee; eighth; Charles E. Knox (carpenter, 49, Berwick, ME) and Mary E. Chesley (34, Tamworth)
son [Darcy D.], b. 4/16/1904 in Ossipee; tenth; Charles E. Knox (sectionman, 53, Berwick, ME) and Mary E. Chesley (38, Tamworth)
Arlene E., b. 12/26/1931; third; Roy W. Knox (Ossipee) and ----- (Worcester, MA)
Avonne, b. 10/9/1927; first; ----- (Ossipee) and Florence Knox (Sanbornville)
Candace Sara, b. 2/1/1946; first; Charlotte S. Knox (Worcester, MA)

Charles, b. 3/5/1899 in Ossipee; tenth; Charles Knox (laborer, 33, Ossipee) and Carrie Templeton (33, Ossipee)

Charles Edward, b. 5/13/1925; first; Perley Knox (Ossipee) and Nellie Knight (Sandwich)

Dwight E., b. 9/30/1928; second; Darcy D. Knox (Ossipee) and Myrtle F. Vousden (Kent, England)

Gwendoline F., b. 8/21/1928; second; Roy W. Knox (Ossipee) and Sara E. Cather (Worcester, MA)

Hazel Godfrey, b. 12/25/1900 in Ossipee; second; Manville E. Knox (farmer, 33, Ossipee) and Mabel F. Thompson (22, Salisbury)

Olin A., b. 6/6/1886; Charles E. Knox (NH) and Mary E. Chesley (ME) (1959)

Rosemae C., b. 4/15/1927; first; Charles Knox (Ossipee) and Agnes Wasson (Ossipee)

Stanley, b. 4/2/1918; fourth; Earl S. Knox (insurance agt., Ossipee) and Eva Bickford (Rochester); residence - Rochester

KOKEL,
Austin Richard, b. 10/27/1981; Richard Henry Kokel and Jane Elizabeth Sobol

KONDRAT,
Jason Morgan, b. 10/20/1977; Thomas Zigmund Kondrat and Elaine Shelly Farrar

KOREN,
Abigail Rachel, b. 7/14/1999 in Ossipee; Daniel J. Koren and Leanne K. Koren

Daniel Joel, II, b. 8/6/1997 in Ossipee; Daniel Joel Koren and Leanne Howe

KRAFTON,
Jennifer Ann, b. 9/11/1994 in Wolfeboro; Brian G. Krafton and Pamela J. Stache

KRAMER,
Howard Grant, b. 1/23/1939; second; Robert G. Kramer (Portsmouth) and Beryl Moulton (Ossipee)

Lisle Page, b. 2/5/1936; first; Robert G. Kramer (Portsmouth) and Beryl M. Moulton (Ossipee)

Penny, b. 1/4/1958; second; Lisle P. Kramer (Wolfeboro) and Geraldine Minnerly (Norwalk, CT)

Ted Moulton, b. 9/25/1941; third; Robert Grant Kramer (Portsmouth) and Beryl Moulton (Ossipee)

KRUTILEK,
Kaylee Laurel, b. 10/9/2001 in Concord; Eric Krutilek and Tanya Krutilek

KUELL,
Kevin Robert, b. 12/11/1992; Robert William Kuell and Anne Marie Baker
Ryan William, b. 2/12/1991; Robert William Kuell and Anne Marie Baker

LALANCETTE,
Kaitlyn Mae, b. 5/4/1988; William E. Lalancette and Laurenn G. Wade

LAMB,
Starr Lynn, b. 8/4/1997 in Wolfeboro; Shawn Joseph Lamb and Michele Joan Tobin

LAMIE,
Lawrence B., b. 3/2/1936; George Tuft (Middleton) and Alexina M. Lamie (Sanbornville)

LAMONTAGNE,
son, b. 9/14/1893 in Ossipee; second; J. LaMontagne (laborer, Canada) and Alvira Boutcher (Halifax, Canada)
daughter, b. 3/23/1902 in Ossipee; first; Joseph Lamontagne (barber, 30, Canada) and Viola Goodwin (22, Madison)

LAMPER,
John, b. 7/22/1966; fourth; Norman R. Lamper and Edith L. Davis

LAMPSON,
son, b. 3/2/1905 in Ossipee; fourth; David Lampson (farmer, Newfane, VT) and Ida Whynot (NS)

LANCIAUX,
Christian Alain, b. 12/23/1984; Alain Maurice Lanciaux and Lorraine Patricia Pelletier
Michel Jean, b. 11/5/1986; Alain M. Lanciaux and Lorraine P. Pelletier

LANDER,
Kellie Lynn, b. 7/21/1995 in Wolfeboro; William Peter Lander and Susan Marie McCrossin
Megan Kathleen, b. 1/26/1993 in Wolfeboro; William Peter Lander and Susan Marie McCrossin

LAPETE,
Eric Ryan, b. 10/22/1987; Stephen C. Lapete and Beth A. Scogin

LAPOINTE,
Veronica M., b. 1/10/1943; first; Raymond E. LaPointe (St. Johnsbury, VT) and Doris M. Hayden (Burlington, VT)

LAROSA,
Jillian Theresa, b. 1/15/1986; Douglas John LaRosa and Judith Marie Varney
Sarah Jean, b. 3/2/1989; Douglas John LaRosa and Judith Marie Varney

LARRABEE,
Dennis Edwin, b. 10/11/1956; first; Donald E. Larrabee (NH) and Joyce B. Eldridge (NH)
Diane E., b. 9/13/1960; second; Donald E. Larrabee and Joyce B. Eldridge

LARSEN,
Jessica Nicole, b. 5/17/1995 in Dover; Mark James Larsen and Holly Marie Hudak

LAVOIE,
Madison Rose, b. 10/11/2001 in N. Conway; Arron Lavoie and Dorrie Lavoie

LAWS,
David W., b. 4/18/1957; first; David H. Laws (NH) and Barbara L. Butler (Washington, DC)
Martha E., b. 8/14/1948; third; Clifford W. Laws (Lynn, MA) and Elizabeth Atwood (Pelham)

LAZAROVICH,
Anthony Alan, b. 9/29/1985; Roger Alan Lazarovich and Janice Lynn Christopher

LEAHY,
Stefan James, b. 1/11/1986; Kevin John Leahy and Cheryl Ann Baldwin

LEAVITT,
son, b. 8/22/1899 in Ossipee; fourth; W. A. Leavitt (salesman, 38, Effingham) and Ada Maud Pease (28, Boston, MA)
Ernest Morton, b. 3/11/1938; first; Harry M. Leavitt (Parsonsfield) and Marguerite Huckins (Ctr. Ossipee)
Laurie A., b. 9/11/1965; second; Ernest M. Leavitt and Mary A. Bellerose
Mathew Kenneth, b. 3/17/1983; Kenneth Charles Leavitt and Eileen Mary Byrt
Scott M., b. 5/1/1964; first; Ernest Leavitt and Mary Bellerose

Seth Francis, b. 4/25/1978; Kenneth Charles Leavitt and Eileen Mary Byrt

LEE,
Jane G., b. 8/19/1924; first; Arthur Lee (Canada) and Beatrice Raymond (Canada)

LEGAULT,
Crystal Ann, b. 8/4/1992; Paul Emile Legault and Christine Elizabeth Schule

LEGENDRE,
Dennis, b. 5/1/1947; first; Emile J. Legendre (Berlin) and Irene I. Holbrook (Ctr. Ossipee)
Jeffrey Michael, b. 9/29/1974; Dennis Emile Legendre and Susan Patricia Christiansen
Marcella Jean, b. 11/13/1949; second; Emile Legendre (Berlin) and Irene Holbrook (Ossipee)
Maureen Mae, b. 4/23/1957; third; Emile J. Legendre (NH) and Irene I. Holbrook (NH)

LEGERE,
Nicholas Adam, b. 6/4/1989; Glenn Samuel Legere and Michelle Ann Baillargeon

LEHMAN,
Benjamin James, b. 7/14/1998 in Wolfeboro; James William Lehman and Maureen Patricia Russo

LEIGHTON,
Cynthia Gail, b. 12/1/1951; first; Hugh Leighton (ME) and Laura Hodgdon (NH)

LEMAY,
Robert Holden, b. 3/4/1991; Shawn Jeffrey Lemay and Marlo Ann Watson;
Zachary Allen, b. 4/22/1989; Shawn Jeffrey Lemay and Marlo Ann Watson

LENNON,
Michael Charles, b. 12/19/1938; first; Charles J. Lennon (Reading) and Miriam E. Meloon (Beverly)

LEONARD,
Kayla Virginia Cheri, b. 9/9/1989; Mark Edward Leonard and Elaine Laura Heighe

LEONE,
Jessica Sharon, b. 10/7/1976; Mark Francis Leone and Laurie Ann Kirch

LESSARD,
Brian Paul, b. 7/21/1980; Chris V. Lessard and Ann Celia Caterino
Joseph Christian, b. 1/26/1983; Chris V. Lessard and Ann Celia Caterino
Shane, b. 11/11/1976; Richard John Lessard and Ann Rochelle Lambert

LESTER,
Kevin John, b. 8/9/1977; John Gregory Lester and Linda Lee Tapper

LEWIS,
daughter, b. 4/13/1893 in Ossipee; second; George Lewis (laborer, Ossipee) and Ema Clough (Effingham)
daughter, b. 11/20/1894 in Ossipee; third; George M. Lewis (farmer, 30, Ossipee) and Emma Clough (20, Ossipee)
Katherine Mae, b. 9/23/1990; Nathaniel Tinker Lewis and Nina Marie Gould
Ryan Andrew, b. 10/17/1987; Nathaniel T. Lewis and Nina M. Gould

LIBBY,
daughter, b. 2/20/1914; second; Robert W. Libbey (sic) (laborer, Tuftonboro) and Helen S. Eldridge (Ossipee)
child [Alfred K.], b. 11/24/1926; fourth; Robert Libby (Tuftonboro) and Helen Eldridge (Ossipee)
child, b. 3/28/1929; eighth; Robert M. Libby (Tuftonboro) and Helen S. Eldridge (Ossipee)
child, b. 1/8/1933; first; Robert M. Libby (Ossipee) and Helen Eldridge (Tuftonboro)
Brenda L., b. 9/19/1959; fourth; Randolph Libby (Porter, ME) and Carol Perry (Bartlett)
Brindall Ann, b. 9/26/1976; Scott Barry Libby and Vanessa Vittum
Christopher Carl, b. 9/3/1975; David Randolph Libby and Darlene April Eldridge
David R., b. 8/31/1955; first; Randolph Libby (ME) and Carole Perry (NH)
Elson L., b. 9/26/1922; first; Frank Libby (farmer, Tuftonboro) and Bernice L. Canney (Ossipee); residence - Tuftonboro
Florence, b. 9/19/1919; Robert Libby (NH) and Helen Libby (NH) (1958)
Floyd Fred, b. 8/12/1936; twelfth; Robert M. Libby (Tuftonboro) and Helen S. Eldridge (Ossipee)
Hope Victoria, b. 3/5/1972; Scott Barry Libby and Vanessa Vittum
Joshua David, b. 10/4/1978; David Randolph Libby and Darlene April Eldridge
Kelly Mae, b. 8/1/1981; Michael Charles Libby and Cynthia Ann Varney

Leonard Burton, b. 2/11/1930; sixth; Herbert Libby (Wolfeboro) and Gladys Shackford (Alfred, ME)
Linda L., b. 9/12/1943; first; Elson L. Libby (Tuftonboro) and Lois F. Sweet (Tamworth)
Marion A., b. 7/13/1920; Scott D. Libby (farmer, Wakefield) and Stella L. Russell (Waterboro)
Michael J., b. 6/18/1959; second; Winfield Libby (Ossipee) and Constance Pineo (Attleboro, MA)
Randolph C., Jr., b. 7/13/1961; fifth; Randolph Libby and Carole A. Perry
Richard Allen, b. 9/17/1956; second; Randolph C. Libby (ME) and Carole A. Perry (NH)
Roland H., b. 10/11/1930; ninth; Robert M. Libby (Tuftonboro) and Helen E. Eldridge (Ossipee)
Sally A., b. 8/6/1964; sixth; Randolph Libby and Carole Perry
Stacey Lee, b. 12/6/1976; Carl Owen Libby and Brenda June Harmon
Stacy Lynn, b. 2/28/1980; Michael Charles Libby and Cynthia Ann Varney
Steven Scott, b. 1/10/1946; third; Raymond S. Libby (Portland, ME) and Dora B. Nason (Strafford)
Susan G., b. 2/2/1947; first; Annie C. Libby (Ossipee)
Susan M., b. 4/18/1963; fifth; Randolph C. Libby and Carole Perry
Tracey Lyn, b. 12/6/1976; Carl Owen Libby and Brenda June Harmon
Wendy L., b. 8/31/1955; first; Winfield Libby (NH) and Constance Pineo (NH)
Winfield J., Jr., b. 12/11/1967; third; Winfield J. Libby and Constance M. Pineo
Zachary Eldridge, b. 5/3/1986; David Randolph Libby and Darlene April Eldridge

LILLIBRIDGE,
Mary Catherine, b. 9/30/1979; William Lillibridge and Mary Catherine Durkin

LITTLEFIELD,
stillborn child, b. 9/6/1939; first; George L. Littlefield (Barnstead) and Clara Eldridge (Ctr. Ossipee)

LOCKWOOD,
David Alan, b. 6/28/1937; third; Nyle Lockwood (Concord) and Doris Parker (Beebe, Quebec)

LOGAN,
Melonie Lynn, b. 1/28/1983; John Peter Logan and Norma Jean Violette

LORD,
son [Carroll W.], b. 2/9/1908 in Ossipee; first; John A. Lord (teamster, Ossipee) and Laura M. Knight (Belfast, ME)
daughter, b. 8/25/1910 in Ossipee; second; John A. Lord (painter, Ossipee) and Florence M. Knight (Ossipee)
son, b. 10/16/1922; sixth; John A. Lord (undertaker, Ossipee) and Laura M. Knights (Belfast, ME)
Arnold J., b. 7/2/1961; seventh; Rolland Lord and Mary E. Burke
Benjamin Tufts, b. 7/17/1984; Brian Charles Lord and Bonnie Louise Rankin
Brian C., b. 1/13/1957; sixth; Rolland Lord (NH) and Mary E. Burke (NS)
Burke Rankin, b. 12/11/1988; Brian Charles Lord and Bonnie Louise Rankin
Charlotte J., b. 1/7/1929; eighth; John A. Lord (Ossipee) and Laura A. Knight (Belfast, ME)
Diane M., b. 2/17/1953; fourth; Rolland Lord (NH) and Mary Burke (Canada)
Edna A., b. 1/21/1921; fifth; John A. Lord (undertaker, Ossipee) and Louise M. Knight (Belfast, ME)
Francis Edwin, b. 5/27/1951; third; Rolland Lord (NH) and Mary Burke (Canada)
Joanne E., b. 4/24/1955; fifth; Rolland Lord (NS) and Mary Burke (NH)
Katrina Pearl, b. 7/27/1992; John Gregory Lord and Kay Ellen Davis
Lindsay Elizabeth, b. 6/22/1984; Francis E. Lord and Ann Flanders
Martha Adelle, b. 4/27/1949; second; Rolland W. Lord (Ossipee) and Mary Bruke (NS)
Mary K., b. 1/23/1925; seventh; John A. Lord (Ossipee) and Laura Knight (Belfast, ME)
Ruth, b. 4/20/1914; fourth; John A. Lord (clerk, Ossipee) and Florence M. Knight (Belfast, ME)
William Scott, b. 7/27/1992; John Gregory Lord and Kay Ellen Davis

LORING,
child, b. 10/25/1892 in Ossipee; third; Elmer Loring (mechanic, Ossipee) and Julia Loring (Ossipee); residence - Moultonville
son [Rupert L.], b. 11/23/1909 in Ossipee; first; Roy E. Loring (clerk, Ossipee) and Helen E. Corson (Somerset, MA)
son [Robert B.], b. 11/8/1914; third; Roy E. Loring (farmer, Ossipee) and Helen Corson (Somerset, MA)
daughter, b. 4/5/1921; sixth; Roy E. Loring (farmer, Ossipee) and Helen E. Corson (Somerset, ME)
child, b. 8/25/1928; seventh; Roy E. Loring (Ossipee) and Helen E. Corson (Somerset, MA)
Dorothy, b. 1/24/1911 in Ossipee; second; Roy Loring (butcher, Ossipee) and Helen Corson (Somerset, MA)

Gail Sandra, b. 11/13/1944; first; J. Milburn Loring (Ctr. Ossipee) and Sadie Elvira Drew (Madison)
Helen Elizabeth, b. 6/28/1950; second; Robert Loring (Ossipee) and Ruth Mitchell (Campton)
John, b. 10/28/1917; first; Chester M. Loring (chauffeur, Ossipee) and Esther E. Pineo (Ossipee)
Russell G., b. 6/11/1947; first; Robert B. Loring (Ctr. Ossipee) and Ruth F. Mitchell (Campton)
Ruth E., b. 4/17/1918; fifth; Roy Loring (laborer, Ossipee) and Helen Corson (Somerset, MA)
Steven M., b. 11/18/1968; Russell G. Loring and Nancy J. Doe
Timothy Roy, b. 10/18/1952; first; David Loring (NH) and Muriel Hodge (NH)

LOUD,
Arthur, b. 5/7/1920; second; Perley W. Loud (farmer, Melrose, MA) and Lena Hodge (Ossipee)
Clarence B., b. 10/13/1929; first; Perley W. Loud (Malden, MA) and Alice Lambert (E. Corinth, ME)
Emma M., b. 10/11/1918; first; Perley W. Loud (farmer, Malden, MA) and Lena M. Hodge (Ossipee)
George W. T., b. 10/13/1929; second; Perley W. Loud (Malden, MA) and Alice Lambert (E. Corinth, ME)
James F., b. 7/24/1968; Simon F. Loud and Nancy J. Libby
James Hilton, b. 9/1/1951; second; Edmund Loud (VT) and Ruth Hilton (MA)
John F., b. 4/21/1947; first; Arthur P. Loud (Ctr. Ossipee) and June F. Chick (Madison)
Jordan McKenzie, b. 10/29/1992; Jonathan Ryer Loud and Dana Lynn Henderson
Jushua Ryer, b. 1/3/1988; Jonathan Ryer Loud and Dana L. Henderson
Nancy, b. 5/29/1949; third; Arthur Loud (Ossipee) and June Chick (Madison)
Shirley Evelyn, b. 6/19/1948; Arthur Loud (Ossipee) and June Chick (Madison)
Simon F., b. 12/22/1943; first; Edmund D. Loud (Norwich, VT) and Ruth G. Hilton (Lawrence, MA)
Tina M., b. 7/27/1967; first; Simon F. Loud and Nancy J. Libby

LOVERING,
Patricia A., b. 5/7/1936; second; Albert R. Lovering (Freedom) and Norma Waldron (Reading, MA)

LOYAS,
Zachary Jonathan, b. 12/22/1988; Robert Loyas and Hazelean Marie Frailey

LUDWIG,
Eric Sean, Jr., b. 10/16/1990; Eric Sean Ludwig and Lisa Marie Alessi

LUKEN,
Joanne C., b. 11/27/1953; first; Charles Luken (NY) and Josephine Van Meter (NY)

LUSCOMB,
Jodi Ann, b. 9/18/1979; Kenneth Keith Luscomb and Patricia Marie Mollica

LUSH,
Travis Charles, b. 6/13/1996 in Wolfeboro; Mark Douglas Lush and Brenda Claire Gehly

LUTTS,
Sabrina Holly, b. 4/12/1981; Richard John Lutts and Francine Beland

LYMAN,
Anthony Gene, b. 5/11/1990; James Scott Lyman and Dale Lee Cairone

LYONS,
daughter, b. 4/23/1950; first; Mack Lyons (Alton) and Deslie White (Ossipee)

MACARTHUR,
Kevin Michael, b. 8/22/1983; Robert Alan MacArthur and Danette Virginia Toma

MACBRIEN,
Constance, b. 10/23/1942; first; Philip MacBrien (Lynn, MA) and Mabel Harmon (Ossipee)

MACDONALD [see McDonald],
Alison Mary, b. 6/20/1991; Edward Joseph MacDonald and Maureen Patricia Harkins
Cynthia L., b. 12/1/1967; third; Franklin R. MacDonald and Linda M. Deatte
Douglas O., b. 10/3/1951; fifth; George MacDonald (NH) and Mary Strang (CT)

Forrest, Jr., b. 8/27/1953; first; Forrest MacDonald (NH) and Barbara Hobbs (NH)
Gale L., b. 3/30/1969; Franklin R. MacDonald and Linda M. Deatte
George O., b. 12/5/1942; George O. MacDonald (Whitefield) and Mary L. Strong (Glastonbury, CT)
Lauren Noelle, b. 11/22/1992; Edward Joseph MacDonald and Maureen Patricia Harkins
Linda Bessie, b. 7/1/1950; fourth; George MacDonald (Whitefield) and Mary Strang (Glastonbury)
Marilyn R., b. 12/10/1948; George MacDonald (Whitefield) and Mary Strang (Glastonbury, CT)
Matthew Oliver, b. 12/26/1986; Douglas O. MacDonald and Sheryl A. MacCabee
Matthew Scott, b. 7/24/1990; Robert Grant MacDonald and Donna Marie Sanborn
Melissa Ann, b. 8/25/1977; Forrest George MacDonald, Jr. and Pamela Jane Atwood
Sarah Aucelia, b. 3/2/1989; Douglas Oliver MacDonald and Sheryl Ann Maccabee
Stephen Douglas, b. 5/11/1983; Douglas Oliver MacDonald and Sheryl Ann Maccabee
Timothy Gene, b. 1/13/1985; Douglas Oliver MacDonald and Sheryl Ann Maccabee
Tina M., b. 2/19/1957; third; Forrest MacDonald (NH) and Barbara Hobbs (NH)

MACELROY,
Katie Jewell, b. 4/5/1989; Robert Wayne MacElroy and Linda Fosgate

MACK,
James Raymond Leopold, b. 10/21/1999 in N. Conway; James Mack and Terri Mack

MADDOX,
Patricia A., b. 8/17/1959; fifth; Otis Maddox (Greer, SC) and Barbara Pare (Somerville, MA)
Robin M., b. 6/9/1957; fourth; Otis H. Maddox (Greer, SC) and Barbara M. Pare (MA)

MADORE,
Andrew Florian, b. 10/27/1994 in Wolfeboro; Roger A. Madore, Sr. and Rosemary J. Fortin

MAILLE,
Sara Ann, b. 2/7/1984; Richard Maille and Cynthia Jean Leger

MAINZER,
Holly McLean, b. 1/4/2000 in Rochester; Kimo Mainzer and Dawnmarie Mainzer

MALAY,
William K., b. 12/15/1947; first; Charles V. Malay (NS) and Arlene Kirkwood (Gorham, ME)

MALLETT,
Rachel Ann, b. 11/2/1999 in Rochester; William Mallett and Pamela Mallett

MANCHESTER,
Kyle Alden, b. 12/1/1992; Milton Scott Manchester and Shelly Marie Heckman
Mathew Alexander, b. 10/23/1997 in Wolfeboro; Milton Scott Manchester and Shelly Marie Heckman

MARATOS,
Peter Jonathan William, b. 5/2/1987; Peter R. Maratos and Connie M. Duchesne

MARIELLO,
Margaret Elizabeth, b. 4/10/1973; Richard E. Mariello, Jr. and Josephine E. Shorey

MARION,
Ethan Greenleaf, b. 12/5/1977; Bradley Harry Marion and Dawn Elaine Tillinghast

MAROTTA,
Damon Richard, II, b. 12/19/1998 in N. Conway; Damon Richard Marotta and Emily Erica Bismarck

MARSTON,
Richard E., b. 5/2/1925; fourteenth; Charles Marston (Cornish, ME) and Nellie Knight (Auburn, ME)

MARTEL,
Eric George, b. 11/29/1990; David Maurice Martel and Laurie Ann McCue

MARTIN,
daughter, b. 10/9/1895 in Ossipee; ninth; Alec Martin (laborer, Canada) and Annie Magill (Lebanon, ME)

Emma Catherine, b. 6/29/1914; first; George Martin (teamster, NB) and
    Lenna Fieck (New York City)
Janice, b. 3/6/1942; second; John Martin (Sandwich) and Frances
    Williamson (Lunenburg, VT)

MASKELL,
Kyle Stanley, b. 12/19/1985; Anthony Albert Maskell and Patricia Ann Cray

MASON,
Dawn M., b. 3/2/1958; second; Clark D. Mason (Providence, RI) and Helen
    M. Griner (Blackshear, GA)
Kurt D., b. 1/18/1960; third; Clark D. Mason and Helen Griner
Sarah Lynn, b. 4/17/1982; Glen Russell Mason and Beverly Lynn Fall

MASSEY,
Zachariah P., b. 3/12/1987; Jeffery P. Massey and Cheryl Lee Marsh

MATTHEWS,
Falon Ann Joyce, b. 2/29/1992; Blaine Philip Matthews and Elaien Myrtle
    Foss

MAY,
John P., b. 6/18/1955; third; William May (VT) and Grethel Preble (MA)
Kelsey Ann, b. 10/17/1996 in Wolfeboro; John P. May and Linda Marie
    Fosgate
Martha A., b. 4/7/1965; fifth; William H. May and Grethel Z. Preble
Matthew E., b. 1/18/1960; fourth; William H. May and Grethel Preble
Melanie, b. 12/23/1947; first; William H. May (Canaan, VT) and Grethel Z.
    Preble (Somerville, MA)
William H., III, b. 1/16/1954; second; William H. May, II (VT) and Grethel
    L. Preble (MA)

McALLISTER,
son, b. 1/14/1890 in Ossipee; fifth; George F. McAllister (lumberman,
    Milford, ME) and Ellen M. Gove (Cornish, ME)

McCONKEY,
Dale Eric, b. 12/13/1990; Mark Edwin McConkey and Carol Marie Lundbert
Jacob Marc, b. 10/9/1992; Mark Edwin McConkey and Carol Marie
    Lundberg
Victoria May, b. 2/9/1996 in N. Conway; Mark Edwin McConkey and Carol
    Marie Lundberg

McDONALD [see MacDonald],
John J., Jr., b. 8/18/1949; first; John McDonald, Sr. (Sanbornville) and Catherine Lewis (Concord)
Mary Ellen, b. 5/6/1935; third; Chester McDonald (Whitefield) and Lila G. Frye (Harrington, ME)
Richard S., b. 10/27/1937; second; George McDonald (Whitefield) and Sybil Martin (Groveton)

McDORMAND,
Derek Charles, b. 2/20/1986; Scott Alan McDormand and Lorraine Mary Jordan
Michael David, b. 2/26/1983; Scott Alan McDormand and Jacqueline Ann Davis

McDUFFEE,
Marjorie Bertha, b. 8/8/1942; Lloyd McDuffee (Tuftonboro) and Louise Sawyer (Beverly, MA)

McFARLANE,
Alexina B., b. 12/4/1951; third; George D. McFarlane (MA) and Janet Gregory (MA)
Ernest G., b. 12/14/1948; second; George D. McFarlane (Cambridge, MA) and Janet M. Gregory (Boston, MA)
Jeffrey G., b. 6/16/1954; fourth; George D. MacFarlane (MA) and Janet M. Gregory (MA)
Mathew Ryan, b. 5/19/1981; Peter Angus McFarlane and Nancy Diana Mitchell
Peter A., b. 8/13/1945; first; George D. McFarlane (Cambridge, MA) and Janet M. Gregory (Boston, MA)

McFARLIN,
Shaun David, b. 6/8/1971; Frederick Marshall McFarlin and Lois Irene Day

McGEE,
child, b. 9/10/1925; first; John McGee (Portland, ME) and Antoinette DeGrace (Berlin)

McINTIRE,
Laura Mae, b. 9/7/1940; first; Kenneth A. McIntire (S. Portland, ME) and Lois M. Greenlaw (Pleasant Ridge, ME)

McINTYRE,
Mary, b. 5/17/1917; eighth; Daniel McIntyre (clergyman, Scotland) and Mary L. Drew (Boston, MA)

Robert R., b. 12/9/1919; ninth; Daniel McIntyre (clergyman, Scotland) and Mary L. Drew (Boston)

McKAY,
Eva, b. 6/29/1900 in Ossipee; third; Henry McKay (millman, 39, NS) and Fannie Dexter (32)
Kirsten Marie, b. 11/10/1987; William S. McKay and Brenda M. Lundberg

McKEAGNEY,
daughter, b. 12/30/1918; third; Hugh McKeagney (laborer, Ireland) and Laura M. Gibson (Boston, MA); residence - Boston, MA

McKENNEY,
child, b. 12/21/1936; fourth; Norris S. McKenney (Cambridge, MA) and Martha L. Hartford (Kingston)
Chad G., b. 6/20/1947; fourth; Wallace G. McKenney (Woolwich, ME) and Margaret I. Honey (Natick, MA)
Leda Louise, b. 3/6/1939; fifth; Norris F. McKenney (Cambridge, MA) and Martha L. McKenney (Kingston)
Stuart John, b. 2/16/1949; first; Carl C. McKenney (Bath, ME) and Mary Whiting (Madison)
Susan M., b. 9/11/1945; third; Wallace A. McKenney (Woolwich, ME) and Margaret I. Haney (Natick, MA)

McLEAN,
son, b. 10/17/1898 in Ossipee; sixth; Hugh McLean (laborer, 30, PEI) and Mary Gillis (30, NS)

McLENDON,
Wyatt Lloyd, b. 10/7/1997 in N. Conway; Eric Harold McClendon, Jr. (sic) and Stephanie Joan Saujon

McMANUS,
Patrick S., b. 10/21/1986; Sean P. McManus and Julie A. McDonald
Ryan Macdonald, b. 5/19/1992; Sean Patrick McManus and Julie Ann Macdonald

McQUADE,
Michael David, b. 4/23/1987; Patrick K. McQuade and Nancy S. Ehler
Timothy John, b. 6/5/1989; Patrick Kevin McQuade and Nancy Suzanne Ehler

McSWAIN,
Kerry D., b. 5/8/1962; second; Marlow McSwain and Carolyn Litchfield

Tammy L., b. 1/3/1964; third; Marlow McSwain and Carolyn Litchfield

MEADER,
Karen D., b. 6/6/1965; second; Donald N. Meader and Barbara G. Staples
Kathryn L., b. 3/8/1964; first; Donald Meader and Barbara Staples
Paul A., b. 8/7/1969; Donald N. Meader and Barbara G. Staples
Philip Allen, b. 9/23/1949; fourth; Frank Meader (Rockland, ME) and Annie Blanchard (Wakefield, MA)

MELANSON,
son, b. 11/11/1947; first; Lois A. Melanson (Grafton)
Elwin Roy, b. 9/8/1938; second; Roy E. Melanson (Wakefield) and Lena A. Arsenault (Moultonville)
Joan Fay, b. 6/27/1937; second; Roy E. Melanson (Wakefield) and Lena A. Arsenault (Moultonville)
Leon Elwin, b. 2/13/1936; first; Roy E. Melanson (Wakefield) and Lena Arsenault (Moultonville)
Omer, Jr., b. 4/22/1926; first; Omer Melanson (Grafton) and Wilma F. Knox (Seabrook)

MELBYE,
Margaret, b. 4/19/1936; third; Gordon H. Melbye (Norfolk, MA) and Mildred Jefferson (Intervale)

MELOON,
son, b. 7/7/1910 in Ossipee; first; Harry Meloon (merchant, Summit, ND) and Minnie Demeritt (Ossipee)
daughter, b. 3/15/1912; second; Harry Meloon (chauffeur) and Minnie Demeritt (Ossipee)
daughter, b. 10/13/1916; first; Arthur P. Meloon (farmer, Effingham) and Mary L. Chadbourne (Chelsea, MA); residence - Effingham
Donald, b. 1/9/1920; second; Calvin Meloon (clerk, SD) and Bernice White (Campton)
Esther Leona, b. 10/3/1913; third; Harry Meloon (machinist, Summit, SD) and Minnie Demerritt (Ossipee)
Marion M., b. 3/30/1921; third; Calvin A. Meloon (clerk, SD) and Bennicort White (Campton)
Naomi Louise, b. 9/2/1945; second; Wilfred C. Meloon (Ossipee) and Margaret L. Simond (Franklin)
Ralph, b. 11/11/1917; second; Walter C. Meloon (garage owner, SD) and Marian A. Hamm (Ossipee)
Ruth L., b. 9/11/1923; fourth; Calvin A. Meloon (SD) and Bernice N. White (Campton)
Wilfred C., b. 7/2/1918; first; Calvin A. Meloon (clerk, Oneida, SD) and Bernice N. White (Campton)

MENSCH,
Jamie Jean, b. 1/26/1995 in Wolfeboro; John Henry Mensch and Karen May Jensen

MENZIES,
Abigail Beth, b. 7/12/1972; Douglas Bruce Menzies and Susan Kathryn Hayes

MERRILL,
Gregory Richard, b. 8/31/1988; Richard F. Merrill and Rhonda L. Varney

MERROW,
daughter, b. 8/4/1888; first; James D. Merrow (farmer, Ossipee) and Annie E. Merrow (Ossipee)
son, b. 1/18/1894 in Ossipee; second; Dana J. Merrow (farmer, 32, Ossipee) and Annie Williams (26, Ossipee)
son, b. 1/8/1895 in Ossipee; second; Charles H. Merrow (laborer, Ossipee) and Annie E. Pinkham (Dover)
son [Howard W.], b. 5/27/1895 in Ossipee; third; Dana J. Merrow (farmer, Ossipee) and Annie E. Williams (Ossipee)
child [Howard], b. 4/7/1896 in Ossipee; fourth; Daniel Morrow (sic) (mechanic, Ossipee) and Ella Silesby (ME)
daughter, b. 3/28/1906 in Ossipee; first; Charles H. Merrow (clerk, Ossipee) and Emma Walker (Ossipee)
son, b. 9/11/1906 in Ossipee; second; Earl T. Merrow (laborer, Clifton, ME) and Flora Templeton (Ossipee)
daughter, b. 12/5/1906 in Ossipee; first; Llewellyn Merrow (laborer, Ossipee) and Florence Nichols (Ossipee)
son [Charles W.], b. 8/13/1907 in Ossipee; second; Charles Merrow (clerk, Ossipee) and Emma Walker (Ossipee)
daughter [Rachel F.], b. 1/26/1910 in Ossipee; fifth; Earle Merrow (laborer, Ossipee) and Flora Templeton (Ossipee)
daughter [Marian M.], b. 6/10/1910 in Ossipee; third; Charles Merrow (laborer, Ossipee) and Emma Walker (Ossipee)
daughter [Lavinia A.], b. 8/19/1913; sixth; Earle T. Merrow (chauffeur, Bangor, ME) and Flora Templeton (Ossipee)
daughter [Phyllis I.], b. 9/4/1916; tenth; Earl T. Merrow (chauffeur, Clifton, ME) and Flora Templeton (Ossipee)
daughter, b. 12/21/1921; second; Howard W. Merrow (farmer, Ossipee) and Gertrude Bickford (Effingham)
daughter, b. 1/2/1922; thirteenth; Earle T. Merrow (chauffeur, Clifton, ME) and Flora Templeton (Ossipee)
daughter [Ann W.], b. 6/26/1936; first; Howard N. Merrow (Ossipee) and Gertrude S. Bickford (Effingham)
child, b. 6/27/1936; first; Alta G. Merrow (Ossipee)

Alison Elizabeth, b. 3/30/1989; Mark Earl Merrow and Saylee Jeannine Downing

Alta G., b. 4/19/1918; first; Howard Merrow (soldier, Ossipee) and G. S. Bickford (Effingham)

Amy O., b. 12/13/1959; second; Lyford A. Merrow (Wolfeboro) and Carmen Osborne (Mt. Clemons, MI)

Barbara, b. 9/9/1917; first; Llewellyn Merrow (farmer, Ossipee) and Margaret Curtin (Ireland)

Dana H., b. 2/17/1933; third; Howard Merrow (Ossipee) and Gertrude Bickford (Effingham)

Daniel Sands, b. 8/27/1941; first; Chester E. Merrow (Ossipee) and Nellie M. Sands (Allegany, NY)

Danielle Marie, b. 3/14/1993 in Wolfeboro; Michael Sands Merrow and Kathleen Margaret Brule

Derek Joseph, b. 2/10/1990; Michael Sands Merrow and Kathleen Margaret Brule

Gertrude, b. 11/8/1907 in Ossipee; second; Earl Merrow (laborer, Cliff, ME) and Flora Templeton (Ossipee)

Harry Charles, b. 3/19/1938; first; Charles W. Merrow (Ossipee) and Louine C. Smart (Ossipee)

Heather W., b. 11/26/1967; second; Dana H. Merrow and Norma A. Cheney

Hilda, b. 11/17/1917; eleventh; Earl Merrow (chauffeur, Clifton, ME) and Flora Templeton (Ossipee)

Howard E., b. 1/12/1965; first; Dana Merrow and Norma A. Cheney

Joe M., b. 2/6/1943; first; Joe Mack Hall (Beattyville, KY) and Ethelda Merrow (Ctr. Ossipee)

Joshua Mark, b. 7/4/1985; Mark Earl Merrow and Saylee Jeannine Downing

Lyford A., III, b. 2/8/1961; third; Lyford A. Merrow II and Carmen Osborne

Lyford Ambrose, 2nd, b. 5/30/1929; first; Parker Merrow (Malden, MA) and Grace Woolley (W. Medford, MA)

Mark E., b. 6/18/1959; first; Earl Merrow (Ossipee) and Agnes Williams (Milton)

Michael S., b. 12/4/1962; first; Daniel Merrow and Donna Templeton

Michelle Ruth, b. 12/11/1970; Daniel Sands Merrow and Donna Marie Templeton

Mitchell, b. 8/17/1966; second; Daniel S. Merrow and Donna M. Templeton

Parker M., 2nd, b. 5/14/1965; fourth; Lyford A. Merrow and Carmen A. Osborne

Ruby, b. 7/12/1915; stillborn; eighth; Earl T. Merrow (chauffeur, Clifton, ME) and Flora Templeton (Ossipee)

Tanya Louise, b. 6/17/1981; Michael Sands Merrow and Tina Louise Wakefield

MESERVE,
Alan Steven, b. 8/17/1988; Steven A. Meserve and Debbie A. Hall
Clifton E., b. 5/31/1921; second; Frank Meserve (lumberman, Freedom) and Ruby Ryer (Acton, ME); residence - Farmington

MILLER,
Jeremy Allen, b. 1/28/1983; Danny William Miller and Brenda Jean Savage
Kristi Anna, b. 7/13/1986; Robert Eugene Miller and Kathleen Ann Eldridge
Robert Charles, b. 11/5/1990; Robert Eugene Miller and Kathleen Ann Eldridge
Ryan Ann, b. 8/26/1981; Warren Edwin Miller and Cynthia Ann Keane
Samantha Jean, b. 6/23/1993 in Wolfeboro; Danny William Miller and Brenda Jean Savage

MILLIGAN,
Deborah L., b. 12/28/1955; third; Roy Milligan (GA) and Dorothy Abbott (NH)
Dennis R., b. 9/13/1957; fourth; Roy T. Milligan (GA) and Dorothy A. Abbott (NH)
Dwight J., b. 2/13/1953; first; Roy Milligan (NH) and Dorothy Abbott (NH)
Kathleen J., b. 7/14/1954; second; Roy T. Milligan (GA) and Dorothy A. Abbott (NH)
Mark B., b. 11/19/1959; fifth; Roy Milligan (GA) and Ruth Bowlend (Wolfeboro)
Melissa A., b. 10/7/1961; sixth; Roy Milligan and Dorothy A. Abbott
Scott P., b. 3/26/1965; eighth; Roy T. Milligan and Dorothy A. Abbott
Stephanie Anne, b. 3/30/1980; Mark B. Milligan and Kimberly Anne Harrison
Suzanne, b. 5/2/1963; seventh; Roy T. Milligan and Dorothy Abbott
Timothy Jason, b. 7/9/1983; Mark Bradford Milligan and Kimberly Anne Harrison

MILLIKEN,
Frances P., b. 8/19/1953; fourth; Walter P. Milliken (MA) and Bernice Kimball (ME)

MITCHELL,
Cassandra Ann, b. 4/8/1993 in Rochester; Steven Arthur Mitchell II and Alicia Ruth Rudolph
Katelyn Rose, b. 1/8/1997 in Wolfeboro; Steven A. Mitchell, II and Alicia Ruth Rudolph
Steven Arthur, III, b. 8/29/1998 in Wolfeboro; Steven A. Mitchell, II and Alicia Ruth Rudolph

MOFFETT,
Amanda Jean, b. 9/9/1988; Brian F. Moffett and Kimberly A. Forbes

MONEYPENNY,
Ann M., b. 3/1/1963; third; Christopher Moneypenny and Mary McEntegart
Patricia M., b. 3/1/1963; fourth; Christopher Moneypenny and Mary McEntegart

MOODY,
child, b. 2/5/1924; second; Henry B. Moody (Albany) and Annie Eastman (Milan)
child, b. 5/29/1930; fifth; Henry A. Moody (Albany) and Annie O. Eastman (Milan)
child, b. 2/24/1935; first; George Henry Moody (Madison) and Elizabeth S. Hobbs (Tamworth)
Eldred, b. 8/1/1917; second; Ernest A. Moody (farmer, Northwood) and Vivan Hobbs (Ossipee)
Florence, b. 7/3/1915; first; Ernest Moody (laborer, Northwood) and Vivian I. Hobbs (Ossipee)
Harley Banks, b. 5/25/1928; fourth; Henry Moody (Albany) and Anna Eastman (Milan)
Lester W., b. 12/18/1904 in Ossipee; first; Peter M. Moody (painter, 22, Albany) and Frances S. Olmstead (34, NB)
Philip, b. 11/23/1924; first; Leslie Moody (Ossipee) and Catherine Finlay (Scotland)
Robert E., b. 6/16/1942; second; George E. Moody (Tamworth) and Elizabeth S. Hobbs (Tamworth)
Stacey Jo, b. 11/15/1989; Robert Glenn Moody and Sandra Jo Navarro

MOORE,
son, b. 5/11/1890 in Ossipee; eleventh; John N. Moore (farmer, Sanford, ME) and Anna A. Moore (Albany)
Robert A., b. 4/19/1933; second; Alvin E. Moore (Malden, MA) and Anna Mullen (Medford, MA)
Shirley May, b. 3/3/1911 in Ossipee; first; Lyle Moore (laborer, Milton) and Rena V. Bean (Ossipee); residence - Milton

MORAN,
Aurelia, b. 1/28/1981; Thomas Bernard Moran and Kazuko McGarry

MORGAN,
Brian Richard, b. 10/13/1989; Richard Harlan Morgan and Linda Marie Butler

Heather Lynn, b. 12/10/1984; Richard Harlan Morgan and Linda Marie Butler
Joseph L., b. 10/8/1967; third; Richard L. Morgan and Phyllis L. Clark

MORRILL,
Christina Marie, b. 11/22/1976; John Howard Morrill and Cynthia Ann Libby
Crystal Rose, b. 7/16/1989; Daniel Paul Morrill, Sr. and Roxanne Dore
Daniel Paul, Jr., b. 4/4/1986; Daniel Paul Morrill and Roxanne Dore
Scott Allen, b. 2/24/1975; John Howard Morrill and Cynthia Ann Libby

MORRIS,
Madelina Virginia, b. 5/1/2000 in Ossipee; George Sierra Morris and Deborah Loisa Allegra

MORTON,
daughter, b. 5/12/1898 in Ossipee; fourth; Harry Morton (40) and Josephine Graves (33, Bartlett)

MOULTON,
son, b. 10/28/1889; R. C. Moulton (undertaker, Ossipee) and Minnie H. Parsons (Freedom)
stillborn child, b. 1/24/1896 in Ossipee; fifth; Charles Moulton (laborer)
Beryl M., b. 12/12/1912; first; L. O. Moulton (merchant, Ossipee) and Laura Page (Orono, ME)
Catherine Judy, b. 7/10/1937; fifth; James L. Moulton (Parsonsfield, ME) and Gladys Haley (Tuftonboro)
Gwenedene May, b. 6/8/1914; second; Lisle O. Moulton (merchant, Ossipee) and Laura J. Page (Orono, ME)
Robert E., II, b. 2/6/1952; first; Robert Moulton (NH) and Muriel Canney (NH)

MUNROE,
daughter, b. 9/4/1931; second; Arthur Munroe (Ossipee) and Gladys Worcester (Woburn, MA)
Arthur C., b. 7/18/1911 in Ossipee; eighth; Charles N. Munroe (farmer, NS) and Annie Helpard (NS)
Brian Earl, b. 1/30/1956; second; Donald A. Munroe (NH) and Avonne E. Knox (NH)

MURPHY,
Christopher Edward Joseph, b. 6/17/1985; Kevin Edward Murphy and April Michelle Perham

Heather Rebecca, b. 10/24/1973; Leo Francis Murphy, Jr. and Nancy Jane Rollins
Helen Louise, b. 10/16/1936; first; John R. Murphy (Dover) and Mary L. Leavitt (Parsonsfield, ME)
Kailyn Loren, b. 6/9/1996 in Laconia; Charles Loren Murphy and Martelle Karole Connolly

MURRAY,
Adelaide Rose, b. 9/18/1994 in N. Conway; Daniel T. Murray and Ann C. Ullman
Zacharia Daniel, b. 11/9/1989; Daniel Thomas Murray and Anne Celeste Ullman

NASON,
Allen J., b. 8/4/1957; first; Ernest J. Nason (NH) and Priscilla M. Russell (NH)
Christopher D., b. 11/12/1965; seventh; Ernest J. Nason and Priscilla M. Russell
Cody Christopher, b. 1/14/1995 in Wolfeboro; Todd Michael Nason and Cynthia Lynette Maggard
Gardner, b. 8/12/1906 in Ossipee; sixth; Gardner Nason (teamster, Standish, ME) and Emma Chesley (Ossipee)
Joseph, b. 12/11/1911 in Ossipee; fourth; Joseph Nason (laborer, Wakefield) and Nellie Carlin (Cambridge, MA)
Karen A., b. 5/8/1960; third; Ernest J. Nason and Priscilla M. Russell
Kayla Rose, b. 10/13/1993 in Wolfeboro; Timothy Wayne Nason and Susan Eliopoulos
Kaylee Shaye, b. 8/17/1998 in Wolfeboro; Todd Michael Nason and Cynthia Lynette Maggard
Lisa L., b. 3/15/1963; fifth; Ernest J. Nason and Priscilla Russell
Ricky D., b. 10/24/1958; second; Ernest J. Nason (Freedom) and Priscella Russell (Wolfeboro)
Tammy L., b. 9/1/1962; second; Irving Nason and Frances Jones
Timothy W., b. 2/5/1962; fourth; Ernest Nason and Priscilla Russell

NASS,
Chandra Naomi, b. 6/28/1978; Michael J. Glick and Victoria Carlotta Nass

NAYLOR,
Kenneth Robert, b. 3/2/1941; third; Maurice Frank Naylor (Cambridge, VT) and Leona Boyce (Wells River, VT)

NELSON,
Amanda Campbell, b. 8/3/1982; James William Nelson and Ruthann Eldridge

Edwin Russell, b. 1/15/1974; Gordon Russell Nelson and Louise Joyce Moody

Florence A., b. 6/29/1960; second; Andy F. Nelson and Dorothy L. Bisbee

Francis A., b. 10/25/1958; first; Andy F. Nelson (Effingham) and Dorothy L. Bisbee (Wolfeboro)

Gordon R., b. 3/27/1943; first; Russell H. Nelson (Freedom) and Rosamond A. Wheeler (Effingham)

Janice A., b. 6/16/1963; fourth; Andy F. Nelson and Dorothy Bisbee

Jessica Lawhorn, b. 10/7/1980; James W. Nelson and Ruthann Eldridge

Lynne A., b. 4/12/1961; first; Gordon Nelson and Gloria Potvin

Mavis A., b. 12/8/1965; fifth; Andy F. Nelson and Dorothy L. Bisbee

Patricia Lea, b. 5/31/1949; first; Bernard Nelson (Winchester) and Helen Slattery (Hatfield, MA)

Peter A., b. 9/19/1961; third; Andy F. Nelson and Dorothy L. Bisbee

NEPOMUCENO,

Leah Marie, b. 4/1/1995 in Laconia; Ronald Kent Nepomucino and Deborah Ann Sutherland

NEVERS,

Thomas John, b. 11/10/1936; third; Kenneth W. Nevers (Salem, MA) and Maude L. Billings (Chicago, IL)

NEWBEGIN,

Alesia Ruth, b. 5/1/1988; Brian K. Newbegin and Leisa M. Dawe

NEWLING,

Seth E., b. 12/10/1891; first; C. A. Newling (laborer, Effingham) and ----- (Barnstead)

NEWRINE,

daughter, b. 11/13/1906 in Ossipee; second; Alex Newrine (laborer, NY) and Eva Dumont (Lawrence, MA)

NIBLET[T],

daughter [Dorothy M.], b. 12/19/1915; fourth; Samuel Niblett (farmer, Lancashire, England) and Margaret Glynn (Quincy, MA)

son, b. 6/25/1921; Samuel Niblett (farmer, England) and Margaret M. Glynn (Roxbury, MA)

Edward J., b. 11/16/1912; second; Samuel Niblett (farmer, England) and Margaret Glynn (Roxbury, MA)

Elizabeth Glynn, b. 5/31/1926; eighth; Samuel Niblet (England) and Margaret M. Glynn (Roxbury, MA)

Evlyn B., b. 2/7/1924; seventh; Samuel Niblett (Cheshire, England) and Margaret M. Glynn (Roxbury, MA)
Samuel, b. 5/25/1918; fifth; Samuel Niblett (farmer, England) and Margaret Glynn (Roxbury, MA)

NICHOLS,
son, b. 2/26/1887; first; Lyford Nichols (farmer, 27, Ossipee) and Emma (22, Ossipee)
son, b. 6/9/1887; first; Alonzo Nichols (laborer, 26, Ossipee) and Martha (25, Bartlett)
son, b. 5/31/1888; fourth; Charles A. Nichols (farmer, Ossipee) and Emma A. Nichols (Moultonboro)
son, b. 3/23/1889; Frank A. Nichols (farmer, Ossipee) and Hellen Drew (Wolfeboro)
daughter, b. 12/5/1892 in Ossipee; eleventh; Elkanah Nichols (farmer, Ossipee) and Eliza Drew (Ossipee)
daughter, b. –/–/1896 in Ossipee; George Nichols (laborer)
daughter, b. 11/28/1897 in Ossipee; third; Alphonso Nichols (labourer, 37, Ossipee) and Anne Andrews (25, Freedom)
stillborn son, b. 2/17/1899 in Ossipee; first; Joseph Nichols (23, Ossipee) and Carrie I. Nute (19, Ossipee)
son, b. 7/11/1903 in Ossipee; fourth; Alphonzo Nichols (laborer, 39, Ossipee) and Annie Andrews (30, Freedom)
son, b. 8/13/1907 in Ossipee; second; Lewis Nichols (laborer, Ossipee) and Hattie Haddock (Ossipee)
daughter, b. 12/31/1910 in Ossipee; first; Roy S. Nichols (carpenter, Ossipee) and Gertrude Philpot (MA)
son, b. 7/27/1913; second; Lester C. Nichols (fireman, Ossipee) and Eva Perkins (Ossipee)
Alice E., b. 3/8/1924; tenth; Louis W. Nichols (Ossipee) and Hattie Haddock (Ossipee)
Alkeenon F., b. 11/11/1910 in Ossipee; second; Fred Nichols (laborer, Ossipee) and ----- (Effingham)
Carolyn A., b. 7/27/1932; second; Ernest Nichols (Ossipee) and Elizabeth Harmon (Ossipee)
Carrie Lynn, b. 1/22/1985; Alan Richard Nichols and Robin Lee White
Cecil A., b. 1/13/1918; sixth; Lewis Nichols (laborer, Ossipee) and Hattie Haddock (Ossipee)
Douglas W., b. 6/8/1957; first; Ronald Nichols (NH) and Edna R. Dore (NH)
Earl, b. 4/30/1920; seventh; Lewis W. Nichols (lumberman, Ossipee) and Hattie Haddock (Ossipee)
Ernest C., b. 1/21/1910 in Ossipee; third; Lewis W. Nichols (laborer, Ossipee) and Hattie Haddock (Ossipee)

Florence, b. 2/14/1923; ninth; Lewis Nichols (Ossipee) and Hattie Haddock (Ossipee)
George Peter, b. 7/29/1941; second; George Everett Nichols and Elizabeth Lowe (Rochester)
Hazel F., b. 6/11/1943; first; Earl E. Nichols (Ossipee) and Pauline D. Evans (Bethel, VT)
Janet Ellen, b. 10/19/1940; third; Ernest C. Nichols (Ossipee) and Elizabeth G. Nichols (Ossipee)
Jennifer Lee, b. 12/6/1976; Alan Richard Nichols and Robin Lee White
Linwood Arthur, b. 5/1/1950; fourth; Linwood Nichols (Wolfeboro) and Virginia Cook (Ossipee)
Louise, b. 2/23/1912; second; Pearl Nichols (laborer, Ossipee) and Julia Tighe (Salmon Falls)
Pearl, b. 4/30/1920; eighth; Lewis W. Nichols (lumberman, Ossipee) and Hattie Haddock (Ossipee)
Roland Douglass, b. 1/8/1937; third; Albert E. Nichols (Ossipee) and Viola Vittum (Sandwich)
Scott Alan, b. 7/10/1978; Alan Richard Nichols and Robin Lee White
Sheila Esther, b. 2/27/1935; first; Linwood Nichols (Ossipee) and Hazel G. Knox (Ossipee)
Virginia May, b. 2/26/1934; fourth; Albert Nichols (Ctr. Ossipee) and Viola Vittum (Sandwich)

NICKERSON,
Charles W., b. 4/17/1932; sixth; Nelson Nickerson (Yarmouth, NS) and Marjorie Johnson (Yarmouth, NS)
David Wendell, b. 4/1/1949; second; Wendell Nickerson (Fryeburg, ME) and Blanche Templeton (Ossipee)
Edward C., b. 11/3/1948; fifth; Nelson Nickerson, Jr. (NS) and Barbara Sharp (New Hampton)
Jonathan N., b. 2/10/1943; third; Nelson E. Nickerson, Jr. (NS) and Barbara J. Sharp (New Hampton)
Judith E., b. 11/4/1942; Wendell A. Nickerson (Madison) and Blanch L. Templeton (Ossipee)
Mary Louise, b. 3/2/1941; first; Nelson Edward Nickerson (Springhaven, NS) and Barbara J. Sharp (New Hampton)

NIHAN,
Thomas James, b. 7/17/1956; second; Lawrence D. Nihan, Jr. (MA) and Laura H. Hodge (NH)

NIILER,
Kurt Andrew, b. 11/9/1994 in Laconia; Craig J. Niiler and Kristine M. Carlson

NOEL,
Nichole Lee, b. 9/18/1981; Paul Robert Noel and Donna Lee LaPlante

NORCROSS,
Alicia Fay, b. 6/2/1989; Barry Lee Norcross and Dorian Mary Laplante

NOVAK,
Michael Patrick, b. 4/24/1981; Paul Robert Novak and Margaret Elizabeth Clark

NOYES,
Abigail Virginia, b. 12/15/1990; Daniel Peter Noyes and Carol Lynne Gerry
Joan Maryanna, b. 3/16/1939; first; John W. Noyes (Plaistow) and Julia Louise Grant (Chelsea, MA)

NUDD,
Anita M., b. 3/31/1954; third; Wallace L. Nudd (NH) and Priscilla M. Eldridge (NH)
Johanna Kay, b. 10/11/1956; fifth; Wallace R. Nudd (NH) and Priscilla M. Eldridge (NH)
Phyllis A., b. 8/5/1960; sixth; Wallace R. Nudd and Priscilla M. Eldridge
Vivian B., b. 2/18/1953; second; Wallace Nudd (NH) and Priscilla Eldridge (NH)
Wallace Raymond, b. 12/24/1950; first; Wallace Nudd (Ctr. Sandwich) and Priscilla Eldridge (Ossipee)
Yuleander H., b. 12/25/1963; seventh; Wallace R. Nudd and Priscilla M. Eldridge

NURI,
Sarah Jessica, b. 7/23/1978; Donald William Nuri and Edith Esther Klein

NUTE,
son [John], b. 4/12/1889; William H. Nute (laborer) and Laura I. Nute (Jackson)
son [James Lester], b. 5/5/1889; Alfred Nute (farmer, Ossipee) and Mary A. Avery (Milton)
Phyllis E., b. 5/8/1921; first; Philip E. Nute (chauffeur, Bartlett) and Dollie M. Fall (Ossipee)

NYSTEDT,
Barbara A., b. 12/8/1965; third; Walter P. Nystedt and Bonnie M. Kirkwood
Jill E., b. 12/14/1962; second; Walter Nystedt and Bonnie Kirkwood

O'BLENES,
Emily Ann, b. 3/23/1990; Robert Scott O'Blenes, Sr. and Melanie Sue Warren

O'BRIEN,
Patrick A., b. 3/8/1962; first; Richard O'Brien and Francine Ramsdell

O'SHEA,
Dillon Shamus, b. 1/5/1990; Peter Henry O'Shea and Kimberly Ann Gagnon
Tatum Justine, b. 12/28/1987; Peter H. O'Shea and Kimberly A. Gagnon

OIKKOLA,
Peter Sherwood, b. 4/17/1977; Peter Albert Oikkola and Ann Sherwood Wiley

OLIVARES-THOMPSON,
Nicholas, b. 7/23/1992; Christopher George Thompson and Kristi Kai Olivares

OLSON,
baby boy, b. 12/7/1973; Allen Lawrence Olson and Mary Susan Lindsay

ORDWAY,
son, b. 4/21/1895 in Ossipee; first; Charles Ordway (mechanic, Epping) and Carrie Nason (Parsonsfield, ME); residence - Epping

ORINO,
David Christopher, b. 1/24/1973; David William Orino and Shirley Elaine Ellrich
Jean Marie, b. 3/10/1970; David William Orino and Shirley Ellrich

OSGOOD,
son, b. 12/7/1893 in Ossipee; first; Samuel Osgood (farmer, Indianapolis, IN) and Lotta Andrews (St. John, NB)

OUELLETTE,
Paul Allen, b. 4/18/1987; Jay Allen Ouellette and Lauralee Ruth Allen

PAGE,
James Phillip, b. 12/3/1944; first; Robert R. Page (N. Branford, CT) and Priscilla M. Moulton (Ossipee)

PALMER,
son, b. 3/13/1889; Frank E. Palmer (pressman, Ossipee) and Mary M. Palmer (Conway)
daughter, b. 7/2/1897 in Ossipee; second; Frank Palmer (laborer, 35, Ossipee) and Mamie Merrow (29, Conway)
Edgar Morton, b. 8/13/1944; second; Harland C. Palmer (W. Ossipee) and June E. Holbrook (Ctr. Ossipee)
Elaine M., b. 7/16/1965; third; Clarence E. Palmer and Dorothy L. Jordan
Grover E., b. 1/2/1919; first; Grover Palmer (machinist, Ossipee) and Eva M. Benge (England)
Harland C., b. 2/12/1922; first; Herbert E. Palmer (laborer, Sandwich) and Gladys M. Eldridge (Ossipee); residence - Tamworth
Jason Russell, b. 12/29/1972; Edgar Morton Palmer and Georgianna Josephine Cotton
Steven E., b. 8/29/1968; Edgar M. Palmer and Georgianna J. Cotton

PAPPAS,
Ashley Margaret, b. 11/24/1987; James W. Pappas and Patricia A. Goodwin

PAQUETTE,
Caroline Elizabeth, b. 4/19/1978; Ronald Thomas Paquette and Elissa Kurth

PARKER,
Chanelle Kristine, b. 8/26/1988; Randall J. Parker and Kristine E. Robiller

PASCOE,
son, b. 8/31/1899 in Ossipee; first; Thomas Pascoe (laborer, 28, Freedom) and Gertrude Davis (19, Ossipee); residence - Freedom
Dorothy, b. 7/20/1928; fourth; William Pascoe (Freedom) and Agnes M. Page (Tamworth)
Gladys G., b. 11/7/1924; third; William H. Pascoe (Freedom) and Agnes Page (Tamworth)
Henry J., b. 9/10/1920; first; William H. Pascoe (aviator, Freedom) and Agnes M. Page (Tamworth)
Richard L., b. 1/6/1922; second; William H. Pascoe (merchant, Freedom) and Agnes M. Page (Tamworth)

PATRIQUIN,
Harriet R., b. 8/13/1924; third; Harry Patriquin (NS) and Anna Pattin (NS)

PATTERSON,
child, b. 3/15/1931; first; George Patterson and Hester A. DeMeritt (Laconia)
Brent, b. 2/27/1965; second; James W. Patterson and Yoshiko Sakai
John, b. 3/2/1966; third; James Patterson and Yoshiko Sakai
Joseph, b. 3/27/1969; James W. Patterson and Yoshiko Sakai

PEABODY,
David Joshua, Jr., b. 11/15/1993 in Wolfeboro; David J. Peabody, Sr. and Diane L. Del Fuoco

PEARE,
Katherine H., b. 4/15/1955; first; Arthur Peare (NH) and Evelyn Eldridge (NH)

PEARSON,
daughter, b. 12/21/1891 in Ossipee; second; Charles L. Pearson (farmer) and -----; residence - Lawrence, MA
Barbara E., b. 2/20/1924; third; George E. Pearson (Saugus, MA) and Ruth Stetson (Malden, MA)
Caroline Elizabeth, b. 8/8/1976; Charles Edward Pearson and Marsay Lee Broucher
Dianne, b. 1/5/1945; second; Donal C. Pearson (Malden, MA) and Ruby Mae Richards (Plymouth)
Matthew Charles, b. 9/28/1979; Charles Edward Pearson and Marsay Lee Braucher
Walter George, b. 9/6/1949; third; Donal Pearson (Malden, MA) and Ruby Richards (Plymouth)

PEASLEE,
Michael Scott, b. 4/15/1975; Charles Hoyt Peaslee and Dorothy Ann Roberts

PEEK,
Gary Michael, b. 4/9/1988; Gary R. Peek and Lisa Lee Nason

PELLETIER,
Angela Renee, b. 6/12/1981; Michel Gerard Pelletier and Vivian Rose Demanche

PENDARVIS,
Daniel Harvey, b. 5/6/1986; Harry Herbert Pendarvis, III and Lorey Lee Emerson

PENNELL,
Roger E., b. 8/3/1955; first; Edwin Pennell (NH) and Betty Drew (NH)

PENNY,
Rupert A., b. 10/16/1904 in Ossipee; fifth; John Penny (laborer) and May Sawyer; residence - Wolfeboro

PEPPER,
Bruce Richard, b. 7/14/2000 in Wolfeboro; Bruce Pepper and Teresa Pepper

PERKINS,
son, b. 6/6/1906 in Ossipee; first; Lydia Perkins (Bartlett)
daughter, b. 8/8/1916; second; Sidney Perkins (farmer, Ossipee) and Blanche Thompson (Ossipee)
Bertie A., b. 11/24/1893 in Ossipee; first; Hiram Perkins (laborer, Ossipee) and Etta Clough (Effingham)
Elnon, b. 9/3/1921; third; Sidney Perkins (chauffeur, Ossipee) and Blanche Thompson (Ossipee)
Gabriel Forest, b. 3/30/1986; Daniel Douglas Perkins and Sally Ann Cornwell
Kate Elizabeth, b. 2/12/1977; Robert Hilton Perkins and Barbara May Hill
Lawrence W., b. 3/18/1915; Sidney Perkins (laborer, Ossipee) and Blanche Thompson (Ossipee)
Rachael Brook, b. 5/3/1982; Daniel Douglas Perkins and Sally Ann Cornwell

PERRY,
Allen S., b. 9/14/1957; first; Stanley A. Perry (NH) and Barbara D. Gouin (NH)
James T., b. 6/9/1960; second; Stanley A. Perry and Barbara D. Gouin
Keith Ernest, b. 1/11/1951; second; Ernest Perry, Jr. (Conway) and Gwendolyn Knox (Ossipee)
Kyle Knox, b. 7/17/1987; Keith E. Perry and Nancy G. Hodges
Michelle Lee, b. 9/20/1973; Allen Stanley Perry and Barbara Jane Berry

PETELL,
Brody Duston, b. 12/24/2000 in N. Conway; Michael Petell and Rebecca Petell

PETERS,
Emily Elizabeth, b. 7/28/1984; Charles Michael Peters and Sharon Rose Blair

PETERSON,
Eric Marc, b. 11/8/1981; Mark Francis Peterson and Lisa June Larkin
Heather June, b. 10/26/1983; Mark Francis Peterson and Lisa June Larkin
Jennifer Jean, b. 10/1/1980; Mark Francis Peterson and Lisa June Larkin

PHILBRICK,
son [Wesley A.], b. 3/20/1910 in Ossipee; fifth; John Philbrick (laborer) and Edith Cook
child, b. 3/7/1925; first; Ellsworth Philbrick (Waterboro, ME) and Celia Sargent (Ossipee)
Richard Lee, b. 4/24/1939; second; Louise Clough (Wolfeboro)
Warren Edgar, b. 5/14/1926; second; Ellsworth Philbrick (Waterboro, ME) and Celia D. Sargent (Ossipee)

PIERCE,
Marie L., b. 7/1/1896 in Ossipee; first; D. Vinton Pierce (real est. agt., Quincy, MA) and Annie Fitzpatrick (Washington, DC); residence - Quincy, MA

PIERRO,
Sabrina Rosamae, b. 3/10/1982; Michael Arthur Pierro and Sheryl Ann Willison

PIKE,
son, b. 1/24/1889; Charles Pike (farmer, Ossipee) and Annie Pike (Effingham)
Barbara Gaye, b. 8/3/1951; third; John Pike (NH) and Alice Woodman (NH)
Catherine F., b. 1/2/1947; second; John E. Pike (Ctr. Ossipee) and Alice M. Abbott (Conway)
John E., b. 1/12/1921; second; Edwin Pike (farmer, Ossipee) and Gladys Davis (Effingham)
Joyce Ann, b. 8/15/1942; John E. Pike (Effingham) and Alice M. Abbott (Conway)
June Arlene, b. 6/9/1940; second; James C. Pike (Wells, ME) and Katherine Fletcher (Shapleigh, ME)
Ralph, b. 3/11/1926; fourth; Herbert Pike (Ossipee) and Jennie Dougherty (Cape Breton)
Ruth G., b. 1/24/1948; third; John Pike (Ctr. Ossipee) and Alice Woodman (Conway)
Wallace P., b. 10/28/1920; third; Herbert J. Pike (laborer, Ossipee) and Alice Dougherty (PEQ)(sic)

PINEO,
Esther E., b. 3/22/1895 in Ossipee; fourth; John L. Pineo (blacksmith, NS) and Charlotte Hammond (Ossipee)

PINKHAM,
Charles A., b. 10/9/1958; first; Charles R. Pinkham (Chesterville, ME) and Frances L. Eldridge (Ossipee)

PIPER,
son, b. 5/4/1893 in Ossipee; third; George H. Piper (laborer, Alton) and Annie K. Clough (Waterboro, ME); residence - Effingham
Marie Rose, b. 6/9/1995 in Wolfeboro; Stephen James Piper and Laurie Mae Gagnon

PITMAN,
daughter, b. 1/8/1907 in Ossipee; first; Frank Pitman (laborer, Bartlett) and Eva P. Perkins (Ossipee)

PLACE,
Hannah Rose, b. 9/1/1998 in Beverly, MA; Harold Place and Janis Peterson-Place

PLANT,
Michael David, b. 2/1/1970; David Albert Plant and Peggy Jean Hill

PLOURDE-MARCOTTE,
Zachary P., b. 3/9/1990; Paul Henry Marcotte and Theresa Ann Plourde

PLUMMER,
Clifton John, b. 9/4/1939; third; Frank H. Plummer (Wakefield) and Ellen P. Pratt (Ossipee)

PORTER,
Allison Kathleen, b. 4/10/1990; David Frederick Porter and Evamarie Ann Barker

POWER,
Mathew Paul, b. 9/1/1983; Paul Girard Power and Sheryl Lynn Downs

POWERS,
Gerard Edwin, Jr., b. 6/11/1934; first; Gerard E. Powers (Swampscott, MA) and Adah Ames (Lynn, MA)
Robert G., b. 11/2/1963; second; Gerard E. Powers, Jr. and Christine Price

PRATT,
Ellen P., b. 1/4/1915; first; John H. Pratt (farmer, Salem, MA) and Clara M. Moulton (Tamworth)

PRESBY,
Adam, b. 12/26/1966; first; Lynn M. Presby and Brenda A. Marsh

PROK[E]Y,
daughter, b. 5/11/1920; first; Larry Prokey (laborer, Russia) and Ethel Banfill (Farmington)
Violet Elsie, b. 2/26/1926; fourth; Larie Proky (Russia) and Ethel Banfill (Farmington)

PURRINGTON,
Anita Elaine, b. 4/14/1950; first; Rainsford Purrington (W. Ossipee) and Lois Melanson (Grafton)
James A., b. 7/26/1947; second; Rainsford Purrington (W. Ossipee) and Jean M. Campbell (Winchester, MA)
Judy Marie, b. 3/3/1951; second; Rainsford Purrington (Ossipee) and Lois Melanson (Grafton)
Ransford D., b. 9/26/1921; third; Daniel C. Purrington (farmer, Conway) and Vivian Hobbs (Ossipee)

PYNE,
John Stuart, IV, b. 1/28/1981; John Stuart Pyne, III and Laina Joy Kirch

QUIGLEY,
Krista Melanie, b. 9/25/1981; William John Quigley and Dorlyn Michelle Bolduc

QUIMBY,
son, b. 5/27/1888; fourth; George W. Quimby (laborer, Moultonboro) and Ellen Quimby (Moultonboro)
son, b. 12/29/1894 in Ossipee; fourth; S. W. Quimby (Moultonboro)
son, b. 12/29/1894 in Ossipee; fifth; S. W. Quimby (Moultonboro)
Diane J., b. 3/25/1954; first; Willard H. Quimby (ME) and Nancy J. Bean (NH)
Donna Marie, b. 6/30/1956; second; Willard H. Quimby (ME) and Nancy Bean (NH)
Michael W., b. 10/25/1958; third; Willard Quimby (Porter, ME) and Nancy J. Bean (Ctr. Ossipee)

RANCOURT,
Leslie Ann, b. 10/2/1975; Robbin Evan Rancourt and Nancy Grover Bissell

RAND,
Clinton Hunt, b. 6/4/1977; Clinton LeShore Rand and Carolyn Jean Hunt
Darlene Marie, b. 3/3/1976; John Arthur Rand and Diane Marie Runyan
Eugene, b. 4/11/1925; fourth; Nathaniel Rand (New Durham) and Mabel Bean (Ossipee)

RASPANTE,
Michael Anthony, b. 8/6/1981; Frank Raspante and Lisa Gaye Tupeck

RATTIE,
Roland Joseph, b. 5/11/1914; first; Joseph M. Rattie (operator "Movies", Canada) and Doris M. King (Bellows Falls, VT); residence - Calais, ME

RAYMOND,
Gary Richard, b. 7/22/1987; Lawrence D. Raymond, III and Carol A. Ward
Jeffrey Harold, b. 6/20/1989; Lawrence Delano Raymond, III and Carol Ann Ward

REED,
David Thomas, b. 5/20/1940; sixth; Frank Eugene Reed (Houlton, ME) and Mildred F. Whiting (Tuftonboro)
Marion C., b. 8/13/1929; first; Frank Reed (Houlton, ME) and Mildred Whiting (Tuftonboro)
Nathan Paul, b. 5/26/1998 in Wolfeboro; Eugene L. Reed, Jr. and Kimberly Estes
Robert A., b. 10/28/1931; second; Frank E. Reed (Houlton, ME) and Mildred Whiting (Tuftonboro)
Thelma L., b. 5/28/1935; Frank E. Reed (ME) and Mildred F. Whiting (NH) (1956)

REINHOLD,
Jessica Jean, b. 6/6/1989; Robert Vincent Reinhold and Margaret Antoinet Maliawco

REISSFELDER,
Margaret L., d. 5/3/1941; fourth; Theodore Reissfelder (Boston, MA) and Pauline Burleigh (Dover)
William Paul, b. 4/27/1939; third; Theodore Reissfelder (Boston, MA) and Pauline F. Burleigh (Dover)

REMICK,
daughter, b. 8/27/1898 in Ossipee; first; Otis D. Remick (blacksmith, 28, Brookfield) and Cora Tibbetts (20, Madison)

son, b. 1/23/1900 in Ossipee; second; Otis D. Remick (blacksmith, 30, Brookfield) and Cora F. Tibbetts (21, Madison)
daughter [Marian E.], b. 5/30/1901 in Ossipee; third; Otis D. Remick (blacksmith, 31, Wakefield) and Cora Tibbetts (23, Madison)
daughter, b. 2/17/1903 in Ossipee; fourth; Otis Remick (blacksmith, 33, Wakefield) and Cora F. Tibbetts (24, Madison)
Elenor May, b. 5/16/1904 in Ossipee; fifth; Otis Remick (blacksmith, 33, Brookfield) and Cora Tibbetts (26, Madison)
Norman, Jr., b. 6/1/1931; first; Norman Remick (Tamworth) and Ethel Evans (Wolfeboro)

REUTER,
Alicia Patricia, b. 9/2/1987; Frederick G. Reuter, Jr. and Debra A. Whitten

RHINES,
Cindy Lee, b. 7/14/1957; first; Irving K. Rhines (NH) and Eleanor M. Eldridge (NH)
Elsie K., b. 10/11/1922; first; Irving C. Rhines (shoemaker, New Durham) and Angie F. Knox (Ossipee); residence - Rochester
Irving Knox, b. 8/11/1925; second; Irving C. Rhines and Angie F. Knox (W. Ossipee)

RHODES,
Matthew Dallas, b. 5/15/1975; Kenneth Charles Rhodes and Jane Elizabeth Baisley

RHYNE,
Taylor Ann, b. 12/13/1992; Jeffrey A. Rhyne and Jennifer June Johnson

RICCI-PERRY,
Alfred, b. 9/11/1989; Paul Robert Perry and June Ricci

RICHARDSON,
daughter, b. 8/13/1896 in Ossipee; ninth; Andrew Richardson (teamster)

RICKARDS,
Sally A., b. 1/28/1948; second; Hanford Rickards and Helen F. Gillis (Laconia)

RICKER,
Eva G., b. 8/8/1892 in Ossipee; first; William Ricker (farmer, Ossipee) and Marion Frazier (NS)

RIDLEY,
Crystal Marie, b. 9/28/1982; Duane Walter Ridley and Annette Lynne Johnson

RILEY,
Adam Tracy, b. 7/4/1974; Ernest Riley, Jr. and Susan Ellen Damon
Cheryl A., b. 7/11/1947; fourth; Ernest G. Riley (Standish, ME) and Beatrice A. Banfill (Sanford, ME)
Constance M., b. 8/1/1943; third; Ernest G. Riley (Standish, ME) and Beatrice Banfill (Sanford, ME)
Daniel Berton, b. 12/30/1940; second; Ernest G. Riley (Standish, ME) and Beatrice A. Banfill (Sanford, ME)
Daniel B., Jr., b. 2/7/1964; first; Daniel Riley and Cheryl Welch
Ernest Granville, Jr., b. 3/12/1939; first; Ernest G. Riley and Beatrice A. Banfill (Sanford, ME)
Franklin Robert, b. 4/16/1949; fifth; Ernest G. Riley (Standish, ME) and Beatrice Banfill (Sanford, ME)
Herbert F., b. 7/17/1942; Herbert F. Riley (Bridgton, ME) and Jeanne A. Morgan (Alton, ME)
John E., b. 3/29/1953; second; Herbert Riley (ME) and Alice Pike (NH)
Joseph Benjamin, b. 2/22/1989; Franklin Robert Riley and Cheryl Cross
Kristine Beatrice, b. 6/14/1973; Ernest Granville Riley and Susan Ellen Damon
Michael S., b. 8/17/1968; Daniel B. Riley and Cheryl J. Welch
Randy A., b. 1/12/1964; third; Herbert Riley and Alice Pike
Ryan Michael, b. 7/6/1991; Michael Scott Riley and Michelle Lee Perry
Scott Everett, b. 10/15/1978; Franklin Robert Riley and Cheryl Ann Cross
Shirley Lee, b. 12/15/1950; first; Herbert Riley (Bridgton, ME) and Alice Pike (Effingham)
William Ernest, b. 3/10/1972; Ernest Granville Riley, Jr. and Susan Ellen Damon

RINEHART,
Elizabeth Rose, b. 10/13/1938; first; Thomas Rinehart (Philadelphia) and Ida Marion Brown (Mountainview)

RINES,
child, b. 9/2/1930; first; Harlan J. Rines (New Durham) and Ruth Snow (Milton, MA)
Benjamin Cutler, b. 10/8/1990; James Franklin Rines and Wanda Lynn Fowler
Cheryl, b. 12/28/1959; second; Irving Rines (Farmington) and Eleanor Eldridge (Ossipee)
James F., b. 12/13/1957; third; Stanley J. Rines (Gorham) and Marilyn J. Davis (NH)

Karen I., b. 11/2/1964; first; Bruce Rines and Marion Barrow
Kathleen M., b. 11/22/1957; Carl Rines (Shelburne) and Barbara Virgilio (Portland, ME) (1958)
Kristine M., b. 7/2/1955; second; Stanley Rines (NH) and Marilyn Davis (NH)
Micaela Nicole, b. 9/19/1992; James Franklin Rines and Wanda Lynn Fowler
Rebecca Lee, b. 10/21/1958; third; Carl Rines (Shelburne) and Barbara Virgilio (Portland, ME)
Stefanie Ann, b. 5/26/1956; first; Carl D. Rines (NH) and Barbara L. Veigilis (ME)

RIPLEY,
Alexandra Christine, b. 6/3/1994 in N. Conway; Shawn P. Ripley and Denise E. Eldridge
John Thomas, b. 5/10/1972; Robert Wayne Ripley and Cheryl Jean Harmon

ROBACHER,
Alex Jeffey, b. 1/10/2000 in Portsmouth; Steven Robacher and Holly Robacher

ROBACKER,
Shayne Paul, b. 4/7/1988; Paul M. Robacker and Kristin A. Bombardier

ROBERTS,
Joanne Constance, b. 3/25/1941; first; Carlyle Berry Roberts (Rochester) and Lillian E. Faulkingham (Salem, MA)
Keith Elwin, b. 7/24/1941; fourth; Russell Wiggin (Ossipee) and Lucy Richards Roberts (Haverhill, MA)
Marilyn Louise, b. 6/17/1935; second; Rufus Roberts (NS) and Ruth Griswold (Keene)
Sean Edward, b. 10/27/1987; David E. Roberts and Debbie M. Carroll
Sharon Elizabeth, b. 8/23/1940; second; Russell Wiggin (Ossipee) and Richards Lucy (Haverhill, MA)

ROBINSON,
Richard Arnold, b. 11/5/1939; first; Thelma L. Robinson (Ashland)

RODGERS,
Terese Marie, b. 8/11/1984; Steven Woodrow Rodgers and Suzanne Marie Simard

ROGERS,
child, b. 9/7/1925; first; Byron Rogers, Jr. (Byfield, MA) and Leona Bean (Wolfeboro)
Byron S., Jr., b. 10/30/1926; second; Byron Rogers (Byfield, ME) and Leona Bean (Wolfeboro)
Francesca Marie, b. 6/24/1998 in Rochester; Norman Foster Rogers and Gina Jo-Ann Barbaro
Lucy L., b. 11/5/1928; third; Byron L. Rogers (Byfield, MA) and Leona Bean (Wolfeboro)
Paul, b. 5/4/1932; fourth; Byron Rogers (Byfield, MA) and Leona Bean (Wolfeboro)
Ronald Peter, b. 9/2/1935; sixth; Byron Rogers (Byfield, MA) and Leona M. Bean (Wolfeboro)

ROLEAU [see Rouleau],
child, b. 5/1/1927; second; George Roleau (Milton) and Inez Eldridge (Ossipee)

ROLES,
son, b. 11/12/1889; John H. Roles (farmer, Ossipee) and Laura A. Dorr (Ossipee)

ROLLINS,
Douglas Adam, b. 3/31/1980; Barry D. Rollins and Leslie Lynn Picard
Laura Lynn, b. 10/7/1976; Barry Dean Rollins and Leslie Lynn Picard
Shana Lynn, b. 3/20/1983; Randy Norman Rollins and Margaret Ellen Martin

ROSS,
son, b. 2/8/1896 in Ossipee; first; Charles I. Ross (33, Ossipee) and Katie D. Bean (23, Tuftonboro)
son, b. 8/26/1899 in Ossipee; second; Charles I. Ross (laborer, 38, Ossipee) and Bernice Poole (31, NS)
daughter [Bernice B.], b. 3/18/1902 in Ossipee; third; Charles I. Ross (painter, 40, Ossipee) and Bernice Poole (33, NS)
Benjamin Carl, b. 8/14/1989; John Carl Ross and Kimberly Gore
Brooke Ryan, b. 6/11/1991; Bryan Scott Ross and Tracey Lynn Emery
Elizabeth Mae, b. 6/27/1993 in Plymouth; Michael Joseph Ross and Stephanie Roseanne Naylor
Robert, b. 7/3/1897 in Ossipee; first; Charles I. Ross (laborer, 36, Ossipee) and Bernice Poole (29, NS)
Robert Lee, b. 8/14/1940; first; Ernest John Ross (Chocorua) and Mary Elizabeth Knox (New York, NY)
Sally, b. 3/2/1955; second; Kenneth Ross (NH) and Hilda Johnson (NH)
Tania Ty, b. 1/26/1989; Bryan Scott Ross and Tracey Lynn Emery

ROSSE,
daughter, b. 6/1/1951; second; Arthur Rosse (NH) and Marcia Severance (NH)
Jeanne Ann, b. 5/5/1950; first; Arthur Rosse (Worcester, MA) and Marcia Severance (Natick, MA)
Marcia Diane, b. 7/8/1952; third; Arthur Rosse (MA) and Marcia Severance (Natick, MA)

ROULEAU,
Marion Louise, b. 8/18/1925; first; George Rouleau (Milton) and Inez Eldridge (Ossipee)

ROUSE,
Christopher Michael, b. 6/9/1988; Donald I. Rouse and Kathleen M. Kennedy
Timothy Joseph, b. 10/20/1981; Donald Irving Rouse and Kathleen Mary Kennedy

ROUSSEAU,
Charles John, IV, b. 4/26/1991; Charles John Rousseau, III and Dayna L. Moran
Mitchell Austin, b. 10/24/1994; Charles John Rousseau, III and Dayna Leslie Moran

ROWELL,
Justin Charles, b. 9/21/1981; Howard Davis Rowell and Susan Elizabeth Hendricks
Milford A., b. 4/27/1933; eleventh; Randolf Rowell (Albany, VT) and Bessie Boyde (Portland, ME)

RUEL,
Emery Walters, b. 5/30/1991; Christopher Alfred Ruel and Lynda Denise Walters

RUFF,
Ashley Alayah, b. 8/22/2001 in Wolfeboro; Joshua Ruff and Kimberly Ruff
Jared Benjamin, b. 6/23/1982; Charles Frederick Ruff and Judith Ann Kalled
Jason Nathanael, b. 1/11/1977; Charles Frederick Ruff III and Judith Ann Kalled
Joshua Andrew, b. 7/28/1978; Charles F. Ruff III and Judith Anne Kalled

RUO,
Samantha Marie, b. 6/19/1997 in Laconia; Robert Michael Ruo and Diana Natalie LaBelle

RUSSELL,
son, b. 3/31/1910 in Ossipee; first; Jack Russell (laborer, Lewiston, ME) and Etta Colby (Ossipee)
son, b. 2/8/1911 in Ossipee; second; John Russell (laborer) and Etta M. Colby (Ossipee)

RUTTER,
Hayley Marie, b. 10/11/1991; Roger David Rutter and Deborah Ann Emerson

RYDER,
April Pearl, b. 1/4/1956; second; Lloyd Ryder (ME) and Ruth Janet Welch (NH)
Belmont L., b. 8/30/1961; third; Lynwood Ryder and Winifred White
Cody Edward, b. 11/26/1994 in Wolfeboro; Belmont L. Ryder and Rhonda L. Varney
Corey Lee, b. 11/28/1985; Belmont Lynwood Ryder and Erin Sue Moody
Gertrude E., b. 11/1/1963; fourth; Lynwood P. Ryder and Winifred White
Glenn P., b. 8/6/1958; fourth; Lloyd W. Ryder (Newburgh, ME) and Ruth J. Welch (W. Ossipee)
Kirk L., b. 12/17/1959; fifth; Lloyd Ryder (Newburg, ME) and Ruth J. Welch (W. Ossipee)
Marie Agnes, b. 7/21/1940; fourth; Perley Almon Ryder (Newburg, ME) and Gertrude E. Kingston (Griswold, ME)
Misty Lyn, b. 3/13/1984; Belmont Lynwood Ryder and Erin Sue Moody
Perley Ace, b. 9/4/1956; first; Lynwood P. Ryder (ME) and Winifred G. White (NH)
Ryan Almon, b. 5/28/1996 in Wolfeboro; Belmont Lynwood Ryder and Rhonda Lee Varney
Sandra L., b. 8/9/1959; second; Lynwood Ryder (Newburg, ME) and Winifred White (Ossipee)
Scott D., b. 1/1/1961; sixth; Lloyd W. Ryder and Ruth J. Welch
Terri Lee, b. 7/29/1957; third; Lloyd W. Ryder (Newburg, ME) and Ruth J. Welch (NH)
Wendy S., b. 7/20/1967; fifth; Lynwood P. Ryder and Winifred G. White
Wendy Sue, b. 2/17/1983; Perley Ace Ryder and Linda Eileen Moody

ST. CYR,
Horald, b. 1/25/1909 in Ossipee; fifth; Alfred St. Cyr (brick mason, Lancaster) and Malrens Blanso (San Camille, Can.)

ST. ONGE,
Ida Alvina, b. 6/20/1939; first; Arnold St. Onge (Montgomery, VT) and Myra Bunnell (Colebrook)

SABINE,
stillborn son, b. 8/23/1907 in Ossipee; first; Herbert Sabine (jeweler, China, ME) and Ida M. Davis (Ossipee)

SACHES,
daughter, b. 10/1/1922; third; Paul Saches (weaver, Lawrence, MA) and Alice Gaukreger (England); residence - Lawrence, MA

SAMPSON,
Katelyn Amanda, b. 9/1/1993 in Wolfeboro; David Albert Sampson and Sandra Joyce Pollock
Paul M., b. 3/16/1934; first; Alfred J. Sampson (Stowe, ME) and Stella V. Demerritt (Stetson, ME)

SANBORN,
son, b. 4/1/1900 in Ossipee; fifth; Herbert Sanborn (laborer) and Maria Sherman; residence - Wolfeboro

SANPHY,
Merry L., b. 10/21/1955; first; Roland Sanphy (NH) and Joanne Welch (NH)

SARGENT,
son [Warren], b. 10/13/1900 in Ossipee; second; Warren E. Sargent (laborer, 39, Chester) and Julia A. Welch (21, Ossipee)
son [Celia D.], b. 5/23/1903 in Ossipee; third; Warren Sargent (laborer, 39, Chichester) and Julia Welch (24, Ossipee)
daughter [Evelyn], b. 6/20/1906 in Ossipee; fourth; Warren E. Sargent (millman, Ossipee) and Julia A. Welch (Ossipee)
Allan W., b. 2/22/1947; third; Gerald W. Sargent (Ossipee) and Rose M. Knox (Ossipee)
Alton E., b. 5/14/1932; second; Erwin Sargent (Porter, ME) and ----- (Ossipee)
Amy Marie, b. 1/21/1979; Alan Wayne Sargent and Cheryl Renee Jones
Brian Alan, b. 10/29/1975; Alan Wayne Sargent and Cheryl Renee Jones
Cathy J., b. 4/9/1962; first; Richard Sargent and Donna Varney
Charles J., b. 3/12/1945; second; Gerald W. Sargent (Ossipee) and Rosemary Knox (Ctr. Ossipee)
Christine, b. 12/31/1965; first; Alan W. Sargent and Carole J. Duchano

Elaine L., b. 7/29/1948; fourth; Gerald W. Sargent (Ctr. Ossipee) and
	Rosemae Knox (Ctr. Ossipee)
Gerald Walter, b. 3/3/1928; first; Erwin Sargent (Porter, ME) and Edna
	Eldridge (Ossipee)
Glen A., b. 7/20/1963; first; Norman G. Sargent and Donna Craigue
Jeffrey Everett, b. 7/30/1971; Everett Sargent and Shirley Ann Eldridge
Joseph C., II, b. 8/21/1968; Joseph C. Sargent and Rosemarie A. English
Mary, b. 2/28/1913; first; Clarence Sargent (carpenter, Beverly, MA) and
	Ethel Abbott (Ossipee)
Nicole Adele, b. 10/25/1971; Norman Gerald Sargent and Donna Elizabeth
	Craigue
Norman Gerald, b. 1/29/1944; first; Gerald W. Sargent (Porter, ME) and
	Rosemay C. Knox (Ossipee)
Patricia L., b. 3/13/1959; second; Alton Sargent (Ossipee) and Mary
	Weeks (Ctr. Conway)
Richard L., Jr., b. 7/5/1969; Richard L. Sargent and Donna M. Varney
Sarah Jane, b. 1/9/1976; Richard L. Sargent and Donna L. Carney
Wayne A., b. 5/30/1964; first; Alan Sargent and Carole Duchano

SATCHFIELD,
Brian Andrew, b. 12/24/1989; Peter Alan Satchfield and Beverly Joyce
	Christman

SAUNDERS,
Daniel Brian, b. 8/2/1984; David Leslie Saunders and Cindy Lee Berg
Edna Muriel, b. 9/8/1924; second; William C. Saunders (England) and
	Elizabeth Vousden (England)
George M., b. 6/27/1955; first; George Saunders (NC) and Theresa
	Waterman (ME)

SAVAGE,
Jessica Lynne, b. 9/23/1983; Daniel Steven Drew and Diane Lynn Savage

SAVARY,
Devan Isaac, b. 10/17/1991; Richard Aden Savary and Sonya Marie
	Nelson

SAVORY,
daughter, b. 10/4/1916; eighth; Edgar E. Savory (laborer, Marblehead, MA)
	and Carrie E. Bailey (Peabody, MA)
David B., b. 1/9/1912; sixth; Edgar Savory (laborer, Marblehead, MA) and
	Carrie Borley (Peabody, MA)

SAWYER,
daughter, b. 7/7/1899 in Ossipee; first; Dora Sawyer
son, b. 2/25/1917; first; Charlotte A. Sawyer (Ossipee)
Jacob Anthony Browne, b. 8/5/1985; Matthew Thomas Sawyer and Cheryl Marie Andrea
Mary J., b. 5/30/1955; fourth; Hayes Sawyer, Jr. (NH) and Ann McHugh (NH)
Matthew T., b. 1/25/1961; sixth; Hayes W. Sawyer and Ann J. McHugh
Matthew Thomas, Jr., b. 8/2/1982; Matthew Thomas Sawyer and Cheryl Marie Andrea
Michael, b. 2/1/1966; seventh; Hayes W. Sawyer and Ann J. McHugh
Susan M., b. 5/7/1957; fifth; Hayes W. Sawyer (NH) and Ann J. McHugh (NH)
Velma, b. 10/13/1905 in Ossipee; first; Philip Sawyer (laborer, 23, VT) and Minnie Knox (16, Albany); residence - Conway
Wayne Clifford, Jr., b. 4/26/1993; Wayne Clifford Sawyer and Denise Irene Emerson

SCALA,
Joseph Daniel, b. 10/24/1997 in Wolfeboro; Dino Anthony Scala and Beth Hayes

SCEGGEL[L],
daughter, b. 11/4/1894 in Ossipee; first; George O. Sceggell (farmer, 49, Ossipee) and Addie Lewis (20, Ossipee)
daughter, b. 10/17/1896 in Ossipee; second; George Sceggell (farmer, Ossipee) and Addie Lewis (Ossipee)
son, b. 6/29/1910 in Ossipee; second; Benjamin Sceggel (laborer, Ossipee) and Edna Demeritt (Ossipee)
stillborn son, b. 8/4/1913; third; Benjamin Sceggel (laborer, Ossipee) and Edna M. Demerritt (Conway)
Howard, b. 2/14/1905 in Ossipee; first; Benjamin P. Sceggell (laborer, 37, Ossipee) and Edna M. Demeritt (21, Conway)

SCHOEN,
Dale G., b. 3/2/1954; first; Charles R. Schoen (ME) and Francena M. Daughter (ME)

SCHOSSOW,
Sophia Louise Servais, b. 7/22/1985; Paul William Schossow and Sondra Louise Servais

SCHWAB,
daughter, b. 6/6/1902 in Ossipee; sixth; John M. Schwab (farmer, 44, Austria) and Ruth Gascoigne (39, England)

SCHWARTZ,
Collin Raye, b. 5/19/1998 in Wolfeboro; Peter Glen Schwartz and Angela Marie Champney
Scott Daniel, b. 8/7/1971; Richard Schwartz and Cynthia Lynn Dale

SCOTT,
son, b. 5/11/1900 in Ossipee; eighth; Edward J. Scott (station agent, 35, Moncton, NB) and Argie E. Yeaton (31, Alfred, ME)
son, b. 12/8/1903 in Ossipee; tenth; Edward J. Scott (station master, 39, Moncton, NB) and Argie E. Yeaton (35, Alfred, ME)
daughter, b. 3/27/1906 in Ossipee; eleventh; Edward J. Scott (station master, Moncton, NB) and Argie E. Yeaton (Alfred, ME)
daughter, b. 2/11/1910 in Ossipee; eleventh; Edward J. Scott (station agent, NB) and Argie E. Yeaton (Alfred, ME)
Charles W., b. 7/21/1904 in Ossipee; fourth; Lewis W. Scott (farmer, 26, Sunapee) and May U. Scott (26, Sutton)
Maranda Lee, b. 3/18/1992; Randall Llewellyn Scott and Donna Lou Smith

SEAMANS,
Robert M., b. 2/3/1969; David A. Seamans and Gloria J. Varney
Starr L., b. 12/29/1963; first; Richard E. Seamans and Brenda E. Libby

SEELEY,
Samuel Raymond, b. 12/19/1998 in N. Conway; Raymond Harold Seeley and Susan Jean Gaudet

SEGOUIN [see Seguin],
Pauline Joyce, b. 12/1/1937; third; Armand Segouin (Berlin) and Beatrice Dupont (Canada)

SEGUIN [see Segouin],
Allen L., b. 10/21/1948; second; Roger K. Seguin (Alexandria) and Mary Eldridge (Ossipee)
Ashley Elizabeth, b. 8/21/1988; Bruce E. Seguin, Jr. and Justine A. Stuart
Chelsea Rae, b. 4/16/1990; Elwin Bruce Seguin, Jr. and Justine Ann Stuart
Colby Allen, b. 11/16/1986; Elwyn Bruce Seguin, Jr. and Justine Ann Stuart
Donna-Lee Ann, b. 11/12/1983; Elwyn Bruce Seguin, Jr. and Justine Ann Stuart

Nathan Douglas, b. 9/19/1984; Bruce Elwyn Seguin, Jr. and Justine Ann Stuart

SEIBEL,
Hannah Marsay, b. 12/6/1991; Richard Moritz Seibel III and Charlene Adams
Kimberly Faye, b. 9/28/1986; Richard M. Seibel, III and Charlene Adams

SENECAL,
Katelyn Victoria, b. 9/6/2000 in N. Conway; Craig Senecal and Kristine Senecal

SERPA,
Ruarri Michael, b. 7/22/1988; Michael J. Serpa and Donna M. Maguire

SHACKFORD,
Alison Ruth, b. 12/9/2001 in Wolfeboro; Stephen Shackford and Syndra Shackford
Cameron Taylor, b. 5/21/1999 in Wolfeboro; Scott Alan Shackford and Jennifer Hollie Zwearcan Shackford
Darlene F., b. 9/6/1963; first; Ernest E. Shackford, Jr. and June White
Mariah Jean, b. 2/5/2001 in Wolfeboro; Scott Shackford and Jennifer Shackford
Scott A., b. 11/14/1968; Ernest E. Shackford, Jr. and June E. White
Stephen E., b. 4/5/1967; second; Ernest E. Shackford and June E. White

SHAHEEN,
Elizabeth S., b. 11/1/1986; Daniel B. Shaheen and Janice E. Pierro
Rebecca Bruce, b. 6/7/1989; Daniel Bryce Shaheen and Janice Elaine Pierro
Sarah Jane, b. 4/11/1985; Daniel Bryce Shaheen and Janice Elaine Pierro

SHANNON,
Allen W., b. 10/5/1955; second; Guy Shannon (NH) and Mavis Wiggin
Edwin S., b. 4/2/1961; fifth; Guy Shannon and Mavis Wiggin
Guy E., Jr., b. 10/23/1959; fourth; Guy Shannon (Tuftonboro) and Mavis Wiggin (Ossipee)
James Edward, b. 10/16/1952; first; Guy Shannon (Tuftonboro) and Mavis Wiggin (Ossipee)
Terry Lee, b. 6/16/1958; third; Guy E. Shannon (Tuftonboro) and Mavis L. Wiggin (Ossipee)

SHAW,
Ruth A., b. 10/12/1893 in Ossipee; fifth; David F. Shaw (farmer, Saco, ME) and Celia Shaw (Ossipee)

SHEEHAN,
Erin Marie, b. 6/3/1983; Richard Francis Sheehan and Pauline Ruth Penney

SHORTRIDGE,
child, b. 1/2/1900 in Ossipee; second; Everett Shortridge (farmer, Ossipee) and Alice Thompson (Ossipee)

SIAS,
daughter [Alice], b. 8/31/1890 in Ossipee; first; Newell P. Sias (farmer, Ossipee) and Etta Bertwell (Ossipee)
daughter [Gladys], b. 7/27/1892 in Ossipee; second; Newell P. Sias (merchant, Ossipee) and Etta Bertwell (Ossipee)
son [Louie T.], b. 7/6/1893 in Ossipee; third; Newell P. Sias (merchant, Ossipee) and Eda Bertwell (Ossipee)
daughter [Marian], b. 2/12/1896 in Ossipee; fifth; Newell P. Sias (merchant, 32, Ossipee) and Etta Burtwell (28, Ossipee)
Annie Grace, b. 10/18/1894 in Ossipee; fourth; Newell P. Sias (merchant, 31, Ossipee) and Etta Bertwell (27, Ossipee)
Oscar B., b. 2/24/1898 in Ossipee; sixth; Newell P. Sias (merchant, 36, Ossipee) and Etta Bertwell (32, Ossipee)

SICO,
Caroline Dolly, b. 2/5/1990; Paul Stephen Sico and Colleen Sullivan

SIGOUIN,
Theresa Carmen, b. 10/8/1937; first; Albert Sigouin (Berlin) and Bella Duquette (Barford, Quebec)

SIMPSON,
Avery Ryan, b. 5/11/1995 in Wolfeboro; Guy Austin Simpson and Kim Breckley
Guy A., b. 9/16/1969; Harry A. Simpson, Jr. and Susan J. Eldridge
Harry Allen, b. 2/24/1972; Harry Austin Simpson and Susan Jane Eldridge

SINCLAIR,
son, b. 1/12/1899 in Ossipee; second; W. C. Sinclair (agent, Ossipee) and Lucy Drew (Wakefield)
Phillip R., b. 11/4/1895 in Ossipee; first; William C. Sinclair (station agt., Ossipee) and Lucy Drew (Union)

SINCORNNEZE,
son, b. 5/17/1895 in Ossipee; fifth; F. B. Sincornneze (stone cutter) and Pasepaulina; residence - County Farm

SKEHAN,
Erin Keller, b. 12/9/1988; Joseph Skehan and Kellie Jay Hodge

SKELLEY,
Douglas Carl, Jr., b. 7/20/1982; Douglas Carl Skelley and Sheila Emily Maddock

SKOFIELD,
daughter, b. 5/11/1892 in Ossipee; second; Fred H. Skofield (clerk, Amity, ME) and Ruth E. Skofield (Maple Pl., ME)

SLUDER,
Joseph Allan, b. 2/23/1981; Ricky K. Sluder and Barbara Arlene Connor

SMART,
son, b. 11/28/1903 in Ossipee; first; Charles E. Smart (millman, 23, Ossipee) and Mildred M. Blazo (26, Parsonsfield, ME)
Dorothy, b. 10/18/1903 in Ossipee; fourth; Nathaniel Smart (laborer, Gilmanton) and Margaret Hayde (Newburyport, MA)
Helen, b. 9/17/1906 in Ossipee; first; Harry P. Smart (millman, Ossipee) and Harriet Colomy (Farmington)
Jessica Lyn, b. 3/28/1976; William Herbert Smart and Rolynda Louise Crafts
Loraine, b. 4/7/1912; second; Harry P. Smart (millman, Ossipee) and Harriet Colomy (Farmington)
Mildred Martha, b. 7/1/1927; first; Edward C. Smart (Ossipee) and Beatrice Gile (Freedom)

SMITH,
son, b. 3/28/1889; Austin E. Smith (laborer) and Lizzie E. Smith (Ossipee)
son, b. 9/12/1905 in Ossipee; third; Austin E. Smith (laborer, 42, Moultonboro) and Addie Lewis (30, Ossipee)
daughter, b. 4/5/1906 in Ossipee; second; Leroy Smith (sawyer) and Ella Stone
daughter, b. 9/8/1913; second; Ford Smith (stage driver, Ossipee) and Marion Smith (Tamworth)
Albert E., b. 10/30/1919; fifth; Charles E. Smith (laborer, Stow, ME) and Charlotte Sawyer (Ossipee)
Chelley Jean, b. 1/8/1988; Kenneth B. Smith and Debora A. Piper

Cody James, b. 8/6/1996 in Wolfeboro; Michael William Smith and Mary Ellen Milliken
Daniel Paul, b. 2/10/1986; Kenneth Bruce Smith and Deborah Ann Piper
Ellsworth Irving, b. 8/1/1935; first; Ellsworth Smith and Margaret Irvine (St. John, NB)
Ford J., b. 1/3/1891; Melvin Smith and Laura Welch (1960)
Gregory Brian, b. 8/2/1984; Kenneth Bruce Smith and Deborah Ann Piper
Jeremiah Stephen, b. 6/14/1976; Stephen Comstock Smith and Pamela Noel
Lahra, b. 3/31/1974; Stephen Comstock Smith and Pamela Noel
Meredith P., Jr., b. 9/17/1946; first; Meredith P. Smith (PA) and Leda L. Yarnell (Ashland, PA)
Myrtle, b. 10/30/1919; fourth; Charles E. Smith (laborer, Stow, ME) and Charlotte Sawyer (Ossipee)
Nancy Lewis, b. 1/8/1936; second; Clifton Edward Smith (Cliftondale, MA) and Bertha May Riley (Poland, ME)
Richard James, b. 2/18/1938; second; Arthur Burton Smith (Effingham) and Orra E. Moulton (Tuftonboro)
Shanti, b. 3/6/1973; Stephen Comstock Smith and Pamela Noel
Sheri L., b. 3/9/1961; first; Richard L. Smith and Jo-Ann E. Hill
Teajah Keiara, b. 9/26/2001 in N. Conway; Jermaine Smith and Shela Smith
Violet L., b. 10/2/1912; first; Ford J. Smith (teamster, Ossipee) and Marion White (Campton)
Violet May, b. 9/10/1925; fifth; Charles E. Smith (Stowe, ME) and Charlotte Sawyer (Ossipee)

SNOW,
daughter [Pauline], b. 2/22/1909 in Ossipee; first; Elbridge Snow (laborer, Milton, MA) and Eva M. Williams (Ossipee)
son, b. 12/12/1910 in Ossipee; second; Elbridge E. Snow (laborer, Milton, MA) and Eva M. Williams (Ossipee)
Kammy L., b. 3/1/1962; second; Kenneth Snow and Nancy Whiting
Kenneth Arnold, b. 1/19/1938; third; Wilton Snow (Ctr. Ossipee) and Ruth Harriet French (Ctr. Ossipee)
Linda Lee, b. 6/15/1952; first; Wilton Snow (NH) and Marion Abbott (NH)
Michaella Joanne Bean, b. 2/5/1997 in Wolfeboro; Michael Donn Snow and Nichole Ruby Bean
Paul, b. 9/17/1917; third; Elbridge E. Snow (farmer, Milton, MA) and Eva Williams (Ossipee)

SORDIFF,
Anthony Stephen, b. 8/23/1991; Stephen Anthony Sordiff and Carla Jean Hartford

SORELL,
Ames O., III, b. 5/26/1969; Ames O. Sorell, Jr. and Marlene W. Potter

SOUCY,
Norman J., b. 4/20/1932; first; Marie A. Soucy (Canada)

SPARKS,
Bernie G., III, b. 3/19/1954; first; Bernie G. Sparks, Jr. (MA) and Shirley E. Moody (ME)
Cheryl Ann, b. 6/19/1956; second; Bernie G. Sparks, Jr. (MA) and Shirley E. Moody (MA)
Kathie Elaine, b. 7/10/1951; first; Bernie Sparks (Lynn, MA) and Elaine Henry (Bartlett)

SPIEWAK,
Richard J., b. 7/14/1942; Andrew A. Spiewak (Manchester) and Ruth E. Wilson (Portsmouth)

SPRAGUE,
Basil, b. 12/27/1917; second; Arthur L. Sprague (laborer, Effingham) and Grace Brownell (Ossipee)

STANLEY,
Darrell S., b. 3/30/1967; fourth; Harold L. Stanley and Ina M. Harmon
James Edward, b. 4/21/1975; James Stanley and Donna Marie Robinson

STAPLES,
son, b. 4/16/1915; first; Irving Staples (clerk, Ossipee) and Lottie White (Ossipee)
Williard J., b. 10/3/1923; first; Irvin E. Staples (Ossipee) and Sarah Hughes (Ireland)

STEARNS,
son, b. 2/10/1887; first; Edwin H. Stearns (farmer, 41, Ossipee) and Lucy B. (35, Hamilton, MA)

STEIN,
Janice Dorothy, b. 8/13/1952; second; Walter Stein (Jersey City, NJ) and Dorothy Rapp (Jersey City, NJ)

STETSON,
Susan M., b. 8/22/1955; first; Clarence Stetson (ME) and Helen Snow (NH)

STEVENS,
daughter, b. 8/1/1888; second; Edward H. Stevens (farmer, Ossipee) and Lucy B. Stevens (Hamilton)
Brian James, b. 1/13/1991; James Richard Stevens and Deborah Churchill
George, b. 6/23/1920; second; Howard Stevens (hotel clerk, Effingham) and Gladys Eldridge (Ossipee)
Grace M., b. 5/11/1893 in Ossipee; third; E. M. Stevens (farmer, Ossipee) and Lucy Smith (Hamilton, MA)
Katherine Elizabeth, b. 6/29/1992; James Richard Stevens and Deborah Alice Churchill

STEWART,
daughter, b. 12/2/1889; Henry Stewart (farmer, Wolfeboro) and Lucinda Stewart (Cornish, ME)
Barbara R., b. 7/15/1927; Elizabeth Zimmer
Herbert W., b. 7/11/1910 in Ossipee; second; Herbert Stewart (laborer, E. Lebanon, ME) and Lulu Brown (Dover)

STILLINGS,
daughter, b. 11/1/4/1893 in Ossipee; third; Frank Stillings (farmer, Ossipee) and Cora Boardman (Ossipee)
Edwin L., b. 3/11/1898 in Ossipee; fourth; Frank O. Stillings (farmer, 34, Alton) and Cora E. Bean (33, Tuftonboro)
Elwin F., b. 10/15/1948; third; Edwin L. Stillings (Ossipee) and Agnes M. Whitten (Wolfeboro)

STIRRUP,
Michael Pye, b. 4/18/1949; second; Joseph B. Stirrup (Fall River, MA) and Claire Cohen (Melrose, MA)

STOCKBRIDGE,
Angela Marie, b. 7/27/1990; Richard Carter Stockbridge, II and Pamela Joy Wood
Dennie M., b. 4/23/1949; fourth; Willard Stockbridge (Wolfeboro) and Lavinia Merrow (Ossipee)
Glenn R., b. 7/29/1960; first; Roland C. Stockbridge and Loretta M. Woodbury
John J., b. 6/7/1952; first; Willard Stockbridge, Jr. (Wolfeboro) and Julia O'Neill (Memphis, TN)
Melissa A., b. 4/12/1967; first; Richard C. Stockbridge and Grace A. Barranco
Michael Joseph, b. 12/31/1976; Richard Carter Stockbridge and Grace Agnes Barranco
Richard C., 2nd, b. 1/23/1969; Richard C. Stockbridge and Grace A. Barranco

Robert Allan, b. 12/10/1950; first; Willard Stockbridge, Jr. (Wolfeboro) and Julia O'Neill (TN)
Robin Nicole, b. 5/11/1993 in Wolfeboro; Richard Carter Stockbridge, II and Pamela Joy Wood
Sandra M., b. 4/13/1969; Roland C. Stockbridge and Loretta M. Woodbury
Wayne C., b. 11/6/1962; second; Roland Stockbridge and Loretta Woodbury

STOCKTON,
Aliya Brianna, b. 2/13/2001 in Wolfeboro; William Stockton and Beth Stockton
Brandon William Timothy, b. 11/21/1994 in Wolfeboro; William T. Stockton and Beth A. Hines

STODDARD,
Diane Carolyn, b. 12/16/1951; first; Donald Stoddard (MA) and Maude Gordon (Wolfeboro)
Jane Lisbeth, b. 12/28/1952; second; Donald Stoddard (Melrose, MA) and Maude Gordan (Wolfeboro)

STONE,
Cynthia Ann, b. 12/5/1952; Philip Stone (ME) and Irene Leso (ME)
David P., b. 9/29/1964; sixth; Philip Stone and Irene Lesso
Douglas B., b. 7/21/1960; first; Bruce L. Stone and Ruth W. Staples
Jenica Ari, b. 2/19/1988; Arthur G. Stone and Ariovalda M. Machado

STOUT,
Jacob Wesley, b. 7/23/1993 in Wolfeboro; David Allen Stout and Cynthia Mae Cochrane
Jeramiah Corey, b. 2/17/1988; David A. Stout and Cynthia M. Cochrane
Joel Allen, b. 4/1/1995 in Wolfeboro; David Allen Stout and Cynthia Mae Cochrane

STRONG,
Ian Campbell, b. 10/5/1991; John Mercer Strong and Piper Ann Burns
Ralph Elmore, b. 12/18/1940; third; Ralph E. Torsey (Winthrop, ME) and Beatrice R. T. Strong (Lewiston, ME)

STUART,
Cody Jackson, b. 7/6/1992; Edward John Stuart and Vanessa Mae Armstrong
Dalton James, b. 7/6/1992; Edward John Stuart and Vanessa Mae Armstrong

Edward John, Jr., b. 9/9/1990; Edward John Stuart and Vanessa Mae
  Armstrong

STURTEVANT,
James Jeffrey, b. 6/7/1991; Jeffrey Charles Sturtevant and Terry Lynn Carr

SULLIVAN,
Katie Ann, b. 10/5/1982; Edward Joseph Sullivan and MaryAnn Judith
  Engel
Kendyl Ann, b. 2/6/1990; Brendan Maurice Sullivan and Katherine Luanne
  Meader
Patrick Sean, b. 11/4/1978; Edward Joseph Sullivan and Mary Ann Judith
  Engel
Timothy Michael, b. 12/3/1980; Edward Joseph Sullivan and Mary Ann
  Judith Engel

SWANSBURG,
Nicholas Stephen, b. 7/18/1998 in N. Conway; Stephen Gerard Swansburg
  and Sacha Miai Eldridge

SWEET,
Lesley Gail, b. 9/5/1951; second; Leslie Sweet (NH) and Muriel Seiffert
  (MA)

SWEETZER,
son, b. 8/13/1904 in Ossipee; first; George H. Sweetzer (laborer) and
  Bessie Ainsworth (Hardwick, VT, 18)

SWINERTON,
Gloria, b. 6/7/1933; second; Richard Swinerton (Milton) and Laura
  Duchano (Sanbornville)

SYKES,
Sterling Thomas, b. 8/12/1988; Franklin T. Sykes and Catherine J.
  Swansburg

SYLVAIN,
Donald Joseph, b. 4/21/1993 in Wolfeboro; Roy Clifford Sylvain and Lynn
  Marie Watson

SZEWCZYK,
Sarah Jean, b. 10/31/1989; John Szewczyk and Wendy Susan Wickman

TALLMAN,
Ethel Frances, b. 7/17/1941; third; Harry Taylor Tallman (Bangor, ME) and Doris Marion Brooks (Wolfeboro)
Ethel Mae, b. 5/27/1940; third; Harry T. Tallman (Bangor, ME) and Doris Marion Brooks (Wolfeboro)

TAMOSUNAS,
Amy Beth, b. 8/5/1982; Paul Alix Tamosunas and Adele Joan Anderson

TAPPAN,
Phyllis Ann, b. 11/14/1934; first; Edwin E. Tappan (Wolfeboro) and Ruth E. Dugan (Somerville, MA)
Winifred Dorothy, b. 6/2/1934; second; George Tappan (IA) and Minnie Lewis (Wakefield)

TAYLOR,
David Gray, b. 3/11/1936; second; Chester Taylor (Somerville, MA) and Edwina Rudd (Milton Mills)
Florence R., b. 1/25/1918; third; Walter Taylor (laborer, Parsonsfield, ME) and Lona Cutting (Effingham); residence - Effingham
Kimberly Beth, b. 7/29/1982; Jeffrey Scot Taylor and Desira Lee Syvinski

TEBBETTS [see Tibbitts],
son, b. 3/20/1887; third; Charles Tebbetts (painter, 31, Portsmouth) and Lucy A. (28, Bethlehem)
daughter, b. 7/18/1888; fourth; Charles Tebbetts (painter, Portsmouth) and Lucy A. Tebbetts (Bethlehem)
daughter, b. 6/17/1890 in Ossipee; first; Ada Tebbetts; County Pauper
daughter, b. 5/14/1892 in Ossipee; sixth; Charles Tebbetts (laborer) and Lucy A. Hoyt (Littleton)

TEMPLETON,
son, b. 10/12/1916; first; Ahial Templeton (laborer, Ossipee) and Arthena Eldridge (Ossipee)
child, b. 10/2/1927; first; John Templeton (Ossipee) and Louise Abbott (Ossipee)
Ahial, b. 10/19/1897 in Ossipee; eighth; Ahial Templeton (farmer, 66, Washington) and Effie Williams (28, Ossipee)
Arthur W., Jr., b. 11/12/1951; second; Arthur Templeton (NH) and Marion Wheeler (MA)
Blanche, b. 8/1/1918; second; Abiel Templeton (lumberman, Ossipee) and Arthena Eldridge (Ossipee)
Donna M., b. 10/2/1943; second; Ralph R. Templeton (Ossipee) and Ruth D. Bodge (Ossipee)

Ira, b. 8/10/1887; Ahiel Templeton (NH) and Effie Williams (NH) (1953)
Joyce Elizabeth, b. 12/22/1938; first; Ralph R. Templeton (Ossipee) and
Ruth D. Bodge (Ossipee)
Ralph, b. 12/24/1919; third; Ahiel Templeton (laborer, Ossipee) and
Arteena Eldridge (Ossipee)
Ralph C., b. 10/8/1951; third; Ralph Templeton (NH) and Ruth Bodge (NH)
Sandra Ann, b. 4/24/1946; first; Arthur W. Templeton (Ossipee) and
Marion Wheeler (Brockton, MA)

TERRIO,
daughter, b. 11/15/1915; second; Frank Terrio (farmer, Weymouth, MA)
and Susan H. Perkins (Lowell, MA)

TEXEIRA,
Barbara Olla, b. 1/30/1988; Eugene D. Texeira and Carolyn E. Brown

THERIAULT,
Matthew Tyler, b. 8/3/1991; Robert Philip Theriault and Darlene Ann
Eldridge
Samantha Megan, b. 7/3/1997 in N. Conway; Robert Philip Theriault and
Darlene Ann Eldridge

THIBADEAU [see Thibodeau],
John, b. 1/22/1933; fourth; Carroll Thibadeau (Conway) and Ruth Brown
(Portland, ME)

THIBODEAU [see Thibadeau],
child, b. 2/10/1932; third; Carroll H. Thibodeau (Conway) and Ruth H.
Browne (Portland, ME)
Carl Lawrence, b. 9/7/1930; second; Carroll Thibodeau (Conway) and
Ruth Browne (Portland, ME)
Wayne Wilfred, b. 2/21/1940; third; Fred Thibodeau (St. Albans, VT) and
Ellen Delorier (Lowell, MA)

THINAULT,
daughter, b. 2/10/1909 in Ossipee; eighth; Henry Thinault (carpenter,
Grandanse, NB) and Sarah Hachy (Belmont); residence - Conway

THOMAS,
Rebecca R., b. 12/11/1965; fifth; Marvin L. Thomas and Edna R. Dore
Ricky W., b. 11/27/1963; fourth; Marvin L. Thomas and Edna Dore

THOMPSON,
daughter, b. 6/9/1899 in Ossipee; first; Chauncey Thompson (sectionhand, 20, Union) and Winifred Hatch (18, Madison)
daughter, b. 4/20/1902 in Ossipee; second; Chauncy Thompson (printer, 23, Union) and Winifred Hatch (22, Madison)
daughter [Dorothy H.], b. 6/7/1902 in Ossipee; first; Charles A. Thompson (dealer in lumber, 33, Ossipee) and Sadie Abbott (26, Ossipee)
Blanche E., b. 5/6/1893 in Ossipee; first; J. W. Thompson (carpenter, Tuftonboro) and L. E. Chadborne (Ossipee)
Cameron William, b. 12/14/1976; James Bailey Thompson and Melanie May
Darlene J., b. 3/31/1967; fifth; Richard B. Thompson and Jo-Ann E. Hill
James B., b. 1/21/1948; third; Herbert Thompson (Effingham) and Florence E. Bailey (Alexandria)
Jane, b. 5/17/1946; second; Herbert E. Thompson (Effingham) and Florence E. Bailey (Alexandria)
Jeneen Meleda, b. 7/17/1972; John Edward Thompson and Constance Meleda Riley
Lucille May, b. 3/15/1939; first; Wendell S. Thompson (Ctr. Ossipee) and Frances M. Nelson (Granite)
Richard B., II, b. 10/17/1964; fourth; Richard Thompson and Jo-Ann Hill
Ronald S., b. 11/8/1965; fourth; Richard B. Thompson and Jo-Ann E. Hill
Ryan Garfield, b. 12/27/1973; James Bailey Thompson and Melanie May
Wendy Snow, b. 12/20/1941; second; Wendell S. Thompson (Effingham) and Frances Mathie Meloon (Granite)

THURSTON,
Alfred John, Jr., b. 7/29/1950; first; Alfred Thurston (Tamworth) and Jean Chase (Wolfeboro)
Christopher Michel, b. 9/22/1984; Michel Robert Thurston and Susan Marie Lane
Daniel S., b. 8/17/1962; fifth; Daniel Thurston and Ellen Smith
Edwin P., b. 1/11/1954; third; Alfred J. Thurston (NH) and Jeanne Maude Chase (NH)
Frances Myrtle, b. 4/2/1937; second; Parker Thurston (Effingham) and Madeline Eldridge (Ossipee)
John Olin, b. 4/26/1970; John Thurston and Lorraine Ann Lord
Larry Carroll, b. 12/11/1951; second; Alfred Thurston (NH) and Jeanne Chase (NH)
Michael Douglas, b. 12/13/1956; second; Douglas L. Thurston (NH) and Lenora M. Berry (NH)
Rebecca Lynn, b. 5/14/1952; first; Douglas Thurston (NH) and Lenora Berry (NH)
Sandra J., b. 8/19/1961; fourth; Daniel Thurston and Ellen D. Thurston
Thomas O., b. 7/18/1964; sixth; Daniel Thurston and Ellen Smith

Wyatt James, b. 1/2/1989; Peter Donald Thurston and Mary Rose Whiting

TIARY,
stillborn son, b. 1/11/1915; first; Frank Tiary (NS) and Susan Bogus (Lowell, MA)

TIBBITTS [see Tebbetts],
daughter, b. 3/29/1894 in Ossipee; seventh; Charles Tibbitts (mason, Ossipee) and Lucy Hoyt (Littleton)

TILLINGHAST,
D. Lance, b. 6/20/1954; second; David C. Tillinghast (NH) and Marilyn J. Raymond (ME)
David C., b. 10/29/1932; second; Louis Tillinghast (Webster, MA) and Iris Haynes (Sanbornville)
David Samuel, b. 10/28/1995 in Wolfeboro; N. Adam Tillinghast and Winifred Marie Hehl
N. Adam, b. 1/2/1961; third; David C. Tillinghast and Marilyn Raymond

TITUS,
Amanda Rose, b. 4/4/1994 in Wolfeboro; Gary W. Titus and Margaret A. Arneen

TOBEY,
stillborn son, b. 6/6/1893 in Ossipee; second; M. P. Tobey (clergyman, Kittery) and Jane Collins (Kittery, ME)

TOBIN,
Valerie Lynn, b. 8/21/1995 in N. Conway; Edwin Francis Tobin and Terri Lynn Bernaby

TOZIER,
Destinyann E., b. 1/13/1987; Randy David Tozier and Gwenda LeAnn Bougher
Emily Marie, b. 10/9/1996 in N. Conway; Christopher Gordon Tozier and Lisa Marie Parker

TREPANIER,
Michael Henry, b. 2/11/1999 in Wolfeboro; Robert Charles Trepanier and Martha Jane Trepanier

TROTT,
son [Chester M.], b. 9/25/1910 in Ossipee; first; Leander M. Trott (storekeeper, Portland, ME) and Hazel M. Cook (Wakefield)

TUCKER,
daughter, b. 10/27/1897 in Ossipee; first; Wilber Tucker (farmer, Ossipee) and Addie Templeton (17, Ossipee)
son, b. 8/30/1899 in Ossipee; second; Wilbur Tucker (farmer) and Addie Templeton (Ossipee)
son, b. 7/9/1900 in Ossipee; third; Wilber Tucker (farmer, Ossipee) and Addie Templeton (20, Ossipee)
Martha F., b. 10/16/1916; fourth; Wilbur H. Tucker (farmer, Ossipee) and Addie B. Templeton (Ossipee)

TUTTLE,
Gregory Allan, b. 10/25/1982; Randal Charles Tuttle and Pamela Jean Hooper
Lori Jean, b. 9/16/1987; Randal C. Tuttle and Pamela J. Hooper
Ryan Charles, b. 9/27/1985; Randel Charles Tuttle and Pamela Jean Hooper

TYLER,
David S., b. 6/3/1958; first; Raymond E. Tyler (Albany) and Eleanor A. McCarty (Boston, MA)
Irene F., b. 6/10/1960; second; Raymond E. Tyler and Eleanor A. McCarty
Mark R., b. 7/24/1964; third; Raymond Tyler and Eleanor McCarty
Megan Lynn, b. 2/3/1992; David Scott Tyler and Bobbi Lynn Johnson

UPSON,
Kristopher Aaron, b. 1/9/1992; Paul David Upson and Joyce Ellen Murdock

VALLEY,
Brandon Robert, b. 9/25/1981; Robert Wayne Valley and Vivian Blanche Nudd
Debra Jean, b. 3/6/1956; second; Paul G. Valley (NH) and Lois A. Welch (NH)
Jerry B., b. 1/4/1962; third; Paul Valley and Lois Welch
Joshua Brandon, b. 11/27/1986; Jerry B. Valley and Lise Helene Lessard
Priscilla Heather Mae, b. 7/17/1978; Robert Wayne Valley and Vivian Blanche Nudd
Wayne Ellis Paul, b. 1/27/1980; Robert Wayne Valley and Vivian Blanche Nudd

VAN DYKE,
Jessica Marie, b. 3/8/1978; Douglas Alan Van Dyke and Dorothy Patricia Murphy

VAN TASSEL,
Jan, b. 4/3/1966; first; Jan Van Tassel and Linda Johnson
Jennifer Naomie, b. 3/16/1974; Baron Jeffrey Van Tassel and Judith Weeks
Laura Lee, b. 2/6/1975; Jan Whittemore Van Tassel and Ellen Frances Nason
Michelle Elizabeth, b. 9/30/1973; Jan Whittemore Van Tassel and Ellen Frances Nason
Steven Allen, b. 4/19/1971; Jan W. Van Tassel and Linda Lou Johnson

VARNEY,
son, b. 12/12/1903 in Ossipee; second; Frank E. Varney (laborer, 31, Porter, ME) and Etta Flanders (18, Freedom)
Barbara A., b. 2/4/1947; fourth; Harold M. Varney (Laconia) and Viola A. Eldridge (Ossipee)
Bruce Wayne, b. 5/29/1946; fourth; Ernest R. Varney (Berwick, ME) and Ethel V. Chase (Effingham)
Chad Allen, b. 1/27/1978; David Allen Varney, Sr. and Sandra Yvonne Dow
David A., b. 8/2/1943; third; Ernest R. Varney and Ethel V. Chase (Effingham)
David A., Jr., b. 4/22/1965; first; David A. Varney, Sr. and Sandra Y. Dow
Donna Louise, b. 2/5/1944; second; Harold M. Varney (Laconia) and Viola Ann Eldridge (Ossipee)
Edgar G., b. 8/30/1948; fifth; Harold M. Varney (Laconia) and Viola A. Eldridge (Ossipee)
Frank Wayne, II, b. 5/10/1991; Frank Wayne Varney and Denise Elaine Eldridge
Gloria Jane, b. 11/8/1950; seventh; Harold Varney (Laconia) and Viola Eldridge (Ossipee)
Jackson Rayan, b. 6/26/1994 in Wolfeboro; Frank W. Varney and Jennifer R. Ouellette
Mary Elizabeth, b. 10/26/1949; sixth; Harold Varney (NH) and Viola Eldridge (NH)
Patricia E., b. 5/2/1948; fifth; Ernest R. Varney (Berwick, ME) and Ethel V. Chase (Effingham Falls)
Ronald E., b. 11/2/1945; third; Harold M. Varney (Laconia) and Viola A. Eldridge (Ossipee)
Wendy L., b. 3/2/1968; David A. Varney and Sandra Y. Dow

VEILLEUX,
Jeremy P., b. 2/28/1969; Henry J. Veilleux and Kathleen P. Cantara

VENO,
son, b. 11/15/1889; Samuel Veno (lumberman, Ossipee) and Alice Veno (Ossipee)
son, b. 1/28/1891 in Ossipee; seventh; Joseph Veno (lumberman, Canada) and ----- (Canada)
son, b. 1/28/1898 in Ossipee; fifth; Samuel Veno (laborer, 25, Quebec) and Alice Comeau (27, NS)
daughter, b. 3/15/1899 in Ossipee; tenth; Samuel Veno (laborer, 36, Quebec) and Alice Comeau (28, NS)
son, b. 10/31/1901 in Ossipee; twelfth; Sam Veno (laborer, 40, Canada) and Alice Comeau (30, NS)
daughter, b. 3/11/1903 in Ossipee; thirteenth; Sam Veno (laborer, 41, Canada) and Alice Comeau (32, NS)
Hazel A., b. 3/13/1900; Samuel Veno (Canada) and Alice Comeau (NS) (1956)
Lena Mae, b. 2/25/1897; Samuel Veno (Canada) and Alice Comeau (NS) (1956)

VERVILLE,
Rachel Ann, b. 1/25/1992; David Parkinson Verville and Carol Ann Kempton

VEZINA,
Amy Marie, b. 10/1/1977; Roger Lionel Vezina and Marie Louise Lareau

VIGNEAULT,
Crystal Lynn, b. 8/22/1970; William Arthur Vigneault and Peggy Ann Fisher

VINCENT,
Deirdre Jan, b. 7/31/1977; Michael Keith Vincent and Janice Carrie White

VINTON,
daughter, b. 8/29/1960; fifth; Robert W. Vinton and Elizabeth Allen
Robert Allen, b. 5/18/1956; fourth; Robert W. Vinton (MA) and Elizabeth Allen (CT)
Roberta E., b. 9/18/1954; fourth; Robert W. Vinton (MA) and Elizabeth Allen (CT)

VITTUM,
child, b. 8/4/1932; fourth; Viola D. Vittum (Tamworth)
Natalie Alice, b. 10/18/1937; fourth; Merton Vittum (Tamworth) and Rachael Merrow (Ossipee)

Paula J., b. 12/28/1943; fifth; Merton C. Vittum (Tamworth) and Rachel F. Merrow (Ctr. Ossipee)

VIVEIROS,
Amanda Leigh, b. 3/21/1990; Joseph Carvalho Viveiros and Wanda Marie Anthony
Joseph Carvalho, III, b. 12/18/1988; Joseph Carvalho Viveiros, Jr. and Wanda Marie Anthony

WADE,
William J., b. 11/7/1964; sixth; Carroll Wade and Elizabeth Gagne

WAGENFELD,
Carole Ann, b. 1/19/1940; second; Henry W. Wagenfeld (Swampscott, MA) and Janice F. Holbrook (Ossipee)
Delores A., b. 10/31/1948; fourth; Kenneth B. Wagenfeld (Saugus, MA) and Velma Emack (Ossipee)
Donna M., b. 1/9/1943; third; Henry Wagenfeld, Jr. (Swampscott, MA) and Janice Holbrook (Ctr. Ossipee)
Sandra Diane, b. 11/9/1937; first; Henry Wagenfeld (Swampscott, MA) and Janice Holbrook (Ossipee)

WAKEFIELD,
Roger W., b. 4/22/1936; first; Wilfred C. Wakefield (Sandwich) and Frances E. Buxton (Somerville, MA)

WALDRIP,
Morgan Eleanor, b. 9/25/2000 in Portsmouth; Kevin Waldrip and Elizabeth Waldrip

WALKER,
son, b. 2/14/1887; ninth; John P. Walker (farmer, 49, Frankfort, ME) and Aurilla Palmer (39, Plymouth, ME)
daughter, b. 5/22/1897 in Ossipee; first; Benjamin Walker (farmer, 26, Troy, ME) and Clara Collins (19, Ossipee)
son, b. 3/23/1899 in Ossipee; second; Benjamin Walker (farmer, Ossipee) and Clara Ames (Ossipee)
Clifford Ames, b. 4/16/1972; Thomas Richard Walker, Sr. and Brenda Dawn Mitton
Cordelia Grace, b. 1/9/1998 in Rochester; Charles Walker and Judith Walker
Erin Stacie, b. 5/6/1970; Samuel Bruce Walker and Lucille Murill Soucy
Luke Alexander, b. 12/28/2001 in Wolfeboro; Clifford Walker and Lynette Walker

Tanya Dawn, b. 7/13/1970; Thomas Richard Walker, Sr. and Brenda Dawn Mitton

WALLACE,
Eda, b. 11/12/1899 in Ossipee; first; Charles L. Wallace (laborer, 42, Ossipee) and Harriett Hurd (39, Boston, MA)

WANNER,
Jacqueline M., b. 3/20/1963; fourth; Wayne A. Wanner and Muriel Hubbard

WANSOR,
Lee Douglas, b. 4/23/1949; fourth; Charles Wansor (Long Island, NY) and Lillian Tully (New York, NY)

WARBURTON,
David C., b. 8/24/1936; first; N. Calvin Warburton (Lynn, MA) and Janice O. Fetch (Lynn, MA)
Natalie Rae, b. 3/13/1938; second; Calvin Warburton (Lynn) and Anna Janice Fitch (Lynn)

WARD,
Gary R., b. 10/30/1959; second; Ralph Ward (Effingham) and Rachel Allard (Porter, ME)
Joanne R., b. 9/6/1958; first; Ralph A. Ward (Effingham) and Rachel V. Allard (Porter, ME)
Laurie Ann, b. 12/27/1960; third; Ralph A. Ward and Rachel V. Allard

WASHBURN,
Stacy A., b. 10/26/1971; Harry L. Washburn and Janet Gail Blais

WASSON,
daughter, b. 7/4/1899 in Ossipee; second; Joseph Wasson (laborer, 34, NB) and Josie Colby (18, Ossipee)
son [Clarence W.], b. 4/10/1901 in Ossipee; third; Joseph Wasson (laborer, 37, NB) and Josie Colby (21, Moultonboro)
daughter [Agnes], b. 6/21/1903 in Ossipee; fourth; Joseph Wasson (laborer, 30, NB) and Josie Colby (23, Moultonboro)
son [Leslie], b. 11/16/1911 in Ossipee; sixth; Joseph Wasson (laborer, NB) and Josie Colby (Ossipee)
son [Andrew], b. 2/21/1916; Joseph Wasson (millman, NB) and Josie Colby (Ossipee)
Andrew, Jr., b. 10/13/1949; fourth; Andrew Wasson (Ossipee) and Mildred Haley (Wolfeboro)

Danny, b. 8/6/1937; first; Andrew Wasson (Ossipee) and Mildred Haley (Wolfeboro)
Evelyn, b. 9/20/1913; seventh; Joseph Wasson (laborer, NB) and Josie Colby (Ossipee)
Joseph Dale, b. 3/20/1976; Andrew Wasson and Linda Marie Norton
Leslie Albert, b. 11/8/1956; first; Leslie Wasson (NH) and Virginia M. Nichols (NH)
Lillian F., b. 9/11/1920; ninth; Joseph Wasson (mechanic, Chatham, NB) and Josie Colby (Ossipee)

WATSON,
Patricia Ann, b. 7/22/1938; fourth; Eleanor S. Hamilton (Brownfield, ME)

WEBB,
Kenneth Harry, b. 12/10/1946; first; Kenneth Lee Webb (Belmont, MA) and Dorothy M. Wormstead (Lynn, MA)

WEBSTER,
Charles Stanley, b. 10/21/1956; second; Charles F. Webster (NH) and Thelma A. Bower (MA)
Steven W., b. 11/26/1958; third; Charles F. Webster (N. Conway) and Thelma A. Bower (Beverly, MA)

WEEDEN,
Jonathan David, b. 5/25/1988; Daniel Thomas Weeden and Karen M. Jensen

WEEKS,
daughter, b. 6/26/1900 in Ossipee; third; Frank S. Weeks (physician, 29, Porter, ME) and Minnie L. Weeks (25, Porter, ME)
daughter, b. 6/8/1901 in Ossipee; fourth; Frank S. Weeks (physician, 36, Porter, ME) and Minnie Alley (27, Porter, ME)
Abigale Jane, b. 5/25/2000 in Portland, ME; Scott Weeks and Julie Weeks
Betty Jean, b. 2/23/1948; first; Kenneth W. Weeks (Milton) and Ruby M. Eldridge (Ossipee)
Taylor Morgan, b. 8/22/1997 in Wolfeboro; Scott Edward Weeks and Julie Dawn Gorman

WEISSMAN,
Michael John, Jr., b. 4/15/1988; Michael J. Weissman and Melodie A. Sylvester

WELCH,
daughter, b. 12/5/1887; seventh; Peter Welch (farmer, 62, Ossipee) and Cora B. (31, Ossipee)
daughter, b. 1/30/1888; Lyford A. Welch (laborer, Ossipee) and Elizabeth A. Welch (Ossipee)
stillborn daughter, b. 3/7/1890 in Ossipee; seventh; John S. Welch (laborer, Ossipee) and Almira Knox (Ossipee)
son, b. 7/28/1892 in Ossipee; first; Paul Welch, Jr. (farmer, Ossipee) and Sarah Goodwin (Eaton)
son, b. 6/19/1894 in Ossipee; ninth; Peter Welch (farmer, 70, Ossipee) and Cora Kimball (36, Parsonsfield)
daughter, b. 9/28/1895 in Ossipee; first; Alice Welch
daughter, b. 10/28/1897 in Ossipee; Peter Welch
son, b. 6/21/1899 in Ossipee; first; James Welch (farmer, Ossipee) and Mabel Shultz
daughter, b. 10/21/1900 in Ossipee; second; Edville O. Welch (farmer, 33, Ossipee) and Eliza Whittiker (32, Conway)
son [Cyrus], b. 6/5/1901 in Ossipee; first; Walter S. Welch (laborer, 24, Ossipee) and Cora Davis (20, Ossipee)
daughter, b. 6/10/1901 in Ossipee; first; Moses Welch (laborer, 23, Ossipee) and Mildred Eldridge (15, Ossipee)
son, b. 10/30/1902 in Ossipee; third; Orrin E. Welch (farmer, 40, Ossipee) and Jennie Bean (35, Ossipee)
daughter [Agnes B.], b. 2/11/1903 in Ossipee; tenth; Silas Welch (laborer, 44, Ossipee) and Emma Templeton (39, Ossipee)
stillborn daughter, b. 1/19/1905 in Ossipee; eleventh; Silas Welch (laborer, 46, Ossipee) and Emma Templeton (39, Ossipee)
son, b. 5/8/1907 in Ossipee; third; W. S. Welch (blacksmith, Ossipee) and Cora B. Davis (Ossipee)
son, b. 1/22/1909 in Ossipee; twelfth; ----- and Emma Templeton (Ossipee)
son, b. 1/15/1910 in Ossipee; first; Granville Welch (laborer, Ossipee) and Amanda Williams (Ossipee)
daughter, b. 3/22/1910 in Ossipee; fourth; Walter S. Welch (blacksmith, Ossipee) and Cora B. Davis (Ossipee)
son, b. 4/27/1910 in Ossipee; second; Moses Welch (laborer, Ossipee) and Millie Eldridge (Ossipee)
son, b. 8/19/1911 in Ossipee; second; George Welch (teamster, Ossipee) and Lizzie B. Davis (Effingham)
son, b. 1/14/1913; first; James Welch (millman, Ossipee) and Gertrude Eldridge (Ossipee); residence - Tamworth
son, b. 10/5/1913; third; George Welch (teamster, Ossipee) and Lizzie Davis (Effingham)
son, b. 4/19/1914; second; Sidney Welch (laborer, Ossipee) and Eva Eldridge (Ossipee)

daughter, b. 6/29/1914; second; James Welch (millman, Ossipee) and Gertrude Eldridge (Ossipee)
daughter, b. 11/19/1916; fourth; George Welch (laborer, Ossipee) and Lizzie Davis (Effingham)
son, b. 4/21/1922; second; Leon Welch (trackman, Ossipee) and Mertie Williams (Freedom)
child, b. 4/4/1923; fourth; Bennie Welch (Ossipee) and Idella Eldridge (Ossipee)
child, b. 8/22/1928; sixth; Ben Welch (Ossipee) and Idella Eldridge (Ossipee)
child, b. 8/21/1931; fifth; Leon J. Welch (Ossipee) and Emma DeMerrett (Lebanon, ME)
daughter, b. 6/10/1934; seventh; Ben Welch (Ossipee) and Della Eldridge (Ossipee)
son, b. 3/20/1942; Kenneth W. Welch (Ossipee) and Ruth E. Pearson (Malden, MA)
Agnes, b. 7/12/1917; second; Bennie Welch (laborer, Ossipee) and Idella Eldridge (Ossipee)
Althea D., b. 4/12/1936; Robert Welch (NH) and Marion Drew (NH) (1955)
Bertha M., b. 7/13/1891; Silas S. Welch (NH) and Emma F. Templeton (NH) (1956)
Cheryl Jean, b. 8/5/1946; first; Evelyn L. Welch (Milton)
Cynthia Marie, b. 11/7/1949; second; Roland Welch (Ossipee) and Ethelda Merrow (Ossipee)
Douglass A., b. 5/28/1945; fifth; Lawrence Welch (Ctr. Ossipee) and Winifred D. Brown (Portland, ME)
Ford John, b. 5/25/1892; John Welch (NH) and Caroline Templeton (1952)
George, b. 8/12/1883; Moses P. Welch (Ossipee) and Sarah Welch (Ossipee) (1948)
Herman L., b. 3/18/1883; Peter Welch (Ossipee) and Cora B. Kimball (Parsonsfield, ME) (1948)
James Martin, b. 4/21/1938; third; Carroll C. Welch (Ctr. Ossipee) and Sara E. Scruton (Farmington)
Judith Fay, b. 1/5/1940; fourth; Lawrence E. Welch (Ossipee) and Dorothy W. Brown (S. Portland, ME)
Lawrence O., b. 12/3/1931; first; Lawrence Welch (Ossipee) and Dorothy Brown (S. Portland, ME)
Marion, b. 7/6/1915; first; Benjamin F. Welch (teamster, Ossipee) and Della Eldridge (Ossipee)
Minnie F., b. 6/17/1901; James Welch (NH) and Mabel Schultz (MA) (1956)
Paul, b. 5/24/1926; fifth; Ben Welch (Ossipee) and Idella Eldridge (Ossipee)
Pauline S., b. 10/27/1931; second; Robert E. Welch (Ossipee) and Marion L. Drew (Sanbornville)

Philip W., b. 8/13/1933; second; Lawrence Welch (Ossipee) and Dorothy Browne (Portland, ME)
Robert Harrison, b. 5/9/1934; third; Robert E. Welch (Ossipee) and Marion Drew (Sanbornville)
Roland Martin, b. 3/8/1952; fourth; Roland Welch (NH) and Ethelda Merrow (NH)
Ruth J., b. 7/29/1934; third; Lawrence Welch (Ossipee) and Dorothy Brown (S. Portland, ME)
Susan Betsy, b. 1/27/1951; third; Roland Welch (Ossipee) and Ethelda Merrow (Ossipee)
Sylvia, b. 4/23/1919; third; Bennie Welch (laborer, Ossipee) and Idella Eldridge (Ossipee)
Walter Scott, 2nd, b. 9/16/1929; first; Carroll C. Welch (Ossipee) and Elizabeth Scruton (Farmington)

WENTWORTH,
son, b. 5/3/1887; ninth; George E. Wentworth (laborer, 45, Lowell, MA) and Susan F. (36, Falmouth, ME)
stillborn son, b. 9/25/1888; third; Daniel Wentworth (farmer, Jackson) and Nancy Wentworth (Bartlett)
Fred K., b. 1/6/1943; third; Gordon C. Wentworth (Somersworth) and Nina I. Farrand (Nottingham)

WEYMOUTH,
son, b. 4/25/1912; first; Guy Weymouth (Wakefield) and Ethel Eldridge (Ossipee)
Agnes, b. 2/5/1917; fourth; Guy E. Weymouth (lumber maker, Sanbornville) and Ethel M. Williams (Ossipee)
Clayton W., b. 9/27/1924; seventh; Guy Weymouth (Wakefield) and Ethel M. Eldridge (Ossipee)
Lena Viola, b. 4/19/1913; second; Guy F. Weymouth (laborer, Wakefield) and Ethel Eldridge (Ossipee)
Lizzette A., b. 11/16/1919; fifth; Guy Weymouth (lumber marker, Sanbornville) and Ethel M. Eldridge (Ossipee)
Olive M., b. 3/15/1922; sixth; Guy Weymouth (mill operative, Wakefield) and Ethel M. Eldridge (Ossipee); residence - Freedom

WHEELER,
Philip James, b. 1/11/1936; first; Fred K. Wheeler (Newbury, VT) and Ruth Olga Pike (Portland, ME)

WHITE,
son, b. 8/5/1888; first; Scott L. White (weaver, Ossipee) and Cate B. White (NS)

son, b. 4/9/1889; Charles W. White (farmer, Ossipee) and Cytheria A. White (Tamworth)
stillborn daughter, b. 5/11/1892 in Ossipee; first; Charles A. White (merchant, Ossipee) and Emma J. White (Ossipee)
daughter, b. 3/31/1895 in Ossipee; first; Lowenstein L. White (laborer, Haverhill, MA) and Lizzie A. Pascoe (Freedom)
son, b. 12/18/1896 in Ossipee; second; Lowenstein L. White (bag. master, 24, Haverhill, MA) and Elizabeth A. Pascoe (20, Freedom)
son [Walter G.], b. 4/19/1899 in Ossipee; third; Lowenstein White (baggagemaster, 26, Ossipee) and Lizzie A. Pascoe (21, Freedom); residence - Freedom
daughter, b. 4/25/1919; first; James White (laborer) and Mabel Bean (Ossipee)
child, b. 9/27/1922; first; Belmont White (Ossipee) and Grace Eldridge (Ossipee)
daughter, b. 10/14/1932; sixth; Belmont White (Ossipee) and Grace Eldridge (Ossipee)
Allan, b. 10/24/1928; fourth; Belmont White (Ossipee) and Grace Eldridge (Ossipee)
Anita E., b. 9/10/1943; first; Harold E. White (Ctr. Ossipee) and Frances A. Dow (Ctr. Ossipee)
Beulah, b. 9/4/1930; fourth; Belmont A. White (Ossipee) and Grace B. Eldridge (Ossipee)
Charles Edward, b. 2/21/1952; fourth; Ervin White (NH) and Mildred Smart (NH)
Charles Ivan, b. 4/9/1928; first; Kenwood C. White (Ossipee) and Winnie Chamberlin (Wolfeboro)
Chris A., b. 6/21/1955; first; Norman White (NH) and Joyce Deatte (NH)
David Harold, b. 6/18/1952; fourth; Harold White (NH) and Frances Dow (NH)
Deslie, b. 5/31/1924; first; Chester White (Ossipee) and Avis E. Knox (Boston, MA)
Doris J., b. 2/18/1948; second; Ervin W. White (Ctr. Ossipee) and Mildred Smart (N. Conway)
Edward Charles, b. 12/9/1976; Ervin Scott White and Sharon Kaye Hebert
Eleanor L., b. 6/26/1929; second; Kenwood C. White (Ossipee) and Winnie Chamberlin (Wolfeboro)
Eric Christopher, b. 9/1/1974; Ronald Kenneth White and Bonita Joyce Boyd
Ervin, b. 1/31/1915; first; Mott H. White (laborer, Ossipee) and Mary M. White (NS)
Ervin Scott, b. 8/5/1944; first; Ervin W. White (Ctr. Ossipee) and Mildred M. Smart (Conway)
Geraldine, b. 7/18/1936; Belmont White (Ossipee) and Grace B. Eldridge (Ossipee)

Granville, b. 2/10/1891; Scott White (NH) and Reufina Welch (NH) (1959)
Helen M., b. 5/9/1955; fifth; Ervin White (NH) and Mildred Smart (NH)
Janice Carrie, b. 12/27/1956; fifth; Harold E. White (NH) and Frances A. Dow (NH)
Jeremy Gordon, b. 1/23/1978; Gordon Ellis White and Rosemary Bean
John H., b. 1/3/1969; Ervin W. White and Mildred M. Smart
June Elizabeth, b. 6/25/1940; tenth; Belmont White (Ossipee) and Grace Eldridge (Ossipee)
Kathleen G., b. 2/11/1945; second; Harold E. White (Ctr. Ossipee) and Frances Arlene Dow (Ctr. Ossipee)
Keith Gordon, b. 8/10/1975; Gordon Ellis White and Rosemary Bean
Kenwood, b. 2/2/1902 in Ossipee; second; Charles A. White (merchant, 47, Ossipee) and Emma J. Palmer (43, Ossipee)
Lucinda Elizabeth, b. 6/17/1950; third; Ervin White (Ossipee) and Mildred Smart (Conway)
Marcia A., b. 7/7/1932; third; Kenwood C. White (Ossipee) and Winifred Chamberlin (Wolfeboro)
Marie Elaine, b. 4/24/1944; first; Fred J. White (Wellington, ME) and Irene Lois Eldridge (W. Ossipee)
Marilyn J., b. 7/12/1947; third; Harrold E. White (Ctr. Ossipee) and Frances A. Dow (Ctr. Ossipee)
Natalie Nan, b. 7/13/1913; first; Virgil D. White (auto dealer, Ossipee) and Marguerite A. Graves (Fitchburg, MA)
Nicholas James, b. 2/18/1990; Valerie Margaret Emerson
Norman, b. 10/22/1934; sixth; Belmont A. White (Ossipee) and Grace B. Eldridge (Ossipee)
Penny L., b. 9/28/1961; third; Norman L. White and Joyce Deatte
Peter Alan, b. 4/17/1988; Chris A. White and Nancy M. Lewis
Robin Lee, b. 6/16/1957; second; Norman White (NH) and Joyce M. Deatte (NH)
Rodney, Jr., b. 6/12/1966; first; Rodney White and Linda M. Eldridge
Rusty E., b. 11/1/1964; first; Ervin White and Sharon Hebert
Rusty Ervin, Jr., b. 5/24/1995 in N. Conway; Rusty Ervin White Sr. and Wendy Sue Lariviere
Ruth E., b. 7/22/1931; first; Andrew M. White (Dana, MA) and Ethel Haines (Peabody, MA)
Samantha Joelle, b. 8/14/1986; John David White and Robyn Jackson
Sarah Grace, b. 4/27/1983; Chris Alan White and Nancy Marie Lewis
Tammy L., b. 8/25/1963; sixth; Ervin W. White and Mildred Smart
Wendy L., b. 6/26/1968; Ervin S. White and Sharon K. Hebert

WHITING,
Amanda Marguerite, b. 9/12/1987; Jeffrey Lee Whiting and Theresa Lynn Woodward

Amy P., b. 12/3/1943; second; Charles C. Whiting (Tuftonboro) and Addie
P. Dore (Wolfeboro)
Barbara H., b. 8/31/1958; fifth; Russell Whiting (Ossipee) and Helen
Eldridge (Ossipee)
Carl, b. 6/3/1919; sixth; Leon L. Whiting (farmer, Tamworth) and Mary R.
Francis (Cambridge, MA)
Clyde, b. 8/16/1913; fifth; Leon Whiting (teamster, Ossipee)
Duane M., b. 9/28/1948; second; Russell F. Whiting (Ossipee) and Helen
S. Eldridge (Ossipee)
Eric Leon, b. 3/23/1927; first; Richard Whiting (Ossipee) and Ada L.
Erickson (Oxford, ME)
Joenne F., b. 9/11/1947; third; Charles C. Whiting (Tuftonboro) and Addie
P. Dore (Wolfeboro)
Justin Alexander, b. 1/9/1989; Jeffrey Lee Whiting and Theresa Lynn
Woodward
Kurt Joseph James, b. 10/29/1993 in Rochester; Robert C. Whiting and
Arleen Claire Demers
Leon, b. 8/7/1915; fifth; Leon L. Whiting (farmer, Tamworth) and Mollie
Francis (Cambridge, MA)
Linda May, b. 9/21/1949; third; Russell Whiting (Ossipee) and Helen
Eldridge (Ossipee)
Mary R., b. 9/7/1957; fourth; Russell Whiting (NS) and Helen S. Eldridge
(NH)
Nancy Ann, b. 7/5/1943; first; Roger W. Whiting (Ossipee) and Virginia P.
Palmer (W. Ossipee)
Raymond Charles, b. 9/8/1935; first; Charles C. Whiting (Ossipee) and
Addie P. Dore (N. Wolfeboro)
Richard P., b. 9/10/1967; seventh; Russell F. Whiting and Helen S.
Eldridge
Robert Craigue, b. 1/14/1951; third; Russell Whiting (Ossipee) and Helen
Eldridge (Ossipee)
Roger, b. 8/8/1921; seventh; Leon Whiting (farmer, Tamworth) and Mary
Francis (Cambridge, MA)
Russell F., b. 4/30/1927; eighth; Leon L. Whiting (Tamworth) and Mary R.
Francis (Cambridge, MA)
Russell Ford, b. 8/26/1945; first; Russell F. Whiting (Ossipee) and Sadie
Helen Eldridge (Ctr. Ossipee)
Stanley, b. 6/11/1929; ninth; Leon L. Whiting (Tamworth) and Mary
Frances (Cambridge, MA)
Steven G., b. 2/10/1962; sixth; Russell Whiting and Helen Eldridge

WHITNEY,
Carolyn Ann, b. 5/8/1989; Peter Mark Whitney, Jr. and Susan Marie
Sawyer

Christopher Peter, b. 7/9/1994 in Wolfeboro; Peter M. Whitney, Jr. and
Susan M. Sawyer
George A., Jr., b. 9/27/1927; first; George A. Whitney (S. Berwick, ME)
and Hazel Bean (Ossipee) (1942)

WHITTEMORE,
son, b. 3/7/1947; second; James F. Whittemore (NY) and Madeline E.
Foster (Wolfeboro)
James E., b. 4/17/1952; first; James Whittemore (NY) and Bertha Brown
(NH)

WHITTEN,
Florence Mildred, b. 12/4/1938; first; Jesse James Dore (Wolfeboro) and
Phoebe C. Whitten (Tuftonboro)
June Beverly, b. 2/10/1929; second; George Whitten (Wakefield) and
Hazel Bean (Ossipee)

WHITTIER,
daughter, b. 8/9/1887; first; Andrew J. Whittier (laborer, 21, Wolfeboro)
and Adah L. (19, Uxbridge, MA)
Amy, b. 3/26/1978; Richard Whittier and Valerie O. O'Brien

WIGGIN,
daughter, b. 4/4/1902 in Ossipee; first; Edwin Wiggin (laborer, 20,
Ossipee) and Abbie E. Welch (23, Ossipee)
daughter, b. 6/23/1903 in Ossipee; second; Edwin Wiggin (laborer, 21,
Ossipee) and Abbie Welch (24, Ossipee)
daughter, b. 8/8/1907 in Ossipee; fourth; Edwin Wiggin (laborer, Ossipee)
and Abbie Welch (Ossipee)
daughter [Leah M.], b. 12/22/1907 in Ossipee; first; Jerry Wiggin (laborer,
Ossipee) and Laura O. Snow (Milton, MA)
son [Shirley W.], b. 12/12/1909 in Ossipee; second; Jerry Wiggin (laborer,
Ossipee) and Laura Snow (Milton)
daughter, b. 5/22/1913; fifth; Edward Wiggin (millman, Ossipee) and
Abbie Welch (Ossipee)
son [Russell C.], b. 8/4/1916; third; Jerry Wiggin (laborer, Ossipee) and
Laura Snow (Milton, MA)
daughter [Catherine], b. 11/30/1918; fourth; Jerry Wiggin (laborer,
Ossipee) and Laura Snow (Milton, MA)
daughter, b. 8/10/1921; sixth; Jerry Wiggin (trackman, Ossipee) and Laura
Snow (Milton, MA)
Amanda L., b. 10/21/1986; Jerry B. Wiggin, II and Patricia A. Evans
Ann M., b. 4/13/1963; first; Jerry B. Wiggin and Linda Dore
Brian Adam, b. 11/13/1987; Jerry B. Wiggin II and Patricia A. Evans

Claire Marilyn, b. 11/13/1944; fourth; Russell E. Wiggin (Ctr. Ossipee) and
    Lucy Mabel Richards (Haverhill, MA)
Craig H., b. 3/22/1960; first; Harold H. Wiggin and Marilyn J. Mudgett
De'anna Leeanne, b. 4/12/1991; Jerry Bruce Wiggin and Patricia Ann
    Evans
Deana Mae, b. 9/9/1971; Jerry Bruce Wiggin and Linda Lee Dore
Estella May, b. 5/21/1899 in Ossipee; second; Charles Wiggin (farmer,
    Ossipee) and Effie Bennett
Esther B., b. 12/14/1895 in Ossipee; first; Arthur H. Wiggin (lawyer,
    Ossipee) and Harriet M. Wiggin (Waterbury, ME)
Hazel, b. 7/7/1894 in Ossipee; first; Charles A. Wiggin (farmer, 30,
    Ossipee) and Effie Bennett (28, Ossipee)
Jerry Bruce, b. 11/8/1944; third; Shirley W. Wiggin (Ctr. Ossipee) and
    Ethel Iola Harmon (Ossipee)
Marie Eunice, b. 5/30/1941; second; Shirley Weston Wiggin (Ossipee) and
    Ethel Iola Harmon (Ossipee)
Marjorie, b. 6/22/1904 in Ossipee; third; Edwin E. Wiggin (laborer, 23,
    Ossipee) and Abby E. Nichols (24, Ossipee)
Mavis L., b. 11/5/1932; first; Shirley W. Wiggin (Ossipee) and Ethel
    Harmon (Ossipee)
Philip Drew, b. 7/10/1925; fourth; Roscoe Wiggin (Acton, ME) and Nelly
    Drew (Tamworth)
Terri L., b. 4/10/1963; second; Harold H. Wiggin and Marilyn Mudgett

WILBUR,
Klara April, b, 6/4/1999 in Rochester; Joseph Wilbur and Lisa Wilbur

WILCOX,
Bonnie Mae, b. 2/28/1945; first; Herbert L. Wilcox (Quincy, MA) and
    Virginia Arlene Cox (Ctr. Ossipee)
Edith Louise, b. 8/31/1946; second; Herbert Wilcox (Quincy, MA) and
    Virginia A. Cook (Ossipee)
Karen C., b. 2/6/1942; second; Herbert L. Wilcox (Quincy, MA) and Helen
    L. Olden (Laconia)

WILDER,
Elsie Belden, b. 9/8/1891; George Wilder (NH) and Carrie Yeaton (NH)
    (1951)

WILEY,
Kate Elizabeth, b. 1/16/1980; David Conant Wiley and Joan Theresa
    Forgette

WILKINS,
son [Elmer L.], b. 4/7/1906 in Ossipee; fourth; ----- Wilkins (farmer, Ossipee) and Dora Sawyer (Ossipee); parent's color - "dark and white"
son, b. 12/16/1907 in Ossipee; color - "C"; Erlin C. Wilkins (farmer, Ossipee) and Dora Sawyer (Ossipee)
son [Olin M.], b. 9/21/1908 in Ossipee; second; Frank Wilkins (farmer, Freedom) and Lucy M. Roles (Ossipee)
Debra G., b. 2/25/1952; fourth; Lyford Wilkins (NH) and Pauline Evans (VT)
Irene E., b. 2/16/1933; fourth; Leslie Wilkins (Wolfeboro) and Geraldine Abbott (Ossipee)
Lloyd Almon, b. 4/8/1930; third; Leslie O. Wilkins (Wolfeboro) and Geraldine Abbott (Ossipee)
Lloyd W., b. 11/13/1968; Lloyd A. Wilkins and Catherine F. Pike

WILKINSON,
Mary-Jo, b. 2/3/1967; third; Maurice F. Wilkinson and Ellen F. Knowles
Nancy Ellen, b. 12/21/1970; Maurice Francis Wilkinson and Ellen Furlong Knowles

WILLAND,
son, b. 11/7/1894 in Ossipee; second; Leander Willand (farmer, Ossipee) and Emma Hanson (Ossipee)

WILLARD,
Hannah Elizabeth, b. 3/20/1997 in N. Conway; Scott Gordon Willard and Amy Susan Hughes
Kyle Robert, b. 12/28/1999 in N. Conway; Scott Willard and Amy Willard

WILLETTE,
Aaron Joshua, b. 10/23/1996 in Wolfeboro; Randy Scott Willette and Corina Jane Scherer
Shayla Marie, b. 4/2/1994 in Wolfeboro; Randy S. Willette and Corina J. Scherer
Tyler Stanley, b. 10/16/1990; Randy Scott Willette and Corina Jane Willette

WILLEY,
Glenn A., b. 12/9/1931; fifth; Evan H. Willey (N. Conway) and Louise Spencer (Albany, NY)

WILLIAMS,
daughter, b. 9/10/1897 in Ossipee; fifth; Lorenzo Williams (laborer, 37, Effingham) and Abby Williams (30, Ossipee)
son, b. 10/12/1898 in Ossipee; seventh; Frank P. Williams (farmer, 32, Ossipee) and Sarah J. Eldridge (31, Ossipee)
son, b. 8/24/1905 in Ossipee; ninth; Frank Williams (laborer, 39, Ossipee) and Jennie Eldridge (38, Ossipee)
daughter, b. 2/2/1908 in Ossipee; eleventh; Frank Williams (Ossipee) and Jennie Eldridge (Ossipee)
daughter, b. 3/8/1911 in Ossipee; first; Cornelius Williams (shoemaker, Wakefield) and Elizabeth Snow (Milton, MA); residence - Sanbornville
Belinda, b. 10/23/1958; third; Richard Williams (Milton) and Margie Williams (Ctr. Ossipee)
Bertha M., b. 7/4/1903; Frank P. Williams and Sarah J. Eldridge (1960)
Bruce E., b. 8/19/1953; first; Richard Williams (NH) and Margie Williams (NH)
David Alan, b. 10/19/1951; third; Perley Williams (NH) and Evelyn Welch (NH)
David Jay, b. 6/16/1993 in N. Conway; Jason Odell Williams and Jennifer Marie Noble
Donna Darleen, b. 3/31/1950; third; Charles Williams (NH) and Hope N. Jackson (NH)
Gail E., b. 3/12/1964; seventh; Perley Williams and Evelyn Welch
Herbert L., b. 10/20/1896; Frank Williams and Sarah Eldridge (1962)
Jacqueline J., b. 4/5/1949; second; Charles Williams (NH) and Hope Jackson (NH)
Jason Odell, b. 7/6/1971; David Alan Williams and Brenda Joyce Eldridge
Jayne J., b. 7/15/1958; fifth; Charles Williams, Jr. (Milton) and Hope Jackson (Rochester)
Kelly Bea, b. 3/22/1984; Barry Richard Williams and Patricia Louise Vose
Kennett, b. 4/1/1923; fourth; Prest Williams (Berwick, ME) and Ethel M. Hurd (Dover)
Kerry D., b. 5/18/1955; fourth; Perley Williams (NH) and Evelyn Welch (NH)
Lizzie A., b. 10/16/1901 in Ossipee; second; Lorenzo Williams (laborer, 41. Effingham) and Abbie Nichols (36, Ossipee)
Lori J., b. 8/19/1959; sixth; Perley Williams (Ossipee) and Evelyn Welch (Milton)
Lynn P., b. 8/16/1957; fifth; Perley J. Williams (NH) and Evelyn L. Welch (NH)
Margie L., b. 8/15/1933; Willis Williams (Ossipee) and Hilda Merrow (Ossipee)
Melvin Frank, b. 11/12/1937; eighth; Jefferson Williams (Ossipee) and Cora Dunn (Dorchester)

Nancy Elaine, b. 4/26/1950; second; Perley Williams (Ossipee) and Evelyn Welch (Milton)
Perley J., b. 7/29/1916; third; Perley N. Williams (mill man, Tuftonboro) and Marjorie Cosgrove (Dover)
Phylis, b. 9/23/1917; third; Prent Williams (laborer, Berwick, ME) and Ethel Hurd (Dover)
Reginald E., b. 7/7/1928; second; Perley Williams (Tuftonboro) and Verna Merrow (Ossipee)
Sandra S., b. 11/20/1953; third; Charles Williams, Jr. (NH) and Hope Jackson (NH)
Shaber, b. 6/21/1897 in Ossipee; fourth; William Williams (farmer, 39, Ossipee) and Susie Welch (29, Ossipee)
Sherri Lynn, b. 12/17/1974; Theodore Thomas Williams and Barbara Ann Alden
Theodore T., b. 9/8/1944; first; Charles J. Williams (Milton) and Hope M. Jackson (Rochester)
Travis Courtney, b. 11/2/1975; David Alan Williams and Brenda Joyce Eldridge
Waldo John, b. 4/30/1929; first; John Williams (Ossipee) and Juanita Knox (Hampton)
Willis Newman, b. 5/25/1914; second; Perley N. Williams (millman, Tuftonboro) and Margaret Cosgrove (Dover)

WILSON,
Bradley Brian, b. 11/14/1998 in Wolfeboro; Brian Kevin Wilson and Terri Lea Carlton
Katherine Taylor, b. 2/23/2001 in Portland, ME; Michael Wilson and Lisa Wilson
Lynn Marie, b. 12/10/1983; Calvin Warren Wilson and Cheryl Lynn Gaulzetti
Warren Earle, b. 10/31/1981; Calvin Warren Wilson and Cheryl Lynn Gaulzetti

WIMS,
Edward Malachi, b. 8/11/1999 in Rochester; David Wims and Jeannette Wims

WINKLEY [see Winsley],
daughter, b. 3/13/1916; second; Ervin M. Winkley (mason, Dover) and Bessie M. Abbott (Ossipee)
Mark Dwight, b. 4/30/1939; first; Mark A. Winkley (Ossipee) and May Trask Sawyer (Beverly, MA)

WINSLEY [see Winkley],
son, b. 5/22/1912; first; Irving M. Winsley (mason, Dover) and Bessie M. Abbott (Ossipee)

WINSOR,
Alicia Susan, b. 3/3/1993 in N. Conway; Scott Richard Winsor and Debra Jean Coderre

WOOD,
son, b. 1/12/1899 in Ossipee; third; Frank Wood (farmer) and Eliza Speedy
stillborn daughter, b. 6/17/1903 in Ossipee; fourth; Frank Wood (farmer, Ossipee) and Eliza Speedy (NB)
Ida M., b. 5/5/1895 in Ossipee; second; Frank Wood (farmer, Ossipee) and Eliza Spinney
Wayne Thomas, b. 12/12/1940; Frances Rita Wood (Concord, MA)

WOODARD,
Steven Christopher, b. 2/5/1970; John Berten Woodard and Carolyn Louise Bye

WOODMAN,
daughter, b. 7/2/1914; first; Herman E. Woodman (teamster, Wakefield) and Susie V. Wiggin (Ossipee); residence - Wakefield
son, b. 3/30/1916; second; Herman Woodman (teamster, Wakefield) and Susie V. Wiggin (Ossipee)
daughter, b. 5/30/1917; third; Herman Woodman (laborer, Wakefield) and Susie Wiggin (Ossipee)

WOODWARD,
son, b. 5/20/1918; A. C. Woodward (farmer, Townsend, MA) and Anna M. Davis (Reading, VT)
Melissa Lee, b. 9/24/1975; John Shurman Woodward and Theresa Lee Boewe

WORMWOOD,
Clifton, b. 1/20/1899 in Ossipee; second; Herbert Wormwood (25, Ossipee) and Minnie Tibbetts (24, Madison)

WRIGHT,
Carrie Anne, b. 12/17/1981; Mark Edward Wright and Jane Moffett

YARBROUGH,
Daniele Marie, b. 5/1/1994 in N. Conway; Dale Yarbrough and Sarah E. Greene

YORK,
Mia Paige, b. 10/20/2000 in Laconia; Peter York and Lisa York
Nancy Ruth, b. 2/19/1940; second; Renslow W. York (Smyrna Mills, ME) and Shirley T. Adams (Haverhill, MA)

YOUNG,
Bruce William, b. 8/23/1944; second; Hammond A. Young (Acworth) and Hazel K. Philbrick (N. Newport)

ZAWLOCKI,
Emily Katherine, b. 7/22/1989; Richard John Zawlocki and Joan Schlemmer

ZIMMER,
John Baptist, b. 1/28/1940; second; Oswald J. Zimmer (Walpole, MA) and Sylvia M. Eldridge (Ossipee)
Mary Joanne, b. 1/28/1940; third; Oswald J. Zimmer (Walpole, MA) and Sylvia M. Eldridge (Ossipee)
Linda R., b. 4/4/1948; first; William J. Zimmer (W. Ossipee) and Rose P. Avery (Holderness)
William J., b. 4/3/1931; first; Joseph Zimmer (Boston, MA) and Sylvia Eldridge (Ossipee)

UNKNOWN SURNAME,
child, b. –/–/1896 in Ossipee; first; "French Girl" listed as mother

MARRIAGES

AABERG,
Philip M. Lou Ann **Lucke** 4/3/1970 in Wolfeboro; H - b. 4/8/1949; W - b. 8/27/1949

ABBOTT,
Almon F. of Ossipee m. Mary A. **Dorr** of Ossipee 4/28/1888 in Ossipee; H - 25, laborer, b. Ossipee, s/o Jacob Abbott (Ossipee); W - 25, housekeeper, b. Ossipee, d/o Herman R. Dorr (Ossipee)
Carroll G. of Ossipee m. Bertha M. **Page** of Tamworth 9/27/1933 in Farmington; H - 26, laborer; W - 21, at home
David m. Renee J. **Abbott** 8/16/1986; H - b. 6/6/1962; W - b. 2/14/1964
David W. m. Renee J. **Hamel** 8/14/1982 in Ctr. Ossipee; H - b. 6/6/1962; W - b. 2/14/1964
Donald W. m. Robyn J. **White** 7/11/1987; H - b. 8/6/1959; W - b. 1/22/1963
Ernest G. of Ossipee m. Ruth M. **Elliott** of Ossipee 1/27/1927 in Ossipee; H - 38, laborer; W - 26, housekeeper
Ernest Guy of Ossipee m. Etta M. **Colby** of Ossipee 2/1/1917 in Ossipee; H - 28, mill man, b. Ossipee, s/o Lyford Abbott (Ossipee) and Etta Ward (Ossipee); W - 22, housewife, 2nd, b. Ossipee, d/o Daniel Colby (Ossipee) and Josie Evans (Ossipee)
Everett m. Brenda **Nellenback** 6/29/1968 in Sanbornville; H - b. 5/8/1949; W - b. 8/1/1949
Frank L. of Ossipee m. Florence M. **Witham** of Brookfield 10/27/1898 in Wolfeboro; H - 32, farmer, b. Ossipee, s/o James Abbott (deceased) and Lavina Abbott (deceased); W - 20, maid, b. Brookfield, d/o James E. Witham (Brookfield) and Dorcas Witham (Brookfield)
George E. of Ctr. Ossipee m. June L. **Hodge** of Ctr. Ossipee 6/24/1951 in Moultonville; H - 21, factory worker; W - 21, at home
George H. of Ossipee m. Jennie B. **Champion** of Effingham 3/5/1887 in Ossipee; H - 22, laborer, b. Ossipee, s/o Jacob Abbott and Harriett; W - 23, housekeeper, b. Effingham, d/o Lorenzo Champion and Sobrina
Guy L. of Ossipee m. Fannie A. **Templeton** of Ossipee 11/23/1907 in Ossipee; H - 21, laborer, b. Ossipee, s/o Lyford A. Abbott (Ossipee, sawyer) and Etta Ward (Ossipee, housewife); W - 17, maid, b. Ossipee, d/o Charles Templeton (Ossipee, farmer) and Roberline Johnson (Ossipee, housewife)
Harry V. m. Gladis F. **Shortridge** 12/25/1915 in Ossipee; H - 22, teamster, b. Ossipee, s/o Lyford A. Abbott (Ossipee); W - 22, domestic, b. Wakefield, d/o Everett Shortridge (Ossipee)
Harry V. of Ossipee m. Agnes M. **Knox** of Ossipee 3/4/1933 in Ossipee; H - 39, laborer; W - 29, housewife

Jacob N. of Ossipee m. Jessie B. **Ainsworth** of Ossipee 6/1/1907 in Ossipee; H - 26, farmer, b. Ossipee, s/o Jacob Abbott (Ossipee) and Harriet N. Fernald (Ossipee, housewife); W - 17, maid, d/o Charles W. Ainsworth (teamster) and Nellie Alexander (housewife)

Joseph C. of Ossipee m. Hattie M. **Abbott** of Ossipee 7/28/1895 in Ossipee; H - 31, farmer, b. Ossipee, s/o Lemuel Abbott (deceased) and Abbie Abbott (deceased); W - 21, maid, b. Ossipee, d/o Albert Abbott (Ossipee, farmer) and Allie Hammond (Ossipee, housewife)

Ray M. m. Eva C. **Page** 1/2/1921 in Tamworth; H - 30, fireman, b. Ossipee, s/o Lyford A. Abbott (sawyer) and Etta Ward (housewife); W - 18, housewife, b. Tamworth, d/o Arthur C. Page (blacksmith) and Mary A. Remick (housewife)

Wade of Ossipee m. Josephine **Eldridge** of Ossipee 5/5/1917 in Ossipee; H - 21, mill man, b. Ossipee, s/o Lyford L. Abbott (Ossipee) and Etta Ward (Ossipee); W - 17, housework, b. Ossipee, d/o Everett Eldridge (Ossipee) and Nettie Pike (Ossipee)

William G. of Ossipee m. Grace E. **Williams** of Ossipee 2/22/1901 in Effingham; H - 34, farmer, b. Ossipee, s/o Jacob Abbott (Ossipee, farmer) and Harriet Abbott (Ossipee, housewife); W - 21, maid, b. Ossipee, d/o John Williams (Ossipee, farmer) and Harriet Williams (Ossipee, housewife)

ADAIR,
Christopher J. of Moultonboro m. Rose M. **Muise** of Ossipee 11/10/2000

ADAMS,
Gary m. Roberta G. **Borey** 12/18/1987; H - b. 4/18/1943; W - b. 3/23/1946

ADDISON,
Jeffrey m. Cynthia E. **Morley** 7/1/1969 in Ctr. Ossipee; H - b. 1/31/1946; W - b. 6/20/1947

ADJUTANT,
Chester of Moultonville m. Maude **Ames** of S. Tamworth 9/23/1934 in Moultonville; H - 21, laborer; W - 21, at home

Chester Willard of Ossipee m. Marjorie Alice **Harmon** of Madison 3/29/1941 in Porter, ME; H - 28, laborer; W - 20, at home

Matthew A. m. Deana M. **Wiggin** 2/25/1989; H - b. 2/10/1971; W - b. 9/9/1971

Norman M. of Ossipee m. Lisa M. **Carpenter** of Ossipee 9/5/1998

Randy Martin m. Ann Marie **Wiggin** 4/21/1979 in Ossipee; H - b. 12/15/1957; W - b. 4/13/1963

AFES,
Abe of Lewiston, ME m. Eve **Bancroft** of Auburn, ME 11/23/1935 in Ctr. Ossipee; H - 34, salesman; W - 26, at home

AHEARN,
Patrick D. m. Susan B. **Sanders** 8/8/1982 in Ossipee; H - b. 2/1/1956; W - b. 12/12/1954

AINSWORTH,
Michael E. m. Linda G. **Johnson** 6/17/1978 in Franconia; H - b. 6/29/1953; W - b. 3/31/1956
Wallace of Ossipee m. Alice B. **Harmon** of Ossipee 4/27/1912 in Ossipee; H - 19, teamster, b. Stowe, VT, s/o Charles W. Ainsworth (Callis, VT); W - 17, b. Brookfield, d/o John M. Harmon (Freedom)

ALBEE,
Everett S. of Wolfeboro m. Meredith I. **Severance** of Ossipee 8/5/1949 in Laconia; H - 21, bulldozer; W - 16, at home

ALBRIGHT,
Russell Alan m. Iris Marian **Allen** 7/4/1992 in Ctr. Ossipee

ALDRICH,
Thomas W. of Ossipee m. Emma J. **Eldridge** of Ossipee 1/24/1933 in Ossipee; H - 51, laborer; W - 56, housewife

ALLARD,
Cyrus of Conway m. Belle **Sargent** of Ossipee 12/12/1911 in Ossipee; H - 48, millman, 2nd, b. Conway, s/o Peter Allard (NB); W - 18, maid, b. Ossipee, d/o Everett Sargent (Ossipee, farmer)

ALLEN,
Henry W. of Ossipee m. Abbie T. **Hoxie** of Portsmouth 9/20/1919 in Dover; H - 62, grain dealer, b. Ossipee, s/o Elisha P. Allen (Ossipee) and Eunice Beacham (Ossipee); W - 40, dressmaker, b. Carver, MA, d/o Isaac Shaw (Carver, MA) and Ruth A. Westgate (Carver, MA)
James R. m. Jane L. **Dempsey** 12/6/1986; H - b. 11/27/1955; W - b. 6/21/1954
Thomas S. m. Jeanie M. **Rowe** 7/26/1991; H - b. 7/1/1964; W - b. 11/6/1964
William m. Jennifer **Klitgaard** 10/10/1987; H - b. 6/25/1957; W - b. 11/14/1952

ALLEY,
George of Conway m. Emily M. **Welch** of W. Ossipee 4/12/1958 in Conway; H - 19, forester; W - 18, secretary
Nahum M. of Ctr. Conway m. Virginia B. **Girouard** of Claremont 5/31/1954 in Conway; H - 43, superintendent; W - 33

ALLMAN,
Barnard of Revere, MA m. Betty **Baker** of Beachmont, MA 7/20/1935 in Ctr. Ossipee; H - 23, salesman; W - 23, at home

ALMSTEDT,
Harry W. m. Kelly J. **Fracasso** 10/10/1987; H - b. 11/28/1964; W - b. 7/23/1965

ALTOMARE,
Frank Vincent of Ctr. Ossipee m. Kimberlee Ann (Primus) **Kimball** of Ctr. Ossipee 7/9/1994

ALWARD,
David A. m. Deborah L. **Buck** 8/6/1983 in Ossipee; H - b. 4/7/1958; W - b. 11/16/1959
John E. m. Carol A. **Paige** 10/28/1972 in Ossipee; H - b. 7/8/1950; W - b. 8/11/1953

AMES,
Daniel V. m. Martha A. **Dorr** of Ossipee 11/6/1887 in Ossipee; H - 27, s/o Asa Ames (Ossipee) and Catherine; W - 25, b. Ossipee
James Ronald m. Laura Lee **Van Tassel** 12/21/1992 in Ossipee
James W. of Tamworth m. Joanne **Stoddard** of Ctr. Ossipee 7/1/1950 in Chocorua; H - 18, lumbering; W - 17, at home
Ralph R. of Tamworth m. Ferne **Hodge** of Ctr. Ossipee 11/19/1953 in Ctr. Ossipee; H - 18, farmer; W - 19, at home
Roger Stanley m. Sandra Lee **Ryder** 2/19/1977 in Ossipee; H - b. 10/17/1956; W - b. 8/9/1959

ANDERSON,
David Edward, Jr. m. Cheryl Lynn **Bean** 6/2/1979 in Ossipee; H - b. 8/7/1951; W - b. 11/6/1959
George Creedon of Ossipee m. Alice Rita **Mazza** of Portland, ME 4/30/1949 in Ctr. Ossipee; H - 34, truck driver; W - 27, at home

ANDREA,
Robert A. m. Janice M. **Bourgault** 9/20/1986; H - b. 10/4/1964; W - b. 5/3/1964

ANDREWS,
Austin D. of Ossipee m. Alice P. **Young** of Ossipee 9/18/1909 in Ossipee;
H - 30, farmer, b. MA, s/o Cyrus A. Andrews (W. Paris, ME, farmer);
W - 19, teacher, b. Ossipee, d/o Arthur P. Young (Ossipee, farmer)

ANGELL,
John Q. of Ossipee m. Nettie F. **Hodge** of Ossipee 3/15/1923 in Barre, VT;
H - 53, b. Randolph, VT; W - 46, b. Ossipee

ANNABLE,
George I. of Lynn, MA m. Cora M. **Thorne** of Lynn, MA 8/31/1925 in
Ossipee; H - 47, b. Bury, PQ; W - 40, b. St. John, NB

ANTHONY,
Jeffery M. m. Kimberly A. **Lang** 4/16/1988; H - b. 11/18/1967; W - b. 6/30/1967
Mark James m. Bernadette Marie **Edwards** 5/12/1989; H - b. 5/18/1967; W - b. 3/21/1970
Robert W. m. Valerie A. **Hartford** 7/2/1985; H - b. 10/9/1963; W - b. 4/28/1966
Terrance Lee m. Lori Ruth **Weeman** 8/20/1988; H - b. 7/23/1945; W - b. 8/6/1962

ANTOGNONI,
John Joseph, Jr. m. Louise H. **Cottone** 3/5/1988; H - b. 6/24/1954; W - b. 9/22/1953

APPLETON,
Scott Thomas of Ossipee m. Tiffanie Marie **Capone** of Ossipee 5/24/1997

APPLIN,
Stephen m. Dianne **Pearson** 5/4/1968 in Durham; H - b. 2/6/1945; W - b. 1/5/1945

APRIL,
Cornelius F. m. Patricia D. **Kavlivas** 5/6/1972 in Ossipee; H - b. 3/27/1925; W - b. 10/16/1940

ARCHAMBEAULT,
Arthur W. of Newmarket m. Marie C. **Colby** of Ctr. Ossipee 6/30/1956 in
Newmarket; H - 23, shoe worker; W - 19, shoe worker

ARCISZ,
Joseph m. Gloria **Kahl** 1/17/1964 in Ctr. Ossipee; H - 48, salesman; W - 32, teacher

ARMITAGE,
Richard T. m. Janice M. **Eldridge** 10/4/1969 in Ossipee; H - b. 12/6/1948; W - b. 5/8/1949

ARMSTRONG,
Dwight C. of Ossipee m. Jessica G. **Lorenz** of Moultonboro 10/6/2001
James P. m. Paulette J. **Royea** 6/14/1980 in Ossipee; H - b. 11/5/1949; W - b. 3/7/1957
Robert Thomas m. Barbara C. **Gridley** 10/12/1985; H - b. 5/3/1920; W - b. 2/27/1925

ARNOLD,
Harry Willis of Keene m. Pauline Tina **Meloon** of Ctr. Ossipee 11/11/1937 in Seabrook; H - 29, interviewer; W - 26, stenographer
William F. of Ossipee m. Alice E. **Stacy** of Madison 1/17/1917 in Madison; H - 28, farmer, b. Milbury, MA, s/o David Arnold and Grace Arnold; W - 25, housework, b. Madison, d/o Almond Stacy (Madison) and Mary J. Pascoe (Newton Center)

ARONOWITZ,
Saul A. of Portland, ME m. Lourdes A. **Cahoon** of Portland, ME 6/29/1960 in Ossipee; H - 37, salesman; W - 37, clerk

ARSANAL,
Leon of Ossipee m. Sadie **Nichols** of Ossipee 8/24/1896 in Ossipee; H - 29, laborer, b. PEI, s/o Sylvester Arsanal (PEI, laborer) and Lucy Arsanal (PEI, housekeeper); W - 22, housemaid, 2nd, b. Ossipee, d/o Ahial Templeton (Ossipee, farmer) and Effie Templeton (Ossipee, housekeeper)

ASPINALL,
George W. of Tamworth m. Gloria V. **Boucher** of W. Ossipee 10/9/1953 in Ctr. Ossipee; H - 25, lineman; W - 18, at home

ATKINSON,
Gordon H. of New York City m. Katharine **Fletcher** of Ossipee 9/2/1923 in Ossipee; H - 26, b. England; W - 24, b. Portland, ME

ATWOOD,
John E. m. Pauline G. **Noel** 9/6/1975 in Ossipee; H - b. 1/8/1911; W - b. 10/31/1923

AUBREY,
Fred R. of Ossipee m. Vera M. **Colbath** of Sanbornville 7/21/1928 in Ossipee; H - 43, horseman; W - 44, housemaid
John M. m. Karen A. **Kinder** 9/7/1984; H - b. 9/6/1949; W - b. 10/9/1957

AUDERER,
Albert F., III m. Lynn P. **Williams** 9/23/1978 in Ossipee; H - b. 3/22/1948; W - b. 8/6/1957

AUGENTI,
Jordan B. m. Carol A. **Sprague** 4/8/1972 in Ossipee; H - b. 1/26/1950; W - b. 12/17/1950

AVERY,
Carroll W. of Salem, MA m. Helen F. **Smart** of Ossipee 8/18/1931 in Ossipee; H - 26, mech. engineer; W - 25, school teacher
Earl Ernest of Plymouth m. Helen Avalve **Helme** of Ctr. Ossipee 9/10/1939 in Plymouth; H - 26, salesman; W - 20, waitress
Guy of Ctr. Ossipee m. Viola D. **Nichols** of Ctr. Ossipee 10/24/1955 in Wolfeboro; H - 52, logging; W - 55, housewife
Lewis T. m. Ruth M. **Dore** 4/3/1982 in Ossipee; H - b. 8/9/1958; W - b. 3/9/1965
Lewis Tracy of Ctr. Ossipee m. Kathleen Suzanne (Boyd) **Harrington** of Ctr. Ossipee 8/9/1996
Stephen of Laconia m. Phebe F. **Whitehouse** of Ossipee 7/9/1893 in Tuftonboro; H - 51, optician, b. Rumney, s/o Caleb Avery (Rumney) and Lucinda (Ellsworth); W - 52, housewife, b. Effingham, d/o Isaac Hanson (Madbury) and Sarah (Effingham)

AZENEDO,
Adelino of Norton, MA m. Norma **Curran** of Norton, MA 7/1/1955 in Ctr. Ossipee; H - 21, machine oper.; W - 18

BACON,
Raymond W. of Malden, MA m. Madolyn **Murphy** of Medford, MA 10/13/1935 in Ctr. Ossipee; H - 31, machinist; W - 29, clerk
Robert F. of Freedom m. Kelly April **Pittman** of Freedom 6/26/1999

BAGGE,
Mark Alan of Halifax, MA m. Helen V. **McGavin** of Halifax, MA 9/14/1996

BAGLEY,
Ralph E. m. Audrey G. **Merrow** 9/25/1916 in Ossipee; H - 22, painter, b. Nashua, s/o Elno Bagley (Bristol); W - 24, clerk, b. Ossipee, d/o Elmer E. Merrow (Ossipee)

BAILEY,
Allan MacB. of Avon, MA m. V. Mae **Fitzgerald** of Stoughton, MA 6/10/1944 in Ossipee; H - 39, salesman; W - 38, winder
Charles T. of Kittery, ME m. Almeda F. **Collins** of Kittery, ME 7/11/1894 in Ossipee; H - 30, carpenter, b. Kittery, ME, s/o Joseph Bailey (Kittery, ME) and Lucy Trefeton (Kittery, ME, housewife); W - 29, housewife, b. Kittery, ME, d/o Abner Collins (Kittery, ME, captain) and Elizabeth Weeks (Kittery, ME)

BAILLARGEON,
Donald R. of Ossipee m. Tammy Jean **Tozier** of Ossipee 11/24/1994

BAKER,
Christopher E. of W. Ossipee m. Samantha L. **Emerson** of W. Ossipee 9/11/1999
Howard P., Jr. of Wolfeboro m. Carole A. **Wagenfeld** of Ctr. Ossipee 9/9/1961 in Ctr. Ossipee; H - 24, US Coast Guard; W - 21, secretary
Mathers of Providence, RI m. Carol B. **Golden** of Providence, RI 5/5/1959 in Ctr. Ossipee; H - 27, sales; W - 22, actress
Ray m. Candace **Fitzsimmons** 7/11/1964 in W. Ossipee; H - 21, car washer; W - 18, none
William J., Jr. m. Catherine M. **Chickering** 4/13/1985; H - b. 4/12/1949; W - b. 7/23/1953

BALDWIN,
Fred W. of Prentiss m. Ella F. **Yeaton** of Rollinsford 4/19/1892 in Tamworth; H - 34, farmer, b. Prentiss, s/o John F. Baldwin and Melissa Baldwin (Winterport, ME, housewife); W - 34, domestic, b. Rollinsford, d/o Joseph W. Yeaton (Rollinsford, carpenter) and Lauretta Yeaton (Palmer, ME, housewife)

BALUTA,
Walter James m. Jeanne M. **Willess** of Ctr. Ossipee 9/19/1992

BANFIELD,
Charles Willis of Freedom m. Florence Wiggin **Lord** of Ossipee 4/22/1944 in Ossipee; H - 36, US Army; W - 33, bookkeeper

BANFILL,
Ernest B. of Ossipee m. Florence C. **Simms** of Ossipee 9/12/1922 in Sanbornville; H - 21, mechanic, b. Berwick, ME, s/o William Banfill (Madison, butcher) and Rosa LaForge (Quebec, housewife); W - 21, housework, b. Wolfeboro, d/o George Simms (Haverhill, MA, mechanic) and Harriet L. Getto (Tuftonboro, housewife)

BARBER,
Charles Newell, Jr. m. Sherri Ann **Hebert** 12/14/1991; H - b. 3/4/1962; W - b. 3/16/1969
Gary J. m. Kathleen P. **Grimes** 1/3/1981 in Ossipee; H - b. 10/24/1953; W - b. 11/7/1953

BARBIERI,
James R. m. Diane M. **Scripture** 1/21/1984; H - b. 7/21/1963; W - b. 9/13/1964

BARDWELL,
John D. of York, ME m. Lucille **Thompson** of Ossipee 9/7/1958 in Ossipee; H - 27, teacher; W - 19, student

BARIL,
Joseph T. of Ossipee m. Elise **Savigny** of Ossipee 4/6/1918 in Conway; H - 29, teamster, b. Suncook, s/o Leon Baril (Canada) and Orilca Lambert (Canada); W - 28, housework, b. Canada, d/o Antoine Savigny (Canada)

BARNARD,
Matthew Hetcher m. Heather Ruth **Gridley** 7/27/1991; H - b. 2/22/1969; W - b. 1/24/1969
Roy S. of Maynard, MA m. Elaine S. **Joyal** of Maynard, MA 11/9/1963 in Ossipee; H - 35, supt.; W - 22, clerk
Stephen m. Cynthia **Magoon** 8/21/1966 in Ctr. Ossipee; H - 21, student; W - 21, IBM

BARRON,
Roy Amos of Ossipee m. Karen Therese (Roach) **Gaudet** of Ossipee 10/9/1999

BARTER,
Herbert W. of Ctr. Ossipee m. Nancy E. **Hilton** of Ctr. Ossipee 8/11/1950 in Moultonville; H - 24, printer; W - 16, at home
Leiton of Ctr. Ossipee m. Pauline **Taylor** of Ctr. Sandwich 9/30/1955 in Laconia; H - 24, printer; W - 19, at home

BARTON,
Alan E. m. Susan W. **Hatch** 7/10/1982 in Conway; H - b. 10/18/1941; W - b. 11/5/1952
Arthur Clinton M. Janice Mae **Allen** 2/9/1974 in Ossipee; H - b. 11/2/1915; W - b. 4/4/1936
Frederick M. Mary **Varney** 12/21/1966 in W. Ossipee; H - 21, painter; W - 17, student
Llewellyn, Jr. of S. Portland, ME m. Christine E. **Cole** of Portland, ME 8/1/1936 in Chocorua; H - 31. chauffeur; W - 26, clerk
Stephen D. m. Evelyn G. **Moore** of Ossipee 2/16/1957 in Ossipee; H - 21, laborer; W - 22

BASTON,
John Edward of Ossipee m. Cynthia May (Gonyer) **Grant** of Ossipee 6/15/1994

BATES,
Donald C. of Brockton, MA m. Jean S. **Davis** of Brockton, MA 5/24/1952 in Ossipee; H - 21, Navy; W - 21, secretary

BAXTER,
Ralph Edmond of Brooklyn, NY m. Lois **Huckins** of Ctr. Ossipee 10/7/1939 in Ctr. Ossipee; H - 28, doctor of medicine; W - 22, secretary

BEACH,
Oscar, Jr. of Attleboro, MA m. Barbara J. **Strychorz** of Pawtucket, RI 2/2/1963 in Ctr. Ossipee; H - 27, landscaping; W - 21, stone setter

BEACHAM,
John E. of Ossipee m. Winnifred F. **Thurston** of Newbury, VT 10/21/1902 in Haverhill; H - 59, real estate, 2nd, b. Wolfeboro, s/o Simon Beacham (Ossipee, farmer) and Louisa W. Young (Tuftonboro, housewife); W - 39, book keeper, 2nd, b. Newbury, d/o Mrs. S. T. Quint

BEAM,
Jonathan Jewett of Grand Rapids, MI m. Susan Dearborn **Ness** of Grand Rapids, MI 12/16/1995

BEAN,
Charles L. of Ossipee m. Addie S. **Nichols** of Ossipee 7/23/1898 in Ossipee; H - 39, farmer, 2nd, divorced, b. Ossipee, s/o John Bean (Ossipee, farmer) and Sarah Bean (deceased); W - 33, maid, 2nd, b.

Ossipee, d/o Joseph Glidden (deceased) and Elizabeth Glidden (deceased)
Charles S. of Ossipee m. Clara B. **Abbott** of Ossipee 11/27/1887 in Ossipee; H - 30, laborer, b. Ossipee, s/o Stephen Bean (Ossipee) and Martha J.; W - 18, housekeeper, b. Ossipee, d/o Charles F. Abbott and Martha D. (Ossipee)
Clyde L., Jr. of Ctr. Ossipee m. Joyce L. **Reed** of Tuftonboro 11/10/1956 in Melvin Village; H - 21, machinist; W - 18, at home
Ernest C. of Ossipee m. Ethel M. **Brownell** of Ossipee 3/6/1900 in Milton; H - 19, laborer, b. Ossipee, s/o Fred E. Bean (Ossipee, farmer) and Ida V. Bean (Ossipee, housewife); W - 18, maid, b. Ossipee, d/o Benjamin Brownell (Ossipee, farmer) and Ida Brownell (Ossipee, housewife)
Ernest M. of Ossipee m. Marion M. **Welch** of Ossipee 10/10/1930 in Rockland, ME; H - 23, laborer; W - 15, at home
Fred E. m. Ida V. **Dorr** of Ossipee 7/4/1887 in Ossipee; H - 25; W - 20
Fred E. of Ossipee m. Anna **Nichols** of Ossipee 4/11/1892 in Ctr. Ossipee; H - 22, farmer, b. Ossipee, s/o Henry Bean (Eaton, farmer) and Victoria Bean (Eaton, housewife); W - 18, domestic, b. Ossipee, d/o Edwin Nichols (Ossipee, farmer) and Caroline Nichols (Ossipee, housewife)
Harold of Ossipee m. Cora B. **York** of Rochester 3/10/1923 in Ossipee; H - 18, b. Ossipee; W - 18, b. Barrington
Herbert L. of Ossipee m. Iantha E. **Knowles** of Sandwich 12/25/1889 in Sandwich; H - 30, farmer, b. Ossipee, s/o Stephen Bean (Ossipee); W - 2?, housekeeper, b. Moultonboro, d/o John B. Knowles (Manchester)
Lawrence of Scarboro, ME m. Claire F. **Gallant** of Portland, ME 8/2/1959 in Ctr. Ossipee; H - 34, truck driver; W - 21, housewife
Leland H. of Ossipee m. Addie G. **Dore** of Ossipee 5/15/1909 in Ossipee; H - 19, student, b. Ossipee, s/o Charles S. Bean (Ossipee, farmer); W - 17, domestic, b. Wolfeboro, d/o George W. Dore (Ossipee, farmer)
Raymond F. of Amarillo, TX m. Olive A. **Strom** of Amarillo, TX 7/23/1957 in Ossipee; H - 54, retired Navy officer; W - 33, bookkeeper
Robert E. m. Beverly **Westover** 5/6/1967 in Ossipee; H - 34; W - 19
William Cody m. Christina J. **Porcella** 8/25/1990; H - b. 1/18/1964; W - b. 8/18/1969

BEANE,
William E. of Exeter m. Ellen F. **Godfrey** of Ctr. Ossipee 6/16/1956 in Exeter; H - 20, student; W - 19, student

BEATS,
John M. m. Stora L. **Montgomery** 6/7/1986; H - b. 5/1/1965; W - b. 6/28/1966

BEAUDRY,
Brian E. of Ossipee m. Anne W. **Mwangi** of Nashua 12/5/1997

BEAUFORD,
Linwood A. of Auburn, ME m. Elizabeth A. **Corey** of Auburn, ME 3/16/1951 in Ctr. Ossipee; H - 44, shipper; W - 50, housekeeper

BEAULIEU,
Leo Peter of Ossipee m. Claire Lee **Carson** of Ossipee 10/17/1940 in Ossipee; H - 21, shoeworker; W - 17, shoeworker

BEAUPRE,
Kenneth of Franklin m. Priscilla **Copp** of Ossipee 7/7/1962 in Franklin; H - 28, teacher; W - 24, secretary

BECKWITH,
Brian Derek of Ctr. Ossipee m. Loralie Ann Wedge **Brown** of Ctr. Ossipee 12/24/1998

BEDLEY,
John Freeman m. Deborah Jean **Libby** 3/31/1973 in Wolfeboro; H - b. 11/29/1955; W - b. 11/17/1955
Michael Dean of Ossipee m. Brandi Anne **Piper** of Ossipee 7/20/1996

BELL,
Jeremy Moure of Seattle, WA m. Elizabeth Alexandra **Pratt** of Seattle, WA 9/11/1999
William m. Myrtle M. **Slinger** 7/10/1915 in Ossipee; H - 24, teamster, b. Hanson, MA, s/o Charles C. Bell (Digby, NS); W - 22, stitching, b. Rockland, MA, d/o John M. Slinger (Chicago, IL)
William R. m. Patricia J. **Hatch** 6/11/1983 in Ossipee; H - b. 11/22/1950; W - b. 1/12/1960

BELVILLE,
Paul C. m. Josephine **Della Pelle** 11/24/1985; H - b. 5/24/1950; W - b. 5/14/1959

BEMIS,
Robert m. Suzanne **Lafreniere** 11/19/1966 in Ctr. Ossipee; H - 23, clerk; W - 21, receptionist

BENGE,
Arthur E. of Ossipee m. Gladys E. **Welch** of Ossipee 1/1/1929 in Wolfeboro; H - 25, printer; W - 26, book keeper

BENISH,
Richard Christopher of Ossipee m. Colleen Sahrann McCullough **MacDonald** of Ossipee 11/3/2001

BENNETT,
Edward G. of Waterville, VT m. Carol A. **McCuin** of Belvidere, VT 9/20/1963 in Ctr. Ossipee; H - 25, farmer; W - 22, nurse
Sumner L. of Ossipee m. Rosa A. **Wood** of Effingham 1/31/1903 in Effingham; H - 20, watchman, b. Ossipee, s/o Elden Bennett (Sandwich, farmer) and Ella Tewksbury (Tamworth, housewife); W - 24, maid, b. Freedom, d/o James Wood (Canada, laborer) and Dora Frauinar (Canada, housewife)

BENWAY,
Frederick M. m. Donna C. **Potter** 6/28/1986; H - b. 6/15/1968; W - b. 9/8/1961

BERGERON,
Donald E. of Sanbornville m. Donna S. **Downie** of Ossipee 2/29/2000
Gerald R. m. Gayle M. **Contois** 5/6/1989; H - b. 3/4/1950; W - b. 5/23/1964

BERNARDO,
Sonny m. Kerry Anne **DeGloria** 5/30/1992 in Conway

BERRY,
Craig Joseph of Haverhill, MA m. Carla Jean Hartford **Sordiff** of Haverhill, MA 7/4/2001
David A. of Ctr. Ossipee m. Eva M. **Hamel** of Ctr. Ossipee 9/9/1961 in Ctr. Ossipee; H - 23, lineman; W - 18, waitress
Duane Ernest m. Pammy Ann **Eldridge** 6/10/1989; H - b. 8/6/1970; W - b. 6/17/1965
Duane Herman m. Donna Elaine **Alden** 4/14/1970 in Ossipee; H - b. 1/16/1952; W - b. 11/7/1951
Duane Herman m. Barbara **Ferrante** 8/27/1991; H - b. 1/16/1952; W - b. 3/19/1947
Ernest of Ossipee m. Phyllis **Merrow** of Ossipee 9/28/1931 in Ossipee; H - 23, laborer; W - 16, at home
Ernest M., Jr. of Ctr. Ossipee m. Eva J. **Abbott** of Ctr. Ossipee 9/25/1954 in Ctr. Ossipee; H - 18, garage work; W - 18, secretary

Gordon D. m. Gloria F. **Abbott** 10/18/1969 in Ctr. Ossipee; H - b. 2/15/1942; W - b. 5/9/1944

Herman D. of Ossipee m. Margaret A. **Holley** of Boston 4/15/1901 in Ctr. Ossipee; H - 24, laborer, b. Tamworth, s/o Henry C. Berry (Tamworth, farmer) and Fannie Berry (Parsonsfield, housewife); W - 26, maid, b. Ireland, d/o —— (Ireland, deceased)

John Adrian of Ctr. Ossipee m. Jennifer Lee **Nichols** of Ctr. Ossipee 10/14/1995

John M. m. Gaye E. **Varney** 8/17/1972 in Tuftonboro; H - b. 10/21/1946; W - b. 10/12/1944

Raymond A. of W. Ossipee m. Charlotte E. **Eldridge** of Tamworth 6/3/1950 in Moultonville; H - 20, painter; W - 19, at home

BERTON,
Robert E. m. Frances L. **Davis** 5/5/1973 in Ossipee; H - b. 7/22/1927; W - b. 9/5/1912

BERTRAM,
Carl J. m. Carmen Jean **White** 6/23/1972 in Ossipee; H - b. 2/19/1926; W - b. 7/5/1945

BETHELL,
Russell Edward m. Jennifer Lee **Carruthers** 12/24/1990; H - b. 12/5/1971; W - b. 8/6/1972

BETTS,
George R. of Gardiner, ME m. Frances **Howard** of Gardiner, ME 7/10/1946 in Ossipee; H - 21, clerk; W - 21, nurse

BIBBER,
Orville R. m. Lillian A. **Butler** 11/20/1976 in Ossipee; H - b. 12/6/1941; W - b. 12/20/1931

BICKFORD,
Belmont E. of Ossipee m. Dora **Bickford** of Ossipee 1/16/1897 in Ossipee; H - 36, farmer, b. Ossipee, s/o Edward R. Bickford (farmer) and Melissa Thompson (Ossipee, housekeeper); W - 16, housemaid, b. Bartlett, d/o Henry Bickford (Bartlett, laborer) and Ida Cook (Fryeburg, housekeeper)

Carroll m. Elizabeth **Keniston** 8/2/1968 in Ctr. Ossipee; H - b. 6/18/1942; W - b. 4/10/1939

Charles H. of Ossipee m. Sarah I. **Wiggin** of Ossipee 4/9/1899 in Tuftonboro; H - 49, farmer, b. Ossipee, s/o Stephen Bickford (farmer)

and Hannah Young (housewife); W - 41, maid, b. E. Boston, d/o
John L. Wiggin (sailor) and Mary A. Wiggin (housewife)

Wilbur C. of Ossipee m. Angela L. **Gilman** of Pottstown, PA 7/24/1937 in
Ctr. Ossipee; H - 38, farmer; W - 43, at home

BIERWEILER,
Donald C. of Ossipee m. Annie E. **Clark** of Wolfeboro 10/7/1948 in Ctr.
Ossipee; H - 24, mechanic; W - 27, technician

BILLINGS,
Condict Moore m. Debra Ann **Jones** 11/12/1989; H - b. 3/1/1943; W - b.
4/15/1955

BILODEAU,
Herbert G. m. Kathryn E. **Hinckley** 4/24/1982 in Ossipee; H - b.
12/18/1961; W - b. 1/1/1963

BISBEE,
Chester A. of Ossipee m. Roberta G. **Bean** of Ossipee 7/17/1912 in
Ossipee; H - 28, merchant, b. ME, s/o Roscoe Bisbee (Saco, ME); W
- 30, b. Tuftonboro, s/o George O. Bean (Moultonboro)

Chester A. of Ossipee m. Mildred E. **Beckman** of Effingham 7/12/1932 in
Ossipee; H - 48, carpenter; W - 29, housekeeper

Wilbur m. Mary R. **Gosselin** 4/30/1975 in Ossipee; H - b. 10/25/1902; W -
b. 5/29/1913

BLAIR,
Brian K. m. Nancy L. **Floria** 10/28/1972 in Ossipee; H - b. 9/27/1952; W -
b. 2/5/1953

Francis Charles of Melrose, MA m. Beatrice A. **Beckwith** of Boston, MA
6/18/1949 in Ctr. Ossipee; H - 30, railway clerk; W - 32, physical
therapist

BLAIS,
Roger m. Eva **Anderson** 7/29/1964 in Ctr. Ossipee; H - 39, brick mfg.; W
- 37, office work

BLAISDELL,
Erving A. of Ossipee m. Jennie M. **Linscott** of Effingham 5/12/1894 in
Effingham; H - 23, laborer, b. Boston, MA, s/o Hosea Blaisdell; W -
19, housemaid, b. Porter, ME, d/o James Linscott

BLAKE,
Daniel Richard m. Alice Susan **Davis** 5/10/1991; H - b. 5/20/1970; W - b. 2/12/1970
Percy A. of Madison m. Esther R. **Gilman** of Madison 12/9/1951 in Madison; H - 61, RR agent; W - 44, store prop.
Perley E. of Milford, CT m. Helen K. **Nadeau** of Woodmont, CT 6/23/1948 in Ctr. Ossipee; H - 42, contractor; W - 32, welder
Richard F. of Seekonk, MA m. Maureen **Hatch** of Pawtucket, RI 3/12/1959 in Ctr. Ossipee; H - 22, laborer; W - 18, none
Richard M. m. Marilyn J. **White** 8/3/1969 in Ctr. Ossipee; H - b. 12/5/1946; W - b. 7/12/1947
Simon of Ossipee m. Mabel E. **Fall** of Ossipee 1/12/1893 in Ctr. Ossipee; H - 33, farmer, b. Ossipee, s/o Thomas J. Blake and Sarah (Ossipee); W - 20, b. Ossipee, d/o Frank Fall (Ossipee) and Emma (Ossipee)
William of Portland, ME m. Carole **Higgins** of Portland, ME 8/11/1958 in Ossipee; H - 20, Navy; W - 19, none

BLANKE,
Dennis m. Kathryn **Breault** 12/31/1966 in Ctr. Ossipee; H - 21, Navy; W - 18, none

BLEYLE,
Donald A. m. Patricia F. **Snyer** 1/4/1981 in Ctr. Ossipee; H - b. 9/6/1927; W - b. 8/28/1930

BLOIS,
William, Jr. m. Arlene **McKenzie** 8/20/1964 in Ctr. Ossipee; H - 40, produce; W - 49, none

BLOUIN,
Francis X. of Somerville, MA m. Dagny D. **Dube** of Ctr. Ossipee 9/3/1951 in Wolfeboro; H - 25, shipper; W - 21, student
Paul S. of Auburn, ME m. Jean E. **Hodgkins** of Auburn, ME 8/8/1950 in Ctr. Ossipee; H - 19, station att.; W - 16, at home

BOARDMAN,
Carlos of W. Ossipee m. Natalie A. **Plant** of W. Ossipee 1/16/1952 in Ctr. Ossipee; H - 45, mill hand; W - 27, housekeeper
Forest E. m. Ada M. **Wentworth** 11/8/1915 in Tuftonboro; H - 30, laborer, b. Camden, s/o Joseph E. Boardman (Camden, ME); W - 19, domestic, 2nd, b. Tuftonboro, d/o Frank I. Wentworth (Tuftonboro)
Fred B. of Amesbury, MA m. Cora Ada S. **Feltham** of Amesbury, MA 8/3/1903 in Ossipee; H - 27, clerk, b. Amesbury, MA, s/o Leonard

Boardman (Amesbury, MA, mechanic) and Ada J. Tucker (Stillwater, ME, housekeeper); W - 25, school teacher, b. Amesbury, MA, d/o James H. Feltham (England, hatter) and Laura E. Sidelinger (Union, ME, housewife)

BOATMAN,
Lawrence of Portsmouth m. Margaret A. **Dore** of Ctr. Ossipee 3/6/1960 in Wolfeboro; H - 19, Air Force; W - 17, shoe shop

BODGE,
Walter C. of Ossipee m. Maud F. **Hanson** of Ossipee 1/1/1901 in Ossipee; H - 24, laborer, b. Tuftonboro, s/o James L. Bodge (Moultonboro, deceased) and Betsey H. Bodge (deceased); W - 18, maid, b. Ossipee, d/o James Hanson (Ossipee, farmer) and Affey A. Hanson (Ossipee, housewife)

BODURTHA,
Richard Sheldon m. Susan Marie **Peck** 7/15/1988; H - b. 11/24/1952; W - b. 8/31/1944

BOEHM,
Donald W. of Ctr. Ossipee m. Deborah A. **Neenan** of Ctr. Ossipee 10/14/1995

BOGARD,
Nelson of Newton, IL m. Barbara H. **Senior** of Newport, RI 11/10/1946 in Conway; H - 21, US Navy; W - 19, at home

BOISSE,
Victor E. of Manchester m. Charlotte J. **Lord** of W. Ossipee 10/21/1950 in Wolfeboro; H - 28, Navy; W - 26, nurse

BOISVERT,
Paul Joseph m. Deborah Jean **Black** 3/20/1993 in Rochester
Robert R. m. Joanna K. **Nudd** 10/18/1975 in Ossipee; H - b. 5/20/1957; W - b. 10/11/1956

BOLDUC,
Douglas G. m. Marilyn R. **Bolduc** 9/7/1985; H - b. 5/30/1962; W - b. 3/23/1952

BOLTON,
James M. of Ctr. Ossipee m. Wanda R. Merchant **Roberts** of Ctr. Ossipee 6/23/2001

BOOTHBY,
Robert H. of Saco, ME m. Alice **Witham** of Sebago Lake, ME 7/3/1937 in Freedom; H - 24, machinist; W - 18, at home

BORDEN,
Harold F. of Water Village m. Doris R. **McNeil** of Ormond Beach, FL 4/10/1956 in Ctr. Ossipee; H - 37, writer; W - 32, dental tech.

BOSTON,
Herman D., Jr. of Sanford, ME m. Lucy L. **Rogers** of Ossipee 9/8/1946 in Ossipee; H - 25, warehouse man; W - 17, waitress

BOUCHER,
Ernest J., Jr. of W. Ossipee m. Constance M. **LeBlanc** of Ctr. Ossipee 5/30/1953 in Ctr. Ossipee; H - 24, clerk; W - 21, bookkeeper

BOUCHICAS,
Grant Paul m. Doris Mary **Sheehan** 8/21/1989; H - b. 6/19/1967; W - b. 2/4/1960

BOURGAULT,
Daniel R. m. Lynn M. **Shannon** 9/10/1983 in Ossipee; H - b. 7/10/1962; W - b. 5/26/1965

BOURGEOIS,
Robert Paul, Jr. of Effingham m. Mary Beth Joy **Kenney** of Ctr. Ossipee 6/16/2001

BOUTIN,
Bruce Kyle m. Janie Elizabeth **Bugden** 11/19/1988; H - b. 11/27/1961; W - b. 11/5/1962
Harold of Ossipee m. Patricia **Boyd** of Tamworth 12/7/1962 in Tamworth; H - 35, waiter; W - 32, housewife
Raymond Paul m. Robin Anita **Pohl** 9/30/1978 in Ossipee; H - b. 8/28/1952; W - b. 10/30/1956
Raymond Paul, II of Manchester m. Angela Nanette **Ames** of Manchester 7/8/2001

BOUTWELL,
Roswell Murray of Effingham m. Anna Pauline **McMinn** of Effingham 8/26/1941 in Ossipee; H - 53, insurance agt.; W - 28, secretary

BOVA,
Paul Anthony m. Deborah J. **Farrell** 3/31/1989; H - b. 12/5/1959; W - b. 11/29/1960

BOWE,
Richard, Jr. of Wolfeboro m. Joan **Noyes** of Ctr. Ossipee 7/15/1962 in Wolfeboro; H - 24, real estate broker; W - 23, teacher

BOWEN,
Walter M. of Rochester m. Patricia A. **Loring** of Ctr. Ossipee 11/21/1957 in Ctr. Ossipee; H - 23, laborer; W - 23, secretary

BOWER,
Theodore H. of Boston, MA m. Dorothy E. **Ross** of Boston, MA 7/6/1951 in Ctr. Ossipee; H - 49, layout man; W - 35, at home

BOWERS,
Howard L. of Ossipee m. Beatrice I. **Davis** of Ossipee 12/24/1917 in Ossipee; H - 28, lumberman, b. NS, s/o Carl Bowers (NS) and Carrie Bowers (NS); W - 19, housework, b. Effingham, d/o Frank Davis (Effingham) and Marsha Judkins (Freedom)

BOWMAN,
Richard D. of Beverly, MA m. Dorothea **Colbert** of Salem, MA 8/28/1937 in Union; H - 26, market man; W - 26, teacher

BRACK,
Albert, Jr. of Ossipee m. Ruthann **Letteney** of Wolfeboro 9/24/1958 in Wolfeboro; H - 19, secretary; W - 17, home

BRACKETT,
James A. of Boston m. Ona L. **Hanson** of Ossipee 12/20/1919 in Ossipee; H - 52, lawyer, b. Boston, s/o Benjamin Brackett (Tewksbury, MA) and Sarah Small (Hampton, ME); W - 31, hotel business, b. Boston, d/o Frank Hanson (Ossipee) and Lillian E. Patrell (Springfield, MA)
Timothy Edward of Sanbornville m. Jeneen Meleda **Thompson** of Ossipee 9/10/1994

BRADEW,
John R. of Cornish, ME m. Etta R. **Weeks** of E. Parsonsfield 10/15/1926 in Ctr. Ossipee; H - 31, b. Cornish; W - 19, b. E. Parsonsfield

BRADLEY,
Charles H. of Ossipee m. Edith **Richardson** of Wakefield 11/26/1914 in Ossipee; H - 35, b. Newbury, MA, s/o Thomas G. Bradley; W - 41, housekeeper, b. Walton, MA, d/o A. Maynard Richardson (S. Boston, MA)
Edwin Keiffer, III m. Michele Marie **Duchesne** 12/20/1988; H - b. 1/10/1962; W - b. 4/27/1967
Harold of Haverhill, MA m. Mabel M. **Crouse** of Haverhill, MA 10/10/1936 in Ossipee; H - 46, cook; W - 22, at home
Joseph L. m. Patricia A. **Blomstrom** 8/16/1970 in Ossipee; H - b. 6/7/1941; W - b. 12/31/1947

BRADSTREET,
Charles O. of Ossipee m. Helen M. **Campbell** of Ossipee 4/29/1946 in Ossipee; H - 41, gas sta. att.; W - 43, waitress

BRALCZYK,
Stanley Adam of Ctr. Ossipee m. Robin Lynn **Bralczyk** of Ctr. Ossipee 6/24/1999

BRANNON,
Daniel E. of Indianapolis, IN m. Janice M. **Reynolds** of S. Paris, ME 1/28/1961 in Ctr. Ossipee; H - 21, US Navy; W - 21, nurse

BRENNAN,
Thomas P. m. Alice W. **Smith** 8/27/1983 in Ossipee; H - b. 3/5/1957; W - b. 8/18/1956

BRESNAHAN,
Brian D. m. Karie L. **Shannon** 4/3/1982 in Ossipee; H - b. 8/5/1947; W - b. 10/28/1959

BRETON,
Donald Henry m. Stephanie Anne **Alexander** 7/16/1993 in Concord

BRETT,
Warren T. of Framingham, MA m. Barbara J. **Bisbee** of Ossipee 12/3/1953 in Moultonville; H - 25, G.M.C.; W - 16, at home

BRISBIN,
Charles E. of Readfield, ME m. Hazel M. **Richardson** of GA 11/8/1950 in Ctr. Ossipee; H - 74, merchant; W - 53, housewife

BRITTON,
Raymond F. m. Margaret L. **Boissey** 5/22/1967 in Ctr. Ossipee; H - 46, machinist; W - 43

BRODEUR,
Michael Richard m. Anne R. **Currier** 9/4/1971 in Ossipee; H - b. 11/6/1947; W - b. 12/10/1947

BRODIE,
Edward William of Haverhill, MA m. Jennie Bell **Worster** of Haverhill, MA 6/2/1943 in Ossipee; H - 83, retired; W - 60, housewife

BRODRICK,
Charles H. of Wolfeboro m. Pearl B. **Morton** of Ossipee 7/16/1960 in Ossipee; H - 69, retired; W - 63, housewife

BRONSCOMBE,
Harold H. of E. Newport, ME m. Barbara R. **Colby** of Plymouth, ME 9/4/1934 in Effingham Falls; H - 36, auto mech.; W - 22, at home

BROOKS,
Gary F. of Ossipee m. Cindy L. (LaVoice) **Brooks** of Ossipee 12/31/1996
Harold V. m. Cheryl E. **Morrill** 3/7/1981 in Ossipee; H - b. 12/3/1935; W - b. 6/8/1945
Richard W. of Holliston, MA m. Dorothy E. **Burke** of Holliston, MA 11/9/1963 in Ctr. Ossipee; H - 22, landcaper; W - 22, secretary

BROTHERS,
Elmer Wayne of Ossipee m. Esther Geraldine **Ames** of Tamworth 1/29/1949 in Ctr. Ossipee; H - 20, mill worker; W - 22, stenographer
Lawrence of Ossipee m. Beatrice E. **Palmer** of Ossipee 6/29/1927 in Ossipee; H - 23, laborer; W - 19, at home
Stanley Neal m. Diane L. **Aleksa** 1/21/1978 in Ossipee; H - b. 9/2/1953; W - b. 4/17/1956

BROUGH,
Dale R. of Attleboro, MA m. Deborah J. **Williams** of Attleboro, MA 7/30/1955 in Ctr. Ossipee; H - 20, toolmaker; W - 18

BROUGHTON,
Robert Edwin m. Eleanor Lorraine **Moylan** 6/2/1990; H - b. 3/7/1938; W - b. 7/6/1933

BROWN,
Albert W. of Kittery, ME m. Marion L. **Hutchins** of Kittery, ME 8/25/1932 in Laconia; H - 22, clerk; W - 21, stenographer
Charles M. of Ossipee m. Nellie M. **Smith** of Ossipee 7/4/1888 in Ossipee; H - 20, laborer, b. Madison, s/o John M. Brown; W - 26, housekeeper
Christopher Ralph m. Tracey Lynn **Hodgkins** 5/1/1993 in Jackson
Clyde H. of Ossipee m. Lucinda E. **Nason** of Wakefield 1/11/1923 in Ossipee; H - 22, b. Ossipee; W - 17, b. Brookfield
Donald K. m. Eleanor L. **Iverson** 11/24/1985; H - b. 5/26/1925; W - b. 7/22/1921
Fred B. of Ossipee m. Edna A. **Dame** of Ossipee 5/5/1894 in Ossipee; H - 24, farmer, b. Tuftonboro, s/o John H. Brown (Tuftonboro, wheelwright) and Celeste Williams (Tuftonboro, housewife); W - 24, housewife, b. Ossipee, d/o William Dame (Ossipee, blacksmith) and Carrie Peavy (Ossipee, housewife)
Isaac, Jr. m. Linda J. **Dufresne** 3/9/1969 in Ctr. Ossipee; H - b. 1/25/1947; W - b. 5/30/1947
John F., Jr. of Milton, MA m. Gladys G. **Pascoe** of Ossipee 9/27/1921 in Whittier; H - 36, salesman, b. Freedom, s/o John F. Brown (E. Douglas, MA) and Alice Rogerson (E. Douglas, MA); W - 52, teacher, b. Wolfeboro, d/o Henry J. Pascoe (Corpas Hill, VT) and Annie L. Laughlin (Freedom)
Keith J. m. Stacie J. **Robinson** 10/5/1991; H - b. 1/17/1964; W - b. 3/22/1970
Lawrence F. of Lewiston, ME m. Eva **Shephard** of Bath, ME 4/29/1950 in Ossipee; H - 31, engineer; W - 24, nurse
Michael A. m. Carol L. **Sacca** 8/13/1983 in Ossipee; H - b. 7/30/1946; W - b. 9/2/1950
Reginald P. m. Marilyn E. **Chase** 5/15/1978 in Ossipee; H - b. 8/15/1948; W - b. 11/26/1955
Richard Eugene of Ossipee m. Naomi Ruth **Ennis** of Pocomoke City, MD 9/18/1945 in Ossipee; H - 21, US Navy; W - 24, beautician
Richard S. of Ossipee m. June F. **Varney** of Wolfeboro 5/30/1954 in N. Hampton; H - 26, shipwright; W - 25, secretary
Robert C. of Ossipee m. Patricia A. **Chase** of Penacook 1/15/1955 in Penacook; H - 19, truck driver; W - 19, secretary
Scott Michael m. Sandra May **Stockbridge** 7/28/1990; H - b. 7/27/1971; W - b. 4/13/1969
Steven Lawrence of Effingham m. Tammy Marie **Willess** of Effingham 8/29/1998
Tom H. of Ossipee m. Bessie M. **Pease** of Freedom 11/21/1896 in Freedom; H - 21, painter, b. Ossipee, s/o Herbert H. Brown (deceased) and Charlotte J. Brown (Ossipee, housewife); W - 19,

dressmaker, b. Freedom, d/o Alonzo Pease (Freedom, tailor) and Mary J. Pease (Freedom, housewife)
Walter S. of Freeport, ME m. Lena V. **Moore** of Freeport, ME 7/22/1937 in Moultonville; H - 50, shoe cutter; W - 39, shoe stitcher
William H. of Madison m. Mabel R. **Shultz** of Albany 2/18/1909 in Ossipee; H - 27, blacksmith, 2nd, b. Madison, s/o Royal P. Brown (Islesboro, ME, sea captain); W - 29, housekeeper, b. Boston, MA, d/o Alfred Shultz (N. Chesterfield, farmer)
William H. of W. Ossipee m. Myrtle Blanche **Smith** of Jackson 11/4/1935 in Contoocook; H - 23, mill worker; W - 18, tel. operator

BROWNE,
William H. of Ossipee m. Frances E. **Osgood** of Ossipee 5/17/1933 in Ossipee; H - 21, mill laborer; W - 23, shoe shop

BROWNELL,
Bryan Keith of Ctr. Ossipee m. Michelle Lee **Gale** of Ctr. Ossipee 9/22/2001
Clifford R. of Ossipee m. Barbara **Merrow** of Ossipee 2/12/1933 in Ossipee; H - 19, at home; W - 15, at home
Clifford R. of Ctr. Ossipee m. Marion B. **Beane** of Ctr. Ossipee 7/25/1948 in Tamworth; H - 34, truck driver; W - 33, telephone oper.
Edwin P. of Ctr. Ossipee m. Ingrid M. **Hinz** of Ctr. Ossipee 2/8/1959 in Ctr. Ossipee; H - 25, body shop; W - 32, housekeeper
Harold L. of Wolfeboro m. Patricia E. **Hersey** of Ossipee 6/27/1959 in Wolfeboro; H - 19, Marine Corp.; W - 18, waitress
Keith W. m. Barbara G. **Pike** 12/9/1967 in Ctr. Ossipee; H - 20, carpenter; W - 16, student
Michael D. m. Ginger D. **Crowley** 10/17/1987; H - b. 1/9/1959; W - b. 8/13/1962

BRUDNICK,
Bernard B. of New York City, NY m. Eve **Krieger** of New York City, NY 8/5/1946 in Ossipee; H - 29, personnel mgr.; W - 28, supervisor

BRYANT,
Almon O. of Ossipee m. Daisy B. **Bisbee** of Ossipee 12/7/1898 in Effingham; H - 24, laborer, b. Effingham, s/o Samuel P. Bryant (Effingham, farmer) and Eunice Bryant (Freedom, housewife); W - 21, maid, b. Effingham, d/o Roscoe Bisbee (Saco, farmer) and Lydia A. Bisbee (Effingham, housewife)
Almon O. of Ossipee m. Elva **Welch** of Ossipee 10/24/1909 in Ossipee; H - 35, laborer, 2nd, b. Effingham, s/o Samuel B. Bryant (Effingham,

farmer); W - 26, domestic, 2nd, b. Ossipee, d/o Lyford Welch (Ossipee, farmer)
Floyd G. of Tilton m. Lillian B. **Currier** of Granite 8/6/1934 in Granite; H - 24, teacher; W - 20, at home
James M. of Somersworth m. Ida E. **Brown** of Somersworth 9/26/1906 in Portsmouth; H - 56, shoemaker, 2nd, b. Somersworth, s/o S. D. Bryant (Ireland, shoemaker) and Mary E. Faye (Berwick, ME, housewife); W - 46, maid, 2nd, b. Portsmouth, d/o John Brown (Portsmouth, sailor) and Caroline Stokeman (Germany, housewife)
Loren Earl of Ossipee m. Beulah P. **Merryfield** of Ossipee 7/19/1940 in Ossipee; H - 24, laborer; W - 18, child's nurse

BUCHIKOS,
Andrew Don of Ossipee m. Renee Sandra **Jones** of Ossipee 8/28/1999
William Allen m. Lesly M. **Walker** 5/14/1988; H - b. 10/22/1950; W - b. 10/19/1960
William Allen, Jr. m. Wanda Lee **Nichols** 12/21/1991; H - b. 2/28/1972; W - b. 9/14/1972

BUCK,
Leaman H. of Cumberland Ctr., ME m. Beulah B. **Hicks** of Cumberland Ctr., ME 12/8/1956 in Ctr. Ossipee; H - 57, mill worker; W - 51, housekeeper

BUDROE,
Edward H. of Chocorua m. Barbara **Eldridge** of Ossipee 10/2/1948 in Ctr. Ossipee; H - 18, truck driver; W - 19, at home

BUELOCK,
Gary E. of S. Portland, ME m. Loretta A. **Gibbs** 6/26/1963 in Ctr. Ossipee; H - 30, salesman; W - 24, salesgirl

BUESSER,
William Ronal, Jr. of Cornish, ME m. Susan M. **Talarico** of Cornish, ME 4/30/1999

BUMP,
Richard T. of Geneva, NY m. Penelope G. **Burrell** of Rehoboth, MA 7/5/1963 in Ctr. Ossipee; H - 21, US Army; W - 18, student

BUNKER,
Frank Eldred of Ossipee m. Charlotte Isabell **Lewis** of Portland, ME 11/28/1943 in Gilford; H - 38, mill man; W - 21, hair dresser

BURCH,
David m. Joyce K. **Hinders** 3/23/1987; H - b. 1/24/1940; W - b. 1/10/1944

BURKE,
John F. of Ossipee m. Rose C. **Stewart** of Charlestown, MA 6/21/1953 in Ctr. Ossipee; H - 44, chauffeur; W - 42, supervisor
Stephen G. m. Maureen F. **MacDougall** 9/5/1982 in Concord; H - b. 4/10/1956; W - b. 6/27/1959

BURLEIGH,
Charles J. of Ossipee m. Julia F. **Pray** of Ossipee 11/27/1893 in Water Village; H - 30, farmer, b. Ossipee, s/o Samuel Burleigh (Ossipee) and Mary (Wolfeboro); W - 36, teacher, b. Tuftonboro, d/o William N. Roberts (Tuftonboro) and Mary Jackson (Eaton)

BURLISON,
George Stephen m. Gale Lynn **Smith** 7/2/1993 in Wakefield

BURNS,
Stephen W. of New Gloucester, ME m. Ruth B. **Reck** of Bridgton, ME 12/4/1948 in Moultonville; H - 41, instructor; W - 42, housewife

BURT,
Harrison, Jr. m. Jeannette **Garnett** 5/23/1964 in Ctr. Ossipee; H - 38, truck driver; W - 26, none

BURTON,
Thomas P. of Bismarck, ND m. Sandra D. **Wagenfeld** of Ctr. Ossipee 5/28/1960 in Ctr. Ossipee; H - 25, M.D.; W - 22, nurse

BURTWELL,
Albert A. of Ossipee m. Nettie M. **Hanson** of Ossipee 4/23/1896 in Ossipee; H - 30, farmer, b. Ossipee, s/o Robertson Bertwell (sic) and Susan J. Bertwell; W - 20, housekeeper, b. Ossipee, d/o James Hanson (Ossipee, farmer) and Aphia Hanson (Ossipee, housewife)

BUSCH,
Roger H. of Fridley, MN m. Priscilla L. **Jack** of Ctr. Ossipee 10/12/1954 in Ctr. Ossipee; H - 23, student; W - 19, office clerk

BUSH,
Michael Mark, Sr. of Ossipee m. Bobbi Jo **Johnson** of Ossipee 6/23/1996

BUSHMAN,
Richard J. of Ctr. Ossipee m. Lois E. (Oxner) **Beaton** of Ctr. Ossipee 6/25/1995
Robert J. of Ossipee m. Kelley A. **McBride** of Ossipee 3/29/1999

BUSWELL,
Edgar L. of Long Beach, CA m. Martha M. **Anderson** of Long Beach, CA 10/14/1948 in Ctr. Ossipee; H - 47, US Government; W - 50, housekeeper
Ellis W. of Ossipee m. Pauline E. **Warren** of Wolfeboro 4/12/1927 in Ctr. Ossipee; H - 17, lineman; W - 19, stenographer
Isaac L. of Ossipee m. Catherine **Clancy** of Ossipee 3/30/1936 in Chocorua; H - 24, laborer; W - 15
Lester G. of Ossipee m. Blanche M. **Eldridge** of Ossipee 9/7/1909 in Ossipee; H - 28, teacher, b. Ossipee, s/o Ellis U. Buswell (Ossipee, carpenter); W - 23, teacher, b. Ossipee, d/o J. Frank Eldridge (Ossipee, jobber)
Shirl E. of Ossipee m. Laura B. **Nickerson** of Ossipee 7/1/1925 in Ossipee; H - 25, b. Ossipee; W - 20, b. NS
Walter of Ossipee m. Leler B. **Locke** of Ossipee 1/12/1900 in Haverhill, MA; H - 27, carpenter, b. Ossipee, s/o E. U. Buswell (Ossipee, carpenter) and Mary A. Buswell (Ossipee, housewife); W - 18, maid, b. Franconia, d/o C. H. Locke (Canterbury, carpenter) and Sarah Locke (Haverhill, housewife)

BUTLER,
Craig Martin of Ctr. Ossipee m. Deborah Marie (Lane) **Warren** of Ctr. Ossipee 4/28/1994
Edward T. m. Stacey A. **Connolly** 4/27/1985; H - b. 12/14/1964; W - b. 2/7/1965
John P., Jr. m. Karen M. **Dow** 10/26/1985; H - b. 10/12/1946; W - b. 3/10/1958
Kenneth A. of Middleton m. Catherine V. **Buchanan** of Ossipee 6/20/1961 in Ossipee; H - 18, sole layer; W - 17, none

BUTTERFIELD,
Kenneth A. of Hiram, ME m. Abbie E. **Hilton** of Bridgton, ME 11/7/1937 in Ctr. Ossipee; H - 27, garage business; W - 23, clerk

BUTTON,
Kenneth Russell of Ctr. Ossipee m. Helen Mane **King** of Ctr. Ossipee 9/8/2001

BUZZELL,
Frank of Ossipee m. Fannie **Canney** of Wolfeboro 1/25/1888 in Ossipee; H - 20, laborer, b. Parsonsfield, ME, s/o D. F. Buzzell (Effingham); W - 21, housekeeper, b. Wolfeboro
Frank of Ossipee m. Elvena E. **Downs** of Orwell, VT 2/14/1891 in Ossipee; H - 23, laborer, b. Parsonsfield, s/o D. F. Buswell (sic) (Effingham) and Lydia A. (Parsonsfield); W - 22, housework, b. Orwell, VT, d/o Peter Orwell (sic) (Canada) and Victoria (Canada)

BYERS,
Richard S. m. Martha Frances **Lussier** 5/22/1971 in Ossipee; H - b. 1/4/1923; W - b. 10/2/1934

CADE,
Erick Darin m. Dawn Elizabeth **Reed** 12/15/1990; H - b. 7/11/1967; W - b. 4/17/1968

CAMERON,
Bruce H. m. Anita M. **Nudd** 7/17/1993 in W. Ossipee
Paul E. m. Cindy L. **Harbison** 7/24/1986; H - b. 3/24/1946; W - b. 5/23/1962

CAMIRE,
Robert R. m. Linda M. **Bushey** 4/23/1977 in Rochester; H - b. 1/26/1948; W - b. 10/19/1947

CAMPBELL,
Forest F. of Rochester m. Winifred **Eldridge** of Ossipee 8/25/1928 in Ossipee; H - 24, laborer; W - 18, at home
John S. of Providence, RI m. Nancy **Ruselewicz** of Pawtucket, RI 9/8/1960 in Ossipee; H - 62, engineer; W - 35, clerk
Michael B. m. Carolyn B. **McNally** 10/31/1965 in Ctr. Ossipee; H - 21, none; W - 18, none
William of Ossipee m. Barbara **Grant** of Ossipee 10/26/1958 in Ossipee; H - 53, farmer; W - 44, none
William of Ossipee m. Claira **Pirozzi** of Bedford 3/24/1962 in Concord; H - 22, student; W - 21, student

CAMPION,
Edwin J., Jr. m. Patricia Anne **Chevalier** 12/28/1991; H - b. 1/20/1959; W - b. 7/9/1963

CANFIELD,
Gilbert Andrew m. Bethany Lynn **Hayford** 1/20/1990; H - b. 10/27/1969; E - b. 7/20/1970

CANNEY,
Christopher S. m. Jo-Anne M. **Davis** 7/3/1974 in Tamworth; H - b. 10/1/1955; W - b. 2/7/1956
Forrest F. of Ossipee m. Roxanna **Philbrick** of Ossipee 1/1/1919 in Ossipee; H - 24, laborer, b. Ossipee, s/o Fred M. Canney (Ossipee) and Emma F. Hilton (Ossipee); W - 21, housework, b. Limerick, ME, d/o Alfred Philbrick (Conway) and Elsie C. Drown (Waterboro, ME)
J. H. of Ossipee m. Edith **Connor** of Ossipee 7/13/1892 in Moultonville; H - 32, shoemaker, b. Ossipee, s/o Henry Canney (Ossipee, farmer) and Sarah Canney (Sandwich, housewife); W - 30, housekeeper, b. Ossipee, d/o John B. Connor (Ossipee, carpenter) and Julia Connor (Ossipee, housewife)
James E. of Ossipee m. Carrie **Young** of Ossipee 11/1/1917 in Ossipee; H - 63, farmer, 2nd, b. Ossipee, s/o Wentworth Canney (Ossipee) and Mary Avery (Wolfeboro); W - 49, housework, 3rd, b. Providence, RI, d/o James Ellis (Sunnyside, PEI) and Agnes E. Folsom (Sunnyside, PEI)

CAPITE,
Lawrence M. of Worcester, MA m. Elvira **Botticelli** of Worcester, MA 9/16/1959 in Ctr. Ossipee; H - 38, self employed; W - 26, receptionist

CAPLES,
Richard F. m. Karen M. **Nault** 10/8/1988; H - b. 8/9/1958; W - b. 9/19/1963

CAPRON,
Robert E. m. Laurel W. **McKivergan** 10/3/1986; H - b. 11/13/1962; W - b. 1/23/1963

CARBERG,
Brian Michael m. Wendy Lee **Fowler** 8/17/1993 in Ossipee

CARD,
Joseph M., Jr. m. Barbara **Reardon** 9/25/1966 in Ossipee; H - 46, civil engineer; W - 28, home

CARDARELLI,
Patrick m. Darlene R. **Lawton** 9/22/1984; H - b. 3/17/1960; W - b. 7/31/1963

CARDOZA,
John L. m. Susan R. **Krakowski** 11/11/1981 in Ossipee; H - b. 5/3/1957; W - b. 8/20/1953

CAREY,
Charles of Lynn, MA m. Kate **McAlly** of Aylesford, NS 8/3/1909 in Sanbornville; H - 43, teamster, b. Lynn, MA, s/o William Casey (Aylesford, NS, farmer); W - 32, domestic, b. Aylesford, NS, d/o James McAlley (sic) (Aylesford, NS, farmer)
Steven C. m. Joanne Hazel **Hodge** 6/30/1973 in Ossipee; H - b. 3/4/1953; W - b. 10/23/1952

CARLETON,
Michael William of Ctr. Ossipee m. Heidi Elizabeth **Eldridge** of Ctr. Ossipee 5/25/1996
Robert m. Janice D. **Stein** 2/10/1968 in Meredith; H - b. 8/7/1943; W - b. 8/13/1952

CARLSON,
Donald Irving of Attleboro, MA m. Norma K. **Goode** of Attleboro, MA 5/29/1999
Robert G. of Brookfield m. Jean A. **Davidson** of New Britain, CT 7/28/1961 in Concord; H - 29, engineer; W - 25, teacher

CARPENTER,
Kenneth of Wolfeboro m. Frances **Helphard** of Ossipee 3/8/1958 in Ossipee; H - 23, mechanic; W - 19, home

CARR,
Warren R. of Rochester m. Edna M. **Abbott** of Ctr. Ossipee 6/28/1958 in Ossipee; H - 21, mechanic; W - 18, secretary

CARRO,
Oscar F. of Otisfield, ME m. Helen E. **McKay** of Norway, ME 10/3/1957 in Ctr. Ossipee; H - 44, mechanic; W - 42, stitcher
Paul F. of Otisfield, ME m. Maud E. **Currier** of Otisfield, ME 6/15/1957 in Ossipee; H - 75, laborer; W - 62, housewife

CARRUTHERS,
Richard W. m. Kathleen M. **Rines** 8/25/1985; H - b. 4/30/1955; W - b. 11/22/1957

CARTER,
Charles H. of Ossipee m. Kitty E. **Saunders** of Providence, RI 2/11/1926 in Ossipee; H - 62, b. Ossipee; W - 47, b. Escauaba, MN
Ernest m. Gloria **Tupeck** 5/4/1968 in Ctr. Ossipee; H - b. 11/2/1947; W - b. 2/14/1946
George H. m. Henrietta **Parker** 8/13/1916 in Ossipee; H - 38, collector, b. Somerville, MA, s/o Silas D. Carter (NS); W - 34, housewife, 2nd, b. E. Boston, MA, d/o George Bradley (at sea)

CARVALHO,
Charles John m. Theresa Elizabeth **Massarelli** 9/9/1989; H - b. 12/24/1941; W - b. 5/13/1937

CARVER,
David C. m. Lori A. **Fulcher** 7/11/1987; H - b. 7/15/1960; W - b. 7/13/1962
Dennis E. m. Karen N. **Capach** 7/8/1978 in Ossipee; H - b. 3/21/1958; W - b. 10/20/1961
Warren D. m. Suzanne M. **Holt** 1/19/1985; H - b. 5/20/1965; W - b. 9/10/1955

CASH,
Charles M. of Freedom m. Jacqueline R. **St. Clair** of Ossipee 8/18/1952 in Wolfeboro; H - 23, service man; W - 20, dental assistant

CATLOW,
Milton J. m. Paula M. **Warner** 6/14/1986; H - b. 10/15/1962; W - b. 1/10/1968
Milton J. K. of Concord m. Deirdra A. Ryan **White** of Ossipee 4/26/1997

CATTANEO,
James m. Susan Marie **Morton** 6/28/1975 in Ossipee; H - b. 3/15/1954; W - b. 1/15/1954
John J. m. Blanche M. **Morton** 5/17/1982 in Ossipee; H - b. 11/16/1928; W - b. 5/13/1935

CAULKINS,
Dale C. m. Carol S. **Hodge** 6/27/1980 in Ctr. Ossipee; H - b. 10/20/1939; W - b. 3/23/1936
Thomas Dale m. Sandra Jean **Abbott** 8/25/1979 in Ossipee; H - b. 8/26/1961; W - b. 12/14/1960

CAVERLY,
Daniel G. m. Debora C. **Thoma** 9/26/1981 in Moultonboro; H - b. 3/10/1953; W - b. 7/28/1954

CAYER,
Louis J., II m. Sverena M. **Colwell** 5/6/1988; H - b. 10/21/1947; W - b. 5/6/1969

CELLENNE,
Albert of Tamworth m. Ruth **Loring** of Ctr. Ossipee 1/17/1937 in Farmington; H - 20, laborer; W - 18, household worker

CHADBOURN[E],
H. J. of Ossipee m. Carry B. **Nason** of Ossipee 4/5/1896 in Ossipee; H - 28, laborer, b. Ossipee, s/o Isaac Chadbourne (Effingham, farmer) and Hannah E. Leighton (Ossipee, housekeeper); W - 21, housekeeper, b. Parsonsfield, ME, d/o Benjamin Nason (Parsonsfield, ME, farmer) and Eva Cook (Parsonsfield, ME, housekeeper)
Isaac of Ossipee m. Hattie M. **Osgood** of Parsonsfield, ME 4/6/1890 in Effingham; H - 59, farmer, b. Effingham, s/o Oliver Chadbourn (farmer); W - 40, housekeeper, b. Kittery, ME, d/o Ephraim Billings (Kittery, ME, farmer)

CHALIFOUX,
Armel C. of Salem, MA m. Hilda M. **Atwood** of Marblehead, MA 3/16/1940 in Ossipee; H - 26, lampworker; W - 28, at home

CHAMBERLAIN,
Brian James m. Ann Marie **Plant** 7/27/1991; H - b. 7/1/1964; W - b. 12/18/1958
Deane M. m. Cecily B. **Cowan** 2/3/1972 in Ossipee; H - b. 2/6/1922; W - b. 3/9/1934
Deane M. m. Marjorie E. **Santulli** 7/30/1978 in Alton; H - b. 2/6/1922; W - b. 4/12/1928

CHAMBERLIN,
Charles A. m. Zita M. **Deslauriers** 12/31/1983 in Wolfeboro; H - b. 7/17/1953; W - b. 11/3/1957
Guy H. of Milton m. Verna M. **Woodman** of Ossipee 8/27/1921 in Portsmouth; H - 34, iceman, 2nd, b. Wakefield, s/o Fred M. Chamberlin (Milton) and Grace M. Dicey (Effingham); W - 17, housewife, b. Ossipee, d/o Fred Woodman (NS) and Etta M. Colby (Ossipee)

CHAMIDES,
Robert E. of Providence, RI m. Betty L. **Cartwright** of Providence, RI 6/1/1953 in Ossipee; H - 30, architect; W - 17, interior decorator

CHAMPAGNE,
Craig A. m. Mary Ann **DeFosses** 12/10/1988; H - b. 8/2/1960; W - b. 6/3/1963

CHANDLER,
Henry H. M. of Ossipee m. Winnie N. **Chick** of Ossipee 11/5/1898 in Ossipee; H - 30, farmer, 2nd, divorced, b. Ossipee, s/o James H. Chandler (farmer) and Laura L. Chandler (deceased); W - 20, maid, b. Ossipee, d/o Amasa Chick (Ossipee, farmer) and Lenora Chick (deceased)
Henry M. of Ossipee m. Ida **Bickford** 8/25/1890 in Ossipee; H - 21, farmer, b. Albany, s/o John H. Chandler (Baldwin, ME, tailor); W - 35, housekeeper

CHAO,
San M. of Rochester, NY m. Karen M. **Brooks** of Rochester, NY 8/12/2000

CHAPMAN,
Robert A. m. Bonnie L. **Brouillette** 8/14/1982 in Ossipee; H - b. 7/19/1952; W - b. 2/4/1949

CHASE,
Edwin O. of Ossipee m. Florence E. **Knox** of Ossipee 9/26/1942 in Conway; H - 31, farmer; W - 38, at home
Herbert M. of Springfield, MA m. Florence J. **Miller** of Springfield, MA 10/5/1917 in Wakefield; H - 23, mechanic, b. Ossipee, s/o Winfield S. Chase (Saco) and Elizabeth Townsend (Baldwin, ME); W - 26, seamstress, b. Hanover, d/o Edgar M. Miller (Etna) and Esther J. Everett (Hanover)
John L. of Ossipee m. Susan J. **Chase** of Ossipee 12/3/1913 in Ossipee; H - 80, retired, 3rd, b. Hiram, ME, s/o Gideon Chase (Standish, ME); W - 70, housekeeper, 2nd, b. Stewartstown, d/o George W. Gerry (Biddeford, ME)
Winfield S. of Ossipee m. Lizzie M. **Townsend** of Baldwin, ME 4/8/1892 in Ctr. Ossipee; H - 25, teacher, b. Saco, ME, s/o Melvin B. Chase (Standish, ME, farmer) and Susan J. Chase (Madison, housewife); W - 19, domestic, b. Lynn, MA, d/o John Townsend, Jr. (Lynn, MA, farmer) and Ida M. Townsend (Sebago, ME, housewife)

CHAVAREE,
Marc Anthony m. Linda Ann **Lofredo** 7/6/1991; H - b. 4/15/1963; W - b. 2/7/1954

CHELLMAN,
Chester M. Jerildine **Rines** 7/24/1974 in Ossipee; H - b. 8/11/1952; W - b. 3/30/1952

CHENEY,
John Gordon of Tuftonboro m. Edna Susan **Young** of Ossipee 8/21/1941 in Ossipee; H - 34, farmer; W - 32, teacher

CHESLEY,
George H. of Dover m. Gladys Eldridge **Palmer** of Rochester 9/30/1938 in Milton; H - 42, used car manager; W - 42, at home

Joshua E. of Ossipee m. Minnie C. **Clark** of Tamworth 4/29/1893 in Ctr. Ossipee; H - 24, laborer, b. Eaton, s/o George W. Chesley (Effingham) and Hannah (Tamworth); W - 21, b. Tamworth, d/o Gilman Clark and Laura

CHICK,
Earl of Wakefield m. Mabel B. **Burton** of Wakefield 8/28/1936 in Moultonville; H - 30, mill wright; W - 50, press writer

Frank H. of Ossipee m. Annie **McIsaac** of Boston, MA 1/4/1908 in Ossipee; H - 48, coachman, b. Ossipee, s/o Amasa Chick (Ossipee); W - 34, maid, b. NS, d/o Lenora Wentworth (NS)

Harry W., Jr. m. Donna C. **Floria** 1/17/1981 in Ossipee; H - b. 11/24/1952; W - b. 7/5/1954

CHIVVIS,
Almon m. Helen **Hofmann** 1/8/1964 in Ctr. Ossipee; H - 59, retired; W - 65, housewife

CHOATE,
Richard S. of W. Medway, MA m. Kathryn A. **Seveain** of W. Medway, MA 8/6/1954 in Ctr. Ossipee; H - 26, carpenter; W - 25, waitress

CHRISTIANSEN,
Bruce Maronus m. Sandra Gail **Sargent** 12/4/1976 in Ossipee; H - b. 9/11/1949; W - b. 3/31/1953

CHUTE,
James A. of Ossipee m. Mary I. **Carlton** of Ossipee 10/17/1895 in Ossipee; H - 29, farmer, b. Ossipee, s/o Albion Chute (deceased) and Merabah Roberts (Effingham, housewife); W - 39, housewife, 2nd, b. Orrington, ME, d/o Raymond Smith (deceased) and Roxanna Sprane (Berwick, ME, housewife)

CICCOLO,
Frank M. Ethel **Pray** 2/28/1916 in Ossipee; H - 23, barber, b. Allston, MA, s/o John Ciccolo (Italy); W - 22, teacher, b. Ossipee, d/o John E. Pray (Ossipee)

CINCOTTA,
Eric Joseph m. Louise Annette **Wright** 7/4/1993 in Ossipee

CIOFFI,
Ferdinand F. m. Maria **Snow** 12/31/1969 in Ctr. Ossipee; H - b. ½/1924; W - b. 3/26/1941

CLANCY,
Edward J. of Ossipee m. Verna L. **Merrow** of Ossipee 10/28/1920 in Ossipee; H - 28, mechanic, b. Lynn, MA, s/o Patrick Clancy (Ireland) and Mary Healey (Ireland); W - 18, cook, b. Ossipee, d/o Earle Merrow (Clifton, ME) and Flora D. Templeton (Ossipee)
Reginald E. of Durham m. Carolyn **Fracker** of Durham 12/2/1949 in Durham; H - 21, student; W - 18, student

CLARK,
Bruce C. m. Meredith A. **Harbour** 2/12/1971 in Ossipee; H - b. 6/12/1948; W - b. 5/3/1950
Christopher Travis of Ossipee m. Dani Allyson **Davis** of Ossipee 7/30/1994
Edmund Palmer of Ossipee m. Marjorie Anne **Butler** of Hamden, CT 10/6/1944 in Wolfeboro; H - 40, personnel supervisor; W - 22, secretary
Frank Herbert m. Dorothy Ellen **Adjutant** 8/18/1973 in Ossipee; H - b. 12/3/1951; W - b. 8/13/1955
Robert M. m. Mary P. **Marshall** 10/19/1980 in Ossipee; H - b. 1/2/1940; W - b. 2/14/1941
Robert M. of W. Ossipee m. Carmel Magdialene **Clark** of W. Ossipee 9/27/1999
Russell A. m. Rosa J. **Minkins** 10/23/1980 in Ossipee; H - b. 10/3/1904; W - b. 1/1/1902
William E., Jr. of Charlestown m. Charlotte **Mason** of Ossipee 8/1/1931 in Charlestown; H - 23, mech. engineer; W - 22, school teacher

CLARKE,
Benjamin F. of Ossipee m. Mabel M. **Savary** of Madison 8/15/1923 in Madison; H - 62, b. Damariscotta Mills, ME; W - 47, b. Albany

CLAVIN,
Donald A. of Cranston, RI m. Marilyn F. **Foster** of N. Attleboro, MA 10/11/1963 in Ctr. Ossipee; H - 40, cook; W - 32, waitress

CLEMENTS,
Ralph H. of Melrose, MA m. Dorothy **Wyatt** of Saugus, MA 8/2/1934 in Ctr. Ossipee; H - 25, optometrist; W - 22, R.N.

CLEVELAND,
Robert A. of S. Portland, ME m. Annie E. **McClellan** of S. Portland, ME 4/15/1952 in Ctr. Ossipee; H - 38, pipefitter; W - 45, housekeeper
William McKay of Ctr. Ossipee m. Gwyneth Lori **Johnson** of Ctr. Ossipee 5/20/1995

CLIFFORD,
Arthur C. m. Eleanor M. **Stillings** 7/1/1967 in E. Rochester; H - 22, clergyman; W - 20, factory

CLOUGH,
James F. of Ossipee m. Carrie B. **Wormhood** of Ossipee 11/8/1890 in Ossipee; H - 32, laborer, b. Parsonsfield, ME, s/o Oliver Clough (Parsonsfield, ME, farmer); W - 22, housekeeper, b. Ossipee, d/o Charles P. Wormhood (farmer)
Oren of Ossipee m. Melissa **Leighton** of Ossipee 11/30/1891 in Ossipee; H - 49, farmer, b. Effingham, s/o James Clough (Ossipee) and Sobriety Clough (Ossipee); W - 38, housework, b. Waterboro, d/o Benjamin Carpenter (Ossipee) and Comfort (Ossipee)

CLUFF,
Nakum J. of Kennebunk, ME m. Charlotte B. **Montgomery** of Kennebunk, ME 9/18/1932 in Ossipee; H - 52, farmer; W - 22, at home

COATES,
Benjamin L., III of Ossipee m. Nancy Jean **White** of Ossipee 6/27/1998
Dennis John of Ctr. Ossipee m. Toby Leigh **Billings** of Ctr. Ossipee 3/28/1998
Dennis John of Ctr. Ossipee m. Jamie Marie **Eldridge** of Ctr. Ossipee 8/17/2001

COE,
William A. of Silver Lake m. Euel E. **McFee** of Jamaica Plain, MA 5/13/1946 in Tamworth; H - 34, engineer; W - 31, dental asst.

COGSWELL,
Richard L. of Ctr. Ossipee m. Candy Ann (Stevens) **Bliss** of Ctr. Ossipee 9/28/1996

COLBY,
Arthur of Ossipee m. Edith **Goodbury** of Rochester 9/12/1936 in Rochester; H - 21, day laborer; W - 19, housekeeper
Daniel of Ossipee m. Mary J. **Evans** of Ossipee 6/29/1910 in Ossipee; H - 40, laborer, 2nd, b. Ossipee, s/o Arthur Colby (Ossipee, farmer) and Harriet Elliott; W - 34, domestic, b. Ossipee, d/o John W. Evans (Ossipee) and Mary J. Welch (Ossipee)
David of Ossipee m. Lavinia **Welch** of Ossipee 5/2/1887 in Ossipee; H - 18, laborer, b. Ossipee; W - 18, housekeeper, b. Ossipee
Luther of Ossipee m. Mary **White** of Ossipee 6/21/1900 in Ossipee; H - 48, farmer, 2nd, b. Ossipee, s/o Daniel Colby (Moultonboro, farmer) and Mary E. Colby (Moultonboro, housewife); W - 43, housekeeper, 2nd, b. Ossipee, d/o Lyford Williams (Effingham, farmer) and Lydia Williams (Effingham, housewife)
Plummer of Ossipee m. Etta **Woodman** of Ossipee 4/1/1913 in Ossipee; H - 40, laborer, b. Tuftonborough, s/o Arthur Colby; W - 22, housekeeper, 2nd, b. Ossipee, d/o Fred Bean
Ralph of Ossipee m. Minnie P. **Fall** of Ossipee 12/25/1898 in Ossipee; H - 19, farmer, b. Ossipee, s/o Sarah Colby (Ossipee, housewife); W - 16, maid, b. Ossipee, d/o Plummer Fall (Ossipee, laborer) and Nellie M. Fall (Ossipee, housewife)
Royal of Ctr. Ossipee m. Florence **Littlefield** of Rochester 12/24/1934 in Rochester; H - 21, laborer; W - 19, housekeeper
Royal P. of Ctr. Ossipee m. Louise B. **White** of Tamworth 6/11/1955 in Ctr. Ossipee; H - 41, laborer; W - 44, housekeeper
William of Ossipee m. Josephena **Brown** of Ossipee 5/16/1887 in Ossipee; H - 28, laborer; W - 14, housekeeper

COLE,
Carl of Norton, MA m. Beverly **Booth** of Attleboro, MA 1/24/1961 in Ossipee; H - 36, manager; W - 23, none
Charles of Cornish, ME m. Nellie **Johnson** of Cape Elizabeth, ME 3/31/1909 in Ossipee; H - 39, laborer, b. Cornish, ME, s/o James B. Cole (Cornish, ME, laborer); W - 41, housekeeper, 2nd, b. Norway, ME, d/o John Pike (Cape Elizabeth, ME, laborer)
Donald G. of Portland, ME m. Claudia C. **Wildes** of Portland, ME 4/18/1950 in Ossipee; H - 31, soldier; W - 30, waitress
James H. of Ossipee m. Jennett **Huckins** of Bartlett 1/24/1891 in Ossipee; H - 42, farmer, b. Cornish, ME, s/o Asa Cole and Desire (Limerick); W - 48, housework, b. Bartlett

Roy of Ossipee m. Amanda M. **Dziedzic** of Rochester 6/12/1999

COLLIER,
Simon D. m. Evette **Nathan** 9/18/1965 in Ctr. Ossipee; H - 43, USN; W - 31, housewife

COLMAN,
Nathaniel of Newington m. Thelma **Harvey** of Epping 11/23/1935 in Ctr. Ossipee; H - 24, carpenter; W - 24, clerk

COLPITTS,
Robert W. m. Mollie **McRae** 5/25/1974 in Ossipee; H - b. 12/18/1938; W - b. 12/16/1937

COMEAU,
Phillip Joseph of Rumney m. Sylvia Marie **Zimmer** of W. Ossipee 5/15/1943 in Rumney; H - 42, contractor; W - 31, housework
Ulysse m. Marie **Dugas** 11/19/1966 in Conway; H - 67, none; W - 68, none

CONITER,
Charles m. Susan **Libby** 8/20/1966 in Ossipee; H - 26, IBM; W - 19, clerk

CONLEY,
Norman G. m. Donna J. **Cousens** 11/14/1965 in Ctr. Ossipee; H - 24, student; W - 25, nurse

CONLON,
Frederick E. m. Ruth Mae **Deuley** 9/17/1971 in Ossipee; H - b. 6/1/1935; W - b. 12/3/1932
Frederick E. m. Marjorie R. **Goodwin** 7/24/1977 in Ossipee; H - b. 6/1/1935; W - b. 11/6/1936

CONNER,
Albert H. of Ossipee m. Carolyn **Langley** of Ossipee 6/18/1933 in Farmington; H - 26, millman; W - 23, at home
Arthur N. of Ossipee m. Mary A. **Pascoe** of Ossipee 6/26/1918 in Ossipee; H - 28, hotelman, b. Ossipee, s/o William Conner (Ossipee) and Annie G. Hodgdon (Stanstead, PQ); W - 32, clerk, b. Freedom, d/o Henry J. Pascoe (Copper Sill, VT) and Annie O. Laughton (Freedom)
Charles E., Jr. of Ossipee m. Elfreda J. **Eldridge** of Ossipee 6/4/1924 in Ossipee; H - 22, b. Exeter; W - 19, b. Ossipee
Donald A. m. Margaret S. **Horn** 6/19/1982 in Ossipee; H - b. 5/15/1936; W - b. 10/21/1938

Earl E. of Ossipee m. Catherine B. **Snow** of Ossipee 6/4/1914 in Ossipee; H - 23, teamster, b. Ossipee, s/o Willie N. Conner (Ossipee); W - 23, clerk, b. Milton, MA, d/o Elbridge B. Snow

Fred E. of Ossipee m. Florence M. **Hodge** of Ossipee 9/8/1895 in Ossipee; H - 24, printer, b. Ossipee, s/o John B. Conner (Ossipee, carpenter) and Julia A. Abbott (Ossipee, housewife); W - 19, maid, b. Ossipee, d/o John C. Hodge (Ossipee, miller) and Laura E. Garland (Ossipee, housewife)

John B. of Ossipee m. Evelyn **Sargent** of Ossipee 1/16/1927 in Ossipee; H - 23, chauffeur; W - 20, at home

Mark Kevin m. Patricia Ann **Weare** 8/4/1990; H - b. 10/24/1953; W - b. 6/20/1953

Michael E. m. Melanie **Brownell** 10/20/1979 in Ossipee; H - b. 9/3/1951; W - b. 2/3/1954

Raymond H. of Ossipee m. Annie L. **Bradbury** of Effingham 11/28/1917 in Ossipee; H - 20, chauffeur, b. Ossipee, s/o Fred E. Conner (Ossipee) and Maude F. Hodge (Ossipee); W - 18, housework, b. Effingham, d/o Frank O. Bradbury (Eaton) and Lillian Taylor (Effingham)

Willie M. of Ossipee m. Addie **Hodgdon** 5/2/1887 in Ossipee; H - 22, laborer, b. Ossipee, s/o Jeremiah Conner (Ossipee) and Lucinda; W - 19, housekeeper

CONNOR,
Jerry m. Barbara **Penna** 3/12/1966 in Ctr. Ossipee; H - 20, Navy; W - 21, clerk

Joseph H. of Ossipee m. Lydia O. **Wingate** of Tuftonboro 12/30/1892 in Ctr. Ossipee; H - 36, farmer, b. Ossipee, s/o Jeremiah Connor (Ossipee, farmer) and Lucinda Connor (Ossipee, housewife); W - 33, teacher, b. Tuftonboro, d/o Daniel S. Wingate (Alton, farmer) and Mary W. Wingate (Tuftonboro, housewife)

Raymond F., Jr. m. Lisa J. **Potter** 8/8/1980 in Ossipee; H - b. 4/12/1957; W - b. 10/11/1962

COOK,
Arthur C. m. Kimberly Ann **Rowell** 12/23/1974 in Ossipee; H - b. 7/17/1954; W - b. 3/22/1957

Arthur E. m. Carole A. **Libby** 3/17/1972 in Pittsfield; H - b. 6/24/1927; W - b. 9/14/1938

Arthur Elwin of Ossipee m. Carolyn Alice **Nichols** of Ossipee 6/24/1949 in Ctr. Ossipee; H - 21, laborer; W - 17, at home

Celon L. of Ossipee m. Edith B. **Abbott** of Wolfeboro 5/27/1933 in Ossipee; H - 33, teamster; W - 32, housekeeper

Clayton R. of Ossipee m. Beatrice M. **Canney** of Ossipee 5/30/1925 in Ossipee; H - 21, b. Ossipee; W - 19, b. Ossipee

Glenn R. of W. Ossipee m. Joanne W. **Sanphy** of Tamworth 2/27/1958 in Ossipee; H - 23, laborer; W - 20, home

James R. B. of Ossipee m. Mima K. **Warring** of Boston 7/5/1911 in Ossipee; H - 59, farmer, 3rd, divorced, b. Conway, s/o Newell Cook (farmer); W - housewife, b. TN, d/o Thomas Warring

Sidney A. of Ossipee m. Hazel **Mattress** of Milton Mills 7/16/1925 in Ossipee; H - 30, b. Effingham; W - 16, b. Milton Mills

Walter R. of Ossipee m. Aner F. **Edwards** of Wolfeboro 7/17/1896 in Ossipee; H - 20, farmer, b. Ossipee, s/o James R. B. Cook (Conway, farmer) and Mary A. Cook (Tamworth, housekeeper); W - 29, housekeeper, 3rd, b. Wolfeboro, d/o Eli B. Canney

COOMBS,
Clarence A. of Freeport, ME m. Florence **MacCullough** of Freeport, ME 4/7/1950 in Moultonville; H - 63, service sta.; W - 59, bookkeeper

James m. Claire **Lanata** 6/25/1964 in Ossipee; H - 47, designer; W - 33, secretary

COPE,
Edward J. of Attleboro, MA m. Florence J. **Morin** of Attleboro, MA 9/27/1933 in Ossipee; H - 32, letter carrier; W - 26, jeweler

COPP,
Daniel B. m. Annie S. **Close** 10/2/1915 in Ossipee; H - 59, teamster, 3rd, b. Hawley, NB, s/o Daniel Copp (Hawley, NB); W - 35, housewife, 2nd, b. St. John, NB, d/o George Bradley (at sea)

Maynard D. of Ossipee m. Nora F. **Eldridge** of Ossipee 4/29/1920 in Ossipee; H - 19, woodsman, b. Orrington, ME, s/o Daniel B. Copp (Sydney, NS) and Mildred Dodge (Orrington, ME); W - 17, housework, b. Ossipee, d/o Everett Eldridge (Ossipee) and Nettie Pike (Ossipee)

Owen of Ossipee m. Rose **Welch** of Ossipee 6/18/1917 in Ossipee; H - 20, teamster, b. Orrington, ME, s/o Daniel B. Copp (NB) and Mildred Dodge; W - 16, housework, b. Ossipee, d/o Moses Welch (Ossipee) and Mildred Eldridge (Ossipee)

Ralph, Jr. of Ctr. Ossipee m. Barbara **Joyce** of Westford, MA 12/22/1962 in Ctr. Ossipee; H - 23, construction; W - 21, nurse aid

Ralph E. of Ossipee m. Louise E. **Nichols** of Ossipee 9/13/1930 in Ossipee; H - 20, laborer; W - 18, at home

CORBIN,
Allen F. of Effingham Falls m. Helen M. **Roth** of Effingham Falls 7/2/1934 in Effingham Falls; H - 27, salesman; W - 31, housekeeper

CORLISS,
Lawrence E. m. Nancy J. **Hodgkins** 8/21/1977 in Ossipee; H - b. 5/28/1932; W - b. 8/9/1938

CORMIER,
Kenneth P. m. Barbara Ann **Peskor** 9/6/1975 in Ossipee; H - b. 6/3/1949; W - b. 10/17/1951

CORNWELL,
Ralph Weld m. Jerilyn Baker **Caraway** 3/17/1973 in Northwood; H - b. 6/3/1936; W - b. 2/6/1947

CORRIVEAU,
Albert m. Patricia **Lambert** 1/23/1966 in Ossipee; H - 22, soldier; W - 18, shipper
Albert Wayne of Taunton, MA m. Patricia Ann (Souza) **Young** of Taunton, MA 8/18/1994
David m. Mary **Frost** 1/15/1966 in Ctr. Ossipee; H - 21; W - 18, bench assembler

COST,
John J. of Wiscasset, ME m. Marilyn **Martin** of Portland, ME 7/28/1958 in Ossipee; H - 23, student; W - 19, student

COSTELLO,
Edward J., Jr. m. Anita L. **McBride** 12/31/1978 in Ossipee; H - b. 4/4/1947; W - b. 9/18/1940

COTE,
Raymond m. Mabel **Austin** 10/14/1966 in Ctr. Ossipee; H - 30, factory; W - 31, none

COTTON,
Dana R., Jr. m. Linda **Cheney** 3/9/1968 in Tuftonboro; H - b. 3/19/1948; W - b. 5/11/1948
Dana R., Jr. m. Diana L. **Boyd** 1/29/1976 in Ossipee; H - b. 3/19/1948; W - b. 10/2/1951
Frederick P., Jr. m. Pamela A. **Doty** 7/15/1989; H - b. 9/17/1940; W - b. 1/1/1948

COUGHLIN,
Edward G. of Ossipee m. Alice L. **Doe** of Ossipee 9/21/1923 in Tamworth; H - 26, b. Portsmouth; W - 22, b. Ossipee

COULTER,
George m. Rose A. **Scripture** 10/10/1987; H - b. 9/10/1960; W - b. 12/19/1958

COURTNEY,
Eric of Wolfeboro m. G. Geraldine **Pascoe** of W. Ossipee 5/8/1945 in Ossipee; H - 25, Army Air Corps; W - 20, at home

COUSINS,
Richard Brian m. Noreen M. **Piche** 5/24/1977 in Ossipee; H - b. 3/9/1957; W - b. 9/19/1957

COUTURE,
David R. m. Joan L. **Palmer** 5/9/1981 in Ossipee; H - b. 8/22/1960; W - b. 9/26/1960

COVITZ,
Julius of Dorchester, MA m. Irene Dorothy **Skeist** of Brighton, MA 7/16/1945 in Ossipee; H - 31, US Army; W - 30, secretary

CRAFT,
Robert N. m. Irene Forsyth **Tyler** 3/2/1979 in Ossipee; H - b. 6/2/1960; W - b. 6/10/1960

CRAGIN,
Allen of Ossipee m. Dorothy **Cate** of Wolfeboro 6/23/1962 in Ctr. Ossipee; H - 20, laborer; W - 18, none
Allen Bruce of Effingham m. Tracy Smith **Hartwell** of Effingham 1/1/2000

CRAIG,
Charles H. of Ossipee m. Muriel H. **Courser** of Lynn, MA 3/14/1936 in Ossipee; H - 28, dairy manager; W - 22, waitress

CRAM,
Raymond C., Jr. of Ossipee m. Margaret I. **Chase** of Laconia 5/20/1961 in Meredith; H - 27, carpenter; W - 22, home

CRAMPA,
Sabino of Boston, MA m. Virginia **Lents** of Charlestown, MA 12/1/1957 in Ctr. Ossipee; H - 48, counterman; W - 32, at home

CRAWFORD,
William H. of Ossipee m. Addie M. **Brown** of Ossipee 6/2/1888 in Ossipee; H - 20, laborer, b. Sebago, s/o George H. Crawford (Falmouth); W - 20, housekeeper, b. Ossipee, d/o John F. Brown (Ossipee)

CREDIT,
Leo R., Jr. m. Jennifer J. **Eaton** 8/24/1991; H - b. 4/1/1965; W - b. 10/5/1966

CRESSEY,
Albert C. m. Kim Y. **Bellini** 9/3/1983 in Ossipee; H - b. 7/13/1951; W - b. 5/8/1963
Frank H. of Portland, ME m. Mary M. **Dwelley** of Portland, ME 4/2/1952 in Ossipee; H - 27, baker; W - 24, packer
Wayne of W. Baldwin, ME m. Beverly **Drew** of Ctr. Ossipee 4/14/1962 in Ctr. Ossipee; H - 19, woodwork; W - 18, none
Wayne L. m. Betsy C. **Drew** 11/25/1972 in Sanbornville; H - b. 12/22/1942; W - b. 4/9/1952
Wayne L. m. Terry L. **Verrill** 2/14/1987; H - b. 12/22/1942; W - b. 3/21/1968

CROOKS,
David m. Annie E. **Brown** 4/6/1916 in Ossipee; H - 32, clerk, b. Scotland, s/o John Crooks (Scotland); W - 32, housekeeper, 2nd, b. Lonsdale, RI, d/o James Ellis (Bangor, ME)

CROSSMAN,
Sanford of Portland, ME m. Lillian J. **Floyd** of Portland, ME 9/20/1895 in Ossipee; H - 25, teamster, b. NB, s/o Westley Crossman (NB, farmer) and Margaret Crossman (NB, housewife); W - 27, maid, b. N. Conway, d/o Hannah Floyd (Brownfield, ME, housewife)

CROWELL,
Gregory Allen of Effingham m. Theresa Evekyn Saltzman **Tozier** of Effingham 8/10/2001

CROWLEY,
Wilfred J. of Ctr. Ossipee m. Marion L. **Sawyer** of Cornish, ME 6/12/1954 in Ctr. Ossipee; H - 25, teacher; W - 23, clerk

CUDE,
Vernon Lee m. Ruth Coral **Woodworth** 10/8/1972 in Freedom; H - b. 9/10/1947; W - b. 7/4/1948

CULLEN,
Dana B. m. Belinda **Williams** 11/20/1983 in Ossipee; H - b. 10/12/1955; W - b. 10/23/1958

CURRAN,
George S., Jr. of Portland, ME m. Norma M. **Smith** of Portland, ME 7/22/1953 in Ctr. Ossipee; H - 21, US Coast Guard; W - 18, secretary

CURRIER,
Cortland A. of Ctr. Ossipee m. Barbara M. **Brownell** of Ctr. Ossipee 10/31/1950 in Ctr. Ossipee; H - 35, mechanic; W - 33, tel. op.
Jesse A. of Madison m. June M. **Lee** of Ossipee 4/23/1959 in Madison; H - 31, mill worker; W - 31, clerk
Jesse A., Jr. of Madison m. Marguerite E. **Valley** of Ctr. Ossipee 6/29/1951 in Ctr. Ossipee; H - 23, laborer; W - 28, factory worker
John M. of Ossipee m. Janet D. **White** of Ossipee 10/5/1946 in Wolfeboro; H - 28, mechanic; W - 31, waitress
William E. of Ossipee m. Florence E. **Hurn** of Ossipee 10/24/1918 in Cambridge; H - 26, asst. patrolman, b. Ashburnham, s/o Eugene Currier (Windsor, VT) and Hattie M. Lovelett (Windsor, VT); W - 38, school teacher, b. Ossipee, d/o John F. Hurn (Freedom) and Mary J. Smith (Freedom)

CURRY,
David W. of Philadelphia, PA m. Ann E. **Pretka** of Lawrence, MA 8/8/1932 in Ossipee; H - 27, assistant mgr.; W - 24, stenographer
John P. m. Judith A. **Gangemi** 7/17/1984; H - b. 12/15/1935; W - b. 1/28/1947

CUSHMAN,
Kevin N. of Madison m. Brenda R. **Day** of Madison 7/15/2000

CUSTEAU,
Frank Eli of Ctr. Ossipee m. Anna Marie **Baldwin** of Ctr. Ossipee 10/30/1996

CUTTING,
Chester H. of Porter, ME m. Persis M. **Murphy** of N. Sebago, ME 8/25/1951 in Ctr. Ossipee; H - 23, painter; W - 30, beautician

CYR,
George F. m. Mary E. **Perry** 2/14/1981 in Ossipee; H - b. 5/6/1919; W - b. 9/28/1919

D'ANDREA,
David Carl of Ossipee m. June M. Lanteigne **Cormier** of Dracut, MA 8/14/1999

DAIGLE,
Paul Michael m. Mary Josephine **Horgan** 7/14/1990; H - b. 9/12/1959; W - b. 10/12/1957

DAILEY,
Roger M. of Glen Ellyn, IL m. Geraldine M. **Wood** of Buxport 4/21/1958 in Ossipee; H - 26, student; W - 32, nurse

DALE,
Arthur J. of Ctr. Ossipee m. Gertrude E. **Richards** of Rochester 10/14/1950 in Ctr. Ossipee; H - 32, stock mgr.; W - 23, nurse

DALES,
Gregory Franklin m. Cassandra Townsend **Curtis** 1/7/1989; h - b. 12/30/1952; W - b. 1/10/1959

DAME,
Charles A. of Ossipee m. Mattie L. **Haley** of Dover 10/3/1892 in Tuftonboro; H - 26, porter, b. Ossipee, s/o William Dame (Ossipee, blacksmith) and Carrie Whitehouse (Ossipee, housewife); W - 25, chambermaid, 2nd, b. Dover, d/o Rufus Haley (Epping, coal dealer) and M. J. Frederick (Alton, housewife)

DAMON,
Christopher Stephen m. Ann Flanders **Lord** 4/25/1992 in Wolfeboro

DANIELS,
Kirk Michael of Ossipee m. Denise Cassandra **Ploof** of Ossipee 10/3/1998

DANOSKY,
E. Robert m. Sherri J. **Smith** 10/1/1983 in Ossipee; H - b. 11/13/1936; W - b. 3/26/1952

DANTZIG,
Henry of Lambertville, NJ m. Lyn **Hurley** of Frenchtown, NJ 8/6/1961 in Ossipee; H - 45, doctor; W - 49, none

DAVIES,
John Anthony m. Wendy Jo **Allegra** 5/5/1990; H - b. 2/9/1965; W - b. 7/22/1968

DAVIS,
Alan G. m. Salma J. **Breed** 2/29/1984; H - b. 1/23/1959; W - b. 8/14/1957
Bert W. of Ossipee m. Minnie B. **Sawyer** of Ossipee 12/22/1906 in Ossipee; H - 24, farmer, 2nd, b. Effingham, s/o Albion H. Davis (Manchester, stone mason) and Sarah Meloon (Ossipee, housewife); W - 17, maid, 2nd, b. Albany, d/o John Knox (Albany, farmer) and Stella Douglass (Albany, housewife)
Clarence E., Jr. of Standish, ME m. Winifred A. **Peavey** of Standish, ME 7/19/1957 in Ossipee; H - 29, blacksmith; W - 18, accountant
Eli N. of Ossipee m. Georgina **Williams** of Ossipee 12/7/1889 in Ossipee; H - 33, farmer, b. Jackson, s/o Jonathan J. Davis (Northwood); W - 19, housekeeper, b. Ossipee, d/o Samuel Williams (Ossipee)
George W. of Ossipee m. Maud S. **Fitzgerald** of Ossipee 12/22/1925 in Ossipee; H - 50, b. Tuftonboro; W - 43, b. Shoreham, VT
John E. of Ossipee m. Constance I. **Wilson** of Ossipee 12/21/1952 in Ctr. Ossipee; H - 27, grain dealer; W - 32, at home
John Thomas of Ossipee m. Judy Lynn **Adams** of Ossipee 10/1/1995
Johnny L., Jr. of Baton Rouge, LA m. Ramona J. **Bunker** of Ossipee 10/20/1956 in Portsmouth; H - 18, Air Force; W - 15
Lawrence B. of Effingham m. Alice M. **Hanson** of Ossipee 7/9/1945 in Ossipee; H - 27, US Army; W - 26, house keeper
Lincoln K. of S. Easton, MA m. Elizabeth H. **Tucker** of Menlo Park, CA 12/9/1961 in Ctr. Ossipee; H - 59, engineer; W - 56, housewife
Otis A. of Farmington, ME m. Shirley G. **Thorne** of Bingham, ME 9/2/1950 in Moultonville; H - 35, teacher; W - 23, teacher
Richard M., Jr. m. Linda M. **Wright** 1/28/1983 in Ossipee; H - b. 9/5/1949; W - b. 8/10/1947
Silas E. of Ossipee m. Elizabeth Ann **Copp** of Ossipee 6/17/1898 in Ossipee; H - 78, farmer, 3rd, b. Warren, ME, s/o Silas Davis (deceased) and Laura Davis (deceased); W - 49, housewife, 3rd, b. E. Burke, ME, d/o Levi Jenkins (deceased) and Dolly Grisnell (deceased)
Silas E. of Effingham m. Laura J. **Nichols** of Ossipee 7/12/1904 in Ossipee; H - 69, farmer, 3rd, b. Warren, ME, s/o Silas Davis (Newcastle, ME, carpenter) and Betsey Keller (Warren, ME, housekeeper); W - 60, housekeeper, 3rd, b. Brunswick, ME, d/o James Cook (farmer)
Stuart B. m. Julie E. **Benker** 9/18/1982 in Ossipee; H - b. 3/26/1958; W - b. 2/5/1959
Walter M. of Ossipee m. Margaret P. **Gale** of Parsonsfield, ME 8/23/1924 in Tamworth; H - 24, b. Malden, MA; W - 19, b. Parsonsfield, ME
Walter M. m. Deborah L. **Dearborn** 6/5/1982 in Freedom; H - b. 1/24/1956; W - b. 2/5/1959

Willard R. of Ctr. Ossipee m. Doris C. **Parker** of Whitefield 10/3/1926 in St. Johnsbury, VT; H - 21, b. Malden, MA; W - 22, b. Whitefield

DAVISON,
Robert L. of Ctr. Ossipee m. Irene F. **Welch** of Ctr. Ossipee 9/25/1950 in Ctr. Ossipee; H - 40, carpenter; W - 19, at home

DAY,
Douglas G. m. Helen M. **White** 9/27/1975 in Ossipee; H - b. 3/15/1956; W - b. 5/9/1955

John F. m. Mabel E. **Turner** 8/26/1915 in Ossipee; H - 30, insurance agent, b. Wesley, ME, s/o Joel D. Day (Wesley, ME); W - 26, private sec., b. Dover, d/o Courtland H. Turner (Brooklyn, NY)

DEARBORN,
John B. of Ossipee m. Mary Gusta **Watson** of Wakefield 10/15/1894 in Ossipee; H - 45, carpenter, b. Saco, ME, s/o Dominicus Dearborn (carpenter) and Margret Lock (Saco, ME); W - 40, seamstress, b. Wakefield, d/o Isaac Watson (farmer) and Etta Tare (Wakefield)

DEBLOIS,
Remi A. of W. Ossipee m. Gertrude F. **Gurneau** of Laconia 10/16/1939 in Laconia; H - 31, painter; W - 28, nurse

DEBUTTS,
Daniel B. of Manchester m. Velma Pearl **Davis** of Ctr. Ossipee 6/29/1940 in Porter, ME; H - 21, paint sprayer; W - 18, at home

DEFREITOS,
Gene of Ashton, RI m. Beverly **Brock** of N. Attleboro, MA 5/6/1958 in Ossipee; H - 21, restaurant; W - 18, office

DEGLORIA,
Robert m. Paula Andrea **Iannone** 3/23/1992 in Ctr. Ossipee

DEIGHAN,
Joseph Henry of Ctr. Ossipee m. Karen Ann **Copp** of Ctr. Ossipee 8/7/1999

DEJONG,
Erik Jacob m. Charlotte Frances **Andrews** 8/4/1990; H - b. 11/22/1956; W - b. 2/8/1970

DELISLE,
Christopher Thomas of Ossipee m. Isabel **Dupuis** of Ossipee 3/3/1999
Maurice E. of Biddeford, ME m. Rose M. **Wilson** of Westbrook, ME 11/8/1961 in Ctr. Ossipee; H - 49, bodywork; W - 19, none

DELK,
David M. m. Devon E. **Eckhoff** 6/28/1969 in Ossipee; H - b. 2/9/1947; W - b. 7/25/1948

DELORY,
Edmund m. Diana Gayle **Wager** 12/22/1974 in Ossipee; H - b. 10/24/1945; W - b. 2/8/1953

DELP,
David Barry m. Diane Marriam **Scripture** 8/21/1993 in Ossipee

DELUCA,
Joseph J. m. Virginia L. **Emmett** 12/31/1986; H - b. 5/14/1934; W - b. 10/17/1954

DEMARCO,
Asher David m. Erin Gray **Jorgenson** 7/14/1993 in Ossipee

DEMERITT,
Charles W. m. Elizabeth H. **Moody** 12/24/1971 in Ossipee; H - b. 9/1/1914; W - b. 7/22/1913
Harlan S. of Ossipee m. Lotta **Andrews** of Ossipee 10/1/1899 in Ossipee; H - 21, laborer, b. Ossipee, s/o Calvin Demeritt (Ossipee, merchant) and Harriet Demeritt (Freeport, housewife); W - 24, housewife, 2nd, b. St. Johns, NB, d/o Austin Andrews and Sarah Andrews (Eastport, housewife)

DENKO,
Roland S. m. Dorothy M. **Messier** 11/29/1965 in Ossipee; H - 31, USMC; W - 26, home

DENNETT,
Frank S. of Attleboro, MA m. Rita W. **Mellon** of Attleboro, MA 12/26/1959 in Ctr. Ossipee; H - 55, chef; W - 45, office

DENNIS,
Charles E. of Manchester m. Elizabeth R. **Brown** of W. Ossipee 9/28/1957 in E. Rochester; H - 21, shoemaker; W - 18, babysitter

DESJARDINS,
Norman H. m. Donna E. **Hollingsworth** 12/29/1983 in Effingham; H - b. 9/15/1953; W - b. 2/3/1955

DESORCY,
Henry G. R. of Pawtucket, RI m. Ruth **Armstrong** of Pawtucket, RI 6/28/1963 in Ctr. Ossipee; H - 24, weaver; W - 20, waitress

DESROSIERS,
Rene Edward m. Jeane P. **Federici** 9/1/1990; H - b. 8/26/1947; W - b. 4/29/1941
Stephen R. m. Nancy B. **Drelick** 12/4/1993 in Ctr. Ossipee

DEVINE,
Bruce L. of Portland, ME m. Barbara A. **Tormay** of Falmouth, ME 9/16/1950 in Ctr. Ossipee; H - 21, shipping clerk; W - 18, typist

DEWITT,
Kirk Hanson m. Lisa Lee **Antognoni** 12/24/1988; H - b. 6/24/1968; W - b. 9/2/1957
Michael E. m. Ingrid D. **Carlson** 1/27/1988; H - b. 12/29/1954; W - b. 5/27/1956

DEYAB,
Richard George m. Nikol Marie **Tebbetts** 11/16/1990; H - b. 10/6/1972; W - b. 11/11/1972

DICEY,
Wendell G. of Tamworth m. Barbara A. **Hickey** of Ctr. Ossipee 12/26/1963 in Ctr. Ossipee; H - 20, construction; W - 19, housekeeper

DICKSON,
Dennis L. of Effingham m. Judy A. Stackpole **Fisichelli** of Wolfeboro 10/26/2001

DIETEL,
Kim E. of Ossipee m. Cynthia A. **Foster** of Ossipee 8/10/1996

DILTZ,
Steven Arnold m. Kirsten Mahalay **Brownell** 8/3/1979 in Ossipee; H - b. 7/4/1961; W - b. 7/8/1961

DIVINCENZO,
Alfred M. Sandra **Gabriele** 8/5/1964 in Ctr. Ossipee; H - 20, press oper.; W - 18, none

DOBSON,
Thomas E. of Augusta, ME m. Helen E. **Hayes** of Augusta, ME 3/30/1932 in Ossipee; H - 33, barber; W - 31, housekeeper

DODDS,
Bert, Jr. m. Nancy **Thompson** 6/8/1968 in Ctr. Ossipee; H - b. 3/25/1945

DOE,
Benjamin F. of Ossipee m. Clarinda **Davis** of Effingham 10/30/1897 in Ossipee; H - 25, laborer, b. Ossipee, s/o Benjamin Doe (deceased) and Emma F. Hall (deceased); W - 16, housemaid, b. Effingham, d/o E. D. Davis (laborer) and Augusta Davis (housekeeper)
Benjamin F. of Ossipee m. Hazel M. **Godfrey** of Freedom 12/24/1947 in Ctr. Ossipee; H - 47, caretaker; W - 47, at home
Frank B., Jr. of Ossipee m. Lona L. **Eaton** of Freedom 7/15/1924 in Freedom; H - 24, b. Ossipee; W - 19, b. Freedom
Walter E. m. Rosalio Ann **LoGalbo** 10/31/1971 in Freedom; H - b. 8/11/1935; W - b. 5/22/1943
Walter E. m. Evelyn J. K. **Howe** 12/19/1986; H - b. 8/11/1935; W - b. 11/19/1939
Walter E., Jr. of Ossipee m. Nancy J. **Taylor** of Ossipee 10/1/1955 in Tamworth; H - 20, garage; W - 20

DOERRER,
Stanley L. m. Anna R. **Fitzpatrick** 8/29/1987; H - b. 11/22/1931; W - b. 8/31/1936

DOLAN,
Gary M. of Ossipee m. Nancy A. (Littlefield) **Morin** of Ossipee 2/11/1995

DORAN,
Craig Even m. Christina Lynn **Labrie** 6/9/1990; H - b. 1/17/1967; W - b. 12/11/1970

DORE,
Charles C. of Ossipee m. Una M. **Moody** of Ossipee 10/29/1898 in Ossipee; H - 39, trader, b. Ossipee, s/o Frank P. Dore (Ossipee, farmer) and Lucy Dore (Salem, MA); W - 20, maid, b. Ossipee, d/o Alonzo Moody (Ossipee, farmer) and Vila Moody (Wolfeboro, housewife)

George Lawrence of Ctr. Ossipee m. Jennifer Anne **Deal** of Hampstead, MA 5/24/1996

George W. m. Linda L. **Britton** of Ctr. Ossipee 2/2/1957 in Ossipee; H - 17, chopper; W - 20, housework

Leon E. of Ossipee m. Mildred **Pratt** of Ossipee 1/21/1913 in Tuftonborough; H - 19, laborer, b. Ossipee, s/o Everett Dore (Ossipee); W - 24, housekeeper, 2nd, b. Wolfeboro, d/o ----- (Ossipee)

Leon E. of Ossipee m. Mildred F. **Davis** of Tuftonboro 9/30/1925 in Tuftonboro; H - 30, b. Ossipee; W - 18, b. Tuftonboro

Leroy H. of Ossipee m. Blanche E. **Davis** of Ossipee 3/28/1908 in Ossipee; H - 19, millman, b. Tuftonboro, s/o Sylvester Dore (Ossipee); W - 19, maid, b. Effingham, d/o Harry E. Davis (Effingham)

Leroy H. m. Emma **Hutchinson** 6/13/1916 in Ossipee; H - 27, carpenter, 2nd, b. Ossipee, s/o Sylvester S. Dore (Ossipee); W - 17, housework, b. Malden, MA, d/o Walter Hutchinson (Ossipee)

Lewis Alvah of Wolfeboro m. Evelyn L. **Eldridge** of Ossipee 1/24/1939 in Wolfeboro; H - 27, laborer; W - 15, at home

Lyford R. of Ctr. Ossipee m. Joan **Sargent** of E. Wolfeboro 1/3/1959 in Wolfeboro; H - 19, mill work; W - 24, none

Lyford R. of Ctr. Ossipee m. Marie A. **Griffin** of Ctr. Ossipee 12/22/1961 in Ctr. Ossipee; H - 22, millwork; W - 24, home

Roger Allen m. Kathryn Viola **Eldridge** 6/17/1989; H - b. 5/19/1961; W - b. 6/13/1957

DORR,
Charles C. m. Carrie R. **Milliken** 11/24/1916 in Ossipee; H - 55, agent, 3rd, b. Salem, MA, s/o Frank P. Dorr (Ossipee); W - 40, housework, 3rd, b. Quebec, d/o ----- Chapman (Canada)

Cyrus H. of Ossipee m. Julia **Canney** of Wolfeboro 12/25/1887 in Ossipee; H - 27, laborer, b. Ossipee, s/o Alvah Dorr and Hannah (Ossipee); W - 17, domestic, b. Wolfeboro, d/o Rhoda Canney (Wolfeboro)

Ervin of Ossipee m. Clara E. **Nute** of Wolfeboro 12/25/1888 in Ossipee; H - 23, laborer, b. Ossipee, s/o Alvah Dorr (Ossipee); W - 28, housekeeper, b. Tuftonboro, d/o Simon Kenney

DOUCETTE,
Richard C. m. Karen Ann **Nason** 7/29/1984; H - b. 3/15/1955; W - b. 5/8/1960

DOUGLAS,
Ernest of Wolfeboro m. Grace **Campbell** of Ossipee 8/19/1962 in Ossipee; H - 22, salesman; W - 21, none
Everett V. of Ossipee m. Nellie J. **Ainsworth** of Ossipee 3/13/1917 in Ossipee; H - 23, lumberman, b. Moultonborough, s/o Perley Douglass (sic) (Bridgton) and Lucinda Day (Porter); W - 19, housework, b. Elmore, VT, d/o Charles Ainsworth (Callis) and Nellie Alexander (Georgeville, Canada)
Haven E. m. Muriel F. **Nelson** 10/6/1979 in Ossipee; H - b. 1/1/1956; W - b. 6/21/1956

DOUGLASS,
Albion of Sebago, ME m. Gertrude **Durrell** of Sebago, ME 6/21/1930 in Ossipee; H - 24, farmer; W - 19, at home

DOVE,
David m. Cynthia **Hill** 5/5/1977 in Seabrook; H - b. 4/8/1915; W - b. 8/20/1934

DOW,
Ellis M. of Ossipee m. Janet R. **Taylor** of Ossipee 4/14/1956 in Ctr. Ossipee; H - 20, millworker; W - 19, at home
Ellis Milton, III m. Carol Susanne **Lessard** 5/19/1990; H - b. 1/5/1956; W - b. 5/9/1964
Rodney Ernest m. Julie Louise **Wheeler** 9/20/1991; H - b. 11/22/1955
Roland Dinsmore of Tuftonboro m. Greta Ellen **May** of Ossipee 8/5/1945 in Ossipee; H - 26, farmer; W - 22, price clerk

DOWNING,
Donald F. of E. Wolfeboro m. Caroline W. **Delk** of Ossipee 8/12/1957 in Bethel, ME; H - 30, mechanic; W - 34, reg. nurse
Geoffrey Alan m. Ellen Marie **Wallace** 8/5/1978 in Ossipee; H - b. 7/3/1959; W - b. 9/16/1959
Joel P. m. Debra J. **Anderson** 1/31/1981 in Ossipee; H - b. 1/11/1961; W - b. 2/23/1960
Joel Paul m. Fern Marie **Muise** 8/8/1992 in Ossipee

DOWNS,
David Wayne of Effingham m. Rebecca Jean Caulkins **Sutton** of Effingham 10/29/1999
James of Andover, MA m. Anne **Forsyth** of Brighton, MA 2/3/1962 in Ossipee; H - 63, analyst; W - 63, secretary
John R. m. Nancy L. **Lemay** 2/26/1982 in Ossipee; H - b. 8/8/1944; W - b. 3/19/1952

Stephen of Ossipee m. Carrie C. **Peavey** of Farmington 5/31/1891 in Ossipee; H - 19, miller, b. Eaton, s/o Elijah Downs (Eaton) and Victoria (Eaton); W - 20, housework, b. Farmington, d/o Benjamin F. Bray (Ossipee) and Mary E. Watson (Farmington)

DOYLE,
Merton G., Jr. of Portland, ME m. Judith A. **Peterson** of Avon, MA 11/14/1959 in Ctr. Ossipee; H - 21, salesman; W - 19, student

DRAKE,
Benjamin M. of Ossipee m. Lizzie L. **Farnham** of Ossipee 11/25/1891 in Ossipee; H - 21, barber, b. Ossipee, s/o Charles L. Drake (Chichester) and Marian (Ossipee); W - 18, housework, b. Ossipee, d/o Eben Farnham (Ossipee) and Eunice L. (Ossipee)
Kenneth of Hanson, MA m. Doris R. **Knapp** of Hanson, MA 5/5/1956 in Ossipee; H - 39, salesman; W - 44

DREW,
Charles of Laconia m. Virginia **Adjutant** of Ctr. Ossipee 9/7/1962 in Ctr. Ossipee; H - 21, Army; W - 21, nurse
Daniel S. m. Diane L. **Savage** 8/28/1982 in Ossipee; H - b. 8/17/1962; W - b. 2/12/1959
Daniel Steven of Ctr. Ossipee m. Terri Lee **Brooks** of Ctr. Ossipee 7/22/1995
Frank of Ossipee m. Loura **Sargent** of Ossipee 4/2/1904 in Ossipee; H - 20, laborer, b. Ossipee, s/o Frank Drew (laborer) and Jennie Eldridge (Ossipee, housewife); W - 27, housewife, 2nd, b. Ossipee, d/o Alpheus Eldridge (Ossipee, laborer) and Dorothy Jenness (housewife)
James L. m. Mary A. **Fenderson** 9/1/1984; H - b. 2/5/1966; W - b. 2/1/1961
John N. of Ossipee m. Eva M. **Whipple** of Ossipee 12/31/1914 in Ossipee; H - 53, farmer, 2nd, b. Tamworth, s/o John D. Drew (Tamworth); W - 53, matron, 3rd, b. Parsonsfield, ME, d/o Elijah Whipple (Parsonsfield, ME)
John N. of Ossipee m. Annie L. **Hasty** of Ossipee 10/4/1921 in Ossipee; H - 60, farmer, 3rd, b. E. Machias, ME, s/o John D. Drew (Tamworth) and Sarah G. Wiggin (Tamworth); W - 52, housekeeper, 3rd, b. Milton, MA, d/o Nelson L. Lawrence (E. Madison, ME) and Anna Watson (Dennysville, ME)
Philip William of Ossipee m. Frances Josie **Eldridge** of Ossipee 5/7/1941 in Sandwich; H - 21, logger; W - 18, at home
Richard S. m. Deidre A. **O'Leary** 10/13/1983 in Ossipee; H - b. 10/19/1953; W - b. 2/16/1961

Richard W. m. Jacqueline R. **Berry** 3/21/1986; H - b. 8/8/1962; W - b. 8/8/1958

Scott Allan of Natick, MA m. Sandra Lee **Buis** of Natick, MA 10/8/1995

Selden E. of Ctr. Ossipee m. Dorothy P. **Buswell** of Ctr. Ossipee 9/25/1953 in Ctr. Ossipee; H - 32, Army; W - 23, at home

Tony P. m. Helen E. **Loring** 8/30/1972 in Wakefield; H - b. 8/23/1938; W - b. 6/28/1950

Wendell of Ctr. Ossipee m. Arlene **LaFreniere** of Wolfeboro 5/26/1962 in Madison; H - 20, mill work; W - 18, none

Wendell R. of Ctr. Ossipee m. Virginia M. **Buzzell** of Steep Falls, ME 5/30/1959 in Ctr. Ossipee; H - 17, truck driver; W - 16, none

DROWN,

Charles H. of Ossipee m. Nettie **Manson** of Jackson 8/20/1898 in Ossipee; H - 30, farmer, b. Eaton, s/o Elijah Drown (Eaton) and Mary A. Goldthread; W - 30, maid, b. Jackson, d/o John Manson (Jackson, farmer)

Joel P. of Ossipee m. Maude **Duntley** of Ossipee 6/5/1917 in Wakefield; H - 22, laborer, b. Ossipee, s/o Elijah Drown (Eaton) and Victoria Littlefield (Brownfield, ME); W - 31, housework, 2nd, b. Fryeburg, ME, d/o Fairfield Gilman and Harriet Gilman

DROWNS,

Leonard Charles of Ossipee m. Marguerite S. **Tappan** of Ossipee 3/5/1945 in Ossipee; H - 22, millman; W - 18, at home

DUBAR,

Charles E. of Portland, ME m. Mildred **Turner** of Auburn, ME 11/16/1942 in Ossipee; H - 22, burner; W - 20, at home

DUBE,

Leo Phillip of Ossipee m. Mrs. Blanche **Crowley** of Newmarket 5/31/1941 in Newmarket; H - 28, truck driver; W - 33, shoe worker

Ralph P. of Ossipee m. Edna E. **White** of Dover 7/4/1942 in Sanbornville; H - 30, dist. of petroleum; W - 30, nurse

DUBOIS,

Lucien P. of Rochester m. Arlene M. **Eldridge** of Ossipee 3/30/1946 in Rochester; H - 30, mill worker; W - 27, furniture factory

Lucien P. m. Hilda Merrow **Williams** 4/28/1972 in Ossipee; H - b. 10/15/1915; W - b. 11/9/1917

Raymond m. Nancy A. **Tuthill** 4/30/1965 in Manchester; H - 25, cook; W - 21, cashier

Wendell of Pembroke, GA m. Janet **Nichols** of Ctr. Ossipee 6/28/1958 in W. Ossipee; H - 21, student; W - 17, student

DUCHANO,
Donald R. m. Donna E. **Brack** 4/8/1967 in Ossipee; H - 33, real estate; W - 24, bank
Omer J. A. of Wakefield m. Muriel Thermas **Wiggin** of Ossipee 10/16/1938 in Wakefield; H - 19, laborer; W - 17, at home

DUCHARME,
Michael Angelo of Boston, MA m. Leslie Anne **Furtado** of Boston, MA 9/6/1997

DUDELSON,
Barry of Ossipee m. Tina B. (Berry) **McKenzie** of Ossipee 1/6/1996

DUDLEY,
Charles W. of Fryeburg, ME m. Beverly F. **Van Fleet** of Rockland, ME 8/21/1953 in Ctr. Ossipee; H - 19, laborer; W - 22, housewife

DUGLAY,
Hugh of Ossipee m. Ethel S. **Merrow** of Ossipee 11/11/1921 in Ossipee; H - 35, clergyman, b. Bluffton, IN, s/o Ausbury Duglay (Churubusco, IN) and Julia A. Freese (Bluffton, IN); W - 34, at home, b. Salem, MA, d/o Edwin A. Merrow (Ossipee) and Edith C. Scher (Salem, MA)

DUNBAR,
Dennis R. of Littleton, CO m. Carole L. (Cormier) **Dolby** of Littleton, CO 8/22/1995
Edward J. of Camden, ME m. Charlotte M. **Gilchrest** of Camden, ME 2/28/1950 in Ctr. Ossipee; H - 31, inspector; W - 26, waitress

DUNFIELD,
Charles W. of Ossipee m. Emily W. **Sinclair** of Ossipee 5/2/1896 in Ossipee; H - 34, miller, 2nd, b. Bradford, s/o William N. Dunfield and Laura E. Dunfield; W - 25, housekeeper, b. Ossipee, d/o Jerry Sinclair and Susie M. Sinclair

DUNHAM,
Morris m. Mary Anne **Powers** 6/17/1968 in Ctr. Ossipee; H - b. 4/29/1946; W - b. 11/30/1948

DUNN,
Walter L. of Allston, MA m. Norine P. **Brennan** of Jamaica Plain, MA 6/16/1953 in Ctr. Ossipee; H - 22, maintenance; W - 18, at home

DUNPHY,
Ralph, Jr. of Old Orchard, ME m. Takako **Watanabe** of Old Orchard, ME 6/10/1958 in Ossipee; H - 28, marine engineer; W - 23, none

DUNTLEY,
Charles A. of Ossipee m. Fanny **Dow** of Ossipee 7/6/1895 in Ossipee; H - 24, miller, b. Manchester, s/o Charles E. Duntly (sic) (Boston, railroad) and Alice Duntly (Goffstown, housewife); W - 14, maid, b. Sandwich, d/o Albion Dow (Moultonboro, farmer) and Mary Dow

DUPUIS,
Alan of Laconia m. Catherine **Moulton** of Ossipee 12/3/1962 in Wolfeboro; H - 23, car salesman; W - 25, medical secretary

DURHAM,
Gary R. m. Carolyn A. **Foster** 8/3/1969 in Ctr. Ossipee; H - b. 3/15/1947; W - b. 2/13/1949

DUTTON,
Albert R. m. Shirley E. **Loud** 2/14/1969 in Ctr. Ossipee; H - b. 1/24/1941; W - b. 6/19/1948

DUVAL,
Bruce m. Corine **Rowbotham** 10/3/1964 in W. Ossipee; H - 27, heelworker; W - 22, shoeworker

DWYER,
James F. of Fulton, NY m. Jane E. **Washburn** of Fulton, NY 10/10/1947 in Ossipee; H - 31, hotel proprietor; W - 28, bookkeeper

DYER,
Allen R. m. Susan K. **Athearn** 6/29/1969 in W. Ossipee; H - b. 11/10/1944; W - b. 7/19/1947

EARLE,
Peter Charles m. Elizabeth A. **Sawyer** 1/17/1971 in Bartlett; H - b. 8/28/1952; W - b. 6/9/1952

EASTMAN,
Clayton W. of Ossipee m. Marion C. **Butler** of Nottingham 10/18/1919 in Nottingham; H - 25, auto mechanic, b. Conway, s/o Fred R. Eastman (Effingham) and Ella M. Eastman (Bartlett); W - 28, stenographer, b. Nottingham, d/o Frank H. Butler (Nottingham) and Euleta Folsom (Epping)
John D., Jr. of Harpswell, ME m. Elizabeth C. **Lelond** of Harpswell, ME 2/14/1963 in Ctr. Ossipee; H - 30, fisherman; W - 37, home
Paul R. of Barnstead m. Jean F. **Abbott** of Ctr. Ossipee 11/26/1957 in Ctr. Ossipee; H - 22, weaver; W - 18, at home

EATON,
Richard T. m. Lelia G. **Scripture** 9/20/1980 in Ossipee; H - b. 2/17/1932; W - b. 6/15/1938

ECKHOFF,
Peter B. m. Elaine M. **Jones** 8/8/1981 in Wolfeboro; H - b. 12/8/1959; W - b. 9/6/1958
Stephen John m. Susan Yvonne **Lampron** 8/20/1977 in Wolfeboro; H - b. 12/2/1957; W - b. 9/29/1955

EDGERLY,
Herman D. of Chocorua m. Natalie N. **White** of W. Ossipee 9/22/1932 in Tamworth; H - 24, at college; W - 19, at home
Russell D. of Ossipee m. Louise **Colby** of Ossipee 2/25/1932 in Ossipee; H - 22, laborer; W - 23, housekeeper

EDSON,
Peter Allen of Rockland, MA m. Christine A. **Higgins** of Rockland, MA 7/10/1994

EDWARDS,
Charles J. of Ossipee m. Cora L. **Smith** of Ossipee 3/30/1889 in Ossipee; H - 24, laborer, b. Effingham, s/o Charles Edwards (Parsonsfield, ME); W - 21, housekeeper, b. Tamworth, d/o John H. Smith (Tamworth)
James C. m. Cheryl L. **DeFreitas** 7/12/1976 in Ossipee; H - b. 1/18/1957; W - b. 12/15/1958
Jimmy Earl m. Angela Susan **Kelley** 1/20/1989; H - b. 4/14/1965; W - b. 3/23/1967
Robert Stanley of Effingham m. Erin Marie **Blackey** of Ctr. Ossipee 7/3/1999

ELA,
Henry P. m. Dawn M. **Eldridge** 9/25/1993 in Ossipee

ELCOCK,
James B. m. Brenda L. **Moyer** 11/15/1986; H - b. 5/11/1944; W - b. 7/30/1964

ELDREDGE [see Eldridge],
Edgar A. of Ctr. Ossipee m. Norma A. **Moulton** of Pittsfield 10/11/1951 in Pittsfield; H - 25, refrig. service; W - 27, teacher
Ivory E. of Ossipee m. Emma **Welch** of Ossipee 9/22/1888 in Ossipee; H - 20, laborer, b. Ossipee, s/o Daniel Eldridge (Ossipee); W - 18, housekeeper, b. Ossipee, d/o Moses P. Welch (Ossipee)
Oren of Ossipee m. Lizzie B. **Williams** of Ossipee 8/10/1891 in Ossipee; H - 21, laborer, b. Ossipee, s/o Daniel Eldredge (Ossipee) and Betsey (Ossipee); W - 16, housework, b. Ossipee, d/o Samuel Williams (Ossipee) and Ester Williams (Ossipee)

ELDRIDGE [see Eldredge],
Alan m. Lucinda **White** 5/4/1968 in Ctr. Ossipee; H - b. 10/1/1948; W - b. 6/17/1950
Alan C. m. Karen Sue **Jones** 6/30/1973 in Ossipee; H - b. 10/1/1948; W - b. 10/24/1955
Alfred P. m. Myrtle L. **Johnson** 7/18/1971 in Ossipee; H - b. 10/12/1947; W - b. 11/27/1950
Alfred S. of Ossipee m. Mildred I. **Welch** of Ossipee 9/9/1927 in Wolfeboro; H - 30, laborer; W - 40, housekeeper
Amos L. of Ossipee m. Emma J. **Hodgdon** of Boston, MA 10/12/1912 in Ossipee; H - 52, millman, b. Ossipee, s/o James Eldridge (Ossipee); W - 44, dressmaker, b. Somersworth, d/o John K. Hodgdon (Lebanon, ME)
Archie m. Emily M. **Garland** 2/1/1970 in Milton; H - b. 7/10/1913; W - b. 2/2/1907
Austin Melvin of Ossipee m. Barbara **Drinkwater** of Ossipee 1/23/1944 in Ctr. Ossipee; H - 21, shipyard worker; W - 19, at home
Bernard H. of Ctr. Ossipee m. Joyce A. **Berry** of Ctr. Ossipee 1/10/1948 in Moultonville; H - 19, laborer; W - 16, at home
Bradley W. m. Deborah L. **Williams** 9/26/1987; H - b. 10/15/1960; W - b. 11/4/1964
Bruce Edward m. Karen Theresa **Bretton** 5/4/1991; H - b. 1/4/1952; H - b. 2/26/1962
Carl Robert m. Kathleen Grace **White** 9/19/1970 in Ossipee; H - b. 2/23/1953; W - b. 2/11/1945
Carl Robert, Jr. m. Carolee **Erickson** 5/22/1993 in Effingham

Carlton O. of Ossipee m. Martha M. **Hayes** of Ossipee 5/16/1948 in Ctr. Ossipee; H - 23, lumberman; W - 19, at home

Carroll H. of Ossipee m. Dorothy Ethel **Prokey** of Ossipee 8/12/1939 in Wolfeboro; H - 23, forestry service; W - 17, at home

Charles, Jr. of Ctr. Ossipee m. Leola **Edwards** of Ctr. Ossipee 6/30/1962 in Ctr. Ossipee; H - 19, mill work; W - 27, mill work

Charles M. of Ossipee m. Nettie L. **Nichols** of Ossipee 9/12/1907 in Ossipee; H - 42, laborer, 3rd, b. Ossipee, s/o Simon Eldridge (Ossipee, farmer) and Robeline Johnson (Ossipee, housewife); W - 26, maid, b. Ossipee, d/o John W. Nichols (Ossipee, farmer) and Thankful Williams (Ossipee, housewife)

Charles P. of Ossipee m. Reba A. **Vittum** of Ossipee 2/21/1942 in Conway; H - 18, laborer; W - 18, at home

Chauncey of Ossipee m. Esther **Adjutant** of Ossipee 4/20/1931 in Tamworth; H - 21, laborer; W - 16, at home

Chester m. Janet E. **Gerry** 7/30/1967 in Ctr. Ossipee; H - 17, student; W - 21, student

Clifford D. m. Hazel E. **Eldridge** 12/6/1969 in Ctr. Ossipee; H - b. 1/23/1898; W - b. 5/21/1904

Clifton of Ctr. Ossipee m. Virginia **Drew** of Steep Falls, ME 7/6/1962 in Ctr. Ossipee; H - 21, truck driver; W - 19, none

Clifton D. of Ossipee m. Etta M. **Abbott** of Ossipee 1/29/1927 in Ossipee; H - 29, laborer; W - 31, housekeeper

Dana of Ossipee m. Susie A. **Wiggin** of Tuftonboro 2/13/1901 in Ossipee; H - 19, laborer, b. Ossipee, s/o Daniel Eldridge (Ossipee, laborer) and Lizzie Eldridge (Ossipee, housewife); W - 21, teacher, b. Tuftonboro, d/o John A. Wiggin (Tuftonboro, farmer) and Abbie Wiggin (Tuftonboro, housewife)

David of Ossipee m. Annie E. **Eldridge** of Ossipee 3/31/1892 in Ossipee Valley; H - 20, farmer, b. Ossipee, s/o Daniel Eldridge (Ossipee, farmer) and Susan Eldridge (Ossipee, housewife); W - 18, housekeeper, b. Ossipee, d/o William Eldridge (Ossipee, farmer) and Rosanna Eldridge (Ossipee, housewife)

Dennis m. Martha **Berry** 6/28/1968 in Ctr. Ossipee; H - b. 9/3/1949; W - b. 11/15/1948

Douglas C. m. Rebecca E. **Deatte** 1/18/1969 in Ossipee; H - b. 6/20/1949; W - b. 8/17/1951

Douglas Clifford m. Ursula Patricia **Rogers** 11/16/1973 in Ossipee; H - b. 6/20/1949; W - b. 3/4/1948

Eben of Ossipee m. Lucy M. **Berry** of Wolfeboro 7/15/1905 in Ossipee; H - 31, millman, b. Ossipee, s/o Henry Eldridge (Freedom) and Emily Nichols (Ossipee, housewife); W - 33, maid, b. Wolfeboro, d/o John Berry (Salem, MA) and Olive Chesley (Alton, deceased)

Edward of Ossipee m. Carrie R. **Wilkins** of Ossipee 1/17/1917 in Ossipee; H - 39, laborer, b. Ossipee, s/o Charles Eldridge (Ossipee) and Mary Nichols (Ossipee); W - 35, housewife, b. Ossipee, d/o Carey Wilkins (VA) and Abbie Cook (Bartlett)

Ernest F. of Ossipee m. Edna M. **Riley** of Baldwin, ME 7/28/1919 in Standish, ME; H - 27, teaming, b. Ossipee, s/o Frank J. Eldridge (Ossipee) and Abbie Hodgdon (Ossipee); W - 19, school teacher, b. Baldwin, ME, d/o Louis A. Riley (Baldwin, ME) and Etta Black (Baldwin, ME)

Eugene A. m . Phyllis A. **Brown** 10/2/1965 in Conway; H - 35, mill hand; W - 33, housewife

Everett S. of Ossipee m. Nettie **Pike** of Ossipee 12/1/1895 in Ossipee; H - farmer, b. Ossipee, s/o Simon Eldridge (Ossipee, deceased) and Roberline Eldridge (Ossipee, housewife); W - maid, b. Ossipee, d/o John Pike (Ossipee, farmer) and Emma Pike (Ossipee, housewife)

Ezra of Ossipee m. Carrie A. **Skillings** of Conway 6/16/1908 in Ossipee; H - 55, farmer, 2nd, b. Ossipee, s/o Daniel Eldridge (Ossipee); W - 39, housekeeper, 2nd, b. Conway, d/o Lorenzo Lamb (Portland)

Fred of Ossipee m. Cora B. **Welch** of Ossipee 2/8/1897 in Ossipee; H - 19, farmer, b. Ossipee, s/o William Eldridge (Ossipee, farmer) and Rosina Eldridge (Ossipee, housekeeper); W - 16, housemaid, b. Ossipee, d/o Silas Welch (Ossipee, farmer) and Emma Welch (Ossipee, housekeeper)

Fred W. of Ossipee m. Dora T. **Sargent** of Ossipee 12/9/1911 in Ossipee; H - 32, laborer, b. Ossipee, s/o William H. Eldridge (Ossipee, farmer); W - 17, housewife, 2nd, widow, b. Ossipee, d/o Everett Sargent (Ossipee, farmer)

George A. of Ossipee m. Bessie **Welch** of Ossipee 1/5/1903 in Ossipee; H - 32, laborer, b. Ossipee, s/o Charles Eldridge (Ossipee, laborer) and Mary Nichols (Ossipee, housewife); W - 18, maid, b. Ossipee, d/o Lyford Welch (Ossipee, farmer) and Lizzie Eldridge (Ossipee, housewife)

George H. of Ossipee m. Ida **Welch** of Ossipee 12/2/1894 in Ossipee; H - 30, farmer, b. Ossipee, s/o Alpheus Eldridge (Ossipee, farmer) and Dorothy Jenness (Meredith, housewife); W - 18, maid, b. Ossipee, d/o John Welch (Ossipee, farmer) and Elmira Welch (Ossipee, housewife)

George M. m. Diane J. **Hall** 4/13/1985; H - b. 10/11/1950; W - b. 12/31/1961

George Michael m. Charmein Jean **Twombly** 9/18/1971 in Madison; H - b. 10/11/1950; W - b. 12/13/1950

Gordon Allen m. Joan Darlene **Berry** 6/17/1975 in Ossipee; H - b. 9/17/1955; W - b. 1/22/1957

Gregory A. m. Judith L. M. **Bowman** 6/2/1979 in Ossipee; H - b. 10/20/1959; W - b. 3/20/1958
Guy, Jr. m. Nancy **Shores** 2/12/1968 in N. Conway; H - b. 4/2/1947; W - b. 1/14/1950
Guy Henry of Ossipee m. Lottie Edith **Moulton** of Ossipee 7/14/1940 in Freedom; H - 18, woodsman; W - 18, at home
Harrison of Ossipee m. Georgia A. **Davis** of Ossipee 5/18/1914 in Ossipee; H - 53, laborer, 2nd, b. Ossipee, s/o Stephen Eldridge (Ossipee); W - 39, housekeeper, 2nd, b. Ossipee, d/o Samuel Williams (Ossipee)
Harry P. of Ossipee m. Marion M. **Tucker** of Freedom 11/14/1923 in Freedom; H - 25, b. Ossipee; W - 23, b. Deerfield
Harry P. of Ossipee m. Vivian H. **Purrington** of Ossipee 12/18/1927 in Ossipee; H - 29, laborer; W - 28, housekeeper
Harry P., Jr. of Ossipee m. Christabell I. **Stacy** of Tamworth 1/18/1946 in Ossipee; H - 18, mill hand; W - 18, at home
Herbert of Ossipee m. Melinda **Littlefield** of Conway 11/6/1900 in Ossipee; H - 20, farmer, b. Ossipee, s/o Harrison Eldridge (Ossipee, farmer) and Laura Eldridge (Freedom, housewife); W - 19, housemaid, b. Conway, d/o George Littlefield (Conway, farmer) and Carrie Littlefield (Conway, housewife)
Herbert W. of Ossipee m. Lillie D. **Welch** of Ossipee 7/3/1898 in Ossipee; H - 22, farmer, b. Ossipee, s/o Simon Eldridge (Ossipee, deceased) and Roberline Eldridge (Ossipee, housewife); W - 17, maid, b. Ossipee, d/o Moses P. Welch (Ossipee, farmer) and Sarah J. Welch (Ossipee, deceased)
Howard J. m. Cora E. **Kirkwood** 6/15/1921 in Ossipee; H - 26, chauffeur, b. Woodstock, NB, s/o James E. Eldridge (hotel proprietor) and Abbie J. Hodgdon (housewife); W - 18, waitress, b. Ossipee, d/o George E. Kirkwood (teaming) and Clara Eldridge (housewife)
Ivory E. of Ossipee m. Annie E. **Eldridge** of Ossipee 11/29/1899 in Ossipee; H - 31, farmer, 2nd, b. Ossipee, s/o Daniel Eldridge (Ossipee, farmer) and Elsie E. Eldridge (Ossipee, housewife); W - 24, maid, b. Ossipee, d/o William Eldridge (Ossipee, farmer) and Rosanna Eldridge (Ossipee, housewife)
James m. Beverly **Budroe** 9/2/1966 in Ctr. Ossipee; H - 21, mill worker; W - 22, mill worker
James m. Kathleen **Hawes** 9/4/1966 in Whittier; H - 19, Army; W - 18, none
James A. m. Patricia A. **Baxter** 9/30/1977 in Ossipee; H - b. 7/26/1947; W - b. 12/4/1956
James Kenneth m. Jennifer Lee **Brooks** 6/19/1993 in Madison
Jeffrey Alan of W. Ossipee m. Jennifer Lynn **Morgan** of Tamworth 3/17/2001

Jeremy Clyde of Ctr. Ossipee m. Dorothy Cora **Brewer** of Tuftonboro 8/20/1994

John Carroll m. Peggy Edith **Adjutant** 4/13/1974 in Ossipee; H - b. 5/8/1949; W - b. 11/28/1955

John Nichols of Ossipee m. Helen M. **Giles** of Ossipee 5/22/1943 in Ctr. Ossipee; H - 28, mill man; W - 24, secretary

Lafayette of Ossipee m. Elva **Welch** of Ossipee 5/16/1899 in Ossipee; H - 19, farmer, b. Ossipee, s/o Daniel Eldridge (Ossipee, farmer) and Lizzie Eldridge (Ossipee, housewife); W - 16, maid, b. Ossipee, d/o Lyford Welch (Ossipee, farmer) and ----- Welch (Ossipee, housewife)

Lafe of Ossipee m. Myrtle **Eldridge** of Ossipee 1/17/1908 in Ossipee; H - 27, laborer, 2nd, b. Ossipee, s/o Daniel Eldridge (Ossipee); W - 17, maid, b. Ossipee, d/o Harrison Eldridge (Ossipee)

Langdon J. m. Alecia M. **Daigneau** 11/18/1978 in Ossipee; H - b. 1/21/1959; W - b. 9/6/1960

Larry E. of Ctr. Ossipee m. Eva Marie **Chesley** of Parsonsfield, ME 7/15/2000

Larry Edward m. Reita Lee **Willey** 3/10/1973 in Ossipee; H - b. 10/4/1949; W - b. 9/7/1949

Lawrence of Ctr. Ossipee m. Reta **Lane** of Ctr. Ossipee 11/7/1936 in Freedom; H - 22, laborer; W - 19, at home

Lawrence J. of Ctr. Ossipee m. Sandra R. **Hamel** of Ctr. Ossipee 1/7/1961 in Ctr. Ossipee; H - 18, none; W - 16, none

Lawrence John, III of Ctr. Ossipee m. Kelly Ann **Carroll** of Ctr. Ossipee 8/4/2001

Lester of Ossipee m. Florence **Varney** of Ossipee 11/4/1925 in Ossipee; H - 18, b. Ossipee; W - 18, b. Berwick, ME

Lester A. of Ossipee m. Ida M. **Sprague** of Ossipee 12/3/1927 in Ossipee; H - 23, laborer; W - 24, house maid

Louis R. of Ossipee m. Mildred I. **Abbott** of Farmington 4/5/1941 in Berwick, ME; H - 35, lumberjack; W - 29, housework

Mark Allen m. Cynthia Ann **Allen** 11/3/1990; H - b. 7/18/1967; W - b. 12/7/1968

Melvin C. of Ossipee m. Mattie D. **Buswell** of Ossipee 4/5/1896 in Ossipee; H - 30, laborer, 2nd, b. Ossipee, s/o Simon Eldridge (Ossipee, farmer) and Roberline Eldridge (Ossipee, housekeeper); W - 20, housekeeper, b. Ossipee, d/o Isaac Buswell (Ossipee, stone cutter) and Jennie M. Buswell (Ossipee, housekeeper)

Michael Norman of Ctr. Ossipee m. Sarah Ann **Maggio** of Ctr. Ossipee 4/19/1997

Neil Gordon of Ctr. Ossipee m. Jennifer Lynn **Thurber** of Ctr. Ossipee 9/16/2000

Newell P. of Ossipee m. Beatrice E. **Brothers** of Ossipee 11/9/1929 in Ossipee; H - 22, laborer; W - 21, housework

Norman F. of Ctr. Ossipee m. Marie E. **Hodge** of Ctr. Ossipee 8/27/1955 in Rochester; H - 22, woodsman; W - 19, mill work
Norman F. m. Jeanette L. **Eldridge** 6/5/1982 in Ossipee; H - b. 8/19/1932; W - b. 4/12/1935
Norman F., Jr. m. Kira Margit **Brownell** 5/29/1974 in Ossipee; H - b. 1/19/1956; W - b. 1/17/1958
Orodon J. of Ossipee m. Lucy C. **Welch** of Ossipee 10/30/1892 in Ctr. Ossipee; H - 30, farmer, b. Ossipee, s/o Simon Eldridge (Ossipee, farmer) and ----- (Ossipee, housewife); W - 18, housewife, b. Ossipee, d/o Moses Welch (Ossipee, farmer) and Sarah Welch (Ossipee, housewife)
Osborn of Ossipee m. Laura **Welch** of Ossipee 3/26/1899 in Ossipee; H - 25, fireman, b. Ossipee, s/o Alpheus Eldridge (Ossipee, laborer) and Dorothy Eldridge (Ossipee, housewife); W - 22, maid, b. Ossipee, d/o John Welch (Ossipee, laborer) and Elmira Welch (Ossipee, housewife)
Perley E. of Ossipee m. Charlotte **Palmer** of Tamworth 9/27/1947 in Tamworth; H - 16, woodworker; W - 16, at home
Perley E. of Ctr. Ossipee m. Rose M. **Dore** of Ctr. Ossipee 5/29/1959 in Ctr. Ossipee; H - 68, trackman; W - 42, housewife
Perlie E. of Ossipee m. Margaret **Templeton** of Ossipee 11/26/1911 in Ossipee; H - 20, laborer, b. Ossipee, s/o Ivory E. Eldridge (Ossipee, deceased); W - 16, b. Ossipee, d/o Ahial Templeton (Washington, DC, laborer)
Ralph C. of Ctr. Ossipee m. Marguerite R. **Eldridge** of Ctr. Ossipee 6/23/1956 in Chocorua; H - 39, clerk; W - 40
Ralph Charles of Ossipee m. Marguerite Ruth **Winkley** of Ossipee 3/30/1940 in Ossipee; H - 23, mill worker; W - 24, at home
Philip Wayne m. Diane **Ballou** 8/25/1973 in Ossipee; H - b. 5/23/1954; W - b. 12/17/1954
Raymond C. of Ossipee m. Etta M. **Eldridge** of Ossipee 9/17/1919 in Ossipee; H - 20, farner, b. Ossipee, s/o P. J. Eldridge (Ossipee) and Emma P. Welch (Ossipee); W - 17, housework, b. Ossipee, d/o George Eldridge (Ossipee) and Ida Welch (Ossipee)
Richard C. of Ctr. Ossipee m. Sandra L. **Charles** of Ctr. Ossipee 1/19/1963 in Ctr. Ossipee; H - 19, mill work; W - 17, none
Ritchie of Ctr. Ossipee m. Virginia **Eldridge** of Tamworth 4/10/1947 in Tamworth; H - 25, millworker; W - 23, at home
Ritchie m. Christobell **Elliott** 7/18/1964 in Ctr. Ossipee; H - 42, mill; W - 36, mill
Robert W. of Ossipee m. Eva M. **Judkins** of Effingham 8/21/1948 in Moultonville; H - 19, lumbering; W - 18, at home
Robert W. m. Brenda E. **Corrow** 7/16/1979 in Laconia; H - b. 1/30/1929; W - b. 5/29/1947

Rodney H. of Ctr. Ossipee m. Sharon A. **Eldridge** of Wolfeboro 8/23/1963 in Ctr. Ossipee; H - 20, woods; W - 19, none

Rodney Herbert, Jr. m. Caroline Jennifer **Bickford** 12/19/1992 in Ctr. Ossipee

Roy of Ossipee m. Virginia P. **Whiting** of Ossipee 2/14/1946 in Ossipee; H - 19, laborer; W - 21, housewife

Roy of Ctr. Ossipee m. Jean M. **Purrington** of Ctr. Ossipee 8/10/1948 in Rochester; H - 21, millworker; W - 22, waitress

Roy Everett of Ossipee m. Lillian Amy **Dore** of Wolfeboro 6/29/1944 in Wolfeboro; H - 23, lumberman; W - 20, at home

Scott O. m. Abbie J. **Davis** 1/30/1916 in Ossipee; H - 21, laborer, b. Ossipee, s/o Oren Eldridge (Ossipee); W - 19, domestic, b. Ossipee, d/o Alvah Davis (Ossipee)

Stanley m. Mary A. **Hebert** 7/16/1965 in Ctr. Ossipee; H - 19, lumbering; W - 14, none

Stephen L. m. Sharon M. **Runci** 5/17/1986; H - b. 4/22/1962; W - b. 4/11/1966

Tedd m. Arlene **Kosker** 8/24/1964 in Ctr. Ossipee; H - 20, glass; W - 18, typist

Tedd O. of Ctr. Ossipee m. Sharon A. **Charles** of Wolfeboro 12/15/1961 in Ctr. Ossipee; H - 17, wood; W - 18, none

Timothy Edwin of Ctr. Ossipee m. Jessica Jane **Johnson** of Effingham 7/26/1997

Timothy W. of Ctr. Ossipee m. Karen B. **Eldridge** of Ctr. Ossipee 4/29/2000

Timothy Wayne m. Karen Beth **Savage** 12/3/1988; H - b. 4/11/1969; W - b. 5/22/1961

W. Clayton of Ossipee m. Stella M. **Cragin** of Effingham 3/4/1961 in Ossipee; H - 58, state work; W - 60, housekeeper

Walter B. of Natick, MA m. Ada A. **Wallace** of Natick, MA 6/23/1917; H - 40, merchant, b. Natick, MA, s/o Allen J. Eldridge (Natick, MA) and Martha J. Loker (Natick, MA); W - 35, saleslady, b. Doaktown, NB, d/o William Wallace (Doaktown, NB) and Frances Wallace (Nashuaak, NB)

Walter C. of Ossipee m. Peggy A. **Anthony** of Tamworth 10/30/1999

Wayne Alan m. Jessika Jean **Moulton** 7/27/1991; H - b. 1/17/1966; W - b. 10/30/1974

Wendell R. of Ctr. Ossipee m. Virginia L. **Lewis** of Kezar Falls, ME 12/30/1961 in W. Ossipee; H - 22, USA; W - seamstress

Wendell R. m. Brenda E. **Seamans** 7/1/1992 in Pittsburg

Wesley E. of W. Ossipee m. Geraldine **White** of Ctr. Ossipee 6/15/1957 in W. Ossipee; H - 30, bus driver; W - 20, at home

Wilber A. of Ossipee m. Annette M. **Eastman** of Bartlett 6/12/1892 in Conway; H - 20, barber, b. Ossipee, s/o Charles Eldridge (Ossipee, farmer) and Mary Eldridge (Ossipee, housewife); W - 20, domestic, b. Bartlett, d/o Calvin Eastman (Bartlett, farmer)

Wilbur of Ossipee m. Myrtle M. **Templeton** of Ossipee 9/16/1908 in Ossipee; H - 27, laborer, b. Ossipee, s/o Samuel Wallace (Ossipee); W - 19, maid, b. Ossipee, d/o Ahial Templeton (Ossipee)

Wilbur F. of Ossipee m. Florence I. **Cook** of Ossipee 4/3/1900 in Ossipee; H - 21, laborer, b. Ossipee, s/o Solomon F. Abbott (Ossipee, farmer) and Marilla Abbott (deceased, housewife); W - 18, maid, b. Ossipee, d/o James R. B. Cook (Ossipee, farmer) and Mary A. Cook (Ossipee, housewife)

William H. of Ctr. Ossipee m. Elizabeth M. **Moore** of Ctr. Ossipee 1/22/1954 in Tamworth; H - 25, logger; W - 16, at home

William I. m. Deanna L. **Drake** 2/21/1987; H - b. 12/5/1968; W - b. 11/25/1966

Willie R. of Ossipee m. Mabel **Welch** of Ossipee 10/20/1892 in Ctr. Ossipee; H - 22, farmer, b. Ossipee, s/o A. Eldridge (Ossipee, farmer) and Dorothy Eldridge (Meredith, housewife); W - 19, seamstress, b. Ossipee, d/o John Welch (Ossipee, farmer) and Elmira Welch (Ossipee, housewife)

Willie R. m. Cora B. **Williams** 12/5/1916 in Ossipee; H - 46, farmer, 2nd, b. Ossipee, s/o Alpheus Eldridge (Ossipee); W - 16, housework, b. Ossipee, d/o Frank Williams (Ossipee) (see following entry)

Willis R. of Ossipee m. Cora B. **Williams** of Ossipee 4/15/1917 in Ossipee; H - 46, farmer, 2nd, b. Ossipee, s/o Alpheus Eldridge (Ossipee) and Dorothy Jenness (Meredith); W - 16, housework, b. Ossipee, d/o Frank Williams (Ossipee) and Janny Williams (Ossipee) (see preceding entry)

Woodbury M. of Ossipee m. Addie B. **Templeton** of Ossipee 3/11/1896 in Ossipee; H - 29, laborer, 2nd, b. Ossipee, s/o Alpheus Eldridge (Ossipee, farmer) and Dorothy Eldridge (housekeeper); W - 15, housekeeper, b. Ossipee, d/o Charles Templeton (Ossipee, farmer) and Roberline Templeton (housekeeper)

Woodbury M. of Ossipee m. Dora B. **White** of Ossipee 7/10/1898 in Ossipee; H - 31, farmer, 3rd, divorced, b. Ossipee, s/o Alpheus Eldridge (Ossipee, farmer) and Dorothy Eldridge (housewife); W - 16, maid, b. Ossipee, d/o William H. White (Ossipee, farmer) and Mary E. White (Ossipee, housewife)

ELEASON,
Philip of Brunswick, ME m. Imelda **Cloutier** of Portland, ME 6/30/1928 in Ossipee; H - 22, bookkeeper; W - 23, stenographer

ELLIOTT,
Charles L. m. Claire L. **Scungio** 11/5/1965 in Ctr. Ossipee; H - 38, polisher; W - 31, housewife
Harry Herman of Wolfeboro m. Catherine L. **Wiggin** of Ossipee 1/15/1939 in Rochester; H - 31, truck driver; W - 20, shoe operator
Thomas m. Barbara **Hilton** 12/22/1966 in Ctr. Ossipee; H - 19, Army; W - 18, none

ELLIS,
Edward Earl, II of Ctr. Ossipee m. Donna Marie **Grow** of Ctr. Ossipee 7/22/1995

ELWELL,
Royce E. of Bowdoinham, ME m. Ethel H. **Vaughan** of N. Yarmouth, ME 11/17/1937 in Moultonville; H - 35, laborer; W - 18, housework
William Berry of Ossipee m. Jennifer Lee **Strehlow** of Ossipee 2/23/2001

EMACK,
Lester E. of Effingham m. Erma M. **Gile** of Ossipee 3/31/1929 in Chocorua; H - 25, laborer; W - 24, stenographer
William H. m. Eva **Perkins** 1/29/1921 in Ossipee; H - 22, mechanic, b. Effingham, s/o Duncan Emack (timberman) and Grace Hussey (housewife); W - 30, housekeeper, 3rd, b. Parsonsfield, ME, d/o Charles Perkins (farmer) and Emma Eldridge (housewife)

EMANUS,
Shawn Michael of Effingham m. Billijo Frances **Mandile** of Effingham 6/4/2000

EMERSON,
Alan D. of Moultonboro m. Brenda E. **Eldridge** of Ctr. Ossipee 10/8/1960 in Ossipee; H - 17, student; W - 15, none
Everett C. of Ossipee m. Nettie M. **Bertwell** of Ossipee 6/3/1917 in Ossipee; H - 24, farmer, b. Effingham, s/o Amos W. Emerson (Effingham) and Nettie M. Clough (Ossipee); W - 38, housework, 2nd, b. Ossipee, d/o James Hanson (Ossipee) and Abbie Dore (Ossipee)
Levi W. of Ossipee m. Bernice **Hamm** of Ossipee 12/14/1918 in Ossipee; H - 18, section hand, b. Effingham, s/o Amos W. Emerson (Effingham) and Nettie Clough (Effingham); W - 22, housework, b. Ossipee, d/o Alpheus J. Hamm (Ossipee) and Mary Wentworth (Wakefield)
Ralph W. of Ossipee m. Shirley E. **Harmon** of Ctr. Ossipee 6/23/1956 in Laconia; H - 40, mechanic; W - 25, housekeeper

Ralph W. m. Mavis L. **Shannon** 7/29/1972 in Tuftonboro; H - b. 2/13/1916; W - b. 11/5/1932

EMERY,
Anthony D. of Ossipee m. Ina M. **Drew** of Tuftonboro 4/13/1902 in Tuftonboro; H - 32, farmer, b. Bartlett, s/o Stephen Emery (Bartlett, farmer) and Margaret Dana (Madison, housewife); W - 18, maid, b. Tuftonboro, d/o Freeman Drew (Tuftonboro, stone cutter) and Mary E. Quint (Freedom, housewife)
Cheston R. of Ossipee m. Cora **Hersey** of Tuftonboro 9/21/1902 in Wolfeboro; H - 34, laborer, b. Bartlett, s/o Stephen Emery (Bartlett, farmer) and Margaret Dana (Shapleigh, housewife); W - 33, maid, b. Tuftonboro, d/o Peter Hersey (carpenter) and Mary Weeks (Ossipee, housewife)
Louis M. of Ossipee m. Carrie L. **Clay** of Ossipee 1/1/1887 in Ctr. Ossipee; H - 23, laborer, b. Parsonsfield, ME, s/o Nicholas Emery (Tuftonboro) and Louisa F. (Ossipee); W - 21, seamstress, b. Ossipee, d/o Arthur Clay and Olive C. (Ossipee)
Walter G. of Cornish, ME m. Maud E. **Meserve** of Cornish, ME 8/1/1949 in Ctr. Ossipee; H - 51, farmer; W - 43, housekeeper

EMMONS,
Theodore E. m. Virginia L. **Eldridge** 9/14/1985; H - b. 9/2/1958; W - b. 10/14/1956

ENGSTROM,
Earl of Ossipee m. Albertta M. **Glidden** of Newfield, ME 12/22/1900 in Newfield, ME; H - 39, stonemason, b. Sweden, s/o Carl Engstrom (Sweden, carpenter) and Helena Engstrom (Sweden, housewife); W - 31, housemaid, 2nd, b. Saco, ME, d/o Samuel O. Moore (Brownfield, ME, farmer) and Lucy M. Moore (Limerick, ME, housewife)

ENLOE,
John Darrell m. Dorothy Ann **Ferreira** 5/25/1970 in Ossipee; H - b. 12/29/1947; W - b. 9/15/1947

ERICKSON,
Leigh Frederick m. Debbie Lee **Fisher** 7/29/1972 in Effingham; H - b. 8/12/1934; W - b. 9/28/1952

ERLANDER,
Carl Eric m. Pauline Burleigh **Reisfelder** 11/10/1990; H - b. 3/31/1914; W - b. 10/10/1909

ETTER,
Earl Francis of Ossipee m. Elizabeth K. **Trecarten** of Bartlett 4/7/1944 in Ctr. Ossipee; H - 37, printing foreman; W - 23, stenographer

EVANS,
Arthur W., III m. Carol **St. Onge** 10/10/1986; H - b. 4/26/1958; W - b. 11/6/1962
Elmer E., Jr. of Ossipee m. Jeanette B. **Kaminsky** of Ossipee 5/2/1946 in Wolfeboro; H - 19, B&M RR; W - 20, housewife
Frank E. of Portland, ME m. Evelyn **Dow** of Portland, ME 1/29/1928 in Tuftonboro; H - 29, painter; W - 32, nurse
Gordon B. of Tamworth m. Marilyn A. **Larrabee** of Tamworth 10/30/1953 in Wolfeboro; H - 23, truck driver; W - 20, mill worker

EVERITT,
Frederic Wallace of Glendale, CA m. Muria Eldridge **Nelson** of Glendale, CA 8/7/1999

EVITTS,
J. Earle of Ossipee m. Cherie L. **Lensky** of Ossipee 10/18/2001

FALL,
Ausbrey C. of Ossipee m. Mertie B. **Thompson** of Tuftonboro 5/24/1908 in Ossipee; H - 27, painter, b. Ossipee, s/o Plummer F. Fall (Ossipee); W - 24, teacher, b. Tuftonboro, d/o Theoda Thompson (Tuftonboro)
Chauncey C. of Ossipee m. Jennie M. **Thurley** of Ossipee 5/26/1904 in Ossipee; H - 28, laborer, b. Ossipee, s/o George C. Fall (Ossipee, laborer) and Louise C. Nutter (Ossipee, housewife); W - 27, housemaid, 2nd, b. Ossipee, d/o James M. Hilton (Ossipee, laborer) and Emma Chick (Ossipee, housewife)
Clinton H. of Ossipee m. Mildred W. **Price** of Ossipee 3/25/1914 in Ossipee; H - 25, b. Ossipee, s/o George C. Fall (Ossipee); W - 29, teacher, b. Ossipee, d/o John Price
Eli A. of Ossipee m. Cora V. **Moody** of Ossipee 12/26/1893 in Water Village; H - 24, farmer, b. Ossipee, s/o Frank Fall (Ossipee) and Emma (Ossipee); W - 17, b. Ossipee, d/o Alonzo Moody (Ossipee) and Viola (Ossipee)
Miner L. of Ossipee m. Mary E. **Caldwell** of Lee 12/10/1919 in Lee; H - 29, auto repairman, b. Ossipee, s/o George C. Fall (Ossipee) and Louise Nutter (Ossipee); W - 36, school teacher, b. Madbury, d/o William Caldwell (Barrington) and Martha A. Lane (Lee)
Raymond Ernest of Ossipee m. Blanche **Hubert** of Ossipee 12/30/1943 in Ossipee; H - 54, painter; W - 39, hostess

Virgil J. of Ossipee m. Leva M. **Piper** of Tuftonboro 3/24/1907 in Tuftonboro; H - 28, carpenter, b. Ossipee, s/o George C. Fall (Ossipee, boatbuilder) and Louise C. Nutter (Ossipee, housewife); W - 18, maid, b. Tuftonboro, d/o George A. Piper (Tuftonboro, farmer) and Etta Piper (Tuftonboro, housewife)

Willie H. of Ossipee m. Rose M. **Emery** of Ossipee 7/10/1898 in Ossipee; H - 24, farmer, b. Ossipee, s/o George C. Fall (Ossipee, farmer) and Louisa Fall (Ossipee, housewife); W - 18, maid, b. Ossipee, d/o Stephen Emery (Jackson, farmer) and Margaret Emery (Madison, housewife)

FALLER,
William Henry of Huntington, NY m. Dolores **Fletschinger** of New Orleans, LA 7/7/1943 in Ossipee; H - 27, US Coast Guard; W - 26, US Coast Guard

FALLON,
Frank J. of Boston, MA m. Astrid V. **Zinburg** of Boston, MA 9/24/1951 in Ossipee; H - 55, spts. comm.; W - 47, at home

FALLOWS,
Robert E. of Attleboro, MA m. Ann **Morse** of Attleboro, MA 9/10/1955 in Ossipee; H - 35, sprayer; W - 43, waitress

FALTER,
Richard P. of Oakland, ME m. Sharon **Duncan** of Oakland, ME 11/26/1963 in Ctr. Ossipee; H - 24, Navy; W - 18, none

FARINA,
Robert A. m. Tina G. **Carlson** 2/14/1987; H - b. 6/23/1967; W - b. 5/3/1968

Robert Author m. Hellen Margret **Stuart** 6/9/1990; H - b. 6/23/1967; W - b. 6/29/1965

FARIS,
Jeffrey James of Ossipee m. Melissa Lee **Mason** of Ossipee 9/23/1995

FARNHAM,
George A. of Ossipee m. Lilla M. **Plant** of Tamworth 10/13/1905 in Tamworth; H - 30, brakeman, b. Ossipee, s/o Eben C. Farnham (Wakefield) and Eunice Moody (Tamworth); W - 18, maid, b. Tamworth, d/o Joseph Plant and Nellie Plant

FEDCHENKO,
Ronald I. of Detroit, MI m. Jacqueline **Mitchell** of Sebago Lake, ME 6/12/1954 in Ossipee; H - 21, Coast Guard; W - 19, N.E. Tel. & Tel.

FEID,
Norman J. m. Barbara R. **Olsen** 4/1/1967 in Ctr. Ossipee; H - 45, jewelry; W - 39, housewife

FEINBERG,
Maurice of Dorchester, MA m. Ethel H. **Glassman** of Dorchester, MA 7/21/1942 in Ossipee; H - 33, general mgr.; W - 31, pianist

FENDERSON,
Robert E. of W. Ossipee m. Elizabeth M. **Eldridge** of Tamworth 2/1/1961 in Ctr. Ossipee; H - 21, mill work; W - 23, mill work

FERLAND,
George of Portland, ME m. Irene **Bergeron** of Kennebunkport, ME 5/7/1962 in Ctr. Ossipee; H - 33, sales; W - 32, waitress

FERNALD,
Frank A. of Ossipee m. Achsa E. **Hilton** of Ossipee 10/7/1899 in Effingham; H - 26, farmer, b. Ossipee, s/o Tobias Fernald (Ossipee, farmer) and Lavina Fernald (Ossipee, housewife); W - 20, maid, b. Ossipee, d/o James Hilton (Ossipee, farmer) and Emma Hilton (Ossipee, housewife)
Leon F. of Ctr. Ossipee m. Ethel M. **Bean** of Ctr. Ossipee 6/11/1934 in Farmington; H - 30, farmer; W - 29, housekeeper

FERRIS,
Bobby Dean of Ctr. Ossipee m. Paula Fay (Jalbert) **George** of Ctr. Ossipee 4/10/1994

FICKETT,
Daniel A. of Ossipee m. Helen M. **Nickerson** of Albany 3/2/1924 in Ossipee; H - 36, b. Standish, ME; W - 39, b. Albany

FIELDING,
Steven P. m. Sandra R. **Wojcik** 4/13/1991; H - b. 8/9/1950; W - b. 1/31/1959

FILES,
William E. of Gorham, ME m. Pauline M. **Brown** of Portland, ME 12/28/1963 in Ctr. Ossipee; H - 31, welder; W - 41, housework

FINBERG,
William of Windham, ME m. Mary **Herbert** of Windham, ME 5/4/1955 in Ossipee; H - 52, salesman; W - 42

FINN-O'NEIL,
James J. of Ctr. Ossipee m. Cheri Ann **Smith** of Ctr. Ossipee 9/16/1995

FISCHBEIN,
Daniel Walter m. Deborah May **Busch** 1/18/1975 in Ossipee; H - b. 8/30/1955; W - b. 8/5/1955

FISHER,
Harold J. m. Cheri A. **Yeaton** 10/24/1980 in Rochester; H - b. 10/24/1960; W - b. 2/7/1960
Phillip Edward m. Mary June **Dondero** 11/20/1971 in Ossipee; H - b. 10/15/1949; W - b. 6/20/1952
Rodney S. m. Kimberly A. **Harrison** 6/22/1991; H - b. 4/23/1954; W - b. 2/6/1961
Rodney Scott m. Debbie Lee **Eldridge** 9/2/1972 in Effingham; H - b. 8/23/1954; W - b. 8/23/1954
William R. m. Christine M. **Fall** 1/9/1970 in Ossipee; H - b. 5/18/1946; W - b. 12/17/1951

FISHMAN,
Barnett B. of Woburn, MA m. Charlotte G. **Booker** of Woburn, MA 10/22/1937 in Ctr. Ossipee; H - 36, insurance broker; W - 24, at home

FITCH,
Arthur R. of Claremont m. Francella W. **Baker** of W. Ossipee 10/28/1950 in Ctr. Ossipee; H - 19, carpenter; W - 22, artist

FITZPATRICK,
Daniel Joseph of Ctr. Ossipee m. Sibdou Alix Marie-Rachel **Kabore** of Ctr. Ossipee 10/16/1999

FITZSIMMONS,
Henry T. m. Sandra J. **Doe** 9/25/1965 in W. Ossipee; H - 25, butcher; W - 19, office
James W. of W. Ossipee m. Charlotte S. **Knox** of Ossipee 6/22/1957 in Ossipee; H - 39, minister; W - 31, student

FLANAGAN,
Paul of Tamworth m. Hilda **Colby** of Ctr. Ossipee 5/5/1936 in Ossipee; H - 26, waiter; W - 17, unemployed
Paul A. of Ctr. Ossipee m. Irene B. **Gagne** of Conway 1/24/1954 in Conway; H - 44, finisher; W - 25, sander

FLANDERS,
Donald Warren, Jr. of Ctr. Ossipee m. Tressa Jean **Custeau** of Ctr. Ossipee 2/14/1995

FLEMING,
Floyd E. of Ossipee m. Dorothy A. **Brown** of Rochester 4/29/1950 in Rochester; H - 20, mechanic; W - 19, shoe op.

FLETCHER,
James E. m. Jill E. **Nystedt** 8/22/1981 in Ossipee; H - b. 7/31/1960; W - b. 12/14/1962

FLORIA,
Ralph D. m. Marcia A. **Dale** 6/24/1972 in Ossipee; H - b. 4/23/1951; W - b. 3/7/1953

FOGARTY,
John Edward, IV of Ctr. Ossipee m. Juliann Marie **Demers** of Ctr. Ossipee 9/19/1998
Thomas W. m. Holly J. **Flynn** 3/8/1986; H - b. 5/17/1966; W - b. 8/14/1967

FOGG,
George W. of Ossipee m. Carrie B. **Garland** of Wakefield 6/9/1908 in Wakefield; H - 42, farmer, b. Ossipee, s/o Simon Fogg (Ossipee); W - 27, teacher, b. Wakefield, d/o Albert F. Garland (Wakefield)
Michael m. Susan A. **Hayden** 10/3/1969 in Wakefield; H - b. 1/30/1947; W - b. 9/20/1949

FOLLANSBEE,
Joseph A. of W. Ossipee m. Sarah G. **Elliott** of W. Ossipee 7/4/1999

FOLSOM,
John of Ossipee m. Abbie **Sceggel** of Ossipee 12/9/1890 in Ossipee; H - 40, farmer, b. Ossipee, s/o Erastus C. Folsom (Ossipee, farmer); W - 50, housekeeper, b. Ossipee, d/o Moses Nichols
John of Ossipee m. Agnes C. **Ellis** of Providence, RI 11/20/1911 in Ossipee; H - 66, farmer, 2nd, widower, b. Ossipee, s/o Rastus Folsom

(farmer); W - 54, housewife, 2nd, divorced, b. NS, d/o James Russell (deceased)

FONTAINE,
Richard M. Diane **Wood** 12/23/1964 in Ctr. Ossipee; H - 20, pressworker; W - 18, none

FORBES,
Francis of Lynn, MA m. Janet L. **Moody** of Winchester, MA 6/19/1933 in Ossipee; H - 21, painter; W - 19, at home

FORD,
David Brian of Ossipee m. Kathie Mary **Celli** of Ossipee 5/28/1997
Glenn C. of Marshfield, MA m. Shirley M. **Tingley** of Marshfield, MA 5/15/1952 in Ctr. Ossipee; H - 20, laborer; W - 19, at home
Walter J. of Duxbury, MA m. Thelma P. **Garnett** of Brockton, MA 12/1/1953 in Ctr. Ossipee; H - 23, Coast Guard; W - 20, factory

FORSYTHE,
Edwin B., Jr. m. Vicki **Stone** 5/31/1975 in Tamworth; H - b. 6/24/1949; W - b. 9/24/1954

FORTIER,
Albert J. of Ossipee m. Nellie M. **Hobbs** of Tamworth 4/13/1908 in Tamworth; H - 22, teamster, b. Ossipee, s/o Charles S. Fortier (Canada); W - 16, b. Albany, d/o David B. Hobbs (Albany)
William M. of Ossipee m. Helen M. **Ouellette** of Berwick, ME 7/5/1909 in Somersworth; H - 28, laborer, b. Ossipee, s/o Charles S. Fortier (Canada, laborer); W - 25, domestic, b. Canada, d/o Thomas Ouellette (Canada, farmer)

FORTUNE,
Aubra Lain of Memphis, TN m. Rita Meleda **Banfill** of Ossipee 3/26/1953 in Tokyo, Japan; H - 23, Air Force; W - 22, Air Force

FOSS,
Charles L. of Ossipee m. Grace **Townes** of Gonic 7/3/1897 in Ossipee; H - 19, farmer, b. Fryeburg, s/o Delius Foss (Rochester, farmer) and Oraliz Hamlinton (Conway, housekeeper); W - 17, housemaid, b. Weare, d/o Henry Townes (deceased)
Clarence E. of Ossipee m. Minnie **Stewart** of Dover 7/28/1909 in Dover; H - 25, laborer, b. Cornish, ME, s/o Moses W. Foss (Cornish, ME, laborer); W - 18, dressmaker, b. Cornish, ME, d/o Henry Stewart (Cornish, ME, laborer)

Edward P. of Ctr. Ossipee m. Sadie E. (Drew) **Froton** of Ctr. Ossipee 10/23/1996

FOSTER,
Clyde W. of S. Berwick, ME m. Sharon L. **Brackett** of S. Berwick, ME 5/6/1960 in Ctr. Ossipee; H - 20, farm; W - 18, none

FOURNIER,
Michael A. of W. Ossipee m. Pamela J. **Miller** of W. Ossipee 10/24/1998

FOX,
Earle K. of Ossipee m. Phyllis M. **Zimmerman** of Waltham, MA 7/31/1949 in W. Ossipee; H - 46, accountant; W - 37, secretary

FRASER,
Reginald E. of S. Portland, ME m. Wanda F. **Christensen** of Westbrook, ME 2/12/1955 in Ctr. Ossipee; H - 22, mill worker; W - 19, student

FRAZIER,
Thomas L. of N. Attleboro, MA m. Anita A. **Perry** of Attleboro, MA 3/20/1960 in Ctr. Ossipee; H - 25, laborer; W - 20, none

FREDETTE,
Andrew m. Winifred M. **Kmiec** 7/3/1965 in Ctr. Ossipee; H - 34, carpenter; W - 39, none

FREEMAN,
Edwin H. m. Pamela V. **Johnson** 10/23/1971 in Ossipee; H - b. 12/4/1929; W - b. 9/17/1935
George A. of Meredith m. Adelia K. **Nickerson** of Ctr. Ossipee 2/8/1936 in Laconia; H - 24, painter; W - 19, waitress
Norman R., Jr. m. Revel **Paul** 9/17/1977 in Ossipee; H - b. 5/2/1952; W - b. 1/22/1952

FRENCH,
Lewis L., Jr. m. Ida M. **Wiggin** 7/11/1969 in Ctr. Ossipee; H - b. 10/5/1929; W - 3/27/1923

FRENIER,
William of Seekonk, MA m. Virginia **Pierce** of Attleboro, MA 8/13/1958 in Ossipee; H - 19, service; W - 18, student
William F. of Pawtucket, RI m. Nancy A. **Conroy** of S. Attleboro, MA 3/31/1961 in Ctr. Ossipee; H - 22, assembler; W - 21, secretary

FROST,
Arthur W. of S. Miami, FL m. Alice A. **Stewart** of Marblehead, MA 10/8/1930 in Ossipee; H - 41, master plumber; W - 46, candy business
Edwin Carl, Jr. m. Rosalie May **Stanley** 5/16/1975 in Tuftonboro; H - b. 5/17/1951; W - b. 1/19/1953

FROTON,
Wilfred W. m. Sadie E. **Loring** 1/21/1977 in Ossipee; H - b. 2/13/1911; W - b. 3/2/1923

FUENTES,
Edwin of Willimantic, CT m. Jennifer M. **Daley** of Ossipee 4/3/1998

FULLERTON,
Peter Earl m. Susan **Dale** 7/19/1975 in Ossipee; H - b. 11/22/1956; W - b. 7/18/1957
Wayne Ryder m. Theresa L. **Cotton** 12/19/1970 in Ossipee; H - b. 2/24/1951; W - b. 11/3/1951

FURBUSH,
Perry Stanley of Palmyra, ME m. Marion **Thorne** of St. Albans, ME 8/1/1937 in Ctr. Ossipee; H - 25, lawyer; W - 21, school teacher

FURLONG,
Edward Charles, III of Bartlett m. Cheryl A. Feener **Riley** of Ossipee 9/8/1998

FURTADO,
Arthur m. Laurinda **Kirkwood** 6/7/1964 in Conway; H - 19, Navy; W - 19, none
Donald m. Clareen **Pearson** 5/2/1966 in Ctr. Ossipee; H - 22, US Air Force; W - 18, clerk

GAGNE,
Alfred J. of Ossipee m. Frances May **Abbott** of Ossipee 11/18/1945 in Freedom; H - 25, US Army; W - 19, at home
Ernest A. m. Bonnie L. **Ridlon** 4/6/1974 in Wolfeboro; H - b. 4/23/1951; W - b. 12/31/1955
Peter Allen m. Mary Louise **Durgin** 1/27/1973 in Wolfeboro; H - b. 9/29/1946; W - b. 6/25/1948

GAGNI,
Richard H. of Wolfeboro m. Margery K. **ter Weele** of Ctr. Ossipee 8/29/1959 in Ctr. Ossipee; H - 29, teacher; W - 19, student

GAGNON,
Gary Allen, Jr. of Ossipee m. Jessica M. **Van Dyke** of Ossipee 8/9/1997

GALE,
Leonard W. m. Janet L. **Howard** 8/26/1989; H - b. 10/29/1944; W - b. 12/24/1955
Leonard William of Ossipee m. Lesley E. C. **Jorgenson** of Ossipee 1/1/2000
Robert Jay of W. Ossipee m. Beth Ellen **Floria** of W. Ossipee 3/4/2000

GALLAGHER,
Keith William of Ossipee m. Theresa Stella **Goldsmith** of Ossipee 5/10/1941 in Ossipee; H - 18, laborer; W - 16, at home

GALLANT,
Thomas Reed of Ctr. Ossipee m. Meg Alissa **Grant** of Ctr. Ossipee 10/31/1998

GALPIN,
Louis P. of Ossipee m. Annie **Wentworth** of Ossipee 8/3/1901 in Effingham; H - 21, electrician, b. Waterbury, CT, s/o Leslie Galpin (Woodbury, CT, plater) and Mary Christopher (Torrington, CT, housewife); W - 20, maid, b. Ossipee, d/o George E. Wentworth (Wakefield, farmer) and Susan Wentworth (Portland, ME, housewife)

GARDNER,
Arthur of Ossipee m. Nellie A. **Beacham** of Ossipee 5/17/1924 in Wolfeboro; H - 50, b. Canada; W - 49, b. Ossipee

GARIEPY,
Robert m. Patricia **Wilkins** 10/5/1964 in Ossipee; H - 40, landscaper; W - 30, enamel work
Robert A. of Attleboro, MA m. Patricia A. **Wilkins** of Attleboro, MA 7/26/1963 in Ctr. Ossipee; H - 39, landscaper; W - 29, clerk

GARLAND,
Carlton M. of Standish, ME m. Blanche E. **Dyer** of Standish, ME 12/15/1950 in Ctr. Ossipee; H - 33, woodsman; W - 26, at home
Sumner G. of Ossipee m. Bertha E. **Chick** of Effingham 6/4/1901 in Moultonville; H - 50, hotel keeper, 2nd, b. Ossipee, s/o John R.

Garland (Wakefield, farmer) and Hannah F. Garland (Effingham); W - 31, table girl, b. Effingham, d/o J. W. Chick (Effingham, carpenter) and Amanda Chick (Effingham, housewife)

GARLOUGH,
Keith Edward m. Laura Ann **Cook** 8/8/1989; H - b. 9/14/1964; W - b. 7/23/1962

GAUTHIER,
Robert W. of Somerville, MA m. Rosemary **Cooney** of Somerville, MA 8/29/1953 in Ctr. Ossipee; H - 21, machinist; W - 17, clerical worker
Stephen M. m. Raeline **Hamel** 8/30/1985; H - b. 12/5/1961; W - b. 12/12/1962

GAUTREAU,
Scott A. m. Barbara Helen **Whiting** 9/25/1976 in Ossipee; H - b. 2/17/1957; W - b. 8/31/1958

GAUVREAU,
Jon Paul of Tamworth m. Stacy Lynn **Libby** of Tamworth 10/28/2000

GAY,
Ebenezer R. m. Winifred L. **Helfrick** 10/13/1979 in Ossipee; H - b. 2/11/1957; W - b. 9/6/1956

GEAR,
Patrick J., III m. Alicia **Trace** 9/9/1989; H - b. 5/25/1955; W - b. 7/1/1947

GENTHNER,
Frank of Ossipee m. Sarah M. E. **French** of Ossipee 7/10/1913 in Ossipee; H - 22, laborer, b. Rochester, NY, s/o Charles Genthner (Germany); W - 16, at home, b. Dover, d/o Eben French (Exeter)

GETCHELL,
Ralph A. of Cape Elizabeth, ME m. Louise K. **Arnold** of Portland, ME 6/1/1956 in Ossipee; H - 57, surgeon; W - 39, secretary

GETSON,
Donald A. m. Penny Lynn **White** 6/3/1989; H - b. 1/28/1960; W - b. 9/28/1961

GIARDINI,
John E. of Boston, MA m. Nora C. **Searson** of Boston, MA 3/5/1946 in Ossipee; H - 36, room waiter; W - 32, at home

GIBLIN,
Alfred N. of Concord m. Mary K. **Ross** of Ossipee 7/20/1946 in Seabrook; H - 32, salesman; W - 25, at home

GIBSON,
Albert E. of Ossipee m. Mary **Bickford** of Tuftonboro 4/20/1894 in Ossipee; H - 34, farmer, 2nd, widower, b. Chelsea, MA, s/o F. M. Gibson (Eastport, ME, farmer) and Julia A. Wentworth (Wakefield, housewife); W - 31, school teacher, b. Tuftonboro, d/o Isaac C. Bickford (Tuftonboro, farmer) and Deborah Bean (Tuftonboro, housekeeper)
William H., III m. Jill A. **Daley** 8/16/1986; H - b. 8/8/1965; W - b. 10/12/1961

GILBERT,
Francis A. m. Debra L. **Bodwell** 6/24/1982 in Ossipee; H - b. 5/28/1942; W - b. 4/4/1956

GILLIAM,
Raymond J. of Denton, TX m. Barbara J. **Talley** of Auburn, ME 1/19/1963 in Ctr. Ossipee; H - 29, USN; W - 29, housewife

GILMAN,
Edwin F. of Tamworth m. Arlene **Littlefield** of Ossipee 7/10/1943 in Ctr. Ossipee; H - 33, railroad; W - 24, at home
John B. of Ossipee m. Maude E. **Mansur** of Wakefield 12/31/1895 in Ossipee; H - 26, shoemaker, 3rd, b. Ossipee, s/o Israel H. Gilman (Ossipee, farmer) and Mary E. Gilman (Ossipee, housewife); W - 20, housewife, 2nd, b. Wakefield, d/o Herbert S. Mansur (Boston, clergyman) and Lizzie L. Mansur (Wakefield, housewife)

GILPATRICK,
Leon W. of S. Hiram, ME m. Lillian F. **Wasson** of Ctr. Ossipee 6/22/1947 in Moultonville; H - 26, game warden; W - 26, clerk

GLADU,
Richard Clifford of Ossipee m. Laurel Louise (Brown) **Deshaies** of Freedom 5/4/1996
Valmur J. of Lowell, MA m. Mildred L. **Bean** of S. Chelmsford, MA 9/20/1945 in Ossipee; H - 41, discharged vet.; W - 41, insurance agent

GLICK,
Michael J. m. Victoria C. **Nass** 12/6/1980 in Portsmouth; H - b. 9/25/1935; W - b. 10/31/1950

GLIDDEN,
Harley of Ossipee m. Viola **Nichols** of Ossipee 9/15/1927 in Ossipee; H - 19, chauffeur; W - 21, at home
John B. of Ossipee m. Amelia **Stokes** of Ossipee 9/24/1905 in Ossipee; H - 70, farmer, 2nd, b. Effingham, s/o Jerry Glidden (Effingham, farmer) and Betsey Clay (Ossipee, housewife); W - 41, housewife, 2nd, b. Ossipee, d/o Daniel McKenney and Maria Noris (Ossipee)
Robert J. of Wolfeboro m. Jessica Marie **Short** of Ossipee 3/28/1998

GOBEILLE,
William J. m. Bonnie W. **Foley** 8/4/1979 in Ossipee; H - b. 7/28/1937; W - b. 3/6/1945

GOLDEN,
Mark S. m. Jill S. **Charmey** 9/8/1985; H - b. 8/31/1951; W - b. 3/14/1954

GOLDSMITH,
Chester O. of Ossipee m. Stella **Evans** of Wolfeboro 8/31/1924 in Ossipee; H - 23, b. Ossipee; W - 20, b. Wakefield

GOLDTHWAITE,
Keith C. m. Rachelle A. **Hamel** 12/14/1985; H - b. 3/19/1962; W - b. 5/20/1967
Keith Charles m. Laura Marie **Pierni** 9/2/1993 in Madison

GOMES,
Antonio A. m. Carol A. **Leavitt** 11/11/1984; H - b. 10/16/1930; W - b. 6/20/1942

GONYER,
Lewis Eugene of Lancaster m. Nancy J. **Downs** of Ossipee 10/17/1952 in Ctr. Ossipee; H - 24, tree surgeon; W - 17, at home
Thomas Standley of Ctr. Ossipee m. Anstress J. D. **Robinson** of Ctr. Ossipee 7/1/2000

GOODALE,
David m. Leoine **Woodworth** 3/21/1964 in W. Ossipee; H - 51, innkeeper; W - 54, home
David W. m. Mary K. **Bridges** 12/15/1974 in Wakefield; H - b. 9/30/1912; W - b. 5/15/1932

GOODRICH,
Lyman H. of E. Haven, CT m. Edna I. **Reilly** of E. Haven, CT 5/28/1952 in Ctr. Ossipee; H - 68, secretary; W - 50, housekeeper

GOODWIN,
Harold Thomas m. Gina Loreen **Hebert** 2/4/1989; H - b. 1/31/1967; W - b. 7/8/1969

Haven K. m. Anita **Littlefield** 12/–/1972 in Ossipee; H - b. 5/15/1909; W - b. 10/17/1928

John F. of Ossipee m. Bertha **Merrow** of Ossipee 4/21/1898 in Effingham; H - 20, laborer, b. Freedom, s/o Thomas Goodwin (Brownfield, ME, laborer) and Naomi Goodwin (Eaton, housewife); W - 16, maid, b. Ossipee, d/o Daniel W. Merrow (Ossipee, farmer) and Ella Sillsbury (Aurora, ME, housewife)

John F. of Ossipee m. Eva L. **Rattee** of Tamworth 6/16/1903 in Ctr. Ossipee; H - 25, laborer, 2nd, b. Freedom, s/o Thomas Goodwin (Brownfield, ME, soldier) and Naomi Durgin (Eaton, housewife); W - 18, maid, b. Canada, d/o Philip Rattee (Canada, laborer) and Harriet Lamontagne (Canada, housewife)

Thomas of Ossipee m. Naomi **Durgin** of Eaton 4/7/1892 in Ossipee; H - 52, laborer, 2nd, b. Brownfield, ME, s/o Franklin Goodwin (Brownfield, ME) and Abagail Goodwin (Brownfield, ME); W - 34, housekeeper, b. Eaton, d/o Joel Durgin (Eaton) and Margaret Durgin (Eaton, housekeeper)

GOOGOO,
William J. of Ctr. Ossipee m. Muriel A. **Nichols** of Ctr. Ossipee 10/10/1953 in Ctr. Ossipee; H - 31, mill work; W - 18, at home

GORDON,
Peter N. m. Gail S. **Loring** 5/1/1965 in Ossipee; H - 27, salesman; W - 20, secretary

GOSSILIN,
Peter W. of Waltham, MA m. Marjorie **Labor** of Ctr. Ossipee 6/14/1958 in Ossipee; H - 24, laborer; W - 16, school

GOUDEAU,
Ernest E. of Lynn, MA m. Virginia E. **Farley** of Lynn, MA 1/22/1938 in Ossipee; H - 29, salesman; W - 22, shoe worker

GOUIN,
Thornton of Wolfeboro m. Leona **Libby** of Ossipee 6/15/1929 in Ctr. Ossipee; H - 18, millman; W - 16, at home

GOULD,
Lebias R. of Ctr. Tuftonboro m. Barbara J. **Nickerson** of Ossipee 12/31/1949 in Wolfeboro Ctr.; H - 59, wool carder; W - 31, housewife
LeRoy H. of Charlestown, MA m. Eleanor R. **McCarthy** of Charlestown, MA 6/23/1955 in Ctr. Ossipee; H - 42, male nurse; W - 30

GOUMAS,
Timothy J. of Ctr. Ossipee m. Holly Marie **Roberts** of Ctr. Ossipee 10/15/1994

GOVE,
Ralph of Seabrook m. Mary **Spacil** of Newbury, MA 9/7/1952 in Stratham; H - 59, toll collector; W - 56, nurse

GRAHAM,
Richard A., III m. Amanda J. **Chase** 5/31/1986; H - b. 7/3/1958; W - b. 8/12/1963

GRANT,
Henry of Ossipee m. Ruth H. **Hitchcock** of Ossipee 11/7/1930 in Wolfeboro; H - 32, laborer; W - 17, at home
John H. of Ossipee m. Nellie **Carver** of Ossipee 7/2/1887 in Ossipee; H - 22, laborer, b. Berwick, ME; W - 16, housekeeper, b. Ossipee
Kenneth Wilson, Jr. of Ctr. Ossipee m. Ruth Madeliene **Leonard** of Ctr. Ossipee 6/6/1999
Shawn W. of Ctr. Ossipee m. Amy Lynn **Blaine** of Ctr. Ossipee 6/23/2000
Steven D. of Ctr. Ossipee m. Brindall A. **Libby** of Ctr. Ossipee 5/7/1999

GRAVES,
Edward H. of Burlington, MA m. Catherine **Kozachuk** of Burlington, MA 4/2/1954 in Ctr. Ossipee; H - 21, truck driver; W - 16

GRAY,
Donald P. m. Debora **Connor** 12/29/1979 in Tamworth; H - b. 5/2/1959; W - b. 4/21/1961
Douglas A. of Moultonboro m. Elvida B. **Greene** of Ossipee 8/17/1961 in Ossipee; H - 36, none; W - 35, nurse
Edwin John of Rochester m. Ethel Frances **Libby** of Rochester 2/17/1945 in Ossipee; H - 23, woodsman; W - 14, at home
Ivan Ernest, Jr. m. Devra Jean **O'Brien** 11/2/1991; H - b. 1/10/1943; W - b. 10/9/1952
Leslie Austin m. Laura Ann **LeMarche** 5/16/1992 in Wolfeboro

GREEN,
Douglas Mark m. Lauri Sue **Eldridge** 4/27/1991; H - b. 1/12/1959; W - b. 2/11/1969

GREENE,
Clyde F. of VT m. Lorita L. **Hamilton** of Fryeburg, ME 9/29/1951 in Ctr. Ossipee; H - 22, railroad; W - 18, at home

GREENLAW,
Mervyn of S. Portland, ME m. Geraldine **Greenlaw** of S. Portland, ME 12/9/1958 in Ossipee; H - 35, R.R.; W - 29, none

GREGOIRE,
Wayne E. of Ossipee m. Roxanne S. **Dick** of Ossipee 11/18/2000

GREGORIO,
Ralph V. m. Nan S. **Kolzen** 6/11/1983 in Ossipee; H - b. 10/8/1946; W - b. 5/8/1946

GRIDLEY,
Edward P. of Wolfeboro m. Lillian M. **Melanson** of Ossipee 9/15/1935 in Pittsfield; H - 24, caretaker; W - 17, school

GRIFFIN,
Henry A., Jr. of Scarborough, ME m. Beatrice E. **Castelluzzo** of Portland, ME 7/22/1961 in Ossipee; H - 40, electrician; W - 40, secretary
James Michael of Ctr. Ossipee m. Tanya Theresa **Skamarycz** of Ctr. Ossipee 4/9/1999
Paul Vincent of Ctr. Ossipee m. Wendy Elizabeth **Larock** of Ctr. Ossipee 9/23/1997

GRINNELL,
Collin M. m. Tracy E. **Brackett** 8/22/1988; H - b. 10/28/1970; W - b. 5/20/1967

GUARINO,
Robert J. m. Marianne **Daniels** 5/23/1983 in Ossipee; H - b. 9/9/1954; W - b. 2/22/1957

GUL,
Kenneth A. of E. Machias, ME m. Lida **Foss** of E. Machias, ME 11/22/1954 in Ctr. Ossipee; H - 45, state worker; W - 50, motel manager

GUNZEL,
William Skot m. Margery Ethel **Downs** 12/31/1971 in Ossipee; H - b. 10/27/1925; W - b. 9/11/1925

GUPTILL,
Samuel of Ctr. Ossipee m. Marcia G. **Linscott** of Norway, ME 8/1/1936 in Ossipee; H - 39, engineer; W - 37, stitcher

GURLEY,
Fred Arthur, Jr. of Ctr. Ossipee m. Cristin Joy **Harkins** of Ctr. Ossipee 1/1/2000

GUSHA,
Johnathan L. m. Lynne A. **Nelson** 12/18/1982 in Effingham; H - b. 6/11/1963; W - b. 4/12/1961

GUSTAFSON,
Donald R., Jr. m. Sheryl A. **Curtis** 1/16/1987; H - b. 9/16/1957; W - b. 2/5/1966

GUSTAVSON,
F. Gunnar m. Helen **Ebert** 5/18/1967 in Ossipee; H - 68, none; W - 70, none

GUYOTTE,
Alan L. m. Carole A. **Peavey** 4/16/1983 in Ossipee; H - b. 9/35/1951 (sic); W - b. 6/23/1943
Albert F., Jr. m. Cindy L. **Fulcher** 3/16/1983 in Laconia; H - b. 6/21/1959; W - b. 7/8/1955

HACKBARTH,
Frank L. of Brunswick, ME m. Becky Sue **LeCansky** of Auburn, ME 5/22/1956 in Ctr. Ossipee; H - 20, Navy; W - 20, tel. operator

HAGGART,
Lorin Frederick of Ossipee m. Barbara Elizabeth **Pattee** of Plymouth 8/19/1940 in Berlin; H - 27, store manager; W - 21, teacher

HAKALA,
Steven M. m. Teresa A. **Barber** 10/28/1983 in Ossipee; H - b. 6/4/1955; W - b. 4/15/1961

HALE,
Fred A. of Lebanon m. Emily P. **Libby** of Lebanon 2/17/1917 in Ossipee; H - 22, weaver, 2nd, b. Kezar Falls, s/o John W. Hale (Lebanon, ME) and Elvira Thurston (Eaton); W - 19, spooling, b. Lebanon, ME, d/o John Libby (Rochester) and Ida Boyson (Cambridge)

HALEPIS,
Andrew Manuel m. Cheryl Adeline **Riley** 5/1/1976 in Ossipee; H - b. 11/30/1944; W - b. 7/11/1947

HALL,
David C. m. Lisa M. **Taylor** 8/31/1985; H - b. 9/3/1958; W - b. 3/28/1963
Edward J. m. Audrey B. **Hall** 8/20/1984; H - b. 10/28/1909; W - b. 3/21/1912
Herbert E. of Ctr. Ossipee m. Natalie **Vittum** of Ctr. Ossipee 12/13/1956 in Moultonville; H - 20, mill worker; W - 19, secretary
Linwood W. of Bangor, ME m. Phyllis M. **Ames** of Bangor, ME 6/24/1955 in Ctr. Ossipee; H - 22, serviceman; W - 18
Ronald of Pawtucket, RI m. Jeanette **Mailhot** of Pawtucket, RI 3/10/1959 in Ctr. Ossipee; H - 21, weaver; W - 19, none

HALLETT,
Spurge m. Agnes **Ward** 6/19/1965 in Ctr. Ossipee; H - 44, carpenter; W - 55, housewife

HALLOWAY,
Alan O. of Ann Arbor, MI m. Joan A. **Midriff** of Ann Arbor, MI 8/19/1954 in Ossipee; H - 23, machinist helper; W - 21

HALLOWELL,
Ralph E. of Cumberland Mills m. Stella **Barrett** of N. Walpole 2/5/1938 in Ossipee; H - 24, laborer; W - 18, at home

HAMBERGER,
Charles m. Barbara **Janowski** 2/7/1965 in W. Ossipee; H - 19, Army; W - 18, keypunch operator

HAMEL,
William J. of Ctr. Ossipee m. Paula J. **Vittum** of Ctr. Ossipee 6/23/1961 in Ctr. Ossipee; H - 22, steelworker; W - 17, none

HAMILTON,
Charles E., Jr. of S. Portland, ME m. Elaine R. **Raymond** of Ossipee 11/4/1954 in Ctr. Ossipee; H - 23, serviceman; W - 22, salesgirl

HAMM,
Sidney W. of Ossipee m. Edith M. **Jenkins** of Durham 12/15/1914 in Dover; H - 19, b. Ossipee, s/o A. Judson Hamm (Ossipee); W - 19, bookkeeper, b. Durham, d/o Fred E. Jenkins
William B. of Ossipee m. Mabel D. **Mitchell** of Wakefield 2/25/1891 in Ossipee; H - 24, carpenter, b. Ossipee, s/o Hiram Hamm and Mary D.; W - 27, teacher, b. Wakefield, d/o J. R. Mitchell (Middletown) and Harriett L. (Otisfield)

HAMMOND,
Allen D. of Natick, MA m. Barbara L. **Goodrich** of Ossipee 5/12/1951 in Conway; H - 54, insurance; W - 49, at home
Daniel of Ossipee m. Julia M. **Curtis** of Richmond, ME 10/3/1928 in Ossipee; H - 72, farmer; W - 57, housekeeper
George L. of Somersworth m. Annie G. **Stadley** of Somersworth 7/25/1906 in Ossipee; H - 30, salesman, b. Somersworth, s/o Nathan W. Hammond (Berwick, ME, painter) and Rilla Cater (Berwick, ME, housekeeper); W - 23, saleslady, b. Braintree, d/o Edwin B. Stadley (Wells, ME, hotelkeeper) and Mary E. Avery (Wells, ME, housewife)
George R. of Tamworth m. Frances M. **Thurston** of Ctr. Ossipee 10/1/1955 in Ctr. Ossipee; H - 23, truck driver; W - 18, at home
Howard of Ossipee m. Erdine **Eldridge** of Ossipee 4/18/1908 in Ossipee; H - 20, millman, b. Ossipee, s/o Daniel Hammond (Ossipee); W - 17, b. Ossipee, d/o David Eldridge (Ossipee)
Jeffrey David m. Stora Lee **Montgomery** 12/28/1991; H - b. 9/22/1965; W - b. 6/28/1966
Lester of Ossipee m. Mary **Perkins** of Tamworth 11/11/1912 in Ossipee; H - 29, laborer, b. Ossipee, s/o Daniel Hammond (Ossipee); W - 16, housemaid, b. Tamworth, d/o Hiram Perkins (Moultonborough)
Robert J. m. Karen L. **Thompson** 9/9/1989; H - b. 1/9/1945; W - b. 10/4/1964
Walter W. of Ossipee m. Sylvia A. **Cook** of Ossipee 2/28/1927 in Ossipee; H - 32, laborer; W - 39, housekeeper

HAMMONS,
Norris A. of Hallowell, ME m. Gladys B. **Nichols** of Hallowell, ME 7/31/1953 in Ctr. Ossipee; H - 51, salesman; W - 56, bookkeeper

HANER,
Charles E. m. Irene M. **Cowan** 7/1/1972 in Ossipee; H - b. 12/15/1918; W - b. 4/22/1923

HANEY,
Glenn A. of Wallingford, CT m. Marilyn M. **Kelley** of Ctr. Ossipee 9/2/1961 in Wallingford, CT; H - 28, factory worker; W - 26, manager
Keith Douglas m. Eva Marie **O'Grady** 6/18/1977 in Wolfeboro; H - b. 3/9/1954; W - b. 4/8/1955

HANNAH,
Arthur James of Malden, MA m. Diane Ruth **Adams** of Malden, MA 8/16/1997

HANSCOM,
Michael Paul of Wakefield m. Naomi Marion **Woodbury** of Ossipee 3/20/1999

HANSEN,
Neal M. m. Terry L. **Ruland** 8/17/1989; H - b. 7/12/1943; W - b. 11/12/1958
Neil Eric of Westbrook, CT m. Krisha Ann **Fowler** of Westbrook, CT 9/6/1998
Walter C. of Eltingville, NY m. Carol L. **Hubbard** of Mapleton, ME 8/21/1963 in Ctr. Ossipee; H - 20, USAF; W - 19, none

HANSON,
Brian M. m. Pamela Jean **Evans** 6/26/1982 in Ossipee; H - b. 2/3/1955; W - b. 11/28/1956
Hodge Jackson m. Constance Ruggli **Hanson** 6/23/1988; H - b. 10/25/1904; W - b. 12/19/1907
Jacob of Wolfeboro m. Emma F. **Brown** of Ossipee 11/25/1890 in Ossipee; H - farmer, b. Wolfeboro; W - housekeeper, b. Ossipee, d/o James L. Brown (Ossipee, farmer)
Jeremiah of Ossipee m. Lucy L. **Wyman** 2/5/1887 in Ctr. Ossipee
John of Ossipee m. Eunice **Currier** of Ossipee 5/18/1903 in Ossipee; H - 58, farmer, 2nd, b. Ossipee, s/o Stacy D. Hanson (Ossipee, farmer) and Adeline Wood (Ossipee, housekeeper); W - 54, housekeeper, 3rd, b. Ossipee, d/o Jonas Kimball (Ossipee, farmer) and ----- Lear (Ossipee, housekeeper)
Kenneth R. of Ossipee m. Irene E. **Wilkins** of Ctr. Ossipee 5/8/1954 in Ctr. Ossipee; H - 28, truck driver; W - 21, office work
Lewis M. m. Karen **Canney** 3/7/1915 in Ossipee; H - 25, farmer, b. Ossipee, s/o James W. Hanson (Ossipee); W - 22, b. Ossipee, d/o Fred M. Canney

HARBISON,
Cameron C. m. Nancy L. **Bruning** 4/7/1981 in Ossipee; H - b. 4/5/1958; W - b. 8/22/1960
Lance G. m. Cindy Lee **Grames** 4/21/1984; H - b. 9/13/1956; W - b. 5/23/1962
Lance G. of W. Ossipee m. Betty A. **Eldridge** of W. Ossipee 3/5/1994

HARDEN,
Neal C. of Ossipee m. Ida M. **Cobb** of Ossipee 11/18/1919 in Ossipee; H - 41, electrician, b. Kennebunk, ME, s/o Ensworth Harden (Bethel, ME) and Abbie F. Brown (Aetna, ME); W - 43, housewife, b. Farmington, d/o George A. Colomy (Farmington) and Belle Jones (Farmington)

HARDING,
Howard P. of Ossipee m. Cora L. **Saunders** of Ossipee 3/17/1897 in Ossipee; H - 23, teacher, b. Baldwin, ME, s/o Joshua Harding (Baldwin, ME, farmer) and Sarah Huntress (Baldwin, ME, housekeeper); W - 30, housekeeper, b. Ossipee, d/o Daniel Sanders (sic) (Ossipee, farmer) and Eliza Hanscom (Ossipee, housekeeper)

HARDWICK,
Frederick W. of Jamaica Plain, MA m. Marie A. **Dorr** of Jamaica Plain, MA 9/2/1936 in Ossipee; H - 40, candy salesman; W - 33, dental asst.

HARDY,
John A. of Moultonville m. Alice R. **Mattera** of Mansfield, CT 6/16/1934 in Wolfeboro; H - 26, farmer; W - 18, at home

HARFORD,
Thomas Joseph of New York, NY m. Carol Ann **Owerko** of New York, NY 4/8/1996

HARKINS,
James M. m. Deborah K. **Pochelon** 2/19/1983 in Ossipee; H - b. 4/3/1932; W - b. 10/6/1947

HARMON,
Charles M. of Ossipee m. Lizzie M. **Merrow** of Ossipee 6/3/1888 in Wakefield; H - 24, merchant, b. Ossipee, s/o Alonzo Harmon; W - 22, housekeeper, d/o Benjamin Merrow (Haverhill, MA)
Clifford Carroll of Porter, ME m. Kirsten M. **Brownell** of W. Ossipee 2/9/1995
John F. of Ossipee m. Thelma E. **Meserve** of Freedom 3/23/1947 in Ctr. Ossipee; H - 20, student; W - 16, at home

John F. m. Dolores D. **Curtis** 1/29/1981 in Conway; H - b. 11/3/1926; W - b. 3/27/1935

John H. of Ossipee m. Georgia I. **Pearson** of Ossipee 6/15/1913 in Wakefield; H - 24, b. Brookfield, s/o John M. Harmon (Freedom); W - 20, 2nd, b. Madison, d/o John L. Frost (Madison)

John H. of Ossipee m. Ethel J. **Todd** of IA 7/9/1951 in Ctr. Ossipee; H - 62, highway patrol; W - 34, practical nurse

Lloyd W. of Ossipee m. Gertrude **Beacham** of Ossipee 8/24/1912 in Ossipee; H - 22, farmer, b. Ossipee, s/o A. Judson Harmon (Ossipee); W - 20, teacher, b. Ossipee, d/o George A. Beacham (Ossipee)

Ruben S. m. Gladis L. **Sceggell** 3/27/1915 in Ossipee; H - 21, teamster, b. Brookfield, s/o John M. Harmon (Freedom); W - 18, housekeeper, b. Ossipee, d/o George B. Sceggell (Ossipee)

Thomas John m. Margaret Grace **Jones** 3/7/1971 in Ossipee; H - b. 1/1/1953; W - b. 5/27/1952

HARNUM,

Kenneth E. of Brewer, ME m. Dorothy J. **Felician** of Brewer, ME 10/27/1948 in Ctr. Ossipee; H - 36, store mgr.; W - 26, housekeeper

HARRINGTON,

George O. of Somerville, MA m. Eva M. **Durgan** of Ossipee 6/24/1896 in Ossipee; H - 24, clerk, b. Somerville, MA, s/o Nat. D. Harrington and C. Harrington; W - 23, clerk, b. Portland, ME, d/o John E. Durgan (carpenter) and Eva L. Campbell

Warren m. Kathleen S. **Boyd** 10/9/1976 in Ossipee; H - b. 7/3/1946; W - b. 10/22/1956

HARRIS,

Christopher Elliott of W. Ossipee m. Cheryl Lynn **Gerard** of W. Ossipee 4/13/1996

Merle F. m. Beatrice M. **Baker** 8/8/1981 in Ossipee; H - b. 10/9/1916; W - b. 12/15/1917

HARRISON,

James J. of Ossipee m. Marion F. (Best) **Perry** of Tamworth 3/2/1996

Paul Dennis m. Deborah Lynne **Varrell** 8/6/1977 in Freedom; H - b. 7/15/1951; W - b. 7/23/1957

HART,

Lester L. of Westbrook, ME m. Virginia D. **Laffin** of Westbrook, ME 2/19/1952 in Ctr. Ossipee; H - 39, draftsman; W - 43, at home

Stephen Andrew of London, England m. Martha **Cox** of Ossipee 8/27/1994

HARTFORD,
Michael Bruce of Ctr. Ossipee m. Karen Rae **McKusick** of Ctr. Ossipee 1/27/2001
Robert F. m. Martha J. **Smart** 5/27/1978 in Wolfeboro; H - b. 9/6/1955; W - b. 4/11/1957
Robert Francis m. Laura Jeanne **Hedrick** 10/10/1993 in Laconia
Todd R. m. Lisa A. **Ripley** 8/25/1989; H - b. 1/14/1965; W - b. 11/23/1965

HARTMAN,
Michael Alan of Ossipee m. Deborah Louise (Leanna) **LaFerriere** of Ossipee 7/2/1994

HARVEY,
Norman A. of Portland, ME m. June P. **Gagnon** of Portland, ME 9/15/1953 in Ctr. Ossipee; H - 34, clerk; W - 29, cashier
Paul E. m. Pamela D. **Smith** 7/13/1986; H - b. 12/14/1954; W - b. 12/9/1949

HASKELL,
Jobe M. of Ossipee m. Mary L. **McAllister** of Ossipee 12/9/1888 in Ossipee; H - 34, laborer, b. Greenfield, ME, s/o Nathan H. Haskell (Greenbush, ME); W - 25, housekeeper, b. Milford, ME, d/o Emery McAllister (Orono)

HASTING,
Edward E., 2nd of Fryeburg, ME m. Anna Lucille **Murch** of Fryeburg, ME 7/5/1944 in Ctr. Ossipee; H - 21, US Navy; W - 18, student

HATCH,
Charles Stanley m. Mary M. **Bielowski** 5/24/1991; H - b. 9/18/1956; W - b. 1/27/1955
Ellis R. of Rochester m. Anna I. **Hatch** of Ossipee 4/7/1946 in Somersworth; H - 38, lumberman; W - 32, at home
Joseph F. of Bangor, ME m. June E. **Andrews** of Bangor, ME 8/14/1953 in Ctr. Ossipee; H - 30, truck driver; W - 32, waitress

HATT,
Michael D. of Portland, ME m. Susanne M. **Tierney** of Portland, ME 9/2/1961 in Ossipee; H - 23, laborer; W - 21, waitress

HATTENBURG,
Lester J. m. Shirley **Bishop** 8/22/1987; H - b. 1/26/1945; W - b. 9/19/1946
Lester John of Ossipee m. Lisa Dix Unander **Scharin** of Ossipee 7/5/1995

HAYFORD,
Ernest Arthur, Jr. of Ctr. Ossipee m. Shirlee Rivard **Larose** of Ctr. Ossipee 8/7/1999
James E. m. Judith M. **Varney** 3/31/1978 in Ossipee; H - b. 6/28/1953; W - b. 12/17/1960
James Edward m. Cheryl Lee **Tibbetts** 11/24/1990; H - b. 6/28/1953; W - b. 2/26/1966
Jeffrey G. of Ctr. Ossipee m. Marcia H. **Briggs** of Ctr. Ossipee 12/7/1995
John E. of Ossipee m. Elva I. **Nason** of Ossipee 3/16/1920 in Portsmouth; H - 47, machinist, b. Tamworth, s/o Alvin Hayford (Tamworth) and Ella Whiting (Tamworth); W - 33, housework, b. Wakefield, d/o ----- Nason (Conway) and Lucinda Nason (Baldwin, ME)
Paul L. of Tamworth m. Caroline F. **Demeritt** of Ctr. Ossipee 5/28/1950 in Moultonville; H - 22, laborer; W - 19, waitress
Richard K. m. Nancy V. **Fitzsimmons** 1/15/1971 in Ossipee; H - b. 5/23/1932; W - b. 9/1/1947
Timothy Ernest m. Holly Jane **Berry** 2/6/1973 in Ossipee; H - b. 10/24/1954; W - b. 12/24/1956

HEATH,
C. Wilber of Worcester, MA m. Lucy A. **Tripp** of S. Royalston, MA 9/1/1935 in Ctr. Ossipee; H - 25, salesman; W - 24, at home
Gary P. of Eaton m. Edna M. **Knowles** of Ctr. Ossipee 6/6/1959 in Ctr. Ossipee; H - 21, poultry farmer; W - 18, stitcher

HEBERT,
Anthony P. m. Ann M. **Coderre** 7/16/1988; H - b. 12/1/1967; W - b. 5/11/1969
Philip m. Barbara **Varney** 1/8/1966 in W. Ossipee; H - 16, mill; W - 18, mill
Philip L. m. Constance V. **West** 8/27/1976 in Wolfeboro; H - b. 8/31/1949; W - b. 8/27/1957
Timothy L.. m. Deborah L. **Scripture** 9/9/1983 in Ossipee; H - b. 6/28/1952; W - b. 4/25/1961

HECKEL,
Frederick W., IV m. Katherine L. **Fowler** 8/28/1982 in Wolfeboro; H - b. 1/10/1953; W - b. 7/21/1955

HEHL,
Jacob L., Jr. of W. Ossipee m. Barbara J. **White** of Ctr. Ossipee 9/29/1959 in Ctr. Ossipee; H - 31, foreman; W - 27, mill worker

HELME,
Christopher m. Rebecca M. **Eldridge** 10/4/1969 in Ctr. Effingham; H - b. 10/9/1945; W - b. 9/4/1947
David Alvin m. Wenda Snow **Thompson** 3/21/1970 in Ossipee; H - b. 1/16/1949; W - b. 12/20/1941

HEMSLEY,
Linus Sydney m. Susan Gail **Leech** 8/25/1991; H - b. 11/7/1965; W - b. 4/28/1969

HENDERSON,
George Henry m. Tammy Marie **Allen** 9/15/1990; H - b. 5/23/1965; W - b. 11/19/1962
James E. of Gonic m. Caroline A. **Abbott** of Ossipee 11/27/1954 in Ctr. Ossipee; H - 26, shipyard; W - 20, waitress

HERON,
George A. m. Mary M. **Zildjian** 12/30/1973 in Ossipee; H - b. 1/16/1926; W - b. 8/5/1922

HERRICK,
Charles W. m. Jean R. **Wenant** 10/9/1982 in Wolfeboro; H - b. 5/10/1955; W - b. 10/13/1955

HERSEY,
David Allen, Jr. of Ctr. Ossipee m. Kaysee Marie **Dore** of Ctr. Ossipee 9/24/1999
Wayne of Manchester m. Florence **Meloon** of Ossipee 3/25/1946 in Manchester; H - 19, US Sailor; W - 21, governess

HERTEL,
Frederick E., III of Alton m. Marybeth **Hanson** of Alton 2/14/1999

HEWEY,
Arthur B. of Westbrook, ME m. Ina Alice **Abbott** of Ossipee 8/14/1907 in Ossipee; H - 26, machinist, b. Auburn, ME, s/o John B. Hewey (Topsham, machinist) and Laura Ann Baker (Bowdoin, housewife); W - 23, milliner, b. Ossipee, d/o Henry F. Abbott (Ossipee, Reg. of Deeds) and Amanda C. Abbott (Effingham, housewife)

HICKEY,
Arthur A. of Ctr. Ossipee m. Dorothea A. **Thibodeau** of Wolfeboro 10/5/1957 in Wolfeboro; H - 46, real estate; W - 46, nurse

Patrick J. m. Julie A. **Rafko** 10/11/1986; H - b. 1/31/1955; W - b. 1/10/1962
Stephen of Ctr. Ossipee m. Natalie **Rowell** of Chocorua 9/25/1962 in Meredith; H - 27, clerk; W - 29, none
Stephen m. Bonita **Downs** 4/30/1972 in Center Harbor; H - b. 12/13/1935; W - b. 4/24/1945

HICKS,
Roger F. of Cumberland Ctr., ME m. Blanche **Messer** of S. Portland, ME 12/31/1958 in Ossipee; H - 23, sheet metal; W - 23, none

HIDDEN,
Samuel B. m. Dorothy Janice **Stein** 5/8/1970 in Tamworth; H - b. 4/29/1939; W - b. 10/25/1948

HIGGINS,
John D. m. Florence **Tetler** 10/15/1965 in Ctr. Ossipee; H - 58, Western Electric; W - 50, wirewoman

HILBERT,
Mark Russell of Wolfeboro m. Wanda Lee Edwards **Clifford** of Wolfeboro 7/24/1998

HILL,
Bernard R. of Cambridge m. Inez Lizette **Hobbs** of Ossipee 9/8/1914 in N. Conway; H - 31, hardware dealer, b. VT, s/o George K. Hill (Burlington, VT); W - 28, teacher, b. Ossipee, d/o Orodon P. Hobbs (Ossipee)
Dana T. of Ctr. Ossipee m. Katrina Anne **Hedbor** of Ctr. Ossipee 6/30/2001
Harry L. of Ossipee m. Ethel **Ciceolo** of Ossipee 12/9/1922 in Wakefield; H - 45, b. Mason; W - 33, b. Ossipee
Ivan B. of Sweet Home, OR m. Beverly F. **Warren** of Oakland, CA 11/16/1945 in Ossipee; H - 27, at home; W - 23, US Navy
James W., Jr. of Ossipee m. Michelle L. **Naylor** of Ossipee 1/19/1996
John K. of Ossipee m. Dorothy L. **Tibbetts** of Wakefield 9/3/1919 in Ossipee; H - 30, hotel clerk, b. Lynn, MA, s/o Thomas Hill (New Bedford, MA) and Nellie Kearns (S. Dennis, MA); W - 18, student, b. Wakefield, d/o Everett Tibbetts (Brookfield) and Susie Weeks (Wakefield)
Luther F. of Ossipee m. Blanche M. **Merrow** of Ossipee 1/26/1933 in Farmington; H - 26, salesman; W - 43, tel. operator

HILLS,
Charles B. m. Flavelle **Bradley** 3/12/1977 in S. Effingham; H - b. 2/1/1912; W - b. 1/20/1931

HILTON,
Charles R. m. Christia A. **McCue** 8/14/1989; H - b. 12/11/1958; W - b. 1/24/1952
Leonard M. Barbara **Grace** 10/3/1964 in Tamworth; H - 19, carpenter; W - 18, clerk
Newell C. of Ossipee m. Lizzie M. **Webster** of Ossipee 7/20/1902 in Effingham; H - 21, farmer, b. Ossipee, s/o James F. Hilton (Ossipee, farmer) and Emma Chick (Ossipee, housewife); W - 24, maid, b. Tamworth, d/o Horace F. Webster (Tamworth, laborer) and Ada L. Hobbs (Tamworth, housewife)

HINCKLEY,
James E., Jr. of Ctr. Ossipee m. Lisa Lynn **Duquette** of Ctr. Ossipee 8/5/2000

HINCKS,
David of Portland, ME m. Elizabeth **Nelson** of Portland, ME 9/6/1958 in Ossipee; H - 20, USCG; W - 18, student

HINDS,
Edward M. of Ossipee m. Abbie M. **Baker** of Haverhill, MA 4/15/1924 in Danville; H - 60, b. Hampstead; W - 48, b. Haverhill, MA
Kenneth H. of Ossipee m. Margaret I. **Boulanger** of Haverhill, MA 10/20/1929 in Ossipee; H - 25, stock mgr.; W - 21, shop mgr.
Kenneth Henry of Ossipee m. Gwendolyn Hale **Jackson** of Conway 6/28/1941 in Conway; H - 37, stock room mgr.; W - 25, housework

HINES,
Gordon m. Eleanor **Sylvia** 4/1/1966 in Ossipee; H - 45, foreman; W - 25, none

HITCHCOCK,
Howard C. of Wolfeboro Falls m. Hazel B. **Emery** of Wolfeboro Falls 6/6/1931 in Wolfeboro Falls; H - 23, laborer; W - 25, at home
Howard C. of Ctr. Ossipee m. Nina S. **Eldridge** of Ctr. Ossipee 8/29/1959 in Ctr. Ossipee; H - 61, mill worker; W - 51, none
Wilbur T. of Ossipee m. Addie B. **Templeton** of Ossipee 6/16/1898 in Ossipee; H - 25, farmer, b. Ossipee, s/o Porter Hitchcock (deceased) and Lydia Tucker (deceased); W - 17, maid, 2nd, b. Ossipee, d/o

Charles A. Templeton (Ossipee, farmer) and Roberline Jenness (housewife)

HOBBS,
Christopher C. of Ossipee m. Lydia A. **Ladd** of Epping 12/25/1906 in Epping; H - 59, farmer, b. Ossipee, s/o Samuel D. Hobbs (Ossipee, farmer) and Louisa Moody (Ossipee, housewife); W - 41, maid, b. Epping, d/o Daniel B. Ladd (Deerfield, farmer) and Marian S. Jones (Epping, housewife)
Frank O. of Ossipee m. Hattie F. **Eastman** of Tamworth 3/20/1888 in Tamworth; H - 33, laborer, b. Ossipee, s/o Wentworth H. Hobbs (Ossipee); W - 22, housekeeper, b. Albany, d/o Henry Eastman
Thomas of Tamworth m. Beatrice **Drinkwater** of Ossipee 3/19/1945 in Ossipee; H - 27, US Army; W - 26, at home

HODGDON,
Charles E. of N. Conway m. Daisy A. **Dame** of Ossipee 6/2/1928 in Conway; H - 56, grain dealer; W - 44, boarding house
John E. of Ossipee m. Dora G. **Glidden** of Wakefield 6/17/1926 in Sanbornville; H - 78, b. Newburyport; W - 64
John Goebel of S. Weymouth, MA m. Kathrine Christine **Beaton** of S. Weymouth, MA 1/1/1938 in Ossipee; H - 26, insurance agent; W - 32, secretary

HODGE,
Bernard of Ossipee m. Doris M. **Welch** of Ossipee 2/2/1927 in Ossipee; H - 18, laborer; W - 16, at home
Bert N. of Ossipee m. Nettie F. **Loring** of Ossipee 6/6/1896 in Ossipee; H - 23, miller, b. Ossipee, s/o John C. Hodge (Ossipee, miller) and Laura E. Hodge (Ossipee, housewife); W - 19, housemaid, b. Ossipee, d/o George M. Loring (Boston, MA, miller) and Adalaide Loring (Bradford, housewife)
Carleton L. of Ossipee m. Alice M. **Jordon** of Ossipee 10/9/1924 in Tamworth; H - 24, b. Ossipee; W - 18, b. Trenton, ME
Edgar C. of Ossipee m. Carrie L. **Corson** of Milton 5/24/1894 in Sanford, ME; H - 24, shoe maker, b. Ossipee, s/o John C. Hodge (Ossipee, miller) and Laura E. Hodge (Ossipee, housewife); W - 20, shoe maker, b. Lebanon, d/o Munroe Corson (railroad man) and Hannah Corson (housewife)
Elwood N. of Ossipee m. Rachel F. **Merrow** of Ossipee 7/6/1926 in Moultonville; H - 21, b. Ossipee; W - 16, b. Ossipee
Elwood N. m. Barbara A. **Hebert** 2/19/1983 in Ossipee; H - b. 10/25/1959; W - b. 2/4/1947

Eugene W. of Ctr. Ossipee m. Myrtle S. **Langley** of Parsonsfield, ME 6/–/1937 in Effingham Falls; H - 22, trucking; W - 18, house work

Fenton A. of Ctr. Ossipee m. Jennette R. **Eldridge** of W. Baldwin, ME 2/7/1953 in Ctr. Ossipee; H - 20, Navy; W - 19, secretary

Fred of Ossipee m. Bertha **Nichols** of Ossipee 4/24/1897 in Brookfield; H - 22, laborer, b. Ossipee, s/o Samuel Hodge (Ossipee, farmer) and Olive J. Ricker (Ossipee, housekeeper); W - 18, housemaid, b. Ossipee, d/o Charles Nichols (Ossipee, laborer) and Emma Williams (Ossipee, housekeeper)

Gary m. Alice **Fleischer** 10/12/1968 in Ctr. Ossipee; H - b. 12/4/1941; W - b. 7/29/1944

John L. of Ossipee m. Beatrice R. **Milliken** of Limerick, ME 11/14/1931 in Ossipee; H - 24, groceryman; W - 18, at home

Lloyd B. m. Carol M. **Stoddard** of Ctr. Ossipee 2/2/1957 in Ossipee; H - 28, electrician; W - 20

Marcus John of Concord m. Heather Renee **Burton** of Concord 10/18/1998

Wayne of Ctr. Ossipee m. Alice **Hamel** of Ctr. Ossipee 8/18/1962 in Ctr. Ossipee; H - 23, assembly inspector; W - 24, none

HODGSON,
Walter A. m. Phyllis M. **Hoffman** 8/6/1984; H - b. 9/2/1904; W - b. 9/19/1911

HODSDON,
Ervin W. of Ossipee m. Mary L. **Price** of Ossipee 2/25/1917 in Ossipee; H - 53, physician, b. Ossipee, s/o Edward Hodsdon (Ossipee) and Emma Demerritt (Farmington); W - 40, housework, b. Beverly, MA, d/o John Price (Woodstock, NB) and Lilla Merrow (Ossipee)

Grant W. of Ossipee m. Florence E. **Turner** of Malden, MA 7/19/1933 in Ossipee; H - 31, tax collector; W - 33, teacher

HOFFMAN,
Evan John m. Penny Rose **Thibault** 10/24/1992 in Ossipee

HOGAN,
Roland B., Jr. m. Brenda T. **Gould** 12/30/1987; H - b. 6/23/1921; W - b. 3/24/1929

HOLBROOK,
Clement M. of Ossipee m. Mary F. **Berry** of Ossipee 6/21/1919 in Ossipee; H - 21, baggage master, b. Mendon, MA, s/o Morton Holbrook (Mendon, MA) and Cora B. St. John (Montpelier, VT); W -

18, scholar, b. Ossipee, d/o Herman D. Berry (Tamworth) and Margaret Holley (Ireland)

HOLLADAY,
Eric James of Ctr. Ossipee m. Rachel Ailene (Smith) **Emond** of Seabrook 10/28/1995

HOLLIHAN,
Richard Allen of Ossipee m. Margaret Winifred **Leslie** of Lynn, MA 2/14/1995

HOLLOWAY,
Cedric P. of Ossipee m. Norma E. **Young** of Lincolnsville, ME 10/14/1927 in Conway; H - 24, farmer; W - 21, at home

HOLMES,
Chester W. of Ossipee m. Dorothy **Husband** of Moultonboro 11/7/1932 in Ossipee; H - 37, chauffeur; W - 23, waitress
Curtis J. of Intervale m. Cindy Lee **Rhines** of Ctr. Ossipee 4/18/1998

HOLMSTROM,
Donald m. Jane **Small** 6/13/1964 in Ctr. Ossipee; H - 22, student; W - 21, none

HOOPER,
Allen m. Ruth **Cooter** 4/16/1966 in Wolfeboro; H - 23, carpenter; W - 22, nurses aid
David Russell m. Cathy J. **Sargent** 9/8/1979 in Ossipee; H - b. 9/11/1961; W - b. 4/9/1962
Howard A. of Carroll m. Frances L. **Riley** of Ossipee 7/9/1944 in Wolfeboro; H - 29, US Army; W - 18, laundress

HORMELL,
Glenn D. of Ossipee m. Charlotte **Bunker** of Ossipee 2/14/1959 in Ossipee; H - 25, USAF; W - 36, clerk

HORNE,
C. Archie of Haverhill, MA m. Annie M. **Smart** of Ossipee 12/26/1901 in Ctr. Ossipee; H - 28, bank teller, b. Haverhill, MA, s/o E. Frank Horne (Alton, janitor) and Malvina Blanchard (Haverhill, MA, housewife); W - 24, teacher, b. Ossipee, d/o Charles H. Smart (Campton, manufacturer) and Helen A. Folsom (Tamworth, housewife)
Geoffrey C. of Belmont, MA m. Matilda S. **Pinkham** of Watertown, MA 5/24/1934 in Ctr. Ossipee; H - 57, retired; W - 30, stenog.

Harry E. of Ossipee m. Elizabeth **Snow** of Ossipee 10/15/1913 in Freedom; H - 28, laborer, b. Berwick, ME, s/o Charles H. Horne (Bristol); W - 32, b. Milton, MA, d/o Elbridge Snow (Milton, MA)
Robert Glen, Jr. m. Sarah L. **Althoff** 1/20/1989; H - b. 9/4/1966; W - b. 10/30/1967

HORRIGAN,
John M. of Ashland m. Lillian **Drake** of Ossipee 8/9/1890 in Ossipee; H - 26, spinner, b. E. Andover, s/o Michael Horrigan (Boston, MA, pipe maker); W - 18, weaver, b. Wolfeboro, d/o Charles L. Drake (Chichester, laborer)

HOUGH,
John K. of Ossipee m. Theodora **Constantaris** of Ossipee 3/1/1997

HOWARD,
David Paul, II of Ctr. Ossipee m. Rachelle Alice **Hamel** of Ctr. Ossipee 7/23/1994
Sumner M. of N. Wilbraham, MA m. Kathryn G. **DeWolfe** of Portland, ME 7/16/1922 in Ossipee; H - 26, salesman, b. Worthington, MA, s/o Fred L. Howard (N. Chester, MA, retired) and Harriet Merritt (Templeton, MA, housewife); W - 29, cashier, 2nd, b. Portland, ME, d/o ----- Walsh (Portland, ME, retired)

HOWE,
Henry W. of Rochester m. Leonora H. **Wasson** of Ossipee 6/28/1919 in Rochester; H - 18, shoemaker, b. Wakefield, s/o George W. Howe (ND) and Hattie L. Blouing (Canada); W - 19, shoemaker, b. Ossipee, d/o Joseph Wasson (St. John, NB) and Josephine Colby (Ossipee)

HOWELL,
Roy Russell, Jr. m. Annette Mary **Blair** 1/11/1974 in Ossipee; H - b. 1/3/1950; W - b. 7/3/1950

HOWES,
Edward C. of Reading, MA m. Avis P. **Van Dyke** of Peabody, MA 10/13/1960 in Ctr. Ossipee; H - 52, farmer; W - 48, housewife
Edward C. m. Evelyn L. **Young** 1/3/1972 in Ossipee; H - b. 10/12/1907; W - b. 1/2/1906

HOWLAND,
Densmore of Franconia m. Annie **Demeritt** of Ossipee 10/5/1901 in Ossipee; H - 21, salesman, b. Franconia, s/o H. W. Howland (Lisbon,

farmer) and Jennie L. Howland (Groton, housewife); W - 21, dressmaker, b. Ossipee, d/o Calvin S. Demeritt (Ossipee, merchant) and Harriet O. Demeritt (Freeport, housewife)

HOY,
Eugene J. of Portland, ME m. Kathryn **Merchant** of Cambridge, MA 6/7/1948 in Ctr. Ossipee; H - 25, student; W - 23, secretary

HUCKINS,
Ernest L. of Ossipee m. Jane Topliff **Merrow** of Freedom 3/16/1904 in Freedom; H - 21, merchant, b. Freedom, s/o Simon O. Huckins (Freedom, lumberman) and Nellie J. Harmon (Freedom); W - 21, housekeeper, b. Freedom, d/o Edward T. Merrow (Acton, ME) and Nancy T. Baker (Cornish, ME, housekeeper)
Wesley E. of Ossipee m. Sharon Lyn **Avery** of Ossipee 3/7/1998

HUDSON,
David M. of Ossipee m. Michelle Ann **Bartels** of Ossipee 10/11/1997

HUFF,
Herbert Raymond m. Carmen Del Bosque **Ayer** 2/29/1992 in Ossipee

HULTZEN,
Claud H. of Auburn, ME m. Elinor L. **Schultz** of Milford, CT 6/7/1950 in Moultonville; H - 50, executive; W - 27, housewife

HUMPHREY,
John S. of Swampscott, MA m. Doris E. **Green** of Swampscott, MA 6/18/1932 in Ossipee; H - 24, plant foreman; W - 25, at home

HUNT,
Earle A. of New York City, NY m. Marie W. **Archer** of Portland, ME 8/26/1946 in Ossipee; H - 57, clerk; W - 63, housewife

HUNTER,
Leslie m. Louise **Howard** 4/17/1964 in Ctr. Ossipee; H - 60, foreman; W - 39, none

HUNTINGTON,
Benjamin F., Jr. m. Esther L. **Bickford** 3/18/1983 in Moultonboro; H - b. 8/12/1948; W - b. 1/27/1952

HUNTLEY,
William G. m. Judith L. **Goodblood** 5/29/1982 in Ossipee; H - b. 7/28/1949; W - b. 6/21/1950

HURD,
Arnold of Tamworth m. Beverly A. **Bean** of Ctr. Ossipee 10/19/1956 in Ctr. Ossipee; H - 19, farmer; W - 18
Howard E. of Ctr. Ossipee m. Sandra G. **Foster** of Amherst, MA 7/21/1999
William A. of Ossipee m. Hazel A. **Davey** of Sandwich 12/5/1921 in Whittier; H - 24, laborer, b. Ossipee, s/o Aaron Hurd (Freedom) and Emma Danforth (Boston, MA); W - 22, housewife, b. Sandwich, d/o George H. Davey (Sandwich) and Jennie Vittum (Sandwich)

HURLIMAN,
Patrick J. m. Judy E. **Cotton** 3/6/1972 in Wolfeboro; H - b. 2/2/1950; W - b. 11/3/1951

HURN,
Fred of Ossipee m. Florence E. **Loring** of Ossipee 4/12/1905 in Ossipee; H - 28, blacksmith, b. Charlestown, s/o John F. Hurn (Freedom, farmer) and Jennie M. Smith (Freedom, housewife); W - 21, maid, b. Ossipee, d/o Elmer S. Loring (Ossipee, butcher) and Julia J. Chapman (Merrickville, ON, housewife)

HUSSEY,
Brian Keith of Ossipee m. Cassandra Jean **Closson** of Ossipee 12/31/1996
William B. of Ossipee m. Idella M. **Conner** of Ossipee 7/4/1918 in N. Conway; H - 22, chauffeur, b. Effingham, s/o Joseph E. Hussey (Limington, ME) and Mary E. Tarbox (Parsonsfield, ME); W - 21, school teacher, b. Ossipee, d/o William Conner (Ossipee) and Annie G. Hodgdon (Stanstead, PQ)

HUTCHINS,
Albert G. m. Julie M. **Harris** 3/9/1985; H - b. 7/31/1962; W - b. 11/1/1963
George R. of Wolfeboro m. Inez E. **Foss** of Tuftonboro 5/3/1903 in Ossipee; H - 25, farmer, b. Wakefield, s/o Charles Hutchins (Brunswick, ME, carpenter) and Sadie S. Stevens (Brunswick, ME, housewife); W - 17, maid, b. Tuftonboro, d/o Fred Foss (Tuftonboro, farmer) and Anna Foss (Tuftonboro, housewife)
M. B. of Dover m. Alice **Walker** of Granite 11/25/1902 in Ossipee; H - 41, veterinary surgeon, 2nd, b. NY, s/o Levi Hutchins (Bangor, retired) and Sarah Hutchins (Germany); W - 25, maid, b. Woodman, d/o

John P. Walker (deceased) and Aurilla Walker (Plymouth, ME, housewife)

HUTCHINSON,
Clifford Chandler, Jr. of W. Ossipee m. Merri Ellen Gilpatrick **Day** of W. Ossipee 6/23/2001

HYLAND,
Arthur C. of Ossipee m. Margaret **Sebel** of Bath, ME 7/8/1946 in Cornish, ME; H - 38, shipyard; W - 35, at home

INGRAHAM,
William W. of Augusta, ME m. Priscilla **Woodward** of Augusta, ME 7/7/1953 in Ctr. Ossipee; H - 23, student; W - 24, stenographer

JACK,
Guy E. of Ossipee m. Gladys F. **Abbott** of Ossipee 3/15/1933 in Conway; H - 42, undertaker; W - 35, housewife

JACKSON,
Charles W. of Ossipee m. Florence S. **Mitchell** of Effingham 3/3/1912 in Moultonville; H - 21, laborer, b. Reading, MA, s/o Charles A. Jackson (Lebanon, ME); W - 23, b. NY, d/o F. Mitchell (NY)
Ronald of Ctr. Ossipee m. Doris **Wheeler** of Ctr. Effingham 1/23/1937 in S. Tamworth; H - 17, laborer; W - 17, at home
William L. of Ossipee m. Reta M. **Nichols** of Ossipee 4/17/1914 in Ossipee; H - 35, barber, 2nd, b. Windsor, ME, s/o S. F. C. Jackson (Windsor, ME); W - 25, b. Ossipee, d/o Lafayette Nichols (Ossipee)

JACOBSON,
Thomas S. of Ossipee m. Annie C. **Libby** of Ossipee 12/25/1949 in Tuftonboro; H - 22, dairy worker; W - 23, domestic

JACOBUS,
Ralph of Belmont, ME m. Phyllis **Davenport** of Niagara Falls, NY 9/13/1947 in Ctr. Ossipee; H - 44, farmer; W - 35, housewife

JAGEMANN,
Philip m. Lynda **Hayford** 9/14/1968 in Ctr. Ossipee; H - b. 5/16/1947; W - b. 4/17/1949

JANCATERINO,
Wayne S. m. Eileen P. **McCool** 8/24/1985; H - b. 5/13/1951; W - b. 3/14/1955

JAWORSKI,
William J. m. Tammy L. **Lunt** 6/22/1985; H - b. 11/30/1964; W - b. 9/1/1965

JEFFERDS,
Harry B. of Windham, ME m. Carole A. **Cleary** of Portland, ME 8/22/1956 in Ossipee; H - 22; W - 18, secretary

JENNESS,
Harvey of Ctr. Ossipee m. Marie E. **Wiggin** of Ctr. Ossipee 1/31/1959 in Ctr. Ossipee; H - 24, laborer; W - 17, none
John of Ossipee m. Florence **Dyer** of W. Baldwin, ME 11/11/1933 in Ossipee; H - 20, laborer; W - 19, at home
Lorenzo W. of Ossipee m. Emma B. **Jenness** of Ossipee 10/3/1912 in Ossipee; H - 76, carpenter, b. Plymouth, s/o Benjamin Jenness (Boothby, ME); W - 56, housewife, b. Wolfeboro, d/o S. Wentworth (Milton)
Matthias of Wolfeboro m. Bell **Moody** of Wolfeboro 5/18/1896 in Wolfeboro; H - 46, farmer, 2nd, b. Meredith, s/o Jno. R. Jenness (Meredith, farmer) and Mary J. Jenness (Moultonboro, housekeeper); W - 32, housekeeper, 2nd, b. New Durham, d/o Sylvester Berry and Mary Berry (Sandwich, housekeeper)
Wayne H. m. Margaret E. **Eldridge** 6/28/1986; H - b. 5/2/1961; W - b. 7/12/1956

JEWETT,
Lawrence H. of Biddeford, ME m. Marion G. **Gramazio** of Biddeford, ME 9/13/1949 in Ossipee; H - 32, salesman; W - 24, domestic

JILLETTE,
Arthur G., Jr. of Stoneham, MA m. Janet D. **White** of Ossipee 6/25/1960 in Ossipee; H - 23, student; W - 23, teacher

JODLOWSKI,
Christopher Thomas of Tuckahoe, NY m. Sheila Marie **Prudhomme** of Tuckahoe, NY 10/9/1998

JOHNSON,
A. Hollis of Hopedale, MA m. Frances M. **Gill** of Melrose, MA 7/18/1937 in W. Ossipee; H - 21, engineer; W - 22, at home
Carl J. M. of Ossipee m. Esther C. **Peterson** of S. Newbury 8/1/1924 in Ossipee; H - 22, b. Sweden; W - 20, b. Wethersfield, CT
Chester F., Jr. m. Ann Louise **Gagnon** 9/20/1975 in Ossipee; H - b. 3/2/1937; W - b. 9/21/1951

Christopher A. of Ossipee m. Katherine A. **DiPaulo** of Ossipee 10/29/1994
Dale Grover of Conway m. Shawnda Lee **Burby** of Conway 2/15/1998
Dennis M. Brenda A. **Chionchio** 7/24/1967 in Ctr. Ossipee; H - 22, Air Force; W - 19, office
Donald E. of S. Portland, ME m. Jane **Gould** of Ossipee 5/29/1954 in Ossipee; H - 23, photo; W - 22
Donald Harry m. Marsha Ellen **Murphy** 3/10/1973 in Ossipee; H - b. 1/12/1951; W - b. 2/14/1955
Earl B. of Rochester m. Florence H. **Eldridge** of Ctr. Ossipee 8/13/1961 in Ctr. Ossipee; H - 53, carpenter; W - 43, teacher
Forrest Roger m. Linda M. **Plummer** 8/12/1971 in Conway; H - b. 9/27/1951; W - b. 9/26/1951
Kevin Boyd of Ossipee m. Eliza Spring **Huntress** of Ossipee 7/25/1998
Lawrence P., Jr. m. Jane W. **Moriarty** 9/27/1986; H - b. 5/10/1960; W - b. 4/8/1962
Victor m. Zella J. **Gallagher** 8/5/1970 in Ossipee; H - b. 6/12/1915; W - b. 3/13/1923

JOHNSTON,
George M. of N. Conway m. Dorothy **Wormstead** of Ctr. Ossipee 12/20/1942 in Ossipee; H - 20, telephone lineman; W - 20, school teacher
Kirk E. m. Gail A. **Nelson** 4/5/1986; H - b. 12/13/1960; W - b. 4/20/1967
Richard A. m. Patricia A. **Sanfacon** 7/10/1984; H - b. 3/14/1953; W - b. 5/22/1956

JONES,
Chester William of Effingham m. Phyllis Mildred **Hanson** of Ossipee 9/6/1940 in Ossipee; H - 21, painter; W - 16, student
David H. m. Patricia J. **Reardon** 12/8/1990; H - b. 10/25/1950; W - b. 6/4/1949
Kenneth A., Jr. m. Linda Mary **Fisher** 4/20/1991; H - b. 11/14/1946; W - b. 12/3/1946
Leon C. m. Gertrude **Ricker** 7/22/1916 in Ossipee; H - 24, painter, b. Effingham, s/o Albion D. Jones (Newfield, ME); W - 23, housekeeper, b. Ossipee, d/o William Ricker (Ossipee)
Michael R. m. Kathleen Jane **Fogarty** 9/8/1979 in Chocorua; H - b. 9/11/1956; W - b. 10/3/1958
Roger Arthur m. Deborah Jean **Bryant** 8/23/1975 in Ossipee; H - b. 4/29/1944; W - b. 8/31/1955
Taylor of Ossipee m. Jean **Fletcher** of Ossipee 1/22/1948 in Ctr. Ossipee; H - 56, druggist; W - 35, housekeeper
William Thomas of Ctr. Ossipee m. Patsy Marie (Palmer) **Morgan** of Ctr. Ossipee 9/24/1994

JONSSON,
Harry m. Patricia **Cotton** 10/26/1968 in Ctr. Ossipee; H - b. 9/8/1943; W - b. 11/26/1946

JORDAN,
Harry M. of Ctr. Ossipee m. Gloria M. **Cutting** of Kezar Falls, ME 7/1/1950 in Kezar Falls, ME; H - 19, factory emp.; W - 17, at home
Kenneth of Ossipee m. Olena R. **Bilodeau** of Wolfeboro 5/28/1948 in Wolfeboro; H - 20, millworker; W - 19, shoeworker
Ralph Stanley of Ossipee m. Edith M. J. **Huber** of Malden, MA 10/20/1943 in Ctr. Ossipee; H - 19, US Navy; W - 20, office helper

JORDEN,
Paul Neal m. Linda Jo **Elliott** 2/13/1990; H - b. 11/21/1956; W - b. 5/30/1964

JUDKINS,
Thomas of Effingham m. Dorothy A. **Eldridge** of Ctr. Ossipee 10/4/1954 in Ctr. Ossipee; H - 22, lumberman; W - 15, dish washer

JUNKINS,
Robert L. of Portland, ME m. Shirley I. **Montefesco** of S. Portland, ME 12/10/1952 in Ctr. Ossipee; H - 25, operator; W - 29, housewife

KALINUK,
John Douglas m. Irene M. **Trottier** 5/22/1980 in Ossipee; H - b. 10/22/1940; W - b. 5/17/1946

KANE,
Thomas F. of Cambridge, MA m. Bernice T. **Wilkins** of Ashland 9/20/1952 in Ossipee; H - 53, mechanic; W - 41, office work

KAPLAN,
Morton D. of Augusta, ME m. Judith **Burleigh** of Augusta, ME 7/16/1948 in Ctr. Ossipee; H - 23, store business; W - 18, secretary
Sheldon N. of Taunton, MA m. Harriet **Librak** of Fall River, MA 2/21/1952 in Ossipee; H - 20, student; W - 19, student

KAZANJIAN,
Ralph E. m. Patricia E. **McCoy** 8/16/1980 in Moultonville; H - b. 12/17/1937; W - b. 4/16/1951

KEEFE,
James W. of Ossipee m. Grace A. **Chute** of Ossipee 11/19/1895 in Ossipee; H - 22, farmer, b. Boston, s/o John J. Keefe (deceased) and Elizabeth Dunn (deceased); W - 22, maid, b. Effingham, d/o Albion Chute (deceased) and Merabah Chute (Effingham, housewife)

KEITH,
Harold Merritt of Ossipee m. Rita Alia **Beaulieu** of Rochester 9/17/1938 in Gonic; H - 26, express driver; W - 21, mill operative
Lewis Edward of Lynn, MA m. Inez Frances **Cutter** of Winthrop, MA 6/10/1911 in Ossipee; H - 24, merchant, b. Lynn, MA, s/o Ira Bliss Keith (Haverlock, ME, retired); W - 19, d/o Edward F. Cutter

KELLEY,
Francis Joseph, Jr. of Ctr. Ossipee m. Julie Jo **Dansingburg** of Ctr. Ossipee 7/11/1998
Howard m. Permelia **Eldridge** 2/17/1968 in Ctr. Ossipee; H - b. 12/3/1930; W - b. 9/17/1943
Phillip H. of Franklin m. Marion M. **Merrow** of Ossipee 10/5/1930 in Ossipee; H - 23, electrician; W - 20, at home
Thomas m. Carolyn **Tracy** 12/15/1964 in Ossipee; H - 30, USCG; W - 34, none

KELLOGG,
Peter J. of Portland, ME m. Gloria J. **Gibbons** of Portland, ME 8/11/1961 in Ctr. Ossipee; H - 23, salesman; W - 20, secretary

KELLY,
Ralph m. Judith **Wasson** 8/20/1966 in Ossipee; H - 29, mechanic; W - 23, payroll clerk

KENDALL,
Alvin J. of Ossipee m. Nancy L. **Craigue** of Wolfeboro 4/7/1954 in Ossipee; H - 27; W - 19, student

KENNARD,
Benjamin F. of Dover m. Edna Esther **Lord** of Ossipee 12/14/1945 in Keene; H - 33, cabinet maker; W - 24, teacher
Raymond S. of Ossipee m. Ruth E. **Pearson** of Ossipee 7/13/1946 in Ossipee; H - 28, steel moulder; W - 25, at home

KENNY,
Thomas Patrick, IV of Ctr. Ossipee m. Michelle E. **Van Tassel** of Ctr. Ossipee 6/3/1995

KENT,
James F. of Waterboro, ME m. Agatha **Roberts** of Sanford, ME 6/4/1933 in Ossipee; H - 25, grainman; W - 25, secretarial

KENYON,
Johnathan Daniel m. Carol Lynn **Adjutant** 6/24/1978 in Ossipee; H - b. 10/28/1957; W - b. 6/18/1960

KESLAR,
David Allen m. Heather Lynn **Kinmond** 6/10/1990; H - b. 1/30/1968; W - b. 6/21/1968

KEYES,
William C. m. Rebecca **Knapp** 3/24/1979 in Wolfeboro; H - b. 8/19/1943; W - b. 8/3/1956
William Charles m. Donna Carol **Floria** 7/20/1974 in Ossipee; H - b. 8/19/1943; W - b. 7/5/1954

KEYTE,
John B. m. Norma M. **Bailey** 1/14/1974 in Ossipee; H - b. 7/14/1932; W - b. 6/28/1942

KILLACKEY,
James, III m. Dalinda **Peers** 12/7/1968 in Ctr. Ossipee; H - b. 8/17/1948; W - b. 8/11/1948

KILLEHER,
Paul Joseph m. Susan Lynne **Davis** 6/29/1991; H - b. 2/9/1960; W - b. 8/8/1962

KIMBALL,
Albert E. of Malden, MA m. Beatrice **Huckins** of Ossipee 9/14/1929 in Ossipee; H - 24, salesman; W - 23, at home
George of Bridgton, ME m. Marilyn **Lombard** of Westbrook, ME 7/8/1958 in Ossipee; H - 20, salesman; W - 21, secretary
Robert H. of Ctr. Ossipee m. Barbara A. **Feary** of Tamworth 10/5/1963 in Tamworth; H - 26, RBM operator; W - 25, social worker

KING,
Arthur J. m. Doris M. **Hickman** 6/24/1983 in Conway; H - b. 11/10/1931; W - b. 4/21/1935
Benjamin Stewart of W. Ossipee m. Jennifer Harriet **Ball** of W. Ossipee 9/13/1997

Henry of Ossipee m. Mary **Ross** of Ossipee 10/28/1908 in Ossipee; H - 54, painter, b. Ossipee, s/o J. F. King (Shelburne Falls, MA); W - 59, housework, 2nd, b. Ossipee, d/o Amasa Moody (Ossipee)

KINMOND,
Scott D. m. Kimberly E. **Currier** 10/22/1983 in Holderness; H - b. 9/2/1964; W - b. 11/16/1961
Scott David m. Anne Marie **Fogarty** 10/17/1992 in Ossipee

KIRBY,
Todd A. m. Terri L. **Varrell** 9/25/1982 in Madison; H - b. 10/4/1961; W - b. 4/19/1959

KIRKWOOD,
Dana G. m. Bessie **Phillips** 1/31/1921 in Ossipee; H - 21, teamster, b. Ossipee, s/o George E. Kirkwood (teamster) and Clara Eldridge (housewife); W - 20, housemaid, b. Scotland, d/o Alexander E. Phillips (carpenter) and Margaret D. Phillips (housewife)
Dane C. m. Joanne M. **Brown** 9/2/1982 in Rochester; H - b. 1/9/1957; W - b. 6/8/1957
George T. of Ossipee m. Clara S. **Staples** of Ossipee 5/13/1917 in Ossipee; H - 37, teamster, b. Nashua, s/o William Kirkwood (Fall River, MA) and Cora Cilley (Nottingham); W - 49, housework, 2nd, b. Ossipee, d/o Daniel Eldridge (Ossipee) and Susan Eldridge (Ossipee)
Lawrence Dana of Ossipee m. Mary Knight **Lord** of Ossipee 2/18/1941 in S. Tamworth; H - 19, soldier; W - 16, at home

KLEIN,
Larry Louis m. Kristine M. **Rines** 4/15/1978 in Ossipee; H - b. 9/28/1955; W - b. 7/2/1955

KNAPP,
Archie Fred, Jr. of Kittery, ME m. Alberta G. **Baston** of Portland, ME 9/10/1949 in Ctr. Ossipee; H - 32, draftsman; W - 29, nurse

KNIGHT,
Chester of Holliston, MA m. Mary E. **Payne** of Holliston, MA 6/29/1929 in Ctr. Ossipee; H - 29, painter; W - 20, pricing clerk
George F. m. Elaine E. **Nelson** 8/30/1980 in Ossipee; H - b. 7/14/1946; W - b. 6/8/1949
William Ray, Jr. of Brownsville, OR m. Gale Lynn **Smith** of Ctr. Ossipee 2/17/1996

KNOWLES,
George E. of Ctr. Ossipee m. Cora V. **Craigue** of Wolfeboro 7/15/1956 in Wolfeboro; H - 21, engineer; W - 20, tel. operator
Herbert L. of Ctr. Ossipee m. Grace E. **Abbott** of Ctr. Ossipee 3/22/1953 in Ctr. Ossipee; H - 73, sawyer; W - 72, housewife
Robert W. m. Barbara A. **Schmottlach** 12/26/1980 in Ctr. Ossipee; H - b. 9/14/1931; W - b. 3/16/1930

KNOWLTON,
Francis H. of Auburn, ME m. Velma L. **Lewis** of Lewiston, ME 5/18/1946 in Ossipee; H - 27, lineman; W - 34, reporter
George C. of Gloucester, MA m. Eva F. **McLellan** of Gloucester, MA 11/5/1909 in Ossipee; H - 24, mason, b. Gloucester, MA, s/o George M. Knowlton (Gloucester, MA, engineer); W - 23, teacher, b. Gloucester, MA, d/o James A. McLellan (Gloucester, MA, blacksmith)

KNOX,
Alva W. of Ossipee m. Francis M. **Whitney** of Ossipee 8/21/1891 in Tamworth; H - 34, railroad, b. Ossipee, s/o E. R. Knox (Ossipee) and L. B. (Lebanon); W - 24, dressmaker, b. Parsonsfield, d/o H. Whiting (sic) (Parsonsfield) and M. (Providence)
Charles of Ossipee m. Agnes **Wasson** of Ossipee 9/8/1926 in Ctr. Ossipee; H - 27, b. Ossipee; W - 23, b. Ossipee
Charles L. of Ossipee m. Carrie **Welch** of Ossipee 8/31/1894 in Ossipee; H - 31, farmer, b. Ossipee, s/o Thomas Knox (Ossipee, farmer) and Hannah Welch (housewife); W - 30, maid, b. Ossipee, d/o Ahiel Templeton (farmer) and Miriam Nichols (Ossipee, housewife)
Darcy D. of W. Boylston, MA m. Myrtle F. **Vousden** of Ossipee 3/12/1927 in Putnam, CT; H - 22, painter; W - 18, nurse
Dwight E. of Ctr. Ossipee m. Rita E. **Noble** of Amsterdam, NY 5/29/1959 in Ctr. Ossipee; H - 30, teacher; W - 29, singer
Edward C. of Ossipee m. Alice E. **Smith** of Wolfeboro 11/5/1922 in Ossipee; H - 22, farmer, b. Ossipee, s/o Charles E. Knox (Ossipee, farmer) and Mary E. Chesley (Ossipee, housewife); W - 15, housework, b. Dover, d/o Perley A. Smith (Ossipee, blacksmith)
Edward C. of Ossipee m. Elaine E. **Herbert** of Wolfeboro 7/25/1946 in Wolfeboro; H - 22, forestry; W - 18, at home
Herbert E. of Ossipee m. Emma N. **Tewksbury** of Tamworth 11/5/1889 in Madison; H - 31, farmer, b. Ossipee, s/o Ephriam Knox (Ossipee); W - 21, housekeeper, b. Tamworth, d/o William W. Tewksbury (Tamworth)
Lawrence J., Jr. m. Janine A. **Collette** 7/13/1991; H - b. 2/16/1959; W - b. 8/3/1962

Olin A. of Ossipee m. Mabelle E. **White** of Ossipee 2/19/1913 in Ossipee; H - 26, clerk, b. Ossipee, s/o Charles E. Knox (Berwick, ME); W - 18, at home, b. Ossipee, d/o Lowenstein L. White (Haverhill, MA)

Olin A. of Ossipee m. Winifred E. **Brown** of N. Conway 7/30/1927 in N. Conway; H - 41, foreman; W - 41, housekeeper

Olin A. of W. Ossipee m. Beatrice C. **Moore** of W. Ossipee 6/4/1956 in Melvin Village; H - 69, plant supt.; W - 46, housework

KNYCH,
Mathew m. Mary **McLean** 1/6/1968 in Ctr. Ossipee; H - b. 9/18/1920; W - b. 12/15/1916

KOHLER,
John C. of Ossipee m. Nina **Dawson** of KY 8/14/1948 in Moultonville; H - 36, mill foreman; W - 31, drum sander oper.

John C. of W. Ossipee m. Rose E. **LeClair** of E. Rochester 3/29/1956 in Rochester; H - 42, mill foreman; W - 37, housewife

KOOB,
John of Cambridge, MA m. Judith **Leining** of W. Halifax, VT 7/30/1962 in Ossipee; H - 25, student; W - 23, student

KORTEJARVI-ELOVAARA,
Arnold m. Adiela **Grajales** 6/18/1984; H - b. 6/8/1939; W - b. 7/10/1951

KRAMER,
Howard Gray of Ossipee m. Ruth Frances **Smith** of Malden, MA 8/13/1940 in Tamworth; H - 25, lumber grader; W - 22, teacher

L. Page m. Anne M. **Jennison** 10/12/1980 in Ossipee; H - b. 2/5/1936; W - b. 6/22/1941

Peter H. G. of Ossipee m. Sylvia A. **Weldon** of Pittsfield 7/13/1963 in Pittsfield; H - 24, teacher; W - 24, teacher

Robert G. of Ossipee m. Beryl M. **Moulton** of Ossipee 11/5/1933 in Wakefield; H - 22, clerk; W - 20, at home

KRASOW,
Bernard m. Penny **Van Meir** 4/9/1968 in Ossipee; H - b. ½/1927; W - b. 6/24/1946

KRUTILEK,
Eric Edward of Wolfeboro m. Tanya Marie **Belliveau** of Wolfeboro 9/12/1999

KUELL,
Robert William m. Anne Marie **Baker** 9/8/1990; H - b. 8/7/1966; W - b. 1/11/1965

KUHNER,
William of Providence, RI m. Lena E. **Joen** of Providence, RI 8/2/1935 in Ctr. Ossipee; H - 49, mfg. of jewelry; W - 28, not any

LAASE,
Francis W. m. Ellen P. **Hickey** 7/12/1969 in Ctr. Ossipee; H - b. 10/27/1939; W - b. 6/27/1942

LABONTE,
Albert E. m. Barbara A. **Nunn** 12/6/1980 in Hooksett; H - b. 8/7/1931; W - b. 7/19/1954

LABOR,
Dewey m. Josephine **Sulia** 3/6/1969 in Ctr. Ossipee; H - b. 11/3/1935; W - b. 12/21/1935

LACASSA,
Rodolphe of Attleboro, MA m. LaVerna **Inman** of Attleboro, MA 10/24/1959 in Ctr. Ossipee; H - 53, shipper; W - 54, jeweler

LACASSE,
Randolph m. Nelsina **Peace** 8/28/1966 in Wakefield; H - 59, shipper; W - 54, press

LACONTE,
Donald William m. Debra Jane **Burns** 7/4/1993 in Ossipee

LAFAVORE,
Steven P. of W. Ossipee m. Brenda W. (Welch) **Bedford** of W. Ossipee 2/24/1996

LAFONTAINE,
Lawrence m. Christine L. **Graffam** 4/11/1969 in W. Ossipee; H - b. 6/4/1949; W - b. 5/19/1949

LAJOIE,
Aldore S. of Augusta, ME m. Marilyn L. **Hammons** of Augusta, ME 11/17/1946 in Ossipee; H - 21, GI student; W - 18, clerk

LAMB,
Fred of Cleburne, TX m. Myrtle A. **West** of Cleburne, TX 12/9/1960 in Ctr. Ossipee; H - 60, machinist; W - 60, none

LAMONTAGNE,
Joseph of Ossipee m. Viola **Goodwin** of Ossipee 6/14/1897 in Ossipee; H - 27, barber, 2nd, b. Halifax, s/o Fred Lamontagne (Halifax, farmer) and Phel'mne Thatcher (Halifax, housekeeper); W - 18, housemaid, b. Ossipee, d/o Thomas Goodwin (laborer) and Naomi Durgan (Eaton, housekeeper)
Joseph I. m. Georgiana **Bergeron** 3/25/1916 in Somersworth; H - 46, barber, 3rd, b. Canada, s/o Fred Lamontagne (NS); W - 43, housework, 2nd, b. Canada, d/o Andrew Nadeau (Orono, ME)

LAMPRON,
Richard J. of Wolfeboro m. Margaret L. **Reissfelder** of Ctr. Ossipee 5/14/1960 in Ossipee; H - 21, Sprague Electric; W - 18, clerk

LANDRY,
Arthur W. of Revere, MA m. Genevieve **Templeton** of Ctr. Ossipee 8/22/1936 in Seabrook; H - 35, steel worker; W - 36, none

LANGLOIS,
Gregg O. of Ossipee m. Michelle I. **Joubert** of Ossipee 5/15/1999
Leon m. Marion **Rogers** 8/22/1966 in Ctr. Ossipee; H - 59, cook; W - 62, none

LAPAR,
William H. R. m. Sonya R. **Maddock** 2/20/1988; H - b. 4/17/1963; W - b. 7/28/1967

LAPORTI,
Arthur J. of Attleboro, MA m. Mildred **Gochman** of Attleboro, MA 12/18/1954 in Ctr. Ossipee; H - 25, bartender; W - 28, jeweler

LAROSA,
Douglas J. m. Judith M. **Hayford** 7/13/1985; H - b. 7/28/1958; W - b. 12/17/1960

LARRABEE,
Clinton L., III of Sanbornville m. Gail M. Buss **Calderone** of Sanbornville 9/13/1998
Dennis E. m. Darlene F. **Shackford** 6/15/1983 in W. Ossipee; H - b. 10/11/1956; W - b. 9/6/1963

Dennis Edwin m. Patricia Helena **Bugden** 5/2/1993 in W. Ossipee
Donald E. of S. Tamworth m. Joyce B. **Eldridge** of W. Ossipee 6/15/1954 in Ctr. Ossipee; H - 24, mill; W - 24, clerk
Winfield J. of Litchfield, ME m. Cora D. **Larrabee** of Ossipee 8/18/1903 in Ctr. Ossipee; H - 21, laborer, b. Litchfield, s/o Isaac Larrabee (Litchfield, ME, farmer) and Minnie Stewart (Lewiston, ME, housekeeper); W - 30, milliner, b. Greene, ME, d/o Charles H. Larrabee (Greene, ME, farmer) and Martha A. Larrabee (Ossipee, housewife)

LASSARS,
Mitchell T. m. Deborah A. **Emerson** 6/25/1976 in Tuftonboro; H - b. 8/25/1957; W - b. 1/31/1957

LASSITER,
Thomas Michael of Saugus, MA m. Cynthia Sue (Mathes) **Luce** of Zanesville, OH 2/12/1996

LAVALLEE,
Bryan J. of Effingham m. Vicky A. Stanley **Stuart** of Effingham 7/14/2001

LAVALLEY,
John W., Jr. of Attleboro, MA m. Jeannett **Morcotte** of Taunton, MA 11/20/1954 in Ctr. Ossipee; H - 28, sprayer; W - 20, bench worker

LAWLER,
Henry J. of Ossipee m. Ella F. **Young** of Sandown 9/1/1917 in Sandown; H - 34, contractor, b. Brookfield, MA, s/o William Lawler (Ireland) and Alice Kelley (Ireland); W - 25, nurse, b. Sandown, d/o Charles H. Young (Winchendon, MA) and Mrytie L. Sleeper (Sandown)

LEAHY,
Kevin J. m. Cheryl A. **Baldwin** 6/30/1985; H - b. 6/4/1959; W - b. 1/4/1956

LEAVITT,
Harry M. of Ossipee m. Marguerite **Huckins** of Ossipee 11/11/1932 in Wolfeboro; H - 24, sheriff; W - 23, bookkeeper
Scott M. m. Cynthia M. **Cochrane** 2/14/1983 in Ossipee; H - b. 5/1/1964; W - b. 5/23/1966

LECLAIR,
Edgar G. of Boston, MA m. Mildred I. **Melville** of W. Somerville, MA 8/31/1932 in Ossipee; H - 32, R.R. fireman; W - 30, at home

LEE,
William, Jr. m. Josephine **Imondi** 11/30/1968 in Ossipee; H - b. 3/20/1944; W - b. 4/20/1943

LEEMAN,
Albert W., Sr. m. Yvonne C. **Merrill** 9/2/1982 in Gorham; H - b. 1/18/1935; W - b. 5/21/1939

LEGASPI,
Romeo m. Judith **Powers** 12/24/1964 in Ctr. Ossipee; H - 37, USN; W - 25, saleslady

LEGAULT,
Paul E. m. Christine E. **Schule** 9/28/1991; H - b. 1/18/1970; W - b. 12/24/1969

LEGENDRE,
Emile J. of Ossipee m. Irene **Holbrook** of Ossipee 10/12/1946 in Ossipee; H - 25, mechanic; W - 23, at home
Kenneth Emile m. Faith Hope **Mohs** of New York 8/5/2001

LEIGH,
William C. of New York City, NY m. Ardis **Neff** of New York City, NY 8/20/1946 in Ossipee; H - 45, lecturer; W - 31, sales rep.

LEMAY,
Shawn J. m. Marlo A. **Watson** 7/25/1987; H - b. 1/25/1968; W - b. 6/20/1968

LEMIEUX,
James A. m. Deborah A. **Engel** 9/8/1984; H - b. 12/14/1950; W - b. 2/26/1950

LENNON,
Charles J. of Ctr. Ossipee m. Miriam E. **Meloon** of Ctr. Ossipee 10/9/1937 in Sanbornville; H - 29, printer; W - 23, stenographer

LEONARD,
Jason Charles of Wakefield, MA m. Karen Ann **White** of Wakefield, MA 2/13/1999
Stanley R. of Medway, MA m. Evelyn **Fetzer** of N. Attleboro, MA 4/19/1954 in Ctr. Ossipee; H - 24, carpenter; W - 26, jeweler

LESTER,
John Gregory m. Linda Lee **Tapper** 8/21/1976 in S. Eaton; H - b. 2/2/1955; W - b. 1/23/1956

LETELLIER,
Kevin Ronald of Manchester m. Patricia Jean **Quinn** of Ossipee 7/11/1998

LEVESQUE,
Philip D. m. Kathryn R. **Rushton** 5/15/1987; H - b. 2/21/1948; W - b. 2/16/1956
Raymond E. of Portland, ME m. Audrey J. **London** of Portland, ME 6/22/1952 in Ossipee; H - 21, USMC; W - 20, office clerk

LEWIS,
Joseph W. of Lynn, MA m. Ethel **Newhall** of Lynn, MA 9/1/1912 in Ossipee; H - 24, civ. engineer, b. Lynn, MA, s/o Charles E. Lewis (Lynn, MA); W - 24, b. Lynn, MA, d/o James E. Newhall (Lynn, MA)
Stephen E. m. Catherine M. **Baker** 8/22/1987; H - b. 9/26/1951; W - b. 7/23/1953

LIBBY,
Alan D. m. Doreen C. **Sargent** 5/18/1977 in Ossipee; H - b. 12/21/1956; W - b. 4/16/1956
Alan D. of Tuftonboro m. Sherry L. **Hyslop** of Tuftonboro 8/21/1999
Carl D. m. Brenda J. **Ripley** 9/3/1975 in Ossipee; H - b. 4/17/1938; W - b. 8/4/1947
Charlie Paul of W. Ossipee m. Trina Louise **Leone** of W. Ossipee 9/24/1994
David Randolph m. Darlene April **Eldridge** 12/21/1974 in Ossipee; H - b. 8/31/1955; W - b. 4/11/1958
Dean J. m. Holly J. **Hayford** 5/4/1987; H - b. 3/31/1959; W - b. 12/24/1956
Donald of Ossipee m. Josephine L. **Paul** of Milton 10/16/1954 in Milton; H - 25, tannery; W - 21, shoe maker
Edward C. of Kezar Falls, ME m. Avis L. **Eldridge** of Ossipee 9/27/1947 in Ctr. Ossipee; H - 21, laborer; W - 16, laundress
Edward C. of Porter, ME m. Patricia A. **Taylor** of Ctr. Ossipee 8/14/1954 in Ctr. Ossipee; H - 28, lumber; W - 19, waitress
Elson of Ossipee m. Lois F. **Sweet** of Tamworth 10/31/1942 in Tamworth; H - 20, ship fitter; W - 16, at home
Ernest L. of Milton m. Ruth M. **Libby** of Ossipee 7/20/1930 in Lebanon, ME; H - 21, motion picture; W - 16, at home
Floyd F. of Ossipee m. Nancy A. **Pineo** of Wolfeboro 2/21/1959 in Wolfeboro; H - 22, laborer; W - 19, helper

Frank, Jr. of Tuftonboro m. Bernice L. **Canney** of Ossipee 4/4/1920 in Ossipee; H - 27, mail carrier, b. Tuftonboro, s/o Frank Libby (Tuftonboro) and Lucy Haley (Tuftonboro); W - 17, housework, b. Ossipee, d/o Frank Canney (Ossipee) and Emma F. Hilton (Ossipee)

Joseph W. m. Denise P. **McNulty** 3/27/1982 in Alton; H - b. 10/7/1962; W - b. 9/18/1963

Keith W. m. Sandra J. **Caulkins** 7/11/1987; H - b. 11/30/1960; W - b. 12/14/1960

Michael C. m. Cynthia Ann **Varney** 2/18/1977 in Ossipee; H - b. 8/25/1957; W - b. 11/27/1959

Paul G. m. April P. **Ryder** 7/26/1975 in Tamworth; H - b. 7/25/1954; W - b. 1/4/1956

Randolph C. of Porter, ME m. Carole A. **Perry** of Ctr. Ossipee 10/15/1954 in Ctr. Ossipee; H - 16, logging; W - 15

Randolph C. m. Carolyn A. **Cook** 2/25/1972 in Conway; H - b. 1/23/1938; W - b. 7/27/1932

Robert Carlton of Water Village m. Hazel Verna **McKenney** of Water Village 6/4/1939 in Wolfeboro; H - 18, general work; W - 22, housework

Roland H. of Ossipee m. Frances H. **Estes** of Wolfeboro 7/18/1952 in Melvin Village; H - 21, Air Force; W - 18, nurses aid

William L. of Freedom m. Frances L. **Woodman** of Parsonsfield, ME 5/18/1939 in Freedom; H - 28, poultry; W - 24, housework

LIEBERT,
Scott A. m. Carol Lynne **Christiansen** 4/14/1978 in Ossipee; H - b. 2/4/1958; W - b. 4/20/1947

LIMA,
Manuel J. of Attleboro, MA m. Phyllis L. **White** of Attleboro, MA 11/11/1959 in Ctr. Ossipee; H - 35, bartender; W - 31, packer

LINDSAY,
Raymond N. of Boston, MA m. Laura E. **Mulcahy** of Boston, MA 8/14/1943 in Ctr. Ossipee; H - 54, machinist; W - 53, under clerk

William D. of Boston, MA m. Elenor L. **Dunlaps** of Boston, MA 9/3/1921 in Dover; H - 24, clerk, b. Boston, MA, s/o William H. Lindsay (Scotland) and Annie Tyre (Scotland); W - 24, at home, b. Milton, MA, d/o William H. Dunlay (sic) (Boston, MA) and Annie J. Hutchinson (NB)

LITTELL,
Robert E. of Wakefield, MA m. Irene M. **Gaudet** of Lynn, MA 5/15/1959 in Ctr. Ossipee; H - 34, serviceman; W - 22, home

LITTLE ELK,
Myron S. of Weymouth, MA m. Shelly J. **Winn** of Weymouth, MA 10/23/1998

LITTLEFIELD,
Clifton S. of Rochester m. Arlene **Eldridge** of Ctr. Ossipee 11/14/1936 in Rochester; H - 23, chef; W - 18, housework
George F. of Ossipee m. Victoria **Drown** of Ossipee 6/2/1907 in Ossipee; H - 54, farmer, 2nd, b. Madison, s/o Enoch Littlefield and Mary Mills; W - 54, housewife, 2nd, b. Eaton
George L. of Ossipee m. Clara **Eldridge** of Ossipee 12/31/1938 in Lebanon, ME; H - 28, electrician; W - 22, at home
Orace m. Elizabeth **Williams** 12/18/1964 in Ctr. Ossipee; H - 53, carpenter; W - 52, matron
Wilmer L. of Barnstead m. Cyrena P. **Abbott** of Moultonville 6/20/1936 in Moultonville; H - 24, furniture factory; W - 32, nurse maid
Wilmer L. m. Dorothy W. **Byers** 11/10/1986; H - b. 1/10/1912; W - b. 6/26/1923

LITWHILER,
Sterling T. of Mahoney City, PA m. Thurley M. **Libby** of Ossipee 7/6/1955 in Ossipee; H - 21, teacher; W - 20, waitress

LOCKE,
Charles Ray of Ossipee m. Georgia M. **Goldsmith** of Ossipee 10/27/1907 in Ossipee; H - 20, brakeman, b. Franconia, s/o Charles H. Locke (Lisbon, carpenter) and Sarah Clark; W - 20, maid, b. Ossipee, d/o George Goldsmith and Mary Watson (Ossipee, housewife)
Frank E. of Ossipee m. Abbie E. **Nute** of Ossipee 3/31/1900 in Ossipee; H - 25, laborer, b. Bath, s/o Charles H. Locke (Lisbon, carpenter) and Sarah E. Locke (Haverhill, housewife); W - 32, maid, 3rd, b. Ossipee, d/o George W. Nute (Ossipee, soldier) and Sarah E. Nute (Ossipee, housewife)
S. Ellsworth of Sanbornville m. Flora **Thibeault** of Ctr. Ossipee 1/27/1940 in Porter, ME; H - 33, mechanic; W - 26, at home

LOGAN,
Adam W. of Revere, MA m. Florence O. **Sheppard** of Lynn, MA 7/16/1954 in Ossipee; H - 30, inspector; W - 25, clerk

LOLIO,
Thomas m. Karen **Cowley** 7/25/1964 in Ctr. Ossipee; H - 20, laborer; W - 18, none

LOMBARDO,
Eugene of Scarsdale, NY m. Lois G. **Nelson** of Mamaroneck, NY 7/26/1956 in Ctr. Ossipee; H - 29, painter; W - 32, waitress

LORD,
Arnold J. m. Pamela J. **Gauthier** 8/27/1981 in Chocorua; W - b. 7/2/1961; W - b. 1/28/1962
Brian C. m. Bonnie L. **Rankin** 7/24/1982 in Wolfeboro; H - b. 1/13/1957; W - b. 8/13/1953
Edwin F. of Tamworth m. Evaline A. **Flagg** of Ossipee 8/31/1896 in Alton Bay; H - 45, farmer, 2nd, b. Tamworth, s/o Alvah Lord (deceased) and Betsy Lord (Ossipee, housekeeper); W - 20, housekeeper, b. Boston, MA, d/o Thomas B. Flagg (deceased) and Lydia M. Flagg (Cornish, ME, housekeeper)
Francis E. m. Ann **Flanders** 10/29/1977 in Ossipee; H - b. 5/27/1951; W - b. 2/4/1954
Francis Edwin of W. Ossipee m. Kathleen Mary **Harte** of W. Ossipee 11/4/1995
John A. of Ossipee m. Laura May **Knight** of Belfast, ME 5/18/1907 in Wakefield; H - 21, teamster, b. Ossipee, s/o William H. Lord (Ossipee, carpenter) and Sarah Edna Wiggin (Ossipee, housewife); W - 20, maid, b. Belfast, ME, d/o Henry F. Knight (Belfast, ME, carpenter) and Viola J. Carter (Ossipee)
John William m. Susan L. **Henry** 6/27/1970 in CT; H - b. 8/2/1947; W - b. 6/19/1948
Lester W. of Ossipee m. Rena A. **Thompson** of Andover, MA 10/22/1906 in Andover; H - 32, physician, b. Tamworth, s/o Edwin F. Lord (Tamworth, farmer) and Julia A. Hodsdon (Moultonboro); W - 27, nurse, b. Lawrence, MA, d/o Joseph Thompson (England, pattern maker) and Margaret Kenyon (England, housekeeper)
Michael C. m. Sharon A. **Richardson** 2/5/1970 in Effingham; H - b. 8/18/1948; W - b. 6/15/1951

LORETTA,
Allen T. m. Irene F. **Craft** 6/20/1987; H - b. 12/23/1964; W - b. 6/10/1960

LORING,
Chester M. m. Esther E. **Pineo** 11/25/1916 in Ossipee; H - 22, chauffeur, b. Ossipee, s/o Elmer E. Loring (Ossipee); W - 21, clerk, b. Ossipee, d/o Inglis L. Pineo (NS)
Chester M. of Ctr. Ossipee m. Violet Mae C. **Perry** of Ctr. Ossipee 7/13/1945 in Ossipee; H - 52, chauffeur; W - 38, housewife
David F. of Ctr. Ossipee m. Muriel E. **Hodge** of Ctr. Ossipee 8/17/1951 in Moultonville; H - 22, Army; W - 24, at home

George M. of Ossipee m. Rosanna **Greenleaf** of N. Andover 11/14/1899 in Milton Mills; H - 61, mechanic, 2nd, b. Boston, MA, s/o George Loring (Boston, mason) and Juliette Loring (Boston, teacher); W - 61, dressmaker, 2nd, b. W. Fairlee, VT, d/o Thomas Scott (deceased) and Mary Scott (deceased)

James Milburn of Ossipee m. Sadie Elvira **Drew** of Ossipee 9/22/1941 in Raymond; H - 24, truck driver; W - 18, waitress

Robert Bancroft of Ossipee m. Ruth Frances **Mitchell** of Ossipee 6/15/1940 in Raymond; H - 25, laborer; W - 23, school teacher

Russell G. m. Nancy J. **Doe** 12/5/1965 in Wakefield; H - 18, laborer; W - 17, student

Russell George m. Mary Louise **Brooks** 1/26/1974 in Wakefield; H - b. 6/11/947; W - b. 12/13/1946

LOUD,
Arthur P. of Ossipee m. June F. **Chick** of Silver Lake 10/12/1946 in Seabrook; H - 26, mechanic; W - 26, secretary

Clarence B. of Ctr. Ossipee m. Marilyn J. **Whipple** of Tamworth 12/29/1956 in Ossipee; H - 27, mill worker; W - 23, nurse

Clarence B. m. Dorothy F. **Locke** 8/14/1981 in Ossipee; H - b. 10/13/1929; W - b. 1/6/1932

Edmund D'Arcy of Ctr. Ossipee m. Ruth Griffin **Hilton** of Tamworth 4/17/1943 in Moultonboro; H - 27, journalist; W - 20, housework

Grover Cleveland of Ossipee m. Eva Fall **Blake** of Ossipee 8/14/1913 in Ossipee; H - 22, instructor, b. Malden, MA, s/o Clarence B. Loud (Plymouth, ME); W - 20, teacher, b. Ossipee, d/o Simon Blake (Ossipee)

Perley W. of Ossipee m. Lena M. **Hodge** of Rochester 4/7/1917 in Rochester; H - 23, farmer, b. Malden, MA, s/o Clarance B. Loud (Plymouth, ME) and Julia M. Curtis (Stanstead, PQ); W - 19, housework, b. Ossipee, d/o Fred Hodge (Ossipee) and Bertha Nichols (Effingham)

Simon F. m. Nancy J. **Libby** 2/25/1967 in Ctr. Ossipee; H - 23, mill; W - 16, none

Simon F. m. Beverly A. **Cressey** 11/25/1972 in Sanbornville; H - b. 12/22/1943; W - b. 9/17/1943

LOUKAS,
Kane L. m. Kathryn M. **Boyden** 9/28/1986; H - b. 1/7/1957; W - b. 5/7/1958

LOVEJOY,
Bert A. m. Annie B. **Ross** 10/9/1915 in Ossipee; H - 40, liveryman, b. Lancaster, s/o Austin S. Lovejoy (Lancaster); W - 40, dressmaker, 2nd, b. Ossipee, d/o James Eldridge (Ossipee)

LOWE,
John D., II m. Betty A. **Porter** 3/14/1987; H - b. 8/17/1928; W - b. 6/28/1942

LOWELL,
George R. of Freeport, ME m. Virginia M. **Brown** of Freeport, ME 3/18/1950 in Ctr. Ossipee; H - 21, truck driver; W - 20, bookkeeper

LOZIER,
Anthany m. Blanche E. **Dore** 7/25/1915 in Ossipee; H - 23, laborer, b. Carroquet, NB, s/o Raymond Lozier (Carroquet, NB); W - 25, housewife, 2nd, b. Effingham, d/o Harry E. Davis (Ossipee)

LUCIER,
Arthur George of Northfield m. Iva Verna **Andrews** of Ossipee 8/12/1938 in Wolfeboro; H - 24, leather worker; W - 22, secretary

LUCY,
Mark Barton m. Mary Knox **Weismann** 7/17/1993 in N. Conway

LUIS,
Donald W. m. Deborah L. **Scripture** 3/7/1989; H - b. 12/15/1944; W - b. 4/25/1961

LUSCOMB,
Kenneth K. m. Patricia M. **Mollica** 12/3/1977 in Wakefield; H - b. 10/4/1954; W - b. 8/20/1957

LYMAN,
Gene Richard m. Cottie Arlene **Kosse** 7/13/1989; H - b. 2/11/1963; W - b. 5/8/1967
James S. m. Dale L. **Cairone** 10/1/1988; H - b. 2/15/1961; W - b. 10/14/1958

LYNCH,
Mary (sic) W. m. Joanne B. **Baldwin** 10/15/1983 in Hampton; H - b. 10/25/1958; W - b. 6/18/1960

LYON,
William H. m. Rose-Marie **Bourgault** 1/10/1981 in Ossipee; H - b. 8/13/1960; W - b. 6/27/1961

MACBRIEN,
Philip James of Brookfield m. Mabel Frances **Harmon** of Ossipee 7/23/1938 in Effingham; H - 21, laborer; W - 18, waitress

MACCHINIS,
Walter B. of E. Wolfeboro m. Annie M. **Lane** of Ossipee 11/25/1933 in Milton; H - 27, shoe shop; W - 26, nurse

MACDONALD,
Albert m. Eva **Bertulli** 2/29/1964 in Ctr. Ossipee; H - 21, office worker; W - 20, office worker
Douglas O. m. Sheryl A. **Maccabee** 7/28/1981 in Rochester; H - b. 10/3/1951; W - b. 1/19/1960
Forrest G. of Ctr. Ossipee m. Barbara M. **Hobbs** of Tamworth 4/7/1951 in Tamworth; H - 19, agriculture; W - 18, housekeeper
Franklin m. Linda **Deatte** 8/24/1964 in Ctr. Ossipee; H - 19, Navy; W - 19, none

MACGARVEY,
George E. of Chelsea, MA m. Mildred I. **Holman** of Melrose, MA 5/28/1938 in Ossipee; H - 24, investigator; W - 21, salesman

MACHUCK,
Elexander of Conway m. Agnes V. **Eldridge** of Ossipee 8/8/1942 in Conway; H - 53, laborer; W - 28, housewife

MACIVER,
Douglas S. m. Karen D. **Meader** 8/27/1983 in Ossipee; H - b. 12/24/1956; W - b. 6/6/1965

MACK,
James Leroy m. Terri L. **Brooks** 5/24/1991; H - b. 3/8/1956; W - b. 2/23/1957
Robert M. of Wolfeboro m. Tonita E. **Buchanan** of Ossipee 9/1/1956 in Ossipee; H - 21, shipper; W - 17, at home

MACPHEE,
Neil of Ossipee m. Patricia **Hoover** of Ossipee 7/17/1948 in Freedom; H - 29, sawyer; W - 30, bank clerk

MADER,
Richard T. m. Georgiana J. **Palmer** 8/25/1978 in Ossipee; H - b. 5/15/1946; W - b. 4/8/1949

MAGEE,
James F. of Tuftonboro m. Beatrice **Brown** of Water Village 8/9/1933 in Ossipee; H - 45, caretaker; W - 23, at home

MAGNUSON,
Henry A. m. Janet P. **Howard** 7/3/1970 in Ossipee; H - b. 5/12/1928; W - b. 10/16/1947

MAHONEY,
Daniel F. m. Carol A. **Latini** 12/29/1985; H - b. 11/21/1949; W - b. 12/23/1951
John Wells, Jr. m. Virginia Lane **Goodrich** 8/25/1973 in Chocorua; H - b. 11/10/1943; W - b. 10/12/1949
Joseph F. of Boston, MA m. Ida C. **Henderson** of Boston, MA 7/30/1910 in Ossipee; H - 21, farmer, b. Canada, s/o John Mahoney (Canada) and Elizabeth Mahoney (Canada, housekeeper); W - 18, maid, b. Tamworth, d/o Edwin D. Henderson (Tamworth, farmer) and Ada E. Henderson (Madison, housewife)

MAILLE,
Richard m. Cynthia J. **Leger** 10/8/1983 in Ossipee; H - b. 7/13/1947; W - b. 3/21/1958

MAINE,
Raymond R. m. Dorothy H. **Thompson** 10/11/1969 in Ossipee; H - b. 3/13/1895; W - b. 6/7/1902

MALAY,
William K. m. Judith A. **Hooper** 5/10/1969 in Wolfeboro; H - b. 12/15/1947; W - b. 9/26/1948

MALIAWCO,
John Frank m. Maryann **Caton** 5/17/1989; H - b. 5/5/1963; W - b. 2/15/1964

MALLETT,
William L. of Ctr. Ossipee m. Pamela A. **Kagel** of Ctr. Ossipee 7/24/1999

MANDIGO,
Keith Arthur m. Elaine Linda **Sargent** 1/12/1973 in Wolfeboro; H - b. 11/23/1949; W - b. 7/29/1948

MANNING,
Francis J., Jr. of Andover, MA m. Arvilla F. **Prescott** of Andover, MA 9/6/1950 in Moultonville; H - 24, plastic insp.; W - 16, at home

MANSFIELD,
Leroy B. m. Ida L. **Mansfield** 2/29/1988; H - b. 7/29/1920; W - b. 5/2/1936

MARCOW,
Frank of Ossipee m. Mary **Arsenault** of Ossipee 9/23/1901 in Ossipee; H - 24, laborer, b. Canada, s/o Philis Marcow (Canada, laborer) and Obeline Marcow (Canada, housewife); W - 19,maid, b. PEI, d/o Levi Arsenault (PEI, laborer) and Lucy Arsenault (PEI, housewife)

MARION,
Bradley H. m. Dawn E. **Tillinghast** 6/13/1976 in Ossipee; H - b. 10/15/1953; W - b. 5/19/1953

MARR,
Russell B. m. Carol A. **Stroker** 9/28/1965 in Ossipee; H - 21, USAF; W - 20, clerk

MARRONE,
Michael G. of Ashburnham, MA m. Caroline E. **Mahoney** of Westminster, MA 11/3/1950 in Ctr. Ossipee; H - 40, manager; W - 28, bookkeeper

MARTEL,
David Maurice m. Laurie Ann **Comtois** 5/19/1990; H - b. 10/22/1960; W - b. 8/2/1961

MARTIN,
Blaine of Lenoir, NC m. Gloria **Chiusano** of Plymouth, MA 11/6/1962 in Ctr. Ossipee; H - 28, USAF; W - 32, home
Edward D. m. Karen L. **Harris** 9/18/1982 in Ossipee; H - b. 1/12/1962; W - b. 6/3/1962
Frances of Boston, MA m. Dorothy L. **Loring** of Ctr. Ossipee 10/6/1934 in Wolfeboro; H - 25, teacher; W - 23, at home
John A. m. Deborah A. **Bausch** 8/28/1993 in Ossipee
John P. m. Nancy **See** 9/3/1981 in Conway; H - b. 12/20/1934; W - b. 11/18/1952

Leopold of Ossipee m. Josie **Colby** of Ossipee 10/31/1892 in Moultonville; H - 23, chopper, b. Canada, s/o Peter Martin (Quebec, laborer) and Mary Martin (Quebec, housewife); W - 19, housekeeper, 2nd, b. Moultonboro, d/o John Brown (Ossipee, laborer) and ----- (Eaton, housewife)

MARTINSON,
Timothy Francis m. Bonnie L. **Goldsmith** 8/23/1992 in Ossipee

MASON,
Donald Ralph of Auburn, ME m. Frances Irma **Merrow** of Ossipee 10/5/1941 in Ossipee; H - 21, radio engineer; W - 19, at home
Steven A. m. Mara **Cohen** 10/9/1981 in Ossipee; H - b. 10/9/1953; W - b. 5/5/1950
William of Ossipee m. Susie Mildred **Meloon** of Ossipee 9/16/1900 in Ossipee; H - 39, engineer, 2nd, b. Waxford, Canada, s/o John Mason (Roudon, Canada, farmer) and Rose Mason; W - 32, dressmaker, 2nd, b. Effingham, d/o John F. Meloon (Effingham, merchant) and Sarah E. Meloon (Effingham, housewife)

MASSEY,
Gordon R. m. Melissa H. **Brackett** 7/28/1984; H - b. 5/7/1957; W - b. 9/29/1959

MASTERS,
Dennis Irving m. Marianne Patricia **Jordan** 9/11/1993 in Ctr. Ossipee

MATHES,
J. W. of Wakefield m. Fannie **Welch** of Ossipee 8/30/1898 in Ossipee; H - 72, farmer, b. Ossipee, s/o Joseph S. Mathews (sic) (deceased) and Polly Bickford (deceased); W - 42, maid, b. Ossipee, d/o Peter Welch (deceased)

MATTHEWS,
Bryn C. of Toronto, Canada m. Mary E. **Cooley** of Ossipee 8/31/1963 in Wolfeboro; H - 24, TV director; W - 20, student

MATTINGLY,
Matthew John of Ctr. Ossipee m. Mindy Lee **LeBlanc** of Ctr. Ossipee 6/10/2000

MAUZY,
Whitfield, Jr. of Tiajirona, OK m. Abigail **Macomber** of Boston, MA 2/5/1955 in Ossipee; H - 28, engineer; W - 26, editor

MAY,
John P. m. Linda Marie **Ebel** 10/21/1978 in Wolfeboro; H - b. 6/18/1955; W - b. 9/13/1958
John P. of Ctr. Ossipee m. Linda F. (Fosgate) **MacElroy** of Ctr. Ossipee 2/11/1995
William H., Jr. of Ossipee m. Grethel Zenaida **Preble** of Wakefield, MA 6/12/1945 in Ossipee; H - 24, US Army; W - 24, school teacher

MAYO,
Dennis E. m. Beverly E. **Douglas** 10/14/1967 in Ctr. Ossipee; H - 21, laborer; W - 20, office clerk

MAZZONE,
Gaetano m. Constance J. **Sands** 1/1/1965 in Ossipee; H - 44, foreman; W - 30, none

McCARTHY,
Arthur J. of Cambridge, MA m. Bernadine F. **Lally** of Somerville, MA 7/10/1953 in Ctr. Ossipee; H - 23, trunk maker; W - 23, typist clerk
Bennett D. m. Sandra J. **MacFarlane** 8/11/1979 in Ossipee; H - b. 3/8/1945; W - b. 9/29/1946

McCAULY,
Daniel of Ossipee m. Josephine **Pike** of Ossipee 5/25/1907 in Ossipee; H - 44, millman, b. C.B.N.S., s/o John McCauly (C.B.N.S., shipbuilder) and Mary McRichie (C.B.N.S., housewife); W - 24, teacher, b. Ossipee, d/o John Pike (Ossipee, laborer) and Emma F. Wallace (Ossipee, housewife)

McCLURG,
Dennis m. Kathleen M. **Veitch** 8/7/1965 in Ctr. Ossipee; H - 20, Navy; W - 18, jewelry

McCONNELL,
Zane m. Blanche **Bellavance** 10/9/1965 in Ctr. Ossipee; H - 64, shoemaker; W - 48, seamstress

McCORMICK,
David Braydon of Bernardsville, NJ m. Heather Beth **Johnson** of Bernardsville, NJ 9/15/2001

McCOY,
James m. Kimberly B. **Wells** 10/1/1988; H - b. 9/26/1962; W - b. 7/30/1966

McDONALD,
John J. of Ossipee m. Laura **Mattress** of Ossipee 11/10/1902 in Ossipee; H - 29, laborer, b. PEI, s/o D. R. McDonald (PEI, fireman) and Margaret McDonald (PEI, housewife); W - 17, maid, b. Ossipee, d/o Gilbert Mattress (Ossipee, laborer) and Maria Williams (Ossipee, housewife)

McDORMAND,
Scott A. m. Lorraine M. **Piper** 8/3/1985; H - b. 8/13/1960; W - b. 7/30/1941

McDUFFEE,
Lloyd of Ossipee m. Louise Sawyer **Stillings** of Ossipee 4/21/1941 in S. Tamworth; H - 22, mill worker; W - 33, cook

McFARLANE,
Douglas m. Arlene E. **Moses** 10/18/1980 in Groveton; H - b. 6/14/1914; W - b. 10/18/1914
George Douglas of Ossipee m. Janet Miriam **Gregory** of Ossipee 7/1/1939 in Ossipee; H - 23, bookkeeper; W - 22, nurse
Peter Angus m. Nancy Diane **Mitchell** 8/4/1973 in Tuftonboro; H - b. 8/13/1945; W - b. 3/1/1950

McGOWAN,
Robert F. of Attleboro, MA m. Suzanne M. **Greene** of N. Attleboro, MA 10/14/1963 in Ctr. Ossipee; H - 22, printer; W - 20, hairdresser

McHAN,
Alan Dwayne m. Marie Anastais **Lichorobiec** 3/26/1989; H - b. 9/9/1964; W - b. 9/15/1966

McINTYRE,
Donald G. m. Marjorie A. **Lagro** 6/22/1965 in Ossipee; H - 28, laborer; W - 20, clerk

McKAY,
Alfred M. of Ossipee m. Maud **Abbott** of Wolfeboro 5/25/1909 in Wolfeboro; H - 32, laborer, b. Clyde River, NS, s/o James McKay (Clyde River, NS, farmer); W - 35, housekeeper, 2nd, b. Ossipee, d/o Albert S. Abbott (Ossipee, section hand)

McKENNEY,
Carl C. of Ossipee m. Mary **Whiting** of Conway 10/1/1948 in Effingham Falls; H - 27, tourist business; W - 19, sales clerk

McKINLEY,
Todd Michael of Smithfield, RI m. Margaret B. **Hayes** of Smithfield, RI 7/3/1995

McMAHAN,
Timothy Daniel m. Debra L. **Chase** 7/18/1990; H - b. 8/8/1959; W - b. 9/13/1959

McMANUS,
Sean P. m. Julie Ann **MacDonald** 5/21/1988; H - b. 3/22/1963; W - b. 3/29/1965

McNALLY,
Thomas J. m. Sharon K. **Lucas** 12/19/1981 in Wolfeboro; H - b. 12/29/1957; W - b. 6/22/1953

McNAMARA,
Kyle Westphal of Newburyport, MA m. Michelle Leslie **Bergeron** of Newburyport, MA 9/4/1999

McNALLY,
Robert Norwood, Jr. of Tacoma, WA m. Lara Meredith **Pratt** of Tacoma, WA 8/8/1998

McPHERSON,
Dalton B. of Concord m. Pauline L. **Mason** of Ossipee 8/28/1927 in Ossipee; H - 24, printer; W - 20, at home

McSWIGGIN,
James of Pawtucket, RI m. Janet **Roach** of N. Attleboro, MA 8/8/1958 in Ossipee; H - 22, mason; W - 22, secretary

McVEY,
John of Moncton, NB m. Ada **Templeton** of Ossipee 3/30/1891 in Ossipee; H - 22, laborer, b. Moncton, NB, s/o Peter McVey (St. Johns, NB) and Sarah (Moncton, NB); W - 18, housework, b. Ossipee, d/o Hiel Templeton (Ossipee) and Affie (Ossipee)

MEADER,
Donald N. of Ctr. Ossipee m. Barbara G. **Staples** of Tamworth 8/24/1963 in Tamworth; H - 21, salesman; W - 19, student
Douglas W. m. Nancy R. **Stuart** 4/29/1973 in Ossipee; H - b. 3/9/1939; W - b. 7/19/1940

John M. of Rochester m. Freida M. E. **Abbott** of Potsdam, NY 11/21/1931 in Rochester; H - 21, mill apprentice; W - 19, nurse

MEDICH,
Benjamin Oddmund of Lawrenceville, NJ m. Catherine Mary **Stearns** of W. Trenton, NJ 5/29/1999

MEEHAN,
Todd Leon of Ctr. Ossipee m. Amelia Joyce **Leach** of Ctr. Ossipee 6/5/1998

MEISNER,
John Peter m. Cheryl Ann **Baldwin** 4/27/1991; H - b. 9/1/1953; W - b. 1/4/1956

MELANDER,
Karl m. Khadiga **Mohamed** 7/16/1974 in Ossipee; H - b. 9/2/1952; W - b. 6/10/1953

MELANSON,
Omer of Ossipee m. Wilma F. **Knox** of Ossipee 11/1/1925 in Sanbornville; H - 23, b. Grafton; W - 20, b. Seabrook

MELOON,
Calvin A. m. Bernice N. **White** 11/21/1915 in Ossipee; H - 20, clerk, b. Orneda, SD, s/o Walter N. Meloon (Portsmouth); W - 19, domestic, b. Campton, d/o Lyman C. White (Canton, NY)
Walter C. of Effingham m. Marion A. **Hamm** of Ossipee 4/17/1914 in Ossipee; H - 21, carpenter, b. SD, s/o Walter N. Meloon (Portsmouth); W - 21, b. Ossipee, d/o A. Judson Hamm

MENNIE,
William m. Deborah **Marsh** 8/27/1966 in Ctr. Ossipee; H - 20, Navy; W - 19, clerk

MENSCH,
John Henery of Ctr. Ossipee m. Karn May (Jensen) **Weeden** of Ctr. Ossipee 8/20/1994

MENZIES,
Douglas B. m. Susan K. **Hayes** 9/27/1969 in Hooksett; H - b. 2/10/1949; W - b. 5/15/1950

MERCHANT,
George R. m. Antoinette T. **Cautone** 5/24/1986; H - b. 9/16/1958; W - b. 12/23/1961

MERRILL,
C. Eugene of Ossipee m. Phyllis D. **Pascoe** of Freedom 1/22/1900 in Chocorua; H - 25, engineer, b. Concord, s/o I. J. Merrill (Barnstead, farmer) and Ella Cater (Pittsfield, housewife); W - 18, maid, b. Freedom, d/o Henry Pascoe (England, miner) and Philemon Pascoe (Canada, housewife)
Elmer B. of Clifton, NJ m. Minnie **Wiegel** of Clifton, NJ 7/26/1955 in Ossipee; H - 60, af. insp.; W - 35, clerk
Maurice E. of Ossipee m. Annette S. **Prescott** of Franklin 6/28/1933 in Franklin; H - 27, electrician; W - 21, at home
Michael M. m. Kathryn E. **Hinckley** 12/23/1984; H - b. 8/26/1960; W - b. 1/1/1963
Richard F. m. Rhonda L. **Varney** 5/1/1988; H - b. 9/14/1970; W - b. 4/24/1968

MERROW,
Charles H. of Ossipee m. Emma S. **Walker** of Ossipee 6/7/1905 in Ossipee; H - 38, clerk, 2nd, b. Ossipee, s/o James Merrow (Ossipee, farmer) and Caroline Wingate (Wakefield, housewife); W - 24, maid, b. Ossipee, d/o John Walker (Ossipee) and Arvilla Walker (Bangor, ME, housewife)
Charles W. of Ossipee m. Louine C. **Smart** of Ossipee 10/20/1934 in Danvers, MA; H - 27, P.O. clerk; W - 22, stenog.
Dana H. of Ctr. Ossipee m. Norma A. **Cheney** of Tuftonboro 9/17/1960 in Melvin Village; H - 27, driller; W - 20, secretary
Daniel S. of Ctr. Ossipee m. Donna M. **Templeton** of Ctr. Ossipee 6/22/1961 in Ctr. Ossipee; H - 19, USAF; W - 17, school
Earl T. of Ossipee m. Flora B. **Templeton** of Ossipee 8/15/1905 in Ossipee; H - 21, laborer, 2nd, b. Clifton, ME, s/o Daniel Merrow (Ossipee, farmer) and Ella Silsby (Aurora, ME, housewife); W - 20, maid, b. Ossipee, d/o Ahial Templeton (Ossipee, farmer) and Effie Williams (Ossipee, housewife)
Earl T. of Ossipee m. Nellie P. **May** of Ossipee 4/21/1946 in Sandwich; H - 61, millman; W - 48, at home
Earl T., Jr. of Ossipee m. Agnes S. **Williams** of Tamworth 10/30/1948 in Conway; H - 28, garage business; W - 24, at home
Fred D. of Ossipee m. Francis M. **Waitt** of Saugus, MA 10/12/1928 in Saugus, MA; H - 34, painter; W - 19, stenographer
Harold K. of Hyde Park, MA m. Sara Louise **McLauthlin** of Ossipee 6/28/1913 in Ossipee; H - 31, mechanical engineer, b. Boston, MA,

s/o Charles E. A. Merrow (Ossipee); W - 33, b. E. Bridgewater, MA, d/o Martin P. McLaughlin (Duxbury, MA)
Harry Charles of Ossipee m. Lucy Thompson **Smith** of Ossipee 9/27/1997
Howard Earl m. Clemmie Belle **Pike** 6/24/1989; H - b. 1/12/1965; W - b. 3/8/1965
Howard W. of Ossipee m. Gertrude S. **Bickford** of Ossipee 6/23/1917 in Ossipee; H - 22, farmer, b. Ossipee, s/o Dana J. Merrow (Ossipee) and Annie E. Williams (Ossipee); W - 18, housework, b. Effingham, d/o Ray Bickford (New Haven, CT) and Susie G. Shaw (Dover)
Lafayette M. m. Blanche **Macdonald** 8/31/1916 in Ossipee; H - 31, clerk, b. Ossipee, s/o Elmer E. Merrow (Ossipee); W - 30, pianist, b. Newton, MA, d/o Joseph C. Macdonald (NB)
Llewellyn G. of Ossipee m. Florence E. **Nichols** of Ossipee 2/24/1906 in Ossipee; H - 19, milling, b. Ossipee, s/o Daniel W. Merrow (Ossipee, carpenter) and Ella B. Silsby (Ossipee, housewife); W - 17, maid, b. Ossipee, d/o Charles Nichols (Ossipee, farmer) and Addie Glidden (Tamworth, housewife)
Llewellyn G. m. Margaret M. **Curtin** 9/19/1915 in Ossipee; H - 29, laborer, 2nd, b. Ossipee, s/o Daniel W. Merrow (Ossipee); W - 21, waitress, b. Ireland, d/o Timothy Curtin (Ireland)
Mark E. m. Saylee J. **Downing** 10/1/1983 in Ossipee; H - b. 6/18/1959; W - b. 4/17/1964
Mark H. of Sanford, ME m. Eolyn N. **Moody** of Ossipee 5/10/1902 in Moultonville; H - 20, weaver, b. Aurora, ME, s/o Daniel Merrow (Ossipee, fireman) and Ella Silsby (Aurora, ME, housewife); W - 17, maid, b. Ossipee, d/o Alonzo Moody (Ossipee, farmer) and Viola Moody (Wolfeboro, housekeeper)
Mark H. of Ossipee m. Alice J. **Hobbs** of Ossipee 4/12/1911 in Ossipee; H - 29, plumber, 2nd, divorced, b. Ossipee, s/o Daniel W. Merrow (Ossipee, carpenter); W - 36, teacher, b. Ossipee, d/o Frank K. Hobbs (Ossipee, deceased)
Michael S. m. Kathleen M. **Brule** 8/8/1986; H - b. 12/4/1962; W - b. 3/9/1967
Michael Sands m. Tina Louise **Wakefield** 2/20/1981 in Ossipee; H - b. 12/4/1962; W - b. 1/16/1963
Mitchell Paul of Ossipee m. Suzanne Linda **Parshley** of Wolfeboro Falls 8/18/1996

MERRY,
Ronald Bruce m. Deborah Leigh **Milligan** 8/16/1975 in Ossipee; H - b. 7/14/1954; W - b. 12/28/1955

MERTENS,
Edward, II m. Laurie **Shea** 4/6/1968 in Ctr. Ossipee; H - b. 12/11/1949; W - b. 10/20/1949

MESERVE,
Alan m. Doris **White** 5/21/1966 in Ossipee; H - 18, armed services; W - 18, stitcher
Charlie of Ossipee m. Dora L. **McLucas** of Brownfield, ME 5/8/1912 in N. Conway; H - 21, laborer, b. Bartlett, s/o Joseph C. Meserve (Barnstead); W - 25, housework, b. Baldwin, ME, d/o Lyman McLucas (Brownfield, ME)
Scott White m. Danielle Marie **Pochelon** 12/7/1991; H - b. 12/6/1971; W - b. 8/18/1970
Scott White of Ctr. Ossipee m. Katy Lee **Voegtlin** of Ctr. Ossipee 8/23/2001
Steven Alan m. Debra Ann **Hall** 6/11/1988; H - b. 10/24/1968; W - b. 3/26/1968

MESERVY,
Richard m. Joanne C. **Stone** 6/26/1965 in Ctr. Ossipee; H - 23, pipefitter; W - 34, none

MESSINA,
Joseph A. of Methuen, MA m. Eleanor A. **DeCesare** of Haverhill, MA 11/2/1957 in Ossipee; H - 21, clerk; W - 20, tester

MEYER,
Edward E. m. Carol R. **Nagy** 12/29/1983 in Ossipee; H - b. 11/16/1945; W - b. 5/22/1955

MICHAEL,
Edward C. of E. Milton, MA m. Edith D. **Cummings** of E. Milton, MA 9/1/1924 in Ossipee; H - 40, b. Boston, MA; W - 37, b. Somerville, MA

MICHAUD,
Chanel L. m. Irene E. **Lafreniere** 8/4/1986; H - b. 10/10/1935; W - b. 1/5/1947
Joseph of Ossipee m. Florida **Perron** of Ossipee 11/22/1931 in Ossipee; H - 52, laborer; W - 46, housekeeper

MILLER,
Danny W. m. Brenda J. **Savage** 10/23/1982 in Ossipee; H - b. 6/21/1962; W - b. 9/5/1964

James Joseph m. Marie Eunice **Janness** 2/9/1974 in Ossipee; H - b. 8/14/1938; W - b. 5/30/1942

Robert E. m. Kathleen A. **Eldridge** 8/11/1984; H - b. 1/15/1961; W - b. 11/3/1961

MILLIGAN,

Dwight J. m. Amanda J. **Stevens** 8/1/1987; H - b. 2/13/1953; W - b. 2/22/1964

Dwight James m. Debra Ann **Belknap** 9/11/1977 in Wolfeboro; H - b. 2/13/1953; W - b. 9/6/1955

Roy T. of Ctr. Ossipee m. Dorothy A. **Abbott** of Wolfeboro 7/4/1952 in Ctr. Barnstead; H - 27, barber; W - 18, home

MILLIKEN,

George of Portland, ME m. Theresa **Conley** of Portland, ME 6/26/1948 in Ossipee; H - 28, student; W - 19, desk clerk

MILLS,

William F. m. Cora E. **Heath** 3/10/1921 in Ossipee; H - 61, farmer, 3rd, b. Hudson, MA, s/o George P. Mills (farmer) and Roberta Hunting; W - 43, teacher, 2nd, b. Pepperell, MA, d/o Frank W. Heath (shoemaker) and Ellen Nichols

MILNE,

Roland E. m. Charlotte M. **Spinney** 11/6/1976 in Ossipee; H - b. 2/24/1925; W - b. 6/1/1933

Roland E. m. Charlotte M. **Spinney** 8/10/1982 in Ossipee; H - b. 2/24/1925; W - b. 6/1/1933

MILTON,

William M. m. Irma H. **Varin** 9/1/1975 in Ossipee; H - b. 2/16/1915; W - b. 12/7/1925

MIRKOVSKY,

Frank of Lynn, MA m. Jane V. **Bailey** of Lynn, MA 7/21/1945 in Ctr. Sandwich; H - 68, draftsman; W - 69, housewife

MISIASZEK,

Robert Alan m. Patricia Lily **Descoteaux** 3/24/1989; H - b. 5/7/1952; W - b. 6/4/1956

MITCHELL,

David Leon m. Winifred G. **Hahn** 7/23/1989; H - b. 8/11/1941; W - b. 4/11/1938

Robert Dean of W. Ossipee m. Robin Jane (Cruikshank) **Morse** of W. Ossipee 9/24/1994

MOLLER,
G. Christian of Malden, MA m. Dorothy E. **Smith** of Melrose, MA 9/17/1932 in Ossipee; H - 25, public acct.; W - 21, secretary

MONACO,
Vincent of Marblehead, MA m. Ruth M. **Libby** of Boston, MA 6/18/1951 in Ctr. Ossipee; H - 49, barber; W - 37, waitress

MONFET,
Michael E. of Ctr. Ossipee m. Melissa L. **Woodward** of Ctr. Ossipee 8/21/1999

MONROE,
Donald of Ossipee m. Avonne **Knox** of Ossipee 8/14/1948 in Ossipee; H - 18, US Navy; W - 20, packer

MONTGOMERY,
Jonathan E. m. Michelle L. **Walters** 10/22/1988; H - b. 10/18/1967; W - b. 7/25/1969
Jonathan E. of Ctr. Ossipee m. Janet Lee **Larson** of Blackwood, NJ 7/29/1995

MOODY,
Clayton of Effingham m. Elizabeth G. **Nichols** of Ctr. Ossipee 12/22/1961 in Ctr. Ossipee; H - 46, carpenter; W - 48, factory
Edwin of Ossipee m. Mary J. **Brown** of Ossipee 3/19/1887 in Wolfeboro; H - 32, laborer, b. Tamworth, s/o Joseph Moody (Strafford) and Hannah; W - 38, housekeeper, b. Ossipee, d/o M. H. Hayes (Eaton) and Nancy Glidden
George A. of Ossipee m. Lepha A. **Sanborn** of Tamworth 7/17/1897 in N. Conway; H - 35, blacksmith, 2nd, b. Wolfeboro, s/o George Moody (Sandwich, farmer) and Nancy Moody; W - 24, tailoress, b. Tamworth, d/o John W. Sanborn (Tamworth, farmer) and Lewsite Sanborn (Tamworth, housekeeper)
Henry B. of Ossipee m. Anna O. **Eastman** of Ossipee 6/20/1923 in Wakefield; H - 49, b. Albany; W - 25, b. Milan
Leslie of Ossipee m. Linnie R. **Eldridge** of Ossipee 10/15/1910 in Ossipee; H - 36, farmer, b. Ossipee, s/o Bartlett Moody (Ossipee, farmer) and Sarah A. Nutter (Ossipee, housewife); W - 21, maid, b. Freedom, d/o Bertwell E. Eldridge (Freedom, laborer) and Melissie A. Moody (Tamworth)

Leslie of Ossipee m. Catherine A. **Finlayson** of Boston, MA 5/20/1922 in Ossipee; H - 47, farmer, 2nd, b. Ossipee, s/o Bartlett Moody (Ossipee, farmer) and Sarah A. Nutter (Ossipee, housewife); W - 43, nurse, b. Scotland, d/o Archibald Finlayson (Scotland, retired) and Mary Fairbairn (Scotland, housewife)

Nathaniel E. of Ossipee m. Bessie A. **Durant** of Ossipee 9/22/1927 in Tamworth; H - 46, merchant; W - 33, housekeeper

Oscar L. of Ossipee m. Eleanor P. **Quint** of Conway 2/14/1900 in Conway; H - 33, blacksmith, 2nd, b. Ossipee, s/o George W. Moody (Tuftonboro, farmer) and Nancy Quint (Ossipee, housewife); W - 21, maid, b. Conway, d/o Haven Quint (Conway, lumber dealer) and Nettie Wilder (Conway, housewife)

Roger of Wolfeboro m. Virginia C. **Haney** of Ossipee 7/11/1953 in Ossipee; H - 24, Navy; W - 26, secretary

Wayne of Portland, ME m. Joyce **Pike** of Ctr. Ossipee 9/29/1962 in cts; H -22, oil burner serviceman; W - 20, hairdresser

William H. of Ossipee m. Dora E. **Davis** of Ossipee 12/29/1892 in Wolfeboro Jct.; H - 26, brakeman, 2nd, b. Tamworth, s/o George H. Moody (Tamworth, farmer) and Mary A. Moody (Ossipee, housewife); W - 20, housemaid, b. Ossipee, d/o Joseph Davis (Ossipee, farmer) and L. Davis (Ossipee, housewife)

MOOERS,
Gary m. Susan D. **Knisley** 6/28/1969; H - b. 1/25/1945; W - b. 12/25/1950

MOORE,
Arthur H. of Brookline, MA m. Minnie D. **Thomas** of Somerville, MA 8/21/1929 in Ossipee; H - 57, book keeper; W - 52, at home

Duane B. m. Patricia A. **Duggan** 10/9/1982 in Ossipee; H - b. 12/16/1954; W - b. 10/6/1953

Fred of Cambridge, MA m. Beatrice Colby **Thurston** of Effingham 8/15/1937 in Chocorua; H - 49, truck driver; W - 31, at home

Harwood Barrows of NY m. Marie Estelle **White** of Ossipee 10/22/1949 in Ctr. Ossipee; H - 21, student; W - 20, at home

Orion O. of S. Windham, ME m. Eva F. **Anderson** of Pownal, ME 4/10/1960 in Ctr. Ossipee; H - 30, truck driver; W - 33, none

MOREAU,
Ronald A. m. Sharon R. **Welch** 6/15/1985; H - b. 4/19/1954; W - b. 3/25/1950

MORGAN,
Edward R. of Wolfeboro m. Patsy M. **Palmer** of Ctr. Ossipee 6/25/1960 in Wolfeboro; H - 21, truck driver; W - 17, secretary

Edward R., Jr. m. Sawai **Walker** 4/22/1985; H - b. 6/15/1961; W - b. 5/15/1953
Richard H. m. Linda M. **Butler** 6/2/1984; H - b. 5/7/1963; W - b. 6/13/1967

MORIN,
Andrew H. m. Barbara A. **Moore** of Ossipee 2/16/1957 in Ossipee; H - 21, laborer; W - 18

MORLEY,
Clarence C. of Lynn, MA m. Ethel M. **Pauling** of Danvers, MA 5/19/1957 in Tamworth; H - 55, builder; W - 37, at home

MORRILL,
Clarence E. of Rochester m. Mildred L. **Hitchcock** of Ossipee 11/27/1926 in Rochester; H - 25, b. Rochester; W - 18, b. Ossipee
Glenn E. m. Yuleander H. **Nudd** 4/17/1982 in Ossipee; H - b. 5/27/1962; W - b. 12/25/1963
Leonard W. of Ossipee m. Francis L. **Wiggin** of Conway 1/22/1942 in Conway; H - 21, mill worker; W - 18, housework

MORRISON,
James B. of Westbrook, ME m. Natalie Christine **Miller** of Auburn, ME 2/20/1940 in Ossipee; H - 48, physician; W - 29, beautician
Lyman of Ossipee m. Clara **Hutchinson** of Rumney 9/12/1917 in Chocorua; H - 64, peddler, 3rd, b. Groton, s/o Francis Morrison (Groton) and Catherine Welch (Groton); W - 59, housework, 3rd, b. Moultonboro, d/o John Knowles (Thornton) and Betsy J. Morrill (Moultonboro)

MORROW,
John Gordon of Ctr. Ossipee m. Winnie C. **White** of Ctr. Ossipee 8/18/1935 in Plymouth; H - 37, carpenter; W - 32, housewife

MORSE,
Clarence E. of Attleboro, MA m. Lorraine L. **Titus** of Attleboro, MA 10/17/1959 in Ctr. Ossipee; H - 36, machinist; W - 31, housewife
Frederick George of Providence, RI m. Sandra Ann (Capraro) **Lutrario** of Providence, RI 6/10/1995

MORTON,
Gerald L. of Portland, ME m. Elaine M. **Whitten** of Portland, ME 11/23/1952 in Ctr. Ossipee; H - 25, mechanic; W - 22, babysitter
Gerrald L. of S. Portland, ME m. Patricia M. **Spencer** of Portland, ME 10/31/1947 in Ctr. Ossipee; H - 21, US Navy; W - 18, at home

MOTTAU,
Michael Thomas of San Jose, CA m. Ellen Louise **Jones** of San Jose, CA 9/26/1999

MOULTON,
Darwin M. Linda Marie **Corson** 6/28/1980 in Wolfeboro; H - b. 7/16/1957; W - b. 10/28/1958
Frederick of Ossipee m. Nellie I. **Whitten** of Tuftonboro 9/1/1912 in Tuftonboro; H - 53, farmer, b. Bartlett, s/o Levi Moulton (Bartlett); W - 44, housewife, b. Bartlett, d/o Calvin Hoyt (Tuftonboro)
Harley E. of Ossipee m. Gladys P. **Hitchcock** of Ossipee 10/22/1924 in Ossipee; H - 36, b. Sandwich; W - 19, b. Ossipee
James Ernest of Ossipee m. Maude Lillian **Adjutant** of Tamworth 11/10/1941 in Ossipee; H - 22, woodsman; W - 28, housewife
Lyle O. of Ossipee m. Laura J. **Page** of Ossipee 2/27/1912 in Ossipee; H - 25, b. Ossipee, s/o Ansbury Moulton (Ossipee); W - 26, nurse, b. Orono, ME, d/o Frank Page (Harmony, ME)
Otis of Moultonboro m. Hazel M. **Whitten** of Ctr. Ossipee 6/2/1934 in Moultonboro; H - 27, laborer; W - 24, housekeeper

MOYER,
Glen Alexander of Waltham, MA m. Evangeline Blomstrom **Bradley** of Brookline, MA 6/16/2001

MUNROE,
Arthur C. of Ossipee m. Gladys L. **Worster** of Ossipee 1/28/1928 in Rochester; H - 16, laborer; W - 16, at home
Richard A. of Ossipee m. Charlotte C. **Corson** of Wolfeboro 12/25/1945 in Wolfeboro; H - 17, student; W - 17, at home

MURDOCK,
James W. m. Cynthia P. **Smith** 7/24/1982 in Ossipee; H - b. 1/21/1957; W - b. 6/22/1959

MURPHY,
Charles J., III of Ossipee m. Nicole M. **Marchand** of Lawrence, MA 7/9/1995
Charles Loren m. Martelle Karole **McNulty** 9/11/1993 in Ctr. Ossipee
Daniel F. of Ossipee m. Lisa A. **Nardello** of Ossipee 1/30/1998
John R. of Ossipee m. Mary L. **Leavitt** of Ossipee 6/14/1932 in Sanbornville; H - 35, gas & oil; W - 25, at home
Kevin E. m. April M. **Perham** 4/13/1985; H - b. 3/30/1959; W - b. 4/3/1967
Mark C. of Tuftonboro m. Kelly Whiting **Stout** of Ossipee 6/29/1997

MYLER,
Earl E. of Bangor, ME m. Iva L. **Tardiff** of Bangor, ME 1/13/1958 in Ossipee; H - 43, retail; W - 45, none

NAISMITH,
Donald G., Jr. of Ossipee m. Jane M. **Corriveault** of Ossipee 2/4/1996

NAPPI,
Nicholas M. of Portland, ME m. Jean M. **Tinney** of Portland, ME 2/20/1960 in Ossipee; H - 41, salesman; W - 29, instructor

NASON,
Alan m. Rebecca J. **Whiting** 10/27/1978 in Effingham; H - b. 8/4/1957; W - b. 12/17/1959

Benjamin m. Dorothy A. **Eldridge** 10/23/1915 in Tamworth; H - 65, farmer, 3rd, b. Wakefield, s/o Aron Nason (Wakefield); W - 69, housework, 2nd, b. Meredith, d/o Jonathan P. Jenness (Meredith)

Edward J. m. Tina M. **Sargent** 8/24/1985; H - b. 1/18/1964; W - b. 5/26/1965

Ernest R. of Sanbornville m. Meredith J. **Cook** of Ctr. Ossipee 8/31/1957 in W. Ossipee; H - 19, US Navy; W - 19, secretary

Gardner M. of Ossipee m. Cora B. **Chesley** of Ossipee 12/8/1891 in Ossipee; H - 27, laborer, b. Standish, s/o J. H. Nason (Denmark, ME) and Harriett (Standish, ME); W - 19, housework, b. Parsonsfield, d/o George W. Chesley and Ann (Madison)

Henry W., Jr. of Pittsfield, ME m. Arlene M. **Shannon** of S. Portland, ME 5/21/1947 in Ossipee; H - 19, student; W - 16, student

Joseph F. of Ossipee m. Nellie A. **Carlin** of Ossipee 4/15/1917 in Ossipee; H - 68, laborer, 2nd, b. Urkefield, s/o Aaron Nason (Wakefield) and Mary Bean (Ossipee); W - 50, housework, 2nd, b. Cambridge, MA, d/o Dennis Carlin (Kingston)

Justin E. of Chicago, IL m. Rose E. **Ham** of Ossipee 11/22/1920 in Ossipee; H - 62, student, b. Tamworth, s/o Larkin D. Mason (sic) (Tamworth) and Catherine Staples (Lebanon, ME); W - 54, housekeeper, b. Ossipee, d/o John G. Ham (Great Falls) and Nancy Sanborn (Freedom)

Michael m. Shirley L. **Riley** 8/19/1967 in Ossipee; H - 18, laborer; W - 16, none

Ricky D. of Lee m. Kirsten M. **Harmon** of Ossipee 7/14/2001

Timothy Wayne m. Susan **Eliopoulos** 1/11/1990; H - b. 2/5/1962; W - b. 1/3/1962

Todd Michael m. Cynthia Lynette **Maggard** 6/1/1990; H - b. 6/23/1967; W - b. 3/21/1971

NATHAN [see Nathon],
Ronald of Duxbury, MA m. Evitte **Grave** of Kingston, MA 7/15/1956 in Ctr. Ossipee; H - 23, clerk; W - 21, clerk

NATHON [see Nathan],
John G. of Duxbury, MA m. Louise M. **Doten** of Plymouth, MA 7/9/1958 in Ossipee; H - 34, seaman; W - 27, secretary
Ronald W. of Duxbury, MA m. Carolann **Glennon** of Duxbury, MA 10/17/1963 in Ctr. Ossipee; H - 31, clerk; W - 25, none

NEAL,
George A. of Ossipee m. Leonora L. **Severence** of Ossipee 11/5/1921 in Ossipee; H - 47, farmer, b. Ossipee, s/o Tyler R. Neal (Brookfield) and Mary E. Kenerson (Ossipee); W - 48, housewife, 2nd, b. Augusta, ME, d/o Alonzo P. Small (Gray, ME) and Henrietta Allen (Gray, ME)

NEERGAARD,
John H., Jr. m. Laurel A. **Evans** 11/28/1985; H - b. 7/18/1940; W - b. 3/7/1957

NEESE,
Leonard m. Gloria **Taylor** 10/21/1966 in Ossipee; H - 47, advertising; W - 29, secretary

NELSON,
Andy F. of Ctr. Ossipee m. Dorothy L. **Bisbee** of Ossipee 7/19/1953 in Tuftonboro; H - 37, laborer; W - 19, at home
Edwin Russell of Ctr. Ossipee m. Karen Lyn **Tice** of Freedom 6/22/1995
Gordon R. of Ossipee m. Gloria J. **Potvin** of Brighton, MA 11/12/1960 in Ossipee; H - 17, mill; W - 15, none
Harry of Ossipee m. Arvilla **Nichols** of Ossipee 2/18/1907 in Ossipee; H - 22, laborer, b. Newport, RI, s/o Fred Nelson (Denmark, ME, farmer) and Carrie Sorenson (Denmark, housewife); W - 24, maid, 2nd, b. Ossipee, d/o Charles Templeton (Ossipee, farmer) and Roberline Johnson (Ossipee, housewife)
James Earl m. Ann Marie **Nellenback** 6/6/1971 in Sandwich; H - b. 12/12/1951; W - b. 6/9/1950
Ralph E. of S. Paris, ME m. Barbara A. **Morris** of W. Ossipee 5/12/1956 in Conway; H - 19, tannery work; W - 18, fountain
Wayne Edward m. Irene Mae **Adjutant** 1/23/1971 in Ossipee; H - b. 3/15/1949; W - b. 3/20/1951

NEUMAN,
Lloyd L. of Kennebunkport m. Edith A. **Andrews** of N. Jay, ME 6/30/1928 in Ossipee; H - 25, carpenter; W - 23, at home

NEVERS,
Joseph W. of Ossipee m. Mary L. **Hamlin** of Milan 9/11/1954 in Milan; H - 24, airline term. mgr.; W - 21, at home
Thomas J. of Ossipee m. Carole **Chadwick** of Exeter 6/21/1958 in Durham; H - 21, student; W - 21, student

NEVIUS,
George Booker m. April **Bunker** 2/19/1991; H - b. 3/29/1948; W - b. 4/20/1959

NEWBERRY,
Frederick H. of Detroit, MI m. Henrietta **Potter** of Bath, ME 10/25/1946 in Ossipee; H - 68, physician; W - 51, clerk

NEWCOMB,
Charles S. of Lake Worth, FL m. Louise E. **Ribas** of Lake Worth, FL 9/6/1960 in Ossipee; H - 82, retired; W - 67, housewife

NEWCOMBE,
Roy E. m. Mary Margaret **Clayman** 8/25/1979 in Ossipee; H - b. 6/28/1908; W - b. 12/9/1907

NEWELL,
William Francis of Ctr. Ossipee m. Jacqueline Leona **Brooks** of Ctr. Ossipee 10/7/1995

NEWHOOK,
John G. of Malden, MA m. Esther P. **Dunn** of Malden, MA 9/20/1930 in Ossipee; H - 33, draftsman; W - 24, at home

NEWMAN,
Steven J. of Ctr. Ossipee m. Dinice Marie **Kennedy** of Ctr. Ossipee 2/14/1999

NEWTON,
David Frederick of Ossipee m. Judi Kristine **Gilbreath** of N. Grosvenordale, CT 10/8/1994

NIBLETT,
Charles L. of Wolfeboro m. Tiffany J. **Eckhoff** of Ossipee 9/6/1961 in Ossipee; H - 18, student; W - 17, home

Samuel of Ossipee m. Margarett M. **Glynn** of Ossipee 10/26/1910 in Wakefield; H - 34, farmer, b. England, s/o Edward J. Niblett (England) and Jane Abell (England); W - 21, maid, b. Roxbury, MA, d/o Thomas F. Glynn (Brockton, MA, blacksmith) and Kate Monyhan (housewife)

NICHOLS,
Alan R. m. Robin L. **White** 8/16/1975 in Ossipee; H - b. 10/19/1953; W - b. 6/16/1957

Allie of Ossipee m. Viola **Green** of Ossipee 1/21/1934 in Ctr. Ossipee; H - 35, mill hand; W - 34, housekeeper

Alphonzo of Ossipee m. Annie **Andrews** of Freedom 10/10/1896 in Freedom; H - 35, laborer, 2nd, b. Ossipee, s/o Amos Nichols (Ossipee, farmer) and Hannah Nichols (Ossipee, housewife)

Cecil A. of Ctr. Ossipee m. Doris M. **Rasquin** of Ctr. Ossipee 6/8/1953 in Moultonville; H - 36, mill worker; W - 29, at home

Charles A. of Ossipee m. Clara **Doe** of Ossipee 11/20/1926 in Ctr. Ossipee; H - 36, b. Ossipee; W - 42, b. Ossipee

Clyde R. of Wolfeboro m. Florence E. **Hamm** of Ossipee 11/18/1925 in Ossipee; H - 24, b. Effingham; W - 18, b. Ossipee

Earl Eugene of Ossipee m. Pauline Delmore **Evans** of Ossipee 12/21/1941 in Ossipee; H - 21, truck driver; W - 17, at home

Ebenezer of Ossipee m. Hannah **Adagent** of Ossipee 11/17/1887 in Ossipee; H - 73, farmer, b. Ossipee, s/o James Nichols and Lydia; W - 61, housekeeper, b. Ossipee, d/o James Welch and Lydia

Ernest C. of Ossipee m. Elizabeth G. **Harmon** of Ossipee 9/24/1931 in Ossipee; H - 21, mill man; W - 18, at home

Ernest C. of Wakefield m. Bertha A. **Harmon** of Ossipee 10/10/1947 in Wakefield; H - 37, sawyer; W - 28, at home

Frank of Ossipee m. Sadie **Templeton** of Ossipee 8/31/1888 in Ossipee; H - 22, laborer, b. Ossipee, s/o Wentworth Nichols (Ossipee); W - 17, housekeeper, b. Ossipee, d/o Ahiel Templeton (Ossipee)

George A. of Ossipee m. Cora **Thurston** of Eaton 10/29/1888 in Ossipee; H - 18, currier, b. Ossipee, s/o Amos Nichols (Ossipee); W - 17, housekeeper, b. Eaton, d/o Daniel Thurston (Eaton)

George E., Jr. of Freedom m. Elizabeth Lowe **Yuill** of Ctr. Ossipee 7/3/1940 in Porter, ME; H - 28, mechanic; W - 30, beauty parlor prop.

John A. of Ossipee m. Lydia **Griffin** of Ossipee 11/7/1893 in Ctr. Ossipee; H - 53, farmer, b. Ossipee, s/o James L. Nichols and Mary; W - 38, housewife, b. Dummer, d/o Elijah Griffin (Wolfeboro) and Lydia (Ossipee)

Joseph A. of Ossipee m. Carrie E. **Nute** of Wakefield 11/7/1898 in Ossipee; H - 23, laborer, b. Ossipee, s/o Frank A. Nichols (Ossipee, farmer) and Eliza Drew (Wolfeboro, housewife); W - 18, maid, b. Ossipee, d/o George W. Nute (Boston, farmer) and Sarah Nute (Ossipee, housewife)

Lewis W. of Ctr. Ossipee m. Ruth **Bidwell** of Ctr. Ossipee 2/15/1936 in Ctr. Ossipee; H - 50, millman; W - 42, domestic

Lewis Wesley of Ossipee m. Minnie Etta **McDuffee** of Ossipee 10/4/1941 in S. Tamworth; H - 56, mill man; W - 53, housewife

Linwood C. of Ossipee m. Virginia A. **Wilcox** of Ossipee 12/21/1949 in Ctr. Ossipee; H - 18, laborer; W - 23, housewife

Louis W. of Ossipee m. Hattie **Haddock** of Ossipee 6/18/1905 in Ossipee; H - 20, laborer, b. Ossipee, s/o Charles Nichols (Ossipee, deceased) and Hattie Glidden (Tamworth, housekeeper); W - 18, maid, b. Ossipee, d/o George Haddock (Ossipee, laborer) and Julia Hill (Bartlett, deceased)

Lucian P. of Ossipee m. Bernice M. **Welch** of Ossipee 12/3/1910 in Wakefield; H - 30, blacksmith, 2nd, b. Ossipee, s/o Almon J. Nichols (Ossipee) and Lavinia E. Williams (Ossipee); W - 20, domestic, b. Ossipee, d/o Oren E. Welch (Ossipee, farmer) and Jennie Bean (Ossipee, housewife)

Lucien P. of Ossipee m. Georgie B. **Hinkley** of Ossipee 7/10/1902 in New Bedford; H - 26, blacksmith, b. Ossipee, s/o Almon F. Nichols (Ossipee, laborer) and Corena Nichols (Moultonboro, housewife); W - 28, book keeper, b. Ossipee, d/o Seth B. Hinkley (deceased) and Sarah B. Hinkley (housewife)

Moses C. of Ossipee m. Arvilla **Templeton** of Ossipee 3/20/1904 in Ossipee; H - 25, laborer, b. Ossipee, s/o Frank A. Nichols (Ossipee, laborer) and Eliza Drew (housewife); W - 20, housewife, b. Ossipee, d/o Charles Templeton (laborer) and Roberline Johnson (housewife)

Olen of Effingham m. Georgia A. **Dore** of Ossipee 1/6/1907 in Ossipee; H - 21, teamster, b. Ossipee, s/o Charles A. Nichols (Ossipee, farmer) and Emma Williams (Effingham, housewife); W - 18, maid, b. Tuftonboro, d/o George W. Dore (Wolfeboro, farmer) and Lydia A. Stillings (Wolfeboro, housewife)

Perley O. of Ossipee m. Maud **Wasson** of Tamworth 9/12/1931 in Ossipee; H - 44, farmer; W - 41, waitress

Ronald D. of Ctr. Ossipee m. Edna R. **Dore** of Ctr. Ossipee 11/5/1955 in Ctr. Ossipee; H - 18, mill work; W - 17, at home

Roy S. of Ossipee m. Margaret **Collins** of Cambridge, MA 5/5/1922 in Ossipee; H - 29, chauffeur, 2nd, b. Ossipee, s/o Lafayette E. Nichols (Ossipee, farmer) and Susie E. Morgan (Beverly, MA, housewife); W

- 26, attendant, b. England, d/o Timothy Collins (England, quarryman) and Julia Murphy (Ireland, housewife)

NICKERSON,
Alfred J. of Ossipee m. Gladys B. **Hawkes** of Winchester, MA 5/11/1934 in Winchester, MA; H - 50, salesman; W - 31, clerk
Lawrence E. of S. Tamworth m. Geraldine **Pascoe** of Ossipee 9/5/1943 in Tamworth; H - 24, ship builder; W - 18, clerk
Nelson E. of Ossipee m. Bernice I. **Mills** of Ossipee 9/21/1942 in Ossipee; H - 64, boatmaker; W - 53, nurse
Nelson E. of Ctr. Ossipee m. Pearle L. **Tewksbury** of Ctr. Ossipee 3/14/1951 in Ossipee; H - 73, boat builder; W - 31, nurse
Nelson S., Jr. of Ossipee m. Barbara J. **Sharp** of Wolfeboro 1/10/1937 in Wolfeboro; H - 23, boat builder; W - 18, maid
Norman G. m. Marion L. **Nesbitt** 7/9/1967 in Ctr. Ossipee; H - 67, retired; W - 58, teacher

NIHAN,
Lawrence D., Jr. of Effingham m. Laura H. **Hodge** of Ctr. Ossipee 12/1/1951 in Wolfeboro; H - 22, farmer; W - 19, at home

NOKE,
Herbert E. of Waltham, MA m. Theresa F. **Lynch** of Leominster, MA 3/28/1952 in Ctr. Ossipee; H - 25, mechanic; W - 26, reg. nurse

NORTHRUP,
Norman L. of Ctr. Ossipee m. Deborah K. **Woodbury** of Ctr. Ossipee 7/11/1999

NORTON,
Thomas Michael m. Linda M. **Nitz** 10/21/1973 in Ossipee; H - b. 8/13/1951; W - b. 2/13/1952

NOYES,
Derek S. of Ctr. Ossipee m. Kimberly A. **Burke** of Ctr. Ossipee 8/18/2001
John m. Agnes **Shayowitz** 10/26/1968 in Tamworth; H - b. 3/6/1896; W - b. 6/17/1897

NUDD,
Wallace, Jr. of W. Ossipee m. Priscilla M. **Eldridge** of W. Ossipee 10/28/1950 in Moultonville; H - 21, lumbering; W - 18, cook
Wallace R., Jr. m. Jane **Thompson** 7/8/1978 in Ossipee; H - b. 12/24/1950; W - b. 5/17/1946

NURI,
Donald W. m. Edith E. **Klem** 3/5/1977 in Tuftonboro; H - b. 2/6/1945; W - b. 4/17/1949

NUTE,
Charles G. of Wolfeboro m. Abbie M. **Young** of Ossipee 10/26/1890 in Ossipee; H - 41, farmer, b. Wolfeboro, s/o Samuel Nute (Wolfeboro, farmer); W - 32, housekeeper, b. Ossipee, d/o Thomas C. Young

NUTTER,
Leonard R. of Ossipee m. Annie M. **Abbott** of Ossipee 6/17/1889 in Ossipee; H - 25, farmer, b. Ossipee, s/o Moses C. Nutter (Ossipee); W - 20, housekeeper, b. Ossipee, d/o Jacob Abbott (Ossipee)

NYSTEDT,
Walter of W. Ossipee m. Bonnie **Kirkwood** of W. Ossipee 5/5/1962 in Ctr. Ossipee; H - 23, aircraft mechanic; W - 20, waitress

O'BLENES,
Edgar m. Dawn **Teabeault** 4/2/1966 in Ctr. Ossipee; H - 20, factory; W - 20, none

O'BRIEN,
David Robert of Belchertown, MA m. Abby Beth **Lanphear** of Belchertown, MA 4/18/1998

O'CONNOR,
Michael Patrick m. Patricia Marie **LeClair** 8/11/1989; H - b. 2/10/1953; W - b. 1/22/1959

O'HARRE,
John of Ossipee m. Jane **Morrison** of Ossipee 7/2/1913 in Ossipee; H - 50, watchman, b. Ireland, s/o John O'Haree (Ireland); W - 45, b. George Morrison

O'HEARN,
Douglas J. m. Lisa T. **Harrison** 7/9/1983 in Wakefield; H - b. 11/24/1960; W - b. 6/1/1965

O'MALLEY,
Edward Francis of Dorchester, MA m. Marie T. F. **Fournier** of Medford, MA 7/10/1938 in Conway; H - 31, foreman; W - 24, office clerk

O'NEAL,
Sean C. of Effingham m. Trisha C. **King** of Effingham 12/25/2001

O'ROURKE,
Robert m. Karen R. **Hinchey** 5/2/1987; H - b. 5/16/1957; W - b. 9/24/1960

O'SULLIVAN,
Charles H. m. Margaret **Palmer** 6/5/1965 in Ctr. Ossipee; H - 21, US Army; W - 17, student

OLCOTT,
George A. of N. Arbington m. Lena **Walker** of Harrison, ME 11/12/1889 in Ossipee; H - 21, shoemaker, b. S. Waymouth (sic), s/o John Orcott (sic) (N. Abington); W - 22, domestic, b. Harrison, ME, d/o Edward Walker (Harrison, ME)

OLIVEIRA,
Richard m. Marilyn **Penna** 10/19/1968 in Ossipee; H - b. 12/26/1945; W - b. 3/9/1946

OLSEN,
Robert m. Diane **Olsen** 10/14/1966 in Ctr. Ossipee; H - 36, painter; W - 28, housewife

OLSON,
Robert A. of Duxbury, MA m. Diane M. **Reid** of Plymouth, MA 5/20/1955 in Ctr. Ossipee; H - 24, Marines; W - 18

OPPEDISANO,
Joseph A. of Woodbury, NJ m. Jean C. **Laidlaw** of Woodbury, NJ 10/9/1954 in Ctr. Ossipee; H - 36, welder; W - 26, clerk

OSBEN,
Jesse H. of N. Conway m. Hattie **Sedequist** of Ossipee 1/11/1890 in N. Conway; H - 30, laborer, b. Bridgewater, NS, s/o Henry Orben (sic) and Albertha Orben; W - 28, housekeeper, b. NS

OSGOOD,
Gerald of Portland, ME m. Margaret **Davis** of Ctr. Ossipee 5/11/1962 in Ctr. Ossipee; H - 52, equip. operator; W - 56, housekeeper

OTT,
Archie of Sebago Lake, ME m. Adelaide **Sweeney** of Sebago Lake, ME 10/31/1958 in Ossipee; H - 30, US Air Force; W - 30, none

PAGE,
Frank L. of Wolfeboro m. Annie E. **Tibbitts** of Ossipee 10/28/1896 in Brookfield; H - 32, farmer, 2nd, b. Harmony, ME, s/o Elden D. Page (deceased) and Lorinda Clark (Harmony, housekeeper); W - 21, housekeeper, 2nd, b. Portland, ME, d/o Thayer Trott (Portland, ME, farmer) and Emma E. Trott (Wakefield, housekeeper)
Robert Reginald of Wolfeboro m. Priscilla May **Moulton** of Ossipee 12/21/1938 in Wolfeboro; H - 29, teacher; W - 24, at home

PAGONIS,
John of Jamaica, NY m. Ruth **Shea** of Springfield G., NY 3/26/1958 in Ossipee; H - 23, welder; W - 20, bank teller

PAIGE,
Mark m. Laura Lee **Cammett** 4/12/1986; H - b. 10/2/1941; W - b. 4/17/1933

PAINE,
Timothy Edward m. Susan Ann **Moore** 7/8/1991; H - b. 6/8/1957; W - b. 6/22/1959

PALERMO,
Vincent P., Jr. m. Elizabeth A. **Jones** 6/29/1985; H - b. 12/10/1963; W - b. 4/24/1961

PALMER,
Clarence E. of Tamworth m. Dorothy L. **Jordon** of Ctr. Ossipee 5/21/1954 in Ctr. Ossipee; H - 20, sprayer; W - 21, sprayer
Edgar m. Georgiana **Cotton** 5/18/1968 in Ctr. Ossipee; H - b. 8/13/1944; W - b. 4/8/1949
Frank E. of Ossipee m. Mary M. **Merrow** of Ossipee 10/27/1888 in Ossipee; H - 27, laborer, b. Ossipee, s/o Joseph F. Palmer; W - 20, housekeeper, b. Eaton, d/o Benjamin F. Merrow
Harland C. of Tamworth m. June E. **Holbrook** of Ctr. Ossipee 6/27/1942 in Tamworth; H - 19, woodsman; W - 16, at home
Joseph B. of Cranston, RI m. Clara E. **Reynolds** of NC 5/9/1953 in Ctr. Ossipee; H - 19, student; W - 18, student
Lawrence T. m. Dolores C. **Moulton** 5/25/1985; H - b. 12/20/1956; W - b. 3/29/1956
Osmer of Rochester m. Gladys M. **Stevens** of W. Ossipee 7/31/1929 in S. Tamworth; H - 46, salesman; W - 37, waitress
Richard Orrin of Ossipee m. Verna Gertrude **Ham** of Ossipee 8/29/1940 in Portsmouth; H - 28, architect; W - 21, teacher
Robert C. m. Denise R. **Roy** 7/21/1985; H - b. 1/21/1958; W - b. 1/26/1958

PALMISANO,
Carmine C. m. Alice R. **DiPaolo** 3/13/1982 in Ossipee; H - b. 8/24/1929; W - b. 8/1/1947

PANNO,
Wayne F. m. Lynne M. **Palmer** 7/6/1986; H - b. 1/18/1966; W - b. 4/9/1962

PARABOSCHI,
John Lawrence of Deltona, FL m. Donna Jeanne Manore **Tressell** of Deltona, FL 7/3/2001

PARASKOS,
Joshua David of Penacook m. Nicole Ann **Duguay** of Penacook 9/5/1998

PARKER,
John of Ossipee m. Ruth **Pike** of Ossipee 11/21/1930 in Ossipee; H - 20, plant man; W - 17, at home
Larry Raymond of Fryeburg, ME m. Jacqueline Mary Bomaster **Waggener** of Fryeburg, ME 10/13/2001

PARKHURST,
Walter R. of Wolfeboro m. Lisa A. Welch **Parkhurst** of Ossipee 9/23/2000

PARKS,
Robert W. m. Elizabeth R. **Pearson** 8/28/1965 in Ctr. Ossipee; H - 27, trucker; W - 25, student

PARSONS,
Bruce W. m. Elaine S. **Butler** 1/4/1967 in Ctr. Ossipee; H - 20, Navy; W - 20, electronic tester
John M. m. Celia A. **Meloon** 6/14/1916 in Ossipee; H - 64, mechanic, 2nd, b. Freedom, s/o John Parsons (Henniker); W - 63, housekeeper, 2nd, b. Madison, d/o Stephen Flanders (Madison)
Roscoe Myron of Augusta, ME m. Carolyn Hamlin **Weeks** of Fairfield, ME 7/13/1945 in Ossipee; H - 36, accountant; W - 38, tel. operator

PASCOE,
William H. of Ossipee m. Agnes M. **Page** of Tamworth 10/22/1919 in Ossipee; H - 20, merchant, b. Freedom, s/o Harry Pascoe, Jr. (Corprus Hill, VT) and Annie Laughton (Freedom); W - 20, school teacher, b. Tamworth, d/o Edgar Page (Tamworth) and Grace A. Davis (Tamworth)

PATTEN,
John C. of Wolfeboro m. JoLinda L. **Remington** of Ossipee 9/16/2000

PATTERSON,
William of Ossipee m. Gail **Adjutant** of Wolfeboro 8/5/1963 in Wolfeboro Falls; H - 20, mechanic; W - 17, home

PATTISON,
David E., Jr. of Ossipee m. Deborah A. **Porter** of Ossipee 12/31/1998

PATULSKI,
Mark P. m. Jennifer H. **Petrzak** 10/4/1986; H - b. 1/30/1951; W - b. 4/22/1939

PAVLUVCIK,
Arthur J. m. Marcia **McCarthy** 4/15/1989; H - b. 7/7/1935; W - b. 2/7/1943

PEABODY,
David Joshua m. Diane Laura **Delfuoco** 7/19/1992 in Chocorua
William B. m. Judith V. H. **Chase** 1/31/1987; H - b. 10/1/1946; W - b. 4/12/1943

PEARE,
Arthur G. of Ctr. Ossipee m. Evelyn M. **Eldridge** of Tuftonboro 4/24/1954 in Tuftonboro; H - 29, mill; W - 21, at home

PEARL,
Michael J. of Marshfield, MA m. Carolyn A. **Damon** of Scituate, MA 6/23/1951 in Ctr. Ossipee; H - 20, Army; W - 20, secretary
Michael J. of Marshfield, MA m. Juanita **Kelley** of Marshfield, MA 7/7/1956 in Ctr. Ossipee; H - 25, electronic; W - 18

PEARSON,
Donal C. of Ctr. Ossipee m. Ruby M. **Richards** of Ctr. Ossipee 6/21/1942 in Ctr. Ossipee; H - 20, mill man; W - 22, teacher
Walter G. m. Virginia E. **Janek** 1/29/1972 in Wolfeboro; H - b. 9/6/1949; W - b. 9/9/1950

PEAVEY,
Benjamin F. of Ossipee m. Mary F. **Meader** of Tuftonboro 10/30/1892 in Tuftonboro; H - 62, farmer, 4th, b. Tuftonboro, s/o E. Peavey (Tuftonboro) and Abigail Peavey (Dover); W - 52, housekeeper, 3rd, b. Ossipee, d/o Orin J. Brown (Tuftonboro) and Sarah Walker (Ossipee)

PECUNIES,
Russell Quentin of Ctr. Ossipee m. June F. (Averill) **Lunt** of Ctr. Ossipee 12/1/1996

PEEK,
Gary R. m. Lisa L. **Nason** 6/28/1986; H - b. 4/15/1955; W - b. 3/15/1963

PELLERIN,
Gerald Joseph of Ossipee m. Eleanor Marie **Reynolds** of Ossipee 7/11/1998

PELLETIER,
Louis P. J. of Ctr. Ossipee m. Sadie Elvira Drew **Foss** of Sanbornville 8/17/2000

PENDLETON,
Lawrence M. m. Rose C. **Burke** 10/1/1983 in Wolfeboro; H - b. 7/8/1911; W - b. 10/9/1910

PEPPER,
Bruce Richard of Ctr. Ossipee m. Teresa Lyn **Williams** of Ctr. Ossipee 8/12/1997

PERKINS,
Daniel B. m. Sally Ann **Cornwell** 7/5/1980 in Sandwich; H - b. 11/3/1951; W - b. 10/19/1957
Sidney L. of Ossipee m. Blanche G. **Thompson** of Ossipee 8/2/1914 in Wakefield; H - 25, farmer, b. Ossipee, s/o Charles Perkins (Meredith); W - 21, b. Ossipee, d/o John Thompson (Tuftonboro)

PERREAULT,
Andre J. m. Martha J. **Perreault** 12/31/1985; H - b. 5/3/1943; W - b. 5/27/1945

PERREN,
William of Ossipee m. Cora **Clough** of Ossipee 4/21/1903 in Ossipee; H - 20, lumbering, b. NB, s/o Alfred Perren (NS, deceased) and Rebecca Rattee (NS, housewife); W - 20, maid, b. Ossipee, d/o Albion Clough (Ossipee, lumbering) and Olive Clough (Ossipee, housewife)

PERRON,
Amey of Waltham, MA m. Ada **Templeton** of Ossipee 9/20/1896 in Ossipee; H - 23, millman, b. Canada, s/o Andrew Perron (Canada, farmer) and Agness Gognon (Canada, housekeeper); W - 20,

housekeeper, 2nd, b. Ossipee, d/o Ahial Templeton (Ossipee, farmer) and Effie Templeton (Ossipee, housekeeper)
Raymond A., II m. Marcia A. **Pilant** 2/5/1988; H - b. 10/15/1954; W - b. 12/28/1946

PERRY,
Allen S. m. Barbara J. **Berry** 5/23/1973 in Ossipee; H - b. 9/14/1957; W - b. 8/6/1953
Donald John of Ctr. Ossipee m. Donna Marie **Fillipon** of Ctr. Ossipee 8/8/1998
Ernest A., Jr. of Ossipee m. Gwendolyn **Knox** of Ossipee 12/21/1948 in Ctr. Ossipee; H - 19, US Navy; W - 20, telephone op.
Gary R. m. Jean C. **Kolinek** 7/1/1967 in W. Ossipee; H - 17, public works; W - 21, service rep., NT & T Co.
Gary R. m. Kathleen J. **Milligan** 8/3/1972 in Pittsfield; H - b. 12/19/1949; W - b. 7/14/1954
Gary Roy m. Doreen Connie **Libby** 1/1/1989; H - b. 12/10/1949; W - b. 4/16/1956
Herbert L. of Attleboro, MA m. Mildred J. **Bennett** of Attleboro, MA 7/29/1929 in Ctr. Ossipee; H - 26, foreman; W - 23, designer
James T. of Ctr. Ossipee m. Jennifer L. **Josephson** of Ctr. Ossipee 7/17/1999
Keith E. m. Nancy G. **Hodges** 9/18/1982 in Melvin Village; H - b. 1/11/1951; W - b. 3/7/1951
Paul Robert m. June **Ricci** 10/23/1988; H - b. 5/22/1962; W - b. 12/10/1962
Stanley A. of Ctr. Ossipee m. Barbara D. **Gouin** of Tuftonboro 1/26/1957 in Ctr. Ossipee; H - 22, mill worker; W - 17, at home

PETERS,
Charles Michael m. Georgia Elaine **Freeman** 8/12/1989; H - b. 2/15/1951; W - b. 6/6/1944
Charles Michael m. Nancy Ellen **Quinland** 7/20/1991; H - b. 2/15/1951; W - b. 3/20/1947
Charles R., Jr. of Dover, MA m. Betty A. **Harkness** of Walpole, MA 8/10/1963 in Ctr. Ossipee; H - 28, accountant; W - 29, teacher

PETERSON,
David Charles m. Tina Marie **Stanton** 5/2/1992 in Ctr. Ossipee
Thomas F. of Portland, ME m. Joanne C. **Whitten** of Portland, ME 12/31/1961 in Ctr. Ossipee; H - 31, salesman; W - 21, cashier

PETTER,
John B. of Holden, MA m. Elizabeth **Geiler** of Cambridge, MA 11/18/1950 in Ctr. Ossipee; H - 31, doctor; W - 26, lab. tech.

PETTIS,
Steven Daniel m. Marie Frances **Arsenault** 6/18/1988; H - b. 8/20/1956; W - b. 7/16/1953

PHILBRICK,
Edward T. of Raymond, ME m. Frances K. **Grant** of Raymond, ME 6/26/1949 in Ctr. Ossipee; H - 54, lumbering; W - 55, tourist camps
Ellsworth of Ossipee m. Celia D. **Sargent** of Ossipee 11/11/1924 in Conway; H - 25, b. Waterboro, ME; W - 21, b. Ossipee
Wesley of Wolfeboro m. Louise **Clough** of Wolfeboro 5/25/1933 in Ossipee; H - 23, laborer; W - 26, shoe shop

PHILLIPS,
George Robert m. Elmalee **Shortt** 3/12/1989; H - b. 2/13/1946; W - b. 11/1/1954

PICE,
Thomas E. P. of Wellesley, MA m. Margaret **Van Darl** of Cambridge, MA 9/1/1930 in Ossipee; H - 35, retired; W - 26, at home

PICKETT,
Harry A. of Salem, MA m. Isadore **Brown** of Salem, MA 10/17/1928 in Ossipee; H - 56, clerk; W - 55, cashier

PIERRO,
Carmine M. m. Maureen M. **LeGendre** 11/26/1983 in Ossipee; H - b. 9/21/1947; W - b. 4/23/1957

PIKE,
Donald L. of Norton, MA m. Marguerite **Pelletier** of Attleboro, MA 7/15/1954 in Ctr. Ossipee; H - 29, jewelry; W - 34, jewelry
Edwin of Ossipee m. Clara **Wiggin** of Ossipee 1/21/1899 in Ossipee; H - 24, farmer, b. Ossipee, s/o John W. Pike (Ossipee, farmer) and Emma Pike (Ossipee, housewife); W - 17, maid, b. Ossipee, d/o William Wiggin (Moultonboro, farmer) and Sophia Wiggin (Ossipee, housewife)
John I. of Ossipee m. Lillian M. **Bendin** of Portland, ME 8/18/1923 in Freedom; H - 33, b. Ossipee; W - 23, b. Bangor, ME

PILKINGTON,
Samuel S. of Winchester, MA m. Mary **Glidden** of Ossipee 5/3/1946 in Ossipee; H - 25, US Navy; W - 24, at home

PIMENTAL,
George m. Ruth **DiGiovanni** 5/29/1967 in Ctr. Ossipee; H - 34, machinist; W - 35

PINARD,
Russell C. of Ossipee m. Mary **Kolonovich** of Hull, MA 11/23/1959 in Wolfeboro; H - 36, USN; W - 41, waitress
Russell C. m. Anita R. **Pinard** 6/30/1984; H - b. 2/2/1924; W - b. 9/19/1925

PINKHAM,
Charles R. of Ctr. Ossipee m. Frances L. **Eldredge** of Ctr. Ossipee 8/22/1953 in Ctr. Ossipee; H - 32, teacher; W - 29, teacher

PIPER,
E. Perley of Wolfeboro m. Ethel B. **Prokey** of Ossipee 11/7/1943 in Sanbornville; H - 75, store manager; W - 40, at home
Frank F. of Lee m. Marjorie **Sabine** of Ossipee 9/20/1930 in Ossipee; H - 21, plumber; W - 20, at home

PLANTE,
Wilfred of Ossipee m. Janet Elizabeth **Tatham** of Ossipee 10/22/1939 in Ctr. Ossipee; H - 22, meat cutter; W - 18, at home

PLASTRIDGE,
Clement Henry m. Constance Lola **Davis** 3/30/1976 in Laconia; H - b. 7/5/1914; W - b. 6/17/1919

PLUMMER,
Clarence R. of Ossipee m. Mabel **Nute** of Ossipee 11/3/1945 in Dover; H - 52, farmer; W - 44, housewife
Clinton E. m. Lois Elizabeth **Winckler** 12/11/1970 in Ossipee; H - b. 5/22/1934; W - b. 4/15/1928
Stephen Jon of Effingham m. Melissa Eleanor **Jones** of Ossipee 3/31/1998

POCHELON,
Allen G. m. Deborah J. **Kirkwood** 10/15/1965 in Ctr. Ossipee; H - 23, tree expert; W - 18, home

POISSON,
Norman R. of Ctr. Ossipee m. Sheila Ebert **Durgan** of Ctr. Ossipee 9/15/1997

POLLARD,
Hughe M. of Oxford, ME m. Leora C. **Stratton** of Portland, ME 7/27/1956 in Ossipee; H - 36, mechanic; W - 35, secretary

POLLINI,
Jay Michael m. Wenda Marie **Morgan** 10/3/1992 in Ossipee

PONT,
William Joseph m. Laura Helen **Beardsley** 6/9/1974 in Wolfeboro; H - b. 12/23/1945; W - b. 3/12/1949

POPE,
Francis of NY m. Laura S. **Porter** of NY 8/9/1909 in Rochester; H - 42, lawyer, 2nd, b. India, s/o John F. Pope (Chicago, civil engineer); W - 37, editor, b. Covington, KY, d/o William H. Porter (America, merchant)
Gordon A. m. Beatrice I. **Freeman** 9/29/1986; H - b. 4/1/1917; W - b. 9/16/1919

POPHAM,
William of Haverhill, MA m. Patricia **Phinney** of Haverhill, MA 4/29/1956 in Ctr. Ossipee; H - 29, truck driver; W - 22

POTTER,
Albert M. m. Susan A. **Eagan** 10/21/1989; H - b. 1/31/1958; W - b. 7/28/1963
Albert M. of Ossipee m. Isabel C. **Cunha** of Lowell, MA 8/19/2001
John A. of Raymond m. Ella L. **Robinson** of Ossipee 7/28/1910 in Ossipee; H - 20, machinist, b. Raymond, s/o Will Potter (farmer) and ----- Welch; W - 17, student, b. Deerfield, d/o John D. Robinson (Manchester, farmer) and Martha B. Hartford (Deerfield, housewife)

POULIOT,
Eugene of Attleboro, MA m. Alice **Lewis** of Pawtucket, RI 7/6/1962 in Ossipee; H - 48, maintenance; W - 49, housewife
Joseph of Plainville, MA m. Cynthia **Anuseevize** of Norwood, MA ½/1959 in Ctr. Ossipee; H - 24, truck driver; W - 19, none

POWELL,
Benjamin M. of Fordyce, AR m. Nancy W. **Mathews** of Ossipee 7/23/1955 in Ctr. Ossipee; H - 36, US Navy; W - 33, at home

POWERS,
Albert E. of Windham, ME m. Judith M. **Beal** of Windham, ME 3/27/1960 in Ctr. Ossipee; H - 24, body shop; W - 20, none

PRATT,
Charles Henry of Ossipee m. Eva Agnes **Eldridge** of Ossipee 11/24/1913 in Boston, MA; H - 43, farmer, b. Salem, MA, s/o John W. Pratt; W - 35, asst. librarian, b. Boston, MA, d/o Stephen S. Eldridge
John H. of Ossipee m. Clara M. **Moulton** of Ossipee 12/25/1912 in Ossipee; H - 32, farmer, b. Salem, MA, s/o John Pratt (Salem, MA); W - 21, housework, b. Tamworth, d/o Albert P. Moulton (Moultonboro)

PRAY,
John E. of Ctr. Ossipee m. Edith **Hayford** of S. Tamworth 9/26/1891 in Tamworth; H - 22, s/o Asa Pray (Ossipee) and Mary; W - 20, d/o Abijah Hayford (Tamworth)

PREBLE,
Edward A. of Plymouth, MA m. Minnie R. **Setz** of Boston, MA 7/19/1952 in Ossipee; H - 81, editor; W - 67, at home

PRIBILA,
John Stephen m. Gail Irene **Magidsen** 1/19/1991; H - b. 9/15/1942; W - b. 9/12/1952

PRICE,
Larry F. of Ctr. Ossipee m. Lisa A. **Joseph** of Ctr. Ossipee 11/17/2001
Leaston L., III m. Donna M. **Lemay** 11/15/1987; H - b. 8/21/1960; W - b. 11/13/1961

PROKEY,
Larry P. of Ossipee m. Ethel M. **Banfill** of Ossipee 4/27/1920 in Ossipee; H - 22, woodsman, b. Russia, s/o Peter Prokey (Russia) and Rona Prokey (Russia); W - 13, housework, b. Farmington, d/o William Banfill (Conway) and Rosie Laforge (Canada)
Richard Ernest of Rochester m. Esther Lona **Day** of Ossipee 2/12/1949 in Moultonville; H - 21, brakeman; W - 18, at home

PROVOST,
William B. m. Barbara F. **Provost** 8/22/1969 in Ctr. Ossipee; H - b. 1/30/1917; W - b. 5/26/1929

PURKIS,
John D. m. Susan Carol **Blair** 8/25/1979 in Ossipee; H - b. 7/26/1952; W - b. 1/15/1955

PURRINGTON,
Rainsford D. of W. Ossipee m. Lois A. **Melanson** of W. Ossipee 3/4/1950 in Conway; H - 28, woodsman; W - 20, factory worker

PYNE,
John S., III m. Laina J. **Kirch** 10/6/1979 in Effingham; H - b. 8/19/1955; W - b. 11/8/1959

QUIMBY,
Willard H. m. Patricia L. **Whitten** 11/3/1989; H - b. 10/19/1937; W - b. 10/6/1939

QUIROS,
Edin Chavarria of Myrtle Beach, SC m. Deborah Phaup **Harris** of Myrtle Beach, SC 10/16/1999

RAND,
Clinton LeShore m. Carolyn Jean **Hunt** 7/25/1976 in Tamworth; H - b. 4/7/1941; W - b. 5/11/1948
Roger W. m. Gail M. **Smith** 2/24/1991; H - b. 12/5/1934; W - b. 7/12/1956

RANDALL,
Raymond Ansel, Jr. m. Laurie Ann **Kirch** 10/9/1993 in Wolfeboro

RANKIN,
Norman Frisco, Jr. m. Jean M. **Jones** 1/18/1974 in Ossipee; H - b. 10/4/1935; W - b. 12/17/1934

RASPANTE,
Frank m. Lisa G. **Tupeck** 4/12/1980 in Wolfeboro; H - b. 1/5/1951; W - b. 7/21/1960

RASQUIN,
John R. of Freedom m. Doris M. **Pare** of Ctr. Ossipee 11/23/1951 in Ctr. Ossipee; H - 35, student; W - 27, at home

RATTEE,
Felix of Ossipee m. Mary R. **Tinkham** of Ossipee 12/5/1903 in Farmington; H - 37, laborer, 2nd, b. Canada, s/o John Rattee (Canada, farmer) and Delina Rattee (Canada, housewife); W - 36, housekeeper, b. NS, d/o Charles Doliver (NS, farmer) and Annie Doliver (NS, housewife)

RAWDING,
Robert B. of Framingham, MA m. Athlene M. **Rawding** of Cullman, AL 8/23/1954 in Ossipee; H - 23, truck driver; W - 23, housewife

RAY,
Arthur of N. Attleboro, MA m. Joanne **Blocklock** of Plainville, MA 3/9/1956 in Ctr. Ossipee; H - 42, stock clerk; W - 38, press operator
Arthur J. of Chartley, MA m. Mertie E. **Wheaton** of Attleboro, MA 1/26/1956 in Ctr. Ossipee; H - 18, footpress; W - 18

REDLON,
Charles H. of Ossipee m. Delia H. **Walker** of Ossipee 7/3/1888 in Ossipee; H - 19, weaver, b. Hiram, ME, s/o Jacob Redlon (Hiram, ME); W - 16, weaver, b. Porter, ME, d/o John E. Walker
Thomas P. of Ossipee m. Sarah A. **Locklin** of Sweden, ME 10/20/1888 in Ossipee; H - 25, cooper, b. S. Hiram, ME, s/o Jacob Redlon (S. Hiram, ME); W - 20, housekeeper, b. Sweden, ME, d/o Robert Locklin (Sweden, ME)

REDMAN,
Edward L. of Clifton, ME m. Mildred P. **Delano** of Bangor, ME 10/5/1942 in Ctr. Ossipee; H - 51, chemical eng.; W - 43, beautician

REED,
Charles S., Jr. m. Carolee **Ross** 6/15/1991; H - b. 6/25/1939; W - b. 12/5/1941
Edgar of N. Shapleigh, ME m. Mabel C. **Folsom** of Ossipee 6/12/1887 in Malden, MA; H - 21, b. N. Shapleigh, ME, s/o Edward Reed and Sarah A.; W - 19, b. Ossipee, d/o John W. Folsom and Annie
Richard E. of Augusta, ME m. Dorothy Mae **Watts** of Augusta, ME 11/12/1949 in Ctr. Ossipee; H - 44, commissioner; W - 22, stenographer

REGGIE,
Michael C. of Carlstadt, NJ m. Cristina **Saracino** of Cliffside Park, NJ 10/3/1999

REILLY,
Robert J. m. Pearl M. **Center** 5/27/1977 in Ossipee; H - b. 9/25/1910; W - b. 11/6/1908

REINHOLD,
Robert V., Jr. m. Margaret A. **Brown** 10/15/1988; H - b. 2/5/1956; W - b. 3/10/1960

REISSFELDER,
Theodore of Ossipee m. Pauline **Burleigh** of Ossipee 2/21/1931 in Ctr. Tuftonboro; H - 25, clerk; W - 21, stenographer
William m. Bernice **Downs** 10/5/1968 in Ctr. Ossipee; H - b. 4/27/1939; W - b. 9/20/1944

REIZER,
Edward C. m. Marie L. **Lindley** 5/20/1972 in Ossipee; H - b. 12/20/1943; W - b. 9/2/1949

REJDA,
Larry Keith of Ossipee m. Jane L. Russell **Allen** of Ossipee 10/24/1998

REMICK,
Otis D. of Ossipee m. Cora F. **Tibbetts** of Ossipee 12/20/1896 in Ossipee; H - 26, blacksmith, b. Brookfield, s/o Mark Remick (Kittery, ME, stone mason) and Helener Remick (Boston, MA, housewife); W - 18, housemaid, b. Madison, d/o Stephen R. Tibbetts (Madison, farmer) and Mary Tibbetts (deceased)

REMINGTON,
Kenneth K. of Harrington, DE m. Carol **Conner** of Ossipee 6/8/2001

RENBENS,
Maurice of Brookline, MA m. Ruth **Barenholtz** of Brookline, MA 2/22/1956 in Ossipee; H - 43, real estate; W - 38, secretary

REPASY,
Paul V. m. Lucinda A. **Wardwell** 2/12/1967 in Conway; H - 40, signs comm. art; W - 19, housewife

RHINES,
Irving K. of W. Ossipee m. Eleanor M. **Eldredge** of Tamworth 6/16/1955 in Ctr. Sandwich; H - 29, mach. operator; W - 24, nurse aid

RHOADES,
Donald Estes of Winslow, ME m. Evelyn Irene **Olssen** of Skowhegan, ME 6/14/1936 in Ctr. Ossipee; H - 23, paper maker; W - 20, house maid

RICCI,
Joseph, Jr. of Portland, ME m. Jeannette **Quimby** of Portland, ME 11/26/1960 in Ctr. Ossipee; H - 20, fishman; W - 19, clerk

RICE,
Lawrence J., Jr. of Ctr. Ossipee m. Lori Ann **DeLuca** of Ctr. Ossipee 7/16/1994

RICH,
Charles E. of Lynn, MA m. Mary E. **Hodsdon** of Ossipee 4/15/1907 in Ossipee; H - 33, physician, b. N. Palmer, ME, s/o Edwin A. Rich and Mary A. Blackstone; W - 28, maid, b. Ossipee, d/o Arthur L. Hodsdon (Ossipee) and Charlotte Grant (Ossipee, housewife)

RICHARDSON,
Frank of Ossipee m. Rose O. **Conner** of Dover 12/27/1948 in Salem; H - 48, marine engineer; W - 42, bookkeeper
George E. of Lancaster, MA m. Carolyn **Porter** of Pasadena, CA 9/1/1932 in Ossipee; H - 21, electrical eng.; W - 19, at home

RICKER,
George M. of Berwick, ME m. Bertha **Wiggin** of Milton Mills 9/19/1933 in Conway; H - 26, lumberman; W - 25, mill work
Martin V. of Ossipee m. Maria A. **Hammond** of Wolfeboro 8/24/1905 in Weirs; H - 65, farmer, 3rd, b. Ossipee, s/o Hiram S. Ricker (Berwick, ME, farmer) and Irene Chick (Ossipee, housewife); W - 62, housekeeper, 4th, b. Parsonsfield, ME, d/o Daniel Kimball (Tamworth, farmer) and Susan Brown (Ossipee, housewife)

RIETH,
Arthur W. of Needham, MA m. Suzanne H. **Sticklin** of Wellesley Hills, MA 7/29/1950 in Moultonville; H - 24, optician; W - 20, at home

RILEY,
Daniel B. of Ossipee m. Cheryl J. **Welch** of Ctr. Ossipee 2/9/1963 in Ossipee; H - 22, logger; W - 16, school
Daniel B., Jr. m. Cheryl Anne **Feener** 9/23/1989; H - b. 2/7/1964; W - b. 10/17/1953
Ernest G., Jr. m. Susan E. **Damon** 12/27/1969 in Alton; H - b. 3/12/1939; W - b. 12/15/1946

Ernest Granville of Ossipee m. Beatrice A. **Banfill** of Tuftonboro 9/24/1938 in Wakefield; H - 22, laborer; W - 16, at home
Herbert F. of Ossipee m. Jeanne Adele **Morgan** of Wolfeboro 12/20/1941 in Wolfeboro; H - 18, laborer; W - 16, at home
Herbert F. of Ossipee m. Alice M. **Pike** of Ossipee 10/11/1950 in Ctr. Ossipee; H - 27, garage worker; W - 23, waitress
Michael Scott of Ctr. Ossipee m. Michelle Lee **Perry** of Ctr. Ossipee 9/21/1996
Thomas J. of Ossipee m. Heather N. **Hudson** of Manhattan, NY 1/22/2000
William Ernest m. Donna Elizabeth **Magee** 6/20/1992 in Ossipee

RINES,
Bruce E. of Ctr. Ossipee m. Marion A. **Barrow** of Ctr. Ossipee 12/28/1963 in Wolfeboro; H - 20, mechanic; W - 20, secretary
Carl D. of Ctr. Ossipee m. Barbara L. **Virgilio** of S. Portland, ME 10/1/1955 in Wolfeboro; H - 20, auto mechanic; W - 21, nurse
George W. of Ossipee m. Emma **Cole** of Ossipee 9/20/1890 in Ossipee; H - 26, laborer, b. New Durham, s/o Charles Rines (farmer); W - 40, housekeeper, b. Brookfield, d/o Joseph Cole (Ossipee, farmer)
James Franklin of Ossipee m. Brooke Willett **Glidden** of Ossipee 10/1/1999
Mark F. of Ctr. Ossipee m. Shirley E. **Wilson** of Dover 7/7/1951 in Dover; H - 22, teacher; W - 17, secretary
Stanley J. m. Marilyn J. **Rines** 11/26/1977 in Brookfield; H - b. 6/29/1927; W - b. 7/15/1931
Stanley Joseph of Ctr. Ossipee m. Marilyn Joanne **Davis** of Freedom 10/7/1950 in Ctr. Ossipee; H - 23, mechanic; W - 19, telephone op.

RING,
Eugene Vincent m. Christina Atwood **Day** 8/14/1993 in Ossipee
John E., Jr. m. Sydney J. Day **Bronson** 8/25/1984; H - b. 5/6/1949; W - b. 2/11/1955

RIORDAN,
John E. of New York, NY m. Charlotte **Kaliakotas** of New York, NY 6/7/1963 in Ctr. Ossipee; H - 22, welder; W - 38, telephone operator

RIPLEY,
Shawn Patrick m. Denise Elaine **Eldridge** 8/28/1993 in Tamworth

RITCEY,
Robert M. m. Joyce I. **Benker** 12/17/1977 in Ossipee; H - b. 3/18/1949; W - b. 4/25/1956

RITCHOTTE,
Paul Edward m. Louise Theresa **Greene** 9/4/1970 in Ossipee; H - b. 1/5/1940; W - b. 1/30/1944

RIVARD,
Aime Leo, Jr. m. Crystal Cheri **Zavorotny** 12/24/1992 in Ossipee

RIVERA,
Robert Richard of Ctr. Ossipee m. Lisa **Cooper** of Ctr. Ossipee 1/7/2001

RIVERS,
Joseph of Ossipee m. Katie **Clark** of Wolfeboro 6/11/1902 in Ossipee; H - 46, laborer, b. Canada, s/o John Rivers (Champlain, farmer) and Mary Dupray (Canada, housewife); W - 48, maid, 3rd, d/o Charles Gilman (farmer) and Carrie Gilman (housewife)

RIZZO,
Robert Kroell m. Kable Witz **Bonfoey** 7/11/1992 in Ossipee

ROBACHER,
Steven James of Ctr. Ossipee m. Holly Ruth **Morford** of Ctr. Ossipee 5/23/1998

ROBBINS,
Samuel M. of Ossipee m. Isabelle **Walker** of Porter, ME 1/17/1888 in Ossipee; H - 52, painter, b. Middlefield, s/o Jobe Robbins (Middlefield); W - 42, housekeeper, b. Sandwich, d/o Alpheus S. Gilpatrick (Porter, ME)

ROBERT,
Todd Allen m. Laurel Ann **Canney** 8/4/1990; H - b. 3/10/1971; W - b. 1/28/1971

ROBERTS,
Frank of Lynn, MA m. Cordelia **Goldsmith** of Ossipee 6/5/1895 in Ossipee; H - 64, ice dealer, 2nd, b. Tamworth, s/o Daniel Roberts and Sally Roberts; W - 59, housewife, b. Ossipee, d/o Daniel Goldsmith (Ossipee, farmer) and Mary J. Sias (Ossipee)
Lawrence M. of E. Parsonsfield m. Harriett E. **Weeks** of E. Parsonsfield 6/23/1926 in Ossipee; H - 23, b. E. Parsonsfield; W - 24, b. E. Parsonsfield
Maynard M. of Cumberland, ME m. June P. **Emery** of Scarboro, ME 9/15/1959 in Ctr. Ossipee; H - 37, truck driver; W - 32, none

Roland, Jr. of Waterboro, ME m. Marjorie **Day** of Waterboro, ME 5/20/1934 in Ctr. Ossipee; H - 24, laborer; W - 19, at home
Thomas Earl, III m. Suzanne **Branin** 5/29/1977 in Wolfeboro; H - b. 4/4/1953; W - b. 3/25/1955

ROBERTSON,
Charles W. m. Doris S. **Goerner** 9/7/1982 in Ossipee; H - b. 12/7/1920; W - b. 5/2/1949

ROBINSON,
Aaron R. of Mattapan, MA m. Shirley M. **Davis** of Mattapan, MA 11/21/1933 in Nashua; H - 36, cloth cutter; W - 28, stenographer
James P. m. Mary J. **Hannah** 9/26/1987; H - b. 12/26/1956; W - b. 9/23/1959

RODEN,
Thomas C. of Pelham m. Ruth A. **Koehler** of Lowell, MA 8/25/1946 in Ossipee; H - 27, minister; W - 20, hairdresser

ROGERS,
Byron L., Jr. of Ossipee m. Leona M. **Bean** of Ossipee 10/27/1924 in Ossipee; H - 20, b. Newbury, MA; W - 17, b. Wolfeboro
Irving M. of Bartlett m. Addie M. **Palmer** of W. Ossipee 8/15/1936 in Effingham; H - 36, farmer; W - 27, housekeeper

ROLLINS,
Barry Dean m. Leslie Lynn **Picard** 5/10/1973 in Madison; H - b. 11/23/1949; W - b. 11/29/1951
Leonard H. m. Grace E. **Price** 4/12/1921 in Laconia; H - 36, machinist, b. Ossipee, s/o Frank O. Rollins (shoe cobbler) and Imogene G. Hardy (housewife); W - 26, attendant, b. Pepperell, MA, d/o John Price (carpenter) and Lilla Merrow (housewife)

ROLLO,
Fred m. Wanda **Shottek** 8/19/1966 in Ossipee; H - 48, despatcher; W - 40, office
John A. of Ctr. Falls, RI m. Sandra L. **Sullivan** of Pawtucket, RI 11/3/1960 in Ossipee; H - 20, US Navy; W - 19, bookkeeper

ROMANO,
Anthony D. m. Karen L. **Davis** 9/25/1965 in Ctr. Ossipee; H - 20, USMC; W - 19, waitress

ROMANS,
William A. of Baltimore, MD m. Agnes C. **Fields** of Portland, ME 4/6/1946 in Ossipee; H - 21, US Navy; W - 19, none

ROOT,
Steven C. m. Karen E. **Ebel** 9/11/1982 in Ossipee; H - b. 1/25/1955; W - b. 10/14/1954

ROSE,
Edward of Boston, MA m. Anna **Pollen** of Roxbury, MA 8/8/1932 in Ossipee; H - 24, traffic mgr.; W - 23, bookkeeper
Harold, Jr. m. Kathleen A. **Chill** 8/31/1965 in Ctr. Ossipee; H - 25, carpenter; W - 19, sales

ROSS,
Bryan S. m. Tracey L. **Emery** 7/26/1986; H - b. 5/22/1964; W - b. 8/31/1965
Ernest John of Chocorua m. Mary Elizabeth **Knox** of Ossipee 4/6/1940 in Ossipee; H - 19, laborer; W - 18, at home
John E. of Milford, ME m. Annie B. **Eldridge** of Ossipee 9/30/1893 in Meredith; H - 29, millman, b. Milford, ME, s/o W. H. Ross (on the ocean) and Lydia (Kennebeck, ME); W - 23, housewife, b. Ossipee, d/o James Eldridge (Ossipee) and Martha (Ossipee)
Lawrence Elliott of Ctr. Ossipee m. Giovanna C. (Dorne) **Button** of Ctr. Ossipee 10/5/1996
William H. of Ossipee m. Frances M. **Shortridge** of Ossipee 12/24/1921 in Tamworth; H - 22, laborer, b. Ossipee, s/o Onslow S. Ross (Tamworth) and Hattie Moody (Tamworth); W - 21, school teacher, b. Ossipee, d/o Everett Shortridge (Wolfeboro) and Alice J. Thompson (Ossipee)

ROULEAU,
George L. of Milton m. Inez E. **Eldridge** of W. Ossipee 5/30/1925 in Tamworth; H - 21, b. Milton; W - 18, b. W. Ossipee

ROVA,
Enos L. of Ossipee m. Bertha M. **Bodnar** of Merit Island, FL 9/10/1960 in Ossipee; H - 65, carpenter; W - 59, none
Paul E. of Ctr. Ossipee m. Beverly M. **Armon** of Salem 12/30/1945 in Salem, MA; H - 21, US Army; W - 21, secretary

ROWELL,
Howard D. m. Susan E. **Hendricks** 2/28/1981 in Wolfeboro; H - b. 6/3/1955; W - b. 8/8/1962

ROY,
Normand of Pawtucket, RI m. Diane **Simoneau** of Rehoboth, MA 1/30/1962 in Ossipee; H - 23, truck driver; W - 18, turner

ROYEA,
Christopher Paul of Ctr. Ossipee m. Tammy M. Lepelley **Byers** of Ctr. Ossipee 10/24/1998

RUDOLPH,
Gerald Floyd of Ossipee m. Mary Alice **Libby** of Ossipee 10/10/1943 in Ctr. Ossipee; H - 21, soldier; W - 20, nurse's aid

RUMERY,
Newell P. of Augusta, ME m. Jean W. **Bilodeau** of Augusta, ME 11/6/1950 in Ctr. Ossipee; H - 38, clerk; W - 22, housewife

RUMLEY,
Ronny Ray of W. Ossipee m. Cindy Ann **Barnicoat** of W. Ossipee 10/5/1997

RUSSELL,
Alan James of Ctr. Ossipee m. Suzanne (Maggio) **Berube** of Ctr. Ossipee 8/17/1996
Clyde E. of Effingham m. Sylvia **Welch** of Ossipee 8/2/1937 in Effingham Falls; H - 24, laborer; W - 18, at home

RUTHERFORD,
Lester J. of Plymouth m. Mavis E. **Knox** of Ossipee 9/3/1949 in Ctr. Ossipee; H - 24, gas attendant; W - 22, student

RUTTER,
Roger David of Ossipee m. Joy Lee Ayoubee **Bovee** of Ossipee 6/23/2000

RYAN,
Frank of Everett, MA m. Mary **Ryan** of Everett, MA 10/8/1962 in Ctr. Ossipee; H - 68, retired; W - 64, retired
Thomas of Fredericton, NB m. Mertie L. **Davis** of Ossipee 6/5/1894 in Conway; H - 26, mason, b. Fredericton, NB, s/o William Ryan (mason); W - 18, maid, b. Ossipee, d/o Joseph Davis (farmer)
Thomas J. m. Jacqueline L. **Albin** 5/11/1973 in Ossipee; H - b. 1/1/1944; W - b. 5/30/1940
William A. of Ossipee m. Mary T. **Halloran** of Ossipee 4/9/1946 in Ossipee; H - 23, warehouse man; W - 19, at home

RYDER,
Belmont L. m. Erin S. **Moody** 7/25/1985; H - b. 8/30/1961; W - b. 7/16/1967
Belmont Lynwood of Ctr. Ossipee m. Rhonda Lee (Varney) **Merrill** of Ctr. Ossipee 4/23/1994
Lloyd W. of Tamworth m. Ruth J. **Welch** of Ctr. Ossipee 8/22/1952 in Ctr. Ossipee; H - 17, lumbering; W - 18, housework
Lynwood P. of S. Tamworth m. Winifred G. **White** of Ctr. Ossipee 6/25/1955 in Chocorua; H - 18, woodman; W - 17
Lynwood P. m. Beverly A. **Eldridge** 11/11/1978 in Ossipee; H - b. 9/5/1936; W - b. 10/26/1945
Perley A. m. Linda E. **Long** 2/4/1983 in Ossipee; H - b. 9/4/1956; W - b. 12/8/1952

ST. LAURENT,
Norman J. of Canton, ME m. Maude E. **Dyke** of Canton, ME 8/9/1950 in Ctr. Ossipee; H - 22, laborer; W - 18, at home

SAMPSON,
Alfred J. of Ossipee m. Stella V. **DeMerritt** of Ossipee 6/1/1932 in Ossipee; H - 19, laborer; W - 21, at home

SANBORN,
Herbert of Ossipee m. Maria **Sherman** of Ossipee 6/11/1896 in Ossipee; H - 35, farmer, b. Sandwich, s/o ----- (deceased) and Nancy L. Sanborn (Sandwich, housekeeper); W - 26, housekeeper, b. Conway, d/o ----- Sherman (Conway, laborer) and Mrs. Sherman (Conway, housekeeper)
Orin of Brookfield m. Mary D. **Nutter** of Brookfield 5/31/1932 in Ossipee; H - 56, laborer; W - 56, housekeeper
Orin F. of Ossipee m. Sadie M. **Hudson** of Ossipee 8/16/1949 in Ctr. Ossipee; H - 75, retired; W - 53, housekeeper
Raymond m. Dianne J. **Kelley** 1/20/1965 in Ctr. Ossipee; H - 21, clerk; W - 18, none
Scott A. m. Christine A. **Kamal** 2/10/1992 in Ossipee

SANDERS,
Harold W. of Ossipee m. Lucia M. **Greenfield** of Rochester 9/17/1910 in Ossipee; H - 21, farmer, b. Somerville, MA, s/o Charles L. Sanders (Ossipee, farmer) and Clara W. Wentworth (Ossipee, housewife); W - 19, maid, b. Rochester, d/o George E. Greenfield (Rochester, coal dealer) and Delia Morrill (Rochester, housewife)
Obed of Ossipee m. Nancy E. **Grant** of Wolfeboro 3/2/1889 in Ossipee; H - 72, farmer, b. Ossipee, s/o William Sanders; W - 59, housekeeper

Ralph E. of Ossipee m. Margie E. **Meader** of Conway 1/11/1960 in Conway; H - 38, civil engineer; W - 31, home

SANDO,
Thomas N. m. Patricia Mae **Pecoraro** 7/17/1976 in Ossipee; H - b. 4/6/1934; W - b. 12/11/1951

SANPHY,
Roland M. of Conway m. Joanne H. **Welch** of Ctr. Ossipee 9/1/1955 in Ossipee; H - 21, restaurant; W - 18, waitress

SANTOS,
Andrew Keith m. Heide Susanne **Riek** 12/31/1985; H - b. 10/16/1964; W - b. 8/13/1964

SANTUCCI,
George P. of Mansfield, MA m. Simonne **Miclette** of Mansfield, MA 7/8/1957 in Ossipee; H - 38, operator; W - 44, cloth insp.

SARGENT,
Alan Wayne m. Cheryl Renee **Carlton** 7/14/1974 in Ossipee; H - b. 2/22/1947; W - b. 10/8/1954
Alton E. of Ossipee m. Mary E. **Weeks** of Effingham 8/27/1955 in Ctr. Ossipee; H - 23, lumbering; W - 19
Clarence R. of Danvers, MA m. Ethel F. **Abbott** of Ossipee 5/22/1912 in Ossipee; H - 34, carpenter, b. Beverly, MA, s/o R. R. Sargent (Gloucester, MA); W - 22, b. Ossipee, d/o Almon F. Abbott (Ossipee)
David Wayne m. Laurie Ann **Griffin** 7/17/1976 in N. Conway; H - b. 10/1/1956; W - b. 9/12/1957
Everett of Ossipee m. Alice A. **Welch** of Ossipee 8/13/1903 in Ossipee; H - 41, farmer, b. Chichester, s/o Daniel Sargent (Chichester, farmer) and Lucinda Martin (Chichester, housewife); W - 28, maid, b. Ossipee, d/o ---- Welch (carpenter) and Sarepta Parks (Eaton, housewife)
Everett F. of Colchester (sic) m. Laura **Eldridge** of Ossipee 7/1/1891 in Ossipee; H - 27, farmer, b. Chichester, s/o Daniel Sargent and Lucinda; W - 18, housework, b. Ossipee, d/o Alpheus Eldridge (Ossipee) and Dorothy (Meredith)
Frederick E. of Tuftonboro m. Eunice E. **English** of Ctr. Ossipee 7/29/1961 in Wakefield; H - 26, truck driver; W - 18, waitress
Gerald Walter of Ossipee m. Rosemary Caroline **Knox** of Ossipee 10/2/1943 in Freedom; H - 15, woodsman; W - 16, at home
Glen A. of Ossipee m. Jacqueline **McCreadie** of Scotland 1/27/2000

Norman of Ctr. Ossipee m. Donna **Craigue** of Wolfeboro 12/22/1962 in Ctr. Ossipee; H - 18, lumbering; W - 18, none
Norman A. of Ossipee m. Blanche M. **Wheeler** of Effingham 3/12/1954 in Wakefield; H - 41, farmer; W - 41, p. nurse
Richard L. of Effingham Falls m. Donna L. **Varney** of Ctr. Ossipee 6/2/1961 in Ctr. Ossipee; H - mill; W - 17, none
Richard L., Jr. m. Deborah A. **McLaskey** 3/10/1988; H - b. 7/5/1969; W - b. 2/27/1963
Richard Lee, Jr. of Ossipee m. Wendy Leigh **Clough** of Ossipee 7/14/1995
Warren E. of Ossipee m. Julia A. **Welch** of Ossipee 7/27/1893 in Ossipee; H - 28, farmer, b. Chichester, s/o Daniel Sargent (Chichester) and Lucinda; W - 15, housewife, d/o Lyford Eldridge (Ossipee) and Lizzie (Meredith)
Warren E., Jr. of Ctr. Ossipee m. Shirley A. **Eldridge** of Ctr. Ossipee 5/5/1956 in Moultonville; H - 23, Navy; W - 20

SAUNDERS,
Herbert C. of Milton m. Eliza R. **Walker** of Ossipee 3/31/1892 in Ossipee; H - 27, sawyer, 2nd, b. Lowell, MA, s/o J. P. Saunders (Taunton, MA) and S. H. Cummings (Lowell, MA, housewife); W - 20, boxmaker, b. Charlestown, MA, d/o John P. Walker (Thorndike, ME) and Arvilla Walker (Thorndike, ME, housewife)

SAVAGE,
James Francis m. Lynn Barbara **Stanley** 8/28/1993 in Ctr. Ossipee
John C. of White Plains, NY m. Elvera S. **Buechele** of Pittsburgh, PA 7/9/1946 in Ossipee; H - 32, lawyer; W - 27
Richard m. Shirley **Bell** 8/28/1964 in Ctr. Ossipee; H - 21, machinist; W - 18, secretary

SAVARD,
Francis E. of N. Conway m. Edith **Berry** of N. Conway 8/11/1936 in Gorham; H - 21, clerk; W - 21, waitress
Paul Emile of N. Conway m. Madeline **Snow** of Fryeburg, ME 9/11/1937 in Gorham; H - 22, store clerk; W - 23, waitress

SAWTELLE,
James A., Sr. of Ctr. Ossipee m. Lynda Mary-Rose **Dore** of Ctr. Ossipee 4/7/2001

SAWYER,
Hayes W. of Ossipee m. Violet M. **Brown** of Ossipee 11/1/1925 in Ossipee; H - 24, b. Ossipee; W - 26, b. Ossipee

Hayes W., Jr. of Ossipee m. Ann Jane **McHugh** of Wolfeboro 6/3/1950 in Wolfeboro; H - 23, ins. adj.; W - 22, clerical work

Howard P. of Brookfield m. Marie H. **Curtis** of S. Portland 8/30/1961 in Ossipee; H - 69, doctor; W - 60, none

Mathew T. m. Cheryl M. **Andrea** 8/22/1981 in Ossipee; H - b. 1/25/1961; W - b. 10/6/1961

SAYWARD,
Frederick N., Jr. m. Joan **Adams** 3/18/1971 in Ossipee; H - b. 5/4/1932; W - b. 8/6/1930

SCAMMAN,
Aaron Jeffrey m. Darlene Joan **Haskell** 4/1/1992 in Ossipee

SCATES,
Steven Louis of Concord m. Amanda R. (Frias) **Whiting** of Ossipee 12/31/1994

SCEGGEL[L],
Benjamin P. of Ossipee m. Anna M. **Chase** of Ossipee 11/26/1891 in Ossipee; H - 22, laborer, b. Ossipee, s/o Benjamin Sceggel (Ossipee) and Abby Folsom (Ossipee); W - 18, housework, b. Meredith, d/o David Chase (Ossipee) and Ada Sceggell (Ossipee)

Benjamin P. of Ossipee m. Edna N. **Demeritt** of Ossipee 9/28/1901 in Effingham; H - 35, laborer, 2nd, b. Ossipee, s/o Benjamin Sceggel (Ossipee, deceased) and Abbie Sceggel (Ossipee, housewife); W - 18, maid, b. Conway, d/o Daniel Demeritt (Liberty, ME, deceased) and Hannah Demeritt (Conway, housewife)

Elisha W. of Ossipee m. Ada J. **Chase** of Ossipee 8/10/1891 in Ossipee; H - 49, farmer, b. Ossipee, s/o Roswell Sceggel (Ossipee) and Hannah (Ossipee); W - 36, housework, b. Center Harbor, d/o George Hardy (Center Harbor)

George O. of Ossipee m. Addie **Lewis** of Ossipee 4/18/1894 in Ossipee; H - 49, farmer, 2nd, widower, b. Ossipee, s/o Moses Sceggell (Ossipee, farmer) and Abbie G. Wentworth (Lebanon, ME, housewife); W - 20, maid, b. Ossipee, d/o Samuel F. Lewis (Ossipee, farmer) and Betsey A. Bean (Acton, ME, housewife)

SCHAIER,
Carl Alfred of Norwood, MA m. Florence M. **Bickford** of Ossipee 10/2/1949 in Ossipee; H - 49, mechanic; W - 49, at home

Warren C. m. Sandra Jean **Roy** 7/18/1970 in Claremont; H - b. 4/23/1946; W - b. 5/3/1947

SCHATZL,
Thomas F. of Quincy, MA m. Mary Elvina **Caines** of Quincy, MA 11/6/1945 in Ossipee; H - 20, milkman; W - 20, lamp decorator

SCHOFIELD,
Gary James m. Dale Bridgette **Gaudreau** 6/25/1990; H - b. 8/8/1953; W - b. 2/10/1951
James Weston of Ossipee m. Rebecca Lee **Allen** of Ossipee 9/11/1999

SCHONSCHIEFF,
Peter of Ossipee m. Alice M. **Russell** of Ossipee 12/3/1934 in N. Conway; H - 30, electrician; W - 39, housekeeper

SCHULER,
Ronald A., Jr. m. Donna L. **Brown** 8/8/1979 in Tamworth; H - b. 10/7/1956; W - b. 1/18/1957

SCHWANN,
William J. of Lincoln, MA m. Lorraine A. **Moulton** of Medford, MA 12/30/1953 in Ctr. Ossipee; H - 40, publisher; W - 31, at home

SCHWARTZ,
Richard m. Cynthia Lynn **Dale** 4/10/1971 in Ossipee; H - b. 7/2/1950; W - b. 7/24/1951

SCHWEINKHARDT,
William L. m. Sharon Ann **Hale** 7/18/1989; H - b. 3/27/1948; W - b. 10/11/1946

SCOLARO,
Ricky A. m. Rose Anne **Ricker** 5/19/1976 in Freedom; H - b. 11/15/1953; W - b. 8/25/1957

SCOTT,
Edmund S. of Billerica, MA m. Shirley A. **Knapp** of Ossipee 3/22/1958 in Ossipee; H - 28, clerk; W - 20, clerk
Elmer A. of Ossipee m. Grace M. **Colby** of Lowell, MA 10/7/1923 in Tamworth; H - 23, b. Ossipee; W - 23, b. Lowell, MA
Ernest E. of Ossipee m. Mary E. **Stevens** of Wakefield 11/8/1913 in Amesbury, MA; H - 27, station agent, b. Springvale, ME, s/o Edward J. Scott (Moncton, NB); W - 23, b. Newfields, ME, d/o Calvert E. Stevens (Newfield, ME)
Harry A. m. Helen S. **Avery** 1/10/1987; H - b. 3/31/1909; W - b. 9/17/1906

Randall Llewellyn m. Donna Lou Smith **Page** 7/16/1988; H - b. 1/19/1956; W - b. 10/12/1966

SEAMANS,
David M. Gloria **Varney** 11/8/1968 in W. Ossipee; H - b. 8/15/1945; W - b. 11/8/1950
Robert Michael of Ossipee m. Stacy Lee **Crapo** of Freedom 9/12/1998

SEAVEY,
Henry H. of Conway m. Dorothy J. **Rines** of Ossipee 10/27/1949 in Fryeburg, ME; H - 20, mechanic; W - 16, at home

SEELY,
Richard G. of Boston, MA m. Janet E. **Lincoln** of Boston, MA 4/24/1953 in Ctr. Ossipee; H - 21, laborer; W - 19, at home

SEGUIN,
Allen L. m. Linda M. **Whiting** 10/28/1967 in Ossipee; H - 19, mechanic; W - 18, waitress
Bruce E., Jr. m. Justine A. **Stuart** 8/27/1983 in Ossipee; H - b. 4/17/1956; W - b. 8/26/1963
Elwyn B. of Ctr. Ossipee m. Patricia E. **Wilson** of Ctr. Ossipee 5/31/1954 in Ctr. Ossipee; H - 21, laborer; W - 19
Roger K. of Conway m. Mary R. **Eldridge** of Ossipee 3/20/1946 in Ossipee; H - 23, lumberjack; W - 21, housekeeper

SEHOCK,
John W. of Bradford m. Thelma **Leighton** of Gilead, ME 11/7/1937 in Moultonville; H - 22, truck driver; W - 25, at home

SEMANSKI,
Alexander E. m. Judith A. **Fazzino** 8/15/1982 in Ossipee; H - b. 3/25/1931; W - b. 12/29/1941

SENECAL,
Robert Charles of Wolfeboro m. Donnamarie McEwen **Breen** of Wolfeboro 9/13/1999

SENIOR,
Walter M., Jr. of Melvin Village m. Mavis Aletta **Keith** of Ossipee 2/24/1940 in Ossipee; H - 21, at school; W - 21, at home

SERPA,
Michael Joseph of Ossipee m. Rebecca Jane Mahtesian **Ghelfi** of Ossipee 8/7/1998

SHACKFORD,
Scott Alan of Ctr. Ossipee m. Jennifer Hollie **Zwearcan** of Ctr. Ossipee 10/25/1997
Stephen Ernest m. Syndra Louise **Morand** 7/18/1992 in Ossipee

SHANNON,
Edwin Shirly of Tamworth m. Ellen Rachel Potter **Coffey** of Tamworth 7/24/1998
Guy E. of Tuftonboro m. Mavis L. **Wiggin** of Ctr. Ossipee 11/18/1950 in Moultonville; H - 24, state emp.; W - 18, at home
James E. m. Nancy Mary **Norton** 10/7/1978 in Tuftonboro; H - b. 10/16/1952; W - b. 6/10/1957
Scott Dominic of Ossipee m. Gabriella Ruth **Garcia** of Ossipee 7/10/1994

SHAW,
Winthrop H. of Limington, ME m. Agness **Sawyer** of Limington, ME 9/9/1896 in Ossipee; H - 66, farmer, 3rd, b. Northwood, s/o John Shaw (deceased) and Polly Taylor (deceased); W - 15, housemaid, b. Limington, d/o Ausborn Sawyer (Limington, farmer) and Emma Sawyer (Limington, housekeeper)

SHAWVER,
Todd Andrew of Rochester m. Tara Joan **Fillipon** of Ossipee 8/27/1994

SHEA,
James Patrick, Jr. of Ossipee m. Denise Catherine **Arsenault** of Ossipee 9/7/1996

SHEAFF,
Ronald F. of Madison m. Janet H. **Dubois** of Ctr. Ossipee 4/11/1959 in Ctr. Ossipee; H - 20, maintenance; W - 18, maid

SHEEHAN,
William Edward of Ctr. Ossipee m. Dianne Currier **Heinrich** of Ctr. Ossipee 8/18/2001

SHELDON,
Walter M. of Malden, MA m. Mary A. **McGann** of Malden, MA 8/21/1924 in Ossipee; H - 27, b. Malden, MA; W - 29, b. Boston, MA

SHERMAN,
Ronald H. of Wakefield, MA m. Ruth H. **Evans** of Malden, MA 7/3/1931 in Ossipee; H - 23, field supervisor; W - 22, clerk

SHINE,
Francis K. m. Lynda **Strasnick** 8/27/1983 in Ossipee; H - b. 9/1/1942; W - b. 6/17/1949

SHOEMAKER,
Lewis W. of Cape Elizabeth, ME m. Lucy V. **McMahon** of Cape Elizabeth, ME 8/15/1949 in Ossipee; H - 42, salesman; W - 41, housewife

SHURE,
Donald Daniel m. Diane Lynn **Hubbard** 6/10/1989; H - b. 1/15/1959; W - b. 4/21/1956

SIAS,
Newell P. of Ossipee m. Etta **Bertwell** of Ossipee 8/4/1889 in Ossipee; H - 26, farmer, b. Ossipee, s/o J. D. Sias; W - 22, housekeeper, b. Ossipee, d/o Roberson Bertwell (Ossipee)
Newell P. of Ossipee m. Frances M. **White** of Weirs 1/9/1914 in Laconia; H - 50, lumberman, 2nd, b. Ossipee, s/o Jonathan D. Sias (Ossipee); W - 33, housewife, 2nd, b. New Hampton, d/o Charles Young

SIDEBOTHAM,
Ronald Edward m. Cottie Arlene **Kosse** 1/27/1990; H - b. 9/2/1960; W - b. 5/8/1967

SIDIK,
Dennis M. m. Jean E. **English** 5/24/1980 in Ossipee; H - b. 11/25/1946; W - b. 9/27/1951

SILVA,
Edward P. m. Barbara **Houle** 11/1/1965 in Ctr. Ossipee; H - 37, cook; W - 42, waitress
Jesse of Washington, DC m. Verna L. **Lowe** of Kalamazoo, MI 7/18/1952 in Ctr. Ossipee; H - 33, laborer; W - 38, at home

SIMMONS,
Donald David m. Jane Louise **Cheney** 8/29/1992 in W. Ossipee

SIMMS,
Clifton of Wolfeboro m. Elsie **Banfill** of Ossipee 4/5/1919 in Sanbornville; H - 21, machinist, b. Wolfeboro, s/o George B. Simms (Haverhill,

MA) and Harriett L. Getts (Tuftonboro); W - 16, housework, b. Franklin, d/o William Banfill (Conway) and Rosa Laforge (Quebec)

SIMONEAU,
Edward J. of Westbrook, ME m. Jean M. **Levesque** of Portland, ME 3/15/1953 in Ossipee; H - 37, laborer; W - 47, waitress

SIMPSON,
Harry A. m. Susan J. **Eldridge** 12/1/1967 in Epping; H - 55, printer; W - 23, printer
Harry Allen m. Helmi M. **Putonen** 9/18/1993 in Chocorua
Trevor D. of Deblois, ME m. Barbara A. **Bates** of Deblois, ME 11/17/1997

SINCLAIR,
George M. of Salem, MA m. Martha H. **Hadley** of Marblehead, MA 7/23/1934 in Ctr. Ossipee; H - 62, R.R. foreman; W - 38, storekeeper
William C. of Ossipee m. Lucy E. **Drew** of Wakefield 5/13/1891 in Wakefield; H - 35, station agent, b. Ossipee, s/o L. D. Sinclair; W - 26, teacher, b. Exeter, d/o George W. Drew and Lydia W. (Union)
William C. m. Belle N. **Wentworth** 12/16/1915 in Union; H - 56, station agent, 2nd, b. Ossipee, s/o Leander D. Sinclair (Essex Jct., VT); W - 50, teacher, b. Newfields, ME, d/o Charles L. Wentworth (Wakefield)

SIZEMORE,
Todd D. m. Pamela J. **Williams** 7/23/1983 in Ossipee; H - b. 9/29/1962; W - b. 12/27/1964

SKEHAN,
Joseph G., Sr. of Effingham m. Priscilla T. Landry **Reny** of Ctr. Ossipee 8/7/1997

SKELLEY,
Douglas C. m. Sheila E. **Maddock** 4/2/1982 in Wolfeboro; H - b. 10/23/1963; W - b. 12/18/1963

SKILLINS,
Ray F. of Ossipee m. Mary C. **Sanphy** of N. Conway 12/12/1925 in Bartlett; H - 29, b. Bartlett; W - 18, b. Princeton, ME

SLOAN,
George W., Jr. m. Janice M. **Garvey** 12/8/1984; H - b. 7/26/1950; W - b. 2/14/1936

SLOANE,
John Edmund m. Karen Mae **Bailey** 3/14/1992 in Ossipee

SLOVER,
Todd Kevin m. Kimberly Dale **Swick** 9/29/1990; H - b. 9/19/1965; W - b. 9/16/1960

SMART,
Austin E. of Ossipee m. Addie **Sceggel** of Ossipee 5/30/1899 in Ossipee; H - 36, laborer, 3rd, b. Moultonboro, s/o George H. Smith (Moultonboro, laborer) and Mary A. Cook (Tamworth, housewife); W - 24, maid, 2nd, b. Ossipee, d/o Samuel Lewis (Ossipee, soldier) and Betsey Lewis (Ossipee, housewife)
Charles E. of Ossipee m. Mildred M. **Blazo** of N. Parsonsfield 6/20/1901 in N. Parsonsfield; H- 20, manufacturer, b. Ossipee, s/o Charles H. Smart (Campton, manufacturer) and Helen H. Folsom (Tamworth, housewife); W - 23, teacher, b. N. Parsonsfield, d/o Daniel O. Blazo (Sandwich, farmer) and Emily Perkins (Eaton, housewife)
Charles E. of Ossipee m. Adeline J. **Marston** of Haverhill, MA 3/17/1924 in Burlington, VT; H - 43, b. Ossipee; W - 42, b. Alburg, VT
Charles R. of Rochester m. Susie E. **Davis** of Ossipee 4/21/1927 in Dover; H - 46, salesman; W - 42, at home
Joshua Steven of Ctr. Ossipee m. Karyn Theresa **White** of Ctr. Ossipee 5/22/1999
Preston B. of Ctr. Ossipee m. Helen Mae **Colomy** of Ctr. Ossipee 9/12/1934 in Ctr. Ossipee; H - 32, attorney; W - 38, teacher

SMITH,
Arthur B. of Ossipee m. Ona E. **Moulton** of Ossipee 8/23/1935 in Wolfeboro; H - 23, laborer; W - 17, domestic
Austin E. of Ossipee m. Ella **Clough** of Ossipee 5/17/1888 in Ossipee; H - 27, laborer, b. Ossipee, s/o George H. Smith (Ossipee); W - 20, housekeeper, b. Ossipee, d/o William H. H. Clough (Ossipee)
Charles H. of Ossipee m. Evylyn D. **Tappan** of Sandwich 12/21/1903 in Moultonboro; H - 45, fur dealer, b. Ossipee, s/o Isaiah Smith (Ossipee, farmer) and Abigail Goldsmith (housewife); W - 18, maid, b. Peabody, MA, d/o Abram E. Tappan (Moultonboro, farmer) and Abbie F. Tappan (Peabody, MA, housewife)
Charlie E. of Fryeburg, ME m. Charlotte **Sawyer** of Ossipee 4/26/1918 in Ossipee; H - 39, farmer, b. Fryeburg, ME, s/o Salmon M. Smith (Fryeburg, ME) and Betsy Nicholson (Bartlett); W - 18, housework, b. Ossipee, d/o Ellen Sawyer (Biddeford, ME)
Chester W., Jr. of Easton, MA m. Faye F. **McCabe** of Avon, MA 4/1/1950 in Ctr. Ossipee; H - 23, moulder; W - 15, at home

Clifton E. of Tuftonboro m. Bertha M. **Riley** of Ossipee 7/14/1932 in Ossipee; H - 22, laborer; W - 18, at home

Dale R. m. Kelly J. **Hunt** 10/27/1984; H - b. 11/24/1962; W - b. 9/15/1966

Daniel Currier of Haverhill, MA m. Dorothy P. **Bohaker** of Haverhill, MA 7/9/1945 in Wolfeboro; H - 58, salesman; W - 38, dental sec.

Daniel E. m. Valerie T. **Berg** 7/27/1985; H - b. 4/28/1963; W - b. 2/17/1964

Earle D. of Portland, ME m. Carlene M. **Goodwin** of Portland, ME 8/4/1950 in Ctr. Ossipee; H - 29, laborer; W - 31, housewife

Edward F. of Newfield, ME m. Grace M. **Eldridge** of Ossipee 12/14/1905 in Ossipee; H - 36, painter, b. Newfield, s/o Hannibal Smith (Newfield, ME) and Almira M. Whitcher (Newfield, ME); W - 16, maid, b. Ossipee, d/o Woodbury Eldridge (Ossipee) and Dora Eldridge (Ossipee)

Ford J. of Ossipee m. Marion E. **White** of Ossipee 1/3/1912 in Ossipee; H - 21, teamster, b. Ossipee, s/o Melvin Smith (Tamworth); W - 21, housework, b. Campton, d/o Lyman P. White (NY)

Frank E. of E. Harpswell, ME m. Eva M. **Dwyer** of Brunswick, ME 9/7/1930 in Ossipee; H - 24, laborer; W - 19, at home

Henry of Portland, ME m. Mary **Hardy** of Portland, ME 2/13/1955 in Ossipee; H - 24, US Army; W - 22

Henry C. of Newfield, ME m. Nancy **Wallace** of Newfield, ME 12/22/1897 in Wolfeboro; H - 35, farmer, b. Newfield, s/o Hanibel Smith (Newfield, farmer) and Almiry Smith (deceased); W - 23, housekeeper, 2nd, b. Wakefield, d/o John Storer (deceased)

Kenneth B. m. Debora A. **Schultz** 6/30/1984; H - b. 3/29/1952; W - b. 11/14/1958

Oney m. Lucille **Thompson** 2/10/1968 in Ctr. Ossipee; H - b. 11/29/1926; W - b. 3/15/1939

Richard C. m. Elizabeth A. **Marconi** 7/22/1989; H - b. 4/12/1930; W - b. 8/11/1949

Richard J. m. Linda M. **MacDonald** 10/6/1984; H - b. 2/18/1938; W - b. 3/26/1945

Richard L. of Tuftonboro m. JoAnn E. **Hill** of Ossipee 9/3/1960 in Ossipee; H - 21, construction; W - 17, waitress

Samuel P. m. Geraldine E. **Graham** 6/21/1980 in Burke, VT; H - b. 10/5/1957; W - b. 8/20/1957

Walter Roy of Tuftonboro m. Cora Emma **Stillings** of Ossipee 2/23/1934 in Brookline, MA; H - 26, laborer; W - 25, at home

SNOW,
Donn H. m. Patricia M. **Cafarillia** 1/17/1987; H - b. 1/18/1953; W - b. 8/8/1949

Elbridge E. of Ossipee m. Eva M. **Williams** of Ossipee 6/13/1908 in
Ossipee; H - 24, laborer, b. Milton, MA, s/o Elbridge G. Snow (PEI);
W - 16, maid, b. Ossipee, d/o Ren Williams (Effingham)
Kenneth of Rockville, CT m. Nancy A. **Whiting** of Ctr. Ossipee 12/10/1960
in Ctr. Ossipee; H - 22, sheetmetal; W - 17, none
Michael Donn of Ossipee m. Nichole Ruby **Bean** of Ossipee 10/29/1994
Robert Milton, Jr. m. Betty Lou **Stocker** 9/25/1977 in Conway; H - b.
10/24/1947; W - b. 11/19/1951
Wilton of Ossipee m. Ruth H. **French** of Ossipee 4/11/1931 in Rochester;
H - 20, plumber's helper; W - 18, at home
Wilton L. of Ossipee m. Marion **Abbott** of Ossipee 1/27/1952 in
Moultonville; H - 20, mill work; W - 21, at home

SODERBERG,
Walter of Baltimore, MD m. Faye C. **Dallmeyer** of Baltimore, MD
8/21/1959 in Wonalancet; H - 28, teacher; W - 23, teacher

SORDIFF,
Stephen Anthony m. Carla J. **Hartford** 6/14/1991; H - b. 2/16/1965; W - b.
1/5/1968

SOUSA,
Francis R. of N. Deighton, MA m. Gail A. **Horton** of Rehoboth, MA
3/22/1963 in Ctr. Ossipee; H - 21, none; W - 18, none

SOUTH,
Albert, Jr. of Old Orchard, ME m. Suzanne **Luebberman** of Old Orchard,
ME 1/19/1962 in Ossipee; H - 61, salesman; W - 29, none

SOUTHERLAND,
David G. m. Kathleen M. **Mahoney** 5/16/1987; H - b. 9/20/1956; W - b.
8/17/1955

SOUZA,
Anthony of Randolph, ME m. Elizabeth **Kelleher** of Randolph, ME
4/19/1938 in Ossipee; H - 37, store clerk; W - 39, office worker

SPAFFORD,
George D. of Plymouth m. Elizabeth A. **Merrill** of Ossipee 6/15/1942 in
Sanbornville; H - 37, US Army; W - 27, school teacher

SPARKS,
Bernie G., Jr. of Ossipee m. Elaine E. **Henry** of Bartlett 10/28/1950 in
Bartlett; H - 25, electrician; W - 16, waitress

Bernie G., Jr. of Ctr. Ossipee m. Shirley E. **Moody** of Rochester 4/18/1953 in Effingham; H - 27, construction worker; W - 20, factory worker

SPAULDING,
Bruce Romeo, Jr. of Porter, ME m. Diana Mary **Hill** of Ossipee 4/24/1999
Dean Norman of Sanford, ME m. Tanya Louise **Merrow** of Sanford, ME 8/26/2000

SPECKMAN,
Robert E. of Tamworth m. Violet D. **Eldridge** of Ctr. Ossipee 9/8/1951 in Ossipee; H - 23, logger; W - 18, at home

SPIEWAK,
Andrew A. of Manchester m. Ruth E. **Wilson** of Ctr. Ossipee 6/16/1942 in Rochester; H - 24, tree surgeon; W - 24, nurse

SPINNEY,
Calvin, Jr. m. Debra **Valley** 8/9/1975 in Ossipee; H - b. 12/23/1947; W - b. 3/6/1956
Philip C. m. Susan D. **MacIver** 7/20/1974 in Tamworth; H - b. 4/29/1949; W - b. 4/8/1954

SPRAGUE,
Ernest M. of Effingham m. Alice **Hoyt** of Ossipee 12/22/1914 in Ossipee; H - 20, teamster, b. Effingham, s/o Charles M. Sprague (Newfield, ME); W - 17, housekeeper, b. Tuftonboro

SPRINCE,
Jeremy Jon of Ctr. Barnstead m. Julie Melinda **Hansell** of Ctr. Barnstead 10/14/2000

STANLEY,
Harold L. of Ossipee m. Ina **Harmon** of Ossipee 9/26/1942 in Ctr. Ossipee; H - 24, lumberman; W - 21, at home

STAPLES,
Ervin E. of Ossipee m. Lottie B. **White** of Ossipee 1/11/1914 in Ossipee; H - 23, clerk, b. Ossipee, s/o Willis I. Staples (Lynn, MA); W - 19, maid, b. Ossipee, d/o Scott L. White (Ossipee)
Ervin E. of Ossipee m. Marion A. **Berry** of Ossipee 3/9/1946 in Wolfeboro; H - 54, chauffeur; W - 46, at home
Herbert E. m. Alice M. **Shortridge** 10/26/1915 in Parsonsfield, ME; H - 25, b. Parsonsfield, ME, s/o John E. Staples (Ossipee); W - 37, housewife, 2nd, b. Ossipee, d/o Thatcher Thompson (Newfield, ME)

John of Ossipee m. Carrie **Young** of Ossipee 11/26/1913 in Ossipee; H - 51, machinist, 3rd, b. Effingham, s/o Christopher Staples; W - 40, 2nd, b. Providence, RI, d/o James Ellis (Sunnyside, PEI)

Willie I. of Ossipee m. Clara **Eldredge** of Ossipee 6/14/1888 in Ossipee; H - 27, mechanic, b. Lynn, MA, s/o H. Q. Staples (Raymond, ME); W - 18, housekeeper, b. Ossipee, d/o Daniel Eldridge (Ossipee)

STARTZ,
August W. of Brockton, MA m. Iris **Webb** of S. Easton, MA 9/13/1941 in Ossipee; H - 51, foreman; W - 23, forelady

STEIN,
Walter m. Bernice A. **Chapman** 2/18/1972 in Ossipee; H - b. 10/19/1920; W - b. 3/8/1920

STETSON,
Clarence E. of Porter, ME m. Helen M. **Snow** of Ctr. Ossipee 7/23/1954 in Porter, ME; H - 25, lumber co. emp.; W - 19, waitress

STEVENS,
David m. Judith M. **Jensen** 5/24/1977 in Ossipee; H - b. 2/13/1940; W - b. 2/3/1942

Howard of Ossipee m. Rosamond L. **Reed** of Wakefield 12/22/1928 in Wolfeboro; H - 42, millman; W - 28, housekeeper

James R. m. Deborah A. **Churchill** 10/14/1988; H - b. 6/6/1949; W - b. 9/10/1957

Kenneth E. of Ossipee m. Gladys M. **Weeks** of Cornish, ME 5/2/1917 in Cornish, ME; H - 36, station agent, b. Morgan, VT, s/o Henry C. Stevens (Stannard, VT) and Mary McDowell (England); W - 24, school teacher, b. Cornish, ME, d/o Joseph S. Weeks (Cornish, ME) and Mercy E. Weeks (Parsonsfield, ME)

STEWART,
Henry of Ossipee m. Betsey **Philbrick** of Tuftonboro 6/16/1895 in Tuftonboro; H - 47, farmer, b. Ossipee, s/o William Stewart and Sally Eldridge; W - 46, housewife, 3rd, b. Green Hill, d/o Newell Cook

Herbert W. of Ossipee m. Lula M. **Brown** of Cornish, ME 3/18/1909 in Ossipee; H - 24, laborer, b. E. Lebanon, ME, s/o Henry Stewart (Biddeford, ME, laborer); W - 16, housekeeper, b. Dover, d/o Charles W. Brown (Dover, laborer)

Leslie D. of Wolfeboro m. Theresa M. **Nalor** of Wolfeboro 11/15/1942 in Wolfeboro; H - 19, teamster; W - 15, maid

Mark F. m. Vickie E. **Betts** 8/22/1981 in Ossipee; H - b. 12/20/1960; W - b. 10/6/1957

Michael J. m. Deborah Gail **Willette** 11/26/1979 in Ossipee; H - b. 3/8/1954; W - b. 10/8/1957
Paul C. m. Angel M. **Cobb** 7/1/1985; H - b. 7/5/1948; W - b. 2/9/1951

STILLINGS,
Frank O. of Ossipee m. Cora E. **Boardman** of Ossipee 9/1/1892 in Water Village; H - 32, carpenter, b. Alton, s/o Ivory Stillings (Ossipee, farmer) and L. P. Stillings (Ossipee, housewife); W - 30, tailoress, 2nd, b. Tuftonboro, d/o Nehemiah Bean (Tuftonboro, farmer) and Rosannah Bean (Moultonboro, housewife)
Frank O. of Ossipee m. Katie M. **Hoyt** of Tuftonboro 4/18/1905 in Ossipee; H - 44, farmer, 2nd, b. Alton, s/o Ivory Stillings (Ossipee, farmer) and Lydia P. Wentworth (Ossipee, housewife); W - 30, maid, 2nd, b. Tuftonboro, d/o George W. Sawyer (Tuftonboro, farmer) and Christine Cate (Brookfield, housewife)
Joseph of Ossipee m. Mabel E. **Morton** of Lowell, MA 4/9/1892 in Lowell, MA; H - 46, farmer, 2nd, b. Ossipee, s/o Ivory Stillings (Ossipee, farmer) and Lydia Stillings (Ossipee, housewife); W - 34, housekeeper, b. Brownfield, ME, d/o Israel R. Morton (Gorham, ME) and Betsey G. Morton (Ossipee, housekeeper)

STILPHEN,
Geoffrey Marc m. Cindy-Lu **Morrill** 9/15/1979 in Wolfeboro; H - b. 11/1/1954; W - b. 9/9/1954

STIMSON,
Mark A. of Portland, ME m. Virginia R. **Klain** of S. Portland, ME 9/10/1949 in Moultonville; H - 23, musician; W - 28, secretary

STOCKBRIDGE,
Glenn R. m. Donna G. **Davis** 6/6/1987; H - b. 7/29/1960; W - b. 6/24/1958
Horatio H. of Wolfeboro m. Melissa **Going** of Ossipee 11/7/1895 in Wolfeboro; H - 34, teamster, 2nd, b. Boston, s/o Harris Stockbridge (deceased) and Lucy F. Colony (deceased); W - 20, maid, 2nd, b. Ossipee, d/o Moses W. Carter and Mary E. Clough (Effingham, housewife)
Richard m. Grace **Barranco** 7/9/1966 in Ctr. Ossipee; H - 26, electrician; W - 27, secretary
Richard C., II m. Pamela Joy **Wood** 12/9/1989; H - b. 1/23/1969; W - b. 7/28/1971
Roland C. of Ctr. Ossipee m. Loretta M. **Woodbury** of Ctr. Ossipee 10/24/1959; H - 19, painter; W - 18, secretary

STOCKMAN,
James Arnold m. Patricia Anne **Fogarty** 7/17/1976 in Tuftonboro; H - b. 11/20/1955; W - b. 2/19/1957

STOCKTON,
Andrew Phillip of Ctr. Ossipee m. Faye Lee **Massey** of Ctr. Ossipee 6/16/1994
William Timothy of Ossipee m. Beth Anne **Hines** of Ossipee 6/4/1994

STODDARD,
Clark M. of Tamworth m. Eleanor M. **Davis** of Ctr. Ossipee 10/22/1960 in N. Haverhill; H - 20, truck driver; W - 24, factory
Donald T. of Ctr. Ossipee m. Maud A. **Gordon** of Tamworth 7/23/1950 in Chocorua; H - 16, at home; W - 16, at home

STOKES,
Jacob of Freedom m. Angeline A. **McKinney** of Ossipee 3/8/1890 in Effingham; H - 28, laborer, b. Stoneham, s/o Jewett C. Stokes (Freedom, farmer); W - 26, housekeeper, b. Ossipee, d/o ----- (Lebanon, farmer)

STONE,
Arthur G. of Ctr. Ossipee m. Ida C. **Bova** of Ctr. Ossipee 2/17/2000

STORER,
Eliot C. of Ossipee m. Florence M. **Wooward** of Malden, MA 9/26/1924 in E. Andover; H - 36, b. Boston, MA; W - 34, b. Franklin

STOUT,
David A. m. Jody B. **Syvinski** 9/11/1982 in Ossipee; H - b. 9/5/1962; W - b. 2/5/1964
David A. m. Cynthia M. **Leavitt** 2/23/1987; H - b. 9/5/1962; W - b. 5/23/1966
William Lester m. Mary Denise **Mitchell** 6/9/1989; H - b. 6/20/1961; W - b. 2/17/1966

STOWERS,
Ronald D. m. Nancy M. **Rochira** 7/20/1990; H - b. 8/25/1946; W - b. 5/1/1944

STOWIK,
Stanley, Jr. m. Patricia Ann **Faucher** 8/5/1978 in Ossipee; H - b. 6/9/1939; W - b. 4/1/1953

STRATTON,
David S. of Avon, MA m. Mildred F. **Morse** of Fairhaven, MA 4/15/1944 in Ctr. Ossipee; H - 55, lawyer; W - 32, clerk

STREETER,
Danna Arnold m. Lee E. **Lawton** 9/18/1989; H - b. 2/17/1949; W - b. 12/20/1953

STRONG,
John Mercer m. Piper Ann **Burns** 6/2/1990; H - b. 10/28/1952; W - b. 12/8/1963

STROUT,
Chester A. m. Linda M. E. **May** 9/20/1987; H - b. 9/21/1948; W - b. 9/13/1958

STUART,
Edward J. m. Vanessa M. **Armstrong** 6/22/1985; H - b. 10/24/1964; W - b. 9/11/1966

STUBBS,
Edward of Portland, ME m. Joan **Carsey** of Portland, ME 2/6/1959 in Ctr. Ossipee; H - 25, mechanic; W - 24, packer
Edward F. of Portland, ME m. Bertha A. **Markey** of Portland, ME 7/9/1960 in Ctr. Ossipee; H - 28, truck driver; W - 34, packer
Linwood m. Mildred **Greenwood** 12/8/1964 in Ctr. Ossipee; H - 28, bus driver; W - 26, sales clerk

STURTEVANT,
Jeffrey Charles m. Terry Lynn **Carr** 6/30/1990; H - b. 4/8/1967; W - b. 5/3/1963

SUDOL,
John S. m. Loretta N. **White** 10/21/1972 in Ossipee; H - b. 8/1/1922; W - b. 2/14/1929

SULLEY,
Thomas F. of Portland, ME m. June D. **Crockett** of W. Ossipee 8/28/1960 in W. Ossipee; H - 31, teacher; W - 28, housewife

SULLIVAN,
Edward J. m. Mary Ann Judith **Engel** 3/19/1978 in N. Conway; H - b. 1/23/1932; W - b. 7/4/1947

Mark Raymond of Ctr. Ossipee m. Patricia Ann Jencks **Bradbury** of Ctr. Ossipee 12/18/1999

SUPRENARD,
Raymond M. Kathleen **McCarthy** 5/13/1966 in Ctr. Ossipee; H - 20, Navy; W - 19, none

SWANSBURG,
Stephen G. of W. Ossipee m. Sacha M. Eldridge **Palmer** of W. Ossipee 5/22/1998

SWANSON,
Charles m. Marjorie **Jacobs** 10/9/1966 in Ossipee; H - 55, none; W - 52, teller
Edward R., Jr. of Ft. Devens, MA m. Jacqueline J. **Coughlin** of Ossipee 3/8/1941 in Fryeburg, ME; H - 23, Roentgenologist; W - 22, at home

SWEARINGIN,
James Edward of Tamworth m. Carrie Grace Graves **Guty** of Tamworth 12/26/1998

SWEET,
Clyde A. of Nahant, MA m. Mary B. **Sias** of Ossipee 12/12/1949 in Sanbornville; H - 73, interior decorator; W - 58, practical nurse

SWEETMAN,
Alfred W. m. Barbara A. **Canavan** 8/30/1985; H - b. 7/10/1949; W - b. 10/2/1963

SWETT,
John W. of Ossipee m. Bessie B. **Lawrence** of New Bedford 11/6/1904 in Ossipee; H - 18, engineer, b. Ossipee, s/o John R. Swett (Ossipee, engineer) and Sarah E. Whitehouse (Ossipee, housekeeper); W - 16, housemaid, b. Ossipee, d/o Edwin Lawrence (Rochester, engineer) and Milly R. Erdine (Ossipee, housekeeper)

SWIFT,
Clyde C. of Gardiner, ME m. Sylvia **Cunningham** of Gardiner, ME 4/12/1952 in Ctr. Ossipee; H - 34, truck driver; W - 18, at home

SWITAJ,
David D. m. Donna F. **Hodge** 6/4/1983 in Ossipee; H - b. 3/25/1960; W - b. 12/30/1961

SYLVAIN,
Roy Clifford m. Lynn Marie **Watson** 6/27/1992 in Ossipee

SYMONDS,
Donald E., Jr. of Hopkinton m. Elaine H. **Doe** of Ctr. Ossipee 7/20/1963 in Hopkinton; H - 31, electrician; W - 24, nurse

SZMYT,
Steven T. of Portsmouth m. Stacey L. **Hazeltine** of Ossipee 8/20/1999

TAEGER,
Glen D. of Salem, MA m. Mary E. (Day) **Hicks** of Salem, MA 7/14/1994

TALLANT,
Daniel Hugh m. Heidemarie **Burke** 5/30/1992 in Exeter

TAPPAN,
Edwin S. of Ossipee m. Ruth E. **Dugan** of Ossipee 7/3/1933 in Sanbornville; H - 24, mechanic; W - 18, at home

TARLING,
Paul m. Sandra **Templeton** 12/4/1966 in Ctr. Ossipee; H - 23, Army; W - 20, hairdresser

TASKER,
Dana J. of Milton m. Lena M. **Spear** of Ossipee 6/12/1901 in Ctr. Ossipee; H - 27, pharmacist, b. Milton, s/o George Tasker (shoe cutter) and Lydia Tasker; W - 25, teacher, b. Ossipee, d/o A. A. Spear (Standish, ME, farmer) and Sarah E. Spear (housewife)
George F. of Ossipee m. Ada L. **Webster** of Tamworth 1/15/1889 in Ossipee; H - 22, laborer, b. Ossipee, s/o Moses S. Tasker (Strafford); W - 33, housekeeper, b. Ossipee, d/o Joseph W. Hobbs (Ossipee)
George F. of Ossipee m. Julia **Sargent** of Ossipee 11/23/1921 in Ossipee; H - 54, merchant, 2nd, b. Ossipee, s/o Moses S. Tasker (Strafford) and Salome Nichols (Ossipee); W - 43, housewife, 2nd, b. Ossipee, d/o Lyford Welch (Ossipee) and Lizzie Eldridge (Meredith)

TAYLOR,
Charles R. of Ossipee m. Verna M. **Bodge** of Ossipee 5/15/1933 in Ossipee; H - 20, laborer; W - 21, at home
Jeffrey S. m. Desira L. **Syvinski** 10/18/1980 in Ossipee; H - b. 6/30/1962; W - b. 1/2/1963
Kenneth W. of Ayer, MA m. Wilma R. **Turner** of Akron, OH 6/6/1959 in Ctr. Ossipee; H - 20, Army; W - 20, none

Lawrence, Jr. of Porter, ME m. Brenda **Taylor** of Ossipee 8/9/1958 in Ossipee; H - 19, truck driver; W - 15, none

Marvin W. of Ossipee m. Carole **Pollender** of Bradford, VT 3/22/1963 in Ctr. Ossipee; H - 18, US Army; W - 22, none

Max R. of W. Burke, VT m. Blanch May **Brown** of W. Burke, VT 9/17/1935 in Ctr. Ossipee; H - 21, mill worker; W - 20, domestic

TEBBETTS,

John F. of Ossipee m. Alice M. **Willey** of Ossipee 12/25/1887 in Ossipee; H - 19, laborer, b. Ossipee, s/o Theodore Tebbetts and Francis (Sanford, ME); W - 20, domestic, b. Ossipee, d/o Robert Willey (Warren, ME)

TEDJOJUWONO,

Stanley N. m. Barbara H. **Gautreau** 11/21/1984; H - b. 6/23/1944; W - b. 8/31/1958

TEMPLE,

Eugene P. of Portland, ME m. Doris A. **Maxwell** of Westbrook, ME 9/17/1961 in Ctr. Ossipee; H - 27, undertaker; W - 26, home

TEMPLETON,

Ahial m. Arthena T. **Eldridge** 7/23/1916 in Ossipee; H - 19, teamster, b. Ossipee, s/o Ahial Templeton (Ossipee); W - 16, housework, b. Ossipee, d/o George H. Eldridge (Ossipee)

Arthur W. of Ossipee m. Marion L. **Wheeler** of Ossipee 7/3/1945 in Wolfeboro; H - 23, mill man; W - 20, mill worker

Arthur Willard, Jr. m. Joy Lee **Hutchins** 4/20/1974 in Wolfeboro; H - b. 11/12/1951; W - b. 8/3/1951

Bert A. of Ossipee m. Annie **Knox** of Ossipee 3/27/1906 in Ossipee; H - 22, laborer, b. Ossipee, s/o Ahial Templeton (Ossipee, farmer) and Effie Williams (Ossipee, housewife); W - 20, maid, b. Ossipee, d/o Freeman Knox (Ossipee, farmer) and Sarah Colby (Ossipee, housewife)

Ira of Ossipee m. Genevieve **Bacigalupo** of Boston, MA 4/30/1929 in Moultonville; H - 41, laborer; W - 29, at home

Ira of Ctr. Ossipee m. Gertrude **Beaudoin** of Ctr. Ossipee 12/1/1951 in N. Conway; H - 64, laborer; W - 58, housekeeper

John of Ossipee m. Louise A. **Abbott** of Ossipee 12/23/1924 in Ossipee; H - 24, b. Ossipee; W - 19, b. Ossipee

TENNEY,

Michael David m. Christine Susan **Foster** 8/17/1991; H - b. 3/20/1970; W - b. 2/10/1970

Michael Warren m. Heather Myra **Curtis** 6/25/1988; H - b. 1/23/1970; W - b. 2/2/1970

Thomas P. m. Katlin K. **Berkner** 3/4/1986; H - b. 6/8/1961; W - b. 8/23/1948

TERMINIELLO,
Domenic W. of Ossipee m. Bridget Marie **Strong** of Concord 8/19/1995

TERRIO,
Robert T. of Canton, MA m. Grace M. **McKenzie** of Westbrook, ME 10/12/1952 in Ctr. Ossipee; H - 28, gunite; W - 27, housewife

TERRY,
Douglass G. m. Linda L. **George** 6/18/1983 in Ossipee; H - b. 1/2/1956; W - b. 1/6/1948

TERSOLO,
Mark Andrew of Peabody, MA m. Sharon Marie **Holloran** of Peabody, MA 8/14/1999

THAYER,
Ray m. Patricia **Berry** 11/21/1964 in Ossipee; H - 36, theater mgr.; W - 25, bookkeeper

THEBERGE,
Leo Armistice, Jr. m. Carol Ann **Augenti** 12/17/1978 in Wolfeboro; H - b. 1/24/1945; W - b. 12/17/1950

THERRIEN,
Craig A. of Ctr. Ossipee m. Lona C. **Ficara** of Boxford, MA 5/12/2001

THISSELL,
Theodore D. of Ossipee m. Gertrude A. **Smith** of Ossipee 11/20/1934 in Effingham Falls; H - 75, farmer; W - 58, housekeeper

THISTLE,
Fred C. of Ossipee m. Gertrude E. **McKinley** of Ossipee 7/16/1921 in Ossipee; H - 29, carpenter, b. Lynn, MA, s/o Mathew Thistle (Newfoundland) and Frances Downs (Newfoundland); W - 26, stenographer, b. Morgan City, LA, d/o John E. McKinley (Scotland) and Lillian E. Griffith (Australia)

THOMAS,
Marvin L. of KY m. Edna R. **Nichols** of Ctr. Ossipee 2/2/1960 in Wolfeboro; H - 21, airman; W - 22, none
Ryan Scott of W. Ossipee m. Jessica Mae **Taylor** of W. Ossipee 8/19/2000

THOMPSON,
Charles A. of Ossipee m. Sadie F. **Abbott** of Ossipee 9/22/1896 in Ossipee; H - 28, wood worker, b. Ossipee, s/o Samuel J. Thompson (Ossipee, wood worker) and Emeline S. Thompson (Ossipee, housekeeper); W - 21, housemaid, b. Ossipee, d/o Jacob Abbott (deceased) and Harriet N. Abbott (Ossipee, housekeeper)
Chauncy W. of Ossipee m. Winnie M. **Hatch** of Ossipee 10/29/1898 in Ossipee; H - 19, laborer, b. Union, s/o Frank A. Thompson and Nellie A. Thompson (deceased); W - 18, maid, b. Ossipee, d/o Simeon W. Hatch (Madison) and Tryphrosa Hatch
Courtland David m. Margo Montgomery **Hobbs** 9/5/1992 in Ossipee
Dana M. m. Cindi Lee **Eldridge** 3/31/1979 in Ossipee; H - b. 5/24/1959; W - b. 9/8/1961
Frank of Ossipee m. Agnes May **Whitten** of Tuftonboro 10/1/1926 in Ctr. Ossipee; H - 46, b. Ossipee; W - 19, b. Tuftonboro
Frank F. of Ossipee m. Cora **Nichols** of Ossipee 7/15/1899 in Ossipee; H - 26, shoemaker, b. Boston, MA, s/o Freeman Thompson (Ossipee, upholsterer) and Jennie Bump; W - 26, housekeeper, 2nd, b. Eaton, d/o Daniel Thurston (farmer)
John Daniel of Randolph, VT m. Emma Louise **Harlow** of Randolph, VT 6/4/1938 in Ossipee; H - 48, chiropractic; W - 41, chiropractic
John W. of Ossipee m. Ida E. **Chadbourn** of Ossipee 4/14/1889 in Effingham; H - 36, engineer, b. Tuftonboro, s/o Thedora Thompson; W - 28, housekeeper, b. Ossipee, d/o Isaac Chadbourn (Ossipee)
Leroy Oscar of Rochester m. Emma Walker **Merrow** of Ossipee 5/15/1943 in Ctr. Ossipee; H - 54, box maker; W - 61, housework
Richard m. Jo-Ann **Smith** 7/12/1964 in Melvin Village; H - 22, lumberman; W - 21, card oper.
Timothy Edward m. Shelly M. **Heckmann** 9/25/1989; H - b. 1/31/1969; W - b. 6/30/1970
Timothy Edward m. Ann Virginia **Northacker** 10/3/1992 in Ossipee
Vernon C. of Limerick, ME m. Lois J. **Strout** of Auburn, ME 9/8/1956 in Ctr. Ossipee; H - 36, farmer; W - 22

THORRELL,
Dennis Carl m. Linda S. **Kula** 7/17/1971 in Manchester; H - b. 9/14/1950; W - b. 7/30/1950

THURBER,
David W. m. Patricia P. **Bigonski** 8/23/1985; H - b. 8/28/1942; W - b. 6/26/1941

THURLEY,
George H., Jr. of Ossipee m. Jennie M. **Hilton** of Ossipee 8/8/1896 in Ossipee; H - 24, farmer, b. Ossipee, s/o George H. Thurley (Ossipee, farmer) and Annie P. Thurley (Ossipee, housekeeper); W - 19, housekeeper, b. Ossipee, d/o James F. Hilton (Ossipee, farmer) and Emma Hilton (Ossipee, housekeeper)

THURSTON,
Carroll E. of Freedom m. Lois G. **Eaton** of Freedom 8/20/1950 in Ctr. Ossipee; H - 50, painter; W - 42, cook
Douglas L. of W. Ossipee m. Lenora M. **Berry** of Ctr. Ossipee 11/10/1951 in Tamworth; H - 17, factory worker; W - 19, at home
John m. Lorraine A. **Lord** 1/11/1970 in Effingham; H - b. 7/29/1950; W - b. 8/2/1951
Larry C. m. Denice M. **Capalbo** 3/10/1973 in Chocorua; H - b. 12/11/1951; W - b. 11/5/1954
Parker of Effingham m. Madeline **Eldridge** of Ossipee 5/30/1935 in Effingham Falls; H - 21, laborer; W - 20, house wife
Peter D. m. Mary R. **Whiting** 6/23/1984; H - b. 9/18/1955; W - b. 9/7/1957

TIBBETTS,
Charles Edwin of Ossipee m. Harriett **Wilkins** of Ossipee 12/31/1943 in Ossipee; H - 29, laborer; W - 39, housewife

TILLINGHAST,
Adam m. Winifred Marie **Hehi** 8/12/1989; H - b. 1/2/1961; W - b. 9/30/1961
Edward H. m. Carla A. **Johns** 6/26/1982 in Alton; H - b. 3/1/1930; W - b. 6/23/1941

TILTON,
Clifford H., Jr. of Ctr. Ossipee m. Marylynn **Ryan** of Tuftonboro 2/29/1956 in Tuftonboro; H - 23, florist; W - 20, nurses' aid
Garrett K. m. Victoria **Powers** 6/6/1987; H - b. 12/9/1961; W - b. 1/20/1961
Leslie H. m. Nancy L. **Sampson** 11/6/1982 in Ossipee; H - b. 5/13/1952; W - b. 12/11/1955

TINSMAN,
Everett m. Nettie **Cushman** 11/19/1966 in Ctr. Ossipee; H - 55, deputy sheriff; W - 54, secretary

TOBIN,
Edward F. of Ctr. Ossipee m. Terri Lynn **Bernaby** of Ctr. Ossipee 9/24/1994

TONER,
Joseph A. m. Teresa A. **Lovett** 11/9/1985; H - b. 6/23/1962; W - b. 6/24/1962

TONKS,
Gerald of Lowell, MA m. Roberta **Locke** of W. Concord, MA 12/19/1958 in Ossipee; H - 25, mechanic; W - 22, nurse

TOOM,
Peep m. Jacquelyn **Thibault** 10/4/1970 in Manchester; H - b. 5/25/1946; W - b. 5/10/1951

TORREY,
Gerald F. m. Edith **Hill** 7/12/1986; H - b. 5/27/1931; W - b. 7/30/1941

TOZIER,
Thomas J. m. Cindy L. **Saunders** 2/14/1986; H - b. 12/19/1963; W - b. 6/9/1957

TREFRY,
Ralph M., Jr. m. Maureen S. **Boewe** 6/28/1988; H - b. 3/4/1950; W - b. 12/26/1961

TREMBLAY,
Donald Philip m. Betty Ann **Parmenter** 4/26/1974 in Ossipee; H - b. 11/10/1928; W - b. 1/2/1933
Gerald Ronald m. Dorothy Charlotte **Hurley** 4/26/1975 in Ossipee; H - b. 2/8/1945; W - b. 11/4/1943
Lionel J. of Ctr. Ossipee m. Helen M. **Breckfill** of Ctr. Ossipee 12/21/1951 in Wolfeboro; H - 32, lumber; W - 24, cook

TREPANIER,
Robert Charles of Ossipee m. Martha Jane **Weyand** of Ossipee 8/23/1997

TRIPP,
Carl E. m. Avis L. **Jones** 10/15/1965 in Ctr. Ossipee; H - 26, factory; W - 30, factory

TRIPPLE,
Charles A. of Ossipee m. Anna L. **Meyers** of Ossipee 3/25/1912 in PA; H - 30, b. Safe Harbor, PA, s/o John J. Tripple (Churchtown, PA); W - 30, housekeeper, b. Germany, d/o Joseph Meyers (Everett, MA)

TROTT,
Howard W. of Lynn, MA m. Lillian M. **McCurdy** of Beverly, MA 7/3/1954 in Ctr. Ossipee; H - 46, inspector; W - 45, R.N.
Wesley H. of Ossipee m. Gladys M. **Chase** of Dennisport, MA 12/10/1913 in Rochester; H - 19, b. Ossipee, s/o Thayer S. Trott (Portland, ME); W - 18, b. Dennisport, MA, d/o Marshall J. Chase (West Horritz)

TROTTIER,
Craig N. m. Irene A. **Abbott** 11/22/1979 in Plaistow; H - b. 11/22/1931; W - b. 5/17/1946

TUCKER,
Ralph Mansfield of Ossipee m. Hester Abbie **Demeritt** of Ossipee 6/1/1943 in Ctr. Ossipee; H - 39, printer; W - 35, nurse

TUCKERMAN,
Leverett S. of Boston, MA m. Miriam E. **Dame** of Boston, MA 9/2/1944 in Ossipee; H - 51, safe deposit clerk; W - 49, asst. buyer

TUDOR,
Thurston Harry m. Kathryn **Knapp** 8/4/1990; H - b. 1/22/1951; W - b. 4/12/1959

TUPECK,
Russell G. m. Mary Patricia **Reckmeyer** 10/16/1982 in Wolfeboro; H - b. 2/13/1958; W - b. 7/9/1960
Steve of Ossipee m. Bernice E. **Ayers** of Tuftonboro 11/13/1921 in Tuftonboro; H - 27, lumberman, b. Russia; W - 15, housewife, b. Tuftonboro, d/o Herbert Ayers (Tuftonboro) and Ina M. Adjutant (Tuftonboro)

TUPPER,
Jackson A. of Durham, ME m. Mary A. **Bourgoin** of Lisbon Falls, ME 9/12/1942 in Ctr. Ossipee; H - 21, mill worker; W - 18, drug store clerk

TURNER,
Cecil Ray of Windham, ME m. Doris Eleanor **Lord** of Windham, ME 5/23/1938 in Ossipee; H - 31, millman; W - 19, housework
Frederick W. of Mt. Vernon, ME m. Helen Irene **Ladd** of Westbrook, ME 6/30/1945; W - 39, supt.; W - 27, office clerk
Walter Scott m. Barbara M. **Maloney** 8/17/1975 in Ossipee; H - b. 5/14/1950; W - b. 12/24/1953

TUTTLE,
Robert V. of Auburn, ME m. Elizabeth E. **McIntosh** of Lewiston, ME 6/24/1937 in Moultonville; H - 24, shoe worker; W - 29, registered nurse

TWOMBLY,
Herbert of Ossipee m. Elizabeth **Velcourt** of Ossipee 11/9/1930 in Ossipee; H - 52, teamster; W - 39, housekeeper

TYLER,
David S. m. Bobbi L. **Johnson** 5/29/1986; H - b. 6/3/1958; W - b. 7/16/1962
Lester Verne of Freedom m. Lillian Norton **Tyler** of Freedom 4/30/1938 in Ossipee; H - 32, farmer; W - 40, retired

ULUOZ,
Abdul K. of Brighton, MA m. Alta **Golodetz** of Cape Elizabeth, ME 11/16/1960 in Ossipee; H - 33, none; W - 26, clerk

URDIALES,
Richardo E. of Tamworth m. Blanche E. **Houle** of Tamworth 8/5/2000

VACCA,
Ralph C. m. Margie L. **Williams** 4/28/1978 in Ossipee; H - b. 7/12/1911; W - b. 8/15/1933

VACCHIANO,
Timothy James of Cornish, ME m. Amy Christine **Charles** of Cornish, ME 12/31/2001

VALENTINE,
Ian Michael of Conway m. Jennifer Lynn **Hamlin** of Brownfield, ME 1/5/1999

VALLEY,
Henry Patrick of Wolfeboro m. Marguerite Elizabeth **Welch** of Ossipee 10/18/1941 in Wolfeboro; H - 23, laborer; W - 18, laborer
Jerry B. m. Lisa H. **Lessard** 6/7/1986; H - b. 1/4/1962; W - b. 1/28/1967
Paul G. of Ctr. Ossipee m. Lois A. **Welch** of Ctr. Ossipee 8/14/1954 in Ctr. Ossipee; H - 30, machinist; W - 20, restaurant
Robert W. m. Vivian B. **Nudd** 2/14/1978 in Ossipee; H - b. 9/2/1953; W - b. 2/18/1953

VALYS,
Keith Joseph of Winthrop, MA m. Renata Pereira **DeLima** of Winthrop, MA 1/12/2001

VAN BLARCOM,
Earle of Ctr. Ossipee m. Lillian M. G. **Samuelson** of Ctr. Ossipee 9/9/2000

VAN DYKE,
Bruce Edwin m. Velma Jean **Hobbs** 1/20/1973 in Wakefield; H - b. 10/28/1948; W - b. 1/19/1950
Douglas A. of Ossipee m. Dorothy P. Murphy **Van Dyke** of Ctr. Barnstead 12/24/1999

VAN TASSEL,
Jan W. m. Ellen F. **Nason** 10/28/1972 in Ossipee; H - b. 2/19/1944; W - b. 1/22/1953
Jan W. m. Donna M. **Stuart** 4/1/1982 in Ossipee; H - b. 2/19/1944; W - b. 6/14/1940

VARNEY,
Bruce m. Margurite E. **Webster** 9/4/1965 in Conway; H - 19, factory worker; W - 18, waitress
David A. of Ctr. Ossipee m. Sandra Y. **Dow** of W. Ossipee 3/30/1963 in Madison; H - 19, mill work; W - 19, none
Edgar George m. Susan Gail **Varney** 10/30/1990; H - b. 8/30/1948; W - b. 7/17/1953
Ernest R. of Ossipee m. Ethel V. **Chase** of Berwick, ME 3/8/1935 in Ossipee; H - 22, laborer; W - 15, housekeeper
Frank W. m. Jennifer R. **Ouellette** 9/3/1993 in Ossipee
Raymond E. of Ctr. Ossipee m. Marie B. **Eaton** of Goffstown 12/14/1957 in Wolfeboro; H - 22, millworker; W - 18, at home
Raymond E. m. Jean L. **Danforth** 5/13/1983 in Ossipee; H - b. 5/27/1935; W - b. 7/19/1932

Ronald E. m. Gaye E. **Robie** 7/3/1965 in Ctr. Ossipee; H - 19, mill; W - 20, none

VEASEY,
Arthur G. of Bradford, MA m. Mabel L. **Hobbs** of Ossipee 7/12/1911 in Ossipee; H - 37, broker, b. Bradford, MA, s/o George D. Veasey (S. Hampton, provision dealer); W - 33, teacher, b. Ossipee, d/o Orodon P. Hobbs (Ossipee, lumber dealer)

VIDETTI,
David M. of Malden, MA m. Kelley A. **Smith** of Malden, MA 7/28/1995

VIGUE,
Gerald A. m. Patricia A. **Switaj** 8/25/1979 in Ossipee; H - b. 4/5/1930; W - b. 1/31/1935
Henry J. of Ossipee m. Velma A. **Glidden** of Wolfeboro 5/25/1946 in Wolfeboro; H - 22, laborer; W - 16, waitress

VILES,
John R. of Ossipee m. Alice M. **Call** of Ossipee 3/11/2000

VILLEIUX,
Wilfred of Ossipee m. Annie **Munroe** of Ossipee 11/26/1923 in Freedom; H - 27, b. Canada; W - 19, b. Effingham

VINCENT,
Michael K. m. Janice Carrie **Whiting** 10/18/1975 in Ossipee; H - b. 3/28/1954; W - b. 12/27/1956

VINTON,
Robert W. of Ctr. Ossipee m. Elizabeth A. **Woodbury** of Salem, MA 7/23/1953 in Ctr. Ossipee; H - 57, retired; W - 37, nurse

VIOLETTE,
Joseph A. of Westbrook, ME m. Virginia E. **Logan** of Portland, ME 5/10/1952 in Moultonville; H - 34, laundry routeman; W - 29, dental assistant

VITTUM,
Brewster Dale m. Cheryl Jean **Ripley** 6/20/1973 in Ossipee; H - b. 9/30/1953; W - b. 4/5/1949
John Thomas of Ctr. Ossipee m. Stacy Lynn **Raymond** of Ctr. Ossipee 12/31/1995

VOTOUR,
Charles of Clinton, MA m. Edith **Bean** of Ctr. Ossipee 1/19/1934 in Ctr. Ossipee; H - 24, laborer; W - 18, at home

WADE,
Robert S. m. Eleanor L. **Caverly** 5/28/1972 in Ossipee; H - b. 5/14/1916; W - b. 12/6/1919

WAGENFELD,
Kenneth B. of Ctr. Ossipee m. Velma P. **DeButts** of Ctr. Ossipee 5/10/1947 in Kezar Falls, ME; H - 26, truck driver; W - 24, tel. operator

WAGSTAFF,
Donald m. Evelyn **Games** 7/14/1966 in Ctr. Ossipee; H - 30, swords; W - 36, press hand
Francis m. Ida **St. Onge** 7/29/1966 in Ctr. Ossipee; H - 52, jewelry worker; W - 52, packing room

WAINIO,
David m. Barbara **Bearse** 2/1/1966 in Ctr. Ossipee; H - 23, Navy; W - 22, book keeper

WAITE,
Robert E. of Augusta, ME m. Myrlice **Robinson** of Bangor, ME 6/2/1949 in Ctr. Ossipee; H - 37, electrician; W - 34, at home

WALDRIP,
Mark James of Ossipee m. Susan Ann **Dodier** of Ossipee 7/29/2000

WALDRON,
William Russell of Exeter m. Amy Arlene **Coukos** of Lynn, MA 7/29/1999

WALKER,
Benjamin B. of Ossipee m. Clara M. **Ames** of Ossipee 1/18/1894 in Ossipee; H - 23, farmer, b. Detroit, ME, s/o John Walker (Thorndike, farmer) and Aurilla Walker (Somersworth, housewife); W - 16, maid, b. Ossipee, d/o John C. Ames (Ossipee, farmer) and Maria Cotton (Lynnville, IL, housewife)
Duane Elwin, Sr. of Effingham m. Cynthia Lee McLeod **Monroe** of Effingham 3/24/2001
Frank L. of Brockton, MA m. Hazel M. **Baker** of Brockton, MA 4/5/1942 in Ossipee; H - 41, machinist; W - 43, tel. operator

WALL,
Roy E. m. Patricia A. **Bryant-Wall** 9/29/1984; H - b. 3/1/1929; W - b. 4/9/1933

WALLACE,
Charles P. of Ossipee m. Mary F. **Geralds** of Wolfeboro 1/19/1891 in Ossipee; H - 32, laborer, b. Ossipee, s/o S. P. Walker (sic) and Mehitable; W - 23, housework, b. Wolfeboro, d/o Charles E. Geralds and Sarah
Charles P. of Newfield, ME m. Harriett L. **Hurd** of Newfield, ME 12/23/1897 in Ossipee; H - 39, laborer, 4th, b. Ossipee, s/o Simeon P. Wallace (Ossipee, farmer) and Mehitoble Wallace (deceased); W - 34, housekeeper, b. Boston, MA, d/o Ivory G. Hurd (deceased) and Josephene Wallace (Ossipee, housekeeper)
Frank W. of Ossipee m. Idella **Clay** of Ossipee 3/19/1887 in Ossipee; H - b. Ossipee, s/o Samuel Wallace and Bethana; W - housekeeper, b. Ossipee, d/o Arthur Clay and Olive
Harry A. of Ossipee m. Susie M. **Meloon** of Ossipee 8/1/1891 in Ossipee; H - 21, salesman, b. Ossipee, s/o S. P. Wallace (Ossipee) and Emily M. (Ossipee); W - housework, b. Ossipee, d/o John F. Meloon (Ossipee) and Sarah (Ossipee)
Harry A. of Ossipee m. Susie **Brooks** of Freedom 11/18/1900 in Freedom; H - 30, clerk, 2nd, b. Ossipee, s/o Simeon Wallace (Ossipee, farmer) and Emily M. Wallace (Ossipee); W - 33, dressmaker, b. Freedom, d/o Silas Brooks (farmer) and Hannah Brooks (housewife)
Irton E. of Natick, MA m. Mary L. **Miller** of Natick, MA 4/7/1917 in Ossipee; H - 42, tinsmith, 2nd, b. Boisetown, NB, s/o William Wallace (Doaktown, NB) and Frances A. Fraser (Nashuaak, NB); W - 31, nurse, b. New Bedford, d/o Edward Chadwick (Edgartown, MA) and Adeline Chadwick (Braintree, MA)
Robert T. m. Leola J. **Eldridge** 4/30/1988; H - b. 8/25/1931; W - b. 8/5/1934
Simeon P. of Ossipee m. Josephene L. **Hurd** of Ossipee 10/21/1897 in Waltham; H - 66, farmer, 3rd, b. Ossipee, s/o Samuel Wallace (deceased) and Dolly Wallace (deceased); W - 59, housekeeper, 2nd

WALSH,
Earle L., Jr. of Wolfeboro m. Ruth L. **Cellemme** of Ctr. Ossipee 6/3/1942 in Wolfeboro; H - 23, US Air Corps; W - 24, waitress
John of Hartsdale, NY m. Evelyn F. **Gooby** of Mt. Vernon, NY 8/2/1933 in Wakefield; H - 33, salesman; W - 25, clerk
Joseph A., Jr. of Concord m. Elizabeth Glenn **Aiton** of Concord 9/26/1998

WALTER,
Glenn Allen m. Dale Frances **Caldwell** 3/31/1973 in Wolfeboro; H - b. 4/22/1951; W - b. 2/16/1964

WANNER,
Wayne of Philadelphia, PA m. Muriel **Manson** of Kittery, ME 10/29/1962 in Ossipee; H - 21, USAF; W - 27, none

WARD,
Melvin Lewis of Dorchester, MA m. Irene Marie **Phelps** of Dorchester, MA 5/18/1945 in Ossipee; H - 32, US Navy; W - 25, US Navy
Stephen Lewis m. Sandra Lee **DeSimone** 6/17/1989; H - b. 11/25/1951; W - b. 2/10/1949

WARNER,
Clarence A. of Huntington, NY m. Margaret D. T. **Jones** of Woodbury, NY 6/19/1961 in Ossipee; H - 57, fuel oil; W - 62, typist

WARREN,
Andre R. of Waterville, ME m. Harriet I. **Baird** of Manchester, ME 8/26/1952 in Ctr. Ossipee; H - 34, engineer; W - 37, clerk

WASSON,
Andrew of Ctr. Ossipee m. Mildred Elizabeth **Haley** of Tuftonboro 2/10/1937 in Farmington; H - 20, clerk; W - 18, student
Clarence of Ossipee m. Louise **Templeton** of Ossipee 7/7/1928 in Ossipee; H - 27, millman; W - 24, at home
Dannie E. of Ctr. Ossipee m. Elizabeth J. **Chase** of Chocorua 5/3/1958 in Chocorua; H - 20, carpenter; W - 17, none
Leslie of Ctr. Ossipee m. Virginia **Nichols** of Ctr. Ossipee 10/30/1955 in Ctr. Ossipee; H - 43, lumbering; W - 21, laborer
Perley J. m. Maude L. **Varney** 9/10/1916 in Laconia; H - 20, laborer, b. Ossipee, s/o Joseph S. Wasson (NB); W - 25, housework, b. Tamworth, d/o George O. Varney (Ossipee)
Perley Joseph of Ossipee m. Hazel Mabel **Merrill** of Ossipee 11/27/1940 in Ossipee; H - 44, truck driver; W - 43, school teacher

WATERBURY,
Edmund P. of Wilmington, VT m. Evelyn M. **Marshall** of Wilmington, VT 10/22/1956 in Ctr. Ossipee; H - 55, retired; W - 37, housewife

WATERHOUSE,
Wayne Meron m. Marianne **Hall** 4/3/1976 in Ossipee; H - b. 8/6/1951; W - b. 1/1/1957

WATKINS,
Arthur E. of Ossipee m. Helen **Jeffries** of Ossipee 12/22/1932 in Ossipee;
H - 45, builder; W - 38, housekeeper

WATSON,
William F. m. Teresa J. **Haggard** 9/30/1982 in Ossipee; H - b. 3/29/1950;
W - b. 3/26/1958

WEBB,
Kenneth Lee of W. Acton, MA m. Dorothy M. **Wormstead** of Ctr. Ossipee
9/1/1945 in Pittsfield; H - 24, US Army; W - 23, teacher
Paul J. of Rochester m. Ruth E. **Walsh** of Ctr. Ossipee 3/15/1950 in
Rochester; H - 23, unemployed; W - 31, housekeeper
Wallace I. of Wolfeboro m. Cora B. **Perry** of Wolfeboro 11/4/1912 in
Ossipee; H - 25, draughtsman, b. England, s/o Henry I. Webb
(England); W - 28

WEBSTER,
Ai M. of Ossipee m. Winnie M. **Nichols** of Effingham 7/18/1902 in
Ossipee; H - 19, teamster, b. Tamworth, s/o Horace F. Webster
(Tamworth, laborer) and Ada L. Hobbs (Tamworth, housewife); W -
19, maid, b. Ossipee, d/o Charles Nichols (Ossipee, farmer) and
Emma Williams (Effingham, housewife)
Charles Francis m. Betty Ann **Anderson** 7/9/1976 in Tuftonboro; H - b.
1/13/1926; W - b. 9/5/1925
Charles M. of Rochester m. Fannie M. **Clough** of Ossipee 7/17/1893 in
Ossipee; H - 26, shoemaker, b. Rochester, s/o A. J. Webster
(Oxford) and E. A. Shorey (Rochester); W - 18, housewife, b.
Ossipee, d/o W. H. Clough and Sarah (Parsonsfield)
Wilbur of Ossipee m. Flossie **Eldridge** of Ossipee 12/13/1902 in Ossipee;
H - 23, laborer, b. Tamworth, s/o Horace Webster (farmer) and Ada
L. Hobbs (Ossipee, housekeeper); W - 17, maid, b. Ossipee, d/o
Daniel Eldridge (Ossipee, laborer) and Lizzie Templeton (Ossipee,
housewife)
Wilbur F. of Ossipee m. Ida M. **Lane** of Ossipee 10/1/1926 in Moultonville;
H - 47, b. Tamworth; W - 45, b. Tamworth
William Frances of Madison m. Pearl Melvina **Bickford** of Ossipee
11/22/1941 in Sanbornville; H - 36, laborer; W - 20, laundress

WEEDEN,
Daniel T. m. Karen M. **Tinkham** 10/25/1986; H - b. 12/10/1951; W - b.
3/25/1953

WEEKS,
Cecil R. of Ossipee m. Bertha L. **Cutting** of Ossipee 2/24/1918 in Ossipee; H - 22, lumberman, b. Porter, ME, s/o Edwin C. Weeks (Porter, ME) and Lillian Drown (Eaton); W - 17, housework, b. Effingham, d/o Sherman Cutting (Weld, ME) and Ida Sanborn (Parsonsfield, ME)
Kenneth W. of Effingham m. Ruby M. **Eldridge** of Ctr. Ossipee 5/10/1947 in Ctr. Ossipee; H - 24, carpenter; W - 20, cook

WEINBRECHT,
Alfred R. of Lynn, MA m. Bertha M. **Carlson** of Lynn, MA 6/19/1933 in Ossipee; H - 23, oil man; W - 21, at home

WEINMAN,
David, 2nd o f New York City, NY m. Elizabeth A. **Fuller** of White Plains, NY 7/28/1946 in Ossipee; H - 37, physician; W - 32, nurse

WELCH,
Alston B. of Ossipee m. Stella **Wiggin** of Ossipee 1/22/1905 in Ossipee; H - 26, farmer, b. Ossipee, s/o Jeremiah Welch (Ossipee, farmer) and Ellen Welch (Ossipee, housewife); W - 20, maid, b. Ossipee, d/o William H. Wiggin (Ossipee, millman) and Sophia Eldridge (Ossipee, housewife)
Bennie F. - Ossipee m. Della **Eldridge** of Ossipee 12/20/1914 in Ossipee; H - 21, laborer, b. Ossipee, s/o Paul Welch (Ossipee); W - 20, housewife, b. Ossipee, d/o George Eldridge (Ossipee)
Carroll C. of Ossipee m. Sara E. **Scruton** of Farmington 9/1/1928 in Ctr. Conway; H - 21, clerk; W - 20, stenographer
Chester R. of Ctr. Ossipee m. Helen M. **Hibbard** of Ctr. Ossipee 9/15/1951 in Ctr. Ossipee; H - 38, laborer; W - 28, factory worker
Douglas A. m. Virginia E. **Roberts** 8/21/1965 in Chocorua; H - 20, salesman; W - 19, secretary
Edville O. of Ossipee m. Eliza A. **Welch** of Ossipee 5/23/1909 in Ossipee; H - 41, laborer, 2nd, b. Ossipee, s/o William H. Welch (Ossipee, farmer); W - 40, maid, 2nd, b. Conway, d/o Charles Whittaker (Conway, farmer)
Edwin P. of Ossipee m. Sylvia M. **Bickford** of Ossipee 9/17/1928 in Ossipee; H - 39, teamster; W - 24, housekeeper
Edwin P. of Ossipee m. Lydia **McNeil** of Conway 12/20/1933 in Ossipee; H - 48, laborer; W - 38, housekeeper
Ernest L. of Ossipee m. Sarah **Helmes** of Ossipee 1/20/1917 in Ossipee; H - 22, laborer, b. Ossipee, s/o Lyford Welch (Ossipee) and Lizzie Eldridge (Ossipee); W - 25, housework, b. Ossipee, d/o Charles Helme and Emma Ames (Ossipee)

Ford J. m. Emma L. **Weymouth** 8/11/1915 in Ossipee; H - 24, laborer, b. Ossipee, s/o John Welch (Ossipee); W - 31, housework, 2nd, b. Shelburne, NS, d/o Robert P. Ryer (Shelburne, NS)

Ford J. of Ossipee m. Helen B. **Keenen** of Ossipee 12/26/1925 in Ossipee; H - 33, b. Ossipee; W - 28, b. Farmington

Ford J., Jr. of Ctr. Ossipee m. Barbara **Tattrie** of Wolfeboro 12/23/1950 in Ctr. Ossipee; H - 24, Navy; W - 19, at home

Ford J., Jr. of Ctr. Ossipee m. Betty J. **Carr** of Tilton 9/29/1956 in Tilton; H - 30, service mgr.; W - 24, stenographer

George of Ossipee m. Lizzie B. **Davis** of Effingham 10/29/1907 in Ossipee; H - 24, laborer, b. Ossipee, s/o Moses P. Welch (Ossipee, lumberman) and Sarah J. Welch (Ossipee, housewife); W - 17, maid, b. Effingham, d/o Ebenezer Davis (farmer) and Augusta Cole (housewife)

James of Ossipee m. Mabel R. **Shultz** of Ossipee 8/1/1898 in Ossipee; H - 27, farmer, b. Ossipee, s/o Peter Welch (Ossipee, farmer) and Cora B. Kimball (Parsonsfield, housewife); W - 19, maid, b. Boston, d/o Albert Shultz (NS, agent) and Ida M. Lovell (Boston, housewife)

John, 3rd of Ossipee m. Lydia M. **Flagg** of Boston, MA 11/19/1887 in Ossipee; H - 52, farmer, b. Ossipee, s/o Silas Welch and Affie (Ossipee); W - 40, housekeeper, b. Ossipee

Kenneth W. of Ctr. Ossipee m. Ruth E. **Pearson** of Ctr. Ossipee 1/10/1942 in Ctr. Ossipee; H - 18, laborer; W - 21, mill worker

Lawrence E. of Ossipee m. Dorothy W. **Brown** of Ossipee 5/17/1931 in Bartlett; H - 21, mill laborer; W - 17, at home

Leland Conrad of Portland, ME m. Violet Hazel **Hooper** of Portland, ME 9/30/1938 in Ossipee; H - 47, box maker; W - 50, housekeeper

Leon J. of Ossipee m. Myrtle **Williams** of Milton 12/22/1919 in Tamworth; H - 25, laborer, b. Ossipee, s/o Orren E. Welch (Ossipee) and Jessie E. Bean (Ossipee); W - 20, housework, b. Tamworth, d/o Justin Williams (Tamworth) and Cora Smart (Tamworth)

Leon J. of Ossipee m. Emma F. **Demerritt** of Ossipee 9/8/1930 in Ossipee; H - 38, laborer; W - 39, housekeeper

Lisle R. of Tuftonboro m. Norma **Colby** of Ctr. Ossipee 7/15/1950 in Moultonville; H - 24, lumber hand; W - 18, nurse maid

Mark C. m. E. Maureen **Whittaker** 6/30/1979 in Ossipee; H - b. 1/7/1933; W - b. 7/24/1942

Maurice C. of Ossipee m. Thelma M. **Chase** of Wolfeboro 10/28/1921 in N. Conway; H - 19, chauffeur, b. Ossipee, s/o Orren E. Welch (Ossipee) and Jennie E. Bean (Ossipee); W - 18, student, b. Augusta, ME, d/o John K. Chase (Wolfeboro) and Ethel M. Bisbee (Wolfeboro)

Maurice C. of Ossipee m. Blanche **Emery** of Tuftonboro 12/3/1925 in Tuftonboro; H - 23, b. Ossipee; W - 26, b. Tuftonboro

Moses of Ossipee m. Mildred **Eldridge** of Ossipee 5/22/1900 in Ossipee; H - 21, laborer, b. Ossipee, s/o Moses P. Welch (Ossipee, farmer) and Sarah J. Welch (Ossipee, housewife); W - 16, maid, b. Ossipee, d/o Charles M. Eldridge (Ossipee, laborer) and Irene M. Eldridge

Orrin E. of Ossipee m. Jennie E. **Bean** of Ossipee 12/8/1890 in Ossipee; H - 27, currier, b. Ossipee, s/o John Welch 3rd (Ossipee, farmer); W - 21, housekeeper, b. Ossipee, d/o John Bean (Ossipee, farmer)

Paul of Ossipee m. Minnie **Nute** of N. Conway 5/8/1899 in N. Conway; H - 25, brakeman, b. Ossipee, s/o Jeremiah Welch (Ossipee, farmer) and Ellen J. Welch (housewife); W - 23, maid, b. Conway, d/o Isaac Nute (flagman) and Harriett Nute (housewife)

Peter P. of Ossipee m. Bertha S. **Merrow** of Ossipee 10/18/1914 in Ossipee; H - 25, laborer, b. Ossipee, s/o Lyford Welch (Ossipee); W - 31, weaver, 2nd, b. Aurora, ME, d/o Daniel A. Merrow (Ossipee)

Peter P. of Ossipee m. Sarah E. **Perry** of Wolfeboro 4/23/1950 in Wolfeboro; H - 60, board sawyer; W - 36, housewife

Preston E. of Ctr. Ossipee m. Laura B. **Buswell** of Ctr. Ossipee 1/17/1958 in Ctr. Ossipee; H - 46, laborer; W - 52, housework

Robert of Ossipee m. Marion **Drew** of Wakefield 7/29/1929 in Union; H - 24, laborer; W - 18, housewife

Robert Roy m. Patricia Lillian **Suicies** 2/8/1991; H - b. 1/14/1958; W - b. 11/16/1960

Robert Roy of N. Sandwich m. Amanda Lee **Drew** of N. Sandwich 11/7/1997

Roland E. of Ctr. Ossipee m. Ethelda **Merrow** of Ctr. Ossipee 11/1/1947 in Moultonville; H - 25, laborer; W - 25, tel. operator

Sidney L. of Ossipee m. Eva **Eldridge** of Ossipee 8/25/1912 in Ossipee; H - 21, laborer, b. Ossipee, s/o Lyford Welch (Ossipee); W - 18, housework, b. Ossipee, d/o David Eldridge

Walter S. of Ossipee m. Cora B. **Davis** of Ossipee 3/2/1899 in Ossipee; H - 22, farmer, b. Ossipee, s/o Jeremiah C. Welch (Ossipee, farmer) and Ellen J. Welch (Ossipee, housewife); W - 18, maid, b. Ossipee, d/o Valentine Davis (Ossipee, farmer) and Abbie J. Davis (deceased)

Willie S. of Ossipee m. Gertie M. **Eldridge** of Ossipee 8/23/1908 in Ossipee; H - 21, laborer, b. Ossipee, s/o Silas Welch (Ossipee); W - 16, maid, b. Ossipee, d/o Orin Eldridge (Ossipee)

WELLINES,
Richard m. Mildred B. **Hicks** 8/24/1977 in Ossipee; H - b. 6/5/1926; W - b. 8/17/1939

WELSH,
Robert of Kingston, PA m. Sophie L. **Sulya** of Augusta, ME 6/18/1954 in Ctr. Ossipee; H - 30, US Navy; W - 22

WENHOLD,
Elmer George m. Alice Mary **Welch** 5/1/1976 in Ossipee; H - b. 4/19/1917; W - b. 7/5/1925

WENTWORTH,
Fred, 2nd m. Susan A. **Randall** 8/20/1965 in N. Conway; H - 22, banker; W - 20, secretary
Gordon C., Jr. of Ossipee m. Jeanne A. **Stocks** of S. Hiram, ME 2/8/1947 in Seabrook; H - 21, student; W - 18, at home
Roger Arthur of Wolfeboro m. Methyl Muriel **Knights** of Wolfeboro 6/12/1938 in Wakefield; H - 21, diesel mechanic; W - 18, housework

WEST,
Carl Stuart, Jr. of Ossipee m. Rebecca Lynne **Randall** of Wolfeboro 5/2/1998
Chester Stuart of Ossipee m. Joyce Annette (Haley) **Macdonald** of Ossipee 7/27/1996

WESTBERRY,
Richard A. of S. Portland, ME m. Sara L. **Littlefield** of S. Portland, ME 6/17/1950 in Ctr. Ossipee; H - 22, marine eng.; W - 20, at home

WESTFALL,
Kurt P. of Ossipee m. Darlene P. **Cheney** of Sanbornville 6/27/1998

WEYMOUTH,
Guy F. of Ossipee m. Ethel M. **Eldridge** of Ossipee 8/30/1911 in Northwood; H - 21, teamster, b. Sanbornville, s/o James F. Weymouth (carpenter); W - 18, maid, b. Ossipee, d/o John P. Eldridge (Ossipee)

WHEELER,
Fred K. of W. Ossipee m. Ruth C. **Parker** of Ctr. Ossipee 2/27/1937 in Farmington; H - 32, mill worker; W - 22, at home
Jan F. m. Jean A. **Hoff** 6/19/1971 in Ossipee; H - b. 8/1/1948; W - b. 2/24/1953

WHIPPLE,
Frank P. of Tamworth m. Marguerite H. **Leavitt** of Ctr. Ossipee 3/8/1953 in Ctr. Ossipee; H - 44, contractor; W - 43, at home

WHITAKER,
Nathan W. of Ossipee m. Ida **Richardson** of Hiram, ME 3/27/1887 in Rochester; H - 17, laborer, s/o Charles Whitaker and Malinda; W - 17, housekeeper, b. Hiram, ME

WHITE,
Belmont A. of Ossipee m. Grace B. **Eldridge** of Ossipee 5/27/1923 in Ossipee; H - 22, b. Ossipee; W - 16, b. Ossipee
Bernard Lee of Ossipee m. Agnes M. **Ponkop** of Ossipee 11/15/1952 in Conway; H - 26, truck driver; W - 33, at home
Bernard Lee m. Marguerite Priscilla **Tilton** 8/20/1976 in Lakeport; H - b. 6/9/1926; W - b. 7/7/1920
Charles E. of Ctr. Ossipee m. Sheryl Dawn **Bliss** of W. Newfield, ME 9/18/1999
Chester A. of Ossipee m. Avis E. **Knox** of Ossipee 7/11/1923 in Sanbornville; H - 22, b. Ossipee; W - 24, b. Boston, MA
Chris A. m. Nancy M. **Lewis** 8/8/1981 in Ossipee; H - b. 6/21/1955; W - b. 8/11/1958
Ernest m. Hazel **Baker** 8/27/1966 in Ctr. Ossipee; H - 85, retired; W - 72, none
Ervin m. Sharon **Hebert** 6/26/1964 in Ctr. Ossipee; H - 19, mill; W - 16, none
Ervin W. m. Celia J. **Burdett** 11/6/1988; H - b. 9/27/1922; W - b. 5/5/1926
Ervin Windefield of Ossipee m. Mildred M. **Smart** of Ossipee 4/15/1944 in Freedom; H - 21, US Army; W - 16, at home
Fred Joseph of Groton m. Irene Lois **Eldridge** of W. Ossipee 10/4/1943 in Rumney; H - 20, mining man; W - 18, at home
Gardner L. of Lexington, MA m. Janet **Downs** of Granite 10/19/1936 in Wolfeboro; H - 21, at training sch.; W - 21, at home
George B. of Ossipee m. Augusta **Champion** of Effingham 9/16/1888 in Effingham; H - 28, merchant, b. Ossipee, s/o Allen A. White; W - 28, dressmaker, b. Effingham, d/o Lorenzo Champion (Effingham)
Gordon Ellis m. Rosemary **Bean** 7/12/1975 in Ossipee; H - b. 5/19/1955; W - b. 1/22/1958
Granville E. of Ossipee m. Amanda **Williams** of Ossipee 1/19/1908 in Ossipee; H - 18, laborer, b. Ossipee, s/o Scott L. White (Ossipee); W - 16, maid, b. Ossipee, d/o Frank R. Williams (Ossipee)
Granville E. of Ossipee m. Ada **Williams** of Ossipee 8/21/1919 in Ossipee; H - 28, woodsman, b. Ossipee, s/o Scott L. White (Ossipee) and Refina B. Welch (Ossipee); W - 20, housework, b. Ossipee, d/o Calbert Williams (Ossipee) and Nellie Nichols (Ossipee)
Granville E. of Ctr. Ossipee m. Bertha B. **Nichols** of Ctr. Ossipee 9/8/1935 in Ctr. Ossipee; H - 40, laborer; W - 30, at home

Harold Eugene of Ossipee m. Frances Arlene **Dow** of Ossipee 3/6/1943 in Ctr. Ossipee; H - 18, mill man; W - 18, at home

James H. of Sanbornville m. Mabel M. **Bean** of Ossipee 9/28/1918 in Ossipee; H - 38, teamster, b. Plainfield, CT, s/o George White (Marlboro) and Carrie Fairchild (Plainfield, CT); W - 16, housework, b. Ossipee, d/o Fred E. Bean (Madison) and Anna Nichols (Ossipee)

Jeremy Gordon of Ctr. Ossipee m. Sarah Jean **Abbott** of Ctr. Ossipee 9/11/1999

John H. of Ctr. Ossipee m. Joanne H. (Hodge) **Carey** of Ctr. Ossipee 7/2/1994

Kenneth F., Jr. m. Jeannette L. **Kirley** 10/24/1967 in Ctr. Ossipee; H - 26, water dept.; W - 36, home

Mayhew O. of Ossipee m. Etta **Colby** of Moultonboro 9/9/1889 in Ossipee; H - 29, farmer, b. Ossipee, s/o Mayhue C. White; W - 16, housekeeper, b. Moultonboro, d/o Luther Colby (Moultonboro)

Mott H. of Ossipee m. Mary M. **Ryer** of Ossipee 5/6/1908 in Ossipee; H - 19, teamster, b. Ossipee, s/o Scott L. White (Ossipee); W - 23, maid, b. NS, d/o Robert Ryer (NS)

Norman L. of Ossipee m. Joyce M. **Deatte** of Tamworth 1/16/1954 in Tamworth; H - 19, lumber; W - 21, mill worker

Rodney A. m. Linda M. **Eldridge** 12/24/1965 in Ctr. Ossipee; H - 37, highway; W - 21, printer

Rusty E. of Ctr. Ossipee m. Wendy S. **LaRiviere** of Ctr. Ossipee 9/24/1994

Scott L. of Ossipee m. Renfina **Welch** of Ossipee 12/28/1902 in Ossipee; H - 35, farmer, 2nd, b. Ossipee, s/o Allen White (Ossipee, merchant) and Elizabeth Lougee (Parsonsfield, ME, seamstress); W - 31, maid, 2nd, b. Ossipee, d/o William Welch (Ossipee, laborer) and Eliza Tibbetts (Ossipee, housewife)

Scott L. m. Rhenfina B. **Colby** 7/9/1916 in Ossipee; H - 49, farmer, 2nd, b. Ossipee, s/o Allen A. White (Ossipee); W - 45, housework, 2nd, b. Ossipee, d/o William H. Welch (Ossipee)

Virgil D. of Ossipee m. Marguerite A. **Graves** of Newport 4/9/1912 in Newport; H - 22, salesman, b. Ossipee, s/o Charles White (Ossipee); W - 23, teacher, b. Fitchburg, MA, d/o Selfred R. Graves (Boston, MA)

Walter G. of Ossipee m. Estella M. **Wiggin** of Tamworth 10/1/1921 in Ossipee; H - 22, machinist, b. Ossipee, s/o Lowenstein L. White (Haverhill, MA) and Elizabeth L. Pascoe (Freedom); W - 22, teacher, b. Tamworth, d/o Charles A. Wiggin (Ossipee) and Effie M. Bennett (Middleton, MA)

WHITING,
Charles A. of Ossipee m. Lill **Bickford** of Ossipee 11/24/1894 in Ossipee; H - 21, farmer, b. Tamworth, s/o Jerry Whiting; W - 19, maid, b. Ossipee, d/o Henry Bickford (Ossipee, laborer) and Ida Cook (Ossipee, housewife)
Raymond M. Carolyn **Dore** 10/26/1964 in Lakeport; W - 29, factory; W - 24, factory
Richard P. of Ossipee m. Ada P. **Ericsson** of Littleton 8/7/1926 in Littleton; H - 20, b. Ossipee; W - 22, b. Oxford, ME
Robert C. of Ossipee m. Arleen C. (Demers) **Nault** of Ossipee 10/12/1996
Robert Craigue m. Janice Carrie **White** 7/29/1972 in N. Conway; H - b. 1/14/1951; W - b. 12/27/1956
Robert Craigue m. Judith P. **Morgan** 2/26/1977 in Tuftonboro; H - b. 1/14/1951; W - b. 9/12/1953
Roger W. of Ossipee m. Virginia P. **Palmer** of Ossipee 1/24/1942 in Wolfeboro; H - 20, mill man; W - 17, at home
Russell, Jr. m. Herberta **Evans** 6/20/1964 in Ctr. Ossipee; H - 18, laborer; W - 19, home
Russell Ford of Ossipee m. Helen Sadie **Eldridge** of Ossipee 2/28/1945 in Ossipee; H - 19, woodsman; W - 18, at home
Stanley of Ossipee m. Viola **Partridge** of Wolfeboro 12/22/1948 in Moultonville; H - 19, woodsman; W - 19, housewife
Steven G. m. Wendy J. **Cincotta** 5/11/1985; H - b. 12/10/1962; W - b. 2/6/1965

WHITTEMORE,
James F. of Ossipee m. Bertha **Brown** of Ossipee 1/6/1952 in Ctr. Ossipee; H - 26, millwork; W - 16, at home

WHITTINGHAM,
Tim James m. Diane **Veliz** 4/7/1993 in Ctr. Ossipee

WICAL,
Ronald of Rochester, NY m. Linda **Skillo** of Rochester, NY 3/7/1958 in Ossipee; H - 20, lab. tech.; W - 18, office work

WIDGINS,
Lawrence T. of Philadelphia, PA m. Nellie **Horne** of Portland, ME 11/23/1959 in Ctr. Ossipee; H - 29, USAF; W - 24, none

WIGGIN,
Arthur H. of Ossipee m. Harriet M. **Bradeen** of Waterboro, ME 12/25/1893 in Water Village; H - 28, lawyer, b. Ossipee, s/o C. F. Wiggin

(Ossipee) and Villa (Wolfeboro); W - 23, housewife, b. Waterboro, ME, d/o W. N. Bradeen (Waterboro, ME) and Sarah (Waterboro, ME)
Arthur R. of Ossipee m. Arlena G. **Stillings** of Ossipee 6/29/1910 in Ossipee; H - 28, shoemaker, b. E. Rochester, s/o Charles A. Wiggin (Lebanon, ME, teamster) and Abbie Wallingford; W - 18, maid, b. Ossipee, d/o Frank B. Stillings (Ossipee, farmer) and Cora Beane
Charles G. of Ossipee m. Alice M. **Meserve** of Effingham 7/29/1903 in Waterboro, ME; H - 23, school teacher, b. Ossipee, s/o Charles H. Wiggin (Ossipee, wheelwright) and Ella S. Nichols (Ossipee, housewife); W - 20, maid, b. Boston, MA, d/o John Meserve (Kittery, ME, carpenter) and Adelaide Pease (Tamworth)
Edwin of Ossipee m. Abbie **Welch** of Ossipee 4/27/1900 in Ossipee; H - 19, laborer, b. Ossipee, s/o William H. Wiggin (Ossipee, laborer) and Sophia Wiggin (Ossipee, housewife); W - 21, maid, b. Ossipee, d/o Peter Welch (Ossipee, deceased) and Cora B. Welch (Parsonsfield, ME, housewife)
Edwin of Ossipee m. Margaret **Nickerson** of Exeter 9/22/1946 in Moultonboro; H - 63, millman; W - 48, at home
Grover C. of Ossipee m. Velma C. **Meloon** of Ossipee 11/25/1909 in Ossipee; H - 24, R.R. service, b. Ossipee, s/o George P. Wiggin (Ossipee, farmer); W - 22, maid, b. Effingham, d/o Frank Meloon (Ossipee, supt. alms house)
Harry L. of Wakefield m. Mabel **Drowns** of Ossipee 11/21/1900 in Ossipee; H - 19, farmer, b. Tuftonboro, s/o William Wiggin (Wakefield, farmer) and Mary Wiggin (Tuftonboro, housewife); W - 16, housemaid, b. Ossipee, d/o Elijah Drowns (Eaton, farmer) and Victoria Drowns (Eaton, housewife)
Jerry of Ossipee m. Laura O. **Snow** of Ossipee 11/23/1907 in Ossipee; H - 23, laborer, b. Ossipee, s/o Jeremiah Wiggin (Ossipee, carpenter) and Lizzie Welch (Ossipee, housewife); W - 22, maid, b. Milton, MA, d/o Elbridge G. Snow (Milton, MA, laborer) and Jessie McPhee (PEI, housewife)
Jerry B. of Ctr. Ossipee m. Linda L. **Dore** of Ctr. Ossipee 2/15/1963 in Ctr. Ossipee; H - 18, none; W - 15, none
Jerry B. of Ctr. Ossipee m. Donna Jean Lawrence **Randall** of Ctr. Ossipee 7/6/2001
Jerry Bruce, II m. Patricia Ann **Evans** 10/19/1985; H - b. 4/17/1965; W - b. 5/25/1964
Lester A. of Ossipee m. Helen M. **Jewett** of Ossipee 6/26/1912 in Milton; H - 25, livery keeper, b. Tuftonboro, s/o Arthur Wiggin (Tuftonboro); W - 22, b. Milton, d/o Homer Jewett (Milton)
Russell Elvin of Ossipee m. Lucy Mabel **Roberts** of Ossipee 12/20/1941 in Wolfeboro; H - 25, laborer; W - 28, housewife

Shirley of Ossipee m. Ethel **Harmon** of Ossipee 9/9/1932 in Ossipee; H - 22, laborer; W - 17, at home
Virgil T. of Wolfeboro m. Minnie E. **Hurn** of Ossipee 12/23/1923 in Ossipee; H - 38, b. Wolfeboro; W - 39, b. Ossipee
Virgil T. of Ossipee m. Mrs. Ina **Hersey** of Springvale, ME 11/13/1939 in Springvale, ME; H - 54, bricklayer; W - 55, housewife

WILBUR,
Robert M. m. Kathryn J. **Hodgdon** 7/19/1986; H - b. 10/30/1948; W - b. 1/26/1951

WILCOX,
Herbert L. of Ossipee m. Ethel F. **Gray** of Ossipee 7/26/1952 in Ctr. Ossipee; H - 42, plumbers helper; W - 22, hospital employee
Herbert Lyman of Ossipee m. Virginia A. **Cook** of Ossipee 11/25/1944 in Moultonboro; H - 34, plumber's helper; W - 18, at home
Michael William m. Tammy Louise **White** 5/28/1988; H - b. 4/17/1968; W - b. 8/25/1963
Michael William of Ossipee m. Dale Lee (Cairone) **Lyman** of Ossipee 6/22/1996

WILEY,
David C. m. Joan T. **Wilson** 3/26/1978 in Ossipee; H - b. 5/15/1950; W - b. 11/27/1946

WILKESMAN,
Charles R. m. Donna M. **Quimby** 12/27/1975 in Tamworth; H - b. 9/15/1938; W - b. 6/30/1956

WILKINS,
Earlin L. of Ossipee m. Dora M. **Sawyer** of Ossipee 3/19/1917 in Ossipee; H - 21, farmer, b. Ossipee, s/o Carey Wilkins (VA) and Abby I. Cook (Conway); W - 24, housework, b. Saco, ME, d/o Daniel Sawyer and Luella Sawyer
Elmer L. of Ossipee m. Allura **Wakefield** of Tuftonboro 6/29/1929 in Moultonville; H - 23, laborer; W - 23, housewife
Elmer L. of Ossipee m. Agnes J. **Valley** of Wolfeboro 12/1/1963 in Ctr. Ossipee; H - 57, jobber; W - 64, retired
Leslie W. of Ctr. Ossipee m. Verna M. **Taylor** of Ossipee 10/5/1951 in Tamworth; H - 23, state worker; W - 39, housewife
Lloyd A. m. Catherine F. **Pike** 10/21/1967 in Ctr. Ossipee; H - 37, laborer; W - 20, office clerk
Lyford of Ossipee m. Pauline **Nichols** of Ossipee 5/11/1948 in Ossipee; H - 20, laborer; W - 23, housewife

Olif M. of Ossipee m. Louise A. **Fall** of Ossipee 5/29/1930 in Ossipee; H - 22, laborer; W - 23, at home

Olif M. of Ossipee m. Harriet **Schuch** of Ossipee 8/29/1936 in Ossipee; H - 28, farmer; W - 32, housekeeper

WILKINSON,
Ralph of Effingham m. Mildred **Eldridge** of Ossipee 5/4/1930 in Tamworth; H - 20, millman; W - 18, at home

WILLEY,
Gregory m. Reita **Johnson** 12/21/1968 in Concord; H - b. 7/1/1952; W - b. 9/7/1949

WILLIAMS,
Barry R. m. Patricia L. **Vose** 8/29/1981 in Manchester; H - b. 2/15/1956; W - b. 10/8/1955

Bruce E. m. Rose Mary **Willard** 8/20/1977 in Ossipee; H - b. 8/19/1953; W - b. 12/22/1949

David Alan m. Brenda Joyce **Eldridge** 2/2/1971 in Ossipee; H - b. 10/19/1951; W - b. 1/10/1952

Edward H. of Ctr. Ossipee m. Jane M. **Davey** of Meredith 9/24/1960 in Meredith; H - 26, electrician; W - 19, home

G. Richard m. Denese **Carroll** 6/25/1966 in Whittier; H - 21, clerk; W - 18, clerk

George Henry of Wakefield m. Florence B. **Murray** of Ossipee 3/7/1944 in Dover; H - 35, truckman; W - 39, nurse

Ira S. of W. Ossipee m. Blanche E. **Hill** of Haverhill, MA 10/26/1935 in Atkinson; H - 38, carpenter; W - 44, stenographer

John A. of Ossipee m. Juanita **Knox** of Ossipee 12/15/1928 in Ossipee; H - 28, truckman; W - 18, at home

Kerry D. m. Debra L. **Fisher** 10/6/1984; H - b. 5/18/1955; W - b. 8/23/1954

Lance A. of Tuftonboro m. Jill Lynn **Hayford** of Ctr. Ossipee 10/1/1994

Lorenzo of Ossipee m. Abbie M. **Jenness** of Effingham 10/10/1896 in Ossipee; H - 27, farmer, 2nd, b. Effingham, s/o James Williams (Effingham, farmer); W - 30, housekeeper, 2nd, b. Ossipee, d/o Amos Nichols (Ossipee, farmer) and Hannah Nichols (Ossipee, housewife)

Newman P. of Ossipee m. Mary M. **Cuskor** of Dover 1/13/1912 in Dover; H - 21, millman, b. Ossipee, s/o John T. Williams (Ossipee); W - 21, housework, b. Dover, d/o Tom Cuskor

Perley John of Ossipee m. Evelyn Louise **Welch** of Ossipee 4/24/1949 in Ctr. Ossipee; H - 32, woodsman; W - 23, waitress

Print E. m. Ethel M. **Felker** 3/18/1921 in Ossipee; H - 28, stage driver, 2nd, b. Berwick, ME, s/o Archie Williams (belt maker) and Cora Robinson

(housewife); W - 27, housewife, 2nd, b. Dover, d/o Frank Hurd (barber) and Ellen Bonner (spinner)
Richard W. of Tamworth m. Margie L. **Williams** of Ossipee 6/21/1952 in Moultonville; H - 28, farmer; W - 18, at home
Robert of Center Harbor m. Pauline R. **Birge** of Center Harbor 12/12/1953 in Ctr. Ossipee; H - 27, machinist; W - 22, telephone operator
Samuel of Ossipee m. Hattie **Eldridge** of Ossipee 10/8/1892 in Moultonville; H - 23, farmer, b. Ossipee, s/o Samuel Williams (Ossipee, farmer) and Esther Williams (Ossipee, housewife); W - 16, housemaid, b. Ossipee, d/o Daniel Eldridge (Ossipee, farmer) and Elsie Nichols (Ossipee, housewife)
Theodore Thomas m. Barbara Ann **Alden** 10/10/1974 in Tuftonboro; H - b. 9/8/1944; W - b. 9/4/1956
W. Dwaine m. Laurie Ann **Ward** 12/15/1979 in Ossipee; H - b. 8/27/1955; W - b. 12/27/1960
Waldo J. of W. Ossipee m. Beatrice D. **Wilson** of Ctr. Ossipee 10/18/1953 in Ctr. Ossipee; H - 24, mill hand; W - 18, at home
Ward m. Judith **Nickerson** 5/9/1964 in Ctr. Ossipee; H - 31, draftsman; W - 21, secretary
Willis of Ossipee m. Hilda **Merrow** of Ossipee 2/3/1933 in Ossipee; H - 18, laborer; W - 16, at home

WILSON,
Brian K. of W. Ossipee m. Terri L. **Carlton** of W. Ossipee 6/21/1997

WING,
Raymond G. of Newport, ME m. Eva **Curtis** of Newport, ME 4/20/1953 in Ctr. Ossipee; H - 33, self-employed; W - 43, housewife

WINKLEY,
Dana P. m. Robin K. **Lamy** 2/19/1980 in Manchester; H - b. 2/19/1942; W - b. 5/13/1957
Ervin M. of Ossipee m. Bessie M. **Abbott** of Ossipee 6/18/1911 in Ossipee; H - 25, mason, b. Dover, s/o Mark H. Winkley (Strafford, mason); W - 19, housewife, b. Ossipee, d/o George Abbott (Ossipee, laborer)
Mark A. of Ossipee m. May Trask **Sawyer** of Ossipee 10/18/1936 in Moultonville; H - 24, mason tender; W - 22, waitress

WINTHROP,
Paul B. m. Solange M. **Cropeau** 7/5/1986; H - b. 9/4/1945; W - b. 8/24/1946

WONG,
Henry of Portland, ME m. Lenore Beatrice **Tripp** of Portland, ME 6/30/1945 in Ossipee; H - 39, restaurant; W - 23, hairdresser

WOOD,
Francis R. of W. Scarboro, ME m. Geraldine M. **Goode** of Portland, ME 11/7/1955 in Ctr. Ossipee; H - 25, engineer; W - 28, nurse

J. Frank of Ossipee m. Eliza **Speedy** of Ossipee 11/24/1894 in Ossipee; H - 28, farmer, b. Ossipee, s/o Frank Wood (Ossipee, farmer) and Loise Nichols (Ossipee, housewife); W - 23, cook, b. St. Johnsbury, d/o James Speedy (St. Johnsbury, NB, farmer)

Jeffrey D. of Ctr. Ossipee m. Laura M. Chouinard **Steadman** of Ctr. Ossipee 6/18/1998

John F. of Ossipee m. Lizzie M. **Bean** of Ossipee 9/19/1888 in Haverhill, MA; H - 22, laborer, b. Ossipee, s/o Frank Wood (Ossipee); W - 18, housekeeper, b. Ossipee, d/o Frank Bean

John M. of Ossipee m. Ruby R. **Piper** of Wolfeboro 3/5/1957 in Ossipee; H - 65, retired; W - 53

Leslie m. Donna **Rogers** 1/7/1968 in Ossipee; H - b. 1/18/1944; W - b. 6/11/1945

WOODBURY,
Carlton J. of Rochester m. Eva May **Eldridge** of Ossipee 4/10/1941 in Berwick, ME; H - 21, shoe worker; W - 15, at home

WOODILL,
Ryan Kim of Ossipee m. Emily Donna **Clark** of GA 9/17/2000

WOODMAN,
Daniel M. m. Debra S. **Deuso** 11/5/1981 in Ossipee; H - b. 7/25/1957; W - b. 10/21/1960

Frederick of Ossipee m. Ida **Bean** of Ossipee 7/20/1905 in Ossipee; H - 44, laborer, b. Etna, ME, s/o Quincy Woodbury (sic) (Etna, ME) and Lydia B. Dyer (Etna, ME); W - 15, maid, b. Ossipee, d/o Fred Bean and Anna Bean

Oscar W. of Ossipee m. Emma E. **Armstrong** of St. Johns, NS 4/23/1890 in Wakefield; H - 20, farmer, b. Newfield, ME, s/o Jonathan Woodman (Woodman's Mills, merchant); W - 25, housekeeper, b. St. Johns, NS, d/o James Armstrong (St. Johns, NS, farmer)

Oscar W. of Ossipee m. Ella R. **White** of Medford, MA 5/10/1911 in Ossipee; H - 39, farmer, 2nd, divorced, b. Newfield, ME, s/o Jonathan Woodman (farmer); W - 37, housewife, 2nd, widow, b. Boston, d/o James M. Towne (Medford, MA, machinist)

Raymond, Jr. of Auburn, ME m. Jean Forbes **Cooper** of Auburn, ME 6/29/1945 in Ossipee; H - 21, maritime service; W - 18, at home
Richard H. m. Marilyn Judith **Mason** 2/14/1980 in Ossipee; H - b. 8/1/1930; W - b. 11/27/1952
Richard H. m. Bonnie L. **Jenner** 8/10/1985; H - b. 8/1/1930; W - b. 7/11/1948

WOODWARD,
Freeman E. of Tamworth m. Jacqueline L. **Tibbetts** of Ctr. Ossipee 8/29/1963 in Tamworth; H - 21, carpenter; W - 18, home
Harold A. of Concord m. Marion E. **Haynes** of Ctr. Ossipee 7/13/1935 in Wolfeboro; H - 47, manufacturer; W - 33, social worker
Verne E. of Haverhill m. Eleanor M. **Hartford** of W. Ossipee 1/23/1942 in Meredith; H - 23, station agent; W - 20, at home

WORMHOOD,
Chester A. of Sebago, ME m. Hazel L. **Sawyer** of Steep Falls, ME 12/10/1932 in Rochester; H - 38, merchant; W - 21, at home

WORMWOOD,
Lewis N. of Ossipee m. Dora **Crawford** of Ossipee 4/11/1888 in Ossipee; H - 23, laborer, b. Ossipee, s/o Charles P. Wormwood; W - 17, housekeeper, d/o George H. Crawford

WOYTON,
Robert John of Providence, RI m. Cynthia L. **Gwinn** of Norfolk, MA 12/6/1997

WRIGHT,
Leo T. of Lexington, MA m. Helen A. **Ignico** of Lexington, MA 6/10/1951 in Ctr. Ossipee; H - 21, electrician; W - 18, comptometer op.

WYMAN,
Melvin E. of Ossipee m. Idella **Thompson** of Effingham 9/20/1890 in Effingham; H - 28, laborer, b. Ossipee, s/o John Wyman; W - 16, housekeeper, b. Ossipee, d/o Albert Thompson (Ossipee)
Walter H., Jr. of Tamworth m. Ruth P. **Wiggin** of Somersworth 7/23/1950 in Moultonville; H - 20, plumber; W - 23, at home

WYNNE,
Kenneth of Woodbridge, CT m. Patricia J. **Fitzgerald** of Hamden, CT 7/8/1946 in Ossipee; H - 23, student; W - 22, student

YANKOWSKY,
Richard m. Edna **Martin** 2/20/1964 in Ossipee; H - 31, house painter; W - 21, office worker

YEATON,
Mitchell D. m. Gloria A. **Davis** 5/10/1980 in Ctr. Ossipee; H - b. 5/31/1957; W - b. 12/1/1957

YOUNG,
Charles B. of Ossipee m. Addie **Stevens** of Ossipee 3/24/1887 in Ossipee; W - housekeeper, d/o Mark Stevens (Wolfeboro)
Howard E. of Ossipee m. Minnie M. **Frey** of Ossipee 10/5/1904 in Ossipee; H - 31, farmer, b. Ossipee, s/o Arthur P. Young (Ossipee, farmer) and Emma F. Keniston (Ossipee, housewife); W - 34, housekeeper, 2nd, b. Westfield, ME, d/o Cyrus A. Andrews (contractor) and Sarah Bonney (Carleton, NB, housewife)
J. Lester of Ossipee m. Angie B. **Hodgdon** of Ossipee 6/22/1914 in Ossipee; H - 30, carpenter, b. Ossipee, s/o Arthur P. Young (Ossipee); W - 30, housekeeper, 2nd, b. Effingham, d/o William Glidden (Effingham)
Royce A. of Lisbon Falls, ME m. Laura M. **Libby** of Lisbon Falls, ME 4/12/1952 in Ctr. Ossipee; H - 44, machinist; W - 48, sewing in mill
Walter H. of Ossipee m. Margaret E. **Monroe** of Everett, MA 5/23/1905 in Ossipee; H - 36, farmer, b. Ossipee, s/o Joseph Young (Ossipee, farmer) and Hannah Chick (Waterbury, ME); W - 31, maid, b. NS, d/o Samuel Monroe (NS) and Hannah Jenness (NS)

ZALEWSKI,
Stefan C. m. Eileen M. **English** 6/16/1990; H - b. 5/28/1950; W - b. 5/14/1955

ZERVAS,
Arthur A. m. Kathleen J. **Farrell** 1/8/1983 in Freedom; H - b. 7/7/1924; W - b. 2/17/1936

ZIMMER,
O. Joseph of Ossipee m. Sylvia M. **Eldridge** of Ossipee 5/24/1930 in Ossipee; H - 21, laborer; W - 18, at home

ZINCK,
Robert E. of E. Rumford, ME m. Emilienne **Orino** of Rumford, ME 4/10/1951 in Ctr. Ossipee; H - 25, electrician; W - 45, at home

Abbott, Annie M. - Nutter, Leonard R.
Abbott, Bessie M. - Winkley, Ervin W.
Abbott, Caroline A. - Henderson, James E.
Abbott, Clara B. - Bean, Charles S.
Abbott, Cyrena P. - Littlefield, Wilmer L.
Abbott, Dorothy A. - Milligan, Roy T.
Abbott, Edith B. - Cook, Celon L.
Abbott, Edna M. - Carr, Warren R.
Abbott, Ethel F. - Sargent, Clarence R.
Abbott, Etta M. - Eldridge, Clifton D.
Abbott, Eva J. - Berry, Ernest M., Jr.
Abbott, Frances May - Gagne, Alfred J.
Abbott, Freida M. E. - Meader, John M.
Abbott, Gladys F. - Jack, Guy E.
Abbott, Gloria F. - Berry, Gordon D.
Abbott, Grace E. - Knowles, Herbert L.
Abbott, Hattie M. - Abbott, Joseph C.
Abbott, Ina Alice - Hewey, Arthur B.
Abbott, Irene A. - Trottier, Craig N.
Abbott, Jean F. - Eastman, Paul R.
Abbott, Louise A. - Templeton, John
Abbott, Marion - Snow, Wilton L.
Abbott, Maud - McKay, Alfred M.
Abbott, Mildred I. - Eldridge, Louis R.
Abbott, Renee J. - Abbott, David
Abbott, Sadie F. - Thompson, Charles A.
Abbott, Sandra Jean - Caulkins, Thomas Dale
Abbott, Sarah Jean - White, Jeremy Gordon
Adagent, Hannah - Nichols, Ebenezer
Adams, Diane Ruth - Hannah, Arthur James
Adams, Joan - Sayward, Frederick N., Jr.
Adams, Judy Lynn - Davis, John Thomas
Adjutant, Carol Lynn - Kenyon, Johnathan David
Adjutant, Dorothy Ellen - Clark, Frank Herbert
Adjutant, Esther - Eldridge, Chauncey
Adjutant, Gail - Patterson, William
Adjutant, Irene Mae - Nelson, Wayne Edward
Adjutant, Maude Lillian - Moulton, James Ernest
Adjutant, Peggy Edith - Eldridge, John Carroll
Adjutant, Virginia - Drew, Charles
Ainsworth, Jessie B. - Abbott, Jacob N.
Ainsworth, Nellie J. - Douglas, Everett V.
Aiton, Elizabeth Glenn - Walsh, Joseph A., Jr.
Albin, Jacqueline L. - Ryan, Thomas J.
Alden, Barbara Ann - Williams, Theodore Thomas

Alden, Donna Elaine - Berry, Duane Herman
Aleska, Diane L. - Brothers, Stanley Neal
Alexander, Stephanie Anne - Breton, Donald Henry
Allegra, Wendy Jo - Davies, John Anthony
Allen, Cynthia Ann - Eldridge, Mark Allen
Allen, Iris Marian - Albright, Russell Alan
Allen, Jane L. Russell - Rejda, Larry Keith
Allen, Janice Mae - Barton, Arthur Clinton
Allen, Rebecca Lee - Schofield, James Weston
Allen, Tammy Marie - Henderson, George Henry
Althoff, Sarah L. - Horne, Robert Glen, Jr.
Ames, Angela Nanette - Boutin, Raymond Paul, II
Ames, Clara M. - Walker, Benjamin B.
Ames, Esther Gertrude - Brothers, Elmer Wayne
Ames, Maude - Adjutant, Chester
Ames, Phyllis M. - Hall, Linwood W.
Anderson, Betty Ann - Webster, Charles Francis
Anderson, Debra J. - Downing, Joel P.
Anderson, Eva - Blais, Roger
Anderson, Eva F. - Moore, Orion O.
Anderson, Martha M. - Buswell, Edgar L.
Andrea, Cheryl M. - Sawyer, Matthew T.
Andrews, Annie - Nichols, Alphonzo
Andrews, Charlotte Frances - DeJong, Erik Jacob
Andrews, Edith A. - Neuman, Lloyd N.
Andrews, Iva Verna - Lucier, Arthur George
Andrews, June E. - Hatch, Joseph F.
Andrews, Lotta - Demeritt, Harlan S.
Anthony, Peggy A. - Eldridge, Walter C.
Antognoni, Lisa Lee - DeWitt, Kirk Hanson
Anuseevize, Cynthia - Pouliot, Joseph
Archer, Marie W. - Hunt, Earle A.
Armon, Beverly M. - Rova, Paul E.
Armstrong, Emma E. - Woodman, Oscar W.
Armstrong, Ruth - Desorcy, Henry G. R.
Armstrong, Vanessa M. - Stuart, Edward J.
Arnold, Louise K. - Getchell, Ralph A.
Arsenault, Denise Catherine - Shea, James Patrick, Jr.
Arsenault, Marie Frances - Pettis, Steven Daniel
Arsenault, Mary - Marcow, Frank
Athearn, Susan K. - Dyer, Allen R.
Atwood, Hilda M. - Chalifoux, Armel C.
Augenti, Carol Ann - Theberge, Leo Armistice, Jr.
Austin, Mabel - Cote, Raymond
Avery, Helen S. - Scott, Harry A.

Avery, Sharon Lyn - Huckins, Wesley E.
Ayer, Carmen Del Bosque - Huff, Herbert Raymond
Ayers, Bernice E. - Tupeck, Steve

Bacigalupo, Genevieve - Templeton, Ira
Bailey, Jane V. - Mirkovsky, Framk
Bailey, Karen Mae - Sloane, John Edmund
Bailey, Norma M. - Keyte, John B.
Baird, Harriet I. - Warren, Andre R.
Baker, Abbie M. - Hinds, Edward M.
Baker, Anne Marie - Kuell, Robert William
Baker, Beatrice M. - Harris, Merle F.
Baker, Betty - Allman, Barnard
Baker, Catherine M. - Lewis, Stephen E.
Baker, Francella W. - Fitch, Arthur R.
Baker, Hazel - White, Ernest
Baker, Hazel M. - Walker, Frank L.
Baldwin, Anna Marie - Custeau, Frank Eli
Baldwin, Cheryl A. - Leahy, Kevin J.
Baldwin, Cheryl Ann - Meisner, John Peter
Baldwin, Joanne B. - Lynch, Mary W.
Ball, Jennifer Harriet - King, Benjamin Stewart
Ballou, Diane - Eldridge, Philip Wayne
Bancroft, Eve - Afes, Abe
Banfill, Beatrice A. - Riley, Ernest Granville
Banfill, Elsie - Simms, Clifton
Banfill, Ethel M. - Prokey, Larry P.
Banfill, Rita Meleda - Fortune, Aubra Lain
Barber, Teresa A. - Hakala, Steven M.
Barenholtz, Ruth - Renbens, Maurice
Barnicoat, Cindy Ann - Rumley, Ronny Ray
Barranco, Grace - Stockbridge, Richard
Barrett, Stella - Hallowell, Ralph E.
Barrow, Marion A. - Rines, Bruce E.
Bartels, Michelle Ann - Hudson, David M.
Baston, Alberta G. - Knapp, Archie Fred, Jr.
Bates, Barbara A. - Simpson, Trevor D.
Bausch, Deborah A. - Martin, John A.
Baxter, Patricia A. - Eldridge, James A.
Beacham, Gertrude - Harmon, Lloyd W.
Beacham, Nellie A. - Gardner, Arthur
Beal, Judith M. - Powers, Albert E.
Bean, Beverly A. - Hurd, Arnold
Bean, Cheryl Lynn - Andersen, David Edward, Jr.
Bean, Edith - Votour, Charles

Bean, Ethel M. - Fernald, Leon F.
Bean, Ida - Woodman, Frederick
Bean, Jennie E. - Welch, Orrin E.
Bean, Leona M. - Rogers, Byron L., Jr.
Bean, Lizzie M. - Wood, John F.
Bean, Mabel M. - White, James H.
Bean, Marylynn - Tilton, Clifford H., Jr.
Bean, Mildred L. - Gladu, Valmur J.
Bean, Nichole Ruby - Snow, Michael Donn
Bean, Roberta G. - Bisbee, Chester A.
Bean, Rosemary - White, Gordon Ellis
Beane, Marion B. - Brownell, Clifford R.
Beardsley, Laura Helen - Pont, William Joseph
Bearse, Barbara - Wainio, David
Beaton, Kathrine Christine - Hodgdon, John Goebel
Beaton, Lois E. (Oxner) - Bushman, Richard J.
Beaudoin, Gertrude - Templeton, Ira
Beaulieu, Rita Alia - Keith, Harold Merritt
Beckman, Mildred E. - Bisbee, Chester A.
Beckwith, Beatrice A. - Blair, Francis Charles
Bedford, Brenda W. (Welch) - LaFavore, Steven P.
Belknap, Debra Ann - Milligan, Dwight James
Bell, Shirley - Savage, Richard
Bellavance, Blanche - McConnell, Zane
Bellini, Kim Y. - Cressey, Albert C.
Belliveau, Tanya Marie - Krutilek, Eric Edward
Bendin, Lillian M. - Pike, John I.
Benker, Joyce I. - Ritcey, Robert M.
Benker, Julie E. - Davis, Stuart B.
Bennett, Mildred J. - Perry, Herbert L.
Berg, Valerie T. - Smith, Daniel E.
Bergeron, Georgiana - Lamontagne, Joseph I.
Bergeron, Irene - Ferland, George
Bergeron, Michelle Leslie - McNamara, Kyle Westphal
Berkner, Katlin K. - Tenney, Thomas P.
Bernaby, Terri Lynn - Tobin, Edward F.
Berry, Barbara J. - Perry, Allen S.
Berry, Edith - Savard, Francis E.
Berry, Holly Jane - Hayford, Timothy Ernest
Berry, Jacqueline R. - Drew, Richard W.
Berry, Joan Darlene - Eldridge, Gordon Allen
Berry, Joyce A. - Eldridge, Bernard H.
Berry, Lenora M. - Thurston, Douglas L.
Berry, Lucy M. - Eldridge, Eben
Berry, Marion A. - Staples, Ervin E.

Berry, Martha - Eldridge, Dennis
Berry, Mary F. - Holbrook, Clement M.
Berry, Patricia - Thayer, Ray
Bertulli, Eva - MacDonald, Albert
Bertwell, Etta - Sias, Newell P.
Bertwell, Nettie M. - Emerson, Everett C.
Berube, Suzanne (Maggio) - Russell, Alan James
Betts, Vickie E. - Stewart, Mark F.
Bickford, Caroline Jennifer - Eldridge, Rodney Herbert, Jr.
Bickford, Dora - Bickford, Belmont E.
Bickford, Esther L. - Huntington, Benjamin F., Jr.
Bickford, Florence M. - Schaier, Carl Alfred
Bickford, Gertrude S. - Merrow, Howard W.
Bickford, Ida - Chandler, Henry M.
Bickford, Lill - Whiting, Charles A.
Bickford, Mary - Gibson, Albert E.
Bickford, Pearl Melvina - Webster, William Frances
Bickford, Sylvia M. - Welch, Ernest P.
Bidwell, Ruth - Nichols, Lewis W.
Bielowski, Mary M. - Hatch, Charles Stanley
Bigonski, Patricia P. - Thurber, David W.
Billings, Toby Leigh - Coates, Dennis John
Bilodeau, Jean W. - Rumery, Newell P.
Bilodeau, Olena R. - Jordan, Kenneth
Birge, Pauline R. - Williams, Robert
Bisbee, Barbara J. - Brett, Warren T.
Bisbee, Daisy B. - Bryant, Almon O.
Bisbee, Dorothy L. - Nelson, Andy F.
Bishop, Shirley - Hattenburg, Lester E.
Black, Deborah Jean - Boisvert, Paul Joseph
Blackey, Erin Marie - Edwards, Robert Stanley
Blaine, Amy Lynn - Grant, Shawn W.
Blair, Annette Mary - Howell, Roy Russell, Jr.
Blair, Susan Carol - Purkis, John D.
Blake, Eva Fall - Loud, Grover Cleveland
Blazo, Mildred M. - Smart, Charles E.
Bliss, Candy Ann (Stevens) - Cogswell, Richard L.
Bliss, Sheryl Dawn - White, Charles E.
Blocklock, Joanne - Ray, Arthur
Blomstrom, Patricia A. - Bradley, Joseph L.
Boardman, Cora E. - Stillings, Frank O.
Bodge, Verna M. - Taylor, Charles R.
Bodnar, Bertha M. - Rova, Enos L.
Bodwell, Debra L. - Gilbert, Francis A.
Boewe, Maureen S. - Trefry, Ralph M., Jr.

Bohaker, Dorothy P. - Smith, Daniel Currier
Boissey, Margaret L. - Britton, Raymond F.
Bolduc, Marilyn R. - Bolduc, Douglas G.
Bonfoey, Kable Witz - Rizzo, Robert Kroell
Booker, Charlotte G. - Fishman, Barnett B.
Booth, Beverly - Cole, Carl
Borey, Roberta G. - Adams, Gary
Botticelli, Elvira - Capite, Lawrence M.
Boucher, Gloria V. - Aspinall, George W.
Boulanger, Margaret I. - Hinds, Kenneth H.
Bourgault, Janice M. - Andrea, Robert A.
Bourgault, Rose-Marie - Lyon, William H.
Bourgoin, Mary A. - Tupper, Jackson A.
Bova, Ida C. - Stone, Arthur G.
Bovee, Joy Lee Ayoubee - Rutter, Roger David
Bowman, Judith L. M. - Eldridge, Gregory A.
Boyd, Diana L. - Cotton, Dana R., Jr.
Boyd, Kathleen S. - Harrington, Warren
Boyd, Patricia - Boutin, Harold
Boyden, Kathryn M. - Loukas, Kane L.
Brack, Donna E. - Duchano, Donald R.
Brackett, Melissa H. - Massey, Gordon R.
Brackett, Sharon L. - Foster, Clyde W.
Brackett, Tracy E. - Grinnell, Collin M.
Bradbury, Annie L. - Conner, Raymond H.
Bradbury, Patricia Ann Jencks - Sullivan, Mark Raymond
Bradeen, Harriet M. - Wiggin, Arthur H.
Bradley, Evangeline Blomstrom - Moyer, Glen Alexander
Bradley, Flavelle - Hills, Charles B.
Bralczyk, Robin Lynn - Bralczyk, Stanley Adam
Branin, Suzanne - Roberts, Thomas Earl, III
Breault, Kathryn - Blanke, Dennis
Breckfill, Helen M. - Tremblay, Lionel J.
Breed, Saima J. - Davis, Alan G.
Breen, Donnamarie McEwen - Senecal, Robert Charles
Brennan, Norine P. - Dunn, Walter L.
Bretton, Karen Theresa - Eldridge, Bruce Edward
Brewer, Dorothy Cora - Eldridge, Jeremy Clyde
Bridges, Mary K. - Goodale, David W.
Briggs, Marcia H. - Hayford, Jeffrey G.
Britton, Linda L. - Dore, George W.
Brock, Beverly - DeFreitos, Gene
Bronson, Sydney J. Day - Ring, John E., Jr.
Brooks, Cindy L. (LaVoice) - Brooks, Gary F.
Brooks, Jacqueline Leona - Newell, William Francis

Brooks, Jennifer Lee - Eldridge, James Kenneth
Brooks, Karen M. - Chao, San M.
Brooks, Mary Louise - Loring, Russell George
Brooks, Susie - Wallace, Harry A.
Brooks, Terri L. - Mack, James Leroy
Brooks, Terri Lee - Drew, Daniel Steven
Brothers, Beatrice E. - Eldridge, Newell P.
Brouillette, Bonnie L. - Chapman, Robert A.
Brown, Addie M. - Crawford, William H.
Brown, Annie E. - Crooks, David
Brown, Beatrice - Magee, James F.
Brown, Bertha - Whittemore, James F.
Brown, Blanch May - Taylor, Max R.
Brown, Donna L. - Schuler, Ronald A., Jr.
Brown, Dorothy A. - Fleming, Floyd E.
Brown, Dorothy W. - Welch, Lawrence E.
Brown, Elizabeth R. - Dennis, Charles E.
Brown, Emma F. - Hanson, Jacob
Brown, Ida E. - Bryant, James M.
Brown, Isadore - Pickett, Harry A.
Brown, Joanne M. - Kirkwood, Dane C.
Brown, Josephena - Colby, William
Brown, Loralie Ann Wedge - Beckwith, Brian Derek
Brown, Lula M. - Stewart, Herbert W.
Brown, Margaret A. - Reinhold, Robert V., Jr.
Brown, Mary J. - Moody, Edwin
Brown, Pauline M. - Files, William E.
Brown, Phyllis A. - Eldridge, Eugene A.
Brown, Violet M. - Sawyer, Hayes W.
Brown, Virginia M. - Lowell, George R.
Brown, Winifred E. - Knox, Olin A.
Brownell, Barbara M. - Currier, Cortland A.
Brownell, Ethel M. - Bean, Ernest C.
Brownell, Kira Margit - Eldridge, Norman F., Jr.
Brownell, Kirsten M. - Harmon, Clifford Carroll
Brownell, Kirsten Mahalay - Diltz, Steven Arnold
Brownell, Melanie - Conner, Michael E.
Brule, Kathleen M. - Merrow, Michael S.
Bruning, Nancy L. - Harbison, Cameron C.
Bryant, Deborah Jean - Jones, Roger Arthur
Bryant-Wall, Patricia A. - Wall, Roy E.
Buchanan, Catherine V. - Butler, Kenneth A.
Buchanan, Tonita E. - Mack, Robert M.
Buck, Deborah L. - Alward, David A.
Budroe, Beverly - Eldridge, James

Buechele, Elvera S. - Savage, John C.
Bugden, Janie Elizabeth - Boutin, Bruce Kyle
Bugden, Patricia Helena - Larrabee, Dennis Edwin
Buis, Sandra Lee - Drew, Scott Allan
Bunker, April - Nevius, George Booker
Bunker, Charlotte - Hormell, Glenn D.
Bunker, Ramona J. - Davis, Johnny L., Jr.
Burby, Shawnda Lee - Johnson, Dale Grover
Burdett, Celia J. - White, Ervin W.
Burke, Dorothy E. - Brooks, Richard W.
Burke, Heidemarie - Tallant, Daniel Hugh
Burke, Kimberly A. - Noyes, Derek S.
Burke, Rose C. - Pendleton, Lawrence M.
Burleigh, Judith - Kaplan, Morton D.
Burleigh, Pauline - Reissfelder, Theodore
Burns, Debra Jane - Laconte, Donald William
Burns, Piper Ann - Strong, John Mercer
Burrell, Penelope G. - Bump, Richard T.
Burton, Heather Renee - Hodge, Marcus John
Burton, Mabel B. - Chick, Earl
Busch, Deborah May - Fischbein, Daniel Walter
Bushey, Linda M. - Camire, Robert R.
Buswell, Dorothy P. - Drew, Selden E.
Buswell, Laura B. - Welch, Preston E.
Buswell, Mattie D. - Eldridge, Melvin C.
Butler, Elaine S. - Parsons, Bruce W.
Butler, Lillian A. - Bibber, Orville R.
Butler, Linda M. - Morgan, Richard H.
Butler, Marion C. - Eastman, Clayton W.
Butler, Marjorie Anne - Clark, Edmund Palmer
Button, Giovanna C. (Dorne) - Ross, Lawrence Elliott
Buzzell, Virginia M. - Drew, Wendell R.
Byers, Dorothy W. - Littlefield, Wilmer L.
Byers, Tammy M. Lepelley - Royea, Christopher Paul

Cafarillia, Patricia M. - Snow, Donn H.
Cahoon, Lourdes A. - Aronowitz, Saul A.
Caines, Mary Elvina - Schatzl, Thomas F.
Cairone, Dale L. - Lyman, James S.
Calderone, Gail M. Buss - Larrabee, Clinton L., III
Caldwell, Dale Frances - Walter, Glenn Allen
Caldwell, Mary E. - Fall, Miner L.
Call, Alice M. - Viles, John R.
Cammett, Laura Lee - Paige, Mark
Campbell, Grace - Douglas, Ernest

Campbell, Helen M. - Bradstreet, Charles O.
Canavan, Barbara A. - Sweetman, Alfred W.
Canney, Beatrice M. - Cook, Clayton R.
Canney, Bernice L. - Libby, Frank, Jr.
Canney, Fannie - Buzzell, Frank
Canney, Julia - Dorr, Cyrus H.
Canney, Laurel Ann - Robert, Todd Allen
Canney, Karen - Hanson, Lewis M.
Capach, Karen N. - Carver, Dennis E.
Capalbo, Denice M. - Thurston, Larry C.
Capone, Tiffanie Marie - Appleton, Scott Thomas
Caraway, Jerilyn Baker - Cornwell, Ralph Weld
Carey, Joanne H. (Hodge) - White, John H.
Carlin, Nellie A. - Nason, Joseph F.
Carlson, Bertha M. - Weinbrecht, Alfred R.
Carlson, Ingrid D. - DeWitt, Michael E.
Carlson, Tina G. - Farina, Robert A.
Carlton, Cheryl Renee - Sargent, Alan Wayne
Carlton, Mary I. - Chute, James A.
Carlton, Terri L. - Wilson, Brian K.
Carpenter, Lisa M. - Adjutant, Norman M.
Carr, Betty J. - Welch, Ford J., Jr.
Carr, Terry Lynn - Sturtevant, Jeffrey Charles
Carroll, Denese - Williams, G. Richard
Carroll, Kelly Ann - Eldridge, Lawrence John, III
Carruthers, Jennifer Lee - Bethell, Russell Edward
Carsey, Joan - Stubbs, Edward
Carson, Claire Lee - Beaulieu, Leo Peter
Cartwright, Betty L. - Chamides, Robert E.
Carver, Nellie - Grant, John H.
Castelluzzo, Beatrice E. - Griffin, Henry A., Jr.
Cate, Dorothy - Cragin, Allen
Caton, Maryann - Maliawco, John Frank
Caulkins, Sandra J. - Libby, Keith W.
Cautone, Antoinette T. - Merchant, George R.
Caverly, Eleanor L. - Wade, Robert S.
Cellemme, Ruth L. - Walsh, Earle L., Jr.
Celli, Kathie Mary - Ford, David Brian
Center, Pearl M. - Reilly, Robert J.
Chadbourn, Ida E. - Thompson, John W.
Chadwick, Carole - Nevers, Thomas J.
Champion, Augusta - White, George B.
Champion, Jennie B. - Abbott, George H.
Chapman, Bernice A. - Stein, Walter
Charles, Amy Christine - Vacchiano, Timothy James

Charles, Sandra L. - Eldridge, Richard C.
Charles, Sharon A. - Eldridge, Tedd O.
Charney, Jill S. - Golden, Mark S.
Chase, Ada J. - Sceggel, Elisha W.
Chase, Amanda J. - Graham, Richard A., III
Chase, Anna M. - Sceggel, Benjamin P.
Chase, Debra L. - McMahan, Timothy Daniel
Chase, Elizabeth J. - Wasson, Dannie E.
Chase, Ethel V. - Varney, Ernest R.
Chase, Gladys M. - Trott, Wesley H.
Chase, Judith V. H. - Peabody, William B.
Chase, Margaret I. - Cram, Raymond C., Jr.
Chase, Marilyn E. - Brown, Reginald P.
Chase, Patricia A. - Brown, Robert C.
Chase, Susan J. - Chase, John L.
Chase, Thelma M. - Welch, Maurice C.
Cheney, Darlene P. - Westfall, Kurt P.
Cheney, Jane Louise - Simmons, Donald David
Cheney, Linda - Cotton, Dana R., Jr.
Cheney, Norma A. - Merrow, Dana H.
Chesley, Cora B. - Nason, Gardner M.
Chesley, Eva Marie - Eldridge, Larry E.
Chevallier, Patricia Anne - Campion, Edwin J., Jr.
Chick, Bertha E. - Garland, Sumner G.
Chick, June F. - Loud, Arthur P.
Chick, Winnie M. - Chandler, Henry H. M.
Chickering, Catherine M. - Baker, William J., Jr.
Chill, Kathleen A. - Rose, Harold, Jr.
Chionchio, Brenda A. - Johnson, Dennis
Chiusano, Gloria - Martin, Blaine
Christensen, Wanda F. - Fraser, Reginald E.
Christiansen, Carol Lynn - Liebert, Scott A.
Churchill, Deborah A. - Stevens, James R.
Chute, Grace A. - Keefe, James W.
Ciceolo, Ethel - Hill, Harry L.
Cincotta, Wendy J. - Whiting, Steven G.
Clancy, Catherine - Buswell, Isaac L.
Clark, Annie E. - Bierweiler, Donald C.
Clark, Carmel Magdialene - Clark, Robert M.
Clark, Emily Donna - Woodill, Ryan Kim
Clark, Katie - Rivers, Joseph
Clark, Minnie C. - Chesley, Joshua E.
Clay, Carrie L. - Emery, Louis M.
Clay, Idella - Wallace, Frank W.
Clayman, Mary Margaret - Newcombe, Roy E.

Cleary, Carole A. - Jefferds, Harry B.
Clifford, Wanda Lee Edwards - Hilbert, Mark Russell
Close, Annie S. - Copp, Daniel B.
Closson, Cassandra Jean - Hussey, Brian Keith
Clough, Cora - Perren, William
Clough, Ella - Smith, Austin E.
Clough, Fannie M. - Webster, Charles M.
Clough, Louise - Philbrick, Wesley
Clough, Wendy Leigh - Sargent, Richard Lee, Jr.
Cloutier, Imelda - Eleason, Philip
Cobb, Angel M. - Stewart, Paul C.
Cobb, Ida M. - Harden, Neal C.
Cochrane, Cynthia M. - Leavitt, Scott M.
Coderre, Ann M. - Hebert, Anthony P.
Coffey, Ellen Rachel Potter - Shannon, Edwin Shirly
Cohen, Mara - Mason, Steven A.
Colbath, Vera M. - Aubrey, Fred R.
Colbert, Dorothea - Bowman, Richard D.
Colby, Barbara R. - Bronscombe, Harold H.
Colby, Etta - White, Mayhew O.
Colby, Etta M. - Abbott, Ernest Guy
Colby, Grace M. - Scott, Elmer A.
Colby, Hilda - Flanagan, Paul
Colby, Josie - Martin, Leopold
Colby, Louise - Eldridge, Russell D.
Colby, Marie C. - Archambeault, Arthur W.
Colby, Norma - Welch, Lisle R.
Colby, Rhenfina B. - White, Scott L.
Cole, Christine E. - Barton, Llewellyn, Jr.
Cole, Emma - Rines, George W.
Collette, Janine A. - Knox, Lawrence J., Jr.
Collins, Almeda F. - Bailey, Charles T.
Collins, Margaret - Nichols, Roy S.
Colomy, Helen Mae - Smart, Preston B.
Colwell, Sverena M. - Cayer, Louis J., II
Comtois, Laurie Ann - Martel, David Maurice
Conley, Theresa - Milliken, George
Conner, Carol - Remington, Kenneth K.
Conner, Idella M. - Hussey, William B.
Conner, Rose O. - Richardson, Frank
Connolly, Stacey A. - Butler, Edward T.
Connor, Debora - Gray, Donald P.
Connor, Edith - Canney, J. H.
Conroy, Nancy A. - Frenier, William F.
Constantaras, Theodora - Hough, John K.

Contois, Gayle M. - Bergeron, Gerard R.
Cook, Carolyn A. - Libby, Randolph C.
Cook, Florence I. - Eldridge, Wilbur F.
Cook, Laura Ann - Garlough, Keith Edward
Cook, Meredith J. - Nason, Ernest R.
Cook, Sylvia A. - Hammond, Walter W.
Cook, Virginia A. - Wilcox, Herbert Lyman
Cooley, Mary E. - Matthews, Bryn C.
Cooney, Rosemary - Gauthier, Robert W.
Cooper, Jean Forbes - Woodman, Raymond, Jr.
Cooper, Lisa - Rivera, Robert Richard
Cooter, Ruth - Hooper, Allen
Copp, Elizabeth Ann - Davis, Silas E.
Copp, Karen Ann - Deighan, Joseph Henry
Copp, Priscilla - Beaupre, Kenneth
Corey, Elizabeth A. - Beauford, Linwood A.
Cormier, June M. Lanteigne - D'Andrea, David Carl
Cornwell, Sally Ann - Perkins, Daniel B.
Corriveault, Jane M. - Naismith, Donald G., Jr.
Corrow, Brenda E. - Eldridge, Robert W.
Corson, Carrie L. - Hodge, Edgar C.
Corson, Charlotte C. - Munroe, Richard A.
Corson, Linda Marie - Moulton, Darwin
Cotton, Georgiana - Palmer, Edgar
Cotton, Judy E. - Hurliman, Patrick J.
Cotton, Patricia - Jonsson, Harry
Cotton, Theresa L. - Fullerton, Wayne Ryder
Cottone, Louise H. - Antogoni, John Joseph, Jr.
Coughlin, Jacqueline J. - Swanson, Edward R., Jr.
Coukos, Amy Arlene - Waldron, William Russell
Courser, Muriel H. - Craig, Charles H.
Cousens, Donna J. - Conley, Norman G.
Cowan, Cecily B. - Chamberlain, Deane M.
Cowan, Irene M. - Haner, Charles E.
Cowley, Karen - Lolio, Thomas
Cox, Martha - Hart, Steven Andrew
Craft, Irene F. - Loretta, Allen T.
Cragin, Stella M. - Eldridge, W. Clayton
Craigue, Cora V. - Knowles, George E.
Craigue, Donna - Sargent, Norman
Craigue, Nancy L. - Kendall, Alvin J.
Crapo, Stacy Lee - Seamans, Robert Michael
Crawford, Dora - Wormwood, Lewis N.
Cressey, Beverly A. - Loud, Simon F.
Crockett, June D. - Sulley, Thomas F.

Cropeau, Solange M. - Winthrop, Paul B.
Crouse, Mabel M. - Bradley, Harold
Crowley, Blance (Mrs.) - Dube, Leo Phillip
Crowley, Ginger D. - Brownell, Michael D.
Cummings, Edith D. - Michael, Edward C.
Cunha, Isabel C. - Potter, Albert M.
Cunningham, Sylvia - Swift, Clyde C.
Curran, Norma - Azenedo, Adelino
Currier, Anne R. - Brodeur, Michael Richard
Currier, Eunice - Hanson, John
Currier, Kimberly E. - Kinmond, Scott D.
Currier, Lillian B. - Bryant, Floyd G.
Currier, Maud E. - Carro, Paul F.
Curtin, Margaret M. - Merrow, Llewellyn G.
Curtis, Cassandra Townsend - Dales, Gregory Franklin
Curtis, Dolores D. - Harmon, John F.
Curtis, Eva - Wing, Raymond G.
Curtis, Heather Myra - Tenney, Michael Warren
Curtis, Julia M. - Hammond, Daniel
Curtis, Marie H. - Sawyer, Howard P.
Curtis, Sheryl A. - Gustafson, Donald R., Jr.
Cushman, Nettie - Tinsman, Everett
Cuskor, Mary M. - Williams, Newman P.
Custeau, Tressa Jean - Flanders, Donald Warren, Jr.
Cutter, Inez Frances - Keith, Lewis Edward
Cutting, Bertha L. - Weeks, Cecil R.
Cutting, Gloria M. - Jordan, Harry M.

Daigneau, Alecia M. - Eldridge, Langdon J.
Dale, Cynthia Lynn - Schwartz, Richard
Dale, Marcia A. - Floria, Ralph D.
Dale, Susan - Fullerton, Peter Earl
Daley, Jennifer M. - Fuentes, Edwin
Daley, Jill A. - Gibson, William H., III
Dallmeyer, Faye C. - Soderberg, Walter
Dame, Daisy A. - Hodgdon, Charles E.
Dame, Edna A. - Brown, Fred B.
Dame, Miriam E. - Tuckerman, Leverett S.
Damon, Carol A. - Pearl, Michael J.
Damon, Susan E. - Riley, Ernest G., Jr.
Danforth, Jean L. - Varney, Raymond E.
Daniels, Marianne - Guarino, Robert J.
Dansingburg, Julie Jo - Kelley, Francis Joseph, Jr.
Davenport, Phyllis - Jacobus, Ralph
Davey, Hazel A. - Hurd, William A.

Davey, Jane M. - Williams, Edward H.
Davidson, Jean A. - Carlson, Robert G.
Davis, Abbie J. - Eldridge, Scott O.
Davis, Alice Susan - Blake, Daniel Richard
Davis, Beatrice I. - Bowers, Howard L.
Davis, Blanche E. - Dore, Leroy H.
Davis, Clarinda - Doe, Benjamin F.
Davis, Constance Lola - Plastridge, Clement Henry
Davis, Cora B. - Welch, Walter S.
Davis, Dani Allyson - Clark, Christopher Travis
Davis, Donna G. - Stockbridge, Glenn R.
Davis, Dora E. - Moody, William H.
Davis, Eleanor M. - Stoddard, Clark M.
Davis, Frances L. - Berton, Robert E.
Davis, Georgia A. - Eldridge, Harrison
Davis, Gloria A. - Yeaton, Mitchell D.
Davis, Jean S. - Bates, Donald C.
Davis, Jo-Anne M. - Canney, Christopher S.
Davis, Karen L. - Romano, Anthony D.
Davis, Lizzie B. - Welch, George
Davis, Margaret - Osgood, Gerald
Davis, Marilyn Joanne - Rines, Stanley Joseph
Davis, Mertie L. - Ryan, Thomas
Davis, Mildred F. - Dore, Leon E.
Davis, Shirley M. - Robinson, Aaron R.
Davis, Susan Lynne - Killeher, Paul Joseph
Davis, Susie E. - Smart, Charles R.
Davis, Velma Pearl - DeButts, Daniel B.
Dawson, Nina - Kohler, John C.
Day, Brenda R. - Cushman, Kevin N.
Day, Christina Atwood - Ring, Eugene Vincent
Day, Esther Lona - Prokey, Richard Ernest
Day, Marjorie - Roberts, Roland, Jr.
Day, Merri Ellen Gilpatrick - Hutchinson, Clifford Chandler, Jr.
Deal, Jennifer Anne - Dore, George Lawrence
Dearborn, Deborah L. - Davis, Walter M.
Deatte, Joyce M. - White, Norman L.
Deatte, Linda - MacDonald, Franklin
Deatte, Rebecca E. - Eldridge, Douglas C.
DeButts, Velma P. - Wagenfeld, Kenneth B.
DeCesare, Eleanor A. - Messina, Joseph A.
DeFosses, Mary Ann - Champagne, Craig A.
DeFreitas, Cheryl L. - Edwards, James C.
DeGloria, Kerry Anne - Bernardo, Sonny
Delano, Mildred P. - Redman, Edward L.

Delfuoco, Diane Laura - Peabody, David Joshua
DeLima, Renata Pereira - Valys, Keith Joseph
Delk, Caroline W. - Downing, Donald F.
Della Pelle, Josephine - Belville, Paul C.
DeLuca, Lori Ann - Rice, Lawrence J., Jr.
Demeritt, Annie - Howland, Densmore
Demeritt, Caroline F. - Hayford, Paul L.
Demeritt, Hester Abbie - Tucker, Ralph Mansfield
Demerritt, Emma F. - Welch, Leon J.
DeMerritt, Stella V. - Sampson, Alfred J.
Demers, Juliann Marie - Fogarty, John Edward, IV
Dempsey, Jane L. - Allen, James R.
Descoteaux, Patricia Lily - Misiaszek, Robert Alan
Deshaies, Laurel Louise (Brown) - Gladu, Richard Clifford
DeSimone, Sandra Lee - Ward, Stephen Lewis
Deslauriers, Zita M. - Chamberlin, Charles A.
Deuley, Ruth Mae - Conlon, Frederick E.
Deuso, Debra S. - Woodman, Daniel M.
DeWolfe, Kathryn G. - Howard, Sumner M.
Dick, Roxanne S. - Gregoire, Wayne E.
DiGiovanni, Ruth - Pimental, George
DiPaolo, Alice R. - Palmisano, Carmine C.
DiPaulo, Katherine A. - Johnson, Christopher A.
Dodier, Susan Ann - Waldrip, Mark James
Doe, Alice L. - Coughlin, Edward G.
Doe, Clara - Nichols, Charles A.
Doe, Elaine H. - Symonds, Donald F., Jr.
Doe, Nancy J. - Loring, Russell G.
Doe, Sandra J. - Fitzsimmons, Henry T.
Dolby, Carole L. (Cormier) - Dunbar, Dennis R.
Dondero, Mary June - Fisher, Phillip Edward
Dore, Addie G. - Bean, Leland H.
Dore, Blanche E. - Lozier, Anthany
Dore, Carolyn - Whiting, Raymond
Dore, Edna R. - Nichols, Ronald D.
Dore, Georgia A. - Nichols, Olen
Dore, Kaysee Marie - Hersey, David Allen, Jr.
Dore, Lillian Amy - Eldridge, Roy Everett
Dore, Linda L. - Wiggin, Jerry B.
Dore, Lynda Mary-Rose - Sawtelle, James A., Jr.
Dore, Margaret A. - Boatman, Lawrence
Dore, Rose M. - Eldridge, Perley E.
Dore, Ruth M. - Avery, Lewis T.
Dorr, Ida V. - Bean, Fred E.
Dorr, Marie A. - Hardwick, Frederick W.

Dorr, Martha A. - Ames, Daniel V.
Dorr, Mary A. - Abbott, Almon F.
Doten, Louise M. - Nathon, John G.
Doty, Pamela A. - Cotton, Frederick P., Jr.
Douglas, Beverly E. - Mayo, Dennis E.
Dow, Evelyn - Evans, Frank E.
Dow, Fanny - Duntley, Charles A.
Dow, Frances Arlene - White, Harold Eugene
Dow, Karen M. - Butler, John P., Jr.
Dow, Sandra Y. - Varney, David A.
Downie, Donna S. - Bergeron, Donald E.
Downing, Saylee J. - Merrow, Mark E.
Downs, Bernice - Reissfelder, William
Downs, Bonita - Hickey, Stephen
Downs, Elvena E. - Buzzell, Frank
Downs, Janet - White, Gardner L.
Downs, Margery Ellen - Gunzel, William Skot
Downs, Nancy J. - Gonyer, Lewis Eugene
Drake, Deanna L. - Eldridge, William I.
Drake, Lillian - Horrigan, John M.
Drelick, Nancy B. - Desrosiers, Stephen R.
Drew, Amanda Lee - Welch, Robert Roy
Drew, Betsy C. - Cressey, Wayne L.
Drew, Beverly - Cressey, Wayne
Drew, Ina M. - Emery, Anthony D.
Drew, Lucy E. - Sinclair, William C.
Drew, Marion - Welch, Robert
Drew, Sadie Elvira - Loring, James Milburn
Drew, Virginia - Eldridge, Clifton
Drinkwater, Barbara - Eldridge, Austin Melvin
Drinkwater, Beatrice - Hobbs, Thomas
Drown, Victoria - Littlefield, George F.
Drowns, Mabel - Wiggin, Harry L.
Dube, Dagny D. - Blouin, Francis X.
Dubois, Janet H. - Sheaff, Ronald F.
Duchesne, Michele Marie - Bradley, Edwin Kieffer, III
Dufresne, Linda J. - Brown, Isaac, Jr.
Dugan, Ruth E. - Tappan, Edwin S.
Dugas, Marie - Comeau, Ulysse
Duggan, Patricia A. - Moore, Duane B.
Duguay, Nicole Ann - Paraskos, Joshua David
Duncan, Sharon - Falter, Richard F.
Dunlaps, Elenor L. - Lindsay, William D.
Dunn, Esther P. - Newhook, John G.
Duntley, Maude - Drown, Joel P.

Dupuis, Isabel - Delisle, Christopher Thomas
Duquette, Lisa Lynn - Hinckley, James E., Jr.
Durant, Bessie A. - Moody, Nathaniel E.
Durgan, Eva M. - Harrington, George O.
Durgin, Mary Louise - Gagne, Peter Allen
Durgin, Naomi - Goodwin, Thomas
Durgin, Sheila Ebert - Poisson, Norman R.
Durrell, Gertrude - Douglass, Albion
Dwelley, Mary M. - Cressey, Frank H.
Dwyer, Eva M. - Smith, Frank E.
Dyer, Blanche E. - Garland, Carlton M.
Dyer, Florence - Jenness, John
Dyke, Maude E. - St. Laurent, Norman J.
Dziedzic, Amanda M. - Cole, Roy

Eagan, Susan A. - Potter, Albert M.
Eastman, Anna O. - Moody, Henry B.
Eastman, Annette M. - Eldridge, Wilber A.
Eastman, Hattie F. - Hobbs, Frank O.
Eaton, Jennifer J. - Credit, Leo R., Jr.
Eaton, Lois G. - Thurston, Carroll E.
Eaton, Lona L. - Doe, Frank B., Jr.
Eaton, Marie B. - Varney, Raymond E.
Ebel, Karen E. - Root, Steven C.
Ebel, Linda Marie - May, John P.
Ebert, Helen - Gustavson, F, Gunnar
Eckhoff, Devon E. - Delk, David M.
Eckhoff, Tiffany J. - Niblett, Charles L.
Edwards, Aner F. - Cook, Walter R.
Edwards, Bernadette Marie - Anthony, Mark James
Edwards, Leola - Eldridge, Charles, Jr.
Eldredge, Clara - Staples, Willie I.
Eldredge, Eleanor M. - Rhines, Irving K.
Eldredge, Frances L. - Pinkham, Charles R.
Eldridge, Agnes V. - Machuck, Elexander
Eldridge, Annie B. - Ross, John E.
Eldridge, Annie E. - Eldridge, David
Eldridge, Annie E. - Eldridge, Ivory E.
Eldridge, Arlene - Littlefield, Clifton S.
Eldridge, Arlene M. - Dubois, Lucian P.
Eldridge, Arthena T. - Templeton, Ahial
Eldridge, Avis L. - Libby, Edward C.
Eldridge, Barbara - Budroe, Edward H.
Eldridge, Betty A. - Harbison, Lance G.
Eldridge, Beverly A. - Ryder, Lynwood P.

Eldridge, Blanche M. - Buswell, Lester G.
Eldridge, Brenda E. - Emerson, Alan D.
Eldridge, Brenda Joyce - Williams, David Alan
Eldridge, Charlotte E. - Berry, Raymond A.
Eldridge, Cindi Lee - Thompson, Dana M.
Eldridge, Clara - Littlefield, George L.
Eldridge, Darlene April - Libby, David Randolph
Eldridge, Dawn M. - Ela, Henry P.
Eldridge, Debbie Lee - Fisher, Rodney Scott
Eldridge, Della - Welch, Bennie F.
Eldridge, Denise Elaine - Ripley, Shawn Patrick
Eldridge, Dorothy A. - Nason, Benjamin
Eldridge, Dorothy A. - Judkins, Thomas
Eldridge, Elfreda J. - Conner, Charles E., Jr.
Eldridge, Elizabeth M. - Fenderson, Robert M.
Eldridge, Emma J. - Aldrich, Thomas W.
Eldridge, Erdine - Hammond, Howard
Eldridge, Ethel M. - Weymouth, Guy F.
Eldridge, Etta M. - Eldridge, Raymond C.
Eldridge, Eva - Welch, Sidney L.
Eldridge, Eva Agnes - Pratt, Charles Henry
Eldridge, Eva May - Woodbury, Carlton J.
Eldridge, Evelyn L. - Dore, Lewis Alvah
Eldridge, Evelyn M. - Peare, Arthur G.
Eldridge, Florence H. - Johnson, Earl B.
Eldridge, Flossie - Webster, Wilbur
Eldridge, Frances Josie - Drew, Philip William
Eldridge, Gertie M. - Welch, Willie S.
Eldridge, Grace B. - White, Belmont A.
Eldridge, Grace M. - Smith, Edward F.
Eldridge, Hattie - Williams, Samuel
Eldridge, Hazel E. - Eldridge, Clifford D.
Eldridge, Heidi Elizabeth - Carleton, Michael William
Eldridge, Helen Sadie - Whiting, Russell Ford
Eldridge, Inez E. - Rouleau, George L.
Eldridge, Irene Lois - White, Fred Joseph
Eldridge, Jamie Marie - Coates, Dennis John
Eldridge, Janice M. - Armitage, Richard T.
Eldridge, Jeanette L. - Eldridge, Norman F.
Eldridge, Jennette R. - Hodge, Fenton A.
Eldridge, Josephine - Abbott, Wade
Eldridge, Joyce B. - Larrabee, Donald E.
Eldridge, Karen B. - Eldridge, Timothy W.
Eldridge, Kathleen A. - Miller, Robert E.
Eldridge, Kathryn Viola - Dore, Roger Allen

Eldridge, Laura - Sargent, Everett F.
Eldridge, Lauri Sue - Green, Douglas Mark
Eldridge, Leola J. - Wallace, Robert T.
Eldridge, Linda M. - White, Rodney A.
Eldridge, Linnie R. - Moody, Leslie
Eldridge, Madeline - Thurston, Parker
Eldridge, Margaret E. - Jenness, Wayne H.
Eldridge, Marguerite R. - Eldridge, Ralph C.
Eldridge, Mary R. - Seguin, Roger K.
Eldridge, Mildred - Welch, Moses
Eldridge, Mildred - Wilkinson, Ralph
Eldridge, Myrtle - Eldridge, Lafe
Eldridge, Nina S. - Hitchcock, Howard C.
Eldridge, Nora F. - Copp, Maynard D.
Eldridge, Pammy Ann - Berry, Duane Ernest
Eldridge, Permelia - Kelley, Howard
Eldridge, Priscilla M. - Nudd, Wallace, Jr.
Eldridge, Rebecca M. - Helme, Christopher
Eldridge, Ruby M. - Weeks, Kenneth W.
Eldridge, Sharon A. - Eldridge, Rodney H.
Eldridge, Shirley A. - Sargent, Warren E., Jr.
Eldridge, Susan J. - Simpson, Harry A.
Eldridge, Sylvia M. - Zimmer, O. Joseph
Eldridge, Violet D. - Speckman, Robert E.
Eldridge, Virginia - Eldridge, Ritchie
Eldridge, Virginia L. - Emmons, Theodore E.
Eldridge, Winifred - Campbell, Forest F.
Eliopoulos, Susan - Nason, Timothy Wayne
Elliott, Christobel - Eldridge, Ritchie
Elliott, Linda Jo - Jordan, Paul Neal
Elliott, Ruth M. - Abbott, Ernest G.
Elliott, Sarah G. - Follansbee, Joseph A.
Ellis, Agnes C. - Folsom, John
Emerson, Deborah A. - Lassars, Mitchell T.
Emerson, Samantha L. - Baker, Christopher E.
Emery, Blanche - Welch, Maurice C.
Emery, Hazel B. - Hitchcock, Howard C.
Emery, June P. - Roberts, Maynard M.
Emery, Rose M. - Fall, Willie H.
Emery, Tracey L. - Ross, Bryan S.
Emmett, Virginia L. - Deluca, Joseph J.
Emond, Rachel Ailene (Smith) - Holladay, Eric James
Engel, Deborah A. - Lemieux, James A.
Engel, Mary Ann Judith - Sullivan, Edward J.
English, Eileen M. - Zalewski, Stefan C.

English, Eunice E. - Sargent, Frederick E.
English, Jean E. - Sidik, Dennis M.
Ennis, Naomi Ruth - Brown, Richard Eugene
Erickson, Carolee - Eldridge, Carl Robert, Jr.
Ericsson, Ada P. - Whiting, Richard P.
Estes, Frances H. - Libby, Roland H.
Evans, Herberta - Whiting, Russell, Jr.
Evans, Laurel A. - Neergaard, John H., Jr.
Evans, Mary J. - Colby, Daniel
Evans, Pamela Jean - Hanson, Brian M.
Evans, Patricia Ann - Wiggin, Jerry Bruce, II
Evans, Pauline Delmore - Nichols, Earl Eugene
Evans, Ruth H. - Sherman, Ronald H.
Evans, Stella - Goldsmith, Chester O.

Fall, Christine M. - Fisher, William R.
Fall, Louise A. - Wilkins, Olif M.
Fall, Mabel E. - Blake, Simon
Fall, Minnie P. - Colby, Ralph
Farley, Virginia E. - Goudeau, Ernest E.
Farnham, Lizzie L. - Drake, Benjamin M.
Farrell, Deborah J. - Bova, Paul Anthony
Farrell, Kathleen J. - Zervas, Arthur A.
Faucher, Patricia Ann - Stowik, Stanley, Jr.
Fazzino, Judith A. - Semanski, Alexander E.
Feary, Barbara A. - Kimball, Robert H.
Federici, Jeane P. - Desrosiers, Rene Edward
Feener, Cheryl Anne - Riley, Daniel B., Jr.
Felician, Dorothy J. - Harnum, Kenneth E.
Felker, Ethel M. - Williams, Print E.
Feltham, Cora Ada S. - Boardman, Fred B.
Fenderson, Mary A. - Drew, James L.
Ferrante, Barbara - Berry, Duane Herman
Ferreira, Dorothy Ann - Enloe, John Darrell
Fetzer, Evelyn - Leonard, Stanley R.
Ficara, Lona C. - Therrien, Craig A.
Fields, Agnes C. - Romans, William A.
Fillipon, Donna Marie - Perry, Donald John
Fillipon, Tara Joan - Shawver, Todd Andrew
Finlayson, Catherine A. - Moody, Leslie
Fisher, Debbie Lee - Erickson, Leigh Frederick
Fisher, Debra L. - Williams, Kerry D.
Fisher, Linda Mary - Jones, Kenneth A., Jr.
Fisichelli, Judy A. Stackpole - Dickson, Dennis L.
Fitzgerald, Maud S. - Davis, George W.

Fitzgerald, Patricia J. - Wynne, Kenneth
Fitzgerald, V. Mae - Bailey, Allen MacB.
Fitzpatrick, Anna R. - Doerrer, Stanley L.
Fitzsimmons, Candace - Baker, Ray
Fitzsimmons, Nancy V. - Hayford, Richard K.
Flagg, Evaline A. - Lord, Edwin F.
Flagg, Lydia M. - Welch, John, 3rd
Flanders, Ann - Lord, Francis E.
Fleischer, Alice - Hodge, Gary
Fletcher, Jean - Jones, Taylor
Fletcher, Katharine - Atkinson, Gordon H.
Fletschinger, Dolores - Faller, William Henry
Floria, Beth Ellen - Gale, Robert Jay
Floria, Donna C. - Chick, Harry W., Jr.
Floria, Donna Carol - Keyes, William Charles
Floria, Nancy L. - Blair, Brian K.
Floyd, Lillian J. - Crossman, Sanford
Flynn, Holly J. - Fogarty, Thomas W.
Fogarty, Anne Marie - Kinmond, Scott David
Fogarty, Kathleen Jane - Jones, Michael R.
Fogarty, Patricia Anne - Stockman, James Arnold
Foley, Bonnie W. - Gobeille, William J.
Folsom, Mabel C. - Reed, Edgar
Forsyth, Anne - Downs, James
Foss, Inez E. - Hutchins, George R.
Foss, Lida - Gul, Kenneth A.
Foss, Sadie Elvira Drew - Pelletier, Louis P. J.
Foster, Carolyn A. - Durham, Gary R.
Foster, Christine Susan - Tenney, Michael David
Foster, Cynthia A. - Dietel, Kim E.
Foster, Marilyn F. - Clavin, Donald A.
Foster, Sandra G. - Hurd, Howard E.
Fournier, Marie T. F. - O'Malley, Edward Francis
Fowler, Katherine L. - Heckel, Frederick W., IV
Fowler, Krisha Ann - Hansen, Neil Eric
Fowler, Wendy Lee - Carberg, Brian Michael
Fracasso, Kelly J. - Almstedt, Harry W.
Fracker, Carolyn - Clancy, Reginald E.
Freeman, Beatrice I. - Pope, Gordon A.
Freeman, Georgia Elaine - Peters, Charles Michael
French, Ruth H. - Snow, Wilton
French, Sarah M. E. - Genthner, Frank
Frey, Minnie M. - Young, Howard E.
Frost, Mary - Corriveau, David
Froton, Sadie E. (Drew) - Foss, Edward P.

Fulcher, Cindy L. - Guyotte, Albert F., Jr.
Fulcher, Lori A. - Carver, David C.
Fuller, Elizabeth A. - Weinman, David, 2nd
Furtado, Leslie Anne - Ducharme, Michael Angelo

Gabriele, Sandra - DiVincenzo, Alfred
Gagne, Irene B. - Flanagan, Paul A.
Gagnon, Ann Louise - Johnson, Chester F., Jr.
Gagnon, June P. - Harvey, Norman A.
Gale, Margaret P. - Davis, Walter M.
Gale, Michelle Lee - Brownell, Bryan Keith
Gallagher, Zella J. - Johnson, Victor
Gallant, Claire F. - Bean, Lawrence
Games, Evelyn - Wagstaff, Donald
Gangemi, Judith A. - Curry, John P.
Garcia, Gabriella Ruth - Shannon, Scott Dominic
Garland, Carrie B. - Fogg, George W.
Garland, Emily M. - Eldridge, Archie
Garnett, Jeannette - Burt, Harrison, Jr.
Garnett, Thelma P. - Ford, Walter J.
Garvey, Janice M. - Sloan, George W., Jr.
Gaudet, Irene M. - Littell, Robert E.
Gaudet, Karen Therese (Roach) - Barron, Roy Amos
Gaudreau, Dale Bridgette - Schofield, Gary James
Gauthier, Pamela J. - Lord, Arnold J.
Gautreau, Barbara H. - Tedjojuwono, Stanley N.
Geiler, Elizabeth - Petter, John B.
George, Linda L. - Terry, Douglass G.
George, Paula Fay (Jalbert) - Ferris, Bobby Dean
Geralds, Mary F. - Wallace, Charles P.
Gerard, Cheryl Lynn - Harris, Christopher Elliott
Gerry, Janet E. - Eldridge, Chester
Ghelfi, Rebecca Jane Mahtesian - Serpa, Michael Joseph
Gibbons, Gloria J. - Kellogg, Peter J.
Gibbs, Loretta A. - Buelock, Gary R.
Gilbreath, Judi Kristine - Newton, David Frederick
Gilchrest, Charlotte M. - Dunbar, Edward J.
Gile, Beatrice M. - Smart, Edward C.
Gile, Erma M. - Emack, Lester E.
Giles, Helen M. - Eldridge, John Nichols
Gill, Frances M. - Johnson, A. Hollis
Gilman, Angela L. - Bickford, Wilbur C.
Gilman, Esther R. - Blake, Percy A.
Girouard, Virginia B. - Alley, Nahum M.
Glassman, Ethel H. - Feinberg, Maurice

Glennon, Carolann - Nathon, Ronald W.
Glidden, Albertta M. - Engstrom, Earl
Glidden, Brooke Willett - Rines, James Franklin
Glidden, Dora G. - Hodgdon, John E.
Glidden, Mary - Pilkington, Samuel S.
Glidden, Velma A. - Vigue, Henry J.
Glynn, Margarett M. - Niblett, Samuel
Gochman, Mildred - LaPorti, Arthur J.
Godfrey, Ellen F. - Beane, William E.
Godfrey, Hazel M. - Doe, Benjamin F.
Goerner, Doris S. - Robertson, Charles W.
Going, Melissa - Stockbridge, Horatio H.
Golden, Carol B. - Baker, Mathers
Goldsmith, Bonnie L. - Martinson, Timothy Francis
Goldsmith, Cordelia - Roberts, Frank
Goldsmith, Georgia M. - Locke, Charles Ray
Goldsmith, Theresa Stella - Gallagher, Keith William
Golodetz, Alta - Uluos, Abdul K.
Gooby, Evelyn F. - Walsh, John
Goodblood, Judith L. - Huntley, William G.
Goodbury, Edith - Colby, Arthur
Goode, Geraldine M. - Wood, Francis R.
Goode, Norma K. - Carlson, Donald Irving
Goodrich, Barbara L. - Hammond, Allen D.
Goodrich, Virginia Lane - Mahoney, John Wells, Jr.
Goodwin, Carlene M. - Smith, Earle D.
Goodwin, Marjorie R. - Conlon, Frederick E.
Goodwin, Viola - Lamontagne, Joseph
Gordon, Maud A. - Stoddard, Donald T.
Gosselin, Mary R. - Bisbee, Wilbur
Gouin, Barbara D. - Perry, Stanley A.
Gould, Brenda T. - Hogan, Roland B., Jr.
Gould, Jane - Johnson, Donald E.
Grace, Barbara - Hilton, Leonard
Graffam, Christine L. - LaFontaine, Lawrence
Graham, Geraldine E. - Smith, Samuel P.
Grajales, Adiela - Kortejarvi-Elovaara, Arnold
Gramazio, Marion G. - Jewett, Lawrence H.
Grames, Cindy Lee - Harbison, Lance G.
Grant, Barbara - Campbell, William
Grant, Cynthia May (Gonyer) - Baston, John Edward
Grant, Frances K. - Philbrick, Edward T.
Grant, Meg Alissa - Gallant, Thomas Reed
Grant, Nancy E. - Sanders, Obed
Grave, Evitte - Nathan, Ronald

Graves, Marguerite A. - White, Virgil D.
Gray, Ethel F. - Wilcox, Herbert L.
Green, Doris E. - Humphrey, John S.
Green, Viola - Nichols, Allie
Greene, Elvida B. - Gray, Douglas A.
Greene, Louise Theresa - Ritchotte, Paul Edward
Greene, Suzanne M. - McGowan, Robert F.
Greenfield, Lucia M. - Sanders, Harold W.
Greenlaw, Geraldine - Greenlaw, Mervyn
Greenleaf, Rosanna - Loring, George M.
Greenwood, Mildred - Stubbs, Linwood
Gregory, Janet Miriam - McFarlane, George Douglas
Gridley, Barbara C. - Armstrong, Robert Thomas
Gridley, Heather Ruth - Barnard, Matthew Hetcher
Griffin, Laurie Ann - Sargent, David Wayne
Griffin, Lydia - Nichols, John A.
Griffin, Marie A. - Dore, Lyford R.
Grimes, Kathleen P. - Barber, Gary J.
Grow, Donna Marie - Ellis, Edward Earl, II
Gurneau, Gertrude F. - DeBlois, Remi A.
Guty, Carrie Grace Graves - Swearingin, James Edward
Gwinn, Cynthia L. - Woyton, Robert John

Haddock, Hattie - Nichols, Louis W.
Hadley, Martha H. - Sinclair, George M.
Haggard, Teresa J. - Watson, William F.
Hahn, Winifred G. - Mitchell, David Leon
Hale, Sharon Ann - Schweikhardt, William L.
Haley, Mattie L. - Dame, Charles A.
Haley, Mildred Elizabeth - Wasson, Andrew
Hall, Audrey B. - Hall, Edward J.
Hall, Debra Ann - Meserve, Steven Alan
Hall, Diane J. - Eldridge, George M.
Hall, Marianne - Waterhouse, Wayne Meron
Halloran, Mary T. - Ryan, William A.
Ham, Rose E. - Nason, Justin E.
Ham, Verna Gertrude - Palmer, Richard Orrin
Hamel, Alice - Hodge, Wayne
Hamel, Eva M. - Berry, David A.
Hamel, Rachelle A. - Goldthwaite, Keith C.
Hamel, Rachelle Alice - Howard, David Paul, II
Hamel, Raeline - Gauthier, Stephen M.
Hamel, Renee J. - Abbott, David W.
Hamel, Sandra R. - Eldridge, Lawrence J.
Hamilton, Lorita L. - Greene, Clyde F.

Hamlin, Jennifer Lynn - Valentine, Ian Michael
Hamlin, Mary L. - Nevers, Joseph W.
Hamm, Bernice - Emerson, Levi W.
Hamm, Florence E. - Nichols, Clyde R.
Hamm, Marion A. - Meloon, Walter C.
Hammond, Maria A. - Ricker, Martin V.
Hammons, Marjorie L. - Lajoie, Aldore S.
Haney, Virginia C. - Moody, Roger
Hannah, Mary J. - Robinson, James P.
Hansell, Julie Melinda - Sprince, Jeremy Jon
Hanson, Alice M. - Davis, Lawrence B.
Hanson, Constance Ruggli - Hanson, Hodge Jackson
Hanson, Marybeth - Hertel, Frederick E., III
Hanson, Maud F. - Bodge, Walter C.
Hanson, Nettie M. - Burtwell, Albert A.
Hanson, Ona L. - Brackett, James A.
Hanson, Phyllis Mildred - Jones, Chester William
Harbison, Cindy L. - Cameron, Paul E.
Harbour, Meredith A. - Clark, Bruce C.
Hardy, Mary - Smith, Henry
Harkins, Cristin Joy - Gurley, Fred Arthur, Jr.
Harkness, Betty A. - Peters, Charles R., Jr.
Harlow, Emma Louise - Thompson, John Daniel
Harmon, Alice B. - Ainsworth, Wallace
Harmon, Bertha A. - Nichols, Ernest C.
Harmon, Elizabeth G. - Nichols, Ernest C.
Harmon, Ethel - Wiggin, Shirley
Harmon, Ina - Stanley, Harold L.
Harmon, Kirsten M. - Nason, Ricky D.
Harmon, Mabel Frances - MacBrien, Philip James
Harmon, Marjorie Alice - Adjutant, Chester Willard
Harmon, Shirley E. - Emerson, Ralph W.
Harrington, Kathleen Suzanne (Boyd) - Avery, Lewis Tracy
Harris, Deborah Phaup - Quiros, Edin Chavarria
Harris, Julie M. - Hutchins, Albert G.
Harris, Karen L. - Martin, Edward D.
Harrison, Kimberly A. - Fisher, Rodney S.
Harrison, Lisa T. - O'Hearn, Douglas J.
Harte, Kathleen Mary - Lord, Francis Edwin
Hartford, Carla J. - Sordiff, Stephen Anthony
Hartford, Eleanor M. - Woodward, Verne E.
Hartford, Valerie A. - Anthony, Robert W.
Hartwell, Tracy Smith - Cragin, Allen Bruce
Harvey, Thelma - Colman, Nathaniel
Haskell, Darlene Joan - Scamman, Aaron Jeffrey

Hasty, Annie L. - Drew, John N.
Hatch, Anna I. - Hatch, Ellis R.
Hatch, Maureen - Blake, Richard F.
Hatch, Patricia J. - Bell, William R.
Hatch, Susan W. - Barton, Alan E.
Hatch, Winnie M. - Thompson, Chauncy W.
Hawes, Kathleen - Eldridge, James
Hawkes, Gladys B. - Nickerson, Alfred J.
Hayden, Susan A. - Fogg, Michael
Hayes, Helen E. - Dobson, Thomas E.
Hayes, Margaret B. - McKinley, Todd Michael
Hayes, Martha M. - Eldridge, Carlton O.
Hayes, Susan K. - Menzies, Douglas B.
Hayford, Bethany Lynn - Canfield, Gilbert Andrew
Hayford, Edith - Pray, John E.
Hayford, Holly J. - Libby, Dean J.
Hayford, Jill Lynn - Williams, Lance A.
Hayford, Judith M. - LaRosa, Douglas J.
Hayford, Lynda - Jagemann, Philip
Haynes, Marion E. - Woodward, Harold A.
Hazeltine, Stacey L. - Szmyt, Steven T.
Heath, Cora E. - Mills, William F.
Hebert, Barbara A. - Hodge, Elwood N.
Hebert, Gina Loreen - Goodwin, Harold Thomas
Hebert, Mary A. - Eldridge, Stanley
Hebert, Sharon - White, Ervin
Hebert, Sherri Ann - Barber, Charles Newell, Jr.
Heckmann, Shelly M. - Thompson, Timothy Edward
Hedbor, Katrina Anne - Hill, Dana T.
Hedrick, Laura Jeanne - Hartford, Robert Francis
Hehi, Winifred Marie - Tillinghast, Adam
Heinrich, Dianne Currier - Sheehan, William Edward
Helfrick, Winifred L. - Gay, Ebenezer R.
Helme, Helen Avalve - Avery, Earl Ernest
Helmes, Sarah - Welch, Ernest L.
Helphard, Frances - Carpenter, Kenneth
Henderson, Ida C. - Mahoney, Joseph F.
Hendricks, Susan E. - Rowell, Howard D.
Henry, Elaine E. - Sparks, Bernie G., Jr.
Henry, Susan L. - Lord, John William
Herbert, Elaine E. - Knox, Edward C.
Herbert, Mary - Finberg, William
Hersey, Cora - Emery, Cheston R.
Hersey, Patricia E. - Brownell, Harold L.
Hervey, Ina, Mrs. - Wiggin, Virgil T.

Hibbard, Helen M. - Welch, Chester R.
Hickey, Barbara A. - Dicey, Wendell G.
Hickey, Ellen P. - Laase, Francis W.
Hickman, Doris M. - King, Arthur J.
Hicks, Beulah B. - Buck, Leaman H.
Hicks, Mary E. (Day) - Taeger, Glen D.
Hicks, Mildred B. - Wellines, Richard
Higgins, Carole - Blake, William
Higgins, Christine A. - Edson, Peter Allen
Hill, Blanche E. - Williams, Ira S.
Hill, Cynthia - Dove, David
Hill, Diana Mary - Spaulding, Bruce Romeo, Jr.
Hill, Edith - Torrey, Gerald F.
Hill, JoAnn E. - Smith, Richard L.
Hilton, Abbie E. - Butterfield, Kenneth A.
Hilton, Achsa E. - Fernald, Frank A.
Hilton, Barbara - Elliott, Thomas
Hilton, Jennie M. - Thurley, George H., Jr.
Hilton, Nancy E. - Barter, Herbert W.
Hilton, Ruth Griffin - Loud, Edmund D'Arcy
Hinchey, Karen R. - O'Rourke, Robert
Hinckley, Kathryn E. - Bilodeau, Herbert G.
Hinckley, Kathryn E. - Merrill, Michael M.
Hinders, Joyce K. - Burch, David
Hines, Beth Anne - Stockton, William Timothy
Hinkley, Georgie B. - Nichols, Lucien P.
Hinz, Ingrid M. - Brownell, Edwin P.
Hitchcock, Gladys P. - Moulton, Harley E.
Hitchcock, Mildred L. - Morrill, Clarence E.
Hitchcock, Ruth H. - Grant, Henry
Hobbs, Alice J. - Merrow, Mark H.
Hobbs, Barbara M. - MacDonald, Forrest G.
Hobbs, Inez Lizette - Hill, Bernard B.
Hobbs, Mabel L. - Veasey, Arthur G.
Hobbs, Margo Montgomery - Thompson, Courtland David
Hobbs, Nellie M. - Fortier, Albert J.
Hobbs, Velma Jean - Van Dyke, Bruce Edwin
Hodgdon, Addie - Conner, Willie M.
Hodgdon, Angie B. - Young, J. Lester
Hodgdon, Emma J. - Eldridge, Amos L.
Hodgdon, Kathryn J. - Wilbur, Robert M.
Hodge, Carol S. - Caulkins, Dale C.
Hodge, Donna F. - Switaj, David D.
Hodge, Ferne - Ames, Ralph R.
Hodge, Florence M. - Conner, Fred E.

Hodge, Joanne Hazel - Carey, Steven C.
Hodge, June L. - Abbott, George E.
Hodge, Laura H. - Nihan, Lawrence D., Jr.
Hodge, Lena M. - Loud, Perley W.
Hodge, Marie E. - Eldridge, Norman F.
Hodge, Muriel E. - Loring, David F.
Hodge, Nettie F. - Angell, John Q.
Hodges, Nancy G. - Perry, Keith E.
Hodgkins, Jean E. - Blouin, Paul S.
Hodgkins, Nancy J. - Corliss, Lawrence E.
Hodgkins, Tracey Lynn - Brown, Christopher Ralph
Hodsdon, Mary E. - Rich, Charles E.
Hoff, Joan A. - Wheeler, Jan F.
Hoffman, Phyllis M. - Hodgson, Walter A.
Hofmann, Helen - Chivvis, Almon
Holbrook, Irene - Legendre, Emile J.
Holbrook, June E. - Palmer, Harland C.
Holley, Margaret A. - Berry, Herman D.
Hollingsworth, Donna E. - Desjardins, Norman H.
Holloran, Sharon Marie - Tersolo, Mark Andrew
Holman, Mildred I. - MacGarvey, George E.
Holt, Suzanne M. - Carver, Warren D.
Hooper, Judith A. - Malay, William K.
Hooper, Violet Hazel - Welch, Leland Conrad
Hoover, Patricia - MacPhee, Neil
Horgan, Mary Josephine - Daigle, Paul Michael
Horn, Margaret S. - Conner, Donald A.
Horne, Nellie - Widgins, Lawrence T.
Horton, Gail A. - Sousa, Francis R.
Houle, Barbara - Silva, Edward P.
Houle, Blanche E. - Urdiales, Richardo E.
Howard, Frances - Betts, George R.
Howard, Janet L. - Gale, Leonard W.
Howard, Janet P. - Magnuson, Henry A.
Howard, Louise - Hunter, Leslie
Howe, Evelyn J. K. - Doe, Walter E.
Hoxie, Abbie T. - Allen, Henry W.
Hoyt, Alice - Sprague, Ernest M.
Hoyt, Katie M. - Stillings, Frank O.
Hubbard, Carol L. - Hansen, Walter C.
Hubbard, Diane Lynn - Shure, Donald Daniel
Huber, Edith M. J. - Jordan, Ralph Stanley
Hubert, Blanche - Fall, Raymond Ernest
Huckins, Beatrice - Kimball, Albert E.
Huckins, Jennett - Cole, James H.

Huckins, Lois - Baxter, Ralph Edmond
Huckins, Marguerite - Leavitt, Harry M.
Hudson, Heather N. - Riley, Thomas J.
Hudson, Sadie M. - Sanborn, Orin F.
Hunt, Carolyn Jean - Rand, Clinton LeShore
Hunt, Kelly J. - Smith, Dale R.
Huntress, Eliza Spring - Johnson, Kevin Boyd
Hurd, Harriett L. - Wallace, Charles P.
Hurd, Josephene L. - Wallace, Simeon P.
Hurley, Dorothy Charlotte - Tremblay, Gerald Ronald
Hurley, Lyn - Dantzig, Henry
Hurn, Florence E. - Currier, William E.
Hurn, Minnie E. - Wiggin, Virgil T.
Husband, Dorothy - Holmes, Chester W.
Hutchins, Joy Lee - Templeton, Arthur Willard, Jr.
Hutchins, Marion L. - Brown, Albert W.
Hutchinson, Clara - Merrow, Lyman
Hutchinson, Emma - Dore, Leroy H.
Hyslop, Sherry L. - Libby, Alan D.

Iannone, Paula Andrea - DeGloria, Robert
Ignico, Helen A. - Wright, Leo T.
Imondi, Josephine - Lee, William, Jr.
Inman, LaVerna - LaCassa, Rodolphe
Iverson, Eleanor L. - Brown, Donald K.

Jack, Priscilla L. - Busch, Roger H.
Jackson, Gwendolyn Hale - Hinds, Kenneth Harry
Jacobs, Marjorie - Swanson, Charles
Janek, Virginia E. - Pearson, Walter G.
Janness, Marie Eunice - Miller, James Joseph
Janowski, Barbara - Hamberger, Charles
Jeffries, Helen - Watkins, Arthur E.
Jenkins, Edith M. - Hamm, Sidney W.
Jenner, Bonnie L. - Woodman, Richard H.
Jenness, Abbie M. - Williams, Lorenzo
Jenness, Emma B. - Jenness, Lorenzo W.
Jennison, Anne M. - Kramer, L. Page
Jensen, Judith M. - Stevens, David
Jewett, Helen M. - Wiggin, Lester A.
Joen, Lena E. - Kuhner, William
Johns, Carla A. - Tillinghast, Edward A.
Johnson, Bobbi Jo - Bush, Michael Mark, Sr.
Johnson, Bobbi L. - Tyler, David S.
Johnson, Gwyneth Lori - Cleveland, William McKay

Johnson, Heather Beth - McCormick, David Braydon
Johnson, Jessica Jane - Eldridge, Timothy Edwin
Johnson, Linda G. - Ainsworth, Michael E.
Johnson, Myrtle L. - Eldridge, Alfred P.
Johnson, Nellie - Cole, Charles
Johnson, Pamela V. - Freeman, Edwin H.
Johnson, Reita - Willey, Gregory
Jones, Avis L. - Tripp, Carl E.
Jones, Debra Ann - Billings, Condict Moore
Jones, Elaine M. - Eckhoff, Peter B.
Jones, Elizabeth A. - Palmero, Vincent P., Jr.
Jones, Ellen Louise - Mottau, Michael Thomas
Jones, Jean M. - Rankin, Norman Frisco, Jr.
Jones, Karen Sue - Eldridge, Alan C.
Jones, Margaret D. T. - Warner, Clarence A.
Jones, Margaret Grace - Harmon, Thomas John
Jones, Melissa Eleanor - Plummer, Stephen Jon
Jones, Renee Sandra - Buchikos, Andrew Don
Jordan, Marianne Patricia - Masters, Dennis Irving
Jordon, Alice M. - Hodge, Carleton L.
Jordon, Dorothy L. - Palmer, Clarence E.
Jorgenson, Erin Gray - Demarco, Asher David
Jorgenson, Lesley E. C. - Gale, Leonard William
Joseph, Lisa A. - Price, Larry F.
Josephson, Jennifer L. - Perry, James T.
Joubert, Michelle I. - Langlois, Gregg O.
Joyal, Elaine S. - Barnard, Roy S.
Joyce, Barbara - Copp, Ralph, Jr.
Judkins, Eva M. - Eldridge, Robert W.

Kabore, Sibdou Alix Marie-Rachel - Fitzpatrick, Daniel Joseph
Kagel, Pamela A. - Mallett, William L.
Kahl, Gloria - Arcisz, Joseph
Kaliakotas, Charlotte - Riordan, John E.
Kamal, Christine A. - Sanborn, Scott A.
Kaminsky, Jeanette B. - Evans, Elmer E., Jr.
Kavlivas, Patricia D. - April, Cornelius F.
Keenen, Helen B. - Welch, Ford J.
Keith, Mavis Aletta - Senior, Walter M., Jr.
Kelleher, Elizabeth - Souza, Anthony
Kelley, Angela Susan - Edwards, Jimmy Earl
Kelley, Dianne J. - Sanborn, Raymond
Kelley, Juanita - Pearl, Michael J.
Kelley, Marilyn M. - Haney, Glenn A.
Keniston, Elizabeth - Bickford, Carroll

Kennedy, Dinice Marie - Newman, Steven J.
Kenney, Mary Beth Joy - Bourgeois, Robert Paul, Jr.
Kimball, Kimberlee Ann (Primus) - Altomare, Frank Vincent
Kinder, Karen A. - Aubrey, John M.
King, Helen Mane - Button, Kenneth Russell
King, Trisha C. - O'Neal, Sean C.
Kinmond, Heather Lynn - Keslar, David Allen
Kirch, Laina J. - Pyne, John S., III
Kirch, Laurie Ann - Randall, Raymond Ansel, Jr.
Kirkwood, Bonnie - Nystedt, Walter
Kirkwood, Cora E. - Eldridge, Howard J.
Kirkwood, Deborah J. - Pochelon, Allen G.
Kirkwood, Laurinda - Furtado, Arthur
Kirley, Jeannette L. - White, Kenneth F., Jr.
Klain, Virginia R. - Stimson, Mark A.
Klem, Edith E. - Nuri, Donald W.
Klitgaard, Jennifer - Allen, William
Kmiec, Winifred M. - Fredette, Andrew
Knapp, Doris R. - Drake, Kenneth
Knapp, Kathryn - Tudor, Thurston Harry
Knapp, Rebecca - Keyes, William C.
Knapp, Shirley A. - Scott, Edmund S.
Knight, Laura May - Lord, John A.
Knights, Methyl Muriel - Wentworth, Roger Arthur
Knisley, Susan D. - Mooers, Gary
Knowles, Edna M. - Heath, Gary P.
Knowles, Iantha E. - Bean, Herbert L.
Knox, Agnes M. - Abbott, Harry V.
Knox, Annie - Templeton, Bert A.
Knox, Avis E. - White, Chester A.
Knox, Avonne - Monroe, Donald
Knox, Charlotte S. - Fitzsimmons, James W.
Knox, Florence E. - Chase, Edwin O.
Knox, Gwendolyn - Perry, Ernest A., Jr.
Knox, Juanita - Williams, John A.
Knox, Mary Elizabeth - Ross, Ernest John
Knox, Mavis E. - Rutherford, Lester J.
Knox, Rosemay Caroline - Sargent, Gerald Walter
Knox, Wilma F. - Melanson, Omer
Koehler, Ruth A. - Roden, Thomas C.
Kolinek, Jean C. - Perry, Gary R.
Kolonovich, Mary - Pinard, Russell C.
Kolzen, Nan S. - Gregorio, Ralph V.
Kosker, Arlene - Eldridge, Tedd
Kosse, Cottie Arlene - Lyman, Gene Richard

Kosse, Cottie Arlene - Sidebotham, Ronald Edward
Kozachuk, Catherine - Graves, Edward H.
Krakowski, Susan R. - Cardoza, John L.
Krieger, Eve - Brudnick, Bernard B.
Kula, Linda S. - Thorrell, Dennis Carl

Labor, Marjorie - Gossilin, Peter W.
Labrie, Christina Lynn - Doran, Craig Even
Ladd, Helen Irene - Turner, Frederick W.
Ladd, Lydia A. - Hobbs, Christopher C.
LaFerriere, Deborah Louise (Leanna) - Hartman, Michael Alan
Laffin, Virginia D. - Hart, Lester L.
LaFreniere, Arlene - Drew, Wendell
Lafreniere, Irene E. - Michaud, Chanel L.
Lafreniere, Suzanne - Bemis, Robert
Lagro, Marjorie A. - McIntyre, Donald G.
Laidlaw, Jean C. - Oppedisano, Joseph A.
Lally, Bernadine F. - McCarthy, Arthur J.
Lambert, Patricia - Corriveau, Albert
Lampron, Susan Yvonne - Eckhoff, Stephen John
Lamy, Robin K. - Winkley, Dana P.
Lanata, Claire - Coombs, James
Lane, Annie M. - Macchinis, Walter B.
Lane, Ida M. - Webster, Wilbur F.
Lane, Reta - Eldridge, Lawrence
Lang, Kimberly A. - Anthony, Jeffrey M.
Langley, Carolyn - Conner, Albert H.
Langley, Myrtle S. - Hodge, Eugene W.
Lanphear, Abby Beth - O'Brien, David Robert
LaRiviere, Wendy S. - White, Rusty E.
Larock, Wendy Elizabeth - Griffin, Paul Vincent
Larose, Shirlee Rivard - Hayford, Ernest Arthur, Jr.
Larrabee, Cora D. - Larrabee, Winfield J.
Larrabee, Marilyn A. - Evans, Gordon B.
Larson, Janet Lee - Montgomery, Jonathan E.
Latini, Carol A. - Mahoney, Daniel F.
Lawrence, Bessie B. - Swett, John W.
Lawton, Darlene R. - Cardarelli, Patrick
Lawton, Lee E. - Streeter, Danna Arnold
Leach, Amelia Joyce - Meehan, Todd Leon
Leavitt, Carol A. - Gomes, Antonio A.
Leavitt, Cynthia M. - Stout, David A.
Leavitt, Marguerite H. - Whipple, Frank P.
Leavitt, Mary L. - Murphy, John R.
LeBlanc, Constance M. - Boucher, Ernest J., Jr.

LeBlanc, Mindy Lee - Mattingly, Matthew John
LeCansky, Becky Sue - Hackbarth, Frank L.
LeClair, Patricia Marie - O'Connor, Michael Patrick
LeClair, Rose F. - Kohler, John C.
Lee, June M. - Currier, Jesse A.
Leech, Susan Gail - Hemsley, Linus Sydney
LeGendre, Maureen M. - Pierro, Carmine M.
Leger, Cynthia J. - Maille, Richard
Leighton, Melissa - Clough, Oren
Leighton, Thelma - Sehock, John W.
Leining, Judith - Koob, John
Lelond, Elizabeth C. - Eastman, John D., Jr.
LeMarche, Laura Ann - Gray, Leslie Austin
Lemay, Donna M. - Price, Leaston L., III
Lemay, Nancy L. - Downs, John R.
Lensky, Cherie L. - Evitts, J. Earle
Lents, Virginia - Crampa, Sabino
Leonard, Ruth Madeliene - Grant, Kenneth Wilson, Jr.
Leone, Trina Louise - Libby, Charlie Paul
Leslie, Margaret Winifred - Hollihan, Richard Allen
Lessard, Carol Susanne - Dow, Ellis Milton, III
Lessard, Lisa H. - Valley, Jerry B.
Letteney, Ruthanne - Brack, Albert, Jr.
Levesque, Jean M. - Simoneau, Edward J.
Lewis, Addie - Sceggell, George O.
Lewis, Alice - Pouliot, Eugene
Lewis, Charlotte Isabell - Bunker, Frank Eldred
Lewis, Nancy M. - White, Chris A.
Lewis, Velma L. - Knowlton, Francis H.
Lewis, Virginia L. - Eldridge, Wendell R.
Libby, Annie C. - Jacobson, Thomas S.
Libby, Brindall A. - Grant, Steven D.
Libby, Carole A. - Cook, Arthur E.
Libby, Deborah Jean - Bedley, John Freeman
Libby, Doreen Connie - Perry, Gary Roy
Libby, Emily P. - Hale, Fred A.
Libby, Ethel Frances - Gray, Edwin John
Libby, Laura M. - Young, Royce A.
Libby, Leona - Gouin, Thornton
Libby, Mary Alice - Rudolph, Gerald Floyd
Libby, Nancy J. - Loud, Simon F.
Libby, Ruth M. - Libby, Ernest L.
Libby, Ruth M. - Monaco, Vincent
Libby, Stacy Lynn - Gauvreau, Jon Paul
Libby, Susan - Coulter, Charles

Libby, Thurley M. - Litwhiler, Sterling T.
Librak, Harriet - Kaplan, Sheldon N.
Lichorobiec, Marie Anastais - McHan, Alan Dwayne
Lincoln, Janet E. - Seely, Richard G.
Lindley, Marie L. - Reizer, Edward C.
Linscott, Jennie M. - Blaisdell, Erving A.
Linscott, Marcia G. - Guptill, Samuel
Littlefield, Anita - Goodwin, Haven K.
Littlefield, Arlene - Gilman, Edwin F.
Littlefield, Florence - Colby, Royal
Littlefield, Melinda - Eldridge, Herbert
Littlefield, Sara L. - Westberry, Richard A.
Locke, Dorothy F. - Loud, Clarence B.
Locke, Leler B. - Buswell, Walter
Locke, Lori Ann - Aaberg, Philip
Locke, Roberta - Tonks, Gerald
Locklin, Sarah A. - Redlon, Thomas P.
Lofredo, Linda Ann - Chavaree, Marc Anthony
LoGalbo, Rosalio Ann - Doe, Walter E.
Logan, Virginia E. - Violette, Joseph A.
Lombard, Marilyn - Kimball, George
London, Audrey J. - Levesque, Raymond E.
Long, Linda E. - Ryder, Perley A.
Lord, Ann Flanders - Damon, Christopher Stephen
Lord, Charlotte J. - Boisse, Victor E.
Lord, Doris Eleanor - Turner, Cecil Ray
Lord, Edna Esther - Kennard, Benjamin F.
Lord, Florence Wiggin - Banfield, Charles Willis
Lord, Lorraine A. - Thurston, John
Lord, Mary Knight - Kirkwood, Lawrence Dana
Lorenz, Jessica G. - Armstrong, Dwight C.
Loring, Dorothy L. - Martin, Frances
Loring, Florence E. - Hurn, Fred
Loring, Gail S. - Gordon, Peter N.
Loring, Helen E. - Drew, Tony P.
Loring, Nettie F. - Hodge, Bert N.
Loring, Patricia A. - Bowen, Walter M.
Loring, Ruth - Cellenne, Albert
Loring, Sadie E. - Froton, Wilfred W.
Loud, Shirley E. - Dutton, Albert R.
Lovett, Teresa A. - Toner, Joseph A.
Lowe, Verna L. - Silva, Jesse
Lucas, Sharon K. - McNally, Thomas J.
Luce, Cynthia Sue (Mathes) - Lassiter, Thomas Michael
Luebberman, Suzanne - South, Albert, Jr.

Lunt, June F. (Averill) - Pecunies, Russell Quentin
Lunt, Tammy L. - Jaworski, William J.
Lussier, Martha Frances - Byers, Richard S.
Lutrario, Sandra Ann (Capraro) - Morse, Frederick George
Lyman, Dale Lee (Cairone) - Wilcox, Michael William
Lynch, Theresa F. - Noke, Herbert E.

Maccabee, Sheryl A. - MacDonald, Douglas O.
MacCullough, Florence - Coombs, Clarence A.
Macdonald, Blanche - Merrow, Lafayette M.
MacDonald, Colleen Sahrann McCullough - Benish, Richard Carpenter
Macdonald, Joyce Annette (Haley) - West, Chester Stuart
MacDonald, Julie Ann - McManus, Sean P.
MacDonald, Linda M. - Smith, Richard J.
MacDougall, Maureen F. - Burke, Stephen G.
MacElroy, Linda F. (Fosgate) - May, John P.
MacFarlane, Sandra J. - McCarthy, Bennett D.
MacIver, Susan D. - Spinney, Philip C.
Macomber, Abigail - Mauzy, Whitfield, Jr.
Maddock, Sheila E. - Skelley, Douglas C.
Maddock, Sonya R. - Lapar, William H. R.
Magee, Donna Elizabeth - Riley, William Ernest
Maggard, Cynthia Lynette - Nason, Todd Michael
Maggio, Sarah Ann - Eldridge, Michael Norman
Magidsen, Gail Irene - Pribila, John Stephen
Magoon, Cynthia - Barnard, Stephen
Mahoney, Caroline E. - Marrone, Michael G.
Mailhot, Jeanette - Hall, Ronald
Maloney, Barbara M. - Turner, Walter Scott
Maloney, Kathleen M. - Southerland, David G.
Mandile, Billijo Frances - Emanus, Shawn Michael
Mansfield, Ida L. - Mansfield, Leroy B.
Manson, Muriel - Wanner, Wayne
Manson, Nettie - Drown, Charles H.
Mansur, Maude E. - Gilman, John B.
Marchand, Nicole M. - Murphy, Charles J., III
Marconi, Elizabeth A. - Smith, Richard C.
Markley, Bertha A. - Stubbs, Edward F.
Marsh, Deborah - Mennie, William
Marshall, Evelyn M. - Waterbury, Edmund P.
Marshall, Mary P. - Clark, Robert M.
Marston, Adeline J. - Smart, Charles E.
Martin, Edna - Yankowsky, Richard
Martin, Marilyn - Cost, John J.
Mason, Charlotte - Clark, William E., Jr.

Mason, Marilyn Judith - Woodman, Richard H.
Mason, Melissa Lee - Faris, Jeffrey James
Mason, Pauline L. - McPherson, Dalton B.
Massarelli, Theresa Elizabeth - Carvalho, Charles John
Massey, Faye Lee - Stockton, Andrew Phillip
Mathews, Nancy W. - Powell, Benjamin M.
Mattera, Alice R. - Hardy, John A.
Mattress, Hazel - Cook, Sidney A.
Mattress, Laura - McDonald, John J.
Maxwell, Doris A. - Temple, Eugene P.
May, Greta Ellen - Dow, Roland Dinsmore
May, Linda M. E. - Strout, Chester A.
May, Nellie P. - Merrow, Earl T.
Mazza, Alice Rita - Anderson, George Creedon
McAllister, Mary L. - Haskell, Jobe M.
McAlly, Kate - Carey, Charles
McBride, Anita L. - Costello, Edward J., Jr.
McBride, Kelley A. - Bushman, Robert J.
McCabe, Faye F. - Smith, Chester W., Jr.
McCarthy, Eleanor R. - Gould, LeRoy H.
McCarthy, Kathleen - Suprenard, Raymond
McCarthy, Marcia - Pavluvcik, Arthur J.
McClellan, Annie E. - Cleveland, Robert A.
McCool, Eileen P. - Jancaterino, Wayne S.
McCoy, Patricia E. - Kazanjian, Ralph E.
McCreadie, Jacqueline - Sargent, Glen A.
McCue, Christia A. - Hilton, Charles R.
McCuin, Carol A. - Bennett, Edward G.
McCurdy, Lillian M. - Trott, Howard W.
McCusick, Karen Rae - Hartford, Michael Bruce
McDuffee, Minnie Etta - Nichols, Lewis Wesley
McFee, Euel E. - Coe, William A.
McGann, Mary A. - Sheldon, Walter M.
McGavin, Helen V. - Bagge, Mark Alan
McHugh, Ann Jane - Sawyer, Hayes W., Jr.
McIntosh, Elizabeth E. - Tuttle, Robert V.
McIsaac, Annie - Chick, Frank H.
McKay, Helen E. - Carro, Oscar F.
McKenney, Hazel Verna - Libby, Robert Carlton
McKenzie, Arlene - Blois, William, Jr.
McKenzie, Grace M. - Terrio, Robert T.
McKenzie, Tina B. (Berry) - Dudelson, Barry
McKinley, Gertrude E. - Thistle, Fred C.
McKinney, Angelina A. - Stokes, Jacob
McKivergan, Laurel W. - Capron, Robert E.

McLaskey, Deborah A. - Sargent, Richard L., Jr.
McLauthlin, Sara Louise - Merrow, Harold K.
McLean, Mary - Knych, Mathew
McLellan, Eva F. - Knowlton, George C.
McLucas, Dora L. - Meserve, Charlie
McMahon, Lucy V. - Shoemaker, Lewis W.
McMinn, Anna Pauline - Boutwell, Roswell Murray
McNally, Carolyn B. - Campbell, Michael B.
McNeil, Doris R. - Borden, Harold F.
McNeil, Lydia - Welch, Edwin P.
McNulty, Denise P. - Libby, Joseph W.
McNulty, Martelle Karole - Murphy, Charles Loren
McRae, Mollie - Colpitts, Robert W.
Meader, Karen D. - MacIver, Douglas S.
Meader, Margie E. - Sanders, Ralph E.
Meader, Mary F. - Peavey, Benjamin F.
Melanson, Lillian M. - Gridley, Edward P.
Melanson, Lois A. - Purrington, Rainsford D.
Mellon, Rita W. - Dennett, Frank S.
Meloon, Celia A. - Parsons, John M.
Meloon, Florence - Hersey, Wayne
Meloon, Miriam E. - Lennon, Charles J.
Meloon, Pauline Tina - Arnold, Harry Willis
Meloon, Susie M. - Wallace, Harry A.
Meloon, Susie Mildred - Mason, William
Meloon, Velma - Wiggin, Grover C.
Melville, Mildred I. - LeClair, Edgar G.
Merchant, Kathryn - Hoy, Eugene J.
Merrill, Elizabeth A. - Spafford, George D.
Merrill, Hazel Mabel - Wasson, Perley Joseph
Merrill, Rhonda Lee (Varney) - Ryder, Belmont Lynwood
Merrill, Yvonne C. - Leeman, Albert W., Sr.
Merrow, Audrey G. - Bagley, Ralph E.
Merrow, Barbara - Brownell, Clifford R.
Merrow, Bertha - Goodwin, John F.
Merrow, Bertha S. - Welch, Peter P.
Merrow, Blanche M. - Hill, Luther F.
Merrow, Emma Walker - Thompson, Leroy Oscar
Merrow, Ethel S. - Duglay, Hugh
Merrow, Ethelda - Welch, Roland E.
Merrow, Frances Irma - Mason, Donald Ralph
Merrow, Gertrude B. - French, Lewis L.
Merrow, Hilda - Williams, Willis
Merrow, Jane Topliff - Huckins, Ernest L.
Merrow, Lizzie O. - Harmon, Charles M.

Merrow, Marion M. - Kelley, Phillip H.
Merrow, Mary M. - Palmer, Frank E.
Merrow, Phyllis - Berry, Ernest
Merrow, Rachel F. - Hodge, Elwood N.
Merrow, Tanya Louise - Spaulding, Dean Norman
Merrow, Verna L. - Clancy, Edward J.
Merryfield, Beulah P. - Bryant, Loren Earl
Meserve, Alice M. - Wigign, Charles G.
Meserve, Maud E. - Emery, Walter G.
Meserve, Thelma E. - Harmon, John F.
Messer, Blanche - Hicks, Roger F.
Messier, Dorothy M. - Denko, Roland S.
Meyers, Anna L. - Tripple, Charles A.
Miclette, Simonne - Santucci, George P.
Midriff, Joan A. - Halloway, Alan O.
Miller, Florence J. - Chase, Herbert M.
Miller, Mary L. - Wallace, Irton E.
Miller, Natalie Christine - Morrison, James B.
Miller, Pamela J. - Fournier, Michael A.
Milligan, Deborah Leigh - Merry, Ronald Bruce
Milligan, Kathleen J. - Perry, Gary R.
Milliken, Beatrice R. - Hodge, John L.
Milliken, Carrie R. - Dorr, Charles C.
Mills, Bernice I. - Nickerson, Nelson E.
Minkins, Rosa J. - Clark, Russell A.
Mitchell, Florence S. - Jackson, Charles W.
Mitchell, Jacqueline - Fedchenko, Ronald I.
Mitchell, Mabel D. - Hamm, William B.
Mitchell, Mary Denise - Stout, William Lester
Mitchell, Nancy Diane - McFarlane, Peter Angus
Mitchell, Ruth Frances - Loring, Robert Bancroft
Mohamed, Khadiga - Melander, Karl
Mohs, Faith Hope - Legendre, Kenneth Emile
Mollica, Patricia M. - Luscomb, Kenneth K.
Monroe, Cynthia Lee McLeod - Walker, Duane Elwin, Sr.
Monroe, Margaret E. - Young, Walter H.
Montefusco, Shirley I. - Junkins, Robert L.
Montgomery, Charlotte B. - Cluff, Nakum J.
Montgomery, Stora L. - Beats, John M.
Montgomery, Stora Lee - Hammond, Jeffrey David
Moody, Bell - Jenness, Matthias
Moody, Cora V. - Fall, Eli A.
Moody, Elizabeth H. - Demeritt, Charles W.
Moody, Eolyn N. - Merrow, Mark H.
Moody, Erin S. - Ryder, Belmont L.

Moody, Janet L. - Forbes, Francis
Moody, Shirley E. - Sparks, Bernie G., Jr.
Moody, Una M. - Dore, Charles C.
Moore, Barbara A. - Morin, Andrew H.
Moore, Beatrice C. - Knox, Olin A.
Moore, Elizabeth M. - Eldridge, William H.
Moore, Evelyn G. - Barton, Stephen D.
Moore, Lena V. - Brown, Walter S.
Morand, Sandra Louise - Shackford, Stephen Ernest
Morcotte, Jeannett - LaValley, John W., Jr.
Morford, Holly Ruth - Robacher, Steven James
Morgan, Jeanne Adele - Riley, Herbert F.
Morgan, Jennifer Lynn - Eldridge, Jeffrey Alan
Morgan, Judith P. - Whiting, Robert Craigue
Morgan, Patsy Marie (Palmer) - Jones, William Thomas
Morgan, Wenda Marie - Pollini, Jay Michael
Moriarty, Jane W. - Johnson, Lawrence P., Jr.
Morin, Florence J. - Cope, Edward J.
Morin, Nancy A. (Littlefield) - Dolan, Gary M.
Morley, Cynthia E. - Addison, Jeffrey
Morrill, Cheryl E. - Brooks, Harold V.
Morrill, Cindy-Lu - Stilphen, Grgeory Marc
Morris, Barbara A. - Nelson, Ralph E., Jr.
Morrison, Jane - O'Harre, John
Morse, Ann - Fallows, Robert E.
Morse, Mildred F. - Stratton, David S.
Morse, Robin Jane (Cruikshank) - Mitchell, Robert Dean
Morton, Blanche M. - Cattaneo, John J.
Morton, Mabel E. - Stillings, Joseph
Morton, Pearl B. - Brodrick, Charles H.
Morton, Susan Marie - Cattaneo, James
Moses, Arlene E. - McFarlane, Douglas
Moulton, Beryl M. - Kramer, Robert G.
Moulton, Catherine - Dupuis, Alan
Moulton, Clara M. - Pratt, John H.
Moulton, Dolores C. - Palmer, Lawrence T.
Moulton, Jessika Jean - Eldridge, Wayne Alan
Moulton, Lorraine A. - Schwann, William J.
Moulton, Lottie Edith - Eldridge, Guy Henry
Moulton, Norma A. - Eldredge, Edgar A.
Moulton, Ona E. - Smith, Arthur B.
Moulton, Priscilla May - Page, Robert Reginald
Moyer, Brenda L. - Elcock, James B.
Moylan, Eleanor Lorraine - Broughton, Robert Edwin
Muise, Fern Marie - Downing, Joel Paul

Muise, Rose M. - Adair, Christopher J.
Mulcahy, Laura E. - Lindsay, Raymond N.
Munroe, Annie - Villeiux, Wilfred
Murch, Anna Lucille - Hasting, Edward E., 2nd
Murphy, Madolyn - Bacon, Raymond W.
Murphy, Marsha Ellen - Johnson, Donald Harry
Murphy, Persis M. - Cutting, Chester H.
Murray, Florence B. - Williams, George Henry
Mwangi, Anne W. - Beaudry, Brain E.

Nadeau, Helen K. - Blake, Perley E.
Nagy, Carol R. - Meyer, Edward E.
Nalor, Theresa M. - Stewart, Leslie D.
Nardello, Lisa A. - Murphy, Daniel F.
Nason, Carry B. - Chadbourne, H. J.
Nason, Ellen F. - Van Tassel, Jan W.
Nason, Elva I. - Hayford, John E.
Nason, Karen Ann - Doucette, Richard C.
Nason, Lisa L. - Peek, Gary R.
Nason, Lucinda E. - Brown, Clyde H.
Nass, Victoria C. - Glick, Michael J.
Nathan, Evette - Collier, Simon D.
Nault, Arleen C. (Demers) - Whiting, Robert C.
Nault, Karen M. - Caples, Richard F.
Naylor, Michelle L. - Hill, James W., Jr.
Neenan, Deborah A. - Boehm, Donald W.
Neff, Ardis - Leigh, William C.
Nellenback, Ann Marie - Nelson, James Earl
Nellenback, Brenda - Abbott, Everett
Nelson, Elaine E. - Knight, George F.
Nelson, Elizabeth - Hincks, David
Nelson, Gail A. - Johnston, Kirk E.
Nelson, Lois G. - Lombardo, Eugene
Nelson, Lynne A. - Gusha, Johnathan L.
Nelson, Muria Eldridge - Everitt, Frederic Wallace
Nelson, Muriel F. - Douglas, Haven E.
Nesbitt, Marion L. - Nickerson, Norman G.
Ness, Susan Dearborn - Bearn, Jonathan Jewett
Newhall, Ethel - Lewis, Joseph W.
Nichols, Addie S. - Bean, Charles L.
Nichols, Anna - Bean, Fred E.
Nichols, Arvilla - Nelson, Harry
Nichols, Bertha - Hodge, Fred
Nichols, Bertha B. - White, Granville E.
Nichols, Carolyn Alice - Cook, Arthur Elwin

Nichols, Cora - Thompson, Frank F.
Nichols, Edna - Thomas, Marvin L.
Nichols, Elizabeth G. - Moody, Clayton
Nichols, Florence E. - Merrow, Llewellyn G.
Nichols, Gladys B. - Hammons, Norris A.
Nichols, Janet - DuBois, Wendell
Nichols, Jennifer Lee - Berry, John Adrian
Nichols, Laura J. - Davis, Silas E.
Nichols, Louise E. - Copp, Ralph E.
Nichols, Muriel A. - Googoo, William J.
Nichols, Nettie L. - Eldridge, Charles M.
Nichols, Pauline - Wilkins, Lyford
Nichols, Reta M. - Jackson, William L.
Nichols, Sadie - Arsanal, Leon
Nichols, Viola - Glidden, Harley
Nichols, Viola D. - Avery, Guy
Nichols, Virginia - Wasson, Leslie
Nichols, Wanda Lee - Buchikos, William Allen, Jr.
Nichols, Winnie M. - Webster, Ai M.
Nickerson, Adelia K. - Freeman, George A.
Nickerson, Barbara J. - Gould, Lebias R.
Nickerson, Helen M. - Fickett, Daniel A.
Nickerson, Judith - Williams, Ward
Nickerson, Laura B. - Buswell, Shirl E.
Nickerson, Margaret - Wiggin, Edwin
Nitz, Linda M. - Norton, Thomas Michael
Noble, Rita E. - Knox, Dwight E.
Noel, Pauline G. - Atwood, John E.
Northacker, Ann Virginia - Thompson, Timothy Edward
Norton, Nancy Mary - Shannon, James E.
Noyes, Joan - Bowe, Richard, Jr.
Nudd, Anita M. - Cameron, Bruce H.
Nudd, Joanna K. - Boisvert, Robert R.
Nudd, Vivian B. - Valley, Robert W.
Nudd, Yuleander H. - Morrill, Glenn E.
Nunn, Barbara A. - LaBonte, Albert E.
Nute, Abbie E. - Locke, Frank E.
Nute, Carrie E. - Nichols, Joseph A.
Nute, Clara E. - Dore, Ervin
Nute, Mabel - Plummer, Clarence R.
Nute, Minnie - Welch, Paul
Nutter, Mary D. - Sanborn, Orin
Nystedt, Jill E. - Fletcher, James E.

O'Brien, Devra Jean - Gray, Ivan Ernest, Jr.

O'Grady, Eva Marie - Haney, Keith Douglas
O'Leary, Deidre A. - Drew, Richard S.
Olsen, Barbara R. - Feid, Norman J.
Olsen, Diane - Olsen, Robert
Olssen, Evelyn Irene - Rhoades, Donald Estes
Orino, Emilienne - Zinck, Herbert E.
Osgood, Frances E. - Browne, William H.
Osgood, Hattie H. - Chadbourn, Isaac
Ouellette, Helen M. - Fortier, William M.
Ouellette, Jennifer R. - Varney, Frank W.
Owerko, Carol Ann - Harford, Thomas Joseph

Page, Agnes M. - Pascoe, William H.
Page, Bertha M. - Abbott, Carroll G.
Page, Donna Lou Smith - Scott, Randall Llewellyn
Page, Eva C. - Abbott, Ray M.
Page, Laura J. - Moulton, Lyle O.
Paige, Carol A. - Alward, John E.
Palmer, Addie E. - Rogers, Irving M.
Palmer, Beatrice E. - Brothers, Lawrence
Palmer, Charlotte - Eldridge, Perley E.
Palmer, Georgiana J. - Mader, Richard T.
Palmer, Gladys Eldridge - Chesley, George H.
Palmer, Joan L. - Couture, David R.
Palmer, Lynne M. - Panno, Wayne F.
Palmer, Margaret - O'Sullivan, Charles H.
Palmer, Patsy M. - Morgan, Edward R.
Palmer, Sacha M. Eldridge - Swansburg, Stephen G.
Palmer, Virginia P. - Whiting, Roger W.
Pare, Doris M. - Rasquin, John R.
Parker, Doris C. - Davis, Willard R.
Parker, Henrietta - Carter, George H.
Parker, Ruth C. - Wheeler, Fred K.
Parkhurst, Lisa A. Welch - Parkhurst, Walter R.
Parmenter, Betty Ann - Tremblay, Donald Philip
Parshley, Suzanne Linda - Merrow, Mitchell Paul
Partridge, Viola - Whiting, Stanley
Pascoe, G. Geraldine - Courtney, Eric
Pascoe, Geraldine - Nickerson, Lawrence E.
Pascoe, Gladys G. - Brown, John F., Jr.
Pascoe, Mary A. - Conner, Arthur N.
Pascoe, Phyllis D. - Morrill, C. Eugene
Pattee, Barbara Elizabeth - Haggart, Lorin Frederick
Paul, Josephine L. - Libby, Donald
Paul, Revel - Freeman, Norman R., Jr.

Pauling, Ethel M. - Morley, Clarence C.
Payne, Mary E. - Knight, Chester
Peace, Nelsina - Lacasse, Randolph
Pearson, Clareen - Furtado, Donald
Pearson, Dianne - Applin, Stephen
Pearson, Elizabeth R. - Parks, Robert W.
Pearson, Georgia I. - Harmon, John H.
Pearson, Ruth E. - Welch, Kenneth W.
Pearson, Ruth E. - Kennard, Raymond S.
Pease, Bessie M. - Brown, Tom H.
Peavey, Carole A. - Guyotte, Alan L.
Peavey, Carrie C. - Downs, Stephen
Peavey, Winifred A. - Davis, Clarence E., Jr.
Peck, Susan Marie - Bodurtha, Richard Sheldon
Pecoraro, Patricia Mae - Sando, Thomas N.
Peers, Dalinda - Killackey, James, III
Pelletier, Marguerite - Pike, Donald L.
Penna, Barbara - Connor, Jerry
Penna, Marilyn - Oliveira, Richard
Perham, April M. - Murphy, Kevin E.
Perkins, Eva - Emack, William H.
Perkins, Mary - Hammond, Lester
Perreault, Martha J. - Perreault, Andre J.
Perron, Florida - Michaud, Joseph
Perry, Anita A. - Frazier, Thomas L.
Perry, Carole A. - Libby, Randolph C.
Perry, Cora B. - Webb, Wallace I.
Perry, Marion F. (Best) - Harrison, James J.
Perry, Mary E. - Cyr, George F.
Perry, Michelle Lee - Riley, Michael Scott
Perry, Sarah E. - Welch, Peter P.
Perry, Violet Mae C. - Loring, Chester M.
Peskor, Barbara Ann - Cormier, Kenneth P.
Peterson, Esther C. - Johnson, Carl J. M.
Peterson, Judith A. - Doyle, Merton G., Jr.
Petrzak, Jennifer H. - Patulski, Mark P.
Phelps, Irene Marie - Ward, Melvin Lewis
Philbrick, Betsey - Stewart, Henry
Philbrick, Roxanna - Canney, Forrest F.
Phillips, Bessie - Kirkwood, Dana G.
Phinney, Patricia - Popham, William
Picard, Leslie Lynn - Rollins, Barry Dean
Piche, Noreen M. - Cousins, Richard Brian
Pierce, Virginia - Frenier, William
Pierni, Laura Marie - Goldthwaite, Keith Charles

Pike, Alice M. - Riley, Herbert F.
Pike, Barbara G. - Brownell, Keith W.
Pike, Catherine F. - Wilkins, Lloyd A.
Pike, Clemmie Belle - Merrow, Howard Earl
Pike, Josephine - McCauly, Daniel
Pike, Joyce - Moody, Wayne
Pike, Nettie - Eldridge, Everett S.
Pike, Ruth - Parker, John
Pilant, Marcia A. - Perron, Raymond A., II
Pinard, Anita R. - Pinard, Russell C.
Pineo, Esther E. - Loring, Chester M.
Pineo, Nancy A. - Libby, Floyd F.
Pinkham, Matilda S. - Horne, Geoffrey C.
Piper, Brandi Anne - Bedley, Michael Dean
Piper, Leva M. - Fall, Virgil J.
Piper, Lorraine M. - McDormand, Scott A.
Piper, Ruby R. - Wood, John M.
Pirozzi, Claira - Campbell, William
Pittman, Kelly April - Bacon, Robert F.
Plant, Ann Marie - Chamberlain, Brian James
Plant, Lilla M. - Farnham, George A.
Plant, Natalie A. - Boardman, Carlos
Ploof, Denise Cassandra - Daniels, Kirk Michael
Plummer, Linda M. - Johnson, Forrest Roger
Pochelon, Danielle Marie - Meserve, Scott White
Pochelon, Deborah K. - Harkins, James M.
Pohl, Robin Aniat - Boutin, Raymond Paul
Pollen, Anna - Rose, Edward
Pollender, Carole - Taylor, Marvin W.
Ponkop, Agnes M. - White, Bernard Lee
Porcella, Christina J. - Bean, William Cody
Porter, Betty A. - Lowe, John D., II
Porter, Carolyn - Richardson, George E.
Porter, Deborah A. - Pattison, David E., Jr.
Porter, Laura S. - Pope, Francis
Potter, Donna C. - Benway, Frederick M.
Potter, Henrietta - Newberry, Frederick H.
Potter, Lisa J. - Connor, Raymond F., Jr.
Potvin, Gloria J. - Nelson, Gordon R.
Powers, Judith - Legaspi, Romeo
Powers, Mary Anne - Dunham, Morris
Powers, Victoria - Tilton, Garrett K.
Pratt, Elizabeth Alexandra - Bell, Jeremy Moure
Pratt, Lara Meredith - McNally, Robert Norwood, Jr.
Pratt, Mildred - Dore, Leon E.

Pray, Ethel - Ciccolo, Frank
Pray, Julia F. - Burleigh, Charles J.
Preble, Grethel Zenaida - May, William H., Jr.
Prescott, Annette S. - Merrill, Maurice E.
Prescott, Arvilla F. - Manning, Francis J., Jr.
Pretka, Ann E. - Curry, David W.
Price, Grace E. - Rollins, Leonard H.
Price, Mary L. - Hodsdon, Ervin W.
Price, Mildred W. - Fall, Clinton H.
Prokey, Dorothy Ethel - Eldridge, Carroll H.
Prokey, Ethel B. - Piper, E. Perley
Provost, Barbara F. - Provost, William B.
Prudhomme, Sheila Marie - Jodlowski, Christopher Thomas
Purrington, Jean M. - Eldridge, Roy
Purrington, Vivian H. - Eldridge, Harry P.
Putonen, Helmi M. - Simpson, Harry Allen

Quimby, Donna M. - Wilkesman, Charles R.
Quimby, Jeannette - Ricci, Joseph, Jr.
Quinlan, Nancy Ellen - Peters, Charles Michael
Quinn, Patricia Jean - Letellier, Kevin Ronald
Quint, Eleanor P. - Moody, Oscar L.

Rafko, Julie A. - Hickey, Patrick J.
Randall, Donna Jean Lawrence - Wiggin, Jerry B.
Randall, Rebecca Lynne - West, Carl Stuart, Jr.
Randall, Susan E. - Wentworth, Fred, 2nd
Rankin, Bonnie L. - Lord, Brian C.
Rasquin, Doris M. - Nichols, Cecil A.
Rattee, Eva L. - Goodwin, John F.
Rawding, Athlene M. - Rawding, Robert B.
Raymond, Elaine R. - Hamilton, Charles E., Jr.
Raymond, Stacey Lynn - Vittum, John Thomas
Reardon, Barbara - Card, Joseph M., Jr.
Reardon, Patricia J. - Jones, David H.
Reck, Ruth B. - Burns, Stephen W.
Reckmeyer, Mary Patricia - Tupeck, Russell G.
Reed, Dawn Elizabeth - Cade, Erick Darin
Reed, Joyce L. - Bean, Clyde L., Jr.
Reed, Rosamond L. - Stevens, Howard
Reid, Diane M. - Olson, Robert A.
Reilly, Edna I. - Goodrich, Lyman H.
Reisfelder, Pauline Burleigh - Erlander, Carl Eric
Reissfelder, Margaret L. - Lampron, Richard J.
Remington, JoLinda L. - Patten, John C.

Reny, Priscilla T. Landry - Skehan, Joseph G., Jr.
Reynolds, Clara E. - Palmer, Joseph B.
Reynolds, Eleanor Marie - Pellerin, Gerald Joseph
Reynolds, Janice M. - Brannon, Daniel E.
Rhines, Cindy Lee - Holmes, Curtis J.
Ribas, Louise E. - Newcomb, Charles S.
Ricci, June - Perry, Paul Robert
Richards, Gertrude E. - Dale, Arthur J.
Richards, Ruby M. - Pearson, Donal C.
Richardson, Edith - Bradley, Charles H.
Richardson, Hazel M. - Brisbin, Charles E.
Richardson, Ida - Whitaker, Nathan W.
Richardson, Sharon A. - Lord, Michael C.
Ricker, Gertrude - Jones, Leon C.
Ricker, Rose Anne - Scolaro, Ricky A.
Ridlon, Bonnie L. - Gagne, Ernest A.
Riek, Heide Susanne - Santos, Andrew Keith
Riley, Bertha M. - Smith, Clifton E.
Riley, Cheryl A. Feener - Furlong, Edwin Charles, III
Riley, Cheryl Adeline - Halepis, Andrew Manuel
Riley, Edna M. - Eldridge, Ernest F.
Riley, Frances L. - Hooper, Howard A.
Riley, Shirley L. - Nason, Michael
Rines, Dorothy J. - Seavey, Henry H.
Rines, Jerildine - Chellman, Chester
Rines, Kathleen M. - Carruthers, Richard W.
Rines, Kristine M. - Klein, Larry Louis
Rines, Marilyn J. - Rines, Stanley J.
Ripley, Brenda J. - Libby, Earl D.
Ripley, Cheryl Jean - Vittum, Brewster Dale
Ripley, Lisa A. - Hartford, Todd R.
Roach, Janet - McSwiggin, James
Roberson, Stacie J. - Brown, Keith J.
Roberts, Agatha - Kent, James F.
Roberts, Holly Marie - Goumas, Timothy J.
Roberts, Lucy Mabel - Wiggin, Russell Elvin
Roberts, Virginia E. - Welch, Douglas A.
Roberts, Wanda R. Merchant - Bolton, James M.
Robie, Gaye E. - Varney, Ronald E.
Robinson, Anstress J. D. - Gonyer, Thomas Standley
Robinson, Ella L. - Potter, John A.
Robinson, Myrlice - Waite, Robert E.
Rochira, Nancy M. - Stowers, Ronald D.
Rogers, Donna - Wood, Leslie
Rogers, Lucy L. - Boston, Herman D., Jr.

Rogers, Marion - Langlois, Leon
Rogers, Ursula Patricia - Eldridge, Douglas Clifford
Ross, Annie B. - Lovejoy, Bert A.
Ross, Carolee - Reed, Charles S., Jr.
Ross, Dorothy E. - Bower, Theodore H.
Ross, Mary - King, Henry
Ross, Mary K. - Giblin, Alfred N.
Roth, Helen M. - Corbin, Allen F.
Rowbotham, Corine - Duval, Bruce
Rowe, Jeanie M. - Allen, Thomas S.
Rowell, Kimberly Alan - Cook, Arthur C.
Rowell, Natalie - Hickey, Stephen
Roy, Denise R. - Palmer, Robert C.
Roy, Sandra Jean - Scahier, Warren C.
Royea, Paulette J. - Armstrong, James P.
Ruland, Terry L. - Hansen, Neal M.
Runci, Sharon M. - Eldridge, Stephen L.
Ruselewicz, Nancy - Campbell, John S.
Rushton, Kathryn R. - Levesque, Philip D.
Russell, Alice M. - Sconschieff, Peter
Ryan, Mary - Ryan, Frank
Ryder, April P. - Libby, Paul G.
Ryder, Sandra Lee - Ames, Roger Stanley
Ryer, Mary M. - White, Mott H.

St. Clair, Jacqueline R. - Cash, Charles M.
St. Onge, Carol - Evans, Arthur W., III
St. Onge, Ida - Wagstaff, Francis
Sabine, Marjorie - Piper, Frank F.
Sacca, Carol L. - Brown, Michael A.
Sampson, Nancy L. - Tilton, Leslie H.
Samuelson, Lillian M. G. - Van Blarcom, Earle
Sanborn, Lepha A.. - Moody, George A.
Sanders, Susan B. - Ahearn, Patrick D.
Sands, Constance J. - Mazzone, Gaetano
Sanfacon, Patricia A. - Johnston, Richard A.
Sanphy, Joanne W. - Cook, Glenn R.
Sanphy, Mary C. - Skillins, Ray F.
Santulli, Marjorie E. - Chamberlain, Deane M.
Saracino, Cristina - Reggie, Michael C.
Sargent, Belle - Allard, Cyrus
Sargent, Cathy J. - Hooper, David Russell
Sargent, Celia D. - Philbrick, Ellsworth
Sargent, Dora T. - Eldridge, Fred W.
Sargent, Doreen C. - Libby, Alan D.

Sargent, Elaine Linda - Mandigo, Keith Arthur
Sargent, Evelyn - Conner, John B.
Sargent, Joan - Dore, Lyford R.
Sargent, Julia - Tasker, George F.
Sargent, Loura - Drew, Frank
Sargent, Sandra Gail - Christiansen, Bruce Maronus
Sargent, Tina M. - Nason, Edward J.
Saunders, Cindy L. - Tozier, Thomas J.
Saunders, Cora L. - Harding, Howard P.
Saunders, Kitty E. - Carter, Charles H.
Savage, Brenda J. - Miller, Danny W.
Savage, Diane L. - Drew, Daniel S.
Savage, Karen Beth - Eldridge, Timothy Wayne
Savary, Mabel M. - Clarke, Benjamin F.
Savigny, Elise - Baril Joseph T.
Sawyer, Agness - Shaw, Winthrop H.
Sawyer, Charlotte - Smith, Charlie E.
Sawyer, Dora M. - Wilkins, Earlin L.
Sawyer, Elizabeth A. - Earle, Peter Charles
Sawyer, Hazel L. - Wormhood, Chester A.
Sawyer, Marion L. - Crowley, Wilfred J.
Sawyer, May Trask - Winkley, Mark A.
Sawyer, Minnie B. - Davis, Bert W.
Sceggel, Abbie - Folsom, John
Sceggel, Addie - Smith, Austin E.
Sceggell, Gladis L. - Harmon, Ruben S.
Scharin, Lisa Dix Unander - Hattenburg, Lester John
Schmottlach, Barbara A. - Knowles, Robert W.
Schuch, Harriett - Wilkins, Olif M.
Schule, Christine E. - Legault, Paul E.
Schultz, Debora A. - Smith, Kenneth B.
Scripture, Deborah L. - Hebert, Timothy L.
Scripture, Deborah L. - Luis, Donald W.
Scripture, Diane M. - Barbieri, James R.
Scripture, Diane Marriam - Delp, David Barry
Scripture, Lelia G. - Eaton, Richard T.
Scripture, Rose A. - Coulter, George
Scruton, Sara E. - Welch, Carroll C.
Scungio, Claire L. - Elliott, Charles L.
Seamans, Brenda E. - Eldridge, Wendell R.
Searson, Nora C. - Giardini, John E.
Sebel, Margaret - Hyland, Arthur C.
Sedequist, Hattie - Orben, Jesse H.
See, Nancy - Martin, John P.
Senior, Barbara H. - Bogard, Nelson

Setz, Minnie R. - Preble, Edward A.
Seveain, Kathryn A. - Choate, Richard S.
Severance, Meredith I. - Albee, Everett S.
Severence, Leonora L. - Neal, George A.
Shackford, Darlene F. - Larrabee, Dennis E.
Shannon, Arlene M. - Nason, Henry W., Jr.
Shannon, Karen L. - Bresnahan, Brian D.
Shannon, Lynn M. - Bourgault, Daniel R.
Shannon, Mavis L. - Emerson, Ralph W.
Sharp, Barbara J. - Nickerson, Nelson S., Jr.
Shayowitz, Agnes - Noyes, John
Shea, Laurie - Mertens, Edward, II
Shea, Ruth - Pagonis, John
Sheehan, Doris Mary - Bouchicas, Grant Paul
Shephard, Eva - Brown, Lawrence F.
Sheppard, Florence O. - Logan, Adam W.
Sherman, Maria - Sanborn, Herbert
Shores, Nancy - Eldridge, Guy, Jr.
Short, Elmalee - Phillips, George Robert
Short, Jessica Marie - Glidden, Robert J.
Shortridge, Alice M. - Staples, Herbert E.
Shortridge, Frances M. - Ross, William H.
Shortridge, Gladis F. - Abbott, Harry V.
Shottek, Wanda - Rollo, Fred
Shultz, Elinor L. - Hultzen, Claud H.
Shultz, Mabel R. - Welch, James
Shultz, Mabel R. - Brown, William H.
Sias, Mary B. - Sweet, Clyde A.
Simms, Florence C. - Banfill, Ernest B.
Simoneau, Diane - Roy, Normand
Sinclair, Emily W. - Dunfield, Charles W.
Skamaraycz, Tanya Theresa - Griffin, James Michael
Skeist, Irene Dorothy - Covitz, Julius
Skillings, Carrie A. - Eldridge, Ezra
Skillo, Linda - Wical, Ronald
Slinger, Myrtle M. - Bell, William
Small, Jane - Holmstrom, Donald
Smart, Annie M. - Horne, C. Archie
Smart, Helen F. - Avery, Carroll W.
Smart, Louine C. - Merrow, Charles W.
Smart, Martha J. - Hartford, Robert F.
Smart, Mildred M. - White, Ervin Windefield
Smith, Alice E. - Knox, Edward C.
Smith, Alice W. - Brennan, Thomas P.
Smith, Cheri Ann - Finn-O'Neil, James J.

Smith, Cora L. - Edwards, Charles J.
Smith, Cynthia P. - Murdock, James W.
Smith, Dorothy E. - Moller, G. Christian
Smith, Gail M. - Rand, Roger W.
Smith, Gale Lynn - Burlison, George Stephen
Smith, Gale Lynn - Knight, William Ray, Jr.
Smith, Gertrude A. - Thissell, Theodore D.
Smith, Jo-Ann - Thompson, Richard
Smith, Kelley A. - Videtti, David M.
Smith, Lucy Thompson - Merrow, Harry Charles
Smith, Myrtle Blanche - Brown, William H.
Smith, Nellie M. - Brown, Charles M.
Smith, Norma M. - Curran, George S., Jr.
Smith, Pamela D. - Harvey, Paul E.
Smith, Ruth Frances - Kramer, Howard Gray
Smith, Sherri J. - Danosky, E. Robert
Snow, Catherine B. - Conner, Earl E.
Snow, Elizabeth - Horne, Harry E.
Snow, Helen M. - Stetson, Clarence E.
Snow, Laura O. - Wiggin, Jerry
Snow, Madeline - Savard, Paul Emile
Snow, Maria - Cioffi, Ferdinand F.
Snyer, Patricia F. - Bleyle, Donald A.
Sordiff, Carla Jean Hartford - Berry, Craig Joseph
Spacil, Mary - Gove, Ralph
Spear, Lena M. - Tasker, Dana J.
Speedy, Eliza - Wood, J. Frank
Spencer, Patricia M. - Morton, Gerrald L.
Spinney, Charlotte M. - Milne, Roland E.
Spinney, Charlotte M. - Milne, Roland E.
Sprague, Carol A. - Augenti, Jordan B.
Sprague, Ida M. - Eldridge, Lester A.
Stacy, Alice E. - Arnold, William F.
Stacy, Christabell I. - Eldridge, Harry P., Jr.
Stadley, Annie G. - Hammond, George L.
Stanley, Lynn Barbara - Savage, James Francis
Stanley, Rosalie May - Frost, Edwin Carl, Jr.
Stanton, Tina Marie - Peterson, David Charles
Staples, Barbara G. - Meader, Donald N.
Staples, Clara S. - Kirkwood, George T.
Steadman, Laura M. Chouinard - Wood, Jeffrey D.
Stearns, Catherine Mary - Medich, Benjamin Oddmund
Stein, Dorothy Janice - Hidden, Samuel B.
Stein, Janice D. - Carleton, Robert
Stevens, Addie - Young, Charles B.

Stevens, Amanda J. - Milligan, Dwight J.
Stevens, Gladys M. - Palmer, Osmer
Stevens, Mary E. - Scott, Ernest E.
Stewart, Alice A. - Frost, Arthur W.
Stewart, Minnie - Foss, Clarence E.
Stewart, Rose C. - Burke, John F.
Sticklin, Suzanne H. - Rieth, Arthur W.
Stillings, Arlena G. - Wiggin, Arthur R.
Stillings, Cora Emma - Smith, Walter Roy
Stillings, Eleanor M. - Clifford, Arthur C.
Stillings, Louise Sawyer - McDuffee, Lloyd
Stockbridge, Sandra May - Brown, Scott Michael
Stocker, Betty Lou - Snow, Robert Milton, Jr.
Stocks, Jeanne A. - Wentworth, Gordon C., Jr.
Stoddard, Carol M. - Hodge, Lloyd B.
Stoddard, Joanne - Ames, James W.
Stokes, Amelia - Glidden, John B.
Stone, Joanne C. - Meservy, Richard
Stone, Vicki - Forsythe, Edwin B., Jr.
Stout, Kelly Whiting - Murphy, Mark C.
Strasnick, Lynda - Shine, Francis K.
Stratton, Leora C. - Polland, Hughe M.
Strehlow, Jennifer Lee - Elwell, William Berry
Stroker, Carol A. - Marr, Russell R.
Strom, Olive A. - Bean, Raymond F.
Strong, Bridget Marie - Terminiello, Domenic W.
Strout, Lois J. - Thompson, Vernon C.
Strychorz, Barbara J. - Beach, Oscar, Jr.
Stuart, Donna M. - Van Tassel, Jan W.
Stuart, Hellen Margret - Farina, Robert Author
Stuart, Justine A. - Seguin, Bruce E., Jr.
Stuart, Nancy R. - Meader, Douglas W.
Stuart, Vicky A. Stanley - Lavallee, Bruce J.
Suicies, Patricia Lillian - Welch, Robert Roy
Sulia, Josephine - Labor, Dewey
Sulya, Sophie L. - Welsh, Robert
Sullivan, Sandra L. - Rollo, John A.
Sutton, Rebecca Jean Caulkins - Downs, David Wayne
Sweeney, Adelaide - Ott, Archie
Sweet, Lois F. - Libby, Elson
Swick, Kimberly Dale - Slover, Todd Kevin
Switaj, Patricia A. - Vigue, Gerald A.
Sylvia, Eleanor - Hines, Gordon
Syvinski, Desira L. - Taylor, Jeffrey S.
Syvinski, Jody B. - Stout, David A.

Talarico, Susan M. - Buesser, William Ronal, Jr.
Talley, Barbara J. - Gilliam, Raymond J.
Tappan, Evylyn D. - Smith, Charles H.
Tappan, Marguerite S. - Drowns, Leonard Charles
Tapper, Linda Lee - Lester, John Gregory
Tardiff, Iva L. - Myler, Earl E.
Tatham, Janet Elizabeth - Plante, Wilfred
Tattrie, Barbara - Welch, Ford J., Jr.
Taylor, Brenda - Taylor, Lawrence, Jr.
Taylor, Gloria - Neese, Leonard
Taylor, Janet R. - Dow, Ellis M.
Taylor, Jessica Mae - Thomas, Ryan Scott
Taylor, Lisa M. - Hall, David C.
Taylor, Nancy J. - Doe, Walter E., Jr.
Taylor, Patricia A. - Libby, Edward C.
Taylor, Pauline - Barter, Leiton
Taylor, Verna M. - Wilkins, Leslie W.
Tebbetts, Nikol Marie - Deyab, Richard George
Tebeault, Dawn - O'Blenes, Edgar
Templeton, Ada - McVey, John
Templeton, Ada - Perron, Amey
Templeton, Addie B. - Eldridge, Woodbury M.
Templeton, Addie B. - Hitchcock, Wilbur T.
Templeton, Arvilla - Nichols, Moses C.
Templeton, Donna M. - Merrow, Daniel S.
Templeton, Fannie A. - Abbott, Guy L.
Templeton, Flora B. - Merrow, Earl T.
Templeton, Genevieve - Landry, Arthur W.
Templeton, Louise - Wasson, Clarence
Templeton, Margaret - Eldridge, Perlie E.
Templeton, Myrtle M. - Eldridge, Wilbur
Templeton, Sadie - Nichols, Frank
Templeton, Sandra - Tarling, Paul
ter Weele, Margery K. - Gagni, Richard H.
Tetler, Florence - Higgins, John D.
Tewksbury, Emma N. - Knox, Herbert E.
Tewksbury, Pearle L. - Nickerson, Nelson E.
Thibault, Jacquelyn - Toom, Peep
Thibault, Penny Rose - Hoffman, Evan John
Thibeault, Flora - Locke, S. Ellsworth
Thibodeau, Dorothea A. - Hickey, Arthur A.
Thoma, Debora C. - Caverly, Daniel G.
Thomas, Minnie D. - Moore, Arthur H.
Thompson, Blanche G. - Perkins, Sidney L.
Thompson, Dorothy H. - Maine, Raymond R.

Thompson, Idella - Wyman, Melvin E.
Thompson, Jane - Nudd, Wallace R., Jr.
Thompson, Jeneen Meleda - Brackett, Timothy Edward
Thompson, Karen L. - Hammond, Robert J.
Thompson, Lucille - Bardwell, John D.
Thompson, Lucille - Smith, Oney
Thompson, Mertie B. - Fall, Ausbrey C.
Thompson, Nancy - Dodds, Bert, Jr.
Thompson, Rena A. - Lord, Lester W.
Thompson, Wenda Snow - Helme, David Alvin
Thorne, Cora M. - Annable, George I.
Thorne, Marion - Furbush, Perry Stanley
Thorne, Shirley G. - Davis, Otis A.
Thurber, Jennifer Lynn - Eldridge, Neil Gordon
Thurley, Jennie M. - Fall, Chauncey C.
Thurston, Beatrice Colby - Moore, Fred
Thurston, Cora - Nichols, George A.
Thurston, Frances M. - Hammond, George R.
Thurston, Winnifred F. - Beacham, John E.
Tibbetts, Cheryl Lee - Hayford, James Edward
Tibbetts, Cora F. - Remick, Otis D.
Tibbetts, Dorothy L. - Hill, John K.
Tibbetts, Jacqueline L. - Woodward, Freeman E.
Tibbitts, Annie E. - Page, Frank L.
Tice, Karen Lyn - Nelson, Edwin Russell
Tierney, Susanne M. - Hatt, Michael D.
Tillinghast, Dawn E. - Marion, Bradley H.
Tilton, Marguerite Priscilla - White, Bernard Lee
Tingley, Shirley M. - Ford, Glenn C.
Tinkham, Karen M. - Weeden, Daniel T.
Tinkham, Mary R. - Rattee, Felix
Tinney, Jean M. - Nappi, Nicholas M.
Titus, Lorraine L. - Morse, Clarence E.
Todd, Ethel J. - Harmon, John H.
Tormay, Barbara A. - Devine, Bruce L.
Townes, Grace - Foss, Charles L.
Townsend, Lizzie M. - Chase, Winfield S.
Tozier, Tammy Jean - Baillargeon, Donald R.
Tozier, Theresa Evelyn Saltzman - Crowell, Gregory Allen
Trace, Alicia - Gear, Patrick J., III
Tracy, Carolyn - Kelley, Thomas
Trecarten, Elizabeth K. - Etter, Earl Francis
Tressell, Donna Jeanne Manore - Paraboschi, John Lawrence
Tripp, Lenore Beatrice - Wong, Henry
Tripp, Lucy A. - Heath, C. Wilber

Trottier, Irene M. - Kalinuk, John Douglas
Tucker, Elizabeth H. - Davis, Lincoln K.
Tucker, Marion M. - Eldridge, Harry P.
Tupeck, Gloria - Carter, Ernest
Tupeck, Lisa G. - Raspante, Frank
Turner, Florence E. - Hodsdon, Grant W.
Turner, Mabel E. - Day, John F.
Turner, Mildred - Dubar, Charles E.
Turner, Wilma R. - Taylor, Kenneth W.
Tuthill, Nancy A. - DuBois, Raymond
Twombley, Charmein Jean - Eldridge, George Michael
Tyler, Irene Forsyth - Craft, Robert N.
Tyler, Lillian Norton - Tyler, Lester Verne

Valley, Agnes J. - Wilkins, Elmer L.
Valley, Debra - Spinney, Calvin, Jr.
Valley, Marguerite E. - Currier, Jesse A., Jr.
Van Darl, Margaret - Pice, Thomas E. P.
Van Dyke, Avis P. - Howes, Edward C.
Van Dyke, Dorothy P. Murphy - Van Dyke, Douglas A.
Van Dyke, Jessica M. - Gagnon, Gary Allen, Jr.
Van Fleet, Beverley F. - Dudley, Charles W.
Van Meir, Penny - Krasow, Bernard
Van Tassel, Laura Lee - Ames, James Ronald
Van Tassel, Michelle E. - Kenny, Thomas Patrick, IV
Varin, Irma H. - Milton, William M.
Varney, Barbara - Hebert, Philip
Varney, Cynthia Ann - Libby, Michael C.
Varney, Donna L. - Sargent, Richard L.
Varney, Florence - Eldridge, Lester
Varney, Gaye E. - Berry, John M.
Varney, Gloria - Seamans, David
Varney, Judith M. - Hayford, James E.
Varney, June F. - Brown, Richard S.
Varney, Mary - Barton, Frederick
Varney, Maude L. - Wasson, Perley J.
Varney, Rhonda L. - Merrill, Richard F.
Varney, Susan Gail - Varney, Edgar George
Varrell, Deborah Lynne - Harrison, Paul Dennis
Varrell, Terri L. - Kirby, Todd A.
Vaughan, Ethel H. - Elwell, Royce E.
Veitch, Kathleen M. - McClurg, Dennis
Velcourt, Elizabeth - Twombly, Herbert
Veliz, Diane - Whittingham, Tim James
Veriill, Terry L. - Cressey, Wayne L.

Virgilio, Barbara L. - Rines, Carl D.
Vittum, Natalie - Hall, Herbert E.
Vittum, Paula J. - Hamel, William J.
Vittum, Reba A. - Eldridge, Charles P.
Voegtlin, Katy Lee - Meserve, Scott White
Vose, Patricia L. - Williams, Barry R.
Vousden, Myrtle F. - Knox, Darcy D.

Wagenfeld, Carole A. - Baker, Howard P., Jr.
Wagenfeld, Sandra D. - Burton, Thomas P.
Wager, Diane Gayle - Delory, Edmund
Waggener, Jacqueline Mary Bomaster - Parker, Larry Raymond
Waitt, Francis M. - Merrow, Fred D.
Wakefield, Allura - Wilkins, Elmer L.
Wakefield, Tina Louise - Merrow, Michael Sands
Walker, Alice - Hutchins, M. B.
Walker, Delia H. - Redlon, Charles H.
Walker, Eliza R. - Saunders, Herbert C.
Walker, Emma S. - Merrow, Charles H.
Walker, Isabelle - Robbins, Samuel M.
Walker, Lena - Olcott, George A.
Walker, Lesly M. - Buchikos, William Allen
Walker, Sawai - Morgan, Edward R., Jr.
Wallace, Ada A. - Eldridge, Walter B.
Wallace, Ellen Marie - Downing, Geoffrey Alan
Wallace, Nancy - Smith, Henry C.
Walsh, Ruth E. - Welch, Paul J.
Walters, Michelle L. - Montgomery, Jonathan E.
Ward, Agnes - Hallett, Spurge
Ward, Laurie Ann - Williams, H. Dwaine
Wardwell, Lucinda A. - Repasy, Paul V.
Warner, Paula M. - Catlow, Milton J.
Warren, Beverly F. - Hill, Ivan B.
Warren, Deborah Marie (Lane) - Butler, Craig Martin
Warren, Pauline E. - Buswell, Ellis W.
Warring, Mima K. - Cook, James R. B.
Washburn, Jane E. - Dwyer, James F.
Wasson, Agnes - Knox, Charles
Wasson, Judith - Kelly, Ralph
Wasson, Leonora H. - Howe, Henry W.
Wasson, Lillian F. - Gilpatrick, Leon W.
Wasson, Maud - Nichols, Perley O.
Watanabe, Takako - Dunphy, Ralph, Jr.
Watson, Lynn Marie - Sylvain, Roy Clifford
Watson, Marlo A. - Lemay, Shawn J.

Watson, Mary Gusta - Dearborn, John B.
Watts, Dorothy Mae - Reed, Richard E.
Weare, Patricia Ann - Conner, Mark Kevin
Webb, Iris - Startz, August W.
Webster, Ada L. - Tasker, George F.
Webster, Lizzie M. - Hilton, Newell C.
Webster, Margurite E. - Varney, Bruce
Weeden, Karen May (Jensen) - Mensch, John Henery
Weeks, Carolyn Hamlin - Parsons, Roscoe Myron
Weeks, Etta R. - Bradew, John R.
Weeks, Gladys M. - Stevens, Kenneth E.
Weeks, Harriett E. - Roberts, Lawrence M.
Weeks, Mary E. - Sargent, Alton E.
Weeman, Lori Ruth - Anthony, Terrance Lee
Weismann, Mary Knox - Lucy, Mark Barton
Welch, Abbie - Wiggin, Edwin
Welch, Alice A. - Sargent, Everett
Welch, Alice Mary - Wenhold, Elmer George
Welch, Bernice M. - Nichols, Lucian P.
Welch, Bessie - Eldridge, George A.
Welch, Carrie - Knox, Charles L.
Welch, Cheryl J. - Riley, Daniel B.
Welch, Cora B. - Eldridge, Fred
Welch, Doris M. - Hodge, Bernard
Welch, Eliza A. - Welch, Edville O.
Welch, Elva - Eldridge, Lafayette
Welch, Elva - Bryant, Almon O.
Welch, Emily M. - Alley, George
Welch, Emma - Eldredge, Ivory E.
Welch, Evelyn Louise - Williams, Perley John
Welch, Fannie - Mathes, J. W.
Welch, Gladys E. - Benge, Arthur E.
Welch, Ida - Eldridge, George H.
Welch, Irene F. - Davison, Robert L.
Welch, Joanne H. - Sanphy, Roland M.
Welch, Julia A. - Sargent, Warren E.
Welch, Laura - Eldridge, Osborn
Welch, Lavinia - Colby, David
Welch, Lillie D. - Eldridge, Herbert W.
Welch, Lois A. - Valley, Paul G.
Welch, Lucy C. - Eldridge, Orodon J.
Welch, Mabel - Eldridge, Willie R.
Welch, Marguerite Elizabeth - Valley, Henry Patrick
Welch, Marion M. - Bean, Ernest M.
Welch, Mildred I. - Eldridge, Alfred S.

Welch, Renfina - White, Scott L.
Welch, Rose - Copp, Owen
Welch, Ruth J. - Ryder, Lloyd W.
Welch, Sharon R. - Moreau, Ronald A.
Welch, Sylvia - Russell, Clyde E.
Weldon, Sylvia A. - Kramer, Peter H. G.
Wells, Kimberly B. - McCoy, James
Wenant, Jean R. - Herrick, Charles W.
Wentworth, Ada M. - Boardman, Forest E.
Wentworth, Annie - Galpin, Louis P.
Wentworth, Belle N. - Sinclair, William C.
West, Constance V. - Hebert, Philip L.
West, Myrtle A. - Lamb, Fred
Westover, Beverly - Bean, Robert E.
Weyand, Martha Jane - Trepanier, Robert Charles
Weymouth, Emma L. - Welch, Ford J.
Wheaton, Mertie E. - Ray, Arthur J.
Wheeler, Blanche M. - Sargent, Norman A.
Wheeler, Doris - Jackson, Ronald
Wheeler, Julie Louise - Dow, Rodney Ernest
Wheeler, Marion L. - Templeton, Arthur W.
Whipple, Eva M. - Drew, John N.
Whipple, Marilyn J. - Loud, Clarence B.
White, Barbara J. - Hehl, Jacob L., Jr.
White, Bernice N. - Meloon, Calvin A.
White, Carmen Jean - Bertram, Carl J.
White, Deirdra A. Ryan - Catlow, Milton J. K.
White, Dora B. - Eldridge, Woodbury M.
White, Doris - Merserve, Alan
White, Edna E. - Dube, Ralph P.
White, Ella R. - Woodman, Oscar W.
White, Frances M. - Sias, Newell P.
White, Geraldine - Eldridge, Wesley E.
White, Helen M. - Day, Douglas G.
White, Janet D. - Currier, John M.
White, Janet D. - Jillette, Arthur G., Jr.
White, Janice Carrie - Whiting, Robert Craigue
White, Karen Ann - Leonard, Jason Charles
White, Karyn Theresa - Smart, Joshua Steven
White, Kathleen Grace - Eldridge, Carl Robert
White, Loretta N. - Sudol, John S.
White, Lottie B. - Staples, Ervin E.
White, Louise B. - Colby, Royal P.
White, Lucinda - Eldridge, Alan
White, Mabelle E. - Knox, Olin A.

417

White, Marie Estelle - Moore, Harwood Barrows
White, Marilyn J. - Blake, Richard M.
White, Marion E. - Smith, Ford J.
White, Mary - Colby, Luther
White, Nancy Jean - Coates, Benjamin L., III
White, Natalie N. - Edgerly, Herman D.
White, Penny Lynn - Getson, Donald A.
White, Phyllis L. - Lima, Manuel J.
White, Robin L. - Nichols, Alan R.
White, Robyn J. - Abbott, Donald W.
White, Tammy Louise - Wilcox, Michael William
White, Winifred G. - Ryder, Lynwood P.
White, Winnie C. - Morrow, John Gordon
Whitehouse, Phebe F. - Avery, Stephen
Whiting, Amanda R. (Frias) - Scates, Steven Louis
Whiting, Barbara Helen - Gautreau, Scott A.
Whiting, Janice Carrie - Vincent, Michael K.
Whiting, Linda M. - Seguin, Allen L.
Whiting, Mary - McKenney, Carl C.
Whiting, Mary R. - Thurston, Peter D.
Whiting, Nancy A. - Snow, Kenneth
Whiting, Rebecca J. - Nason, Alan
Whiting, Virginia P. - Eldridge, Roy
Whitney, Francis M. - Knox, Alva W.
Whittaker, E. Maureen - Welch, Mark C.
Whitten, Agnes May - Thompson, Frank
Whitten, Elaine M. - Morton, Gerald L.
Whitten, Hazel M. - Moulton, Otis
Whitten, Joanne C. - Peterson, Thomas F.
Whitten, Nellie I. - Moulton, Frederick
Whitten, Patricia L. - Quimby, Willard H.
Wiegel, Minnie - Merrill, Elmer B.
Wiggin, Ann Marie - Adjutant, Randy Martin
Wiggin, Bertha - Ricker, George M.
Wiggin, Catherine L. - Elliott, Harry Herman
Wiggin, Clara - Pike, Edwin
Wiggin, Deana M. - Adjutant, Matthew A.
Wiggin, Estella M. - White, Walter G.
Wiggin, Francis L. - Morrill, Leonard W.
Wiggin, Ida M. - French, Lewis L., Jr.
Wiggin, Marjorie E. - Jenness, Harvey
Wiggin, Mavis L. - Shannon, Guy E.
Wiggin, Muriel Thermas - Duchano, Omer J. A.
Wiggin, Ruth P. - Wyman, Walter H., Jr.
Wiggin, Sarah I. - Bickford, Charles H.

Wiggin, Stella - Welch, Alston B.
Wiggin, Susie A. - Eldridge, Dana
Wilcox, Virginia A. - Nichols, Linwood C.
Wildes, Claudia C. - Cole, Donald G.
Wilkins, Bernice T. - Kane, Thomas F.
Wilkins, Carrie E. - Eldridge, Edward
Wilkins, Harriett - Tibbetts, Charles Edwin
Wilkins, Irene E. - Hanson, Kenneth R.
Wilkins, Patricia - Gariepy, Robert
Wilkins, Patricia A. - Gariepy, Robert A.
Willard, Rose Mary - Williams, Bruce E.
Willess, Jeanne M. - Baluta, Walter James
Willess, Tammy Marie - Brown, Steven Lawrence
Willette, Deborah Gail - Stewart, Michael J.
Willey, Alice M. - Tebbetts, John F.
Willey, Reita Lee - Eldridge, Larry Edward
Williams, Ada - White, Granville E.
Williams, Agnes S. - Merrow, Earl T., Jr.
Williams, Amanda - White, Granville E.
Williams, Belinda - Cullen, Dana B.
Williams, Cora B. - Eldridge, Willie R.
Williams, Cora B. - Eldridge, Willis R.
Williams, Deborah J. - Brough, Dale R.
Williams, Deborah L. - Eldridge, Bradley W.
Williams, Elizabeth - Littlefield, Orace
Williams, Eva M. - Snow, Elbridge E.
Williams, Georgina - Davis, Eli N.
Williams, Grace E. - Abbott, William G.
Williams, Hilda Merrow - Dubois, Lucien P.
Williams, Lizzie B. - Eldredge, Oren
Williams, Lynn P. - Auderer, Albert F., III
Williams, Margie L. - Williams, Richard W.
Williams, Margie L. - Vacca, Ralph C.
Williams, Myrtle - Welch, Leon J.
Williams, Pamela J. - Sizemore, Todd D.
Williams, Teresa Lyn - Pepper, Bruce Richard
Wilson, Beatrice D. - Williams, Waldo J.
Wilson, Constance I. - Davis, John E.
Wilson, Joan T. - Wiley, David C.
Wilson, Patricia E. - Seguin, Elwyn B.
Wilson, Rose M. - Delisle, Maurice E.
Wilson, Ruth E. - Spiewak, Andrew A.
Wilson, Shirley E. - Rines, Mark F.
Winckler, Lois Elizabeth - Plummer, Clinton E.
Wingate, Lydia O. - Connor, Joseph H.

Winkley, Marguerite Ruth - Eldridge, Ralph Charles
Winn, Shelly J. - Little Elk, Myron S.
Witham, Alice - Boothby, Robert H.
Witham, Florence M. - Abbott, Frank L.
Wojcik, Sandra R. - Fielding, Steven P.
Wood, Diane - Fontaine, Richard
Wood, Geraldine M. - Dailey, Roger M.
Wood, Pamela Joy - Stockbridge, Richard C., II
Wood, Rosa A. - Bennett, Sumner L.
Woodbury, Deborah K. - Northrup, Norman L.
Woodbury, Elizabeth A. - Vinton, Robert W.
Woodbury, Loretta M. - Stockbridge, Roland C.
Woodbury, Naomi Marion - Hanscom, Michael Paul
Woodman, Etta - Colby, Plummer
Woodman, Frances L. - Libby, William L.
Woodman, Verna M. - Chamberlin, Guy H.
Woodward, Melissa L. - Monfet, Michael E.
Woodward, Priscilla - Ingraham, William W.
Woodworth, Leoine - Goodale, David
Woodworth, Ruth Coral - Cude, Vernon Lee
Wooward, Florence M. - Storer, Eliot C.
Wormhood, Carrie B. - Clough, James F.
Wormstead, Dorothy - Johnston, George M.
Wormstead, Dorothy M. - Webb, Kenneth Lee
Worster, Gladys L. - Munroe, Arthur C.
Worster, Jennie Bell - Brodie, Edward William
Wright, Linda M. - Davis, Richard M., Jr.
Wright, Louise Annette - Cincotta, Eric Joseph
Wyatt, Dorothy - Clements, Ralph H.
Wyman, Lucy L. - Hanson, Jeremiah

Yeaton, Cheri A. - Fisher, Harold J.
Yeaton, Ella F. - Baldwin, Fred W.
York, Cora B. - Bean, Harold
Young, Abbie M. - Nute, Charles G.
Young, Alice P. - Andrews, Austin D.
Young, Carrie - Staples, John
Young, Carrie - Canney, James E.
Young, Edna Susan - Cheney, John Gordon
Young, Ella F. - Lawler, Henry J.
Young, Evelyn L. - Howes, Edward C.
Young, Norma E. - Holloway, Cedric P.
Young, Patricia Ann (Souza) - Corriveau, Albert Wayne
Yuill, Elizabeth Lowe - Nichols, George E., Jr.

Zavorotny, Crystal Cheri - Rivard, Aime Leo, Jr.
Zildjian, Mary M. - Heron, George A.
Zimmer, Sylvia Marie - Comeau, Phillip Joseph
Zimmerman, Phyllis W. - Fox, Earle K.
Zinburg, Astrid V. - Fallon, Frank J.
Zwearcan, Jennifer Hollie - Shackford, Scott Alan

DEATHS

ABBOTT,
son, d. 8/19/1888 at –; b. Ossipee; Harrison Abbott and Emma F. Welch
daughter, d. 4/3/1909 at – in Ossipee; b. Ossipee; Jacob Abbott (Ossipee) and Bessie Ainsworth (VT)
A. Clifford, d. 7/18/1897 at 1/1/1 in Ossipee; meningitis; b. Ossipee; Almon F. Abbott (Ossipee) and Mara A. Dore (Ossipee)
Ada Bernice, d. 2/19/1977 at 89 in Ossipee; b. NH
Adelaide A., d. 7/29/1917 at 68/3/4; housework; married; b. Ossipee; Daniel G. Merrow (Ossipee) and Sarah Moody (Ossipee)
Agnes May, d. 6/8/1994 at 90; Joseph Wasson and Josephine Colby
Albert C., d. 10/22/1919 at 76/7/26; farmer; widower; b. Ossipee; Caleb Abbott
Albert S., d. 8/18/1909 at 62/3/20 in Wolfeboro; pericarditis; section hand; b. Ossipee; John F. Abbott (Ossipee) and Lucinda Emerson (Effingham)
Almon F., d. 5/22/1928 at 65/11/21; b. Ossipee; Jacob Abbott and Harriett Abbott
Alta C., d. 2/14/1986 at 90 in Ossipee; b. Chocorua
Asa M., d. 9/2/1894 at 77 in Ossipee; cartis insufficiency; farmer; married
Belle M., d. 11/29/1900 at 40 in Woburn; pneumonia; widow
Benjamin F., d. 5/14/1929 at 89/0/24 in Ossipee; b. Wolfeboro; Nathan Abbott and Betsey Allard
Carroll Guy, d. 2/23/1989 at 81 in Wolfeboro; b. Ossipee
Charles A., d. 6/19/1915 at 41/5/24; musician; married; b. Ossipee; Albert C. Abbott (Ossipee) and Addie Merrow (Ossipee)
Charles W., d. 9/5/1904 at – in Tewksbury, MA; nephritis acute
Daniel, d. 11/1/1906 at 68/3 in Ossipee; pneumonia; blacksmith; married; b. Biddeford, ME; Thomas Abbott and Lydia Files
Edward, d. 4/22/1943 at 74/6 in Ossipee; b. N. Reading, MA; Charles B. Abbott and Martha Hovey
Edwin C., d. 2/21/1931 at 77/4/18 in Melrose, MA; b. Ossipee; Nathan Abbott and Betsy Allard
Eliza A., d. 1/24/1907 at 63/7 in Ossipee; general debility; widow; b. Effingham; John Parsons (Gilmanton) and Hannah Flanders (Madison)
Emily J., d. 8/30/1909 at 76/7/13 in Ossipee; acute bronchitis; visitor; b. Saco, ME; Joseph Lewis (Saco, ME) and Sophronia Rear (Effingham)
Ernest G., d. 3/12/1965 at 76 in Wolfeboro; b. Ctr. Ossipee
Etta M., d. 6/26/1959 at 92 in Ossipee; b. Freedom; Susan Ward
Fannie A., d. 8/30/1972 at 81 in Wolfeboro; b. NH
Frances A., d. 4/21/1934 at 85/7/5 in Sandwich; b. Ossipee; Lewis W. Nute and Harriett Hanson
Frank W., d. 3/16/1906 at 51 in Ossipee; bronchitis; laborer; married; b. Ossipee; John F. Abbott (Ossipee) and Lucinda Emerson (Ossipee)

George H., d. 8/26/1900 at 35/5/3 in Ossipee; heart disease; cabinet maker; married; b. Ossipee; Jacob Abbott (Ossipee) and Harriet Fernald (Ossipee)

Guy L., d. 8/1/1945 at 58/11/9 in Wolfeboro; b. Ossipee; Lyford A. Abbott and Etta M. Lord

Harriet N., d. 1/27/1908 at 67/8/8 in Ossipee; cardiac dropsy; b. Ossipee; John Y. Fernald (Watervlle, ME) and Sally Trickey (Waterville, ME)

Harrison R., d. 2/21/1900 at 61/4/1 in Ossipee; strangulated hernia; farmer; widower; b. Ossipee; Benjamin Abbott and ----- Wiggin

Harry V., d. 3/23/1977 at 83 in Wolfeboro; b. NH

Hattie, d. 11/15/1918 at 20/11/1; single; b. Ossipee; Lyford A. Abbott (Ossipee) and Etta M. Ward (Freedom)

Henry F., d. 5/16/1923 at 76/6/17; b. Ossipee; John Abbott and Joanna Graves

Howard W., d. 2/13/1894 at 22/2/18 in Ossipee; scrof. & heart disease; cabinet maker; single; b. Ossipee; Albert C. Abbott (Ossipee) and Abbie A. Merrow (Ossipee)

Irving Henry, d. 12/21/1996 at 75 in Ctr. Ossipee; Wade Abbott and Josephine Eldridge

Jacob N., d. 7/30/1955 at 74/10/21 in Wolfeboro; b. NH; Jacob Abbott and Harriett Abbott

Jennie B., d. 2/18/1938 at 73/3/7 in Ossipee; b. Effingham; Lorenzo Champion and Sabrina Day

John F., d. 9/17/1895 at 73 in Ossipee; valvular disease heart; farmer; widower

Joseph C., d. 2/29/1944 at 80/3 in Haverhill, MA; b. Ossipee; Limuel Abbott and Abbie Langley

Josephine E., d. 11/23/1964 at 65 in Dover; b. Ossipee

Lemuel, d. 7/31/1904 at 43 in Boston; pyonephrosis; broker; Lemuel Abbott

Lester M., d. 6/18/1958 at 66/10/23 in Ctr. Ossipee; b. Lynn, MA; Lawrence Abbott and Emma Ward

Levonia, d. 2/4/1887 at 81 in Ossipee; domestic; widow; b. Ossipee

Louis F., d. 10/13/1937 at 86/0/6 in Boston, MA

Mary A., d. 11/24/1944 at 84/5/10 in Wolfeboro; b. Ossipee; Herman R. Dore and Sarah E. Dore

Merle C., d. 11/9/1891 at 0/4 in Ossipee; b. Ossipee

Moses, d. 4/29/1920 at 76/4/25; livery; single; b. Ossipee; Frank Abbott (Ossipee)

Nellie M., d. 4/18/1892 at 13 in Ossipee; corea; b. Ossipee; Albert S. Abbott (Ossipee) and Alice Hammond (Ossipee)

Osborne H., d. 10/25/1983 at 99 in Ossipee; b. Tuftonboro

Ruth M., d. 2/4/1950 at 49/9/20 in Wolfeboro; b. Exeter; Charles Elliott and Ida Curtis

Sarah Martel, d. 5/5/1994 at 90; Frank Hannaford and Agnes Martel

Solomon F., d. 7/22/1908 at 62 in Ossipee; arteriosclerosis; farmer; b. Ossipee; Solomon Abbott and Rena -----
Vonia M., d. 4/28/1926 at 71/5; b. Ossipee; Samuel Hodge and Mary C. Hodge
Wade, d. 12/16/1968 at 73 in Hanover; b. NH
Wilbur L., d. 1/20/1956 at 84 in Ossipee; b. Wolfeboro; Ephraim Abbott and Carolyne Moody
William G., d. 7/23/1937 at 70/4/23 in Ossipee; b. Ossipee; Jacob Abbott and Harriet Fernald

ADAMS,
Lorimer S., d. 2/23/1983 at 88 in Ossipee; b. Chagrin Falls, OH
Winnie May, d. 2/4/1972 at 83 in Ossipee; b. NH

ADJUTANT,
Chester, d. 6/3/1972 at 59 in Ossipee; b. NH
Parkman, d. 3/3/1903 at 77/0/10 in Ossipee; disease of prostrate glands; carpenter; widower; b. Tuftonboro; Samuel Adjutant (Ossipee) and Nancy Dore

AIKENS,
Hester J. P., d. 10/14/1941 at 91/3/23 in Ossipee; b. Gilmanton; Burleigh F. Parsons and Elmera Lamprey

AINSWORTH,
son, d. 9/5/1913 at –; b. Ossipee; Wallace Ainsworth (Stow, VT) and Alice Harmon

ALBRO,
Elinor, d. 12/2/1999 at 96 in Ossipee; Albert N. Brise and Maude E. Lapham

ALDEN,
Dorothy D., d. 9/5/1980 at 60 in Ossipee; b. MA

ALDERSON,
Wesley Taylor, d. 1/6/1979 at 94 in Ossipee; b. MA

ALDRICH,
Emma Jane, d. 2/28/1938 at 70/2/7 in Wolfeboro; b. Somersworth; John Calvin Hodgdon and Melinda Hodgdon

ALLARD,
Abner, d. 3/21/1919 at 69/4/21; farmer; married; b. Conway; Henry Allard (Albany) and Fanny Dollof (Conway)
Isaac, d. 12/2/1899 at 78 in Ossipee; apoplexy
James, d. 3/11/1918 at 60/10/4; lumberman; widower; b. Albany; Orlando Allard
Page, d. 8/3/1899 at 78 in Ossipee; paralysis of heart; farmer; widower; b. Madison

ALLEN,
Charles Albert, d. 5/19/1940 at 66/9 in Dover; b. Wakefield; William Allen and Elizabeth Nichols
Elisha P., d. 5/10/1901 at 71 in Ossipee; cerebral apoplexy; hotel keeper; married; b. Ossipee
Ella Frances, d. 2/27/1914 at 62/5; b. Shrewsbury, MA; Calvin Berry (Oxford, MA) and Harriet Conant (Monson, MA)
Esther C., d. 4/19/1982 at 87 in Ossipee; b. Melrose, MA
Eunice, d. 8/10/1894 at – in Ossipee; cerebral hemorhage; single; b. Ossipee
Eunice C., d. 1/23/1922 at 87/5/27 in Ossipee; widow; b. Ossipee; Asa Beacham (Ossipee) and Apha Canney (Ossipee)
George H., d. 4/8/1954 at 90/7/5 in Moultonboro; b. Moultonboro; Charles Allen and Mahitable Whitten
Henry W., d. 11/16/1941 at 84/11/12 in Wolfeboro; b. Ossipee; Elisha P. Allen and C. Beacham
Hila C., d. 3/5/1983 at 87 in Wolfeboro; b. Milford, CT
John J., d. 4/15/1897 at 67 in Ossipee; paralysis of heart
Mary Ann, d. 7/24/1900 at 79 in Ossipee; acute gastritis; housewife; single; b. Ossipee; Daric Allen
Polly, d. 7/8/1887 at 82/6/25 in Ossipee; domestic; widow; b. Ossipee
Polly, d. 1/5/1896 at 84 in Ossipee; marasmus seniles; b. Wakefield
Robert Henry, III, d. 11/19/1989 at 50 in Wolfeboro; b. Winthrop, MA

ALLEY,
Harry W., d. 11/21/1929 at 44/5/15 in Ossipee; b. Madison; Eugene Alley and Sarah Tebbetts

ALLON,
Thomas F., d. 1/18/1957 at 85 in Ossipee; b. Worcester, MA; Archibald Allon and Rebecca Hoddock

ALTENBERN,
Albert W., d. 1/12/1967 at 81 in Ossipee; b. Lena, IL

ALTHAUS,
Ella, d. 5/25/1975 at 80 in Ossipee; b. NY

ALWARD,
Robert Frank, d. 5/21/1983 at 65 in Ossipee; b. Framingham, MA

AMARAL,
Joseph Francis, d. 6/19/1997 at 86 in Ossipee; Emanuel P. Amaral and Maria DePonte

AMBROSE,
Ebenezer W., d. 12/28/1911 at 83/3/2; heart disease; farmer; widower; b. Ossipee; Jno. Ambrose (Ossipee) and Oliver Hodsdon (Ossipee)

AMES,
Barnet, d. 5/9/1918 at 74/3/2; minister; married; b. Holderness; Thomas J. Ames (Holderness) and ----- (Ossipee)
Frank J., d. 11/13/1935 at 68/7/10 in Ossipee; b. Ossipee; Asa Ames and Catherine Knox
Fred W., d. 10/2/1941 at 78/9/24 in Ossipee; b. Machias, ME; John C. Ames and Clarissa Libby
John C., d. 1/13/1931 at 91/5/6 in Ossipee; b. Ossipee; Marston Ames and Clarissa Moulton
Lizzie E., d. 3/10/1913 at 65/10/2; housework; widow; b. Ossipee; Barzella Welch (Ossipee) and Julia Templeton (Hillsboro)
Maria C., d. 3/8/1922 at 66/0/11 in Ossipee; housekeeper; married; b. Lindenville; ----- Cotton
Marston, d. 6/8/1887 ar 87 in Ossipee; farmer; widower; b. Ossipee
Mattie, d. 10/10/1898 at 38/0/2 in Ossipee; venous congestion; housewife; married; b. Ossipee; F. P. Dore
Paul T., d. 11/9/1954 at 0/0/2 in Wolfeboro; b. Wolfeboro; Roy Ames and Lois Connor
Sally, d. 2/23/1894 at 86/4/18 in Wakefield; influenza; housewife; married
Sarah J., d. 8/4/1926 at 79/4; b. Ossipee; Jacob Eldridge and Sarah Welch

AMY,
Renee Owen, d. 3/9/1992 at 83 in Ossipee; b. Johnstown, PA

ANDERSON,
Earle Stanley, d. 4/12/1997 at 96 in Ossipee; Walter Anderson and Evelyn Hicks
Lillian A. M., d. 1/16/1983 at 92 in Ossipee; b. Sweden
Lulu I., d. 12/22/1985 at 72 in Ossipee; b. Gloucester, MA

Olive, d. 4/13/1900 at 85 in Ossipee; pemphigus

ANDREWS,
daughter, d. 6/5/1911 at –; stillborn; b. Ossipee; Austin Andrews (Hampton, NB) and Alice P. Young (Ossipee)
Austin D., d. 4/1/1952 at 73 in Wolfeboro; b. Canada; Austen C. Andrews and Sarah Bonney
Daniel W., d. 8/3/1900 at 75 in Ossipee; aortic incompetency; widower; b. Effingham; ----- (Scarboro, ME) and Betsey Watson (Lee)
Edward C., d. 5/28/1892 at 0/0/2 in Ossipee; icterus; b. Ossipee; E. B. Andrews (Freedom) and Emma A. Burke (Somerville)
Edwin, d. 2/27/1914 at –; laborer; b. Freedom; Thomas Andrews and ----- Watson
Emma A., d. 6/21/1928 at 63/9/21; b. Somerville, MA; Samuel Burke and Caroline Atkinson
Ezekiel B., d. 12/4/1928 at 67/8/25; b. Freedom; Joseph Andrews and Juliette Bennett
Helen, d. 4/17/1904 at 2/7/9 in Ossipee; accidental poisoning; b. Ossipee; E. B. Andrews (Freedom) and Emma Burke (Somerville)
John, d. 3/3/1946 at 66/1/29 in Ossipee; b. Union, CT
Ruth M., d. 5/15/1911 at 11/9/17; pneumonia; student; b. Ossipee; E. B. Andrews (Freedom) and Emma H. Burke (Somerville)

ANGEL,
Nettie F., d. 7/31/1954 at 77/10/20 in Wells, ME; b. Ossipee; George Loring and Adelaide Woodman

ANTHONY,
Arnold G., d. 4/16/1985 at 71 in Ossipee; b. Brownfield, ME
Terrance Lee, d. 7/8/1991 at 45 in Wolfeboro; b. Bridgton, ME
William John, d. 2/24/1974 at 50 in Manchester; b. ME

APPLEBEE,
Albert J., d. 3/8/1982 at 82 in Ossipee; b. Kensington
Esther Mary, d. 3/30/1986 at 89 in Ossipee; b. Milton Mills

ARATA,
Eugene A., d. 2/3/1995 at 85; John Arata and Ismene Neri
Irene L., d. 5/6/1989 at 80 in Portsmouth; b. Lewiston, ME

ARCHIBOLD,
Adeline, d. 10/17/1906 at 76 in Ossipee; paralysis of heart; b. Acton

AREY,
Louis M., d. 12/10/1980 at 90 in Ossipee; b. Portland, ME

ARMSTRONG,
Jack Clarence, d. 11/26/1989 at 12 in Ossipee; b. Wolfeboro
Leroy S., d. 4/12/1946 at 47 in Ossipee; b. Needham, MA; Richard Armstrong and Adoline Flood
Robert T., d. 3/10/1999 in FL; Johnson Armstrong and Anna Corbett

ARSENAULT,
Lawrence J., d. 7/17/1969 at 80 in Ossipee; b. Canada
Leon, d. 3/9/1927 at 58/8/19; b. PEI; Sylvester Arsenault
Sadie, d. 3/13/1938 at 63/10/25 in Ossipee; b. Ossipee; Ahiel Templeton and Effie Williams

ASHER,
Inga Lindberg, d. 1/8/1974 at 85 in Ossipee; b. Norway

ASHOEE,
Mary M., d. 12/27/1904 at 73/9/21 in Ossipee; heart failure; housework; married; b. Ossipee; William Moulton (Wakefield) and Sally Smith (Ossipee)

ASPINWALL,
Elizabeth F., d. 8/6/1972 at 78 in Ossipee; b. Newfoundland

ATHERTON,
Stella, d. 6/17/1925 at 40/2/23; b. Ossipee; William Wiggin and Sophia Eldridge

ATKINS,
Lena Mary, d. 7/6/1989 at 100 in Ossipee; b. Worcester, MA

AUBUCHONT,
Louis A., d. 4/25/1950 at 78/1/5 in Wolfeboro; b. Millbury, MA; Alex Aubuchont and Mary ----

AUSTIN,
Elizabeth B., d. 4/10/1988 at 76 in Ossipee; b. Brooklyn, NY

AVERY,
Arthur J., d. 5/31/1969 at 41 in Ossipee; b. NH
Arthur W., d. 11/8/1955 at 71/6/17 in Ossipee; b. NH; Frank Avery and Abbie Elliotte

Dorcas, d. 8/26/1890 at 80 in Ossipee; Bright's disease; domestic; widow; b. Wolfeboro; Stephen Nute and Annie Nute

Guy L., d. 12/5/1978 at 75 in Ossipee; b. NH

Kenneth Wallace, d. 7/8/1997 at 86 in Ossipee; Alonzo F. Avery and Lillian A. Wallace

Margaret E., d. 1/10/1985 at 74 in Ossipee; b. Wolfeboro

Phoebe, d. 5/12/1932 at 90/5/0 in Ossipee; b. Ossipee; Isaac Hanson and Sarah Leighton

Viola D., d. 5/6/1978 at 78 in Wolfeboro; b. NH

AYERS,

Carrie Sherwood, d. 7/29/1945 at 91/10/16 in Ossipee; b. Roxbury, MA; William N. Heath and Mary Anderson

Edith E., d. 5/1/1972 at 87 in Rochester; b. NH

Ina Mabel, d. 11/7/1973 at 86 in Wolfeboro; b. NH

John, d. 1/28/1895 at 75/0/16 in Ossipee; cerebral softening; farmer; widower; John Ayers (Newburyport) and Mary Ray (Ossipee)

John J., d. 4/11/1935 at 55/1/8 in Ossipee; b. Saranac, NY; Nahum H. Ayers and Sarah Flanders

John M., d. 5/10/1909 at 54/10/4 in Ossipee; general neuritis; farmer; b. Ossipee; John Ayers (Ossipee) and Elizabeth Krunsford (Rockport, MA)

Samson (sic - female), d. 4/19/1900 at 82/5 in Ossipee; hernia; widow; Joshua Roberts

Stephen, d. 7/23/1899 at 84 in Ossipee; old age; farmer; married; b. Greenland; Thomas Ayers

BABB,

Jennie A., d. 6/23/1918 at 43/10/14; housewife; married; b. Ossipee; Isaac Small (Limerick, ME) and Jennie MacKay (Scotland)

BABKIRK,

Dana Michael, d. 1/11/1997 at 37 in Wolfeboro; Maynard L. Babkirk and Maria C. Zangari

BACIGALUPO,

Thomas, d. 2/3/1946 at 66/5/7 in Wolfeboro; b. Italy

BAGLEY,

Audrey M., d. 9/4/1978 at 86 in Wolfeboro; b. NH

Bradbury J., d. 11/22/1981 at 84 in Ossipee; b. Jacksonville, ME

Laura Winship, d. 2/22/1988 at 90 in Wolfeboro; b. Derry

Ralph E., d. 2/8/1918 at 22/6/8; clerk; married; b. Nashua; Elmo Bagley (Groton) and Sadie Sargent (Millbrook)

Sadie, d. 11/10/1954 at 84 in Concord; b. NH; Seneca Sargent and Eliza Ham

BAILEY,
Frances Viola, d. 2/8/1999 at 85 in Ossipee; Herbert Lord and Gertrude Hoyt
Freeman, d. 2/4/1937 at 59/7/24 in Ossipee; b. Jackson; Moses Bailey and Addie Fernald
Mabel F., d. 10/5/1927 at 30/4/22; b. Jackson; Moses Bailey and Addie Fernald
May Bell, d. 4/24/1890 at 0/0/10 in Ossipee; b. Ossipee
Walter L., d. 3/28/1978 at 84 in Ossipee; b. OR

BAIN,
Frederick W., d. 7/5/1985 at 87 in Ossipee; b. Yarmouth, NS

BAKER,
Alice Anne, d. 6/1/1995 at 61; Joseph William Roy and Edith Alice Vaillancourt
Eva, d. 4/2/1973 at 70 in Wolfeboro; b. USA
Frederick, d. 6/22/1973 at 83 in Ossipee; b. MA
Herman C., d. 5/28/1935 at – in Ossipee
Sarah A., d. 2/23/1923 at 80/6/12; b. Orrington, ME; Benjamin Atwood and Lucy Baker

BALDER,
Lucia, d. 8/30/1971 at 88 in Ossipee; b. Spain

BALDWIN,
Olive A., d. 3/18/1909 at 65/0/23 in Ossipee; val. heart disease; housekeeper; b. Ossipee; Leander Sinclair (Essex, VT) and Olive Kimball (Kennebunk, ME)
Rebecca Emily, d. 6/6/1975 at 88 in Ossipee; b. NH

BALLOU,
George, d. 6/4/1930 at 73 in Ossipee; John A. Ballou and Annie Smith

BALZARINI,
Marie Ange, d. 9/30/1996 at 84 in Ossipee; Omer J. Soucy and Mary Louise Dube

BAMFORD,
Clayton F., d. 5/15/1953 at 52/7/22 in Wolfeboro; b. Houlton, ME; David Bamford and Georgie Van Tassel

Cora Hazel, d. 12/26/1995 at 94; Frank Rouse and Minnie E. Hale

BANCROFT,
Mary, d. 12/12/1989 at 99 in Ossipee; b. Teuchl, Austria

BANFIELD,
Rose B., d. 11/16/1978 at 86 in Rochester; b. NY
Stanley M., d. 9/22/1966 at 76 in Ossipee; b. Worcester, MA

BANFILL,
Charles Willis, d. 12/28/1992 at 85 in Ctr. Ossipee; b. Conway
Eliza, d. 11/30/1916 at 71/7/21; housekeeper; married; b. Ossipee; William N. Roberts (Tuftonboro) and Mary Jackson (Eaton)
Florence Lord, d. 3/30/2000 at 89 in Ctr. Ossipee; John Alvah Lord and Laura Mae Knight
Fred R., d. 1/1/1974 at 74 in Wolfeboro; b. NH
Meleda A., d. 6/18/1976 at 78 in Ossipee; b. Canada
Rose A., d. 5/19/1966 in Ossipee; b. Richmond, Canada
William, d. 4/2/1959 at 89 in Ossipee; b. Conway; Charles Banfill and Jane Jackson

BARKER,
Florence Cooke, d. 10/28/1996 at 101 in Ossipee; Richard Cooke and Phoebe Newcomb
Howard P., Sr., d. 10/10/1988 at 79 in Ossipee
William S., d. 9/10/1936 at 75 in Ctr. Ossipee

BARNARD,
Samuel E., d. 7/31/1963 at 83 in Ossipee; b. Salem, MA

BARNES,
Charles R., d. 2/22/1988 at 86 in Ossipee; b. Revere, MA
Ralph Eugene, d. 5/23/1991 at 53 in Ossipee; b. Lowell, MA

BARNHART,
Homer Lee, d. 11/18/1993 at 71 in Wolfeboro

BAROSKI,
Eva, d. 9/11/1995 at 88; Peter Foyder and Mary O'Lear

BARROW,
Loretta A., d. 1/18/1977 at 60 in Wolfeboro; b. MA
Thomas H., Jr., d. 5/19/1978 at 64 in Wolfeboro; b. MA

BARROWS,
Doris, d. 8/13/1921 at 0/11/18 in Ossipee; L. W. Barrows (Bridgewater, VT) and Clara L. Barrows (Lynn, MA)

BARRY,
Frank Wildrick, d. 11/8/1994 at 83; Edward W. Barry and Harriett Findlay

BARSHAW,
Mitchell, d. 2/10/1945 at 83/3/14 in Ossipee; b. Sherbrook, Canada; Mitchell Barshaw and Cegtha Dorr

BARTA,
Eleanor, d. 8/21/1937 at 22/9/7 in Ossipee; b. Needham, MA; William G. Barta and Florence I. Beane

BARTON,
Annie Jane, d. 9/19/1941 at 54/11/14 in Ossipee; b. Hull, England; James Chilvers
Charles Sidney, d. 9/19/1941 at 27/7/4 in Ossipee; b. Beverly, MA; Charles M. Barton and Annie Jane Chilvers

BASTON,
John Edward, d. 9/14/2001 in Ctr. Ossipee; Kenneth Baston and Patricia McJuary

BATCHELDER,
Frank, d. 4/2/1944 at 88/4/29 in Ossipee; b. Conway; John Batchelder and Harriet Kennson

BATTERSBY,
Amalia Anna, d. 6/24/1982 at 89 in Ossipee; b. NY

BAUER,
Harriet, d. 10/24/1996 at 88 in Ossipee; Axel Morck and Harriett Colsen

BAZYLEWICZ,
Walter S., d. 2/6/1986 at 81 in Ossipee; b. Lithuania, Poland

BEACH,
Hazel Libbey, d. 12/20/1985 at 83 in Ossipee; b. Wolfeboro

BEACHAM,
Abigail C. Q., d. 11/29/1892 at 72 in Ossipee; chron. gast. catarrh; housewife; married; b. Ossipee; Samuel Quarles

Alonzo, d. 8/3/1888 at 35; merchant; single; b. Ossipee; Simon Beacham
Annie, d. 10/6/1901 at 54 in Ossipee; over dose of Paris Green; married; b. Ossipee; Lyman Chick
Annie E., d. 10/17/1926 at 85/2/29; b. Ossipee; Asa Beacham and Aphia Canney
Asa, d. 4/5/1895 at 94/6/28 in Ossipee; old age; widower; b. Ossipee; Richard Beacham and Hannah Pitman
Asa, d. 5/10/1920 at 72/10/7; farmer; married; b. Ossipee; Moses Beacham (Ossipee) and Sarah Bennett (Tuftonboro)
Ernest W., d. 1/11/1917 at 41/6/7; liveryman; single; b. Ossipee; John E. Beacham (Ossipee) and Annie E. Chick (Ossipee)
Hannah, d. 2/18/1889 at 70; domestic; widow; b. Wolfeboro
John E., d. 7/2/1918 at 75/6/18; farmer; married; b. Wolfeboro; Simon F. Beacham (Ossipee) and Louisa W. Young (Tuftonboro)
Sarah, d. 5/11/1909 at 70/2/4 in Ossipee; paralysis heart; housekeeper; b. Ossipee; Simon Beacham (Ossipee) and Lovye W. Young (Tuftonboro)
Simeon F., d. 5/24/1893 at 86/1 in Ossipee; farmer; widower; b. Ossipee; R. Beacham (Ossipee) and Hannah Pitman (Ossipee)
Sophia M., d. 1/28/1926 at 52/5/10; b. Wolfeboro; Mark Avery and Dorcas Nute
Winifred E., d. 3/27/1951 at 88/4/12 in Haverhill, MA; b. VT; Union Durant and Sophia Randall

BEAN,
daughter, d. 8/16/1894 at 0/0/0 in Ossipee; stillborn; b. Ossipee; Charles S. Bean (Ossipee) and Clara Abbott (Wolfeboro)
child, d. 4/5/1932 at – in Ossipee; b. Ossipee; Ernest D. Bean and Marion Welch
Ada, d. 4/12/1936 at 87/11/13 in Ossipee; b. Chatham; Joseph Ware and Mary Jane Chick
Addie, d. 5/31/1955 at 90 in Concord; b. NH; Joseph Glidden and Elizabeth Johnson
Anna G., d. 1/16/1952 at 77/3/0 in Moultonboro; b. Ossipee; ----- Nichols and Caroline Eldridge
Beatrice Pearl, d. 1/10/1994 at 90; Charles Converse and Annie Angus
Carlyn V., d. 6/7/2000 in Manchester; Wilbur Freethy and Lula Kenney
Charles L., d. 6/14/1922 at 63/2/6 in Ossipee; farmer; married; b. Ossipee; John Bean (Ossipee) and Sarah Welch (Ossipee)
Charles S., d. 1/19/1911 at 53/5/16; pneumonia; farmer; married; b. Tuftonboro; Stephen Bean (Tuftonboro) and Martha J. Abbott (Ossipee)
Clara B., d. 11/19/1958 at 86 in Wolfeboro; b. Ossipee; Charles Abbott and Almira Richardson
Clyde, Sr., d. 11/6/1966 at 54 in Wolfeboro; b. Ossipee

Dana H., d. 7/7/1951 at 86/6/19 in Ossipee; b. Ossipee; Stephen Bean and Martha Abbott

Ella F., d. 4/27/1941 at 87/6/3 in Ossipee; b. Ossipee; Elisha Hanson and Dorcas Hanson

Ernest D., Jr., d. 5/23/1935 at 3/1 in Moultonville; b. Moultonville; Ernest D. Bean and Marion M. Welch

Frank John, Sr., d. 11/28/2000 at 95 in Ossipee; John Bean and Clara Horne

Fred E., d. 4/4/1934 at 72/1/17 in Ossipee; b. Ossipee; Stephen Bean and Mary A. Abbott

Fred E., d. 2/9/1940 at 69/10/20 in Rochester; b. Eaton; Henry Bean and Victoria Harriman

George E., d. 6/9/1912 at 33/9/8

George F., d. 2/19/1900 at 71/7/15 in Tuftonboro; cystitis; farmer; married; b. Tuftonboro; James Bean

Harold, d. 11/14/1960 at 56 in Ossipee; b. Ossipee

Horace, d. 8/10/1904 at – in Rochester; accident; brakeman

Ira G., d. 12/26/1920 at 63/5/6; farmer; married; b. Tuftonboro; George F. Bean (Tuftonboro) and Sarah F. Abbott (Tuftonboro)

Irving T., d. 7/6/1902 at 36/6/4 in Ossipee; pulmonary tuberculosis; shoecutter; married; b. Ossipee; Thomas M. Bean and Joanna White

Joanna, d. 10/4/1900 at – in Haverhill; cancer breast; married

John, d. 12/21/1906 at 76/9/3 in Ossipee; abscess of antrum; farmer; widower; John Bean (Ossipee) and Lydia Welch (Ossipee)

Joseph, d. 2/18/1934 at 76/0/3 in Ossipee; b. Canada

Joseph B., d. 5/19/1954 at 89 in Ossipee; b. N. Haverhill

Lena, d. 3/6/1899 at 0/8/24 in Ossipee; tonsilitis; b. Ossipee; Fred Bean (Eaton) and Georgina Nichols (Ossipee)

Lillian Mae, d. 8/7/1938 at 0/0/25 in Ossipee; b. Wolfeboro; Clyde Bean and Hazel Downing

Luella J., d. 1/4/1930 at 44/11 in Boston, MA; b. Ossipee; Edward Willand and Betsy Brown

Margaret, d. 4/23/1943 at 1/10/12 in Wolfeboro; b. Wolfeboro; Ernest Bean and Marion Welch

Martha J., d. 12/11/1910 at 78/3/25 in Ossipee; heart disease mitral; housewife; widow; b. Ossipee; Solomon Abbott (Ossipee) and Dorcas Chick (Ossipee)

Mary E., d. 10/6/1888 at 31; domestic; single; b. Tuftonboro; Nehemiah Bean and Rosanah Bean

Mary Fredline, d. 2/23/1989 at 78 in Ossipee; b. Amesbury, MA

Maud, d. 1/9/1898 at 2/0/28 in Ossipee; measles; b. Ossipee; Fred Bean (Eaton) and Annie Nichols (Ossipee)

Milton L. H., d. 9/5/1981 at 75 in Ossipee; b. Tuftonboro

Raymond, d. 5/19/1980 at 82 in Ossipee; b. NH

Sarah F., d. 10/23/1903 at 70/6/16 in Tuftonboro; chronic gastritis; housewife; widow; b. Sandwich; Gafton Abbott and Catherine Frye

Shirley, d. 8/24/1911 at 0/6/21; cholera infantum; b. Ossipee; Lisle Moore (Milton) and Rena Bean (Ossipee)

BEANE,
George O., d. 3/8/1925 at 76/3/5; b. Moultonboro; H. Beane and R. Horn

BEAUPRE,
Gordon A., d. 12/8/2001 in Wolfeboro; Arnold Beaupre and Mabel Russell

BECKETT,
Marguerite May, d. 8/19/2000 at 74 in Ossipee; Arthur Saybe and Lea Robinson

BECKMAN,
Mabel L., d. 7/18/1963 at 84 in Ossipee; b. W. Newfield, ME

BEDELL,
Frank, d. 12/18/1898 at 51 in Ossipee; marasmus; married; b. Conway

BELANGER,
Jo-Ann, d. 2/18/1999 at 57 in Wolfeboro; Leigh Hughes and Cecile Gagnon

BELDING,
Ella Octavia, d. 7/4/1984 at 94 in Ossipee; b. Italy

BELL,
Bruce K., d. 2/23/1986 at 50 in Ossipee; b. E. Conway
Denise Elizabeth, d. 1/24/1997 at 41 in Lebanon; Roger K. Bickford and Agnes Ryan
Robert Charles, d. 4/17/1996 at 23 in Dover; Robert Lee Bell and Lucinda White

BELLEFEUILLE,
Albert, d. 4/26/1957 at 47 in Hanover; b. Manchester; Albert Bellefeuille and Lucy Avery

BELLEROSE,
Arthur W., d. 7/23/1990 at 71 in Hanover; b. Lincoln

BEMIS,
Grace Lowd, d. 1/23/1977 at 45 in Ossipee; b. NH

BENGE,
Arthur E., d. 7/15/1970 at 65 in Wolfeboro; b. MA
Benjamin, d. 10/3/1946 at 84/7/1 in Ossipee; b. Sussex, England; David Benge and Elizabeth Benge
Gladys W., d. 1/21/1982 at 79 in Wolfeboro; b. Ossipee

BENKER,
Florence Frieda, d. 10/4/1994 at 67; George R. Gordon and Florence Crawford

BENNETT,
son, d. 11/4/1908 at 0/0/1 in Ossipee; premature birth; b. Ossipee; A. Bennett and Lilla -----
son, d. 5/24/1939 at 0/0/7 in Wolfeboro; b. Wolfeboro; Russell E. Bennett and Gretchen E. Goldsmith
Charles, d. 2/24/1969 at 97 in Ossipee; b. NH
Elden, d. 10/10/1906 at 55/11 in Ossipee; arterio sclerosis; farmer; married; b. Sandwich; Abner Bennett (Sandwich) and Sally Worthing
Eleanor G., d. 1/31/1965 at 74 in Ossipee; b. Boston, MA
Ella A., d. 11/15/1930 at 82/11/5 in Ossipee; b. Tamworth; Joseph Tewksbury and Naomi Head
Gaynelle Ardenia, d. 5/6/1998 in Ossipee; Lewis E. Bennett and Alice M. Stevens
Hester Rose, d. 12/13/1992 at 91 in Ossipee; b. Alton
James M., d. 10/30/1906 at 67 in Ossipee; enteritis; single; b. Albany
Jennie W., d. 1/2/1903 at 27/7 in Portland; pulmonary tuberculosis; married
Maurice P., d. 1/3/1979 at 95 in Ossipee; b. NH
Olin E., d. 7/10/1915 at 45
Rose A., d. 10/2/1944 at 66/0/14 in Ossipee; b. Freedom; James Wood and Francenia Dube
Russell E., d. 9/11/2001 in Laconia; Sumner Bennett and Rose Wood
Sumner L., d. 7/17/1950 at 68 in Wolfeboro; b. Ossipee; Alden Bennett and Ella Tewksbury

BENOIT,
Jeannette Mary, d. 8/20/1994 at 70; Arthur Burgess, Sr. and Maud Hanson

BENTON,
Harold E., d. 2/18/1968 at 68 in Ossipee; b. NH

BENZING,
Constance Louise, d. 2/4/1989 at 81 in Ossipee; b. Salt Lake City, UT

BERRY,
Alice E., d. 7/6/1970 at 77 in Ossipee; b. NH
Dwight W., d. 8/25/1957 at 12 in Laconia; b. Wolfeboro; Ernest Berry and Phyllis Merrow
Ernest M., Sr., d. 7/1/1989 at 80 in Wolfeboro; b. Ossipee
Florence E., d. 12/12/1977 at 72 in Ossipee; b. NH
George, d. 4/14/1930 at 72 in Ossipee; b. Sandwich
Gladys Mable, d. 12/17/1996 at 90 in W. Ossipee; John P. Eldridge and Emma P. Welch
Hardy W., d. 12/3/1928 at 43/0/21; b. NS; Charles Berry and Emma Tamper
Henry E., d. 7/22/1952 at 48/10/8 in Ossipee; b. Ossipee; Herman Berry and Margarete Holly
Henry S., d. 3/21/1914 at 66/4/26; cook; b. Tamworth; Daniel Berry (Tamworth) and Irene Hyde
Irene Agnes, d. 2/7/1909 at 3/2/2 in Ossipee; la grippe; b. Ossipee; Herman Berry (Tamworth) and Margaret Hodge (Ireland)
Leonard, d. 11/26/1911 at 56; valvular dis. of heart; married; b. Wells, ME
Margaret H., d. 11/5/1945 at 72/3/9 in Ossipee; b. Waterford, Ireland; Morris Holly
Phyllis M., d. 6/15/1976 at 59 in Wolfeboro; b. NH
Ralph, d. 1/17/1983 at 84 in Ossipee; b. Conway
Raymond Elliott, d. 10/26/1985 at 75 in N. Conway; b. Tamworth
Sarah E., d. 6/5/1919 at 59/10/1; housework; single; b. Portland, ME; William M. Berry (ME) and Mary Deland (Portland, ME)
Sarah J., d. 4/6/1930 at 79 in Ossipee; b. Alton; George D. Garland and Mary J. Bickford
Teresa E., d. 10/11/1977 at 66 in Wolfeboro; b. NH

BERTON,
Frances L., d. 8/8/1975 at 62 in Laconia; b. NH
Robert E., d. 4/28/1974 at 46 in Ossipee; b. MA

BERTWELL,
Abbie E., d. 7/9/1914 at –
Ann M., d. 12/19/1887 at 60 in Ossipee; domestic; married; b. Ossipee
George, d. 9/25/1894 at – in Ossipee; softening of the brain; single; b. Ossipee; Robinson Bertwell (England) and Hannah Dickey (Acworth)
Robinson, d. 10/25/1891 at 80 in Ossipee; farmer; widower; ----- (England) and ----- (Ossipee)

BERZETY,
Ethel Gertrude, d. 6/4/1989 at 80 in N. Conway; b. Yonkers, NY

BEYER,
William G., d. 7/8/1965 at 34 in Ossipee; b. Bellerose, NY

BEYERSTEDT,
Fred J., d. 11/21/1973 at 65 in Wolfeboro; b. WI

BEZANSON,
George V., d. 5/14/1965 at 94 in Ossipee; b. Halifax, NS

BICKFORD,
son, d. 5/25/1898 at 0/0/1 in Ossipee; premature birth; b. Ossipee; Belmont Bickford and Dora Bickford
Alonzo, d. 12/17/1922 at 69/2/20 in Concord; farmer; widower; b. Ossipee; Stephen Bickford (Somersworth) and Hannah Young
Angela L., d. 6/14/1957 at 62 in Dover; b. Pottstown, PA; Peter Richter and Amelia -----
Ann F., d. 5/22/1922 at 76/10/26 in Ossipee; housewife; married; b. Ossipee; Hollis Emerson (VT) and Mercy Abbott (Ossipee)
Belmont E., d. 4/14/1935 at 75/2/21 in Ossipee; b. Ossipee; Edward R. Bickford and Melissa Thompson
Blanche I., d. 7/31/1999 at 91 in Ossipee; Perley A. Jenness and Blanche I. Weeks
Charles, d. 2/15/1918 at 69; farmer; married; b. Ossipee; Stephen Bickford and Hannah Young
Edith C., d. 2/22/2001 in Wolfeboro; William Brown and Mable Schultz
Edward B., d. 10/13/1904 at 85/5 in Ossipee; old age; farmer; widower; b. Ossipee; John Bickford (Somersworth) and Rachel Austin (Somersworth)
Eleanor Helen, d. 2/2/1998 in Ossipee; Luther Kenney and Helen Lucy
Emma, d. 12/24/1887 at 35 in Ossipee; domestic; married; b. Ossipee; John F. Abbott (Ossipee)
Grace E., d. 1/19/1990 at 98 in Ossipee; b. Wells, ME
Harry E., d. 4/25/1949 at 71 in Wolfeboro; b. Gonic; Daniel C. Bickford and Sarah B. Downing
James, d. 3/4/1894 at 81 in Ossipee; cerebral hemorrhage; widower; b. Ossipee
Leon, d. 9/22/1973 at 62 in Ossipee; b. NH
Lucy G., d. 7/9/1908 at 11/5/1 in Ossipee; convulsions; b. Ossipee; George Bickford (Tamworth) and Edith Cook (Wolfeboro)
Melissa, d. 4/3/1896 at 73/9/26 in Ossipee; apoplexy; housekeeper; married; Samuel Thompson
Rosanna, d. 1/21/1902 at 73 in Ossipee; caranoma altesi; housewife; widow; b. Moultonboro; Ebenezer Horne (Moultonboro) and Annie ----- (Moultonboro)
Stella Crawford, d. 9/26/1988 at 93 in Ossipee; b. N. Holderness

Stephen, d. 6/13/1898 at 85 in Ossipee; regurgitation; farmer; married; b. Dover; James Bickford

BIERWEILER,
Elizabeth Agnes, d. 10/18/1977 at 84 in Rochester; b. Canada
Frederick, d. 2/10/1976 at 84 in Rochester; b. MA
Mark C., d. 9/13/2000 in Wolfeboro; Robert Bierweiler and Barbara Conery

BIGGS,
Charles Robert, d. 2/7/1984 at 91 in Ossipee; b. Wakefield, MA
Isabelle L., d. 1/25/1975 at 81 in Ossipee; b. MA
Robert Goodhue, d. 6/16/1994 at 73; Charles R. Biggs and Isabelle Lowell

BILADEAU,
John, d. 8/18/1889 at 0/2/6; b. Ossipee; John Biladeau and Naitiessie Lewis

BILAPKA,
Helen M., d. 4/29/1987 at 83 in Ossipee; b. Brighton, MA

BILLINGS,
Debra A., d. 10/15/1998 in Laconia; Clarence R. Plummer, Jr. and Louise Underhill

BISBEE,
Chester A., d. 10/31/1967 at 84 in Wolfeboro; b. Parsonsfield, ME
Mary R., d. 6/29/1987 at 74 in Wolfeboro; b. Alfred, ME
Mildred E., d. 1/23/1981 at 77 in Wolfeboro; b. Newburyport, MA
Roberta G., d. 2/3/1931 at 49/4/2 in Lawrence, MA; b. Ossipee; Oscar Goldsmith and Ella F. Bean
Roscoe A., d. 9/14/1919 at 80/4/5; farmer; widower; b. Saco, ME; E. Bisbee and A. Brayton (Eaton)
Wilbur, d. 2/29/1976 at 73 in Wolfeboro; b. NH

BISSON,
Juliette Theresa, d. 5/22/1996 at 62 in Ossipee; Oliva Dusseault and Clarinia Gagnon

BLACKEY,
Albert R., d. 5/21/1925 at 90/5/13; b. Meredith; John Blackey and Betsey Bryant
Daniel, d. 9/6/1922 at 73/4/5 in Ossipee; farmer; single; b. Sandwich; Ira Blackey (VT) and Sarah Smart (NH)

Elsa, d. 9/4/1890 at 74 in Ossipee; exhaustion from insanity; widow; b. Linden, VT

Julia A., d. 2/8/1925 at 86; b. Moultonboro; Henry Smith and Sarah Goodwin

Samuel, d. 3/1/1890 at 72 in Ossipee; enteritis; domestic (sic); married; b. Sandwich

BLAIR,
Robert, Jr., d. 9/27/1922 at 42 in Ossipee; postmaster; married; b. Ireland; Robert Blair (Ireland) and Mary A. Dunlap (Ireland)

BLAISDELL,
Gertie, d. 10/4/1894 at 0/0/15 in Ossipee; pneumonia; Irving Blaisdell (Boston) and Jennie Linscott (Porter, ME)

BLAKE,
Kenneth, d. 5/11/1970 at 21 in Portland; b. ME
Mabel E., d. 12/7/1966 at 93 in Ossipee; b. Ossipee
Mayra Mae, d. 11/11/1989 at 96 in Ossipee; b. Waltham, MA
Pauline C., d. 11/2/1981 at 59 in Wolfeboro; b. Biddeford, ME
Sarah, d. –/–/1897 at 76 in Ossipee; bronchitis and heart disease
Simon, d. 5/16/1929 at 70/1/19 in Ossipee; b. Ossipee; Thomas J. Blake and Sarah Williams

BLAKELEY,
Acil, d. 6/8/1966 at 86 in Wolfeboro; b. NS
Florence M., d. 5/17/1963 at 58 in Wolfeboro; b. Framingham, MA

BLAKELY,
Lila L., d. 10/21/1959 at 93 in Ossipee; b. Reading, MI; Amos Bartholomew and Abbie Van Buren

BLANCHARD,
William A., d. 8/3/1943 at 69/5/24 in Wolfeboro; b. Keene; ----- Blanchard and Mamie Smith

BLOMSTROM,
Oscar M., d. 2/10/1989 at 81 in Wolfeboro; b. Westwood, MA

BLOOD,
Mary, d. 4/9/1890 at 70 in Ossipee; dysentery; domestic; widow; b. Ossipee

BLY,
Charles, d. 6/9/1967 at 81 in Ossipee; b. Brentwood

BOARDMAN,
Forrest C., d. 9/3/1971 at 85 in Wolfeboro; b. ME

BODGE,
Abbie M., d. 6/20/1955 at 90/7/2 in Somerville, MA; b. ME; James Crowley and Nancy Wiggin
James, d. 11/20/1938 at 75/10/15 in Ossipee; b. Ossipee; James S. Bodge and Betsy H. Goodwin
Maude F., d. 5/18/1947 at 62/7/18 in Ossipee; b. Ossipee; James Hanson and Apphia Dore
Walter, d. 8/2/1955 at 78 in Wolfeboro; b. NH; James Goodwin and Betsy Goodwin

BODWELL,
daughter, d. 10/25/1960 at – in Wolfeboro; b. Wolfeboro
Emily F., d. 9/9/1984 at 59 in Wolfeboro; b. Effingham

BOEHME,
Joseph Thomas, d. 9/9/2000 at 89 in Ossipee; Edmund Boehme and Charlotte Robbins

BONNEY,
Catherine, d. 5/4/1912 at 82/0/29; housekeeper; married; b. NB; John Tracy (NB) and Elizabeth Bailey (NB)
David D., d. 4/26/1915 at 92/7/16; mill operator; married; b. Cutler, ME; Abiel Bonney and Mary Sparks

BOOMER,
Jane H., d. 9/23/1975 at 87 in Wolfeboro; b. MA
Stephen Henry, d. 12/23/1989 at 95 in Wolfeboro; b. Westbrook, ME

BORG,
Lillian, d. 11/22/1991 at 82 in Wolfeboro; b. Phillipston, MA

BORGATTI,
Lorraine E., d. 10/15/2000 in Wolfeboro; Angelo Borgatti and Albina Bouley

BORGES,
Ralph A., d. 6/4/1987 at 74 in Wolfeboro; b. Whitman, MA

BOSTON,
Will F., d. 10/23/1959 at 75 in Ossipee; b. Brookfield; Henry Boston and Susan Drew

BOTTING,
Edmund H., d. 12/11/1988 at 58 in Ossipee; b. Ashland, ME

BOUCHER,
Ernest J., d. 6/30/1955 at 78 in Laconia; b. Canada; Julius Boucher
Ernest J., d. 12/10/1979 at 73 in Concord; b. MA
Stanley Julias, d. 5/21/1985 at 80 in Ossipee; b. Pelham

BOUCHICAS,
Paul George, d. 2/27/1999 at 84 in Ossipee; George Buchikos and Maude Hamel

BOURQUE,
Viola L., d. 2/17/1988 at 87 in Ossipee; b. Halifax, NS

BOUSQUET,
Ellen, d. 1/15/1955 at 85/3/15 in Ossipee; b. Valcourt, PQ; Warren Woodward
Herve, d. 8/24/1984 at 85 in Ctr. Ossipee; b. Suncook
Joseph O., d. 10/15/1951 at 82 in Concord; b. Canada; Frank Bousquet and Emelia Stebbins
Peter S., d. 8/20/1960 at 59 in Manchester; b. Allentown

BOUTIN,
Harold Raymond, d. 8/22/1989 at 62 in Wolfeboro; b. Dover

BOWERS,
Karen M., d. 8/22/1975 at 6 weeks in Ossipee; b. MA

BOWLEND,
Lillian M., d. 2/6/1972 at 84 in Ossipee; b. NY

BOWLEY,
Edgar F., d. 3/1/1933 at 62/5/15 in Ossipee; b. Wakefield

BOYCE,
Charles S., d. 2/21/1960 at 89 in Ossipee; b. Stoneham, MA

BOYD,
Harry L., d. 8/10/2001 in Ossipee; ----- Boyd

BOYLE,
Francis W., d. 6/8/1977 at 69 in Wolfeboro; b. MA

BRACK,
Albert P., d. 10/4/1973 at 77 in Ossipee; b. MA
Cora F., d. 5/26/1975 at 60 in Wolfeboro; b. NY

BRACKETT,
Ada Gertrude, d. 11/8/1974 at 96 in Ossipee; b. NH
Bertha Leona, d. 4/7/1977 at 69 in Ossipee; b. ME

BRADBURY,
Frank O., d. 4/19/1943 at 81/11/18 in Ossipee; b. Eaton; Fred E. Bradbury and Martha Watson
Lillian Cecelia, d. 9/4/1940 at 72/8/9 in Ossipee; b. Effingham; Charles Taylor and Mary E. Pray

BRADFORD,
Exilda M., d. 8/19/1985 at 76 in Wolfeboro; b. Waterville, ME
William H., d. 12/18/1982 at 79 in Wolfeboro; b. Wolfeboro

BRADLEY,
Edwin K., Jr., d. 3/9/1979 at 48 in Conway; b. PA
George, d. 9/4/1912 at 67; farmer; married; b. St. John, NB; George Bradley

BRAHM,
Walter J., d. 10/9/1980 at 72 in Wolfeboro; b. MA

BRAINERD,
Flora D., d. 11/3/1996 at 71 in Portland, ME; Joseph Coppeta and Emilia Zona

BRANT,
Frank, d. 3/20/1944 at 78/8/25 in Ossipee; b. Weymouth, MA

BRASIER,
Everett H., d. 5/28/1968 at 72 in Wolfeboro; b. ME
Helen Hovey, d. 6/22/1949 at 79 in Wolfeboro; b. Abbott, ME; Thomas Hovey and Maria Works
Margaret Ann, d. 1/16/1998 in Medway, MA; Stephen McDonald and Margaret Keenan

BREED,
John L., d. 11/8/1999 in Ossipee; Frank Breed and Belle Chapman
Vera M., d. 11/2/2001 in Ossipee; Frederick Schultz and Maude Splaine

BRETT,
Lionel M., d. 7/13/1967 at 79 in Ossipee; b. Boston, MA

BREWSTER,
Annie Irene, d. 1/22/1984 at 90 in Ossipee; b. Fredericton, NB

BRIAR,
George, d. 12/27/1895 at 40 in Ossipee; hepatic cirrhosis; carpenter; married

BRIDGES,
John S., d. 9/4/1931 at 62/4/7 in Ossipee; b. Castine, ME; John R. Bridges and Nancy Ann Black

BRIGGS,
Albert E., d. 3/9/1950 at 78/4/26 in Wolfeboro; b. W. Dighton, MA; John A. Briggs and Mary Ellen Talbot
Alma M., d. 10/2/1946 at 72/9/2 in Ossipee; b. NS; John Brown and ----- Sanford
Arthur, d. 7/26/1952 at 76 in Ossipee; b. Wolfeboro; George Briggs and Ada Brown
Everett, d. 8/25/1961 at 84 in Ossipee; b. Wolfeboro

BRISSETTE,
Arlene Clayton, d. 2/12/1995 at 80; George H. Browne and Virginia Clayton

BROLIN,
Charles, d. 2/10/1998 in Ossipee

BROOK,
Edith M., d. 5/4/1983 at 103 in Ossipee; b. Saugus, MA

BROOKS,
Annie J., d. 5/12/1958 at 78 in Rochester; b. England; William Harrison and Margaret Carrick
Arthur, d. 7/16/1946 at 78/5/29 in Ossipee; b. Freedom; Charles H. Brooks and Hannah Moore
Arthur A., d. 10/21/1956 at 66/9/2 in Ossipee; b. Amherst, NS; Frederick Brooks and Rebecca Greene

Gardner, d. 10/27/1916 at 85/10/13; none [occupation]; widower; b. Ossipee; John Brooks

Grace Knowles, d. 6/4/1997 at 91 in Wolfeboro; Josiah A. Knowles and Avis Tufts

Jessie E., d. 9/26/1986 in ME; b. 10/1913

Myrtle E., d. 11/22/1968 at 74 in Wolfeboro; b. MA

Willard Wilfred, d. 2/1/1997 at 75 in Wolfeboro; Ralph Brooks and Hattie Stuart

William, d. 11/1/1955 at 71 in Farmington; b. England; Daniel Brooks and Comfort Marsh

BROWN,
Addie Priscilla, d. 9/4/1975 at 79 in Ossipee; b. ME
Adelbert L., d. 7/12/1955 at 79 in Rochester; b. NY
Angie E., d. 7/1/1949 at 77/10/16 in Ossipee; b. Freedom; William Moses and Sarah J. Wilkinson
Anna M., d. 6/10/1955 at 80 in Union; b. England; Daniel Brooks and Comfort Marsh
Archie D., d. 12/23/1977 at 79 in Ossipee; b. NH
Arthur M., d. 5/20/1962 at 83 in Wolfeboro; b. Fremont
Benjamin O., d. 2/19/1905 at 75 in Ossipee; cancer lower jaw; single; b. Ossipee; Adam T. Brown and Alice Hipson
Bernard N., d. 7/1/1985 at 89 in Ossipee; b. Tuftonboro
Bessie M., d. 7/16/1947 at 68/7 in Ossipee; b. Freedom; Alonzo Pease and Mary Jane Moses
Betsey E. W., d. 1/18/1908 at 90/6/11 in Ossipee; cerebral hemorrhage; housewife; b. Brookfield; Eliphalet Willey and Sally Henderson
Caroline, d. 7/14/1919 at 83/8/29; housekeeper; widow; b. Tuftonboro; Kinsley L. Wiggin (Tuftonboro) and ----- Demerritt (Tuftonboro)
Carroll Grant, d. 11/13/1990 at 84 in Ossipee; b. Sandwich
Charles L., d. 1/25/1909 at 57/5/9 in Ossipee; paralysis of heart; farmer; b. Ossipee; J. Loring Brown (Ossipee) and Hannah E. Hersey (Tuftonboro)
Charles W., d. 6/7/1985 at 91 in Ossipee; b. Ipswich, MA
Claire I., d. 4/17/1983 at 55 in Portsmouth; b. Andover, MA
Clyde Herbert, d. 3/21/1993 at 92 in Wolfeboro
Dan, d. 6/5/1952 at 82/4/3 in Ossipee; b. Portland, ME; Royal Brown and Cristy Ward
Dana J., d. 11/18/1940 at 81/5/10 in Ossipee; b. Ossipee; Jacob F. Brown and Betsey Willey
David, d. 1/28/1929 at 85 in Ossipee; b. Sandwich; Stephen Brown and Mary Brier
Edmund K., d. 12/3/1954 at 90 in Concord; b. Ossipee; Edmund Brown
Edna A., d. 12/24/1940 at 71/8/12 in Ossipee; b. Ossipee; William Dame and Carrie Dame

Elizabeth P., d. 6/20/1954 at 79/0/11 in Wolfeboro; b. Wenham, MA
Ellen, d. 4/19/1939 at 84/7/3 in Ossipee; b. Strafford, ME; Elden Hayes and Abigail Pitman
Ellsworth E., d. 1/12/1981 at 51 in Ossipee; b. Brownfield, ME
Elmer, d. 3/4/1974 at 85 in Ossipee; b. NH
Eugene F., d. 12/2/1931 at 84/11/14 in Ossipee; b. Ossipee; Jacob F. Brown and Betsy E. Willey
Francis K., d. 1/31/1892 at 75 in Ossipee; pneumonia; farmer; married; b. Ossipee; Adam T. Brown
Fred, d. 5/25/1944 at 74/8/9 in Ossipee; b. Ossipee; John Brown and Cellestia Willard
Fred H., d. 2/3/1955 at 75 in Somersworth; b. NH; Dana Brown and Nellie Allen
Fred R., d. 9/21/1944 at 65/10/4 in Westmoreland; b. Ossipee; Francis Brown and Sarah Wentworth
George W., d. 4/13/1953 at 86 in Wakefield; b. Tamworth
Gertie M., d. 5/23/1888 at 15/0; b. Ossipee; Herbert Brown and Charlotte Harmon
Harry R., d. 6/13/1962 at 77 in Wolfeboro; b. Ossipee
James L., d. 7/21/1903 at 85/4/11 in Ossipee; inflammation of bladder; farmer; widower; b. Ossipee
John M., d. 12/23/1923 at 77/4/28; b. Northwood; John F. Brown and ----- Carter
Judigh Berry, d. 7/26/1997 at 63 in W. Ossipee; Wendell H. Berry and Eleanor Stedman
Leslie, d. 7/4/1950 at 45 in Concord; b. CT; Leslie Sargent and Etta Hanson
Levi W., d. 6/3/1915 at 81/3/10; farmer; married; b. Ossipee; James Brown (Ossipee) and Rebecca Pray (Brownfield, ME)
Lowel, d. 5/19/1918 at 74; b. Ossipee
Lucinda W., d. 7/10/1958 at 77 in Wolfeboro; b. Boston, MA; William Crosby and Ida Blanchard
Mabel F., d. 1/31/1963 at 89 in Ossipee; b. Portland, ME
Margaret, d. 1/2/1892 at 79/5 in Ossipee; la grippe; housewife; widow; b. Ossipee
Mary E., d. 8/23/1919 at 70/7/18; housewife; married; b. Ossipee; Thomas Peavey (Ossipee) and Deborah Sherburn (Rochester)
Mary J., d. 2/6/1903 at 46 in Ossipee; cerebral softening; single; b. Ossipee; Benjamin C. Brown
Muriel G., d. 10/5/1918 at 17/2/29; scholar; single; b. Ossipee; Tom H. Brown (Ossipee) and Bessie Pease (Freedom)
Nancy J., d. 8/3/1978 at 22 in Hanover; b. NH
Nellie A., d. 9/19/1951 at 91 in Ossipee; b. Ossipee; Elisha Allen and Eunice Becham

Olive J., d. 10/15/1928 at 82/4/11; b. Ossipee; Hiram S. Ricker and Irene Ricker

Owen, d. 8/28/1891 at 27/0/19 in Ossipee; farmer; single; b. Ossipee; Francis K. Brown (Ossipee) and S. F. Wentworth (Ossipee)

Porter W., d. 2/8/1910 at 82/2 in Ossipee; old age; farmer; single; b. Wolfeboro; Moses P. Brown (Wolfeboro) and Lydia V. Quarles (Ossipee)

Rhoda, d. 9/11/1887 at 76 in Ossipee; housewife; married

Rosie A., d. 5/7/1929 at 75 in Ossipee; b. Tamworth; —— Smith

Sarah, d. 12/4/1925 at 88/9/17; b. Ossipee; Moses W. Brown and Abbgil Peabody

Sarah F., d. 8/–/1913 at 71/9/19

Susan, d. 6/15/1903 at 64 in Ossipee; epileptic convulsions; married; b. Sandwich

Tom H., d. 11/27/1954 at 79 in Wolfeboro; b. Ossipee; Herbert Brown and Charlot Hammond

BROWNELL,
Benjamin F., d. 5/23/1891 at 69 in Ossipee; married; b. Ossipee; Thomas Brownell and Lucy Sherman

Clara L., d. 1/10/1985 at 93 in Wolfeboro; b. Thetford Mines, PQ

Edwin Philip, d. 1/21/1997 at 63 in Ctr. Ossipee; Clifford Raymond Brownell and Barbara Marrow

Harold Parker, d. 9/14/1995 at 79; David Brownell and Clara Parker

Harriet, d. 2/26/1890 at 60 in Ossipee; pneumonia; housewife; married; b. Nantucket, MA

Ingrid Hinz, d. 10/23/1997 at 71 in Ctr. Ossipee; Friedrich Hinz and Else Gollnast

Keith Warren, d. 8/2/1990 at 43 in Wolfeboro; b. Wolfeboro

Martha, d. 3/30/1958 at 84 in Westbrook, ME; b. Ossipee; Daniel Hanson and Martha Clough

BRUGMAN,
Francis A., d. 10/4/1984 at 76 in Ossipee; b. E. Boston, MA

BRYANT,
Almon O., d. 11/15/1964 at 92 in Ossipee; b. Effingham

Alvin, d. 7/1/1891 at 77 in Ossipee; farmer; widower

Elva W., d. 9/10/1959 at 75 in Wolfeboro; b. Ossipee; Lyford Welch and Lizzie Eldridge

James, d. 12/27/1927 at 63; b. Eaton

Josephine S., d. 8/23/1984 at 86 in Ossipee; b. Lawrence, MA

Lester A., d. 2/18/1908 at 3/11/7 in Ossipee; pernicious anemia; b. Ossipee; Almon Bryant (Effingham) and Daisy Bisbee (Effingham)

Perley A., d. 7/31/1966 at 76 in Ossipee; b. Eaton

BRYDEN,
Marjorie Wood, d. 12/12/1978 at 82 in Ossipee; b. MA

BRYSON,
Helen Mary, d. 12/29/1996 at 89 in Ossipee; Albert Ludwig and Clara Beck

BRZEZINSKE,
Joseph J., d. 2/27/1987 at 49 in Wolfeboro; b. Ipswich, MA

BRZEZNSKI,
Edythe Carole, d. 3/29/1988 at 51 in Ossipee; b. Beverly, MA

BUCHANAN,
Ralph Richard, d. 5/2/2001 in Ossipee; John Kotomski and Annie Joiolkoniske

BUCKINGHAM,
Eva Katherine, d. 6/15/1993 at 86 in Ossipee

BUCKLEY,
Diantha, d. 11/9/1914 at 76; b. Stoneham, ME

BUCKMAN,
Fannie P., d. 12/22/1973 at 87 in Ossipee; b. NY

BUCKNAM,
Gilbert, d. 3/13/1919 at 5/5/20; b. Lynn, MA; William L. Bucknam (Lynn, MA) and Mabel C. Fisher (Cambridge, MA)

BUDROE,
daughter, d. 6/21/1910 at 0/0/1 in Ossipee; premature birth; b. Ossipee; Joseph Budroe (Conway) and Bertha Welch (Ossipee)
Walter S., d. 8/19/1985 at 65 in Ossipee; b. Conway

BUMSTEAD,
Mildred F., d. 5/8/1985 at 84 in Ossipee; b. Charlestown, MA

BUNCE,
Marjorie V., d. 2/5/1961 at 58 in Ossipee; b. Chelsea, VT

BUNKER,
Frank E., d. 5/19/1954 at 49 in Ossipee; b. Tamworth; Fred Bunker and Elsie Davis
Laura, d. 7/8/1911 at 48; gastric cancer; married; b. Claremont

Priscilla, d. 2/21/1902 at 65 in Ossipee; fracture femur; housewife; widow

BUNNEY,
Isabelle Marie, d. 8/10/1995 at 82; Peter Nadeau and Corrine Boisvert

BURBANK,
Nathaniel, d. 2/5/1890 at 87 in Ossipee; influenxa with pneumonia; domestic (sic); single; b. Wakefield

BURDETTE,
Frank Elliott, d. 6/23/1987 at 63 in Ossipee; b. Detroit, MI

BURGER,
Arthur T., d. 8/2/1977 at 81 in Laconia; b. NY
Barbara Aiken, d. 3/18/1997 at 86 in Dover; Zoeth A. Sherman and Elsie Rogers

BURGESS,
Lloyd J., d. 3/14/1980 at 69 in Ossipee; b. NH

BURKE,
John F., d. 7/21/1982 at 73 in Wolfeboro; b. Charlestown, MA
Kathleen M., d. 8/8/2001 in Ossipee; John Nelson and Anne Fallon
Mary Adela, d. 12/17/1974 at 82 in Ossipee; b. Canada
Selina Maude, d. 1/4/1988 at 98 in Ossipee; b. Freedom

BURLEIGH,
Arthur S., d. 2/15/1986 at 91 in Ossipee; b. Ossipee
Charles J., d. 3/25/1921 at 57 in Merrimac, MA
Clarissa, d. 12/2/1887 at 73/8 in Ossipee; housewife; widow; b. Wolfeboro
Comfort, d. 2/11/1912 at 80/6/18; b. Ossipee; William Burleigh and Nancy Hodgdon
J. Bradley, d. 5/6/1893 at 77 in Ossipee; carpenter; widower; b. Tuftonboro
Julia, d. 11/15/1911 at 58; syphillis; single; b. Tuftonboro
Julia F., d. 6/25/1913 at 55/11/26; housewife; married; b. Tuftonboro; William N. Roberts (Tuftonboro) and Mary Jackson (Eaton)
Lillian, d. 10/14/1983 at 90 in Ossipee; b. Brooklyn, NY
Mary S., d. 4/2/1895 at 60/7/22 in Ossipee; influenza; housewife; married; b. Wolfeboro; J. W. Bickford (Wolfeboro) and Abra S. Lord (Lebanon)
Samuel, d. 4/6/1896 at – in Ossipee; paralysis of heart; farmer; widower

BURLINGAME,
E. H., d. 8/4/1912 at 75/11; civ. engineer; widower

BURNHAM,
Charles, d. 10/29/1891 at 60 in Ossipee; widower; b. Sandwich

BURNS,
James G., d. 6/25/1995 at 64; Frank Burns and Anna Peck

BUSCH,
Roger H., d. 11/9/2001 in Wolfeboro; Bernard Busch and Margaret Fernholtz

BUSWELL,
daughter, d. 3/29/1971 at – in Wolfeboro; b. NH
Aphia B., d. 8/25/1889 at 0/1/19; b. Ossipee; Isaac Buswell and Jennie M. Gilman
Blanche M., d. 9/3/1986 at 100 in Wolfeboro; b. Ossipee
Catherine C., d. 6/5/1965 at 43 in Wolfeboro; b. Ossipee
Ellis U., d. 8/16/1912 at 65/5/12; carpenter; married; b. Ossipee; Isaac Buswell and Apha Hanson
Evelyn May, d. 2/20/1914 at 0/0/20; b. Ossipee; Walter Buswell (Ossipee) and Lila Locke (Franconia)
Frances Lillian, d. 2/28/1996 at 76 in Ctr. Ossipee; Frank Meserve Sr. and Ruby Ryer
Isaac, d. 4/17/1919 at 69/6/13; stone mason; widower; b. Ossipee; Isaac Buswell (Ossipee) and ----- Hanson (Ossipee)
James, d. 3/14/1891 at – in Ossipee; widower; b. Ossipee
Jennie M., d. 12/9/1916 at 65/5/17; housekeeper; married; b. Ossipee; George F. Gilman (Ossipee) and Mary A. Veazy (Ossipee)
Lester G., d. 10/18/1961 at 80 in Ossipee; b. Ossipee
Mary A., d. 11/9/1931 at 83/5/13 in Ossipee; b. Ossipee; Joseph B. Lewis and Sophronia Lear
Walter, d. 1/29/1932 at 59/2/6 in Ossipee; b. Ossipee; Ellis A. Buswell and Mary A. Lewis

BUTLER,
Agnes A., d. 7/13/1960 at 72 in Laconia; b. Lacross, WI
Edward, d. 6/23/1910 at 70 in Ossipee; senile gangrene; b. Canada
Edwin E., d. 8/28/1955 at 64 in N. Conway; b. NH; Charles Butler and Fannie Miller
Ethel M., d. 10/12/1963 at 88 in Wolfeboro; b. Tuftonboro
Ida V., d. 2/23/1984 at 95 in Ossipee; b. Verplanck, NY

BUTTON,
Deric Frederick, d. 5/28/1999 at 22 in Ossipee; Frederick C. Button and Giovanna C. Dorne

BUZZELL,
Elmira, d. 2/26/1895 at 72 in Ossipee; paralysis of heart; pauper; widow; b. Jackson
Stephen C., d. 5/23/1961 at 79 in Ossipee; b. Stow, ME

CAHILL,
Joseph Francis, d. 8/15/1986 at 88 in Ossipee; b. Boston, MA

CALDER,
Ruth L., d. 3/3/1974 at 59 in Wolfeboro; b. NH

CALHOUN,
John V., d. 4/4/1972 at 85 in Laconia; b. NH
Sybil Pearl, d. 9/11/1995 at 95; William McKeen Sanborn and Etta Mae Wiggin

CALLAN,
Mary Alice, d. 11/24/1996 at 86 in Ossipee; George Bernier and Madeline Litig

CAMERON,
Bruce Halliday, d. 8/2/1993 at 51 in Ossipee

CAMPBELL,
Carolyn, d. 4/5/1966 at 69 in Wolfeboro; b. Boston, MA
George L., d. 1/11/1978 at 83 in Wolfeboro; b. MA
Lemuel, d. 6/11/1939 at 86/5/1 in Wolfeboro; b. NS; Alexander Campbell and Maria L. Mary
Linwood Frank, d. 5/22/2000 at 75 in Ossipee; Clinton W. Campbell and Lucy Ellie Hill
Margaret E., d. 12/27/1938 at 80/8/5 in Wolfeboro; b. McPhersons Mills, NS; John Fraser and Ellen Fraser

CANNEY,
son, d. 3/2/1897 at 0/2/8 in Ossipee; bronchitis; b. Ossipee; Fred M. Canney (Ossipee) and Emma F. Hilton (Ossipee)
son, d. 4/24/1898 at 0/1/5 in Ossipee; convulsions; b. Ossipee; Fred M. Canney (Ossipee) and Emma F. Hilton (Ossipee)
son, d. 8/17/1911 at 1/5; ilio colitis; b. Ossipee; Fred Canney (Ossipee) and Emma F. Hilton (Ossipee)
Carrie, d. 7/29/1942 at 85/3/4 in Ossipee; b. PEI; James Ellis and Agnes Russell
Carrie B., d. 8/1/1914 at 60/0/18; housekeeper; b. Ossipee; Eli Fall (Ossipee) and Eliza Knowles (Samdwich)

Emma F., d. 10/4/1942 at 69/6/2 in Ossipee; b. Ossipee; Smith Hilton and Sarah Bodge
F. Forrest, d. 5/15/1976 at 81 in Laconia; b. NH
Fred M., d. 11/24/1911 at 45; locomotor ataxia; farmer; married; b. Ossipee; Henry Canney (Ossipee) and Sarah Weed
George W., d. 1/20/1910 at 73/7 in Ossipee; pneumonia; farmer; widower; b. Ossipee; Ezra Canney (Tuftonboro) and Mary Nutter (Tuftonboro)
Henry, d. 6/3/1902 at 80/0/14 in Ossipee; cerebral apoplexy; farmer; widower; b. Ossipee; Joshua Canney and Mary -----
Henry, d. 8/27/1908 at 23/11 in Ossipee; pulmonary tuberculosis; b. Everett, MA; Samuel Canney (Ossipee) and Susy Dean (Oxford, ME)
James M., d. 5/28/1891 at 66/11 in Ossipee; millman; widower; b. Ossipee; Barnett Canney and Olive J. Thompson (Ossipee)
John, d. 6/29/1899 at 83/4/12 in Ossipee; mitral regurgitation; widow
Lydia A., d. 10/17/1909 at 77/4/29 in Ossipee; cancer of rectum; housekeeper; b. Somersworth; Solomon Ham (Strafford) and Lydia Gowell (Berwick, ME)
Mary, d. 11/4/1892 at 13/8 in Ossipee; consumption; b. Ossipee; James E. Canney (Ossipee) and Carrie Fall (Ossipee)
Mary A., d. 11/24/1906 at 73/0/13 in Ossipee; cerebral embolism; housewife; married; b. Wolfeboro; Nathaniel Avery (Wolfeboro) and Annie Nute (Wolfeboro)
Sarah A., d. 11/22/1901 at 79/6 in Ossipee; cerebral hemorrhage; married; b. Sandwich; Moses Weed
Wentworth, d. 5/5/1918 at 83; farmer; widower; b. Ossipee; James Canney (Ossipee) and Betsy Beacham (Ossipee)

CANSDALE,
James Harrison, d. 10/6/1994 at 74; James A. Cansdale and Margaret Jane Harrison

CAPELL,
Thomas H., III, d. 7/8/1954 at 6/8/15 in Ossipee; b. Lynn, MA; Thomas H. Capell, Jr. and Catherine Watson

CARBONNEAU,
May, d. 8/14/1974 at 80 in Ossipee; b. NH

CARDOS,
Manuel, Jr., d. 12/30/1996 at 88 in Wolfeboro; Manuel Cardos and Margaret Mellow
Wanda W., d. 3/20/1984 at 71 in Wolfeboro; b. Cambridge, MA

CARDOZA,
Rita B., d. 3/14/2001 in Wolfeboro; Leo Brousseau and Delvina Leclaire

CARLES [see Carter],
Henry C., d. 4/30/1915 at 72/7/9; merchant; widower; b. Ossipee; Sanborn
B. Carter (sic) and Marie Frost (Springvale, ME)

CARLSON,
Robert H., d. 10/8/1985 at 64 in Ossipee; b. New Haven, CT

CARLTON,
Alice M., d. 8/17/1965 at 87 in Ossipee; b. Conway
Bartley A., d. 10/14/1974 at 100 in Wolfeboro; b. VA
Cora B., d. 10/14/1959 at 85 in Ossipee; b. Huntington, VT; Clement St.
    John and Aurila Bachus
Herbert Warren, d. 11/28/1941 at 63/4 in Ossipee; b. Whitefield, ME

CARPENTER,
Louis, d. 6/17/1962 at 74 in Concord; b. Marlboro, MA

CARRO,
Alfred F., d. 8/6/1911 at 0/0/1; cyonosis mana; b. Ossipee; Paul Carro
    (Bangor, ME) and Maud Currier (Gardner, MA)

CARROLL,
William Ignatius, d. 9/5/1972 at 72 in Conway; b. OH

CARROW,
Eric, d. 3/26/1944 at 44/2/11 in Wolfeboro; b. Coventry, VT

CARTER [see Carles],
Alonzo, d. 1/5/1928 at 65; b. Bartlett; Nathaniel Carter and Betsy Brown
Bertha, d. 6/24/1916 at 41; housewife; b. Sandwich; Albert Atwood
    (Sandwich)
Charles Henry, d. 5/30/1938 at 73/9/8 in Wolfeboro; b. Ossipee; Henry
    Clay Carter and Mary Jane Hanson
Emma, d. 1/30/1925 at 59; b. Albany; Jacob Harriman and Sarah Hurd
Harold E., d. 10/18/1982 at 85 in Ossipee; b. Wilmington, MA
I. DeWitt, d. 2/18/1909 at 64 in Ossipee; gun shot accidental; pension
    atty.; b. Ossipee; Sanborn B. Carter (Rochester) and Maria F. Frost
    (Springvale, ME)
James, d. 3/28/1912 at 54; laborer; married; b. Conway
Kathryn E., d. 1/1/1951 at 76 in Wolfeboro; b. MI; John Saunders and
    Harriet Kilton
Mary A. C., d. 1/5/1903 at 72 in Wakefield; widow
Mary J., d. 7/5/1912 at 68/3/6; housewife; married; b. Ossipee; William
    Hanson (Ossipee) and Hannah Abbott (Tuftonboro)

Nettie B., d. 2/7/1903 at 2 in Ossipee; pneumonia; b. Ossipee
William, d. 4/6/1930 at 78/1/21 in Ossipee; b. Newport, VT; William Carter and ----- Whitcomb
Winifred, d. 12/1/2000 at 75 in Ossipee; George Passingham and Margaret Beacon

CARVER,
Eugene T., Jr., d. 11/7/1981 at 55 in Ossipee; b. MA
Joan H., d. 8/25/1987 at 53 in Portland, ME; b. MA
Russell Edward, d. 4/13/1991 at 31 in Ossipee; b. Cambridge, MA

CARVILLE,
Rose Elizabeth, d. 11/23/1973 at 72 in Ossipee; b. MA

CASH,
John H., d. 4/3/1975 at 51 in Wolfeboro; b. ME

CASTINE,
Eugene Howard, d. 1/11/1991 at 56 in Ossipee; b. Proctorsville, VT

CATE,
Dorothea J., d. 2/15/1991 at 78 in Wolfeboro; b. Worcester, MA
Elizabeth E., d. 11/26/1955 at 66/11/29 in Salem, MA; b. MA; George Fletcher and Elvira Marden
George A., d. 8/26/1963 at 86 in Ossipee; b. Dover
Nettie M., d. 11/19/1927 at 58/2/18; b. Wolfeboro

CATTANACH,
John Earle, d. 10/1/2000 at 41 in Ctr. Ossipee; John L. Cattanach and Marilyn Gowell

CAVALLO,
Marion Elizabeth, d. 2/12/2000 at 79 in Ossipee; Arthur P. Meserve and Georgia Noel

CAYEA,
Penny Ann, d. 2/11/2000 at 52 in Ossipee; Douglas Cayea and Virginia Malcolm

CHADBOURN[E],
Chester A., d. 10/12/1889 at 9/8; John Chadbourn and Lydia Chadbourn
John C., d. 6/6/1889 at 50/10/28; laborer; widower; b. Ossipee
W. Irving, d. 8/7/1900 at 24 in Somerville, MA; single

CHADWICK,
Ida A., d. 7/7/1941 at 86/6 in Concord; b. Ossipee; Jacob F. Brown and Bettsy Willie

CHAMBERLAIN,
Annie L., d. 12/12/1954 at 80/3/16 in Ossipee; b. Glasgow, Scotland; James MacDonald and Anne Gutrie
Cora E., d. 4/26/1941 at 73/2/25 in Ossipee; b. Tamworth; David Hayford and Elizabeth Ames
Lester A., d. 8/11/1972 at 97 in Ossipee; b. NH

CHAMBERLIN,
Ivan G., d. 4/4/1936 at 71/9/29 in Ctr. Ossipee; b. Wolfeboro; Joseph W. Chamberlin and Marcia Ann Frost
Joseph W., d. 5/21/1925 at 82/0/4; b. Wolfeboro; John Chamberlin and Lydia Tebbetts
Mary E., d. 2/21/1902 at 78 in Ossipee; adynamia; widow
Othaniel, d. 2/5/1890 at 80 in Ossipee; apoplexy; domestic (sic); widower; b. Conway
Sarah D., d. 12/9/1913 at 66/3/26; housewife; married; b. Moultonboro; Jeremiah Wiggin (NY) and Betsy Williams (Ossipee)

CHAMPAGNE,
Albena M., d. 12/13/1991 at 97 in Ossipee; b. Plymouth

CHAMPION,
Almira C., d. 3/7/1887 at 28 in Ossipee; domestic; single; b. Charleston, VT; Isaac Champion and Nancy
Anna J., d. 10/12/1968 at 80 in Wolfeboro; b. Ireland
Frederick Ryan, d. 9/3/1983 at 81 in Hanover; b. Cambridge, MA
Isaac, d. 1/14/1892 at 61 in Ossipee; bronchitis; farmer; single; b. Effingham; Simeon Champion and Nancy Mead (Burlington, VT)
Margaret H., d. 11/1/2001 in Wolfeboro; John Laforce and Mary Morrow
Sabrina, d. 12/4/1900 at 67/8/20 in Ossipee; paralysis; married; b. Effingham; Thomas S. Day and Charlotte Gentleman
Walter, d. 3/8/1998 in Natick, MA

CHANDLER,
John W., d. 10/13/1923 at 25/0/1; b. Portsmouth; James W. Chandler and Florence B. Morgan
Laura M., d. 4/3/1890 at 44/7/8 in Ossipee; ovarian dropsy; housekeeper; married; b. Ossipee; Stephen W. Ayers and Martha M. Merrell
Minnie V., d. 11/28/1896 at 2/7/5 in Ossipee; intestinal colic; b. Ossipee; H. H. M. Chandler (Albany) and Ida L. Cook (Fryeburg, ME)

CHAPIN,
Lizzie E., d. 6/17/1914 at 46; home duties; b. MA

CHAPMAN,
Eben, d. 12/20/1906 at 85/1 in Ossipee; pneumonia; farmer; widower; b. Milton; Thomas Chapman (Milton) and Elmira Robinson (Milton)
Elinore A., d. 9/6/1988 at 96 in Ossipee; b. Waltham, MA
Florence, d. 2/21/1930 at 66/7/8 in Walford, ON
George C., d. 1/4/1967 at 70 in Ossipee; b. Woburn, MA
Jane G., d. 4/19/1946 at – in Wolfeboro; b. Wolfeboro; John Chapman and Jean Sawyer
Leonard B., d. 2/21/1972 at 91 in Ossipee; b. Canada
Mary J., d. 6/29/1913 at 79; widow; b. Morrickville, ON; James Telford (England) and Catheron Barton (Canada)

CHARETTE,
Harlan D., d. 6/29/1952 at 28/0/25 in Ossipee; b. Rochester; David Charette and Edna I. Ham

CHARLTON,
Florence Gertrude, d. 3/1/1983 at 78 in Ossipee; b. Jackson

CHARPENTIER,
Medora, d. 7/2/1994 at 88; Joseph Levesque and Emma Demaris

CHASE,
Abigail E., d. 10/30/1969 at 64 in Ossipee; b. Irish Sea
Agnes G., d. 5/14/1999 at 72 in Wolfeboro; Walter George and Inez Tewksbury
Arnold D., d. 3/29/1970 at 79 in Ossipee; b. ME
Bertrand, d. 2/12/1968 at 83 in Wolfeboro; b. MA
David D., d. 9/5/2001 in Wolfeboro; David Chase and Jane Thompson
Edwin O., d. 4/1/1981 at 69 in Ossipee; b. Contoocook
Frederica Mark, d. 8/16/1970 at 90 in Ossipee; b. MA
George, d. 7/19/1917 at 53/8/4; farmer; George Clark (sic) (Albany) and Amy Annis (Albany)
Henry L., d. 1/2/1970 at 79 in Ossipee; b. VT
Jennie Foss, d. 6/24/1979 at 91 in Ossipee; b. NH
Leon T., d. 10/18/1957 at 62/2/17 in Ossipee; b. Contoocook; Oscar Chase and Margaret Thornton
Mary S., d. 3/28/1902 at 27/9/11 in Providence; dilation of heart; married
Melville B. C., d. 5/31/1910 at 74/7/12 in Ossipee; pleurisy; machinist; married; b. Hiram, ME; Gideon Chase (Hiram, ME) and Salome Lombard (Hiram, ME)

Oscar, d. 8/5/1961 at 14 in Hanover; b. Portsmouth
Otis Burnham, d. 5/4/1997 at 70 in Wolfeboro; Henry Otis Chase and Leith Ashford

CHEEVER,
Eve Ruth, d. 5/29/1995 at 69; Wesley J. Bruce and Bride Murphy

CHICK,
Charles, d. 12/21/1898 at 39 in Ossipee; facial erysipelas; laborer; married; b. Ossipee; Nathan Chick (Ossipee) and ----- Hyde (Ossipee)
Harriet, d. 9/–/1898 at – in Ossipee; consumption; married; b. Wolfeboro; Samuel Tuttle and Sarah Brown
Harrison, d. 11/18/1895 at 78/0/8 in Ossipee; paralysis
Harry Weston, Sr., d. 1/23/2000 at 82 in Ossipee; Harry Winfield Chick and Helen Blake
Joanna, d. 6/28/1899 at 90 in Ossipee; carcinoma; single
Julia, d. 10/10/1969 at 67 in Ossipee; b. NH
Martha, d. 9/2/1898 at 72/10/22 in Ossipee; apoplexy; housewife; single; b. Ossipee; Samuel Chick (Ossipee) and Marie Goldsmith (Ossipee)
Mary, d. 4/24/1887 at 72/0/11 in Ossipee; housekeeper; married; b. Ossipee
Mary Etta, d. 4/13/1910 at 88/4/12 in Ossipee; pneumonia; housewife; single; b. Ossipee; Samuel Chick (Ossipee) and Mary Goldsmith (Ossipee)
Nathan, d. 5/12/1888 at 76; farmer; widower; b. Ossipee; Samuel Chick and Mary Goldsmith
Pearl M., d. 2/3/1992 at 81 in Ossipee; b. Elizabeth, NJ
Samuel B., d. 9/3/1911 at 74/9/29; typhoid fever; farmer; married; b. ME; Nathan Chick (Ossipee) and ----- Hyde (Ossipee)

CHUBB,
Bessie Edwards, d. 4/10/1973 at 84 in MA; b. MA
Elmer T., d. 3/8/1979 at 92 in Ossipee; b. MA

CHURCHILL,
Anna, d. 10/6/1969 at 79 in Ossipee; b. MA
Grace Elizabeth, d. 5/4/2000 at 93 in Ossipee; Charles Churchill and Melissa Battis

CHUTE,
Albion, d. 9/8/1892 at 65 in Ossipee; rheumatism; farmer; married; b. Otisfield, ME; Daniel Chute (Windham) and Barsheba Maybery (Windham)

CILLEY,
J. K. (male), d. 7/3/1896 at – in Ossipee; opium inebriety; married

CLANCY,
Verna L., d. 4/21/1961 at 59 in Wolfeboro; b. Ossipee

CLARK,
Amelia, d. 3/20/1913 at 73/5/2
Austin F., d. 2/19/1910 at 72/9/7 in Taunton; erysipelas; farmer; married
Cora, d. 10/18/1983 at 82 in Ossipee; b. Chelsea, VT
George A., d. 11/21/1896 at 0/0/21 in Ossipee; diarrhea; b. Ossipee; John H. Clark (NY) and Nellie M. Smith (England)
Gladys M., d. 2/16/1974 at 81 in Ossipee; b. NH
Henrietta Sara, d. 5/16/1941 at 67/10/29 in Ossipee; b. Weathersfield, VT; John Ayer and Mary Cochin
Isabella Carlin, d. 7/17/1997 at 83 in W. Ossipee; John Watt Carlin and Bertha Wilson
James Oliver, Jr., d. 2/9/1996 at 91 in Ossipee; James O. Clark, Sr. and Eleanor Houston
Kate V. C., d. 4/17/1900 at 0/6 in Ossipee; convulsions; b. Ossipee; John N. Clark (Tamworth) and Nellie Smith (England)
Kenneth Malcolm, d. 3/14/1993 at 90 in Ossipee
Maurice V., d. 9/19/1977 at 66 in Ossipee; b. NH
Thomas A., d. 5/17/1944 at 73/6/26 in Wolfeboro; b. Canada; Mathew Clark and Eliza Reed

CLARKE,
Anna E., d. 12/1/1984 at 91 in Ossipee; b. Brookfield
Edmund Palmer, d. 1/8/1979 at 74 in Wolfeboro; b. CT
Otis E., d. 9/15/1936 at 85/9/1 in W. Ossipee; b. Providence, RI

CLARKSON,
Annie Belle, d. 10/9/1978 at 100 in Ossipee; b. MA

CLAY,
Francis Leslie, d. 5/4/1981 at 59 in Salem, MA; b. MA

CLEMONS,
Laura Sarah, d. 12/10/1974 at 93 in Ossipee; b. NH

CLIFFORD,
Arthur Charles, d. 3/30/1988 at 82 in Ossipee; b. Dorchester, MA
Ruth Elizabeth, d. 10/28/1993 at 78 in Wolfeboro

Timothy C., d. 3/1/1922 at 75 in Ossipee; book agent; single; b. Topsham, VT; Absolom Clifford and Susan P. Boynton (Orford)
William, d. 1/19/1910 at 70 in Ossipee; valvular disease of heart; b. Conway

CLOUGH,
Elmira, d. 5/19/1898 at 83 in Ossipee
Frederick, d. 1/19/1891 at 70 in Ossipee; farmer; single; b. Effingham; Benjamin Clough and Sally Granville (Canada)
Harriet, d. 10/16/1892 at 67 in Ossipee; married
Mary, d. 6/6/1900 at 83 in Ossipee; septicemia from submaxillary abscess; widow
Maude C., d. 1/31/1971 at 82 in Ossipee; b. MA
Melissa E., d. 9/29/1908 at 57/0/12 in Ossipee; cerebral hemorrhage; housewife; b. Waterboro, ME; Benjamin Carpenter and Comfort Allen (Bartlett)
Sobriety, d. 7/15/1894 at 75 in Ossipee; gastro enteritis; housewife; married; b. Bartlett; Jacob Allen and Edith Allen

CLOUTMAN,
Edna M., d. 1/1/1979 at 93 in Ossipee; b. NH
William, d. 8/25/1920 at 54; laborer; single; b. Wakefield

CLOWARD,
Davis J., d. 3/1/1968 at 73 in Wolfeboro; b. DE

COBB,
Annie L., d. 12/25/1918 at 76/5/11; housewife; widow; b. Newfield, ME; ---- Chellis
Blanche Irene, d. 10/9/1944 at 71/10/17 in Ossipee; b. S. Chatham
Joseph G., d. 4/6/1915 at 80/3/14; married; b. Limerick, ME; Joshua Cobb (Limerick, ME) and Mary Cook
Walter P., d. 3/31/1916 at 40/1/25; station agent; married; b. Conway; Joseph G. Cobb (Limerick, ME) and Annie L. Chellis (Newfield, ME)

COCHRANE,
Virginia L., d. 6/6/1986 at 70 in Wolfeboro; b. Center Harbor

COHOON,
Catherine V., d. 8/8/1975 at 74 in Ossipee; b. MA

COLBATH,
Gertrude B., d. 1/13/1908 at 22/6 in Ossipee; pulmonary tuberculosis; housewife; b. Farmington; George W. Otis (Farmington) and Clara E. Pinkham (Farmington)
Jonathan, d. 11/4/1932 at 81/2/14 in Ossipee; b. Gilmanton; Mark Colbath and Martha J. Hamm

COLBERT,
Cedric C., d. 2/3/1985 at 78 in Wolfeboro; b. Rindge
Hilda M. S., d. 2/7/1985 at 84 in Wolfeboro; b. Kittery, ME

COLBY,
son, d. 4/21/1894 at 0/0/7 in Moultonboro; premature birth; b. Moultonboro; Luther Colby and Nancy Knox
son, d. 10/26/1899 at – in Ossipee; stillborn; b. Ossipee; Ralph Colby (Ossipee) and Minnie Fall (Ossipee)
Abbie, d. 6/2/1911 at –; stillborn; b. Ossipee; Plummer Colby (Moultonboro) and Etta Bean (Ossipee)
Arthur, d. 1/4/1907 at 62 in Ossipee; valvular disease of heart; laborer; widower; b. Moultonboro; Daniel Colby (Moultonboro) and Mary Williams (Moultonboro)
Arthur C., d. 12/5/1968 at 53 in Wolfeboro; b. NH
Daniel, d. 2/5/1926 at 56; Arthur Colby and Harriet Eldridge
Edward L., d. 8/13/1889 at 0/8; b. Ossipee
Elizabeth B., d. 8/3/1952 at 49/11/19 in Ossipee; b. Deerfield; Samuel J. Haynes and Lillian C. Cram
Enoch, d. 9/22/1914 at 64/0/2; farmer; b. Moultonboro
Etta, d. 3/24/1941 at 50/2/26 in Wolfeboro; b. Ossipee; Fred Bean and Anna Nichols
Florence Littlefield, d. 8/17/1943 at 27/5/0 in Pembroke; b. Oakland, ME; Neil Littlefield and Isabelle Laribee
Harriet, d. 10/25/1898 at 44 in Ossipee; cancer uterine; housewife; married; b. Ossipee; Daniel Eldridge (Ossipee) and Susan Eldridge (Ossipee)
Louise Bertha, d. 3/19/1993 at 87 in Wolfeboro
Mary J., d. 12/17/1958 at 82 in Ossipee; b. Ossipee; John Evans and Mary J. Welch
Nancy, d. 3/21/1897 at – in Ossipee; cardiac dropsy; married
Pearl, d. 2/9/1903 at 19/8/15 in Ossipee; acute gastritis; housewife; married; b. Ossipee; Plummer Fall (Ossipee) and Nellie Ross (Ossipee)
Perle, d. 3/8/1903 at 0/1 in Ossipee; marasmus; b. Ossipee; Ralph Colby (Moultonboro) and Pearl Fall (Ossipee)
Plummer, d. 11/2/1942 at 69/9/0 in Ossipee; b. Ossipee; Arthur Colby and Harriett Eldridge

Robert S., d. 6/7/1945 at 4/3/18 in Tuftonboro; b. Wolfeboro; Royal Colby and Florence Littlefield

Royal Plumer, d. 6/27/1988 at 74 in Ossipee; b. Ossipee

Walter B., d. 8/11/1948 at 27/3/18 in Ossipee; b. Wolfeboro; Ralph Colby and Ida Bean

William, d. 4/10/1924 at 72; b. Moultonboro; Daniel Colby and Mary Williams

COLE,

Comfort J., d. 2/27/1901 at 60 in Ossipee; cancer uterine; housewife; married; b. Bartlett

Desire, d. 1/11/1895 at 89/3/2 in Ossipee; pneumonia; widow; b. Ossipee

Ira, d. 5/31/1946 at 79/0/19 in Wolfeboro; b. Hiram, ME

Isabelle B., d. 2/4/1918 at 0/8/27

James, d. 5/9/1917 at 69; laborer; widower; b. Cornish, ME; A. Cole

Walter L., d. 3/22/1932 at 64/10/19 in Ossipee; b. Milbury, MA; James H. Cole and Jennie O. Wesson

COLEMAN,

Abigail, d. 7/19/1888 at 95; domestic; widow; b. Richmond, ME

Elizabeth Cecelia, d. 10/9/1997 at 84 in Ossipee; Kilburn Adams and Elizabeth Gilbert

Frank, d. 3/4/1928 at 65; b. Barre, MA; Slocum Coleman and Mary Pratt

John J., d. 8/6/1966 at 54 in Ossipee; b. Waltham, MA

COLES,

Catherine D., d. 7/19/1973 at 80 in Ossipee; b. England

Rheta L., d. 9/27/1972 at 86 in Laconia; b. MA

COLFORD,

Kate, d. 12/14/1937 at 66/7/24 in Ossipee; b. NS

COLLINS,

John Francis, d. 10/29/1938 at 60/4/23 in Ossipee; b. Cork, Ireland; James J. Collins and Mary Murray

COLTON,

John A., d. 7/17/1976 at 90 in Ossipee; b. MA

COMEAU,

Joseph A., d. 7/13/1936 at 57/7/10 in Portsmouth; b. Digby Co., NS

Marie Leah, d. 4/13/1976 at 77 in Wolfeboro; b. NS

Maude Grant, d. 10/20/1947 at 70/5/29 in Portsmouth; b. Water Village; John H. Brown and Celestia Willand

COMSTOCK,
Theodore Robinson, d. 5/4/1996 at 76 in Ossipee; William P. Comstock and Mary Rait Robinson

CONDON,
Frank R., d. 4/20/1978 at 72 in Manchester; b. ME
Hazel A., d. 1/8/1945 at 30/1/10 in Wolfeboro; b. Effingham; Arthur L. Sprague and Grace Brownell

CONNARY,
Merlin F., d. 3/24/1985 at 76 in Ossipee; b. Stratford

CONNER [see Connor],
son, d. 1/3/1920 at –; b. Ossipee; Arthur N. Conner (Ossipee) and Mamie Pascoe (Freedom)
Albert H., d. 10/9/1973 at 68 in Wolfeboro; b. NH
Arthur L., d. 9/22/1965 at 75 in Laconia; b. Ossipee
Carolyn Lottie, d. 4/10/1996 at 85 in Ossipee; Allyn A. Langley and Lelia Smith
Charles, d. 11/14/1943 at 41/11/16 in Ossipee; b. Exeter; Edwin Conner and Mary Blake
Earle, d. 4/21/1920 at 28/10/7; butcher; married; b. Ossipee; William Conner (Ossipee) and Annie Hodgdon (Canada)
Edwin C., d. 8/17/1925 at 52/2/8; b. Ossipee; Charles L. Conner and Sarah Garland
Eugene W., d. 5/23/1983 at 73 in Wolfeboro; b. Lexington, MA
Evelyn, d. 2/24/1968 at 61 in Ossipee; b. NH
Gertrude A., d. 3/8/1971 at 58 in Ossipee; b. MA
Glen L., d. 11/26/1961 at 84 in Ossipee; b. Barre, VT
Harlan, d. 9/16/1974 at 63 in Wolfeboro; b. NH
Harry Newton, d. 11/28/1888 at 0/7; b. Ossipee; William N. Conner and Annie Hodgdon
Jeremiah, d. 3/21/1897 at – in Ossipee; paralysis; widower
Joseph H., d. 2/13/1897 at 41/9/6 in Ossipee; pulmonary consumption; married; J. Conner (Ossipee) and Lucinda Hobbs (Ossipee)
Julia A., d. 1/31/1896 at 67/7/12 in Ossipee; valvular disease of the heart; housekeeper; widow; b. Ossipee; Caleb Abbott (Ossipee) and Sarah Ricker (Lebanon, ME)
Lydia N., d. 7/22/1899 at 82/3/10 in Ossipee; angina pectoris; widow; b. Center Harbor; William Payne
Mary A., d. 4/22/1963 at 77 in Ossipee; b. Freedom
Maud, d. 5/17/1898 at 22/3/10 in Ossipee; tuberculosis; housewife; married; b. Ossipee; John C. Hodge and Laura Garland

Richard E. (surname listed as Courier), d. 8/20/1889 at 43/3/25; shoemaker; married; b. Ossipee; Jeremiah Conner and Lucinda Hobbs
Sarah M., d. 9/13/1921 at 80/5/7 in Ossipee; housewife; married; John R. Garland (Wakefield) and Hannah Gile (Effingham)
William B., d. 4/9/1896 at 82/6 in Ossipee; suicide by hanging; civil engineer; married; b. Wakefield; Peaslee B. Conner (Gilmanton) and Eliza Calomy (New Durham)

CONNERS,
Ada, d. 5/16/1969 at 90 in Ossipee; b. NB
Eleanor W., d. 3/11/1981 at 88 in Conway; b. Rockland, NY
Mary Jane, d. 6/24/1983 at 93 in Ossipee; b. Ireland

CONNOR [see Conner],
Charles L., d. 3/20/1932 at 95/8/20 in Ossipee; b. Ossipee; Peasley Connor and Patience Colomy
John B., d. 4/28/1892 at 75/10/18 in Ossipee; lung disease; carpenter; married; b. Wakefield; P. B. Connor (Gilmanton) and Eliza Colomey (New Durham)
John E., d. 6/24/1931 at 0/1/24 in Ossipee; b. Ossipee; John Connor and Evelyn Sargent
William N., d. 12/10/1916 at 51/6/5; hotel prop.; married; b. Ossipee; Jeremiah Connor (Ossipee) and Lucinda Hobbs (Ossipee)

CONNORS,
Paula W., d. 8/5/1957 at 68 in Haverhill; b. Austria; Rudolph Urvantisky and Caroline Witte

CONWAY,
Augusta, d. 11/27/1959 at 78 in Ossipee; b. NS
Howard, d. 3/21/1939 at 55/0/21 in Ossipee; b. Vinal Haven, ME; Willard Conway and Jane Delano

COOK,
daughter, d. 3/10/1891 at – in Ossipee; b. Ossipee; J. R. B. Cook and Mary Ann Ames (Ossipee)
Addie May, d. 3/1/1973 at 76 in Center Harbor; b. NH
Alice Evelyn, d. 3/2/1981 at 92 in Ossipee; b. Albany
Ann, d. 8/13/1890 at 78 in Ossipee; heart disease; domestic; widow; b. Ossipee
Anne F., d. 5/17/1897 at 29/11/22 in Ossipee; septicemia puerperal; housewife; married; b. Wolfeboro; Eli Canney (Wolfeboro) and Sarah Corson (Wolfeboro)
Archie, d. 5/19/1956 at 74 in Wolfeboro; Haven Cook
Arthur E., d. 4/30/1986 at 58 in Wolfeboro; b. Ossipee

Clayton, d. 2/21/1943 at 38/10/17 in Pembroke; b. Ossipee; William Cook and Rose Lewis
Della V., d. 10/27/1981 at 69 in Wolfeboro; b. Newfoundland
Doris E., d. 2/22/1977 at 67 in Wolfeboro; b. NH
Ebenezar, d. 4/20/1922 at 79/11 in Ossipee; teamster; widower; b. Bethel, ME
Forrest C., d. 9/27/1931 at 1/7 in Ossipee; b. Ossipee; Clayton Cook and Beatrice Canney
Hattie A., d. 6/22/1914 at 32; housekeeper; Hiram Philbrick
Henry, d. 7/24/1916 at 86/8/23; none [occupation]; widower; b. Salem, MA; William Cook (Salem) and Eliza Courtney (Gloucester)
Howard E., d. 2/4/1955 at 50 in Dayton, ME; b. NH; Walter Cook and Delia Philbrick
Jemima, d. 3/24/1945 at 78/11/21 in Wolfeboro; b. Belfast, Ireland; Thomas Waring
Jessie P., d. 12/3/1972 at 86 in Ossipee; b. MA
Margaret, d. 7/24/1914 at 81; housekeeper; b. NY; Alexander Green and Martha Hilton
Martha Abigail, d. 4/11/1977 at 88 in Ossipee; b. NH
Mary A., d. 10/23/1909 at 51/2/24 in Ossipee; posioning; b. Ossipee; Asa Ames (Ossipee) and Caroline Knox (Ossipee)
Mary A., d. 12/9/1918 at 73/1/12; housekeeping; married; b. Tamworth
Richard O., d. 1/22/1990 at 83 in Wolfeboro; b. Portland, ME
Sarah Y., d. 2/5/1893 at 77/8 in Ossipee; housewife; widow; b. Wolfeboro; John Young (Newmarket) and Sally Smith
Sidney, d. 12/3/1939 at 41/9/24 in Hanover; b. Ossipee; William J. Cook and Rose Lewis
Walter R., d. 7/16/1944 at 69/2/11 in Ossipee; b. Ossipee; James B. Cook and Addie Jenness
William A., d. 1/27/1937 at 16/11/27 in Wolfeboro; b. Hollis, ME; Walter R. Cook and Addie M. Jenness

COONROD,
Lewis G., Jr., d. 1/1/1981 at 67 in Wolfeboro; b. Savoy, IL

COOPER,
Mildred Frances, d. 8/1/1987 at 74 in Ossipee; b. Salem, MA

COPP,
Arthur C., d. 11/1/1915 at 0/7/9; b. Freedom; Leroy Copp (Bangor, ME) and Rena Bean (Ossipee)
Arthur L., d. 9/9/1942 at 51/2/25 in Rochester; b. Bangor, ME; Daniel Copp and ----- McNorton
Betsy, d. 4/7/1890 at 82 in Ossipee; old age; domestic; single
Byron, d. 4/27/1916 at 76; farmer; widower; b. Wolfeboro

Daniel B., d. 2/28/1924 at 67/6

Francis E., d. 11/30/1921 at 0/3/3; Maynard Copp (Orrington, ME) and Nora Eldridge (Ossipee)

Gladys T., d. 8/8/1975 at 81 in Wolfeboro; b. NH

John, d. 2/2/1890 at 73 in Ossipee; pneumonia; domestic (sic); single; b. Moultonboro

John, d. 12/3/1913 at 76; single; b. Brookfield

Lizzie, d. 1/7/1927 at 33/6/21; b. Ossipee; Frank Wood and Eliza Speedy

Louise N., d. 3/18/1965 at 53 in Wolfeboro; b. Ctr. Ossipee

Mildred W., d. 6/25/1918 at 38/11/18; housewife; married; William Dodge and Amelia Trimm

Nancy, d. 8/–/1890 at – in Ossipee; old age; domestic; married; b. Ossipee

Owen C., d. 10/11/1975 at 78 in Wolfeboro; b. ME

Ralph E., Sr., d. 2/1/1968 at 58 in Ossipee; b. NH

CORE,
Catherine, d. 4/16/1917 at 72/5/13; housewife; single; b. ME; Edmund Eastman and Eliza Ridlon

CORSON,
Abbie, d. 5/13/1912 at 62; widow

Augusta A., d. 11/6/1926 at 79/7/8; b. Biddeford, ME; William Twombley and Sarah Flanders

Charles, d. 1/15/1925 at 80; b. Middleton; Eben Corson

Christopher, d. 2/2/1942 at 57

Eva G., d. 9/10/1928 at 60; b. Wolfeboro

Fred, d. 10/15/1939 at 81 in Ossipee; b. Wolfeboro; William Corson and Hannah Corson

Frederick, d. 11/23/1918 at 64/7; clergyman; married; b. Lebanon, ME; Horatio G. Corson (Lebanon, ME) and Ellen E. Whip (Dover)

COSEBOOM,
Ethel C., d. 3/11/1986 at 98 in Ossipee; b. Keedysville, MD

COTTON,
Clark, d. 7/17/1895 at 28/2/23 in Ossipee; gunshot wound; carpenter; widower; b. Wolfeboro; Brackett Cotton (Wolfeboro) and Susan Cotton (Brookfield)

Dana Russell, Sr., d. 2/8/1999 at 84 in Ossipee; Nathan Pierce Cotton and Edna L. Robbins

Helen Brink, d. 5/20/1988 at 73 in Ossipee; b. New Orleans, LA

Nathan P., d. 12/22/1964 at 81 in Ossipee; b. Cornish, ME

Sarah M., d. 9/18/1897 at 58/10/12 in Ossipee; spinal sclerosis; housewife; married; b. Tuftonboro; John Foss (Strafford) and Sally Hodgdon (Tuftonboro)

COUGHLIN,
Edward G., Jr., d. 4/8/1942 at 17/8/14 in Ossipee; b. W. Ossipee; Edward G. Coughlin and Alice L. Doe
Helen, d. 2/27/1923 at 27/8/9; b. Union; John W. Pike and Eva Thurston

COUSENS,
Florence E., d. 9/17/1964 at 90 in Ossipee; b. Quebec

COVEY,
Uradel P., 3rd, d. 3/10/1980 at 11 in Ossipee; b. NH

COX,
Charlotte A., d. 3/8/1983 at 88 in Ossipee; b. Eliot, ME
Frederic Leo, d. 4/15/1999 at 68 in Ossipee; Reginald Edward Cox and Jane Frawley
Jane F., d. 10/28/1966 at 72 in Ossipee; b. Lowell, MA
Mary Edith, d. 1/1/1963 at 91 in Ossipee; b. Lubec, ME

CRAFT,
Mary A., d. 8/18/1946 at 73/3/17 in Ossipee; b. Galway, Ireland; Martin McInerey and Mary Lindsy

CRAIGUE,
Donald Edwin, d. 5/19/1992 at 74 in Ctr. Ossipee; b. Wolfeboro

CRAM,
Marshall G., d. 2/24/1988 at 28 in Wolfeboro; b. Wolfeboro

CRASSMAN,
Margaret, d. 4/28/1972 at 76 in Wolfeboro; b. NH

CREDIFORD.
Lila I., d. 3/13/1993 at 86 in Ossipee

CREIGHTON,
Susan S., d. 12/26/1888 at 60; domestic; widow; b. Sandwich

CRESSEY,
Betsy C., d. 7/24/1985

CREVIER,
Agnes Theresa, d. 9/16/1996 at 70 in Wolfeboro; Frank J. Perry and Annie C. Richards

CROCKER,
Ronald Edwin, d. 12/26/1970 at 45 in Ossipee; b. NS

CROFT,
Mary M., d. 7/21/1971 at 92 in Wolfeboro; b. VT

CROMBIE,
Lillian F., d. 1/13/1901 at 26/10/24 in Ossipee; uremia; stitcher; married; b. Ossipee; Robert Bertwell (England) and Susan Littlefield (Springvale)

CROOK,
Edna F., d. 11/9/1982 at 80 in Wolfeboro; b. NS

CROSS,
Edgar S., d. 1/27/1942 at 81/5/5 in Ossipee; b. Boston, MA; Martin H. Cross and Rebecca Davidson
Minerva D., d. 7/21/1920 at 58/5/29; housewife; married; J. Davidson (E. Boston)

CROSSMAN,
Everett S., d. 9/22/1960 at 66 in Ossipee; b. Hyde Park, MA
Robert, d. 9/22/1934 at 66/2/20 in Ossipee; b. Taunton, MA; Robert Crossman and Sarah Kane

CROTTE,
Philip, d. 2/24/1914 at 63

CROUSE,
Edgar Freeman, d. 9/2/1978 at 93 in Ossipee; b. NS

CROWLEY,
Grace E., d. 1/14/1954 at 69 in Ossipee; b. Ossipee; Charles Tibbetts and Lucy Hoyt
James, d. 7/1/1893 at 72/9/16 in Ossipee; clergyman; married; b. Cornish, ME; J. Crowley (Cornish, ME) and Mary Ridley (Cornish)
Nancy, d. 11/19/1893 at 69/4/4 in Ossipee; married; b. Moultonboro; J. Wiggin (Wakefield) and Annie Goudy (Ossipee)
Timothy L., d. 12/27/1946 at 52/3/21 in Wolfeboro; John Crowley and Mary Lennahan

CUMMINGS,
Edward, d. 11/2/1926 at 65/6/12; b. Colebrook; Edward N. Cummings and Lucretia F. Merrill
Esther A., d. 10/13/1925 at 84/8/11; b. Jackson; Henry Odway
Phyllis Alfreda, d. 5/24/1993 at 89 in Ossipee

CURRIER,
Adaline, d. 3/31/1895 at 42/0/7 in Ossipee; pneumonia; housewife; single
Barbara M., d. 5/27/2001 in Wolfeboro; Llewellyn Merrow and Margaret Curlin
Benjamin, d. 10/11/1895 at 48 in Ossipee; mitral insufficiency; married
David Lee, d. 2/24/1938 at 0/2/6 in Ossipee; b. Ossipee; Frank A. Currier and Ruth Madeline Morse
Florence E. H., d. 3/20/1949 at 69/10/23 in Laconia; b. NH; John F. Hurn and Jennie Smith
Janet D., d. 7/.5/2001 in Wolfeboro; Ralph Downs and Anne Reed
John, d. 11/30/1934 at 68/3/24 in Ossipee; b. Canada; Duncan Currier and Charlotte McKean
Mabel F., d. 5/11/2001 in Ossipee; Chester Griffin and Hattie Carver
Roland E., d. 4/14/1961 at 60 in Ossipee; b. Tamworth
William E., d. 8/23/1965 at 72 in Laconia; b. MA

CURRY,
Harriet, d. 5/16/1942 at 69/11/12 in Ossipee; b. Milton Mills; Benjamin Goodwin and Emma A. Wentworth
John, d. 10/5/1923 at 75; b. Holderness; William Curry

CURTIS,
Alexandria E., d. 8/25/1997 at 82 in Wolfeboro; John Egnatovich and Sophia -----
Annie M., d. 8/19/1925 at 45/7/8; b. Milton Mills; John Wentworth and Augusta Laskey
Elsie Brown, d. 4/14/1939 at 67/5 in Wolfeboro; b. Lynn, MA; James Brown and Mrs. Henry Wagenfeld
Everett L., d. 2/26/1946 at 69/10/23 in Wolfeboro; b. Farmington; Moses Curtis and Addie Moore
Katherin Anne, d. 5/5/1998 in Ctr. Ossipee; Joseph Champagne and Jaqueline Lassell
Mildred C., d. 7/21/2000 at 96 in Ossipee; Wilber A. Clark and Carra Plaisted
Sarah P., d. 4/5/1981 at 90 in Wolfeboro; b. Danvers, MA
Susannah, d. 1/6/1957 at 77 in Ossipee; b. Newfoundland; James Roberts and Salomi Taylor

CUSHING,
Homer Beattie, Jr., d. 3/31/1996 at 76 in Ossipee; Homer B. Cushing and Nellie Miller

CYR,
George F., d. 11/5/1981 at 62 in Wolfeboro; b. MA

DAKIN,
Anne, d. 5/10/1969 at 89 in Ossipee; b. England

DALE,
Arthur J., d. 6/25/1984 at 66 in Ossipee; b. Sheffield, England
Earl R., d. 12/4/1983 at 86 in Ossipee; b. Shirley, MA
Lottie, d. 5/16/1967 at 81 in Wolfeboro; b. Sheffield, England

DALES,
Jennie M., d. 1/2/1984 at 85 in Ossipee; b. NB

DAME,
Arnold Clarence, d. 8/23/1997 at 91 in Ossipee; J. Harry Dame and Sarah -----
Helen O'Neil, d. 1/11/2001 in Ossipee; James H. O'Neil and Helen O'Connell
Nancy, d. 7/11/1888 at 69; housekeeper; married; b. Canada; John Emerson and Nancy Dearborn
Samuel, d. 1/24/1902 at 82 in Ossipee; cardiac dropsy; farmer; widower; b. Wakefield
Virginia A., d. 4/4/1991 at 78 in Ossipee; b. Union

DAMLIN,
William M., d. 7/5/1956 at 72/7/23 in Ossipee; b. Finland

DANA,
George Henry, d. 9/22/1888 at 0/5; b. Ossipee; John C. Dana and Anga B. Drowns

DANFORTH,
Calvin, d. 3/21/1919 at –; laborer; single
Joseph W., d. 6/21/1964 at 83 in Wolfeboro; b. Boston, MA
Loring, d. 3/7/1890 at 84 in Ossipee; exhaustion; domestic (sic); single; b. Sandwich
Lucy A., d. 6/16/1939 at 77/1/22 in Rochester; b. Effingham; Thomas A. Danforth

469

DAVENPORT,
Herbert, d. 7/19/1935 at 76/10/12 in Ossipee; b. Salisbury; L. D. Davenport
Wilda E., d. 10/23/1985 at 87 in Ossipee; b. S. Berwick, ME

DAVIDIAN,
Harry M., d. 7/19/1949 at 64/11/5 in Ossipee; b. Turkey; Mitchel Davidian and Elizabeth -----

DAVIDSON,
Frances Ray, d. 11/2/1970 at 57 in Ossipee; b. NH

DAVIE,
Gladys M., d. 5/20/1991 at 86 in Ossipee; b. Grafton

DAVIS,
daughter, d. 4/9/1938 at 11 hrs. in Wolfeboro; b. Wolfeboro; Walter M. Davis and Margaret P. Gale
child, d. 4/27/1962 at 24 hrs. in Wolfeboro; b. Wolfeboro
Abbie J., d. 2/7/1888 at 33/3; housekeeper; widow; b. Ossipee
Albion, d. 6/4/1901 at 35 in Ossipee; paralysis spinal; carpenter; married; b. Effingham; John C. Davis (Effingham)
Augusta M., d. 11/24/1948 at 84/10/29 in Ossipee; b. Limerick, ME; ----- and Hannah Edwards
Bertha C., d. 11/22/1975 at 83 in Wolfeboro; b. MA
Brenda W., d. 8/26/1988 at 73 in Wolfeboro; b. Wakefield, MA
Charles E., d. 8/31/1926 at 49/11/3; b. Effingham; Weir T. Davis and Frances Bryant
Charles M., d. 7/11/1890 at 42/6 in Boston, MA; jaundice
Clarence E., d. 9/20/1960 at 79 in Wolfeboro; b. Wakefield
Edward Lemuel, d. 7/27/1997 at 83 in Ossipee; Zabron Alfred Davis and Sarah Candace Middleton
Ella Frances, Mrs., d. 12/11/1944 at 82/6/6 in Wolfeboro; b. Ossipee; John W. Thurley and Esther Ricker
Florence Belle, d. 5/23/1943 at 64/8/16 in Tamworth; b. Ossipee; William Wiggin and Sophia Eldridge
Harry A., d. 3/4/1967 at 74 in Wolfeboro; b. Methuen, MA
Harry E., d. 7/27/1949 at 83/4/21 in Ossipee; b. Effingham; Weire Davis and Frances Bryant
Harry G., d. 1/16/1989 at 78 in Wolfeboro; b. Swampscott, MA
Herbert E., d. 6/5/1929 at 61/8/26 in Ossipee; b. Tamworth; Ellis N. Davis and Rowena Moody
John Everett, d. 8/3/1977 at 52 in Manchester; b. NH\
Julia, d. 5/18/1911 at 58; heart disease; domestic; widow; b. Effingham

Laurette, d. 2/27/1917 at 73/1/25; housework; widow; b. Chatham; Newell W. Cook and Mary Thompson
Mabel Hosmer, d. 9/19/1943 at 67/3/27 in Ossipee; b. Bartlett; Cyrus Hosmer and Alice Gray
Marion G. W., d. 6/6/1971 at 82 in Meredith; b. MA
Nancy L., d. 11/2/1967 at 83 in Wolfeboro; b. Providence, RI
Nester W., d. 3/14/1983 at 74 in Ossipee; b. Chelsea, MA
Ralph T., d. 7/3/1942 at 53/2/9 in Ossipee; b. Ossipee; Albion L. Davis and Ella F. Thurley
Richard, d. 3/21/1971 at 83 in Wolfeboro; b. NH
Roy W., d. 2/9/1966 at 65 in Wolfeboro; b. Ossipee
Shaye Andrew, d. 7/30/1992 at 0/0/9 in Wolfeboro; b. Franklin
Walter M., d. 9/30/1954 at 54 in Wolfeboro; b. Malden, MA; Harry Davis and Mabel Hanson
Walter S., d. 8/26/1963 at 75 in Wolfeboro; b. Effingham
Wilfred Irving, d. 11/1/1983 at 80 in Ossipee; b. Jackson

DAVISON,
Albert P., d. 4/9/1973 at 84 in Ossipee; b. NH

DAY,
Alice M., d. 11/19/1968 at 95 in Ossipee; b. MA
Leon C., d. 9/13/1946 at 48/3/22 in Ossipee; b. Cornish, ME; George E. Day and Hattie Pendexter
Sadie L., d. 6/4/2001 in Franklin; Dean Charles and Evangeline Dyer

DEARBORN,
Annie Collomy, d. 11/13/1985 at 90 in Ossipee; b. Parsonsfield, ME
John, d. 12/4/1899 at 60/3/26 in Ossipee; angina pectoris; carpenter; married; Margaret Locke
Lulu J., d. 10/24/1993 at 89 in Ossipee

DEARBORNE,
Carroll W., d. 7/8/1969 at 74 in Ossipee; b. NH

DEE,
Anne V., d. 10/15/1999 in Wolfeboro; Oren McKiernan and Anna Canon

DELAND,
Mabel, d. 9/27/1924 at 60; b. Wolfeboro

DELLOLIO,
Vincent Antonio, d. 5/25/1997 at 79 in Wolfeboro; Rosario Dellolio and Mary Kaiser

DELORME,
Philip J., d. 7/29/1977

DE MAIANVILLE,
Rose, d. 9/26/1944 at 83/7/21 in Ossipee; b. Canada; George Robinson and Nancy Glose

DEMER[R]ITT,
Charles W., d. 10/19/1987 at 73 in Wolfeboro; b. Laconia
Chester C., d. 3/7/1995 at 75
Elizabeth, d. 9/7/2000 in Wolfeboro; John Harmon and Georgie Frost
Hannah F., d. 4/16/1907 at 57/11 in Ossipee; mitral regurgitation; housewife; widow; b. Ossipee; James Whitiker
Ida A., d. 10/6/1951 at 73/7/4 in Ossipee; b. Gilmanton; Charles Aikens and Hester Parsons
Samuel Edwin, d. 5/3/1939 at 61/7/29 in Ossipee; b. Strafford; John J. Demerritt and Caroline Plimpton

DENNIS,
Ralph L., d. 8/25/1987 at 80 in Wolfeboro; b. Swampscott, MA

DEVER,
Joseph C., d. 12/9/1933 at 19/3/8 in Ossipee; b. Boston, MA; Jessie Dever

DIBONA,
Helen Cheever, d. 12/7/1998 in Ossipee; Frederick A. Lowell and Jennie Mae Conant

DICKINSON,
Ida I., d. 12/11/1989 at 95 in Ossipee; b. Melrose, MA
Johnny R., d. 7/2/2000 in Lebanon; Forrest Dickinson and Leona Avery

DIETZEL,
William H., d. 2/4/1964 at 59 in Wolfeboro; b. Methuen, MA

DILLA,
Katherine R., d. 8/31/1989 at 69 in Ossipee; b. Pittsburgh, PA

DINSMORE,
Dean, d. 1/20/1958 at 91 in Ossipee; b. NH; Warren Dinsmore and Lavinia Thompson
Emma, d. 3/17/1943 at 83/5/19 in Ossipee; b. Milo, ME; Stephen Millett and Abbie Peniga
Hilda Combe, d. 12/17/1977 at 87 in Ossipee; b. RI

DINZEY,
Richard, d. 10/17/1907 at 65 in Ossipee; ataxic paraplegia; single

DIXON,
Ella H., d. 11/4/1993 at 85 in Wolfeboro

DOBBINS,
William, d. 3/2/1994 at 75; Edward Dobbins and Gladys Cotton

DOBLE,
Phineas K., d. 5/5/1914 at 61/9/8; merchant; b. ME; Phineas Doble (ME)
Sarah E., d. 4/18/1921 at 68 in Ossipee; housewife; widow; Daniel G. Merrow (Ossipee) and Sarah Moody (Ossipee)

DODGE,
Elsa, d. 1/7/1919 at 68; housekeeping
Fred H., d. 6/30/1938 at 63/4/14 in Ossipee; b. Royalton, VT

DOE,
daughter, d. 11/19/1903 at 0/0/1 in Ossipee; anaemia; b. Ossipee; Frank B. Doe (Ossipee) and Clarinda Davis (Effingham)
son, d. 11/14/1905 at 0/0/3 in Ossipee; oedema of lungs; b. Ossipee; Frank B. Doe (Ossipee) and Clara Davis (Effingham)
Benjamin F., d. 3/21/1961 at 89 in Ossipee; b. Ossipee
Edgar M., d. 6/21/1931 at 56/0/11 in Ossipee; b; Deerfield
Frank B., Jr., d. 5/15/1974 at 74 in Wolfeboro; b. NH
Hazel M., d. 3/27/1975 at 74 in Wolfeboro; b. NH
Henry H., d. 10/8/1895 at 57 in Ossipee; cerebral hemorrhage; pauper; single; b. Ossipee
Nancy, d. 3/7/1891 at 90 in Ossipee; single; b. Ossipee
Walter E., d. 2/7/1963 at 56 in Wolfeboro; b. Ossipee

DOLAN,
Mildred C., d. 6/25/1987 at 66 in Ossipee; b. Chelsea, MA

DOLIFF,
John, d. 3/7/1914 at 53; laborer

DOLLOFF,
Samuel, d. 7/25/1893 at 90 in Ossipee; inmate; single

DONAHUE,
Carolyn Amanda, d. 12/27/1970 at 61 in Ossipee; b. NH

DONINGER,
Lois Veronica Fielding, d. 8/14/1999 at 81 in Ossipee; Harry Fielding and Anastasia McHloughlin

DONOHUE,
Bridget Mary, d. 1/15/1992 at 90 in Ossipee; b. Ireland

DONOVAN,
Patrick, d. 10/1/1936 at 64/9/28 in Ossipee; b. Ireland; Florenz Donovan and Mary Tulley
Walter D., d. 7/20/1997 at 71 in Wolfeboro; James Donovan and Alice Selfridge

DOOLEY,
Ellen J., d. 6/9/1921 at 62 in Ossipee; housewife; widow; John O'Connell (England) and Mary O'Connell (England)

DORE,
Alvah, d. 7/12/1900 at 77/2 in Ossipee; cancer on face; farmer; married
Carrie R., d. 2/6/1951 at 73/10/8 in Wolfeboro; b. Merrickville, ON; Theodore Chapman and Mary J. -----
Charles E., d. 5/28/1959 at 80 in Wolfeboro; b. Ossipee; John Dore and Rose E. Smith
Clara J., d. 5/6/1895 at 23/1/3 in Ossipee; cholera; single; b. Ossipee; Herman R. Dore (Ossipee) and Sarah E. Dore (Danvers)
Clarence, d. 4/22/1935 at 74/9/19 in Ossipee; b. Ossipee; Frank P. Dore and Lucy Pepper
Doris Vivien, d. 12/4/1971 at 70 in Ossipee; b. NH
Elizabeth, d. 10/26/1980 at 105 in Ossipee; b. Ireland
Evelyn Lettie, d. 6/28/1999 at 76 in Ctr. Ossipee; Fred Eldridge and Dora Sargent
Frank P., d. 10/15/1914 at 78/1/15; housekeeper (sic); b. Ossipee; Beniah Dore (Ossipee) and Hannah Pressey (Ossipee)
Hannah, d. 1/23/1908 at 81/8 in Dover; intestinal nephritis; housewife; b. Ossipee; Isaac Hanson and Mary Church
Herman R., d. 2/1/1920 at 80/11/22; farmer; widower; b. Ossipee; Ezekiel Dore (Wakefield) and Abigail Clark (Wakefield)
Ida M., d. 10/8/1942 at 79/6/27 in Ossipee; b. Baldwin, ME; Calvin Thomas and Martha Wentworth
Jacob C., d. 1/25/1898 at 73 in Ossipee; Brights disease; painter; widower; b. Ossipee; Ezekiel Dore
John Everett, d. 6/12/1928 at 78/0/8; b. Middleton, MA; John C. Dore and Mary Hanson
LeRoy H., d. 2/28/1966 at 78 in Wolfeboro; b. Tuftonboro

Lewis Alvah, d. 2/5/1998 in Ctr. Ossipee; Walter G. Dore and Alter Adjutant

Lucy A., d. 1/11/1936 at 68/0/5 in Ctr. Ossipee; b. Tuftonboro; Henry D. McDuffy and Sarah Cotton

Mary W., d. 9/22/1898 at 80/4 in Ossipee; dysentery; widow; b. Ossipee; Isaac Dore

Rose E., d. 1/22/1934 at 79/5 in Ossipee; b. Limington, ME; Charles A. Smith and Caroline R. Brooks

Sarah E., d. 6/15/1905 at 62/4/26 in Ossipee; meningitis; housewife; married; b. Danvers, MA; John C. Dore and Lewis Hall

Sylvester, d. 3/29/1934 at 67/8/10 in Ossipee; b. Ossipee; Frank P. Dore and Lucy A. Pepper

Walter, d. 5/10/1972 at 87 in Ossipee; b. NH

Wilbur, d. 3/26/1899 at 12/11 in Ossipee; endocarditis; b. Ossipee; John E. Dore (Middleton, MA) and Rose E. Smith (Limington, ME)

William P., d. 12/3/1956 at 82/2/5 in Ossipee; b. Ossipee; Frank P. Dore and Lucy Pepper

DORR,
Hannah P., d. 3/19/1887 at 84 in Ossipee; housekeeper; widow; b. Ossipee

Smith, d. 6/29/1888 at 49/9/8; millman; b. Ossipee; Jonathan Dorr and Mary Goldsmith

DORRER,
Ruth Blanche, d. 1/4/1994 at 86; Edgar E. Aldrich and Verna Tice

DOUCETTE,
Janie Elizabeth, d. 8/3/2001 in Ossipee; Arthur Moulaison and Mary Doucette

DOUGLAS,
Winifred Bell, d. 4/2/1984 at 83 in Ossipee; b. Cornish, ME

DOUGLASS,
Hannah, d. 1/3/1897 at 63/9/28 in Ossipee; bronchitis; widow; b. Sebago, ME; David Jewell and Emmie ----

DOW,
Bessie P., d. 11/24/1983 at 99 in Ossipee; b. Dorchester, MA

Donald E., d. 1/17/1929 at 0/3/26 in Wolfeboro; b. Wolfeboro; Ellis Dow and Agnes Phinney

Ellis M., d. 1/2/1944 at 42/7/14 in Wolfeboro; b. Moultonboro; James Dow and Elizabeth Garland

Gladys B., d. 1/25/1983 at 82 in Ossipee; b. Albany
Meredith J., d. 1/2/1944 at 10/9/25 in Ossipee; b. Ossipee; Ellis Dow and Agnes Phinney
Richard E., d. 12/22/1963 at 57 in Manchester; b. Ashland
Rodney N., d. 7/18/1963 at 14 in Ossipee; b. Rochester
Virginia A., d. 7/21/1926 at 0/0/20; b. Ossipee; Ellis Dow and Agnes Phinney

DOWDEN,
Margaret E., d. 5/13/1991 at 91 in Ossipee; b. Cambridge, MA

DOWELL,
Benjamin, d. 5/12/1937 at 67/9/7 in Ctr. Ossipee; b. Cambridge, MA; John H. Dowell and Sophia Knowles
Walter, d. 2/13/1922 at 60 in Ossipee; mechanic

DOWNING,
Carolyn S., d. 10/8/1962 at 0/5 in Wolfeboro; b. Wolfeboro
Donald F., d. 6/28/1986 at 58 in Ossipee; b. Wolfeboro
Gerda, d. 4/14/1975 at 89 in Ossipee; b. Sweden
Jennie, d. 4/9/1927 at 81
Katresia M., d. 6/26/1967 at – in Center Harbor; b. Conway
Madeline B., d. 12/2/1980 at 70 in Ossipee; b. N. Conway
Stephen Edward, d. 12/28/1991 at 81 in Ossipee; b. Milton

DOWNS,
Carrie W., d. 11/29/1986 at 94 in Ossipee; b. Acton, ME
Esther, d. 2/4/1910 at 75 in Ossipee; la grippe; housewife; widow; b. Ossipee; Silas Welch (Ossipee) and Affie Nichols (Ossipee)
Jonathan, d. 11/6/1900 at 79 in Ossipee; heart disease; single; b. Acton, ME
Melvin G., d. 4/15/1987 at 39 in Wolfeboro; b. S. Effingham

DOYLE,
Albert Russel, d. 4/14/1971 at 63 in Ossipee; b. Washington, DC
Florence Irma, d. 9/30/1984 at 94 in Ossipee; b. Victory, VT

DRAGON,
Benjamin Gerard, d. 11/18/1994 at 7; Bridgette Grogan

DRAKE,
Bradley S., d. 2/9/1949 at 67/8/13 in Ossipee; b. Effingham; John Drake and Julia Hardy

Edith A., d. 10/6/1953 at 79/0/16 in Portland, ME; b. Ossipee; Charles Drake and Belinda Sceggell
Eliza, d. 9/5/1953 at 86 in Laconia; b. Ossipee; Charles Drake and Belinda Sceggell
Mabel E., d. 11/27/1954 at 63 in Eaton; b. Ossipee; George Nichols and Cora Thurston
Mary E., d. 1/21/1919 at 65/4/11; housewife; widow; b. Well, ME; J. B. Littlefield (Well, ME) and Mary F. Smith (Raymond Ctr.)
Sarah A., d. 12/13/1923 at 68/6; b. Tiverton, RI
Sophronia A., d. 12/24/1917 at 66/3/17; housework; widow; b. Ossipee; Joseph Lear (Ossipee) and Sarah Hammond (Ossipee)

DRESSER,
Bert A., d. 3/13/1956 at 80 in Ossipee; b. Turner, ME; Charles Dresser and Celia Fuller

DREW,
Albert R., d. 6/15/1969 at 76 in Wolfeboro; b. NH
Annie L., d. 8/15/1927 at 59/4/2; b. Machias, ME; Nelson Lawrence
Austin F., d. 2/22/1960 at 50 in Wolfeboro; b. Ossipee
Cora E., d. 5/8/1913 at 53/10/24; housewife; married; b. Ossipee; Joseph G. White (Tamworth) and Hannah Devnell (Strafford)
Dorothy P., d. 6/23/1968 at 37 in Laconia; b. NH
Frank, d. 7/30/1925 at 76
Frank, d. 11/12/1942 at 58/6/3 in Tamworth; b. Ossipee; Frank Drew and Sarah J. Eldridge
George, d. 11/23/1943 at 68/0/0 in Ossipee
Jane, d. 11/15/1889 at 83; single; b. Wolfeboro
Lewis, d. 8/26/1893 at 4 in Ossipee; b. Ossipee
Philip William, d. 1/29/1998 in Wolfeboro; William P. Drew and Lena M. Tappan
Selden E., d. 8/8/1984
Walter Bertram, d. 1/16/1974 at 92 in Ossipee; b. NH
Wendell Richard, d. 6/23/1997 at 55 in Wolfeboro; Philip W. Drew and Frances J. Eldridge

DRINKWATER,
Ada M., d. 12/1/1946 at 75/10/11 in Wolfeboro; b. Taunton, MA; George T. Davis and Henrietta Wheeler
Alma B., d. 5/1/1979 at 84 in Ossipee; b. MA
Clyde B., d. 1/20/1988 at 92 in Wolfeboro; b. Taunton, MA

DRISCOLL,
Veronica P., d. 10/20/1970 at 79 in Ossipee; b. MO

DROST,
Kathleen V., d. 6/1/1977 at 73 in Wolfeboro; b. Canada

DROWN,
Charles, d. 10/10/1924 at 74; b. Madison
Elijah G., d. 11/17/1902 at 80 in Ossipee; la grippe; farmer; b. Eaton; Moses Drown and Polly -----
Evelyn D., d. 8/12/1912 at 0/3/19; b. Ossipee; Joel Drown and Mary Gilman
John M., d. 4/19/1966 at 87 in Ossipee; b. Warner
Julia P., d. 1/20/1965 at 85 in Ossipee; b. Warren

DRUGG,
Charles Howard, d. 11/7/1996 at 80 in Ossipee; Clifford Drugg

DUBE,
Francis J. C., d. 4/17/1975 at 70 in Wolfeboro; b. MA
Mary Agnes, d. 1/21/1971 at 78 in Ossipee; b. NY

DUBOIS,
Arlene M., d. 12/8/1969 at 51 in Wolfeboro; b. NH
Hilda M., d. 4/17/1982 at 64 in Wolfeboro; b. Ossipee
Lucien P., d. 8/23/1974 at 58 in Wolfeboro; b. NH

DUCHEMIN,
Frederick Alexander, Jr., d. 5/21/1997 at 83 in Ossipee; Harry J. Duchemin and Ella Dubois

DUCHESNE,
Carol Elizabeth, d. 9/21/1987 at 16 in Ossipee; b. Wolfeboro
Jacqueline Seeckts, d. 7/28/1996 at 55 in Ctr. Ossipee; Ehlert William Seeckts and Jane Taylor

DUFAULT,
Edward N., d. 11/27/1986 at 90 in Ossipee; b. Nashua

DUFFY,
Paul Joseph, Jr., d. 5/20/1998 in Ossipee; Paul Joseph Duffy, Sr. and Virginia Faye Duffy

DUNBAR,
Richard B., d. 5/20/2000 in Concord; Roy Dunbar and Bernice Rogers

DUNFIELD,
Charles W., d. 3/19/1902 at 39 in Ossipee; thoractic aneurism; bag master; married; b. Tamworth

DUNHAM,
Ella B., d. 10/2/1969 at 94 in Wolfeboro; b. Canada
George F., d. 1/12/1951 at 74/5/1 in Wolfeboro; b. Canada; Edwin Dunham and Sara Lamoreaux

DUNLAP,
Barbara M., d. 4/6/1990 at 70 in Wolfeboro; b. Melrose, MA
Iona V., d. 3/24/1982 at 91 in Ossipee; b. Hampton, Canada

DURGIN,
Alonzo E., d. 6/2/1934 at 67/7/8 in Ossipee; b. Freedom; James M. Durgin and Ann Thurston
Charles, d. 10/3/1898 at 0/2 in Ossipee; gastro enteritis; b. Wolfeboro
Charles H., d. 7/29/1890 at 33 in Ossipee; heart disease; laborer; married; b. Ossipee

DURRELL,
John C., d. 9/12/1892 at 73 in Ossipee; heart failure; inmate

DURRETTE,
John Robert, d. 6/29/1978 at 74 in Ossipee; b. VA

DUTTON,
Barbara Hobbs, d. 8/18/1991 at 80 in Ossipee; b. Rochester

DWYER,
Gertrude, d. 7/11/1992 at 89 in N. Conway; b. Medford, MA

DYER,
Nellie, d. 5/12/1904 at 30 in Ossipee; pulmonary tuberculosis; single; b. Wakefield
William H., d. 1/10/1899 at 0/2 in Ossipee; pneumonia; b. Ossipee; Nellie Dyer

EAMES,
Jesse J., d. 10/14/1948 at 68/6/1 in Ossipee; b. Framingham, MA; Edwin A. Eames and Arabella L. Barnes

EARLE,
Carleton Verni, d. 4/13/2001 in Ossipee; ----- and Elmina E. -----

Elmina E., d. 5/15/1987 at 98 in Wolfeboro; b. S. Gardner, MA
Marguerite Fawcett, d. 11/17/1991 at 82 in Ossipee; b. Worcester, MA

EASTMAN,
female, d. 1/26/1899 at 75; influenza
Adam H., d. 2/8/1919 at 70/4/7; laborer; married; b. Conway; Stephen Eastman (Conway) and Dolly Cook (Conway)
Charles, d. 5/26/1935 at 82/5/9 in Ossipee; b. Concord; James H. Eastman and Elisa Nicholson
Claude P., d. 11/16/1962 at 35 in Wolfeboro; b. W. Ossipee
Frances Morton, d. 8/4/1975 at 85 in Ossipee; b. NH
George M., d. 5/12/1934 at 67/9/8 in Ossipee; b. Portland, ME; Sumner Eastman and Philomede Webber
Helen Conklin, d. 12/13/1975 at 73 in Ossipee; b. NY
John E., d. 9/22/1970 at 88 in Ossipee; b. NH
Mary W., d. 8/17/1922 at 75 in Ossipee
Nancy F., d. 4/13/1910 at 81/9/14 in Ossipee; heart failure; widow; b. ME; William Whitney and Olive Parlin
Timothy, d. 4/14/1926 at 90; b. Cooks Island, ME; Henry Eastman and ---- Merriman

EATON,
Bessie E., d. 10/22/1940 at 54/5/17 in Ossipee; b. Kingston; Wallace Tucker and Lettie Tucker
Gilbert D., d. 5/21/1969 at 72 in Wolfeboro; b. England
Mary E., d. 12/17/1924 at 90/1/23; b. Portsmouth; ----- Berry
Richard Thomas, d. 1/18/2001 in Ctr. Ossipee; ----- and Frances Hannah Eaton

EDGERLY,
Frank, d. 7/18/1927 at 75/10; b. Tuftonboro; Albert Edgerly
J. Freeman, d. 5/2/1912 at 65; b. Wolfeboro

EDWARDS,
Charles, d. 12/17/1900 at 77 in Ossipee; pneumonia; farmer; single; b. Effingham
George A., d. 2/21/1930 at 59/10/1 in Ossipee; b. Newfield, ME; George Edwards
Jessie Viola, d. 12/10/1987 at 96 in Ossipee; b. Wolfeboro
John Woodroe, d. 11/15/1998 in Ossipee; Charles Edwards and Agusta West
Leiws E., d. 4/24/1961 at 27 in Wolfeboro; b. Effingham
Mary W., d. 9/21/1984 at 92 in Ossipee; b. Ossipee
Rufus, d. 12/29/1984 at 80 in Ossipee; b. Effingham

EGERT,
Joseph, d. 1/1/1976 at 94 in Ossipee; b. Czechoslovakia

EGLIT,
Christy, d. 3/14/1977 at 96 in Ossipee; b. Latvia

EISENBERG,
Ruth, d. 7/21/1949 at 23/7/15 in Ossipee; b. Westfield, ME; Ephraim Eisenberg and Della R. Prescott

ELAM,
Michael David, d. 9/2/2000 at 44 in Ossipee; Daniel Elam and Louise -----

ELDREDGE,
Olive H., d. 12/23/1951 at 54/4/14 in Wolfeboro; b. E. Hartland, CT; Joseph Holborn and Loetta Searles

ELDRIDGE,
son, d. 4/1/1890 at – in Ossipee; premature birth; b. Ossipee; William Eldridge (Ossipee) and Rosina Eldridge (Ossipee)
child, d. 9/5/1893 at – in Ossipee; O. Eldridge
son, d. 7/3/1898 at 0/0/4 in Ossipee; inanition; b. Ossipee; Orrin Eldridge (Freedom) and Sadie E. Goodwin (Eaton)
daughter, d. 4/27/1899 at 0/0/12 in Ossipee; b. Ossipee; Eliza Eldridge (Ossipee)
daughter, d. 5/7/1899 at 0/0/12 in Ossipee; inanition; b. Ossipee; Eliza Eldridge (Ossipee)
son, b. 8/11/1900 at – in Ossipee; inanition; b. Ossipee; Herbert Eldridge (Ossipee) and Lillie Welch (Ossipee)
son, d. 9/28/1906 at 0/0/11 in Ossipee; stillborn; b. Ossipee; Myrtle Eldridge (Ossipee)
child, d. 7/1/1907 at 0/3/10 in Ossipee; heart trouble; b. Ossipee; George Eldridge (Ossipee) and Ida Welch (Ossipee)
daughter, d. 2/13/1913 at 0/0/1; b. Ossipee; Herbert Eldridge (Ossipee) and Clara Wiggin (Ossipee)
daughter, d. 7/25/1915 at –; b. Ossipee; Herbert Eldridge (Ossipee) and Clara Wiggin
son, d. 5/6/1948 at 3 hrs. in Wolfeboro; b. Wolfeboro; Ahiel Eldridge and Lina Grieshammer
daughter, d. 12/2/1951 at – in Wolfeboro; b. Tamworth; Clyde Eldridge and Eleanor Eldridge
Abbie J., d. 3/5/1945 at 47/4/11 in Laconia; b. Ossipee; Alvah Davis and Florence B. Wiggin

Abbie J., d. 12/2/1949 at 83/9/5 in Ossipee; b. Ossipee; Hiram Hodgdon and Abbie Glidden
Aggie, d. 5/28/1896 at 2/3/18 in Ossipee; asphyxia; b. Ossipee; Ivory Eldridge (Ossipee) and Emma Welch (Ossipee)
Agnes, d. 6/12/1912 at 0/0/13; b. Ossipee; Perley Eldridge (Ossipee) and M. Templeton (Ossipee)
Alfred, d. 3/30/1974 at 73 in Ossipee; b. NH
Alpheus, d. 2/22/1910 at 69/11/29 in Ossipee; pneumonia; b. Ossipee; Jacob Eldridge (Ossipee) and Mary Welch (Ossipee)
Annette M., d. 4/2/1956 at 83/8/14 in Somerville, MA; b. Kearsarge; Calvin Eastman and Almira Eastman
Arthur, d. 5/9/1966 at 69 in Wolfeboro; b. Ossipee
Austin M., d. 5/25/1972 at 49 in Ossipee; b. NH
Bernard, d. 12/21/1926 at 2/9/9; b. Ossipee; Perley Eldridge and Margaret Templeton
Beverly Ann, d. 9/24/1992 at 48 in Union; b. N. Conway
Beverly F., d. 6/4/1973 at 32 in Ossipee; b. NH
Carlton Simon, d. 12/11/1990 at 88 in Wolfeboro; b. Ossipee
Caroline, d. 12/28/1904 at 43/5/23 in Ossipee; cancer of face; housework; married; b. Ossipee; Jonas Kimball (ME) and Margar'te Varney (Ossipee)
Carrie E., d. 10/8/1980 at 99 in N. Conway; b. NH
Charles, d. 5/27/1920 at 76/8/16; farmer; married; b. Ossipee; Stephen Eldridge (Ossipee) and ----- Welch (Ossipee)
Charles M., d. 12/10/1925 at 60/11/12; b. Ossipee; Simon Eldridge and Robline Johnson
Chester C., d. 9/18/1960 at 63 in Ossipee; b. Kearsarge
Clara, d. 12/1/1901 at 18/1/10 in Ossipee; aortic insufficiency; housewife; single; b. Ossipee; Harrison Eldridge (Ossipee) and Olive J. Ricker (Freedom)
Clara, d. 3/21/1961 at 76 in Ossipee; b. Ossipee
Clarence E., d. 7/31/1956 at 51 in Wolfeboro; b. Ossipee; Everett Eldridge and Nettie Pike
Clifford D., d. 11/5/1978 at 80 in Wolfeboro; b. NH
Clyde A., d. 11/30/1970 at 59 in Ossipee; b. NH
Cora, d. 9/23/1900 at 18 in Ossipee; cancer stomach; widow; b. Ossipee; Silas Welch (Ossipee) and Emma Templeton (Ossipee)
Cora, d. 10/13/1992 at 89 in N. Conway; b. Ossipee
Cora B., d. 1/27/1982 at 80 in Conway; b. Ossipee
Daniel, d. 4/5/1896 at 61 in Ossipee; cancer; farmer; married; b. Ossipee; Jacob Eldridge (Ossipee) and Mary Welch (Ossipee)
Daniel, d. 3/29/1910 at 82/0/35 in Ossipee; chronic dementia; farmer; married; b. Ossipee; Jerry Eldridge (Ossipee) and Hannah White
David W., d. 7/19/1999 in Wolfeboro; Wilbur Eldridge and Myrtle Templeton

Dora T., d. 12/2/1932 at 36/11/15 in Ossipee; b. Ossipee; Everett Sargent and Lora Eldridge

Dorothy E., d. 1/27/1974 at 51 in Rochester; b. NH

Edward, d. 1/30/1945 at 80/3/12 in Ossipee; b. Ossipee; Charles Eldridge and Mary Nichols

Eleanor L., d. 2/10/1972 at 53 in Wolfeboro; b. NH

Eliza, d. 9/16/1907 at 38 in Ossipee; cancer of uterus; housewife; married; b. Ossipee; William H. Eldridge (Ossipee)

Ella, d. 10/3/1935 at 63/4/5 in Ossipee; b. Porter, ME; Wilson Howard and Helen Hurd

Elmer O., d. 3/16/1932 at 68/10/0 in Ossipee; b. Ossipee; Daniel Eldridge and Elsie Nichols

Elsah, d. 1/8/1917 at 73/7/7; housework; widow; b. Ossipee; Ebineger Nichols (Ossipee) and Dorcas Welch (Ossipee)

Emily, d. 9/2/1924 at 82/11/19; b. Ossipee; Ebenezar Nichols and Dorcas Welch

Emma P., d. 1/2/1950 at 78/11/4 in Wolfeboro; b. Tuftonboro; Moses Welch and Sarah J. Welch

Ernest H., d. 10/21/1971 at 69 in Ossipee; b. NH

Etta M., d. 3/5/1967 at 72 in Wolfeboro; b. Ossipee

Etta M., d. 2/7/1982 at 79 in Wolfeboro; b. Ossipee

Eugene Atwood, d. 6/16/1992 at 62 in Dover; b. Ossipee

Everett S., d. 10/16/1956 at 83 in Rochester; b. Ossipee; Simon Eldridge and Roberline Johnson

Ezra, d. 3/14/1923 at 77; b. Ossipee; Daniel Eldridge and Susan Moody

Fred W., d. 9/27/1960 at 80 in Wolfeboro; b. Ossipee

George, d. 12/19/1940 at 71/8/9 in Ossipee; b. Ossipee; Charles Eldridge and Mary Nichols

George Henry, d. 4/22/1940 at 75/5/29 in Ossipee; b. Meredith; Elpheus Eldridge and Dorothy Jenness

Georgia, d. 11/4/1965 at 92 in Concord; b. Ossipee

Grover C., d. 4/3/1969 at 87 in Wolfeboro; b. NH

Hannah, d. 7/17/1907 at 75 in Ossipee; apoplexy; housewife; b. Ossipee; ---- Moody

Harold, d. 10/8/1918 at 3/9/14; b. Ossipee; Everett S. Eldridge (Ossipee) and Nettie Pike (Ossipee)

Harold, d. 12/26/1918 at 20/4; laborer; single; b. Ossipee; James P. Eldridge (Ossipee) and Abbie Hodgdon (Ossipee)

Harry P., d. 10/1/1964 at 66 in Wolfeboro; b. Ossipee

Helen, d. 10/19/1930 at 1/9/24 in Ossipee; b. Ossipee; Chester Eldridge and Hazel Eldridge

Herbert W., d. 6/16/1955 at 79/4/9 in Wolfeboro; b. NH; Simon Eldridge and Roberline Johnson

Hiram, d. 3/10/1914 at 78; farmer; b. Ossipee

Howard J., d. 4/5/1984 at 89 in Ossipee; b. Ossipee

Ida, d. 11/29/1965 at 86 in Wolfeboro; b. Ossipee

Isaac, d. 4/4/1887 at 77 in Ossipee; farmer; married; b. Ossipee

Ivory E., d. 2/10/1956 at 89 in Ossipee; b. Ossipee; Daniel Eldridge and Elsie Nichols

J. Frank, d. 4/1/1941 at 78/5/23 in Ossipee; b. Ossipee; James Eldridge and Martha Wallace

James, d. 10/8/1916 at 83/4/4; farmer; widower; b. Ossipee; Jacob Eldridge (Ossipee) and Mary Welch (Ossipee)

Joan M., d. 4/5/1948 at 0/0/1 in Wolfeboro; b. Wolfeboro; Bernard Eldridge and Joyce Berry

John P., d. 3/30/1949 at 78/11/5 in Wolfeboro; b. Ossipee; Simon Eldridge and Robline Johnson

Lafayette, d. 9/2/1956 at 78 in Ossipee; b. Ossipee; Daniel Eldridge and Lizzie Templeton

Laura W., d. 1/18/1952 at 75/10/28 in Ossipee; b. Ossipee; John H. Welch and Elmira Knox

Lawrence J., d. 9/19/1971 at 57 in Laconia; b. NH

Lewis R., d. 8/31/1974 at 67 in Laconia; b. NH

Lizzie, d. 9/26/1913 at 52/9/8; housewife; b. Ossipee; Ahial Templeton (Ossipee) and ----- Nichols (Ossipee)

Lizzie B., d. 1/2/1958 at 80/9/28 in Ossipee; b. Ossipee; Samuel Williams and Esther Welch

Louise C., d. 8/8/1974 at 65 in Ossipee; b. NH

Lucy, d. 2/23/1895 at 0/0/9 in Ossipee; cong. of the lungs; b. Ossipee; Oradon Eldridge (Ossipee) and Lucy Eldridge (Ossipee)

M. L., d. 12/18/1896 at 35 in Ossipee; cerebral hemorrhage; housewife; b. Ossipee

Mabel, d. 10/1/1914 at 40/7/6; basketmaker; b. Ossipee; John Welch (Ossipee) and Elmira Knox (Ossipee)

Margaret C., d. 12/5/1953 at 57 in Ossipee; b. Ossipee; Ahiel Templeton and Effie Williams

Marguerite R., d. 11/26/1981 at 65 in Ossipee; b. Ossipee

Marian E., d. 11/9/1940 at 22/11/6 in Wolfeboro; b. Wolfeboro; Arthur C. Bean and Elizabeth Riley

Martha E., d. 7/13/1907 at 71/3/8 in Ossipee; paralysis; housewife; married; b. Ossipee; Samuel Wallace

Martha M., d. 6/2/1970 at 41 in Wolfeboro; b. MA

Mary, d. 9/2/1921 at 70/4/29 in Ossipee; housewife; widow; Eben Nichols (Ossipee) and Dorcas Wood (Ossipee)

Maude B., d. 9/3/1972 at 75 in Ossipee; b. NH

Maurice S., Pvt., d. 4/14/1944 at 27 in Salisbury, England; b. Ossipee; Everett Eldridge and Nettie Pike (1948)

Maybelle, d. 9/15/1960 at 65 in Concord; b. Ossipee

Mildred I., d. 8/16/1962 at 76 in Ossipee; b. Ossipee

Mrs. Woodbury, d. 10/8/1892 at 20 in Ossipee; consumption; housewife; married

Myrtle, d. 10/9/1918 at 27/7/17; housewife; married; b. Ossipee; Harrison Eldridge (Ossipee) and Laura Eldridge (Freedom)

Myrtle M., d. 6/18/1966 at 77 in Conway; b. Ossipee

Nabby, d. 1/7/1900 at 84/9 in Ossipee; apoplexy; housewife; widow; b. Ossipee; James Welch (Ossipee)

Nettie N., d. 11/4/1969 at 88 in Westbrook; b. NH

Nettie P., d. 5/12/1955 at 75 in Laconia; b. NH; John Pike and Emily Wallace

Newell P., d. 11/20/1965 at 58 in Wolfeboro; b. Ctr. Ossipee

Orin, d. 10/23/1949 at 81 in Wolfeboro; b. Ossipee; Henry Eldridge and Emily Nichols

Orrin, 2nd, d. 4/10/1932 at 61/7/18 in Ossipee; b. Ossipee; Daniel Eldridge and Elsie Nichols

Orville W., d. 11/13/1940 at 48/0/26 in Ossipee; b. Bartlett; William Eldridge and Annette Eastman

Perley E., d. 11/20/1966 at 75 in Wolfeboro; b. Ossipee

Ralph R., d. 9/1/1947 at 70/3/20 in Ossipee; b. Freedom; Eben Eldridge and Arvilla Ward

Raymond C., d. 12/19/1980 at 80 in Ctr. Ossipee; b. Ossipee

Raymond R., d. 5/13/1985 at 61 in Laconia; b. Ossipee

Reba J., d. 8/14/2000 in Lebanon; Herbert Vittum and Alice Clark

Reita L., d. 1/26/1968 at 61 in Wolfeboro; b. NH

Reita Lee, d. 2/25/1996 at 46 in Ctr. Ossipee; Donald E. Johnson and Sylvia York

Rita L., d. 4/29/1977 at 59 in Ossipee; b. NH

Rose M., d. 6/13/1973 at 56 in Ossipee; b. NH

Sarah, d. 9/15/1926 at 51; b. Ossipee; Thomas Goodwin and Naomi Durgin

Scott O., d. 10/6/1968 at 74 in Wolfeboro; b. NH

Stephen, d. 3/2/1891 at 1/40/27 (sic) in Ossipee (see following entry)

Stephen, d. 3/22/1891 at 1/10/27 in Ossipee; b. Ossipee (see preceding entry)

Susan, d. 4/17/1910 at 79/11/17 in Ossipee; pneumonia; housewife; widow; b. Ossipee; Jacob Eldridge (Ossipee) and Nancy Welch (Ossipee)

Susie A., d. 11/2/1972 at 93 in Ossipee; b. NH

Vema, d. 9/7/1898 at 0/7/15 in Ossipee; congestion of lungs; b. Ossipee; Everett Eldridge (Ossipee) and Nettie Pike (Ossipee)

Vivian Hobbs, d. 7/17/1988 at 88 in Wolfeboro; b. W. Ossipee

W. Clayton, d. 11/2/1979 at 76 in Wolfeboro; b. Ossipee

Wendell Richard, d. 6/26/2000 at 61 in Ctr. Ossipee; Raymond Cyrus Eldridge and Etta Eldridge

Wilbur, d. 7/1/1925 at 0/5; b. Ossipee; Wilbur Eldridge and Myrtle Green

Wilbur, d. 2/15/1962 at 80 in Ossipee; b. Ossipee

William H., d. 4/2/1916 at 68; farmer; married; b. Ossipee; Stephen Eldridge (Ossipee) and Hannah Welch (Ossipee)

ELLIOTT,

Frank, d. 9/12/1941 at 65/1/2 in Ossipee; b. Stoneham, MA; Charles Elliott

Henry A., d. 12/12/1992 at 87 in Ossipee; b. E. Alton

Leon F., d. 11/9/1951 at 39/4/1 in Wolfeboro; b. Alton; Frank Elliott and Minnie Groton

Lura, d. 12/12/1940 at 64/2/1 in Ossipee; b. Ossipee; Alfeora Eldridge and Dorothy Eldridge

Luther F., d. 11/23/1955 at 74 in Ossipee; b. NH; Daniel Elliott and Lucy Willowby

ELLIS,

Filomena C., d. 10/25/1987 at 87 in Wolfeboro; b. Somerville, MA

Robert R., d. 11/26/1956 at 66 in Ossipee; b. Eaton; Thomas Ellis and Isabel Thompson

ELWELL,

Joseph E., d. 5/28/1981 at 98 in Ossipee; b. Essex, MA

Lucie, d. 1/11/1969 at 93 in Laconia; b. NH

EMACK,

Alexander D., d. 10/10/1909 at 0/0/12 in Ossipee; cancer of stomach; b. Ossipee; Benjamin Emack (NS) and Flora J. Welch (Ossipee)

Benjamin, d. 7/3/1950 at 75/1/3 in Ossipee; b. Canada; Alexander Emack and Charney Wilson

Emma Madalene, d. 7/10/195 at 91; George K. Gile and Mabel A. Whitcher

Eva P., d. 4/27/1955 at 65/7/22 in Wolfeboro; b. NH; Charles Perkins and Emma Eldridge

John, d. 10/19/1941 at 75/9/19 in Ossipee; b. NB; Alexander Emack and Jane Emack

Lester E., d. 12/20/1962 at 59 in Wolfeboro; b. Parsonsfield, ME

Marion E., d. 9/6/1986 at 61 in Ossipee; b. Wolfeboro

EMERSON,

Amos W., d. 9/21/1944 at 78/7/20 in Wolfeboro; b. Effingham; Bearly Emerson and Mary -----

Charles, d. 4/29/1936 at 86/3/10 in Ossipee; b. Bridgetown, ME; Asia Emerson and Sara Kimball

Lena B., d. 3/9/1935 at 38/6 in Ossipee; b. Lynn, MA; Charles R. Mansfield and Nellie M. Colby

Nettie M., d. 9/12/1956 at 85 in Wolfeboro; b. Effingham; Amos Emerson and Harriet Carpenter
Robert D., d. 10/10/1936 at 0/2 in Wolfeboro; b. Wolfeboro; Ralph W. Emerson and Gertrude Sturtevant

EMERY,
Archie C., d. 6/2/1986 at 77 in Rochester; b. Beverly, MA
Carrie L., d. 4/19/1892 at 26 in Ossipee; atrophic dis.; housekeeper; married; b. Ossipee; Arthur Clay (Ossipee) and Olive Tibbetts
George E., d. 12/11/1939 at 70 in Ossipee
Harry, d. 4/3/1927 at 41; b. NC
Howard E., d. 9/26/1953 at 79/0/1 in Ossipee; b. Moultonboro; Charles Emery and Lucy Haley
James M., d. 5/12/1915 at 72; laborer; widower; b. Bartlett
Lendal B., d. 5/8/1973 at 92 in Wolfeboro; b. NH
Lewis M., d. 5/30/1927 at 65/8/12; b. Parsonsfield; Nicholas Emery and Louisa Canney
Louisa F., d. 10/27/1913 at 77/11/19; housekeeper; married; b. Ossipee; Joshua Emery (Lebanon, ME)
Mary Jane, d. 8/20/1909 at 79 in Ossipee; angina pectoris; transient; b. Ossipee; John T. Emery and Sarah Sawyer
Nickolas, d. 5/20/1914 at 75/11; b. Tuftonboro; John F. Emery and Mary Sawyer
Stephen, d. 3/5/1911 at 65/7; pneumonia; farmer; married; Gilbert Emery (Bartlett) and Nancy Littlefield

EMMETT,
William J., d. 6/9/2001 in Exeter; William Emmett and Margaret Howe

ENGLE,
Alan E., d. 1/6/1976 at 7 in Manchester; b. NH

ENGLISH,
Robert Edward, d. 1/3/1999 at 74 in Ossipee; Philip F. English and Rose Etta Sweeney

ERLANDER,
Carl Eric, d. 9/1/1996 at 82 in Ctr. Ossipee; Hjalmar Erlander and Elizabeth Zatterberg
Mattie Towle, d. 9/23/1988 at 89 in Ossipee; b. Brookfield

ERSKEN,
Israel Lee, d. 7/14/1973 at 16 in Freedom; b. Turkey

ESTES,
Georgia, d. 12/19/1928 at 67/7/5; b. Fairhaven, MA; Timothy Spaulding and Rebecca L. Stewart
Richard Arthur, Sr., d. 2/2/1995 at 77; Arthur Estes and Freda Adjutant

EVANS,
daughter, d. 5/26/1933 at – in Ossipee; b. Ossipee; Frank Evans and Evelyn Dow
Annie L., d. 6/29/1893 at 6/11/26 in Ossipee; b. Ossipee
Annie Pearl Munroe, d. 9/21/1994 at 87; Charles N. Munroe and Annie Helphard
Frederick, d. 8/2/1965 at 52 in Ossipee; b. Lowell, MA
John, d. 7/31/1900 at 87 in Ossipee; old age; laborer; b. Ireland
John R., d. 6/11/1888 at 20/9/24; farmer; married; b. Ossipee; John W. Evans and Mary J. Welch
John W., d. 7/25/1896 at 53/7/8 in Ossipee; anaemice of heart; laborer; single
Olga N., d. 9/9/1982 at 70 in Ossipee; b. Boston, MA

EVENS,
Russell, Jr., d. 10/7/1990 at 79 in Ossipee; b. Malden, MA

FALL,
Ausbrey C., d. 4/13/1974 at 88 in Nashua; b. NH
Eli, d. 2/14/1910 at 92/2/16 in Ossipee; heart disease; farmer; widower; b. Ossipee; Otis Fall (Lebanon, ME) and Elizabeth Pierce
Gordon R., d. 5/16/1963 at 38 in Ossipee; b. Ossipee
Jennie, d. 2/25/1905 at 30 in Ossipee; uraemia; housewife; married; b. Ossipee; J. F. Hilton and A. Hemingway
John, d. 4/9/1890 at 66 in Ossipee; obscure stomach trouble; farmer; married; b. Lebanon, ME; Otis Fall and Elizabeth Pierce
Louisa C., d. 11/25/1915 at 65/2/21; housewife; married; b. Ossipee; Colby Nutter (Ossipee) and Louise Chick (Ossipee)
Lucretia S., d. 12/29/1891 at 54 in Ossipee; housewife; widow; b. Ossipee; Hiram Ricker (Ossipee) and Irina Chick (Ossipee)
Myrtie B., d. 9/23/1959 at 76 in Nashua; b. Tuftonboro; Theodore Thompson and Carry Bodge
Nellie M., d. 4/8/1951 at 90/4/11 in Milford; b. Ossipee; Robert G. Ross and Lidia Moody
Perley D., d. 5/16/1902 at 32/1/3 in Waltham, MA; whooping cough
Plummer F., d. 2/19/1921 at 64/5/29 in Ossipee; weaver; married; John Fall (Laconia) and Lucretia Ricker (Ossipee)
Raymond E., d. 5/2/1961 at 71 in Wolfeboro; b. Ossipee
Willie H., d. 3/3/1913 at 39/3/27; laborer; married; b. Ossipee; George C. Fall (Ossipee) and Louise Nutter (Ossipee)

FARARO,
Maria A., d. 9/23/1986 at 94 in Ossipee; b. New York City

FARENKOPH,
Ann M., d. 10/1/1991 at 82 in Ossipee; b. Brooklyn, NY

FARNHAM,
Lizzie L., d. 8/17/1921 at 69 in Ossipee; hotel manager; widow; Tyler H. Neal (Brookfield) and Mary E. Kenison (Ossipee)

FARRELL,
Annie E., d. 9/13/1978 at 88 in Keene; b. MA

FAWCETT,
Miriam, d. 12/1/2001 in Ossipee; Charles Fawcett and Nancy Bartlett

FECTEAU,
Leon, d. 10/14/1959 at 78 in Ossipee; b. Canada; William Fecteau and Caroline Charland

FEELEY,
John J., d. 10/1/1973 at 83 in Wolfeboro; b. MA

FELCH,
Annie M., d. 7/20/1904 at 48 in Ossipee; tuberculosis; married
Lillian, d. 1/24/1899 at 2 in Ossipee; capillary bronchitis grip; b. Moultonboro

FELKER,
Eleanor E., d. 1/4/1923 at 10/9/15; George Felker and Ethel Hurd

FELLOWS,
Sara, d. 2/18/1923 at 84; b. Barrington

FELTON,
Ethel M., d. 8/4/1952 at 79 in Laconia; b. MA; Charles S. Adams and Adeline Hoptenstall
John Heptonstall, d. 5/10/1940 at 29/4/3 in Ossipee; b. Salem, MA; William S. Felton and Ethel May Adams

FENDERSON,
Robert E., d. 12/12/1970 at 31 in Ossipee; b. ME

FENNERTY,
John W., d. 2/28/1954 at 0/1/12 in Portsmouth; b. Portsmouth; Mark Fennerty and Phyllis Seyman
Mark, d. 7/30/1972 at 66 in Concord; b. ME

FENTON,
Esther Isabel, d. 9/24/1973 at 90; b. NH

FERNALD,
Achsa H., d. 12/29/1961 at 82 in Wolfeboro; b. Ossipee
Ethel M., d. 5/1/2000 in Wolfeboro; Dana Bean and Lucy Dorr
Frank, d. 6/17/1946 at 72/8/19 in Ossipee; b. Ossipee; James Hilton and Emma F. Chick
Gladys Mildred, d. 1/30/1940 at 38/0/20 in Ossipee; b. Ossipee; Frank A. Fernald and Ascha Hilton
Harry, d. 8/14/1970 at 92 in Ossipee; b. NH
John W., d. 12/20/1916 at 73/8/16; farmer; widower; John V. Fernald
Leon F., d. 7/9/1988 at 84 in Wolfeboro; b. Ossipee
Luther Albert, d. 4/15/1939 at 42/5/17 in Ossipee; b. Bartlett; John A. Fernald and Annie Chandler
Mary L., d. 9/5/1967 at 86 in Ossipee; b. Canada
Nancy, d. 4/7/1894 at 55/11/25 in Ossipee; central hemorrhage; housewife; widow
Tobias M., d. 8/2/1900 at 36/3/24 in Ossipee; chronic gastritis; farmer; married; b. Ossipee
Vinnie, d. 10/19/1893 at 5 in Ossipee; b. Ossipee; John Fernald and Nona Jackson
Viola N., d. 11/8/1909 at 62/4 in Tyngsboro; epilepsy; b. Ossipee; Jonathan Jackson (Madison) and A. M. Copp (Ossipee)

FERREN,
John C., d. 3/24/1916 at 79/0/9; farmer; married; b. Freedom; James Ferren (Hampton) and Sallie Woodman (Effingham)

FETTRETCH,
Grace E., d. 7/3/1973 at 83 in Ossipee; b. NY

FETZER,
Anne Mary, d. 9/21/1993 at 96 in Ossipee

FICKETT,
Daniel, d. 2/21/1930 at 47/10 in Effingham; b. Standish, ME; Augustus Fickett and Nellie -----
Helen M., d. 7/23/1960 at 76 in Ossipee; b. Albany

FIELD,
Albion H., d. 1/20/1953 at 76 in Laconia; b. ME; Moses Field and Mary Brehaut
Isabelle, d. 12/12/1950 at 80/6/12 in Moultonboro; b. Scotland; Angus Sillers and Mary -----
Mary J., d. 2/6/1951 at 85 in Moultonboro; b. Cape Elizabeth, ME; Moses Field and Mary Brehaut

FIFIELD,
Charles Russell, Sr., d. 11/26/1998 in Ossipee; George Fifield and Blanche E. Penney

FINNIGAN,
John V., Jr., d. 2/8/1999 at 71 in Ossipee; John V. Finnigan and Rilla Morrison

FISCHBEIN,
Charles David, d. 6/26/1977 at 18 in Ossipee; b. NY

FISHER,
Gale F., d. 6/22/1972 at 85 in Wolfeboro; b. MN
Harriet, d. 1/22/1952 at 87 in Wolfeboro; b. Sheboygan; John Saunders and Harriet Kilton
Peter F., d. 8/26/1977 at 71 in Ossipee; b. Scotland

FISKE,
Maria, d. 11/5/1901 at 88 in Ossipee; old age; widow

FISTERE,
Lois Cudlipp, d. 9/20/1997 at 69 in Ossipee; Albert D. Cudlipp and Reta Niccolls

FITZGERALD,
child, d. 1/4/1925 at 0/0/1; b. Ossipee; Daniel Fitzgerald and Maud Lapost
Daniel C., d. 9/21/1925 at 61; b. Chester, VT

FITZPATRICK,
Joseph, d. 7/21/1970 at 20 in Ossipee; b. MA

FLAMAND,
Mary Mabel, d. 3/18/1999 at 77 in Wolfeboro; William Charles McCarthy and Laura Catherine Foster

FLANAGAN,
Helen, d. 8/8/1939 at 2/11 in Wolfeboro; b. Wolfeboro; Paul Flanagan and Hilda Colby
Marlene A., d. 6/11/1972 at 21 in Ossipee

FLANDERS,
Charles L., d. 10/13/1944 at 60/1/23 in Ossipee; b. Shapleigh, ME; Enoch Flanders and Carrie Hooper
Orlando C., d. 3/10/1929 at 48 in Portland, ME; b. Island Pond, VT; Albert ----
Samuel, d. 8/11/1930 at 78/10/29 in Ossipee; b. Madison; Samuel Flanders and Menza Ryder

FLETCHER,
Harry P., d. 12/9/1975 at 83 in Ossipee; b. ME
Herbert E., d. 11/17/1960 at 77 in Concord; b. Foxcroft, ME
Marguerite, d. 7/31/1957 at 65/10/9 in Ossipee; b. Portland, ME; Joseph Gilkey and Ada True

FLOYD,
George H., d. 7/6/1914 at 71; b. Eaton

FLYNN,
George Henry, Jr., d. 6/19/1996 at 78 in Laconia; George H. Flynn, Sr. and Delia Callahan
Maynard Earl, Jr., d. 3/22/1998 in Ctr. Ossipee; Maynard Earl Flynn, Sr. and Myrtle Lucy -----
Priscilla Ann, d. 4/25/1991 at 61 in Wolfeboro; b. Danvers, MA

FOGARTY,
Carolyn Ann, d. 10/30/1996 at 60 in Wolfeboro; Walter Barnea and Annie White

FOGG,
Albra, d. 8/8/1913 at 54; teacher; single; b. Ossipee; Ebenezer Fogg (Berwick, ME) and Eliza Tibbetts (Ossipee)
Carroll Moulton, d. 12/15/1993 at 70 in Wolfeboro
George W., d. 11/26/1941 at 77/1/21 in Ossipee; b. Ossipee; Simon Fogg and Mary Seaward
Mary Ann, d. 1/10/1890 at 60/5/4 in Ossipee; typhoid pneumonia; housewife; married; b. Ossipee
Richard, d. 2/6/1933 at 0/4/10 in Ossipee; b. Ossipee; Richard A. Fogg and Rose Redell

Simon, d. 1/16/1899 at 82/11/2 in Ossipee; convulsions; farmer; widower; b. Ossipee; Simon Fogg
Willard, d. 12/28/1993 at 88 in Ossipee

FOLEY,
Gertrude Mary Theresa, d. 8/4/1998 in Ossipee; Charles Mansfield and Lillian Buzzell
John C., d. 7/18/1991 at 69 in Ossipee; b. Fitchburg, MA

FOLKINS,
Mary A., d. 4/2/1965 at 86 in Ossipee; b. Chelsea, MA

FOLLANSBEE,
Ernest William, Sr., d. 8/22/1994 at 77; William Frank Follansbee

FOLSOM,
Abbie, d. 5/31/1911 at 75/2/1; mitral insufficiency; housewife; married; b. Ossipee; Moses Nichols (Ossipee) and Eliza Ingalls
Erastus, d. 5/17/1904 at 92/7 in Ossipee; old age; farmer; single
John, d. 4/7/1929 at 83/10/14 in Ossipee; b. Ossipee; Erastus Folsom and Eunice Wood
Loes B., d. 3/25/1896 at 64 in Ossipee; mitral regurgitation; housekeeper; married; Moses Nichols

FOOTE,
Gussei H., d. 11/20/1949 at 78/9/1 in Ossipee; b. Hoboken, NJ; Herman Schmidt and Albertina Koerner

FORD,
Richard Howard, d. 6/29/1997 at 70 in Ossipee; Roy Ford and Edna Ford

FOREST,
Carrie B., d. 3/30/1912 at 31/3/4
Charles, d. 12/15/1900 at 36 in Ossipee; paralysis heart; widower; b. Madison; John Forest

FORMAN,
Helen, d. 4/13/1985 at 91 in Ossipee; b. London, England
Thomas Robert, d. 6/8/1991 at 40 in Ossipee; b. Queens, NY

FORSYTHE,
Nettie Belle, d. 12/30/1992 at 80 in Ossipee; b. Wolfeboro

FORTIER,
John H., d. 5/9/1888 at 5/2/18; b. Ossipee

FOSS,
Charles E., d. 8/12/1969 at 79 in Ossipee; b. NH
Charles Gilbert, d. 11/8/1974 at 85 in Ossipee; b. ME
Florence B., d. 12/26/1969 at 73 in Ossipee; b. NH
John F., d. 3/26/1973 at 84 in Ossipee; b. ME
Lillian, d. 4/29/1888 at 0/6; b. Freedom
Lydia Ann, d. 3/31/1940 at 84/2/18 in Wolfeboro; b. Ossipee; Moses Tasker and Salorney Nichols
Mary Ellen, d. 4/22/1913 at 75
Perry A., d. 12/2/1887 at 31 in Ossipee; laborer; single; b. Tuftonboro; W. H. Foss (Tuftonboro) and Betsey T. Elliott (Tuftonboro)

FOSTER,
Addie M., d. 2/1/1966 at 80 in Ossipee; b. Freedom
Jennie A., d. 8/2/1955 at 95/11/20 in Ossipee; b. MA; William Storey and Sarah Kingston

FOTHERGILL,
Jeffrey C., d. 11/3/1985 at 19 in Ossipee; b. Attleboro, MA
Kristin L., d. 1/8/1982 at 14 in Ossipee; b. Attleboro, MA
Robert Clark, d. 1/8/1982 at 40 in Ossipee; b. Manchester

FOURNIER,
Lillian, d. 7/20/1972 at 92 in Wolfeboro; b. VT

FOX,
Edith, d. 2/6/1943 at 78/3 in Ossipee; b. Bethel, ME; Louis Eames and Martha Porter
Freeman, d. 8/11/1928 at 78; b. Porter, ME; David Fox and Mary Towle
Katherine, d. 1/29/1976 at 85 in Ossipee; b. NY

FRACKER,
Maxine M., d. 2/16/1975 at 74 in Wolfeboro; b. NY

FRANCIS,
Anna R., d. 1/17/1993 at 77 in Ossipee
William A., d. 4/28/1958 at 60 in Rochester; b. Dallas, TX; William Francis and Adelaide Hancock

FRAZEE,
Bert Leroy, d. 5/19/1972 at 83 in Ossipee; b. ME

FREEMAN,
Alexander H., d. 8/21/1996 at 83 in Wolfeboro; Morris Freeman and Pauline Kessler

FREETHY,
Lulu May, d. 6/16/1984 at 87 in Ossipee; b. Wolfeboro

FRENCH,
James R., d. 7/30/1905 at 53 in Ossipee; tuberculosis; single; Almira Lowe
Jennifer R., d. 4/25/1986 at 0/1/18 in Wolfeboro; b. Wolfeboro
Lillian M., d. 1/2/1931 at 38/2/6 in Rochester; b. GA; Cyrill Roy and Hattie Bluin
Prentiss E., d. 5/17/1969 at 86 in Ossipee; b. ME
Ruth Adla, d. 3/14/1997 at 81 in Ossipee; Joseph W. Rye and Mary Alice Jenkinson

FREY,
Charles I., d. 6/12/1903 at 77/2 in Rochester; pulmonary tuberculosis; carpenter; widower; b. Ossipee

FROHOCK,
Blanche J., d. 1/23/1970 at 77 in Wolfeboro; b. Canada
Earl S., d. 2/28/1980 at 87 in Wolfeboro; b. NH

FROST,
Arline Mable, d. 12/22/1998 in Ossipee; Leonard Nowlin and Mildred Humphrey
Bruce Ledyard, d. 4/12/1991 at 87 in Ossipee; b. Sequoit, NY
Colleen Joyce, d. 2/9/1941 at – in Ossipee; b. Ossipee; Randolph Frost and Sadie Hallett
Edwin Carl, Sr., d. 2/17/1997 at 75 in N. Conway; Herbert Frost and Bertha Hurd
Eleanor C., d. 4/4/1971 at 62 in Wolfeboro; b. OH
Ella F., d. 4/24/1895 at 43/3/25 in Ossipee; pulmonary consumption; housewife; widow
Gladys F., d. 11/23/1999 in N. Conway; Everett Shortridge and Alice Thompson
Guy R., d. 9/21/1956 at 63/0/7 in Ossipee; b. Farmington, ME; Charles Frost and Delia Millett
Herbert J., d. 11/3/1982 at 86 in Ossipee; b. Reading, MA
Mildred Rita, d. 9/27/1998 in Ossipee; Frank Barrett Nason and Henrietta McCarg Emery

FROTON,
Angeline E., d. 12/5/1968 at 60 in Wolfeboro; b. NH
Wilfred William, d. 10/20/1995 at 84; William Froton and Mary Elizabeth Muise

FRYE,
David, d. 9/25/1912 at 76
Ivory, d. 12/28/1907 at 78 in Ossipee; general debility; widower; b. Sandwich
Norman William, d. 1/10/1998 in Ossipee; George Frye and Catherine Beyerle

FULLAM,
Arthur Walter, d. 2/19/1996 at 93 in Ossipee; Walter Fullam and Lillian Farrar
Evelyn D., d. 1/29/1973 at 62 in Wolfeboro; b. WY

FULLER,
Edmund J., d. 10/25/1977 at 83 in Ossipee; b. MA
Leo, d. 10/25/1972 at 74 in Conway; b. ME

FURLONG,
Eleanor, d. 3/27/1913 at 76; housekeeper; widow; b. Portland, ME; Andrew J. Lord (Denmark, ME)
Mina W., d. 3/12/1963 at 93 in Ossipee; b. Canada

GAFFNEY,
Mary E., d. 1/20/1887 at 43 in Ossipee; married; b. Ossipee; Nathaniel Grant (Lebanon) and Saphronia M. Hobbs (Norway, ME)

GAGNE,
Alfred, d. 9/20/1977 at 57 in Ossipee; b. NH
Alfred J., d. 8/13/1951 at 62/5/17 in Ossipee; b. Canada; Alfred Gagne
Betty J., d. 6/3/1948 at 0/0/21 in Wolfeboro; b. Wolfeboro; Alfred Gagne and Frances Abbott

GAGNIERE,
Helen Mary, d. 1/12/1971 at 88 in Ossipee; b. NH

GAGNON,
Leopold, d. 6/9/1987 at 64 in Wolfeboro; b. Berwick, ME
Marie Rose, d. 2/10/1995 at 85; Napoleon Bouchette and Rose Parent

GALE,
Bertha M., d. 12/16/1986 in MA; b. 4/1945
Willis D., d. 5/19/1970 at 89 in Ossipee; b. NH

GALLAGHER,
Mary A., d. 11/28/1983 at 88 in Ossipee; b. Providence, RI

GALLANT,
Clifford Paul, d. 7/2/1999 at 71 in Ossipee; Jeremiah Gallant and Mary ----

GALLIGAN,
Helen I., d. 5/6/1983 at 72 in Ossipee; b. Pittsfield, ME

GALVIN,
Gertrude Jeanette, d. 8/11/2001 in Ossipee; Charles P. O'Connell and Gertrude A. Boyes

GAMESTER,
Ruth Marshall, d. 4/19/1997 at 92 in Wolfeboro; Charles H. Marshall and Mary Theresa Harney
Steven Leslie, d. 5/25/2000 at 44 in Ossipee; Robert T. Gamester and Pauline M. Labrie

GANDY,
Lydia, d. 2/5/1891 at 80/5 in Ossipee; housewife; widow; b. Ossipee; George Tasker (Ossipee) and Lydia Winchell

GANNETT,
Eliza, d. 11/8/1922 at 87/6/15 in Ossipee; housewife; widow; b. Sandwich; Samuel Vittum (Sandwich) and Mary Kennison (Albany)

GARDNER,
Addie, d. 9/22/1916 at 36; camp keeper; b. Somersworth; Frank Tonic (Canada)
Annie Drew, d. 1/8/1984 at 95 in Ossipee; b. Taunton, MA
Arthur J., d. 12/13/1954 at 84 in Ossipee; b. Matorn, Canada
Beatrice E., d. 3/21/1905 at 0/2/9 in Ossipee; cyanosis infantile; b. Rowley, MA; Wesley Gardner (Rowley, MA) and Mary Patch (Stowe, MA)
John H., d. 11/4/1969 at 86 in Ossipee; b. MA
Nellie A., d. 2/3/1965 at 90 in Ossipee; b. Ossipee

GARLAND,
Albert B., d. 11/8/1887 at 14/5 in Ossipee; b. Ossipee; Sumner Garland (Ossipee) and Augusta E. Chick (Ossipee)

Bertha E., d. 9/17/1940 at 69/0/16 in Ossipee; b. Effingham; Warren Chick and Hannah Bean
Dexter, d. 8/17/1896 at 87 in Ossipee; cholera morbus; widower
Edna M., d. 10/9/1962 at 86 in Ossipee; b. Moultonboro
Eli, d. 4/4/1899 at 73 in Ossipee; influenza; laborer; married
Fred E., d. 7/25/1984 at 83 in Ossipee; b. Sanbornville
Hannah, d. 5/16/1895 at 82/7/4 in Ossipee; chronic gastritis; housewife; widow; b. Effingham; Samuel Gile (Nottingham) and Eleaner Bean (Nottingham)
Ida Mabel, d. 12/10/1976 at 95 in Ossipee; b. NH
John L., d. 7/19/1968 at 75 in Wolfeboro; b. NH
Sumner G., d. 1/9/1913 at 63/5/10
Verlie E., d. 7/15/1999 in Wolfeboro; Frank Tufts and Fannie Thompson

GARNER,
Ralph Leslie, d. 5/5/1975 at 85 in Ossipee; b. PA
Romaine Sallie, d. 8/15/1979 at 91 in Ossipee; b. PA
Samuel Bronson, d. 1/9/1997 at 82 in Ossipee; Ralph Garner and Romaine Bronson

GARNETT,
Linda Joyce, d. 3/14/1997 at 47 in W. Ossipee; Francis Abbott and Janice Howard

GARRETT,
Benjamin Frank, d. 10/4/2001 in Ossipee; Frank William Garrett and Beryl M. Severance

GARROW,
George R., d. 12/19/1989 at 96 in Ossipee; b. Enosburg, VT
Ruth Frances, d. 4/17/1992 at 82 in Ossipee; b. Reading, MA

GAUTHIER,
Albert J., d. 2/12/1974 at 76 in Ossipee; b. Canada
Gary John, d. 9/21/1987 at 17 in Ossipee; b. Springfield, MA

GAY,
Elizabeth, d. 1/16/1903 at 83 in Ossipee; paralysis heart; housekeeper; widow; b. Wakefield; John Wingate (Wakefield)

GAYVORONSKY,
Gleb, d. 10/13/1999 in Wolfeboro; Alexander Levych and Ludmila Gayvoronsky

GEARWAR,
Esther B., d. 8/25/1980 at 85 in Ossipee; b. CT

GEE,
Peter, d. 10/6/1933 at 78 in Ossipee; b. Canada

GELLER,
Carl W., d. 8/30/1961 at 78 in Wolfeboro; b. Somerville, MA

GENEST,
David J., d. 8/19/1950 at 51 in Ossipee; b. Pittsfield; Oscar Genest and Clarinda Bussier

GEORGE,
Mark, d. 10/15/1907 at 64 in Ossipee; apoplexy

GERRARD,
George, d. 8/26/1947 at 65/8/6 in Ossipee; b. Arbcoth, Scotland; George Gerrard and Mary Fraser

GERRISH,
Helen W., d. 1/26/1990 at 83 in Ossipee; b. Manchester
Nettie L., d. 10/12/1936 at 83/7/22 in Ctr. Ossipee; b. Cornish, ME; Peleg Gerrish and Lydia Chase

GEYER,
Bertha Farr, d. 1/10/1993 at 99 in Ossipee

GIBSON,
Frank W., d. 5/15/1888 at 2/10; b. Ossipee; Albert E. Gibson and Georgie E. Gibson
Frederick M., d. 2/10/1904 at 73/11/6 in Ossipee; heart disease; farmer; married; b. Eastport; Samuel Gilman (sic) and Mary Ham
Julia A., d. 12/30/1917 at 73/1/26

GIFFIN,
Walter Lamont, d. 11/13/1994 at 83; Charles Lamont Giffin and Mary Reese

GILE,
Ernest E., d. 1/25/1964 at 67 in Wolfeboro; b. Charlestown, MA
Guerdon Francis, d. 7/5/1994 at 77; Robert Oscar Gile and Ora Edith Fall

GILES,
Chandler, d. 12/31/1886 at 65 in Ossipee; single; b. Wolfeboro
John T., d. 6/12/1952 at 78/4/27 in Wolfeboro; b. Eaton; John Giles and Ellen Ellis

GILLETT,
Gordon E., d. 2/15/1986 in FL; b. 4/1911

GILLIS,
Hazel May, d. 11/8/1981 at 86 in Ossipee; b. Quincy, MA

GILMAN,
Edmund T., d. 7/9/1925 at 82; b. Tamworth; Ezra Gilman and ----- Patenu
Irene S., d. 8/25/1953 at 34 in Laconia; b. Effingham; Edward Pike and Gladys Davis
Israel H., d. 2/19/1908 at 74/2/11 in Ossipee; apoplexy; farmer; b. Tamworth; Josiah Gilman (Tamworth) and Abigail Hapgood (Tamworth)
John F., d. 9/16/1912 at 74/5/15; farmer; married; b. Denmark, ME; John Gilman and Cyntha Gilman
Mary E., d. 10/26/1911 at 75/10/15; apoplexy; housewife; widow; b. Ossipee; Samuel D. Hobbs (Ossipee) and Louisa Moody (Ossipee)
Mary Ella, d. 7/16/1932 at 77/0/17 in Wolfeboro; b. Ossipee
Nellie May, d. 1/1/1986 at 90 in Ossipee; b. Tamworth
Orestes A., d. 11/15/1954 at 70 in N. Conway; b. Fryeburg, ME; Stephen Gilman and Alemda Small
Stephen, d. 7/17/1926 at 76; b. Baldwin, ME
Winnie, d. 11/10/1961 at 96 in Laconia; b. Water Village

GLIDDEN,
Alice R., d. 1/5/1904 at 87/2/16 in Ossipee; valvular disease of heart; housewife; married; b. Waterboro; Micajah Bean (Waterbury) and Eunice Pike (ME)
Amelia, d. 12/21/1940 at 85/1/8 in Ossipee; b. Ossipee
Beulah L., d. 7/22/1896 at 18 in Ossipee; mitral regurgitation; single; b. MA; N. F. Glidden and Louise Hutchins
Della F., d. 8/11/1950 at 77 in Laconia; b. ME; Eben Beane and Annie Wasgott
Elmer R., d. 8/31/1953 at 63 in Wolfeboro; b. Boston, MA; Elmer R. Glidden and Mary T. Brown
Frank O., d. 1/26/1941 at 80/9/3 in Wolfeboro; b. Calais, ME; Joseph Glidden and Maria Scott
Gertrude, d. 11/20/1983 at 93 in Ossipee; b. Wolfeboro
Harry, d. 8/9/1966 at 88 in Ossipee; b. S. Tamworth

John B., d. 2/13/1911 at 77/2/14; Brights disease; farmer; married; b. Ossipee; Jeremiah Glidden and Betsey Clay

John E., d. 6/20/1941 at 73/7/13 in Wolfeboro; b. Ossipee; Daniel F. Glidden and Mary Goldsmith

Lyle Ernest, d. 9/20/2000 at 80 in Ossipee; Arthur Glidden and Gertrude Chick

Malcolm William, d. 8/8/1996 at 68 in Ossipee; Stanley Glidden and Adeline Goldsmith

Mary E., d. 9/3/1914 at 83; housewife; b. Marblehead, MA; Nathaniel Goldsmith (Marblehead, MA) and Loisa Hyde (Ossipee)

Perlie H., d. 1/12/1911 at 21/7/1; pneumonia; carpenter; single; b. Effingham; Willie M. Glidden (Effingham) and Rosa A. Linscott (Brownfield, ME)

Sara Elizabeth, d. 10/23/1927 at 60/7/15; b. Boston; Frederick H. Grant and Sara E. Quinn

Susan, d. 1/14/1932 at 88/11/1 in Ossipee; b. Effingham; Fineas Glidden and Elizabeth Edgecomb

William M., d. 7/11/1922 at 56/7/8 in Ossipee; married; b. Ossipee; Daniel F. Glidden (Ossipee) and Mary E. Goldsmith (Marblehead, MA)

Willie M., d. 9/6/1925 at 67/0/1; b. Effingham; Vanburn Glidden and Margarette Mitchell

Woodbury, d. 5/18/1929 at 60/6 in Ossipee; b. Alton; Herman Glidden and Maria Harriman

GLIESMAN,
Thomas, d. 4/24/2000 in Manchester; William Gliesman and Grace Clark

GLOVER,
David M., d. 8/23/1946 at – in Ossipee; b. Sandwich

GODFREY,
Alonzo, d. 10/13/1906 at 52/0/5 in Ossipee; valvular disease of heart; single; b. Freedom; Benjamin Godfrey

Sarah A., d. 7/25/1920 at 87/2/13; widow; b. Togus, ME; Gersham A. Cross (Cross Hill, ME) and Mary B. Smart (Monmouth)

GOING,
Warren Elibe, d. 10/2/1996 at 94 in Ossipee; Chester Going and Mary Graves

GOLDSMITH,
Amerette, d. 9/17/1917 at 77/11/11; widow

Charles, d. 4/11/1901 at 50 in Ossipee; cardiac dropsy; single; b. Ossipee

Daniel, d. 8/25/1897 at 96/3/21 in Ossipee; old age; farmer; widower; b. Ossipee; H. Goldsmith and Betsy Roberts

Daniel A., d. 4/21/1912 at 53/4/8; farmer; single; b. Ossipee; George E. Goldsmith (Ossipee) and Emily Gilchrist (Andover, MA)

Dorathy, d. 3/22/1891 at 85 in Ossipee; widow

Emily, d. 10/4/1912 at 83/2/1; widow; b. Andover, MA; Amos Gilchrist

Fred E., d. 10/25/1907 at 44/9/19 in Ossipee; peritonitis; farmer; single; b. Ossipee; George Goldsmith (Ossipee) and Emily Goldsmith (Andover, MA)

George H., d. 7/10/1903 at 42/4/10 in Ossipee; tuberculosis; printer; widower; b. Ossipee; George Goldsmith (Ossipee) and Emily Gilchrist

Hannah F., d. 11/6/1923 at 77/8/17; b. Ossipee; Fred Wiggin and Hannah Gilman

J. L., d. 11/23/1904 at 78/1/19 in Wolfeboro; mitral insufficiency; farmer; married; b. Wolfeboro; Joshua Goldsmith (Ossipee) and Mary Leavitt (Effingham)

Louisa, d. 2/6/1901 at 92 in Ossipee; old age; housewife; widow; Levi Hyde and Louisa Hyde

S., d. 3/1/1919 at 61/2/25; farmer; married; b. Boston, MA; F. L. Goldsmith (Ossipee) and Julia Cram (VT)

William F., d. 3/22/1911 at 82/1/4; weak heart; farmer; married; b. Ossipee; William Goldsmith (Wolfeboro) and Nancy Sceggel (Wolfeboro)

GONYER,
Ralph Henry, d. 6/14/1997 at 60 in Rochester; Henry Richard Gonyer, Sr. and Flora Evelina Morse

GOOD,
Anne T., d. 7/3/1948 at 73/6/5 in Ossipee; b. Boston, MA; Michael Crane and Anne Nerne

GOODALE,
Leoine Hale, d. 9/1/1974 at 64 in Laconia; b. NH

GOODALL,
Carrie, d. 10/31/1970 at 85 in Ossipee; b. MA

GOODEY,
Mary Alice, d. 6/25/1941 at 75/1/2 in Concord; b. MA; Henry D. Casey and ----- Bennett

GOODHUE,
Mary E., d. 2/15/1971 at 60 in Wolfeboro; b. MA

GOODRICH,
Charles W., d. 7/12/1916 at 53; engineer; married; b. Berwick, ME

GOODWIN,
Elvie B., d. 10/28/1972 at 87 in Ossipee; b. MA
Ernest Clayton, d. 9/15/1993 at 92 in Ossipee
Haven K., d. 5/29/1976 at 67 in Wolfeboro; b. NH
John F., d. 5/7/1951 at 73 in Exeter; b. Madison; Thomas Goodwin and Naomi Dugan
Naomi, d. 6/19/1905 at 48/8 in Ossipee; apoplexy; housewife; married; b. Eaton; Joel W. Durgin (Eaton) and M. Roberts (Eaton)
Thomas, d. 1/6/1910 at 69/9/29 in Ossipee; heart disease; retired; widower; b. Madison

GORDON,
Louella C., d. 8/20/1975 at 67 in Ossipee; b. NH

GORENFLO,
Antoinette E., d. 11/28/1977 at 81 in Ossipee; b. DE

GOULD,
Gladys G., d. 4/18/1978 at 73 in Ossipee; b. RI
Harry B., d. 2/7/1987 at 80 in Wolfeboro; b. Roxbury, MA
James, d. 12/4/1923 at 72; b. Quebec

GOUMAS,
Mary Fogg, d. 4/21/1998 in Ossipee; Thomas Fogg and Edith Soderston

GRAF,
John W., d. 1/31/1986 at 40 in Wolfeboro; b. Waterbury, CT

GRAHAM,
Annie M. G., d. 1/25/1971 at 79 in Ossipee; b. NH
Charles, d. 7/13/1901 at 60 in Ossipee; mitral insufficiency; married

GRAMES,
Edward, d. 2/13/1966 at 74 in Ossipee; b. Bartlett
Julia E., d. 11/13/1897 at 5/6 in Ossipee; membranous croup; b. Ossipee; Charles Grames (NS) and Josie Eastman (Bartlett)

GRANT,
Charlott S., d. 12/27/1891 at 83/1/28 in Ossipee; widow; b. Norway, ME; William Hobbs and Cathrine S. Hobbs
Fanny M., d. 12/29/1915 at 76/1/11; none [occupation]; widow

Hattie Delora, d. 1/5/1989 at 86 in Ossipee; b. Bartlett
John Francis, d. 9/15/1944 at 38/4/9 in Laconia; b. Holyoke, MA; John F. Grant and Helen Bulger
Nathaniel, d. 10/5/1889 at 85/5/28; physician; married; b. Lebanon, ME; Edward Grant and Elizabeth Leavitt
Nelson, d. 5/30/1934 at 67/4/21 in Ossipee; b. Jefferson; James Grant
William H., d. 8/23/1906 at 71/9/18 in Ossipee; angina pectoris; physician; married; b. Wakefield; Nathaniel Grant (Lebanon, ME) and Charlotte Hobbs

GRAVES,
Abbie F., d. 6/6/1916 at 68/3/1; housewife; b. Tuftonboro
Delfred R., d. 11/27/1941 at 81/8/23 in Plymouth; b. Boston, MA; Alexis J. Graves and Almira C. Rounsevel
Joanna, d. 9/15/1901 at 79/7/15 in Ossipee; cholera morbus; widow; b. Ossipee; Micajah Bean (Brentwood) and Eunice Pike (Waterboro)

GRAY,
daughter, d. 7/29/1945 at 0/0/0 in Rochester; b. Rochester; Edwin J. Gray and Ethel F. Libby
Ellenora Hastings, d. 3/13/1988 at 95 in Ossipee; b. Ireland
Frank A., d. 6/30/1972 at 88 in Ossipee; b. NH
Harold, d. 9/14/1904 at 0/0/15 in Ossipee; premature birth; b. Ossipee; Walter Gray (Lunenburg, VT) and Etta Mason (Albany)
Harold M., d. 4/3/1950 at 56/2/1 in Ossipee; b. Oldtown, ME; Granville Gray and Lucy White
Irving Priest, d. 12/4/2001 in Ossipee; James E. Gray and Ruth Priest
James C., d. 9/27/1981 at 83 in Laconia; b. Ludlow, VT
Laura, d. 1/29/1925 at 66; Oliver Hurd and Mandy McIntyre
Leah Mae, d. 3/27/1988 at 97 in Ossipee; b. Kearsarge
Louis N., d. 1/26/1980 at 73 in Wolfeboro; b. NH
Sylvia Martha, d. 2/2/1995 at 85; Frederick P. Cram and Annie L. McIntire

GREELEY,
Maude E., d. 2/21/1959 at 74 in Ossipee; b. Hyde Park, MA; John Greeley and Mary Backus

GREEN,
Mary, d. 9/25/1917 at 76; housework; divorced; b. Canada

GREENLAW,
Emma H., d. 3/2/1981 at 98 in Ossipee; b. Strafford

GREENWOOD,
Ellen Beatrice, d. 10/3/1983 at 87 in Ossipee; b. NB

GREGOIRE,
Yvonne, d. 1/25/1960 at 53 in Wolfeboro; b. Berlin

GREGORY,
Albert J., Jr., d. 11/20/1948 at 21/8/15 in Ossipee; b. Newmarket; Albert Gregory and Madeline Connoly

GRENQUIST,
Angelina N., d. 7/2/1961 at 66 in Meredith; b. MA
Otto B., d. 3/31/1962 at 74 in Wolfeboro; b. Portland, ME

GRIDLEY,
Alyce, d. 2/14/1987 at 92 in Wolfeboro; b. Dorchester, MA
Lillian M., d. 7/27/1964 at 46 in Ossipee; b. Wolfeboro

GRIFFIN,
Elijah, d. 5/29/1890 at 87 in Ossipee; old age; farmer; married; b. Ossipee
Grover C., d. 12/21/1968 at 80 in Ossipee; b. ME
Louise May, d. 6/9/1939 at 21/9/10 in Wolfeboro; Harry Nelson and Arvilla Templeton
Lydia, d. 12/1/1902 at 81/10/26 in Ossipee; pulmonary tuberculosis; housewife; widow; b. Ossipee; Joshua Roberts

GRONDAL,
Bror J., d. 5/17/1986 in PA; b. 1/1910
Mildred, d. 5/18/1986 in MA; b. 8/1910

GUENETTE,
Mary J., d. 11/23/1961 at 88 in Wolfeboro; b. Manchester

GUILIANI,
Bruno, d. 2/21/1998 in Ossipee; Giuseppe Guiliani and Catherine Ardesinno

GUPTIL,
Joseph, d. 1/5/1889 at 59/0/2; domestic (sic); single; b. Haverhill; Joseph Guptil and Abigail Currier

GURLEY,
Doris Morse, d. 5/5/1997 at 67 in Ossipee; Fred Monroe Morse and Grace Johnson

GUTHRIE,
Charles Parks, d. 11/28/1979 at 82 in Ossipee; b. NC

HAAG,
Camile W., d. 2/6/1981 at 88 in Ossipee; b. New York, NY

HACKETT,
Norman L., d. 5/4/1979 at 62 in Wolfeboro; b. NH
William, d. 7/25/1944 at 75/3/13 in Ossipee; b. Danvers, MA; William R. Hackett and Olive V. Neaston

HADDOCK,
Georgia, d. 9/20/1917 at 22; single; b. Ossipee; George Haddock and Lucinda Cold (Cornish, ME)

HADLOCK,
Virginia Wentworth, d. 7/11/1988 at 70 in Wolfeboro; b. Malden, MA

HAFFORD,
Ronald Cyrus, d. 10/22/1992 at 0/0/4 in Lebanon; b. Lebanon

HAGON,
Priscella, d. 6/13/1958 at 71 in Wolfeboro; b. Worcester, MA; Richard Powers and Annie Balmer

HAHN,
Arthur G., d. 3/23/1987 at 61 in N. Conway; b. Lynn, MA
Nettie G., d. 1/12/1956 at 82/4 in Ossipee; b. Rochester, NY; George Patterson and Charlotte Patterson
Ruth A., d. 6/14/1985 at 86 in Wolfeboro; b. Rochester, NY

HAINES,
Ada Rendall, d. 11/12/1973 at 97 in Ossipee; b. NH
George, d. 7/22/1962 at 84 in Concord; b. Ossipee
William H., d. 8/23/1913 at 66; none [occupation]; widower; b. Exeter, England

HALE,
Rosanne Belle, d. 4/8/1973 at 75 in Ossipee; b. NH

HALEY,
Albert G., d. 11/6/1977 at 93 in Ossipee; b. MA
Myron, d. 2/15/1966 at 62 in Ossipee; b. Tuftonboro

HALL,
Edith M., d. 11/10/1993 at 93 in Ossipee
Herbert E., d. 5/22/1956 at 50 in Wolfeboro; b. Lawrence, MA; Fred Hall and Grace Nickolson
Lyman, d. 9/28/1927 at –; b. Andover; Andrew J. Hall and Susan J. Bots
Ora A., d. 8/8/1912 at 61

HALLET,
Spurge C., d. 8/2/1988 at 67 in Wolfeboro; b. Conway

HALLETT,
Agnes, d. 3/19/1978 at 67 in Wolfeboro; b. ME
Belle Sargent, d. 7/31/1971 at 78 in Ossipee; b. NH

HALPIN,
Donald B., d. 10/25/21999 in Wolfeboro; Joseph Halpin and Viola Dean

HAM,
Belma M., d. 3/14/1954 at 52 in Saco, ME; b. Ossipee; Walter Cook and Delia Philbrick
Florence, d. 3/23/1999 in Portland, ME; George Haley and Edith Ayers
John G., d. 4/23/1913 at 82; postmaster; married
Mary D., d. 4/5/1888 at 64/5/11; housekeeper; widow; b. Wakefield; William Ham and Mary Roberts
Nancy A., d. 11/18/1919 at 85/2/18; housewife; widow; b. Freedom; William Sanborn and Betsy Taylor
Sarah, d. 2/1/1965 at 88 in Ossipee; b. Jackson
Waldo, d. 10/9/1972 at 86 in Ossipee; b. NH

HAMEL,
Arlene Marion, d. 2/2/1989 at 71 in Wolfeboro; b. Bartlett
William I., d. 6/5/1986 at 75 in Ossipee; b. Franklin

HAMILTON,
Esther L., d. 4/6/1969 at 62 in Ossipee; b. NH
Harry R., d. 1/23/1984 at 88 in Wolfeboro; b. E. Rochester
Mildred S., d. 2/13/1990 at 91 in Ossipee; b. S. Lebanon, ME

HAMLET,
Eliza A., d. 5/7/1936 at 70/0/5 in Ossipee; b. Conway; Matthew Hale and Jane E. Caverley

HAMLIN,
Rena Henrietta, d. 8/10/1974 at 92 in Ossipee; b. NH

HAMM,
Alphonse J., d. 8/20/1924 at 60/3/25; b. Wakefield
Charles E., d. 9/24/1922 at 87/2 in Ossipee; carpenter; widower; b. Strafford; Hiram Hamm (Strafford) and Susan Hall (Strafford)
Hiram B., d. 1/20/1905 at 13/2/8 in Ossipee; chronic Bright's disease; student; b. Ossipee; William B. Hamm (Ossipee) and M. L. Mitchell (Union)
Mabel S., d. 4/6/1942 at 78/2/17 in Ossipee; b. Wakefield; Joseph Mitchell and Harriett Sampson
William B., d. 11/21/1942 at 75/10/23 in Wolfeboro; b. Ossipee; Hiram Hamm and Mary Nutter

HAMMOND,
Abbie, d. 4/29/1918 at 54/7/27; housewife; married; b. Effingham; Aaron Bunker (Effingham) and May Weymouth (Brownfield)
Allen D., d. 4/29/1971 at 74 in Wolfeboro; b. MA
Barbara L., d. 10/27/1985 at 83 in Ossipee; b. Milton, MA
Charlotte Lydia, d. 10/19/1986 at 81 in Ossipee; b. Halifax, NS
David, d. 2/16/1899 at 0/8/25 in Ossipee; b. Ossipee; Daniel Hammond (Ossipee) and Abbie E. Bunker (Effingham)
Edward, d. 1/7/1963 at 91 in Ossipee; b. Ossipee
Erdine, d. 2/22/1909 at 18 in Ossipee; pneumonia; housekeeper; b. Ossipee; David Eldridge (Ossipee) and Eliza Eldridge (Ossipee)
Flora B., d. 8/12/1906 at 16/11 in Ossipee; puerperal convulsions; maid; single; b. Ossipee; Daniel Hammond (Ossipee) and Ella Bunker (Norway, ME)
Lester, d. 10/18/1944 at 61/4/18 in Ossipee; b. Ossipee; Daniel Hammond and Nellie Clough
Mary A., d. 3/18/1934 at 59/10 in Tamworth; b. NS; Hugh MacGilivrary
Nettie M., d. 3/11/1911 at 19/5; peritonitis; single; b. Ossipee; Daniel Harmon (Effingham) and Abbie E. Bunker (Bartlett)
Olive I., d. 8/27/1987 at 97 in Ossipee; b. Medfield, MA
Sylvia S., d. 12/18/1980 at 108 in Ossipee; b. Fryeburg, ME
Upton, d. 10/27/1891 at 75 in Ossipee; brickmaker; widower; b. Ossipee; Thomas Hammond (Ossipee) and Mary Ingalls
Walter W., d. 3/20/1982 at 85 in Ossipee; b. Ossipee
William B., d. 6/13/1924 at 76/2/18; b. Ossipee; David Hammond

HANDY,
Lucy E., d. 5/27/1891 at 46 in Ossipee; housewife; widow; b. Biddeford, ME

HANEY,
Hazel B., d. 4/25/1971 at 68 in Wolfeboro; b. MA

Ralph A., d. 9/10/1959 at 66 in Ossipee; b. Sanbornville; William A. Haney and Abbie A. Avery

HANNAN,
Jason M., d. 9/26/1985 at 28 in Ossipee; b. Worcester, MA

HANSCOM,
Martin, d. 3/26/1925 at 73; b. Jackson; James Hanscom and Mary Martin
Olive, d. 8/27/1907 at 74/10/8 in Ossipee; gangrene; housewife; widow; b. Effingham; John Litcomb and Maria Chase

HANSCOMB,
Bray, d. 8/19/1892 at 75 in Ossipee; consumption; farmer; married; b. Strafford; Jeremiah Hanscam (sic) (Strafford) and Sarah Croaxno (Strafford)

HANSEN,
Lillian C., d. 3/17/1982 at 76 in Ossipee; b. Portland, ME
Linda Jean, d. 11/12/1998 in W. Ossipee; Chester Webster and Hazel Ames
Michael, d. 8/1/1965 at 93 in Ossipee; b. Ettlebruck, Luxembourg

HANSON,
son, d. 5/25/1958 at – in Wolfeboro; b. Wolfeboro; Kenneth Hanson and Irene Wilkins
Afia A., d. 10/28/1914 at 65/5/9; farmer
Annie M., d. 3/26/1933 at 84/10/8 in Ossipee; b. Danvers, MA; George Perkins and Maria Buckley
Arthur, d. 9/25/1976 at 85 in Concord; b. NH
Arvilla, d. 4/7/1930 at 79 in Ossipee; b. Ossipee; Samuel Hobbs and Louise Moody
Benjamin W., d. 6/29/1910 at 69/6/17 in Ossipee; nephritis; farmer; married; b. Brookfield; John Hanson (Brookfield) and Abigail Watson (Ossipee)
Carl Nocona, d. 5/31/2000 at 16 in Ossipee; Peter A. Hanson and Jeannette M. Walsh
Charles A., d. 10/27/1903 at 30/11/5 in Ossipee; valvular disease of heart; farmer; single; b. Ossipee; John Hanson (Ossipee) and Lydia Peavey (Ossipee)
Cyrus, d. 10/25/1888 at 69/6; farmer; widower; b. Gilford; Aaron Hanson
Dorcas L., d. 5/26/1906 at 83/11/2 in Ossipee; old age; housewife; widow; b. Ossipee; Moses Hanson (Ossipee) and Joanna Hanson (Ossipee)
Elisha, d. 5/7/1897 at 76/4 in Ossipee; pneumonia; married; b. Ossipee

Ella, d. 3/6/1906 at 41/3/12 in Ossipee; apoplexy; housewife; married; b. Ossipee; George A. Keniston (Ossipee) and Belle Kimball (Effingham)
Ella Louise, d. 1/20/1943 at 86/11/21 in Larchmont, NY; b. Ossipee; Daniel F. Glidden and Mary E. Goldsmith
Emma, d. 10/9/1898 at 55 in Ossipee; pneumonia; housewife; widow; Loring Brown
Frank S., d. 3/23/1915 at 55/0/10; hotel keeper; married; b. Ossipee; Moses F. Hanson (Ossipee) and Emily Sias
Frank W., d. 9/12/1933 at 58 in Ossipee; b. Stoneham, MA; James A. Hanson and Anna M. Perkins
Frederick Eugene, d. 9/1/1939 at 81/1/25 in Ossipee; b. Ossipee; William Hanson and Hannah Abbott
Greenleaf, d. 9/17/1933 at 92 in Ossipee; b. Wakefield
Greta Spongberg, d. 10/3/1994 at 89; Carl Spongberg and Alvida Fredriks
James, d. 5/29/1904 at 56 in Ossipee; paralysis of heart; clerk; married; b. Eaton
James W., d. 9/28/1925 at 35/3/17; b. Ossipee; Isaac Hanson and Sarah Leighton
Jerry, d. 12/28/1907 at 60/1/6 in Ossipee; mitral insufficiency; farmer; married; b. Ossipee; Stacy D. Hanson (Ossipee) and Adaline Wood (Ossipee)
John, d. 3/2/1921 at 75/11/2 in Ossipee; farmer; widower; Stacey Hanson (Freedom) and Adeline Wood (Freedom)
John F., d. 1/30/1909 at 68/1/12 in Ossipee; gastritis; farmer; b. Ossipee; Isaac Hanson (Effingham) and Sarah Leighton (Effingham)
Karen L., d. 7/24/1965 at 71 in Sanford, ME; b. Ossipee
Kenneth Roland, d. 11/23/1998 in Wolfeboro; Lewis Hanson and Karen Canney
Lettie, d. 12/29/1939 at 70/9 in Ossipee; b. Ossipee; William H. Eldridge and R. Welch
Lewis M., d. 7/20/1976 at 86 in Sanford, ME; b. Ossipee
Lilliam, d. 3/15/1919 at 55/9/11; hotel prop.; widow; b. Springfield, MA; William Patrell (Holyoke, MA) and Etta Hovey (SC)
Lois Marjory, d. 3/11/1982 at 82 in Ossipee; b. Sanbornville
Lydia C., d. 7/7/1901 at 50/1/20 in Ossipee; paralysis of heart; housewife; married; b. Ossipee; Thomas Peavey and Deborah Sherburne (Rochester)
Mary, d. 1/15/1899 at 65 in Ossipee; old age
Mary S., d. 3/7/1929 at 73/10/3 in Wolfeboro
Moses F., d. 12/2/1914 at 80; stable keeper; married; b. Ossipee; William Hanson and Hannah Abbott
Nathan, d. 3/26/1931 at 79/6/21 in Ossipee; b. Ossipee; Erastus Hanson and Nancy Nute

HARDEN,
Neal, d. 12/10/1945 at 66/11/17 in Ctr. Ossipee; b. Kennebunk, ME; Ellsworth Harden and Frances Brown

HARDING,
Frederick William, d. 6/2/1995 at 82; Arthur Harding and Catherine Flynn
Howard P., d. 9/27/1926 at 53/10/30; b. Baldwin, ME; Joshua Harding and Sarah Huntress
Ida C., d. 7/24/1965 at 89 in Gorham; b. Farmington
Viola Sawyer, d. 5/1/1997 at 85 in Wolfeboro; William L. Sawyer and Bertha Trask

HARMON,
son, d. 5/14/1889 at 0/0/3; b. Ossipee; Charles M. Harmond (sic) and Lydia O. Merry
Beatrice G., d. 1/20/1992 at 89 in Ossipee; b. E. Haverhill
Bernard A., d. 9/17/1985
Georgie I., d. 1/1/935 at 41/6/26 in Wolfeboro; b. Madison; John Frost and Bertha Hammond
Gladys Lewis, d. 5/27/1988 at 91 in Ossipee; b. Ossipee
John M., d. 3/11/1946 at 75/9/11 in Ossipee; b. Freedom; Reuben Harmon and Olive M. Harmon
Olive, d. 7/17/1912 at 77/10; widow; b. Freedom; J. Moulton and Hannah Cushion (Freedom)
Reuben S., d. 1/29/1965 at 71 in Wolfeboro; b. Brookfield
Sarah M., d. 2/9/1946 at 82/8/4 in Ossipee; b. Wolfeboro; Samuel Eaton and Elizabeth Berry
Supply, d. 12/23/1944 at 56/4/14 in Ossipee; b. Standish, ME; Herman G. Harmon and Mary E. Wiggin
Thelma Emily, d. 11/23/1977 at 47 in Ossipee; b. NH

HARRIMAN,
Cyrus, d. 4/28/1889 at –; farmer; widower; b. Ossipee
Edna E., d. 5/21/1911 at 0/7/7; b. Boston, MA; ----- Harrison (sic) and Carrie A. Brooks (East Boston)
Elizabeth, d. 11/20/1898 at 77/7/18 in Melrose; hearts disease
Isaac, d. 5/25/1917 at 81/3/26; teamster; widower; b. St. Andrews, NB; I. C. Harrison (sic) and Harriet Hinson
Laura, d. 6/8/1969 at 78 in Ossipee; b. NH
Lottie Belle, d. 9/20/1972 at 95 in Ossipee; b. NH
M. P. (male), d. 3/30/1896 at – in Ossipee; apoplexy; married

HARRIS,
James A., d. 10/20/1978 at 83 in Ossipee; b. MA

HARRISON,
James Robert, d. 4/5/1995 at 71; Clarence J. Harrison and Mary Kidd
Jennifer N., d. 8/4/1979 at 6 in Laconia; b. NH

HART,
Donald B., Jr., d. 12/1/1992 at 63 in Manchester; b. Farmington
Lillian E., d. 7/9/1905 at 0/11 in Ossipee; acute gastritis; b. Boston, MA; Charles J. Hart (Boston, MA)
Walter John, d. 11/28/2001 in Ossipee; Herbert Hart and Maude Ina Calback

HARTE,
William Elliot, d. 7/15/1998 in Wolfeboro; Carl John Harte and Mary Doherty

HARTFORD,
Beryl, d. 12/22/1933 at 4/4/2 in Wolfeboro; b. Ossipee; Daniel Hartford and Nora Knox
Lottie R., d. 8/27/1975 at 96 in S. Paris; b. ME
Nora F., d. 8/12/1966 at 69 in Conway; b. Ossipee

HASKELL,
Edward E., d. 1/20/1939 at 84/8/23 in Ossipee; b. Dover; John S. Haskell and Orinda Cree

HASLETT,
Eliza, d. 4/30/1887 at 80 in Ossipee; housekeeper; single; b. Ossipee

HATCH,
Adelma T., d. 7/14/1974 at 88 in Ossipee; b. NH
Lillian Bertha, d. 12/19/1994 at 71; Walter Nickerson and Bertha Hedlundh
Maud H., d. 11/24/1895 at 1/3/1 in Ossipee; acute bronchitis; Ivory Hatch (Berlin I., ME) and Myra F. Abbott (Berlin I., ME)
Simeon W., d. 5/4/1903 at 76 in Ossipee; valvular disease of heart; farmer; widower; b. Eaton
Tryphosa M., d. 5/10/1928 at 87/10/19

HATHAWAY,
Frances S., d. 3/10/1922 at 78/10/16 in Ossipee; retired; widow; b. Portsmouth; ----- Kingsbury (York, ME) and ----- Abbott (Portsmouth)

HATTENBURG,
Doris E., d. 2/15/1990 at 77 in Wolfeboro; b. Canada

HAUBRIDGE,
Wilhelmina, d. 8/17/1934 at 71/10 in Ossipee; b. Hamburg, Germany

HAUCK,
Charles W., d. 11/15/1989 at 79 in Ossipee; b. Seterritani, PA

HAUGHN,
Constance M., d. 5/31/1974 at 85 in Ossipee; b. VT

HAUSMANN,
Nicole Eve, d. 1/29/1996 at 22 in Ossipee; Miguel Hausmann and Linda Preysler

HAYDEN,
Elizabeth, d. 9/26/1971 at 87 in Ossipee; b. CT
George W., d. 4/20/1951 at 76/7/24 in Wolfeboro; b. Roxbury, MA; Charles Hayden and Frances Butler
Howard P., d. 12/11/1950 at 59/10/16 in Ossipee; b. Avon, MA; Amos Hayden and Ellen Hodgdon

HAYES,
daughter, d. 6/18/1946 at – in Wolfeboro; b. Wolfeboro; Kenneth M. Hayes and Helen Ashe
Della Frances, d. 4/19/1970 at 85 in Ossipee; b. NH
E. W., d. 3/19/1891 at 65 in Ossipee; widower
Kenneth M., d. 2/18/1978 at 64 in Wolfeboro; b. VT
Lucy Edna, d. 2/15/1981 at 90 in Wolfeboro; b. Alton

HAYFORD,
Ernest Arthur, d. 4/1/1978 at 47 in Manchester; b. NH
John A., d. 1/26/1982 at 59 in Wolfeboro; b. Ossipee
Leona M., d. 12/19/1978 at 77 in Ossipee; b. ME

HAYNES,
Verna Elvira, d. 11/5/1994 at 108; Elmer Merrow and Elizabeth Brooks

HAZARD,
Elizabeth Moody Allen, d. 11/7/1971 at 83 in Ossipee; b. MA

HAZLETT,
Alvah, d. 4/4/1903 at 73 in Lynn; cancer; farmer; widower

HEALD,
James, d. 9/11/1932 at 0/2/4 in Ossipee; b. Ossipee; Helen Heald

James N., Sr., d. 8/23/1961 at 90 in Ossipee; b. Dixmont, ME

HEALEY,
Daniel F., d. 7/24/1976 at 42 in Ossipee; b. MA

HEARD,
Howard B., d. 4/24/1967 at 84 in Ossipee; b. Sandwich

HEATH,
Alvin E., d. 11/28/1968 at 62 in Wolfeboro; b. NH
Charles W., d. 9/30/1888 at 63; farmer; married
Clayton Elmer, d. 12/12/2001 in Ossipee; Chester Lewis Heath and Ester Baker
Daniel, d. 5/31/1931 at 82/10/23 in Ossipee; b. Ossipee; Benjamin Heath and Abby Clark
Edwin H., d. 2/1/1942 at 85/1/3 in Ossipee; b. Chatham; Jonathan W. Heath and Catherine M. Burbank
Frank, d. 7/7/1911 at 58; insanity; laborer
Georgiana, d. 1/17/1892 at 40 in Ossipee; pneumonia; housekeeper; widow; b. Ossipee; Asa M. Abbott (Ossipee)
Joseph F., d. 4/29/1908 at 52/1/18 in Ossipee; pneumonia; farmer; b. Roxbury, MA; William Heath (Roxbury, MA) and Mary Sanderson (Boston, MA)
Joseph P., d. 12/7/1915 at 80/10/23; merchant; widower; b. Ossipee; Benjamin Heath (Newfield, ME) and Abbie Clark (Concord)
Lily E., d. 1/19/1969 at 67 in Ossipee; b. England
Mary, d. 3/7/1923 at 80
Mary Leavitt, d. 1/8/1938 at 89/6/4 in Ossipee; b. Ossipee; John R. Garland and Hannah Frances Gile
Mrs. Benjamin, d. 4/25/1891 at 82/4/15 in Ossipee; domestic; widow; b. Concord

HEBERT,
Omer A., d. 12/6/1974 at 60 in VT; b. NH
Sherry Lynn, d. 11/19/1994 at 13; Timothy L. Hebert and Deborah Scripture

HEHL,
Jacob L., Sr., d. 10/22/1959 at 57 in Wolfeboro; b. NY; Louis Hehl and Josephine Cada

HEINRICH,
Richard P., d. 3/1/2000 at 56 in Ctr. Ossipee; Herman Heinrich and Charlotte Koerner

Robert Herman, d. 7/8/1996 at 55 in Laconia; Herman Heinrich and Charlotte Koerner

HELME,
daughter, d. 3/12/1895 at 0/0/12 in Ossipee; scrofula; b. Ossipee; C. W. Helme (Hingham) and Emma Ames (Ossipee)
son, d. 4/25/1900 at – in Ossipee; natural causes; b. Ossipee; Charles W. Helme (Hingham) and Emma J. Helme (Guilford)
son, d. 6/8/1910 at 0/0/1 in Ossipee; marasmus; b. Ossipee; Charles W. Helme and Emma J. Ames (Gilford)
Alvin Fuller, d. 2/10/1989 at 84 in Wolfeboro; b. Ossipee
Charles H., d. 4/20/1985 at 89 in Franconia; b. Ossipee
Charles W., d. 5/8/1914 at 60; farmer
Daniel, d. 6/2/1957 at 64 in Concord; b. Ossipee; Ch. W. Helme and Emma Ames
Emma J., d. 6/8/1910 at 44/5/16 in Ossipee; pleurisy; housewife; married; b. Gilford; Barnet H. Ames (Laconia) and Sarah J. Eldridge (Ossipee)
Stephen, d. 10/28/1913 at 14/7/23; scholar; single; b. Ossipee; Charles W. Helme (RI) and Emma Ames (Ossipee)

HEMANN,
John William, d. 11/9/1983 at 58 in Portsmouth; b. Des Moines, IA

HENDERSON,
Allan H., XIII, d. 7/13/2000 in Dover; Allan Henderson XII and Marguerite Pyburn
Alonzo, d. 2/24/1918 at 67/6/7; laborer; widower; b. Eaton; A. Henderson (Eaton) and Rebecca Carpenter (Eaton)
Hiram, d. 11/7/1912 at 85; farmer; single; b. Eaton
Patience, d. 9/7/1924 at 54/4/10; b. Conway; John Johnson and Mary J. Bean
Sarah J., d. 5/29/1915 at 76/0/13; housewife; widow; b. Brownfield, ME; Adam Wentworth (Brownfield, ME) and Susan Bean (Brownfield, ME)

HENDRICKS,
Elois, d. 5/25/1951 at 77 in Ossipee; b. NY; Joseph LeRock and Mary Brown

HENDRICKSON,
George S., d. 10/30/1976 at 69 in Hanover; b. NY

HENDRY,
Annie M., d. 10/24/1991 at 82 in Wolfeboro; b. Saugus, MA

HERBERT,
Gladys H., d. 11/17/1990 at 92 in Ossipee; b. Efffingham

HERRICK,
Harrison W., d. 10/30/1993 at 73 in Wolfeboro

HERSEY,
Virginia E., d. 12/13/2001 in Wolfeboro; Edwin Hersey and Hattie Springer

HESS,
Eva Marie, d. 1/23/1979 at 77 in Ossipee; b. Germany

HEWEY,
Willis Greene, d. 5/14/1974 at 74 in Ossipee; b. NH

HICKEY,
Alice T., d. 3/8/1956 at 46 in Wolfeboro; b. Berlin; Joseph Tardif and Mary Cantin
Edward P., d. 2/6/1987 at 84 in Ossipee; b. Berlin
James William, d. 4/24/1986 at 80 in Ossipee; b. Boston, MA
Natalie A., d. 2/18/2001 in Wolfeboro; Howard Davis and Caroline Tardiff

HIDDEN,
Samuel H., d. 12/27/1969 at 78 in Ossipee; b. NH

HIGGINS,
Martin P., d. 7/16/1929 at 72 in Ossipee; b. Bangor, ME
Morris, d. 2/27/1964 at 81 in Ossipee; b. Orrington Ctr., ME

HILFRANK,
William L., d. 6/4/1983 at 85 in Ossipee; b. Castleton-on-Hudson, NY

HILL,
Abbie, d. 6/14/1907 at 69 in Ossipee; valvular disease of heart
Anna B., d. 4/1/1965 at 50 in Ossipee; b. Middleton
Eli, d. 4/7/1930 at 81/2/14 in Ossipee; b. Conway; Anguil Hill and Caroline Bean
Elizabeth A., d. 1/3/1975 at 82 in Ossipee; b. ME
Emma, d. 2/26/1915 at 45; laborer; single; b. Bartlett
Etta, d. 12/20/1941 at 75/3/18 in Ossipee; b. Effingham; Thatcher Thompson and Frances Tibbetts
Frances Maude, d. 7/5/1985 at 92 in Ossipee; b. Chatham
Harold Andrew, d. 2/12/1971 at 80 in Ossipee; b. NH

Harold G., d. 2/11/1954 at 50/8/14 in Wolfeboro; b. Tamworth; David Hill and Annie Hill
John K., d. 11/11/1961 at 72 in Wolfeboro; b. Lynn, MA
Leona L., d. 3/19/1970 at 87 in Ossipee; b. MA
Levi, d. 11/20/1897 at 78 in Ossipee; old age; widower; b. Nashua
Martha, d. 10/4/1887 at 63 in Ossipee; housewife; married
Mary, d. 5/31/1939 at 87/1/16 in Ossipee; b. Conway; Ansel Page and Betsey Chase
Robert W., d. 9/13/1917 at 83/4/2; farmer; widower; b. Wolfeboro
Sarah F., d. 12/4/1904 at 55/5 in Ossipee; heart disease; housewife; widow; b. Ossipee; Samuel Tibbetts (Ossipee) and Maria Pinder (Ossipee)
Waldo L., d. 9/8/1976 at 71 in Rochester; b. NH

HILLIARD,
Margaret E., d. 10/28/1974 at 90 in Ossipee; b. Canada

HILLS,
Charles B., d. 3/6/1983 at 71 in Ossipee; b. Evanston, IL

HILTON,
Edith G., d. 4/7/1974 at 91 in Ossipee; b. MA
James F., d. 4/23/1912 at 70/1/27; farmer; married; b. Ossipee; Richard Hilton (Lebanon, ME) and Emma West (Lebanon, ME)
Joseph F., d. 8/27/1922 at 76 in Ossipee; mason; widower; b. Ossipee; Richard Hilton and Eunice Wentworth (Somersworth)
Richard, d. 9/25/1888 at 80/3/20; farmer; widower; b. New Durham; Richard Hilton and Sara Goodwich

HINDS,
Abbie May, d. 1/15/1942 at 58/1/9 in Ossipee; b. Haverhill, MA; Henry Baker and Carrie Dearborn

HITCHCOCK,
Addie B., d. 1/30/1945 at 64/7/19 in Wolfeboro; b. Ossipee; Charles Templeton and Robertine Johnson
Austin C., d. 5/18/1905 at 2/0/16 in Ossipee; bronchitis; b. Ossipee; Wilbur Hitchcock (Ossipee) and Alice Hipson (Ossipee)
Howard C., d. 8/4/1966 at 68 in Wolfeboro; b. Ossipee
Lydia, d. 8/1/1896 at 61 in Ossipee; mitral insufficiency; housekeeper; single; b. Ossipee; Joseph Tucker (Ossipee) and ----- Davis (Wakefield)
Newell W., d. 10/10/1980 at 64 in Epsom; b. NH
Nina E., d. 11/26/1991 at 84 in Ossipee; b. Ossipee

Stanley, d. 3/28/1943 at 24/4/19 in Wolfeboro; b. Ossipee; Wilbur Hitchcock and Abbie B. Templeton
Wilbur T., d. 1/27/1933 at 60/6/18 in Ossipee; b. Ossipee; Porter Hitchcock and Lydia Tucker

HLUSHUK,
Leora E., d. 6/29/1985 at 82 in Ossipee; b. Tuftonboro

HOAG,
Isabel Cossaboom, d. 11/30/1991 at 81 in Ossipee; b. Quincy, MA

HOBART,
Henry, d. 2/28/1903 at 82 in Ossipee; apoplexy; farmer; widower; b. Colebrook

HOBBS,
Catherine M., d. 2/1/1967 at 81 in Ossipee; b. Kent, England
Charles E., d. 4/21/1898 at 39/0/4 in Tamworth; concussion of brain; merchant; married; b. Ossipee; Wentworth Hobbs (Ossipee) and Patience Hall (Holland, VT)
Christine Elzira, d. 2/1/1940 at 85/6/9 in Ossipee; b. Effingham; Jonathon Hobbs and Mary Young
Christopher C., d. 1/22/1927 at 80/1/21; b. Ossipee; Samuel D. Hobbs and Loisa Moody
Don Purcell, d. 6/11/1972 at 92 in Ossipee; b. NH
Dorothy C., d. 4/30/1894 at 82 in Minneapolis; old age ch. indigestion
Frank K., d. 1/4/1906 at 64/2 in Ossipee; uremia; farmer; married; b. Tamworth; Oliver F. Hobbs (Tamworth) and Deborah Jenness (Wolfeboro)
Harry D., d. 12/20/1969 at 64 in Manchester; b. NH
Hattie M., d. 10/14/1974 at 97 in Wolfeboro; b. NH
Herbert W., d. 3/4/1924 at 52/8/2; b. Ossipee; Frank K. Hobbs and Sarah A. Atwood
Joseph P., d. 2/24/1919 at –; blacksmith
Josiah A., d. 6/26/1905 at 41/2/19 in Ossipee; pulmonary phthisis; single; b. Ossipee; J. S. Hobbs (Ossipee) and E. Tibbetts (Madison)
Lydia A., d. 9/11/1936 at 70/10/28 in Ossipee; b. Epping; Daniel B. Ladd and Marian S. Jones
Oliver F., d. 6/18/1895 at 78/2/12 in Ossipee; gastritis; farmer; married; b. Ossipee; Joseph Hobbs (Hampton) and Dolly Cooley (Ossipee)
Orodon P., d. 9/18/1929 at 76/0/18 in Ossipee; b. Ossipee; Oliver F. Hobbs and Deborah Jenness
Sarah, d. 8/14/1910 at 71/11/2 in Ossipee; abdominal cancer; single; b. Ossipee; Samuel D. Hobbs (Ossipee) and Louisa Moody (Ossipee)

Sarah Eva Young, d. 2/5/1940 at 82/10/14 in Ossipee; b. Effingham; Jonathon Hobbs

Wentworth B., d. 1/14/1917 at 75/5/20; farmer; married; b. Ossipee; Larkin D. Hobbs (Ossipee) and D. Hobbs (Effingham)

Wentworth H., d. 5/1/1908 at 84/0/12 in Ossipee; pneumonia; farmer; b. Ossipee; Joseph Hobbs and Dorothy ——

Wilbur, d. 11/7/1972 at 83 in Ossipee; b. MA

HODGDON,

Albert J., d. 5/19/1930 at 80/9/20 in Ossipee; b. Newburyport; Charles Hodgdon and Naomi Roberts

Ebenezer, d. 2/19/1894 at 82/11/17 in Ossipee; apoplexy; farmer; widower; b. Ossipee; Ebenezer Hodgdon (Berwick, ME) and Dorah Wentworth (Berwick, ME)

Forrest Winfield, d. 9/24/1994 at 94; Natt W. Hodgdon and Annie Nicholson

Hiram, d. 1/15/1909 at 84/11/5 in Ossipee; pneumonia; farmer; b. Lebanon, ME; Thomas Hodgdon (Lebanon, ME)

Lucinda, d. 12/31/1919 at 71/3/14; housewife; married; b. Ossipee; Henry C. Abbott (S. Berwick, ME) and Phoebe Bickford (Rochester)

Mary A., d. 11/24/1919 at 83/0/10; housewife; married; b. Townshend, VT; Thomas Higgins (Townshend, VT) and Lucy S. Melendy (Townshend, VT)

Naomi, d. 7/11/1891 at 75/0/21 in Ossipee; housewife; widow; b. Ossipee; John Roberts and P. Wentworth

Octavia, d. 10/4/1912 at 66

Oliver, d. 2/27/1904 at 94/0/12 in Ossipee; senility; shoemaker; widower; b. Lebanon; Thomas Hodgdon (Lebanon) and Annie Tibbetts (ME)

HODGE,

Bernard L., d. 7/30/1981 at 72 in Wolfeboro; b. Ossipee

Bert N., d. 3/12/1937 at 64/3/19 in Moultonville; b. Ossipee; John Hodge and Laura Garland

Bertha, d. 3/3/1958 at 78 in Wolfeboro; b. Effingham; Charles Nichols and Emma Williams

Carrie B., d. 12/1/1901 at 27/2/28 in Ossipee; tuberculosis; married; b. Ossipee; Samuel B. Hodge (Ossipee)

Constance L., d. 5/8/1939 at 0/9/20 in Wolfeboro; b. Ctr. Ossipee; Elwood N. Hodge and Edith M. Bickford

Edith M., d. 4/8/1953 at 44/5/22 in Wolfeboro; b. Dover; Raymond Bickford and Lillian Roy

Elwood N., d. 8/31/1974 at 69 in Wolfeboro; b. NH

Eugene William, d. 5/27/1994 at 81; Bert Hodge and Nettie Loring

Fred, d. 10/29/1946 at 71/1/24 in Ossipee; b. Ossipee; Daniel Hodge and Alice J. Ricker

John C., d. 7/21/1924 at 77/6; b. Ossipee; Samuel Hodge and Mary Chick
John L., d. 10/1/1982 at 75 in Wolfeboro; b. Ossipee
Laura A., d. 11/15/1926 at 66/10/3; b. Ossipee; John Garland and Hannah Gile
Lillian C., d. 6/29/1970 at 85 in Ossipee; b. ME
Mary, d. 6/22/1897 at 81/3 in Ossipee; cerebral hemorrhage; widow; b. Ossipee; Robert Chick
Mary, d. 8/31/1925 at 76; b. Ossipee; Samuel Hodge and Mary Chick
Mira T., d. 6/13/1975 at 88 in Ossipee; b. NH
Nellie B., d. 1/11/1949 at 77 in Wolfeboro; b. Ossipee; John C. Hodge and Laura E. Garland
Peter F., d. 11/18/1915 at 63/2; farmer; single; b. Ossipee; Samuel Hodge (Ossipee) and Mary Chick (Ossipee)
Philip Lee, d. 7/16/1939 at 0/10/28 in Ossipee; b. Laconia; Bernard L. Hodge and Doris Marion Welch
Samuel, d. 3/24/1911 at 70; arterio sclerosis; farmer; divorced; b. Ossipee; Samuel Hodge (Ossipee) and Mary Chick (Ossipee)

HODGES,
Viola Heckman, d. 3/2/1992 at 95 in Ossipee; b. Canada

HODGKINS,
John Fairfield, d. 2/22/1991 at 82 in Wolfeboro; b. Bethel, ME

HODSDON,
Arthur L., d. 2/11/1911 at 69/4/28; multiple sclerosis; retired; married; b. Ossipee; Joseph Hodsdon (Berwick, ME) and Dorcas Lowell (Berwick, ME)
Belinda, d. 1/14/1905 at 72 in Ossipee; influenza; widow; b. Ossipee
Charlotte, d. 12/11/1936 at 92/5/12 in Ctr. Ossipee; b. Ctr. Ossipee; Dr. Nathaniel Grant and Charlotte S. Hobbs
Dorcas G., d. 7/26/1908 at 92/7 in Ossipee; gastritis; housewife; b. Berwick, ME; ----- Gowell (Berwick, ME) and Esther Abbott
Emma B., d. 2/22/1931 at 90/5/10 in Ossipee; b. Farmington; Mark Demeritt and Abigail Leighton
Ervin W., d. 3/15/1930 at 66/11/24 in Ossipee; b. Ossipee; Edward P. Hodsdon and Emma Demeritt
Etta A., d. 5/11/1924 at 76/9/10; b. Ossipee; Joseph Hodsdon and Dorcas Gowell
Frank W., d. 6/11/1932 at 63/11/28 in Ossipee; b. Haverhill, MA; William Hodsdon and Georgia Allen
Herbert A., d. 3/20/1937 at 62/4/2 in Ctr. Ossipee; b. Ossipee; Arthur Hodsdon and Charlotte M. Grant
Ida M., d. 7/12/1954 at 97 in Laconia; b. NH; Col. Joseph Hodsdon and Dorcas Cawell

John W., d. 5/24/1913 at 78/4/20; farmer; single; b. Ossipee; Ebenezer Hodsdon (Ossipee) and Catherine Tuttle (Effingham)
Joseph, d. 4/15/1897 at 80/9/1 in Ossipee; apoplexy; tanner; married; b. Berwick, ME; David Hodsdon (Berwick) and Jane Fogg (Berwick)
Lucy W., d. 7/1/1954 at 81/4/26 in Moultonboro; b. Chatham; Norman Charles and Ester Walker

HOGAN,
Barbara F., d. 1/2/1987 at 62 in Wolfeboro; b. Lynn, MA
Keith D., d. 12/7/1984
Roderick I., d. 10/29/1968 at 72 in Ossipee; b. MA
Stuart A., d. 12/27/1977 at 74 in Ossipee; b. NH

HOILE,
Helen C., d. 5/6/1995 at 99; Eugene Markwith and Minerva Lee Layton

HOLBROOK,
Charles, d. 10/23/1918 at 19/3/1; mechanic; single; b. Mendon, MA; M. A. Holbrook (Mendon, MA) and Cora I. St. John (Plainfield, VT)
Clement M., d. 10/4/1964 at 66 in Ossipee; b. Mendon, MA
Mary F., d. 11/12/1969 at 68 in Ossipee; b. NH

HOLLIHAN,
Donald Wayne, d. 6/4/1977

HOLMAN,
Lillian M., d. 7/12/1983 at 83 in Ossipee; b. Lexington, MA

HOLMES,
Chester Ward, d. 10/12/1974 at 80 in Ossipee; b. MA
Henry Ward, d. 5/6/1943 at 75/7/23 in Wolfeboro; b. Ossipee; Edward Holmes and Sarah Ann Young

HOLMGREN,
Emilie Pope, d. 10/5/1989 at 89 in Ossipee; b. Menlo Park, CA

HOLT,
Donald L., d. 3/28/1997 at 75 in Dover; George W. Holt and Merle -----
George W., d. 3/4/1962 at 68 in Ossipee; b. Danvers, MA

HOOPER,
Arthur Bonn, d. 1/26/1994 at 85; Ray Hooper and Florence Adjutant
Bernice E., d. 12/14/1993 at 90 in Ossipee

Eleanor M., d. 10/28/1998 in Wolfeboro; A. Joseph Houle and Ethel M. Cassava
Ray R., d. 8/2/1961 at 72 in Ossipee; b. Wakefield

HOPKINSON,
Sarah J., d. 12/5/1958 at 63 in Ossipee; b. Saco, ME; Amos Jose

HORMELL,
Charlotte Lewis, d. 6/23/1996 at 72 in Wolfeboro; Walter F. Lewis and Houldah Robbins

HORN,
Ella S., d. 7/11/1935 at 80/5/17 in Somersworth; b. Ossipee; Daniel Nichols and Sarah M. Nichols

HORNE,
son, d. 12/5/1913 at 0/0/1; b. Ossipee; Harry Horne (Tuftonboro) and Lizzie Snow (Milton, MA)
Charles R., d. 12/19/1970 at 73 in Ossipee; b. MA
Chester W., d. 8/10/1963 at 91 in Wolfeboro; b. Shapleigh, ME
Elizabeth, d. 9/17/1976 at 95 in Rochester; b. MA
James F., d. 8/17/1912 at 82
John Elmer, d. 7/17/1999 at 88 in Ossipee; Elmer Horne and Honor -----
Kenneth E., d. 12/3/1979 at 46 in Keene; b. Rochester
Mary A., d. 4/12/1917 at 72; housewife; widow; b. Waltham, MA
W. Ashton, d. 1/22/1937 at 78/11/16 in Moultonville; b. Berwick, ME; Edwin P. Horne and Elizabeth Frost

HOULE,
Armand Joseph, d. 11/12/1983 at 83 in Wolfeboro; b. Cambridge, MA
Ethel M., d. 2/22/1983 at 85 in Laconia; b. Linden, MA

HOUSTON,
John, d. 5/14/2000 at 84 in Ossipee; David Houston and Martha Ellen Fraser

HOWARD,
Dorothy, d. 5/19/1999 at 75 in Ossipee
James, d. 2/23/1923 at 87; b. PEI; Thomas Howard and May Robins

HOWE,
Edward R., d. 11/24/1976 at 69 in Ossipee; b. MA

HOWES,
Avis P., d. 9/9/1964 at 52 in Wolfeboro; b. NS
Edward C., d. 3/5/1981 at 73 in Wolfeboro; b. Melrose, MA

HOWLAND,
Ora A., d. 3/15/1964 at 72 in Ossipee; b. MI

HOYT,
Caleb J., d. 6/27/1900 at 67 in Ossipee; R. R. accident; retired; widower; b. Hampstead; Moses Hoyt (Hampstead) and Hannah Williams (Hampstead)
John Isaac, d. 5/25/1972 at 74 in Ossipee; b. VT
Lenwood S., d. 2/5/1994 at 87; Clarence Hoyt and Jessie Stuart
Sally, d. 12/–/1896 at – in Ossipee; paralysis of the heart

HUBBARD,
Belinda, d. 12/4/1900 at 82 in Ossipee; paralysis heart; married; b. Ossipee
John, d. 1/29/1890 at – in Ossipee; congestion of lungs; domestic (sic); married; b. Ossipee

HUCKINS,
Ernest C., d. 12/22/1946 at 63/9/6 in Ossipee; b. Freedom; Simon O. Huckins and Nettie Harmon
Harry, d. 7/24/1922 at 51 in Ossipee; printer; single; b. Watertown, MA; David L. Huckins (Ossipee) and Sarah F. White (Sandwich)
Jane M., d. 6/26/1956 at 74 in Wolfeboro; b. Freedom; Edward T. Merrow and Nan T. Barker
Simon O., d. 12/12/1933 at 78/0/27 in Ossipee; b. Freedom; Simon Huckins and Cordelia Noble

HUDSON,
Evengeline Eddy, d. 9/22/1975 at 89 in Ossipee; b. IA

HUGHES,
George F., d. 4/1/1971 at 78 in Wolfeboro; b. MA
Lucy C., d. 1/15/1953 at 88 in Ossipee; b. England; John Stephenson and Anne Dover
Mary F., d. 6/28/1972 at 69 in Wolfeboro; b. MA

HULL,
Hulbert Allen, d. 5/20/1991 at 74 in Wolfeboro; b. Newton

HULTEN,
Thure, d. 5/17/1968 at 67 in Laconia; b. Sweden

HUNT,
George, d. 2/19/1908 at 89/11 in Ossipee; pneumonia; b. Salisbury, MA; William Hunt (Sudbury, MA) and Ester Brigham (Sudbury, MA)
Martha E., d. 10/15/1919 at 82/1; widow; William Dane
William A., d. 9/16/1988 at 76 in Wolfeboro; b. Marshfield, MA

HUNTER,
Elsie M., d. 2/.1/1963 at 56 in Wolfeboro; b. Newfoundland
Leslie A., d. 11/1/1982 at 78 in Wolfeboro; b. N. Conway
Lillian M., d. 1/12/1966 at 80 in Ossipee; b. N. Conway
Roxieanna, d. 11/3/2001 in Ossipee; William York and Edna Hurd

HUNTRESS,
Donald R., d. 11/21/1999 at 72 in Ossipee; Eugene E. Huntress and Irma L. Jones

HURD,
son, d. 8/17/1910 at 0/1/23 in Ossipee; cholera infantum; b. Ossipee; Homer H. Hurd (Sanford, ME) and Grace Staples (Parsonsfield, ME)
Albert Wiggin, d. 5/29/1988 at 82 in Ossipee; b. Madison
Alton M., d. 11/25/1944 at 36/8/14 in N. Conway; b. Madison; John Hurd and Dora Emerson
Grace Marian, d. 9/14/1991 at 86 in Ossipee; b. Effingham
Homer H., d. 7/19/1918 at 36/8/13; blacksmith; married; b. Sanford, ME; Charles E. Hurd (Sanford, ME) and Mary Hurd (Sanford, ME)
James, d. 11/16/1940 at 57 in Ossipee; David Hurd and Augusta Judkins
June T., d. 1/26/1998 in Portland, ME; Leon Turner and Clara Jackson
William H., d. 6/7/1921 at 75/9/23 in Ossipee; farmer; widower; Oliver Hurd (Conway) and ----- (Brownfield, ME)

HURN,
Florence E., d. 5/20/1956 at 72 in Wolfeboro; b. Ossipee; Elmer Loring and Julia Chapman
Fred W., d. 1/25/1957 at 80 in Wolfeboro; b. Charlestown, MA; John Hurn and M. J. Hurn
Jennie M., d. 3/10/1906 at 56/4/6 in Ossipee; progressive anemia; housewife; married; b. Madison; Warner Smith and Mary Jackson (Madison)
John F., d. 7/20/1915 at 75/7/29; farmer; widower; b. Freedom; Rubin Hurn (Freedom) and Sally Mattox (Lyman, ME)

HUSBAND,
Raymond W., d. 11/23/1988 at 87 in Wolfeboro; b. Sheldon, VT

HUSE,
George W., d. 8/5/1900 at 46/5/13 in Ossipee; cerebral embolism; hotel keeper; married; b. Manchester; Thomas M. Huse (Fairlee, VT) and Elizabeth Scoby

Johanas, d. 6/5/1896 at 45 in Ossipee; epilepsy

HUSSEY,
John Allen, d. 12/18/1995 at 66; Thomas Hussey and Beatrice Evans

William, d. 10/2/1918 at 22; soldier; married; b. Effingham; Joseph E. Hussey (Limington, ME) and Mary E. Tarbox (Parsonsfield)

HUTCHINS,
son, d. 11/12/1933 at 0/0/3 in Ossipee; b. Ossipee; John C. Davis and Isabelle Hutchins

Augusta, d. 4/2/1941 at 72/0/3 in Wolfeboro; b. Porter, ME; Elias Downs and Sophia A. Rounds

Earl E., d. 9/28/1968 at 50 in Ossipee; b. NH

Eleanor Jeanne, d. 3/21/1996 at 54 in Wolfeboro; Duncan Norris Tozier and Marguerite Cheney

Ernest, d. 6/21/1976 at 71 in Concord; b. NH

Florence, d. 1/28/1958 at 68 in Concord; b. Wakefield; Stephen Hutchins and Elizabeth Wentworth

George, d. 7/29/1920 at 77/11/2; mechanic; widower; b. Lebanon, ME; Simon Hutchins (Wakefield) and Dorothy Farnham

Laura, d. 6/30/1892 at 40 in Ossipee; acute mania; single; Benjamin Hutchins

Mary Louise, d. 4/28/2000 at 79 in Ossipee; Walter B. Boone and Mary Alison Birmingham

Richard, d. 2/16/1895 at 94 in Ossipee; influenza; pauper; single; b. Kittery

Ruth Harrison, d. 6/12/1996 at 93 in Ossipee; George Belonga and Susan Hext

Walter Alan, d. 2/8/1998 in Ossipee; Albert L. Hutchins and Hazel B. Charles

HUTCHINSON,
Harry G., d. 7/31/1938 at 49/2/21 in Ossipee; b. Franklin; Robert Hutchinson and Emma White

HYDE,
Daniel A., d. 3/1/1895 at 72 in Ossipee; paralytic shock; mechanic; widower; b. Ossipee; Levi Hyde (Ossipee) and Mary Gould (Ossipee)

William Alonzo, d. 11/25/1907 at 84/1/11 in Ossipee; cerebral embolism; shoemaker; single; b. Ossipee; William Hyde

INGALLS,
Edward W., d. 3/2/1992 at 57 in Manchester; b. Worcester, MA
Leneler W., d. 2/12/1952 at 73/8/18 in Ossipee; b. Albany; George W. Moody and Mary Agnes Moody

INGEMI,
Marion Maude, d. 5/2/1994 at 61; Jonas Glidden and Evelyn Roberts

IRISH,
Anson P., d. 2/28/1934 at 79/11/25 in Ossipee; b. Lovell, ME; Domonick Irish and Martha Warren

IRONS,
Keith A., d. 8/1/1986 at 6 in Ossipee; b. Salem, MA

IRVINE,
Dorothy Mae, d. 12/11/1990 at 57 in Ossipee; b. Portland, ME

IRVING,
Lenora W., d. 8/15/1970 at 81 in Ossipee; b. NH

JACKSON,
Aver A., d. 1/19/1905 at 43 in Ossipee; influenza; single; b. Dover; Stephen Jackson
Doris Evelyn, d. 12/18/1988 at 69 in Wolfeboro; b. Parsonsfield, ME
Jesse H., d. 7/29/1892 at – in Ossipee; cholera inf.; b. Ossipee; Jesse H. Jackson (Ossipee) and Martha Wiliams (Ossipee)
Jesse H., d. 6/18/1906 at 55 in Ossipee; intestinal obstruction; farmer; married; b. Madison; Jonathan Jackson and Doxy Copp (Effingham)
Jno., d. 11/6/1904 at 83/6/6 in Ossipee; uremia poisoning; farmer; married; b. Madison; Jno. Jackson and Mary Roberts
John, d. 5/21/1935 at 54/5/21 in Ossipee; b. Conway; Sylvester Jackson and Mary Woodman
Martha, d. 7/29/1904 at 67/6/13 in Ossipee; uremia; housekeeper; married; b. Moultonboro; Jeremiah Wiggin (Wakefield) and Elizabeth Williams (Ossipee)
Martha, d. 11/4/1916 at 53; housewife; widow; b. Brownfield, ME; Samuel Williams (Ossipee) and Esther Welch (Ossipee)
Reta N., d. 2/25/1960 at 73 in Wolfeboro; b. Ossipee
Ronald M., d. 9/5/1986 at 66 in Ossipee; b. Augusta, ME
Roxana, d. 12/17/1904 at 85 in Ossipee; old age

Stephen, d. 11/28/1908 at 81 in Ossipee; ewhaustion; b. Madison; Jno. Jackson (NH) and Mary Roberts (NH)

Udoxy, d. 5/3/1913 at 89/2/17; housewife; widow; b. Ossipee; John Copp (Ossipee) and Mary Churchill (Brookfield)

William L., d. 7/11/1952 at 74/1/25 in Ossipee; b. Windsor, ME; George Jackson and Maria Studley

JACOBSEN,
Thomas S., Jr., d. 8/21/1963 at 0/0/1 in Wolfeboro; b. Wolfeboro

JACQUES,
Richard T., d. 6/28/1982 at 69 in Ossipee; b. Ashland

JAHNLE,
Carl George, d. 10/1/1975 at 66 in Gilmanton; b. MA

JANOCH,
Emil, d. 10/31/1973 at 78 in Ossipee; b. Czechoslovakia
Sophie Rada, d. 8/17/1978 at 83 in Ossipee; b. OH

JEDREY,
Joan P., d. 10/8/2001 in Wolfeboro; Joseph Durling and Helen Sullivan

JEFFERS,
Edward, d. 6/29/1980 at 82 in Wolfeboro; b. NH

JENKINS,
Mary Ann, d. 4/20/1949 at 82 in Ossipee; b. England; John Tompson and Martha Smith

JENKS,
Lydia A., d. 9/27/1910 at 68 in Ossipee; Brights disease; widow; b. Boston, MA; Lucius Newell (Needham, MA) and Betsey Burleigh (Wakefield)

JENNESS,
daughter, d. 9/28/1891 at 0/6/24 in Ossipee; Frank Jenness (Union) and Abbie Jenness (Ossipee)

Charles, d. 9/24/1887 at 0/3 in Ossipee; b. Ossipee; Frank Jenness and Abbie

Charles, d. 5/2/1903 at – in Burlington; intestinal obstructions; actor; married

Ellen, d. 1/8/1911 at 67/8/20; mitral insufficiency; housewife; married; George W. Remick (Tamworth)

Emma B., d.4/8/1923 at 75; b. Brookfield; ----- Wentworth and ----- Deland

Jonathan, d. 11/24/1895 at 72 in Ossipee; bronchitis; pauper; b. Meredith
Lena, d. 2/11/1897 at 3 in Ossipee; scarlet fever; Frank Jenness and Abbie Nichols
Lorenzo, d. 6/1/1914 at 78/8/5; b. Tamworth
Luke, d. 11/28/1910 at 92 in Ossipee; digestive and circulatory; married; b. Eaton
Mary J., d. 6/25/1888 at 69; domestic; married; b. Meredith
Sarah B., d. 7/4/1904 at 39 in Wolfeboro; pneumonia; housekeeper; married; b. New Durham; Sylvester Berry and Mary E. Moody

JEROME,
son, d. 3/31/1890 at – in Ossipee; stillborn; b. Ossipee; Robert Jerome (Ossipee) and Hilda Birneir (Ossipee)

JEWETT,
Marion Lloyd, d. 12/21/1976 at 93 in Ossipee; b. ME

JOHANSEN,
Annie O., d. 4/29/1966 at 89 in Ossipee; b. Sweden

JOHANSON,
Otto E., d. 5/16/1970 at 81 in Conway; b. Sweden

JOHNSON,
son, d. 2/11/1909 at – in Ossipee; dead at birth; b. Ossipee; Fanny Johnson
Alice L., d. 5/8/1990 at 88 in Ossipee; b. Rutland, VT
Donald Einar, d. 7/3/1995 at 71; Einar Johnson and Reita Waldron
Edith M., d. 2/27/1992 at 91 in Ossipee; b. N. Collins, NY
Edwin H., d. 3/22/1960 at 84 in Ossipee; b. S. Chatham
George B., d. 11/15/1963 at 92 in Wolfeboro; b. Stockport, England
Georgie, d. 10/14/1934 at 81/6/25 in Ossipee; b. Eaton; Frederick Stewart and Nancy Thompson
Herbert E., d. 9/21/1986 at 78 in Ossipee; b. Everett, MA
Margaret, d. 3/1/1983 at 89 in Ossipee; b. Scranton, PA
Martha C., d. 2/1/1907 at 73 in Ossipee; valvular disease of heart; married
Ralph B., d. 3/14/1988 at 74 in New Britain, CT; b. Wolfeboro
Sylvia York, d. 1/10/1996 at 67 in Wolfeboro; William York and Delia Hatch
Virgil V., d. 2/10/1963 at 86 in Holderness; b. Eugene, OR
Weston A., d. 6/11/1939 at – in Ossipee; b. Stowe, ME; David Johnson
William Dean, d. 9/26/1991 at 54 in Wolfeboro; b. Greensburg, PA

JONES,
Adam H., d. 9/18/2000 in Laconia; David Jones and Debra Plummer
Albert Leon, Jr., d. 6/20/1993 at 69 in Dover
Annie, d. 7/1/1975 at 92 in Wolfeboro; b. Wales
Gertrude R., d. 6/4/1985 at 92 in Ossipee; b. Ossipee
Ida B., d. 6/18/1935 at 49/11/1 in Worcester, MA; b. Boston; George Mason and Nettie Sceggel
Kate, d. 12/14/1903 at 65 in Ossipee; tuberculosis; housewife; single; b. Wakefield
Lamuel, d. 1/28/1924 at 79/4/21; b. China, ME; Noah Jones and Lavinia Hawkes
Nellie, d. 12/22/1946 at 86/10/26 in Tamworth; b. Tamworth; Ismal Gilman and Mary E. Hobbs

JORDAN,
Arthur, d. 6/7/1936 at 14/7/6 in Wolfeboro; b. Bath, ME; Arthur Jordan and Mildred Safford
Arthur F., d. 8/3/1964 at 65 in Wolfeboro; b. Trenton, ME

JOSEPHSON,
Delia, d. 10/24/1974 at 82 in Ossipee; b. Ireland

JOTENJKO,
Frances, d. 8/4/1991 at 80 in Ossipee; b. Austria

JOY,
Edwige M., d. 1/1/1995 at 96; Jean Cyr and Octavie Therrien

JUDKINS,
Lizzie, d. 1/25/1907 at 85 in Ossipee; fracture neck of femur; single; b. Freedom
Roy Earl, d. 8/29/1988 at 59 in Concord; b. Effingham

JUTRAS,
infant, d. 12/26/1941 at -- in Wolfeboro; b. Wolfeboro; Nazaira C. Jutras and Jeanne D. Andrews

KABEARY,
Gerrold P., d. 1/4/1985 at 77 in Ossipee; b. Lakota, ND

KALKO,
Adam, d. 8/9/1937 at 53/11/25 in Ossipee; b. Russia

KALLOCK,
Abby, d. 9/17/1899 at 67 in Canton; angina pectoris; married; L. D. Sinclair (Essex, VT) and Olive Kimball (Kennebunk)

KANE,
John M., d. 8/6/1978 at 76 in Ossipee; b. NH
Thomas, d. 8/24/1965 at 73 in Wolfeboro; b. Newark, NJ

KATZ,
Abraham J., d. 1/13/1971 at 67 in Ossipee; . NY

KAYSER,
John M., d. 11/23/1975 at 62 in Ossipee; b. NY

KEARNEY,
Carrie B., d. 5/10/1971 at 70 in Ossipee; b. Canada

KEATING,
Franklin Henry, d. 7/3/1974 at 79 in Ossipee; b. MA
Loring D., d. 3/13/2001 in Wolfeboro; Franklin Keating and Olga Johnson

KEITH,
R. A. (male), d. 7/31/1898 at 60 in Boston; drowning
William M., d. 6/26/1946 at 61/2/9 in Ossipee; b. Needham, MA; Merritt S. Keith and Ida M. Herring

KELLEY,
Joseph T., d. 1/19/1988 at 65 in Wolfeboro; b. Roxbury, MA
Marion Mildred, d. 12/13/1993 at 83 in Wolfeboro
Wayne G., d. 4/8/1966 at 42 in Ossipee; b. Boston, MA

KELLY,
James Richard, d. 9/14/1994 at 72; Herbert J. Kelly and Beatrice Kane
Louis Masury, Jr., d. 11/4/1996 at 89 in Ossipee; Louis M. Kelly and Florence Kelley
Martha Belle, d. 11/18/1973 at 83 in Ossipee; b. NH
Maurice Edward, d. 12/7/1997 at 87 in Ossipee; John H. Kelly and Marie Cheever
Walter, d. 3/30/1942 at 82/3/11 in Ossipee; b. Conway; Edmond Kelly and Amanda Heath

KENESON,
George A., d. 10/23/1914 at 70/11/13; farmer; b. Ossipee; Solomon Keneson and Hannah Cooley

KENISON,
Hannah S., d. 12/5/1889 at 82; domestic; widow; b. Ossipee; Benjamin Cooley and Susan Avery
Hattie, d. 10/6/1972 at 93 in Ossipee; b. NH
Sarah, d. 4/29/1923 at 81; b. Conway

KENISTON,
George A., d. 12/13/1970 at 86 in Wolfeboro; b. NH
Jesse, d. 2/13/1895 at 81 in Ossipee; influenza; pauper; single; b. Milton
Theodore R., d. 8/21/1975 at 70 in Ossipee; b. NH

KENLY,
Ruth Burdick, d. 8/21/1989 at 90 in Ossipee; b. Newport, RI

KENN,
James A., d. 5/24/1949 at 63/1 in Ossipee; b. Quincy, MA; Alexander Kenn and Susan Borthwick

KENNARD,
Benjamin Franklin, d. 11/18/1992 at 80 in Wolfeboro; b. Nottingham
Laura M., d. 9/26/1969 at 17 in Wolfeboro; b. NH

KENNEFIC,
James, d. 12/17/1945 at 92/0/0 in Ossipee

KENNETT,
George F., d. 4/18/1956 at 79 in Ossipee; b. Effingham; Frank Kennett and Emma Bryant

KENNEY,
James E., d. 11/21/1933 at 81 in Ossipee; b. Ossipee; Wentworth Kenney and L. Avery
Marguerite Anne, d. 1/23/1992 at 88 in Ossipee; b. Hampton Falls

KENNY,
Robert E., d. 4/14/1986 at 70 in Wolfeboro; b. Lancaster

KERR,
Daniel Joseph, Jr., d. 1/18/1997 at 78 in Wolfeboro; Daniel Joseph Kerr, Sr. and Winnifred Agnes Glendon

KERSHAW,
Wilfred W., d. 8/8/1984 at 72 in Wolfeboro; b. Lowell, MA

KEYES,
- Cora L., d. 9/16/1943 at 73/3/7 in Concord; b. Ossipee; Everett F. Keyes and Frances Nutter
- Iola, d. 7/25/1899 at 9/7/5 in Ossipee; abscess of brain; b. Ossipee; Charles Keyes (Ossipee) and Lizzie Chick (Ossipee)
- Lizzie S., d. 10/12/1929 at 78/10/8 in Rochester; b. Ossipee; Samuel Chick and Eliza Carsons

KIMBALL,
- Albert E., d. 1/15/1974 at 68 in Wolfeboro; b. MA
- Arlene B., d. 2/24/1996 at 67 in Wolfeboro; Harry Wadsworth
- Arthur, d. 12/7/1943 at 69/2/3 in Ossipee; b. Rochester; Oliver Kimball and Ellen Littlefield
- Beatrice, d. 6/28/1983 at 76 in Wolfeboro; b. Ossipee
- Charles E., d. 4/27/1955 at 78/4/26 in Ossipee; b. MA; Gardner Kimball and Martha -----
- Ernest Walter, d. 4/6/1992 at 89 in Ossipee; b. Wolfeboro
- Frank, d. 11/27/1923 at 86/5/14; Isaac Kimball and Hannah Foss
- Frank, d. 4/30/1943 at – in Ossipee; Loamia Kimball
- Henry, d. 12/6/1933 at 85/7/8 in Ossipee; b. Wolfeboro; James Kimball and Marguerite Varney
- Horace K., d. 10/26/1929 at 73/10 in Ossipee; b. Porter, ME; Erastus Kimball and ----- Towle
- Idella E., d. 2/25/1888 at 27/3/21; housekeeper; married; b. Canaan; John Waterman
- Inez E., d. 10/25/1973 at 73 in Laconia; b. NH
- Inez Mary, d. 2/23/1999 at 89 in Ossipee; John A. Lee and May Lambert
- Isabelle M., d. 6/27/1913 at 57/2/23
- John Weston, d. 6/21/1983 at 57 in Ossipee; b. Lovell, ME
- Jonas, d. 7/25/1902 at 89/3/2 in Ossipee; apoplexy; farmer; widower; b. Wells, ME
- Loammi, d. 6/11/1894 at 42 in Ossipee; pulmonary tuberculosis; tinsmith; widower; b. Moultonboro; Jonas Kimball (Wells, ME) and Margurett Varney (Ossipee)
- Luella, d. 1/30/1892 at 1/7 in Ossipee; b. Ossipee; Charles P. Kimball (Ossipee) and ----- Williams (Effingham)
- Mattie, d. 8/6/1908 at 66 in Ossipee; cerebral embolism; b. Ossipee
- Nettie, d. 10/7/1889 at 0/0/14; b. Ossipee; Charles P. Kimball and Velner Kimball
- Stanley, d. 4/10/1976 at 76 in Laconia; b. NH
- Viola, d. 12/28/1937 at 83/11/16 in Ossipee; b. Ossipee; Simon Fogg and Viola J. Fogg
- Walter, d. 12/9/1933 at 57/6/18 in Sanford, ME; b. Ossipee; Horace Kimball and Viola Fogg

KING,
son, d. 11/11/1908 at 0/0/1 in Ossipee; cyanosis infantile; b. Ossipee; Hanson King (Springfield) and Mabel Willey (Springfield)
Ada I., d. 1/26/1971 at 101 in Ossipee; b. VT
Fannie, d. 10/1/1952 at 87/1/28 in Wolfeboro; b. MI; Andrew Overbaugh and Mary Gardner
M. Lydia, d. 9/11/1983 at 89 in Wolfeboro; b. Darjehiling, India
Mary Ross, d. 9/3/1909 at 60 in Ossipee; gun shot; housekeeper; b. Ossipee; Amasa Moody (ME) and Mary A. Caverly (ME)

KINNEY,
Mary, d. 3/16/1974 at 93 in Ossipee; b. NH

KINSLEY,
Sybil Mae, d. 7/17/1980 at 92 in Ossipee; b. VT

KIPP,
Helen E., d. 12/7/1985 at 93 in Ossipee; b. Sherbrooke, PQ

KIRCH,
Elsie Mae, d. 9/27/1995 at 64; Leonard Adkins and Ellie Sanders

KIRKWOOD,
Clara S., d. 5/16/1948 at 73/3/2 in Ossipee; b. Ossipee; Daniel Eldridge and Susan Eldridge
Elizabeth Deucher, d. 6/29/1972 at 73 in Ossipee; b. Scotland
George T., d. 6/30/1961 at 81 in Laconia; b. Nottingham
Lawrence Dana, d. 11/13/1993 at 71 in Wolfeboro

KNAPP,
George B., d. 9/20/1974 at 66 in Wolfeboro; b. KS
Robert Allen, d. 1/4/1988 at 28 in Laconia; b. Wolfeboro

KNIGHT,
Ethel Marion, d. 3/31/1983 at 78 in Ossipee; b. Cranston, RI
Henry E., d. 3/8/1915 at 73/8; carpenter; widower; b. Lincolnville, ME; Eben Knight and Sarah Moody

KNOWLES,
Anna Louise, d. 6/8/1999 at 88 in Ctr. Ossipee; John O. Gambell and Annie L. Whalen
Dorothy, d. 6/16/1987 at 76 in Wolfeboro; b. Quincy, MA
Grace W., d. 5/12/1961 at 81 in Laconia; b. Tuftonboro

Herbert L., d. 10/24/1954 at 75 in Laconia; b. ME; Albert Knowles and Joan -----
Philip Earl, d. 1/2/1971 at 68 in Claremont; b. NH
Winslow N., d. 4/28/1987 at 77 in Wolfeboro; b. Everett, MA

KNOWLTON,
Marjorie Ellen, d. 8/23/1998 in Ossipee; Grover Griffin and Alice Ruggles

KNOX,
child, d. 7/24/1898 at 0/7 in Ossipee; bronchitis; b. Ossipee; Charles L. Knox and Carrie Templeton
Alvah W., d. 4/28/1914 at 58/7/4; track foreman; b. Ossipee; Ephraim K. Knox (Ossipee) and Isabella Knox (Ossipee)
Beatrice C., d. 1/15/1983 at 74 in Laconia; b. Ossipee
Blanche, d. 9/16/1898 at 3/7/21 in Ossipee; meningitis; b. Ossipee; Charles L. Knox (Ossipee) and Carrie Templeton (Ossipee)
Carl L., d. 7/31/1966 at 18 in Rochester; b. Rochester
Carrie, d. 3/1/1903 at 36 in Ossipee; tuberculosis of lungs; widow; b. Ossipee; Ahial Templeton (Ossipee) and Elmira Nichols (Ossipee)
Charles E., d. 8/25/1921 at 70/4/30 in Ossipee; carpenter; married; Ephriam Knox (Ossipee)
Charles L., d. 12/30/1898 at 33 in Ossipee; tuberculosis; married; b. Ossipee; Thomas Knox (Ossipee) and Hannah Welch (Ossipee)
Edward C., d. 11/12/1962 at 62 in Tamworth; b. Ossipee
Edward C., Jr., d. 5/18/1964 at 40 in Rochester; b. Freedom
Ephraim K., d. 10/9/1902 at 79/10/3 in Ossipee; cerebral embolism; farmer; married; b. Ossipee
Evelyn Hersey, d. 5/25/1972 at 79 in Ossipee; b. NH
Fay Ora, d. 10/11/1906 at 12/1 in Ossipee; gun shot wound of chest; scholar; single; b. Ossipee; Charles E. Knox (Berwick, ME) and Mary E. Chesley (Tamworth)
Frank W., d. 9/12/1910 at 7/10/12 in Ossipee; b. Rochester; Manville E. Knox (Ossipee) and Mabel Thompson (Salisbury)
Freeman A., d. 1/7/1939 at 79/5/17 in Ossipee; b. Ossipee; W. Thomas Knox and Hannah Welch
Hannah, d. 7/21/1892 at 65 in Ossipee; pulmonary; housewife; married; b. Ossipee; John Welch
Isabella, d. 4/22/1911 at 82/0/20; senility; widow; b. Berwick, ME; William Knox
Mabel F., d. 2/15/1952 at 73 in Wolfeboro; b. Salisbury; Rosto Thompson and Jennie Godfrey
Manville E., d. 5/28/1950 at 83/1/12 in Ossipee; b. Ossipee; Ephraim Knox and Isabella Knox
Myrtle V., d. 11/1/1980 at 71 in Laconia; b. England
Olin A., d. 3/22/1977 at 90 in Ossipee; b. NH

Roy Wesley, d. 5/28/1988 at 86 in Ossipee; b. Ossipee
Sara Ethel, d. 3/5/1997 at 94 in Wolfeboro; George Cather and Annie Chase
Sarah, d. 9/27/1931 at 72 in Ossipee; b. Ossipee; Daniel Colby and Mary Colby
Shirley W., d. 6/11/1952 at 44/5/29 in Ossipee; b. Greenland; Manville Knox and Mabel Thompson
William, d. 3/4/1897 at 33/2/28 in Dover; pneumonia
Winnifred E., d. 3/16/1946 at 64/11/9 in Wolfeboro; b. N. Conway; Alfred L. Sweet and Almira L. Strout

KOHLER,
May T., d. 11/15/1952 at 35/7/23 in Wolfeboro; b. Hart County, KY; John Thompson and Meca Riggs

KOLIN,
Lena A., d. 6/11/1972 at 85 in Ossipee; b. NY

KOLINEK,
Anna, d. 10/28/1972 at 83 in Conway; b. Czechoslovakia

KOSCHALK,
Frances, d. 11/13/1990 at 77 in Ossipee; b. New York, NY

KOSKUBA,
Florence Dube, d. 8/31/1988 at 82 in Wolfeboro; b. Turners Falls, MA

KRAMER,
Robert G., d. 5/14/2001 in Laconia; Otto Kramer and Rena Grant

KRESSLER,
Elizabeth Marie, d. 10/5/1974 at 92 in Ossipee; b. PA

KROELL,
Oscar Robert, d. 2/22/1976 at 93 in Ossipee; b. MO

KRUG,
Frederick Arthur, d. 5/4/1997 at 77 in Wolfeboro; Arthur Krug and Julia Schmitt
Lois Muriel, d. 11/1/1996 at 73 in Ctr. Ossipee; Joseph Hence and Elsie Seadorf

KUNZ,
John H., d. 2/23/1985

KURTH,
John E., d. 7/3/1979 at 88 in Wolfeboro; b. MA
Marguerite R., d. 7/13/1988 at 97 in Ossipee; b. Boston, MA

KUSNIERZ,
Mary E., d. 9/18/1998; Byron Fickett and Jessie Hurd

LABONTE,
Albert Ernest, d. 1/2/1989 at 57 in Wolfeboro; b. Lowell, MA

LABOR,
Hazel A., d. 8/3/1959 at 50 in Wolfeboro; b. Ossipee; Jacob Abbott and Fessie Ainsworth

LABRIE,
Ronald Edward, d. 1/23/1995 at 46; Albert J. Labrie and Faith Cassidy

LACABBE,
Carl, d. 5/21/1911 at 51; tuberculosis; stone cutter; single

LADD,
Anne P., d. 12/10/1937 at 84/3/16 in Ctr. Ossipee; b. Ossipee; Erastus Hanson and Nancy Nute
Byron A., d. 12/2/1974 at 82 in Ossipee; b. MA
Everett W., d. 3/7/1985 at 86 in Ossipee; b. N. Franklin, CT
Irvetta S., d. 11/4/1976 at 86 in Ossipee; b. IA

LAFRANCE,
John R., d. 5/24/1985 at 69 in Wolfeboro; b. Brandon, VT

LAFRENIERE,
Anita Rachel, d. 3/19/1998 in Wolfeboro; Rudolph Simard and Ernestine LaRoche

LAGASSE,
Rene A., d. 1/6/1998 in Ossipee; Alfred LaGasse and Philomene Bourget

LAHTI,
Waino Henry, d. 5/29/1973 at 71 in Ossipee; b. MA

LAING,
Claire M., d. 2/6/1986 at 68 in Wolfeboro; b. Lynn, MA

LAKIN,
Ernest, d. 10/18/1984 at 90 in Ossipee; b. Leicester, England
Frederick Robert, d. 4/15/1985 at 83 in Ossipee; b. Leicester, England

LAMONTAGNE,
Alvina, d. 9/15/1893 at 17 in Ossipee; housewife; married; b. Halifax, Canada
Lenora, d. 4/18/1926 at 34/7/2; b. Tamworth; James Arling and Emma Bickford
Richard, d. 3/26/1913 at 0/2/1/6; b. Milton; Joseph E. Lamontagne (Ossipee) and Lenora B. Clifford (Tamworth)
Richard, d. 2/6/1926 at 1/6/24; b. Tamworth; Henry LaMontagne and Norah Arlin

LAMPER,
Edna L., d. 5/13/1899 at 21/8/19 in Ossipee; pulmonary tuberculosis; single; b. Effingham; Albert B. Lamper (Effingham) and Elvina S. ----- (Freedom)
Elvira S., d. 7/26/1917 at 75/8/7; b. Freedom; James Smith
Gladys, d. 12/15/1973 at 76 in Ossipee; b. NH
Maude Elizabeth, d. 6/15/1987 at 79 in Ossipee; b. Dover

LAMPREY,
Leslie Balch, d. 1/31/1989 at 95 in Wolfeboro; b. Manchester

LANDEAU,
Julia, d. 5/9/1931 at 83 in Ossipee; b. Canada; Abel Landeau and Julia Sandas

LANDRY,
Genevieve, d. 4/26/1991 at 90 in Ossipee; b. Boston, MA

LANE,
Elizabeth M., d. 4/2/1972 at 86 in Ossipee; b. NH

LANEY,
Frank T., d. 7/17/1984 at 69 in Manchester; b. Alton

LANG,
Bessie Katherine, d. 2/17/1987 at 78 in Ossipee; b. Parsonsfield, ME
Joseph W., d. 6/15/1990 at 80 in Wolfeboro; b. Brookfield
Margaret M., d. 4/22/1966 at 79 in Ossipee; b. Beddick, NS
Stephen, d. 9/14/1964 at 80 in Wolfeboro; b. New York, NY

LANGDON,
Bessie, d. 7/14/1985 at 104 in Ossipee; b. Somersworth

LANGLEY,
Joseph, d. 1/31/1918 at 85/5/11; engineer; widower; b. Nottingham

LANGLOIS,
Leon F., d. 2/3/1986 in MA; b. 1/1907

LANOIX,
Rose A., d. 10/8/1973 at 74 in Ossipee; b. ME

LANOUETTE,
William, d. 8/31/1927 at 60/3/7; b. Franklin; John Lanouette and Agnes Rogers

LAPORTE,
Albert E., d. 11/30/1984 at 74 in Ossipee; b. Derry
Mona L., d. 11/24/1984 at 76 in Wolfeboro; b. Peterborough

LARABEE,
Allan F., d. 11/14/1933 at 81/0/29 in Ossipee; b. Albany; James Larabee and Lydia Peabody

LARKIN,
Esther Ellen, d. 9/5/1995 at 101; William Kohler and Emma Doyen

LARLEE,
Donald A., Jr., d. 9/10/1963 at 24 in Ossipee; b. Conway

LAROCHELLE,
Napolean A., d. 12/6/1997 at 71 in Wolfeboro; Michel LaRochelle and Marie Anne Beaudoin

LAROUX,
Arthur, d. 12/7/1961 at 85 in Ossipee; b. Canada

LARRABEE,
Charles H., d. 10/30/1911 at 79/7; farmer; married; b. Greene, ME; Isaac Larabee (Greene, ME) and Rebecca Adams (Greene, ME)
Martha E., d. 1/6/1917 at 86/10/20; none [occupation]; widow; b. Ossipee; ----- Bean (Sanford, ME) and Eunice Murry (Sanford, ME)

LARSON,
Christina, d. 1/3/1920 at 83/9/10; housekeeper; widow; b. Sweden; Pere Larson (Sweden) and Lis Greta (Sweden)
Marie E., d. 9/30/1916 at 49/11/15; housekeeper; single; b. Sweden; Lars P. Larson (Sweden) and Christine Peterson (Sweden)

LATTIE,
Albert, d. 12/10/1928 at 72/6/16; William Lattie
Mary Jane, d. 5/11/1970 at 78 in Gilmanton; b. MA

LAVOY,
Joseph V., d. 12/19/1961 at 79 in Ossipee; b. Freedom

LAWLOR,
Margaret E., d. 1/9/1965 at 80 in Ctr. Ossipee; b. Ogden, NS

LAWRENCE,
Earl A., d. 9/25/1963 at 73 in Wolfeboro; b. Newburyport, MA
Jane A., d. 11/1/1980 at 80 in Ossipee; b. Boston, MA

LAWSON,
Bernard B., d. 3/11/1987 at 85 in Wolfeboro; b. NB

LEAVITT,
Florence G., d. 12/27/1956 at 82 in Rochester; b. Parsonsfield, ME; Simeon Gerrish and Liza Lougee
Harry M., d. 12/27/1946 at 38/5/20 in Wolfeboro; b. Parsonsfield, ME; E. Forrest Leavitt and Florence Garland
Louise, d. 4/24/1944 at 33/0/16 in Ctr. Ossipee; b. Effingham; E. Forrest Leavitt and Florence Gerrish
Nathalie Belcher, d. 10/25/1995 at 79; Lester H. Belcher and Florence May Davy
Rufus, d. 3/15/1927 at 61/2/21; b. Eaton; Calvin L. Leavitt and Ann Drew

LEBLANC,
Joseph, d. 4/9/1947 at 70/9/29 in Wolfeboro; b. Canada
Joseph R., d. 1/12/1962 at 64 in N. Conway; b. NS
Wilfred, d. 9/23/1967 at 74 in Ossipee; b. Canada

LEBROKE,
Charles Franklin, d. 9/13/1974 at 86 in Ossipee; b. NH

LEE,
June G., d. 8/25/1924 at 0/0/3; b. Ossipee; Arthur Lee and Beatrice Raymond

LEGENDRE,
Irene Isabelle, d. 5/11/2001 in Ctr. Ossipee; Clement Holbrook and Mary Berry

LEIGHTON,
Albert W., d. 7/8/1913 at 70/4/4; insurance; widower; b. Ossipee; Charles Leighton (Ossipee) and Sallie Wentworth (Wakefield)
Alice D., d. 6/1/1926 at 72/4/10; b. Tuftonboro; ----- Graves and Abbie Nason
Anna Libby, d. 6/3/1994 at 92; Walter Libby and Mable Lucas
Burt, d. 1/15/1969 at 89 in Ossipee; b. NH
Charles B., d. 10/10/1898 at 43/5/15 in Ossipee; chronic inflammation; farmer; married; b. Ossipee; Charles Leighton (Ossipee) and Sally Wentworth (Wakefield)
George H., d. 11/6/1890 at – in Ossipee; heart disease; farmer; married
Kate C., d. 8/19/1896 at 57/6 in Ossipee; heart disease; housekeeper; b. Buxton, ME; David Smith (Rye) and Mercy Lang (Effingham)
Minnie I., d. 1/20/1954 at 74 in Portsmouth; b. NH; Albert Leighton and Kate Smith

LELAND,
James A., d. 12/19/1986 at 63 in Wolfeboro; b. Glasgow, KY

LEMOINE,
Hazel R., d. 2/19/1984
Wilrose J., d. 2/2/1969 at 74 in Manchester; b. MA

LESSARD,
Bibiane M., d. 6/19/1999 in Lebanon; Napoleon Fontaine and Rose Gibouleau

LEVASSEUR,
Ludger E., d. 1/23/1982 at 75 in Ossipee; b. Laconia

LEVITT,
Bert, d. 1/8/1957 at 83/7/24 in Ossipee; b. Effingham; George Levitt and Narcie Merrill

LEWIS,
Betsy, d. 2/4/1917 at 72; housewife; widow; b. NH

Dorothy A., d. 1/10/1979 at 59 in Wolfeboro; b. NH
Hazen C., d. 6/29/1892 at 58 in Ossipee; syphillis; laborer; married; b. Fryeburg, ME
Mrs., d. 11/24/1895 at 100 in Ossipee; old age; "red"; pauper; b. Old Town, ME
Samuel F., d. 10/4/1900 at 62/7 in Ossipee; Bright's disease; farmer; married; b. Ossipee; Joseph Lewis and Saphronia Lear
Sophronia L., d. 8/17/1889 at 82; domestic; widow; b. Effingham; William Lear
William H., d. 9/9/1888 at 52; farmer; single; b. Saco, ME; Joseph Lewis and Sophronia Lewis

LIBBEY,
James, d. 8/21/1900 at 84 in Ossipee; old age; farmer; b. Porter, ME

LIBBY,
Alfred K., d. 5/9/1942 at 17/3/7 in Ossipee; b. Milton; Robert M. Libby and Helen L. Eldridge
Anne E., d. 2/26/1912 at 54/9/4
Augusta M., d. 8/7/1940 at 77/4/23 in Ossipee; b. Tuftonboro; Andrew Thomas and Martha Ann Bradley
Bernice, d. 3/27/1973 at 69 in Ossipee; b. NH
Carroll Everett, d. 12/7/1991 at 72 in Wolfeboro; b. Freedom
Ernest G., d. 4/13/1976 at 52 in Wolfeboro; b. NH
Floyd Fred, d. 5/1/1996 at 59 in Ossipee; Robert Libby and Helen Eldridge
Frank, d. 7/15/1972 at 79 in Effingham; b. NH
George Edwin, d. 11/28/1996 at 73 in Ctr. Ossipee; George Edwin Libby, Sr. and Angeline Tripp
Mable C., d. 3/30/1960 at 87 in Ossipee; b. Wolfeboro
Randolph C., Jr., d. 2/10/1962 at 0/6 in Wolfeboro; b. Wolfeboro
Robert M., d. 4/1/1978 at 82 in Hanover; b. NH
Scott A., d. 8/14/1974 at 92 in Ossipee; b. NH
Stella, d. 10/30/1973 at 87 in Ossipee; b. ME
Vinnie, d. 4/15/1918 at 1/0/2; b. Ossipee; Robert M. Libby (Tuftonboro) and Helen Eldridge (Ossipee)
Winfield J., Jr., d. 12/11/1967 at 6 hrs. in Wolfeboro; b. Wolfeboro

LIEVI,
Jean C., d. 12/25/1997 at 77 in Wolfeboro; James Quinn and Catherine Mophee

LIGHT,
Albert, d. 4/1/1908 at 5/5/26 in Ossipee; drowning; b. Ossipee; Henry Light (NB) and Nellie Pokey (NB)

LINCOLN,
Edith Brynton, d. 10/10/1979 at 97 in Ossipee; b. MA

LINDELIUS,
Florence Ruth, d. 12/3/1993 at 84 in Ossipee

LINDLEY,
William Thomas, d. 4/14/1999 at 87 in Wolfeboro; Abraham Lindley and Catherine Eckes

LINDSEY,
Ella, d. 4/5/1948 at 61 in Concord

LINEHAN,
David J., d. 4/5/1986 at 64 in Wolfeboro; b. Danvers, MA
Grace Mahan, d. 8/30/1974 at 81 in Ossipee; b. NH
Robert Emmett, d. 11/9/1993 at 75 in Ossipee

LITTELL,
Edith Aileen, d. 1/7/1998 in Ossipee; Edward Athinson Ring and Rilla W. Clark

LITTLEFIELD,
Charles, d. 3/4/1935 at 85/8/11 in Ossipee
Ethel M., d. 3/28/1977 at 80 in Ossipee; b. NH
Marion L., d. 12/6/1968 at 77 in Wolfeboro; b. NH
Muriel Rich, d. 1/23/1985 at 81 in Wolfeboro; b. Boston, MA
Roy A., d. 10/2/1974 at 83 in Ossipee; b. NH

LOCK,
Charles, d. 3/25/1916 at 69; carpenter; widower; b. Canterbury; ----- Lock and Sarah -----

LOCKE,
Sarah, d. 10/2/1907 at 63/5 in Ossipee; cerebral embolism; housewife; married; b. Bath; William Clark and Almira Watters

LOCKWOOD,
G. A., d. 9/29/1901 at 57/9/1 in Ossipee; fatty degeneration heart; clergyman; married; b. Clinton, MI; Clark Lockwood (Norwalk, CT) and Harriet Seymore (Sanesboro, MA)
John A., d. 1/15/1971 at 82 in Ossipee; b. NS

LODICO,
Carmaleen, d. 1/3/1975 at 67 in MA; b. ME

LOGUE,
Bernice Henry, d. 2/23/1974 at 77 in Ossipee; b. NH

LONG,
Leslie R., Jr., d. 9/21/1972 at 71 in Ossipee; b. MA
Ruth Madeline, d. 1/25/1989 at 90 in Ossipee; b. Conway

LOPEZ,
Manuel, d. 3/8/1961 at 81 in Ossipee; b. Spain

LOPEZE,
Marcia, d. 1/19/1891 at 76 in Ossipee; domestic; married

LORD,
Bertrice Marie, d. 1/27/1994 at 77; Robert D. Benson and Alzada L. Fitzgerald
Betsey, d. 1/7/1899 at 83/8/4 in Ossipee; old age; housekeeper; widow; b. Ossipee; Clement Moody (Ossipee) and Mary Moody (Ossipee)
Blanche Jellison, d. 2/26/1987 at 94 in Ossipee; b. Rochester
Carroll W., d. 2/15/1927 at 19/0/0; b. Ossipee; John A. Lord and Laura M. Knight
Effie, d. 7/23/1949 at 75/10/1 in Wolfeboro; b. Ossipee; Francis Lord and Hannah Blaisdell
Flossie W., d. 3/30/1896 at 15/10 in Ossipee; marasmus; single; b. Ossipee; William H. Lord (Tamworth) and Edna S. Wiggin (Ossipee)
Francis N., d. 8/3/1912 at 87/5/25; widower; b. Ossipee; Robert Lord, Jr. (Ossipee) and Nancy Goldsmith (Ossipee)
Frank S., d. 3/28/1937 at 78/11/11 in Ossipee Valley; b. Ossipee; Francis H. Lord and Hannah Blaisdell
Hannah B., d. 3/9/1906 at 70/7/24 in Ossipee; cardiac paralysis; housewife; married; b. Tamworth; Stilson Blaisdell (Tamworth) and Sally Emery (Tamworth)
Ilda Olene, d. 12/15/1995 at 71; Gerald E. Lord and Damie Sapulding
John A., d. 1/4/1952 at 66/2/7 in Ossipee; b. Ossipee; William H. Lord and Sarah E. Lord
Joseph, d. 11/27/1901 at 83 in Ossipee; burn; farmer; widower; b. Madison; Laura Eldridge
Laura M., d. 10/6/1964 at 78 in Wolfeboro; b. Belfast, ME
S. Edna, d. 10/23/1946 at 90/5/20 in Ossipee; b. Ossipee; John G. Wiggin and Louinice E. Merrow

William H., d. 12/24/1928 at 82/8; b. Tamworth; Alvah Lord and Betsey Moody

LORING,
Adelaide L., d. 3/27/1894 at 55/11/25 in Ossipee; gastro enteritis; housewife; married; b. Ossipee; Horace Kimball and Annie Sleeper (Alton)
Chester M., d. 1/9/1969 at 76 in Ossipee; b. NH
Elmer L., d. 5/3/1929 at 67/8/21 in Ossipee; b. Ossipee; George M. Loring and Adelaide Kimball
Emeline A., d. 12/13/1922 at 70/5/14 in Ossipee; b. Clinton, MA; Robert Pratt and Eliza Hersey
George M., d. 9/22/1923 at 84/11/20; b. Boston, MA
Helen E., d. 4/14/1940 at 51/3/28 in Ossipee; b. Samoset, MA; Rev. Frederick Corson and Eva Hardy
James Milburn, d. 7/16/1974 at 57 in Ossipee; b. NH
Julia J., d. 12/30/1937 at 76/10/14 in Ossipee; b. Merricksville, ON; Theodore L. Chapman and Mary Jane Tedford
Marjorie, d. 8/26/1931 at 10/4/21 in Ossipee; b. Ossipee; LeRoy Loring and Helen Corson
Robert B., d. 2/8/1971 at 56 in Wolfeboro; b. NH
Rosanna E., d. 6/5/1905 at 67/1/22 in Ossipee; hepatitis; housekeeper; married; b. Fairlee, VT; Thomas Scott (Scotland) and Mary W. Hanson (Salem, MA)
Roy E., d. 5/1/1950 at 63/11/12 in Stow, MA; b. Ossipee; Elmer Loring and Julia Chapman
Ruth Mitchell, d. 4/28/1993 at 75 in Wolfeboro
Violet Mae, d. 1/12/1998 in Ossipee; William Colbroth and Minnie McLaughlin

LOUD,
Arthur P., d. 1/24/1985 at 64 in Ossipee; b. Ossipee
Clarence B., d. 2/1/1925 at 69/7/19; b. Plymouth, ME; Benjamin Loud and Lydia Bickford
Clarence B., II, d. 1/7/1990 at 60 in Ossipee; b. Ossipee
Edmund D., d. 7/22/1977 at 62 in Wolfeboro; b. VT
Eva Blake, d. 12/20/1988 at 95 in Wolfeboro; b. Ossipee
George W. T., d. 11/6/1929 at 0/0/27 in Boston, MA; b. Ossipee; Perley W. Loud and Alice Lambert
Grover C., d. 8/29/1968 at 77 in Laconia; b. MA
Julia M., d. 7/16/1920 at 64/8/27; housewife; married; b. Canada; Smith Curtis (Canada) and Mary Pond
Perley W., d. 8/13/1963 at 69 in Ossipee; b. Malden, MA

LOVE,
Fred C., d. 2/19/1960 at 74 in Wolfeboro; b. Corsica, PA

LOVERING,
George H., d. 2/1/1917 at 81; merchant; widower; b. Freedom; Dearborn Lovering (Freedom)

LOVETT,
Joseph H., d. 8/12/1917 at 73/11/14; retired; widower; b. Topsfield, MA
Katherine E., d. 3/12/1976 at 85 in Ossipee; b. NY
Louis T., d. 7/22/1973 at 80 in Wolfeboro; b. MA

LOWD,
Leavitt Leon, d. 10/8/1976 at 88 in Ossipee; b. NH

LUNT,
Daniel Edward, Jr., d. 5/15/1989 at 66 in Wolfeboro; b. Portland, ME

LYFORD,
Arlene E., d. 10/4/1996 at 66 in W. Ossipee; Edward F. Jones and Celia Peterson

LYMAN,
Gene Richard, d. 8/16/1989 at 26 in Wolfeboro; b. Hartford, CT

LYON,
Paul E., d. 1/27/1990 at 79 in Ossipee; b. Leominster, MA

LYONS,
daughter, d. 4/23/1950 at 2 hrs. in Ossipee; b. NH; Mark J. Lyons and Deslie White
Benjamin R., d. 2/27/1891 at 73 in Ossipee; farmer; married; b. Stewartstown; William Lyons and Rebecca Bassett
Sally, d. 12/20/1906 at 86/5/9 in Ossipee; senile debility; widow; Mark Wentworth (Wakefield)

MACAULEY,
Daniel, d. 3/14/1941 at 81/5/19 in Ossipee; b. Whycocomaugh, NS; John MacAuley and Mary MacRitchie

MACBRIEN,
Hazel Octavia, d. 2/10/1991 at 79 in Wolfeboro; b. Winchester, MA

MACDONALD,
son, d. 12/7/1942 at 0/0/2 in Wolfeboro; b. Wolfeboro; George O. MacDonald and Mary L. Strong
Agnes J., d. 1/9/1942 at 69 in Ossipee; b. Cambridge, MA; Charles A. Sullivan and Annie O'Brien
Catherine M., d. 8/12/1971 at 49 in Ossipee; b. MA
George O., d. 5/31/1986 at 80 in Wolfeboro; b. Whitefield
Joseph C., d. 1/11/1929 at 67/6/10 in Ossipee; b. NB; Rev. A. MacDonald and Jemina McDonald
Louis Daniel, d. 1/6/1975 at 60 in Ossipee; b. NH
Mary L., d. 8/3/1999 in Wolfeboro; George Strang and Mary Krar
Rose Isabelle, d. 1/18/1971 at 78 in Ossipee; b. NH

MACKENNEY,
George G., d. 1/23/1940 at 64/0/2 in Ossipee; b. Hartford, ME; Samuel MacKenney and Sarah Harris

MACKINNON,
Elizabeth M., d. 11/13/1977 at 66 in Wolfeboro; b. MA
John F., d. 8/19/1965 at 45 in Manchester; b. Somerville, MA

MACLELLAN,
Donald, d. 11/3/1969 at 62 in Manchester; b. MA

MACMILLAN,
Dennis P., d. 11/16/1968 at 19 in Ossipee; b. NJ

MACOMBER,
Harry Theodore, d. 1/9/1998 in Ossipee; Harry P. Macomber and Minnie F. McNay

MADDOCK,
Thelma Mae, d. 2/2/1988 at 80 in Ossipee; b. Portsmouth

MAGEE,
Walter, d. 1/26/1977 at 88 in Ossipee; b. NE

MAGNUSON,
Stanley A., d. 6/2/1983 at 61 in Ossipee; b. Boston, MA

MAGOON,
Ethel Wiggin, d. 3/23/1998 in Wolfeboro; John H. Harmon and Georgie Frost

M. W., d. 6/8/1898 at 76/1/20 in Ossipee; apoplexy; widow; b. Hopkinton; Caleb Clement and Lydia Gile

MAHONEY,
Ida C., d. 9/18/1983 at 91 in Ossipee; b. Tamworth

MAIER,
Elsa, d. 9/4/2000 at 82 in Ossipee; Frederick Maier and Bertha Teschner

MAINEY,
Thomas F., d. 7/25/1973 at 50 in Freedom; b. MA

MALAY,
Arlene Mae, d. 10/28/1992 at 84 in Ossipee; b. Gorham, ME
Charles V., d. 1/20/1973 at 76 in Wolfeboro; b. NS

MALLARD,
H. R., d. 5/12/1900 at 88 in Ossipee; influenza

MALONEY
Thomas P., d. 7/23/1986 at 61 in Ossipee; b. Malden, MA

MANCHESTER,
Charles, d. 9/7/1958 at 57 in Wolfeboro; b. W. Bridgewater; James Manchester and Minnie Folsom

MANNING,
Marian Anita, d. 2/18/1998 in Ossipee; Charles Walker and Ann Baird

MANSON,
Eliza A., d. 4/24/1917 at 74/2/16; housework; widow; b. Conway; Erastus Baker (Bow) and Mary Glines (Eaton)
Jacob, d. 2/17/1895 at 67 in Ossipee; pneumonia; supt. of alms house; married; Jacob Manson (Limington) and Elizabeth Emery
John F., d. 8/30/1909 at 45 in Boston; oedema of lungs and brain; physician; b. Effingham; Jacob Manson (Eaton) and Eliza Baker (Eaton)

MARBLE,
Eva T., d. 9/23/1949 at 77/6/18 in Ossipee; b. Haverhill, MA; Clinton Thom and Isabel Ayer

MARCHAND,
Scott Eliot, d. 12/31/1998 in Ossipee; Robert Edgar Marchand and Evelyn Pearl Minor

MARCHANT,
Mary Ada, d. 11/4/1973 at 101 in Ossipee; b. MA

MARCHI,
Louise, d. 6/8/1969 at 65 in Ossipee; b. MA

MARCON,
Sylvia M., d. 9/4/1913 at 0/2/17; Fred Marcon (Sheffield, VT) and Lila Ainsworth (Montpelier, VT)

MARCOTTE,
Ethel E., d. 10/2/1985 at 102 in Ossipee; b. Raymond

MARDEN,
Edith W., d. 2/13/1975 at 82 in Ossipee; b. NH
Gertrude, d. 7/5/1969 at 98 in Ossipee; b. MA
Mary E., d. 7/18/1963 at 88 in Ossipee; b. Dover

MAREK,
Alyce E., d. 2/5/1988 at 78 in Wolfeboro; b. Effingham

MARIENUS,
William, d. 4/26/1991 at 78 in Wolfeboro; b. Sully, IA

MARR,
George, d. 5/25/1909 at 54 in Ossipee; pul. tuberculosis; stevedore; b/ NS; William Marr (NS) and Hannah Jones (NS)

MARSH,
Gladys M., d. 3/15/1990 at 92 in Ossipee; b. Alton
Mary A., d. 5/15/1956 at 86 in Ossipee; b. Portugal

MARSHALL,
Sidney L., d. 6/8/1984 at 93 in Ossipee; b. Birmingham, England

MARSTON,
Hannah, d. 8/15/1888 at 78; domestic; widow; b. Ossipee; John Roberts
Joseph N., d. 1/13/1928 at 73/10/3; b. Effingham; John Marston and Sarah Davis

Martha, d. 3/6/1936 at 80/2/7 in Ctr. Ossipee; b. St. Paul, MN; Daniel Harmon and Jane Ward
Walter C., d. 4/26/1966 at 81 in Ossipee; b. Effingham

MARTIN,
Alex, d. 8/8/1893 at 48 in Ossipee; laborer; b. Eaton
Catherine Elizabeth, d. 1/18/1992 in Ossipee; b. Brooklyn, NY
Claire L., d. 6/30/2001 in Milton; Eddie St. Cyur and Lucille Martel
Clarence O., d. 5/3/1985 at 86 in Ossipee; b. Brooklyn, NY
Grace, d. 3/17/1973 at 92 in Ossipee; b. ME
Mary P., d. 6/9/1985 at 63 in Wolfeboro; b. Franklin
Pearl, d. 9/5/1991 at 82 in Ossipee; b. Fulton, NY
Vivian I., d. 6/4/1978 at 73 in Ossipee; b. MA

MARTINS,
Rose Marie, d. 10/2/2001 in Ossipee; Peter Costanza and Anna Pusateri

MASON,
Arthur James, d. 5/13/1992 at 82 in Ossipee; b. Boston, MA
Betsey, d. 4/24/1895 at 87 in Ossipee; cerebral congestion; pauper; widow; b. Bartlett
Charles L., d. 3/15/1942 at 63 in Wolfeboro
David S., d. 11/8/1918 at 74; laborer; b. Franklin; Joseph Mason (England)
Harriet D., d. 5/26/1985 at 81 in Wolfeboro; b. Providence, RI
Joanna Folsom, d. 1/6/1938 at 78/8/2 in Ossipee; b. Tamworth; John T. Folsom and Bessie A. Mason
Joseph D., d. 10/22/1940 at 64/4/7 in Ossipee; b. Brownfield, ME
Justin Edwards, d. 8/5/1940 at 83/0/22 in Ossipee; b. Tamworth; Larkin D. Mason and Catherine Staples
Lewis W., d. 1/24/1968 at 45 in Rochester; b. RI
Luther J., d. 11/11/1932 at 68/10/13 in Ossipee; b. Sandwich; Andrew Mason and Hester N. Mason
Richard R., d. 12/19/1984 at 59 in Ossipee; b. S. Tamworth
Rose H., d. 10/11/1936 at 70/0/11 in Ctr. Ossipee; b. Ossipee; John Ham and Nancy Sanborn
Ruth Philbrick, d. 2/27/1994 at 67; Clarence Philbrick and Mary Blanche Mason
Wesley L., d. 7/19/1976 at 78 in Ossipee; b. NH

MASSEY,
Albert Fay, d. 11/11/2001 in Ossipee; William Massey and Barbara Young

MASTERS,
Edith A., d. 10/11/1987 at 42 in Wolfeboro; b. Philadelphia, PA

MASTIN,
Alec, d. 9/27/1932 at – in Ossipee

MATHEWS,
Herbert, d. 10/1/1890 at 33/5 in Ossipee; Bright's disease; laborer; single; b. Wakefield; John W. Mathews and Lizzie Emerson

MATRONI,
Narisco, d. 12/25/1969 at 84 in Ossipee; b. Italy

MATTESON,
Truman Francis, d. 2/8/1994 at 90; Frank Agustus Matteson and Agusta Louise Foote

MATTINGLY,
Matthew John, d. 9/29/2000 at 24 in Ctr. Ossipee; Wilbur L. Mattingly, Jr. and Helen Bertholf

MATTSON,
Jennie Louise, d. 4/27/1983 at 84 in Ossipee; b. Everett, MA

MAXFIELD,
Ruth Southwick, d. 9/3/1973 at 79 in Ossipee; b. MA

MAY,
William Harry, Jr., d. 3/25/1994 at 73; William Harry May and Nellie May Merrow
William Henry, d. 7/7/1943 at 56/11/6 in Ossipee; b. Eden, VT; William E. May and Emma Boyce

MAYERS,
Alice B., d. 7/1/1984 at 89 in Wolfeboro; b. New York City, NY

McALLISTER,
Ellen, d. 1/3/1959 at 81 in Ossipee; b. NS; Daniel Lawlor and Annie Kennedy

McAULEY,
Josephine, d. 5/20/1927 at 44/11/7; b. Ossipee; John W. Pike and Emily F. Wallace

McBRIDE,
Francis Edward, d. 11/11/1971 at 75 in Ossipee; b. RI
Helen I., d. 2/19/1990 at 86 in Ossipee; b. Wolfeboro

Katie M., d. 3/15/1978 at 93 in Ossipee; b. NH

McCARTHY,
John F., d. 12/9/1933 at 19/11/0 in Ossipee; b. Marlboro, MA; Patrick McCarthy

McCARTY,
Patrick, d. 2/19/1914 at 62; laborer; b. Ireland

McCLOUD,
Amelia, d. 4/25/1930 at – in Ossipee; b. Canada; Peter Raymond

McCREARY,
Lylie Mae, d. 5/4/1932 at 40/2/27 in Ossipee; b. Lynn, MA; Charles R. Mansfield and Nellie M. Colby

McCRILLIS,
Margaret, d. 10/26/1969 at 80 in Ossipee; b. NH

McCULLEY,
John F., d. 11/22/1892 at 40 in Ossipee; mechanic; married

McDONALD,
Alice Genevieve, d. 10/25/1990 at 66 in Malden, MA; b. Malden, MA
James Joseph, Jr., d. 2/18/1992 at 79 in Ossipee; b. Belmont, MA
Jay A., d. 1/21/1964 at 0/3 in Wolfeboro; b. Wolfeboro
Jennie L., d. 8/9/1962 at 88 in Ossipee; b. Wolfeboro
John J., d. 2/6/1932 at 58/3/19 in Ossipee; b. Malden, MA; Ronald McDonald and Margaret McDonald

McDUFFEE,
Edwin, d. 3/2/1926 at 63; b. Ossipee; Henry D. McDuffee and Sarah D. Cotton
Gerald Eugene, d. 7/5/1995 at 84; Irving E. McDuffee and Minnie E. Templeton
Irving Eugene, d. 10/2/1940 at 70/10/4 in Tuftonboro; b. Tuftonboro; Henry D. McDuffee and Sara Cotton
Lloyd, d. 7/22/1972 at 54 in Ossipee; b. NH
Martha Boyden, d. 4/1/1998 in Ossipee; Elmer Nelson Boyden and Esther Butler
Sarah, d. 5/3/1904 at 71/7/2 in Tuftonboro; apoplexy; housewife; married; Smith L. Cotton and Hannah Hilton [surname listed as "McDuffy"]

McFARLANE,
Ernest G., d. 3/3/1959 at 10 in Wolfeboro; b. Wolfeboro; G. Douglas McFarlane and Janet Gregory
Janet G., d. 5/22/1980 at 63 in Wolfeboro; b. MA

McGILVRAY,
Daniel, d. 7/5/1914 at 32/4/9; laborer; b. NS

McGINNIS,
Daniel, d. 9/20/1905 at 66 in Ossipee; tuberculosis; farmer; single; b. Scotland B.I.

McGREGOR,
Duncan S., d. 4/9/1933 at 87/0/13 in Ossipee; b. PEI; Joseph McGregor and Isabelle Brown

McINDOE,
Addie L., d. 6/23/1951 at 89 in Wolfeboro; b. Ossipee; Francis Lord and Hannah Blaisdle

McINTIRE,
George H., d. 9/13/1946 at 82/3/6 in Wolfeboro; b. Tuftonboro; Charles McIntire and Mamie Shaw
Julia Emma, d. 3/15/1941 at 83/11/14 in Wolfeboro; b. Tuftonboro; Jonathan Brown and Susan Walker

McKEEN,
Ruth Margaret, d. 12/22/1985 at 90 in Ossipee; b. Fryeburg, ME

McKELLAR,
Robert, d. 12/9/1987 at 90 in Ossipee; b. Greenock, Scotland

McKENNEY,
Cynthia, d. 1/3/1925 at 60; b. Ossipee; Daniel H. McKenney and Lucy Mason
Daniel W., d. 10/13/1910 at 78/9/4 in Ossipee; apoplexy; farmer; widower; b. Ossipee; Daniel McKenney (Lisbon, ME) and Naomi Emerson (Lisbon, ME)
Lucy, d. 3/16/1904 at 64/10 in Ossipee; mitral insufficiency; housewife; married; b. Ossipee; John Noris and Mary Dodge
Norris, d. 5/31/1968 at 78 in Brentwood; b. MA
Otis M., d. 4/20/1932 at 65/0/0 in Ossipee; b. Ossipee; Daniel H. McKenney and Lucy M. Norris

McKENZIE,
Alexander J., d. 6/7/1985 at 70 in Ossipee; b. Shandaken, NY

McKINNON,
James Francis, d. 8/11/1997 at 83 in Wolfeboro; William McKinnon and Kizzie Turcotte
Kathleen Jane, d. 6/16/1999 at 68 in Ctr. Ossipee; Anthony Tobin and Margaret Sullivan
Patricia Violet, d. 4/28/1998 in Ossipee; Everett Stuart and Agnes Shriff

McLAUGHLIN,
Lois Cudhea, d. 2/20/1998 in Ossipee; William Cudhea and Ruby Mae Sanders
Patrick, d. 3/–/1913 at 76
Thomas J., d. 1/25/1973 at 84 in Ossipee; b. NH

McLEAN,
Daniel, d. 3/16/1977 at 66 in Ossipee; b. NY
James, d. 9/18/1898 at 79 in Ossipee; paralysis; widower; b. NS
Neil, d. 7/3/1944 at 83/3/16 in Ossipee; b. Cape Breton, NS

McMAHON,
Tyson J., d. 10/7/1999 in Dover; Donald McMahon and Marguerite Tyson

McMASTER,
Theresa Marion, d. 10/12/2000 at 70 in Ctr. Ossipee; Donald A. McMaster and Sarah Beaton

McNAMARA,
Laura C., d. 11/8/1974 at 86 in Concord; b. MA

McVEY,
John, d. 12/20/1896 at 27 in Ossipee; pulmonary tuberculosis; divorced

MEADER,
Douglas William, d. 7/7/1999 at 60 in Wolfeboro; Frank H. Meader and Annie O. Blanchard
Frank H., d. 3/15/1971 at 67 in Wolfeboro; b. ME
Joan Allen, d. 12/11/1974 at 39 in Ossipee; b. MA

MEEHAN,
Thomas F., d. 1/27/1971 at 85 in Wolfeboro; b. Ireland

MELANSON,
- son, d. 2/14/1936 at 0/0/1 in Wolfeboro; b. Wolfeboro; Roy Melanson and Lena Arsenault
- son, d. 11/16/1947 at 0/0/5 in Wolfeboro; b. Ossipee; Raymond Tibbetts and Lois Melanson

MELOON,
- Bernice N., d. 7/30/1935 at 39/10/16 in Laconia; b. Ossipee; Lyman White and Nellie Oakes
- Charles F., d. 2/8/1956 at 71 in Conway; b. Oneida, SD; Walter Meloon and Apphia Hutching
- Clara L., d. 7/30/1958 at 72 in Winchester; b. Vernon, VT; D. Arnold Streeter and Harriet Snow
- Esther F., d. 5/30/1983 at 84 in Ctr. Ossipee; b. Effingham
- Frank, d. 4/11/1915 at 64/9/18; farmer; married; b. Ossipee; Isiah Meloon (Effingham) and Eliza Kennett (Effingham)
- John F., d. 11/18/1920 at 78/6; painter; widower; b. Effingham; Joseph P. Meloon and Sarah Buswell (Ossipee)
- Mary Chadbourn, d. 12/16/1974 at 93 in Ossipee; b. MA

MELZARD,
- Douglas Ernest, Sr., d. 12/1/2000 at 88 in Ossipee; Charles E. Melzard and Harriett Quimby

MEREDITH,
- Luke James, d. 1/11/2001 in Ossipee; Francis Xavier Meredith and Sheryl Bliss

MERLINO,
- Peter, d. 3/17/1984 at 83 in Wolfeboro; b. Messina, Italy

MERRICK,
- Clayton Milton, Jr., d. 4/10/2000 at 65 in Ossipee; Clayton M. Merrick, Sr. and Mildred Buchanan

MERRIFIELD,
- Stillman, d. 2/18/1958 at 79 in Ossipee; b. ME; Warren Merrifield and Eliza Jose

MERRILL,
- Jennie, d. 12/21/1922 at 69 in Ossipee; housewife; widow; b. Canada; Charles Merrill (Canada) and Deborah Bagley (ME)

MERROW,
daughter, d. 3/23/1906 at 0/0/2 in Ossipee; inanition; b. Ossipee; Charles H. Merrow (Ossipee) and Emma Walker (Ossipee)
son, d. 9/13/1906 at 0/0/29 in Ossipee; inanition; b. Ossipee; Earl F. Merrow (Clifton, ME) and Flora Templeton (Ossipee)
Abbie, d. 6/16/1933 at 81/2/1 in Ossipee; b. Ossipee; Johoneson Dore and Mary Goldsmith
Alice J., d. 6/21/1962 at 88 in Wakefield; b. Ossipee
Ann W., d. 5/25/1958 at 21 in Wolfeboro; b. Wolfeboro; Howard Merrow and Gertrude Bickford
Annie C., d. 5/16/1896 at 21/2/20 in Ossipee; pulmonary phthisis; married
Annie E., d. 7/26/1951 at 83/6/25 in Ossipee; b. Ossipee; John Merrow and Rose Tebbetts
Atwood H., d. 10/1/1912 at 1/2/22; b. Ossipee; Earl T. Merrow (Ossipee) and F. Templeton (Ossipee)
Barbara, d. 1/16/1914 at 1/7; Earl Merrow (Clifton, ME) and Flora Templeton (Ossipee)
Caroline G., d. 6/22/1894 at 2/6/22 in Ossipee; paralysis of brain; b. Ossipee; Charles Merrow and Annie C. Pinkham
Charles, d. 6/11/1932 at 67/7/0 in Ossipee; b. Ossipee; James Merrow and Caroline Wingate
Charles W., d. 7/30/1940 at 32/11/17 in Wolfeboro; b. Ossipee; Charles H. Merrow and Emma Walker
Chester E., d. 2/11/1974 at 67 in Wolfeboro; b. NH
Dana J., d. 6/26/1916 at 53/8/3; farmer; married; b. Ossipee; James Merrow (Wakefield) and Caroline Wingate (Wakefield)
Daniel G., d. 9/3/1890 at – in Ossipee; cordial dropsy; married
Daniel H., d. 6/7/1921 at 64/2/5 in Ossipee; farmer; married; Daniel G. Merrow (Ossipee) and Sarah Moody (Ossipee)
Earl T., d. 2/24/1955 at 70 in Ossipee; b. ME; Daniel Merrow and Ella Silsby
Elizabeth I., d. 1/10/1938 at 78/9/19 in Ossipee; b. Boston, MA; Royal Brooks and Elvira Manson
Elizabeth M., d. 8/5/1949 at 82/11/7 in Ossipee; b. Middleton; Thomas Mitchell and Lydia Perkins
Elizabeth R. M., d. 4/11/1947 at 79/10/2 in Wolfeboro; b. E. Bridgewater, MA; Martin P. McLauthlin and Elizabeth Vincent
Elmer E., d. 2/8/1944 at 81/5/18 in Wolfeboro; b. Ossipee; Daniel G. Merrow and Sarah Moody
Ernest D., d. 12/9/1937 at 65 in Ctr. Ossipee; b. Salem, MA; John A. Merrow and Abbie Dore
Flora, d. 2/20/1945 at 59/7/7 in Laconia; b. Ossipee; Ahiel Templeton and Effie Williams

Florence E., d. 3/31/1910 at 21/1/21 in Ossipee; pleuritis; housewife; married; b. Ossipee; Charles Nichols (Ossipee) and Addie Glidden (Tamworth)

George W., d. 2/13/1894 at 65 in Ossipee; marasmus senilis; single; b. Ossipee

Gertrude Bickford, d. 4/29/1995 at 96; Roy Bickford and Susan J. Shaw

Howard, d. 6/27/1896 at 0/2/20 in Ossipee; renal congestion; b. Ossipee; Daniel Merrow (Ossipee) and Ella Silesby

Howard W., d. 10/5/1952 at 57 in Hartland, VT; b. Ossipee; Dane Merrow and Annie Williams

James, d. 9/9/1905 at 80/10/15 in Ossipee; uremia; carpenter; widower; b. Ossipee; Daniel Merrow (Acton, ME) and Lydia White (Wakefield)

John A., d. 11/13/1925 at 70/2/1; b. Ossipee; Daniel G. Merrow and Sarah Moody

John W., d. 6/24/1887 at 66/5 in Ossipee; merchant; married; b. Ossipee; Robert Merrow (Wakefield) and Lovina Garland (Wakefield)

Josephine, d. 7/23/1937 at 80/9/17 in Wolfeboro; b. Ossipee; Daniel Merrow and Elizabeth Brewster

Lafayette, d. 2/28/1930 at 44/4/18 in Concord; b. Standish, ME; Elmer E. Merrow and Lizzie Brooks

Llewellyn, d. 4/24/1958 at 71 in Ossipee; b. Ossipee; Daniel Merrow and Barbara Silsby

Louine Smart, d. 12/1/1997 at 85 in Ctr. Ossipee; Harry P. Smart and Harriet Colomy

Lydia A., d. 6/11/1888 at 65; housekeeper; widow; b. Ossipee; John Moulton and Susan Davis

Lyford A., d. 7/4/1925 at 59/9/26; b. Ctr. Ossipee; Daniel Merrow and M. Elizabeth Brewster

Margaret C., d. 4/10/1977 at 83 in Wolfeboro; b. Ireland

Maria E., d. 5/30/1913 at –

Mark H., d. 2/13/1935 at 53/8/14 in Cambridge, MA; b. Aurora, ME; Daniel W. Merrow and Ella B. Silsby

Myra J., d. 10/7/1962 at 86 in Ossipee; b. Tamworth

Nan T., d. 9/12/1914 at 59/0/4; b. Cornish, ME; Eben Barker (Cornish, ME) and Ruth Butterfield (Hiram, ME)

Nellie P., d. 7/28/1968 at 70 in Wolfeboro; b. VT

Nellie Sands, d. 12/5/1995 at 92; Frank Sands and Margaret Calahan

Parker M., d. 4/18/1964 at 60 in Wolfeboro; b. Malden, MA

Ralph H., d. 3/20/1947 at 52/3/12 in Wolfeboro; b. Ctr. Ossipee; Charles H. Merrow and Anna Pinkham

Ruby, d. 7/12/1915 at –; b. Bartlett; Earl T. Merrow (Clifton, ME) and Flora Templeton (Ossipee)

Sarah, d. 9/1/1907 at 77/7/1 in Ossipee; chronic bronchitis; housewife; widow; b. Ossipee; Amasa Moody and Mary -----

Sarah M., d. 8/13/1911 at 60/7/14; bronchial pneumonia; housework; single; b. Ossipee; James Merrow (Wakefield) and Caroline Wingate (Wakefield)

MERTENS,
Loretta A., d. 2/28/1968 at 7 hrs., 15 min. in Wolfeboro; b. NH
Margaret M., d. 2/28/1968 at 29 hrs. in Wolfeboro; b. NH

MESERVE,
Albert, d. 9/14/1904 at 68/7/6 in Ossipee; spinal paresis; millman; married; b. Wakefield; Nathaniel Meserve (Ossipee) and Sarah P. Horn (Wakefield)
Charles O., d. 11/9/1945 at 74/0/12 in Ossipee; b. Wakefield; Albert F. Meserve and Frances Hasty
Estelle, d. 3/27/1941 at 71/2/10 in Ossipee; b. Ossipee
Frances A., d. 12/3/1905 at 63/9/20 in Ossipee; dysentery; housekeeper; widow
George W., d. 4/28/1900 at – in Ossipee; chronic diarrhea; married; b. Brookfield
Sarah, d. 1/12/1914 at 81; b. Wolfeboro
William, d. 12/4/1919 at 81/3/4; laborer; widower; b. Brownfield, ME; Joseph Meserve (Limington, ME) and Alvira Ely (Conway)

MESSIER,
Rose Marie, d. 9/8/1992 at 98 in Ossipee; b. N. Grosvenordale, CT

METCALF,
Frank, d. 11/6/1932 at 72/8/5 in Ossipee; b. Lewiston, ME; Charles Metcalf
Marjorie Hardy, d. 4/24/1985 at 80 in Ossipee; b. Haverhill

MEYERS,
Frank, d. 2/10/1948 at 77/7/23 in Ossipee; b. Canada

MICHAUD,
Ethel V., d. 10/12/1969 at 87 in Ossipee; b. ME

MIGRANT,
George E., 3rd, d. 4/10/1981 at 24 in Ossipee; b. Ayer, MA

MILBERRY,
Miriam Elizabeth, d. 1/22/1992 at 82 in Wolfeboro; b. Swampscott, MA

MILES,
Charles S., d. 4/29/1922 at 69/4/17 in Ossipee; reg. of probate; married; b. Madbury; ----- Miles (Sheffield, VT) and Judith Gray (Sheffield, VT)

MILLAR,
Esther Madeline, d. 8/28/2000 at 90 in W. Ossipee; Frederick Bischoff and Elizabeth McCandless

MILLER,
Carroll C., d. 2/21/1998 in Ossipee; Archibald Miller and Elizabeth B. Olive
Doris H., d. 4/15/1998 in Ossipee; Albert W. Stewart and Sadie S. Burkett
Frank E., d. 2/23/1955 at 80 in Laconia; b. MA; Abial Miller and Helen Bickford
Franklin B., Jr., d. 6/27/1971 at 16 in Ossipee; b. MA
Martha, d. 3/12/1969 at 92 in Stoneham; b. NB
Ralph E., d. 6/24/1968 at 71 in Ossipee; b. MA
Rosalind, d. 1/8/1989 at 67 in Wolfeboro; b. Boston, MA

MILLIGAN,
Dennis R., d. 7/26/1977

MILLIKEN,
James, d. 4/15/1910 at 86/5/16 in Ossipee; old age; farmer; married; b. Effingham; Thomas Milliken (Scarboro, ME) and Mary Wedgewood (Effingham)
Lewis J., d. 4/9/1915 at 48/9/16; farmer; married; b. Ossipee; James Miliken (Effingham) and Lydia Hurd (Newton, MA)
Lydia A., d. 12/4/1911 at 78/5; fracture of neck; housewife; widow; b. Newton, MA; Lewis Hurd (Gonic) and ----- Hodgdon (Tuftonboro)
Olive M., d. 10/27/1969 at 87 in Ossipee; b. MA

MILLS,
Tom William, d. 3/19/1994 at 45; Frank C. Mills and Ruth A. Coffin

MISKOVSKY,
Jane B., d. 1/1/1958 at 84 in Wolfeboro; b. Providence, RI; Daniel McDuffee and Elizabeth McDermott

MITCHELL,
Elisabeth, d. 8/20/1999 at 92 in Ossipee; James Gilfeather and Elizabeth Keenan
Karen J., d. 9/28/1978 at 28 in Manchester; b. Ossipee
Leo C., d. 3/16/1985 at 80 in Ossipee; b. Fresno, CA
Woodrow W., d. 7/14/2000 in Wolfeboro; Ross Mitchell and Laura Carter

MIX,
Ella Meta, d. 11/3/1988 at 98 in Ossipee; b. Cambridge, MA

MONOHAN,
Elizabeth J., d. 1/6/1988 at 103 in Ireland; b. Freedom

MONROE [see Munroe],
Annie M., d. 8/16/1916 at 37/4/22; housekeeper; married; b. NS; Henry Hilphard (NS) and Catherine Hilphard (NS)
Charles N., d. 4/21/1910 at 0/6/25 in Ossipee; meningitis; b. Effingham; Norman Monroe
Gertrude, d. 10/15/1910 at 0/2/18 in Ossipee; tuberculosis; b. Ossipee; Norman Monroe and Annie -----
James Albert, d. 9/28/1913 at 0/3/11; b. Ossipee; Norman Monroe (NS) and Annie Helphard (NS)

MONTGOMERY,
Katherine O., d. 4/29/2001 in Ossipee; Simon Oomant and Petronela Arkins

MOODY,
Alden B., d. 4/8/1926 at 62/5; b. Ossipee; Bartlett Moody and Sarah A. Nutter
Alonzo, d. 2/13/1901 at 50/10/3 in Ossipee; cerebral degeneration; farmer; married; b. Sandwich; Jonathan Moody (Parsonsfield) and Sally Frye (Sandwich)
Bartlett, d. 10/3/1919 at 94/6/19; farmer; married; b. Ossipee; Clement Moody and Mary Cooley
Belle A., d. 11/14/1938 at 79/1/17 in Ossipee; b. Ossipee; Allen Smith and Betsy J. Moody
Bessie A., d. 5/24/1978 at 83 in Wolfeboro; b. Scotland
Blanche L., d. 1/13/1969 at 57 in Ossipee; b. ME
Catherine F., d. 4/29/1961 at 82 in Ossipee; b. Scotland
Clayton, d. 5/31/1996 at 80 in Ossipee; Frank Moody and Harriett Marston
Daniel, d. 1/15/1919 at 73/1; laborer; b. Parsonsfield
Eldred, d. 6/26/1919 at 1/10; b. Ossipee; Ernest Moody (Tamworth) and Vivian Hobbs (Ossipee)
Emery, d. 7/15/1936 at 84/3/11 in W. Ossipee; b. Ossipee; Joseph Moody and Hannah Eldridge
Ernest A., d. 5/7/1962 at 74 in Ctr. Ossipee; b. Northwood
Florence M., d. 6/25/1923 at 6/11/22; b.Ossipee; Edwin Moody and Vivian Hobbs
Frank W., d. 4/13/1957 at 73/7/2 in Ossipee; b. Effingham; Francis Moody and Betsey Canney
Fred E., d. 2/9/1935 at 35/04 in Wolfeboro

George W., d. 11/1/1894 at 81/2/26 in Ossipee; senile gangrene; farmer; widower; b. Ossipee; Clement Moody and Mary Moody
Grover T., d. 9/14/1971 at 86 in Wolfeboro; b. NH
Hazel Pearl, d. 9/22/1991 at 92 in Ossipee; b. Jackson
Henry Banks, d. 10/4/1940 at 67/7/24 in Ossipee; b. Albany; George W. Moody and Mary Agnes Doherty
John H., d. 3/1/1953 at 82/9/27 in Wolfeboro; b. Tamworth; William Moody and Lizzie Huntress
Leslie, d. 10/12/1956 at 82/3/12 in Ossipee; b. Ossipee; Bartlett Moody and Sarah Nutter
Linnie, d. 6/28/1916 at 26/10/14; housewife; married; b. Freedom; B. E. Eldridge (Freedom) and Melissa Moody (Tamworth)
Mary F., d. 6/3/1933 at 77/10 in Ossipee; b. Tamworth; Eben Eldridge and Aurilla Ward
Mary R., d. 6/3/1985 at 87 in Wolfeboro; b. New Haven, CT
Mattie B., d. 12/17/1941 at 65/6/13 in Wolfeboro; b. Ossipee; Isaac Buswell and Jennie Gilman
Nathaniel E., d. 10/13/1961 at 81 in Wolfeboro; b. Tamworth
Peter, d. 10/28/1913 at 30/1/6; painter; married; b. Albany; G. A. Moody and A. Kenerson
Robert R., d. 12/21/1969 at 79 in Ossipee; b. ME
Sarah, d. 11/26/1920 at 90/3/29; housewife; widow; b. Ossipee; Nahum Nutter (Farmington) and Esther Horne (Farmington)
Sewell, d. 3/18/1933 at 80/9/18 in Ossipee; b. Ossipee; Joseph A. Moody and Hannah Eldridge
William H., d. 5/28/1939 at 72/11/2 in Ossipee; b. Tamworth; George H. Moody and Mary Ann Hobbs

MOOERS,
Robert Eugene, d. 4/17/1992 at 66 in Ossipee; b. Revere, MA

MOORE,
Annie E., d. 11/9/1961 at 64 in Ossipee; b. Freedom
Edward J., d. 11/18/1969 at 68 in Wolfeboro; b. MA
Flora A., d. 6/4/1902 at 55 in Ossipee; gastritis; housewife; widow; b. Ossipee; Oliver F. Hobbs and Deborah Jenness
Fred, d. 8/9/1975 at 86 in Concord; b. Canada
Maude R., d. 6/13/1983 at 82 in Wolfeboro; b. Boston, MA
Paul Frederick, d. 5/11/1998 in Manchester; Herbert Moore

MORAN,
Michael, d. 7/29/1916 at 45/2; laborer; b. Salem, MA

MOREAU,
Mary Ellen, d. 12/2/1991 at 88 in Ossipee; b. Meriden, CT

MORGAN,
Eleanor H., d. 8/21/1976 at 82 in Ossipee; b. NH
George, d. 7/9/1910 at 64 in Ossipee; mitral insufficiency
Melvin O., d. 6/17/1926 at 76/6/22; b. Wolfeboro; Joseph Morgan
Sarah M., d. 3/29/1976 at 82 in Ossipee

MORRILL,
Clarence Ernest, d. 3/16/1993 at 92 in Ossipee
Harold P., d. 7/10/1900 at 0/10/21 in Ossipee; acute bronchitis; b. N. Windham; Henry W. Morrill (N. Windham) and Maud Lowell (N. Buxton)
Olive, d. 8/20/1985 at 80 in Ossipee; b. Somerville, MA

MORRIS,
Alfred, d. 3/3/1935 at 70/5/17 in Ossipee; b. Portland, ME; Charles Morris and Margaret Garland
Alfred G., d. 3/29/1990 at 90 in Wolfeboro; b. Tuftonboro

MORRISON,
Agnes Rennie, d. 1/18/2000 at 91 in Ossipee; David A. MacCuish and Annie Rennie
Josiah, d. 7/20/1904 at 70 in Ossipee; catarrh of bladder

MORSE,
Bruce C., d. 4/26/2001 in Wolfeboro; Bruce Morse and Evelyn Shafer

MOSHER,
Edith C., d. 12/16/1968 at 74 in Wolfeboro; b. MA

MOTTOLA,
Joseph A., d. 11/19/1987 at 79 in Ossipee; b. Atlantic City, NJ

MOULTON,
infant, d. 1/24/1896 at – in Ossipee; stillborn; Charles Moulton
Ausbry, d. 12/23/1920 at 62/10/29; retired; widower; b. Ossipee; Lewman Moulton and Mary Marston
Enoch, d. 4/8/1919 at 83/9/4; laborer; b. Freedom; Libby Moulton (Freedom) and Lucinda Fogg (Freedom)
George A., d. 3/1/1957 at 64 in Wolfeboro; b. Lakeport; Albert Moulton and Eliza Foss
Gladys Eva, d. 8/16/1993 at 92 in Ossipee
Hannah M., d. 2/2/1933 at 85/9/6 in Newfield, ME; b. Ossipee
Idanelle Thompson, d. 7/13/1979 at 85 in Ossipee; b. MN

James, d. 1/27/1895 at 77 in Ossipee; opium inebriety; farmer; married; b. Newfield; Simon Moulton
James L., d. 7/28/1965 at 76 in Ossipee; b. Parsonsfield, ME
John B., d. 11/10/1905 at 68 in Ossipee; obstruction of bowels; farmer; single; b. Ossipee; John Moulton
Joseph, d. 3/4/1939 at – in Ossipee
Lafayette, d. 12/11/1933 at 76/1/12 in Ossipee; b. Ossipee; Lorenzo D. Moulton and Abigail Merrow
Laura Page, d. 10/22/1975 at 90 in Ossipee; b. ME
Lisle O., d. 8/29/1961 at 75 in Ossipee; b. Ossipee
Lorenzo Dow, d. 6/13/1911 at 28/1/6; tetanus; single; b. Ossipee; L. E. Moulton (Ossipee) and Mattie Manson (Freedom)
Luman G., d. 10/11/1888 at 73; undertaker; married; b. Ossipee; Mark Moulton and Sophia Tibbetts
Maria, d. 11/19/1892 at 60 in Ossipee; pelvic abscess; housewife; b. Tuftonboro; Nathan Whitehouse (Tuftonboro)
Mary, d. 1/1/1905 at 82/9/29 in Ossipee; cerebral congestion; widow; b. Portsmouth; Jeremiah Marston and Mary Hobbs
Mary A., d. 8/25/1901 at 80/6/17 in Ossipee; anaemia; widow; b. Ossipee; James Lord (Ossipee) and Hannah Jones (Beverly)
Minnie H., d. 11/26/1911 at 53/5/16; housewife; married; b. Freedom; John Parsons and Hannah Flanders (Madison)
Nellie J., d. 3/9/1927 at 58/8/8; b. Wolfeboro; Calvin Hoyt and Sally -----
Ona E., d. 2/2/1912 at 55/7/22; housewife; married; b. Conway; James Hamilton (ME) and Ona Coburn (ME)
Rhoda M., d. 3/9/1887 at 49/4/4 in Ossipee; domestic; widow; b. Ossipee; William Moulton (Newfield, ME) and Sally Smith (Ossipee)
William, d. 11/7/1937 at 68/7/13 in Ossipee; b. Detroit, MI; William Moulton

MOYSE,
Ruth TerWilliger, d. 9/16/2000 at 80 in Ossipee; Ira W. TerWilliger and Hazel Armour

MUDGETT,
Annie M., d. 8/30/1980 at 94 in Ossipee; b. MA
Bessie Mae, d. 11/27/1974 at 95 in Ossipee; b. NS
Elwood, d. 4/21/1977 at 58 in Wolfeboro; b. NH
Harriett, d. 3/22/1914 at 87; b. Fryeburg, ME

MUENZNER,
Eva, d. 3/12/1973 at 77 in Wolfeboro; b. MA

MUISE,
Teresa M., d. 4/11/1990 at 89 in Ossipee; b. Wakefield, MA

MULLEN,
Robert H., d. 8/12/1965 at 64 in Ossipee; b. Boston, MA
S. Judson, d. 11/15/1940 at 71/11/6 in Ossipee; b. Weymouth, NS; John Mullen and Madlone Comeau

MUNROE [see Monroe],
Arthur C., d. 8/16/1977 at 66 in Ossipee; b. NH
Brian E., d. 4/24/1958 at 2 in Wolfeboro; b. Wolfeboro; Donald Munroe and Avonne Knox
Charles N., d. 4/22/1946 at 75/0/6 in Ossipee; b. NS; Samuel Munroe and Hannah -----
Emma Louise, d. 3/5/1991 at 93 in Wolfeboro; b. Minot, ME
Maude Mae, d. 11/30/1977 at 85 in Ossipee; b. ME
Terrace R., d. 7/19/1965 at 51 in Ossipee; b. E. Peacham, VT

MURPHY,
James, d. 10/12/1895 at 90 in Ossipee; mitral regurgitation; pauper; widower; b. England
John, d. 1/30/1930 at 66/6 in Ossipee; b. Boston; James Murphy
John R., d. 5/18/1974 at 77 in N. Conway; b. NH
Mary L., d. 10/25/1976 at 70 in Ossipee; b. ME
Patrick, d. 4/20/1953 at 60 in Concord; b. Ireland

MURRAY,
Chester Francis, Sr., d. 2/4/1984 at 79 in Ossipee; b. Lynn, MA
John, d. 2/20/1935 at 62 in Wolfeboro; b. Orangedale, MA; Duncan Murray and Caroline McRickey

MUSKEY,
Stephen Charles, d. 11/1/1976 at 87 in Ossipee; b. Lithuania

MYLIUS,
Marjorie, d. 4/24/1998 in Porter, ME; Louis Mylius and Ethel Crossley

NARY,
George W., Sr., d. 8/29/1971 at 84 in Wolfeboro; b. MA

NASON,
Benjamin, d. 4/29/1918 at 67; farmer; married; b. Parsonsfield
Bruce, d. 2/15/1999 in Wakefield; Lawrence Nason and Marilyn French
Charles H., d. 4/27/1935 at 81/6/11 in Ossipee; b. Ossipee; A. J. Nason and Abbie Hanson
Doris L., d. 5/6/1998 in Ossipee; John Jewell and Emma Mae Thomes
Henrietta Emery, d. 8/2/1974 at 89 in Ossipee; b. NH

Johnnie Willis, d. 5/16/1995 at 73; Willis Linwood Nason and Maude Reed

Lucinda F., d. 10/1/1932 at 87/4/30 in Ossipee; b. Baldwin, ME; Daniel Thorne and Martha Wentworth

Maude E., d. 2/18/1988 at 88 in Ossipee; b. Union

NEAL,

Agnes C., d. 7/20/1981 at 88 in Ossipee; b. Star Prairie, WI

Florence J., d. 4/10/1960 at 65 in Ossipee; b. Reading, MA

George A., d. 8/4/1949 at 77/3/27 in Ossipee; b. Moultonville; Tyler Neal and Mary Kenerson

Harold C., d. 7/29/1965 at 70 in Wolfeboro; b. Malden, MA

Kirk B., d. 6/23/1896 at 59/8 in Ossipee; cerebral hemorrhage; farmer; single; Thomas Neal and Mary Wallingford

Mary E., d. 3/30/1901 at 70/7 in Ossipee; paralysis; housewife; married; b. Brookfield; Solomon Keniston (Brookfield) and Hannah Cooley (Ossipee)

Tyler A., d. 10/6/1909 at 79/6/24 in Ossipee; uraemia; farmer; b. Brookfield; Enoch Neal (Portsmouth) and Betsey Roles (Ossipee)

NEALEY,

Mary, d. 3/17/1932 at 46/2/11 in Ossipee; b. Wakefield; Henry Nealey and Laura Bishop

NEIL,

Arlene Britt, d. 10/29/1997 at 86 in Ossipee; Chester L. Britt and Lizzie Toothacher

NEILSEN,

Maric A., d. 3/16/1991 at 99 in Ossipee; b. Odense, Denmark

NELSON,

Annie A. M., d. 1/24/1894 at 11/10/27 in Ossipee; meningitis; maid; single; b. Newport, RI; Ferdinand Nelson (Denmark) and Caroline Coruson (Denmark)

Arvilla, d. 4/25/1948 at 64/10/7 in Ossipee; b. Ossipee; Charles A. Templeton and Robeline Johnson

Emily E., d. 7/17/1955 at 43 in Wolfeboro; b. OH; James Libby and Elizabeth Mayhiham

Harry F., d. 10/27/1962 at 77 in Wolfeboro; b. Newport, RI

Jessica L., d. 9/21/1981 at 0/11 in Hanover; b. Laconia

Pearl Gay, d. 12/9/1988 at 40 in Ossipee; b. Bangor, ME

Russell H., d. 10/8/1973 at 66 in Wolfeboro; b. NH

NEMETH,
Margaret M., d. 2/15/2000 in Wolfeboro; George Medwick and Rose Kasey

NEWBEGIN,
Leon H., d. 4/14/1991 at 32 in Ossipee; b. Fryeburg, ME
Leon H., d. 3/13/2001 in Ctr. Ossipee; William H. Newbegin and Lottie M. Sargent

NEWCOMB,
Nathan Carsby, d. 10/13/1943 at 77/1/4 in Ossipee; b. Harrison, ME; Simon Newcomb and Mary Richards

NEWHALL,
Urilda J., d. 8/10/1932 at 79/1/27 in Granite; b. Peabody, MA; Nathaniel Putnam and Sallie Galencia

NEWVINE,
Edith, d. 1/18/1907 at 0/2/5 in Ossipee; bronchitis; b. Ossipee; Alex Newvine and Eva -----

NEWMAN,
Olive Ruth, d. 12/7/1997 at 73 in Wolfeboro; Hedley Taylor and Lily Mae Dean

NICHOLS,
son, d. 6/22/1887 at 0/2/2 in Ossipee; b. Ossipee; Alonzo Nichols and Martha J.
daughter, d. 6/29/1893 at 0/0/12 in Ossipee; b. Ossipee; Al. Nichols (Bartlett) and Martha Hill (Conway)
son, d. 2/12/1894 at 0/2 in Ossipee; b. Ossipee; Frank A. Nichols (Ossipee) and Eliza Drew (Ossipee)
son, d. 2/17/1899 at – in Ossipee; puerperal; b. Ossipee; Joseph Nichols (Ossipee) and Carrie Nute (Ossipee)
Abbie A., d. 6/4/1888 at 47/8/23; housekeeper; widow; b. Saco, ME; Upton Harmon and Lydia Jerelison
Ada D., d. 11/9/1932 at 77/9/18 in Ossipee; b. Ossipee; Joseph F. Palmer and Emily M. Merrow
Addie M., d. 8/16/1891 at 0/2/12 in Ossipee; b. Ossipee; Frank A. Nichols (Ossipee) and Eliza Drew (Wolfeboro)
Albert, d. 8/18/1954 at 56/8/20 in Ossipee; b. Ossipee; Alphonzo Nichols and Annie Andrews
Allen, d. 10/28/1909 at 62/10/16 in Effingham; heart disease; hotel keeper; b. Ossipee; Amos Nichols (Ossipee) and Mary White (Ossipee)

Almon J., d. 4/7/1906 at 56/1/8 in Ossipee; heart disease; millman; married; b. Ossipee; Amos Nichols (Ossipee) and Mary White (Ossipee)

Alphonse, d. 5/17/1931 at 69 in Concord; b. Ossipee; Amos Nichols and Hannah Eldridge

Amos, d. 9/30/1905 at 86/7/28 in Ossipee; fracture of femoral neck; laborer; widower; b. Ossipee; James Nichols (Ossipee) and Susan Davis (Moultonboro)

Annie A., d. 6/5/1959 at 85 in Ossipee; b. Freedom; Thomas Andrews and Esther Audway

Bernice, d. 4/8/1961 at 62 in Concord; b. Ossipee

Bertha Alice, d. 6/12/1994 at 75; John H. Harmon and Georgie Frost

Caroline, d. 8/14/1911 at 53/4/3; cholera morbus; housework; married; b. Ossipee; Stephen Eldridge (Ossipee) and Hannah Adjutant (Ossipee)

Carrie I., d. 2/17/1899 at 19 in Ossipee; eclampsia; housewife; married; b. Ossipee; George Nute (Boston) and Sarah Glidden (Ossipee)

Charles, d. 9/3/1891 at 29 in Ossipee; laborer; married; W. Nichols

Clara I., d. 11/26/1928 at 71/0/10; b. Milton; Daniel Fall and Comfort Vining

Clarinda D., d. 1/17/1951 at 69/0/10 in Wolfeboro; b. Effingham; Ebenezar Davis and Augusta Hammond

Clifton S., d. 6/24/1972 at 73 in Ossipee; b. NH

Dana, d. 4/14/1895 at 40/6/28 in Ossipee; Bright's disease; shoemaker; married; b. Ossipee; Amos Nichols (Ossipee) and Mary White (Ossipee)

Ebenezer, d. 8/26/1898 at 86/4/14 in Ossipee; Brights disease; farmer; widower; b. Ossipee; James Nichols (Ossipee) and Lydia White (Ossipee)

Edward, d. 8/3/1912 at 64; laborer; widower

Eliza, d. 4/13/1920 at 61/8/19; housework; b. Wolfeboro; Daniel Drew and Ann Wormwood

Elva, d. 5/22/1924 at 54/8/2; b. Ossipee; Charles W. Tibbetts and Abbie M. Nichols

Elvin W., d. 3/26/1914 at 0/7/29; b. Ossipee; Lester C. Nichols (Ossipee) and Eva Perkins (Ossipee)

Emma F., d. 11/28/1908 at 43/8/23 in Ossipee; septicemia; housewife; b. Ossipee; John Bean (Ossipee) and Sarah Welch (Ossipee)

Ervin W., d. 4/19/1916 at 3/8/3; b. Ossipee; Lewis W. Nichols (Ossipee) and Hattie Haddock (Ossipee)

Flora, d. 1/1/1899 at 49/3/26 in Ossipee; angina pectoris; housewife; married; b. Ossipee; Daniel Eldridge (Ossipee) and Susan Welch (Ossipee)

Florence, d. 1/22/1972 at 64 in Concord; b. NH

Florence V., d. 9/28/1924 at 1/7/15; b. Ossipee; Louis W. Nichols and Hattie Haddock

Frank A., d. 11/7/1922 at 78 in Ossipee; laborer; widower; b. Ossipee

Frank D., d. 6/1/1921 at 66 in Ossipee; farmer; widower; Wentworth Nichols (Ossipee) and Betsy Nichols (Ossipee)

Hannah, d. 2/18/1892 at 73 in Ossipee; pneumonia; housekeeper; widow; b. Ossipee; James Welch

Hattie, d. 6/11/1894 at – in Ossipee; no apparent cause; b. Ossipee; Frank A. Nichols (Ossipee) and Sadie Templeton (Ossipee)

Hattie M., d. 6/15/1932 at 43/10/5 in Ossipee; b. Ossipee; George Haddock and Etta Hill

Hazel K., d. 2/14/1981 at 80 in Wolfeboro; b. Ossipee

Henry C., d. 4/9/1915 at 85/1/8; farmer; widower; b. Ossipee; Richard Nichols (Ossipee) and Annie White (Ossipee)

Henry W., d. 6/15/1931 at 73 in Ossipee; b. Ossipee; Daniel Nichols and Sarah Nichols

Ida, d. 11/12/1943 at 74/0/5 in Ossipee; b. Ossipee; John Nichols and Cordelia Hobbs

John A., d. 11/8/1919 at 79/1/23; farmer; married; b. Ossipee; James A. Nichols (Ossipee) and Mary Lord (Ossipee)

John W., d. 2/25/1896 at 29/2/27 in Ossipee; pulmonary phthisis; clerk; married; b. Ossipee; John A. Nixhols (Ossipee) and Delia J. Hobbs (Ossipee)

John W., d. 4/21/1906 at 67/1/21 in Ossipee; appendicitis; farmer; married; b. Ossipee; William Nichols (Ossipee) and Ellen Williams (Ossipee)

Joseph, d. 12/12/1893 at 45 in Ossipee; laborer; married; b. Ossipee; Eben Welch

Joseph, d. 7/8/1903 at 79/1 in Ossipee; mitral regurgitation; farmer; married; b. Ossipee

Julia M., d. 7/21/1926 at 41/3/29; b. Salmon Falls; Joseph Tighe and Mary Fogarty

Lafayette, d. 8/20/1912 at 52/0/17; farmer; married; b. Ossipee; Amos Nichols (Ossipee) and Mary White (Ossipee)

Lavinia E., d. 7/27/1910 at 63/0/13 in Ossipee; apoplexy; housewife; widow; b. Ossipee; Samuel Williams (Ossipee) and Lizzie Wiggin (Moultonboro)

Lenora, d. 8/21/1899 at 0/10 in Ossipee; whooping cough; b. Ossipee; Charles Nichols (Ossipee) and Emma Williams (Effingham)

Lester C., d. 10/4/1917 at 37/11/16; fireman; divorced; b. Ossipee; Allan A. Nichols (Ossipee) and Helen Crowley (Cornish)

Lewis W., d. 5/10/1967 at 82 in Ossipee; b. Ossipee

Lillian, d. 7/24/1904 at 0/0/15 in Ossipee; marasmus; b. Ossipee; Fred Nichols (Ossipee) and Fidelia Sanborn (Effingham)

Linwood, d. 6/17/1966 at 63 in Ossipee; b. Ossipee

Linwood A., d. 5/14/1950 at 0/0/14 in Wolfeboro; b. Wolfeboro; Linwood Nichols, Jr. and Virginia Cook

Lucian P., d. 12/30/1950 at 72 in Wolfeboro; b. Ossipee; Jet Nichols and Levina Williams

Lydia, d. 5/4/1900 at 69 in Ossipee; cancer bowels; married; b. Ossipee; James Nichols (Ossipee) and Lydia White (Ossipee)

Maude L., d. 10/10/1978 at 88 in Ossipee; b. NH

Minnie E., d. 10/11/1969 at 84 in Wolfeboro; b. NH

Moses C., d. 4/20/1905 at 26 in Ossipee; typhoid fever; laborer; married; b. Ossipee; Frank Nichols (Ossipee) and Addie Templeton (Wolfeboro)

Perley O., d. 6/1/1961 at 74 in Ossipee; b. Ossipee

Plummer, d. 4/11/1945 at 78/1/9 in Ossipee; b. Ossipee; John W. Nichols and Thankful Williams

Robert J., d. 3/12/1947 at 37/1/24 in Wolfeboro; b. Salmon Falls; Perley O. Nichols and Julia Tighe

Roy S., d. 1/6/1951 at 58/4/25 in Wolfeboro; b. Ossipee; Lafayette Nichols and Susan E. Morgan

Seth, d. 5/18/1918 at 74/10/14; laborer; widower; William Nichols (Ossipee) and Ellen Williams (Ossipee)

Susie E., d. 5/12/1932 at 72/2/26 in Beverly, MA; b. Beverly, MA; Mark Morgan and Elizabeth Foss

Thankful, d. 1/9/1920 at 72/3/22; housekeeper; widow; b. Ossipee; Shaber Williams (Ossipee) and Lydia Welch (Ossipee)

Wentworth, d. 1/17/1907 at 83 in Ossipee; la grippe; laborer; widower; b. Ossipee; James Nichols (Ossipee)

William, d. 1/24/1894 at 78/8 in Ossipee; heart disease

NICKERSON,

A. Martin, d. 11/15/1968 at 77 in Wolfeboro; b. NH

Blanche T., d. 4/22/2001 in Wolfeboro; Ahiel Templeton and Arthena Eldridge

Charles, d. 8/1/1936 at 4/8/1 in Wolfeboro; b. Ctr. Ossipee; Nelson Nickerson and Margarete Johnson

Esther, d. 12/27/1946 at 0/9/6 in Ossipee; b. Ossipee; Nelson Nickerson and Barbara Sharp

Irma J., d. 1/10/1944 at 81/0/5 in Tamworth; b. Ossipee; Joshua White

Mertie Addie, d. 8/26/1983 at 83 in Ossipee; b. Tamworth

Nelson E., Jr., d. 11/21/1948 at 35/1/2 in Freedom; b. Spring Haven, NS; Nelson E. Nickerson and Margaret Muise

Nelson E., Sr., d. 10/31/1953 at 75/9/8 in Ossipee; b. NS

Pearl L., d. 10/31/1953 at 33/6/1 in Ossipee; b. Ossipee; Lewis Nichols and Hattie Haddock

Rachael L., d. 6/20/1966 at 77 in Conway; b. Conway

Verna M., d. 2/9/1985 at 62 in Wolfeboro; b. Newport City, VT

Wendell Alley, d. 6/6/1994 at 81; George Nickerson and Erma Alley

Willis E., d. 7/28/1967 at 69 in Wolfeboro; b. Milton

Winfield A., d. 4/14/1974 at 83 in Ossipee; b. NH

NILSEN,
William H., d. 6/25/1987 at 75 in Ossipee; b. Union City, NJ

NOBERT,
Lionel, d. 8/26/1999 at 89 in Ossipee; Leo Nobert and Leticia Perron

NOEL,
Melbourne C., d. 9/2/1993 at 86 in Ossipee
Ruth W., d. 9/24/1994 at 79; Clarence Williams and Nellie Lamprey

NOONAN,
Mildred R., d. 2/28/1988 at 83 in Ossipee; b. Boston, MA

NORMANDEAU,
Marguerite L., d. 8/9/1991 at 78 in Ossipee; b. St. Regis Falls, NY

NORTON,
Lillian M., d. 1/22/1900 at 2 in Ossipee; mitral disease of heart; b. Ossipee

NOYES,
John W., d. 3/28/1975 at 79 in Wolfeboro; b. NH
Julia G., d. 1/1/1968 at 68 in Wolfeboro; b. MA

NUDD,
Wallace Raymond, Sr., d. 2/25/1992 at 62 in Laconia; b. Ctr. Sandwich

NUTE,
Abbie, d. 4/14/1894 at 78 in Ossipee; cardiac paralysis; housewife; married
Alfred H., d. 3/30/1929 at 68/11/23 in Salem, MA; b. Ossipee; James Nute, Jr. and Sarah E. Beacham
Amos, d. 12/26/1914 at 64; laborer; b. Bartlett
Charles, d. 4/15/1955 at 63/0/9 in Ossipee; b. NH; William Nute and Laura -----

Charles A., d. 3/20/1888 at 43/7; single; b. Roxbury, MA; Josiah Nute and Abbie A. Davis
Dellie, d. 5/18/1969 at 84 in Wolfeboro; b. NH
Dennis, d. 12/23/1967 at 81 in Ossipee; b. Bartlett
George K., d. 7/2/1915 at 81; laborer; widower; b. Bartlett
George W., d. 12/27/1908 at 67 in Ossipee; pnuemonia; farmer; b. Boston, MA; ----- Whitmore
Harriet, d. 11/1/1914 at 76/0/24; housekeeper

James, d. 10/5/1891 at 87 in Ossipee; farmer; widower; b. Dover; Thomas Nute (Dover) and Eunice Varney (Dover)

James Lester, d. 3/26/1950 at 60/10/1 in Ossipee; b. Ossipee; Alfred Nute and Mary Avery

James W., d. 9/2/1921 at 81/3/24 in Ossipee; farmer; widower; Charles H. Nute (Sandwich) and Mary A. Welch (Boston, MA)

Jennie L., d. 4/11/1973 at 91 in Ossipee; b. NH

John, d. 3/18/1948 at 58/2/8 in Ossipee; b. Bartlett; William Nute and Laura -----

Lovina, d. 1/20/1888 at 78; domestic; married; b. Ossipee

Lydia A., d. 10/9/1921 at 82/9/6 in Ossipee; widow; Andrew Drew and Lydia Virgia

Sarah A., d. 4/17/1900 at 68/9/5 in Ossipee; meningitis; housewife; widow; b. Ossipee; Richard Beacham (Ossipee) and Sarah Hersey (Tuftonboro)

Sarah A., d. 5/13/1903 at 68/0/6 in Ossipee; mitral insufficiency; married; [? Richard Stillings (Sanford) and Sally Dodge (Ossipee)]

Sarah E., d. 12/14/1908 at 66 in Ossipee; bronchitis; housewife; b. Ossipee; Joseph Glidden (Ossipee) and Mary J. Fields

Thomas, d. 1/5/1911 at 83; apoplexy; farmer; widower; b. Ossipee; James Nute (Wolfeboro) and Mary Nudd (Wolfeboro)

NUTILE,
William, d. 7/26/1980 at 71 in Wolfeboro; b. MA

NUTTER,
Abigail, d. 7/27/1892 at 86 in Ossipee; gastric car.; housewife; married

Elizabeth, d. 2/19/1894 at 89/0/19 in Lawrence; old age

Harriet E., d. 11/16/1937 at 84 in Boston, MA; b. NS; Hugh Elliott

Henry E., d. 10/13/1918 at 32/6/24; farmer; single; b. Boston, MA; Samuel Nutter (Ossipee) and Harriet Elliott (NS)

James E., d. 12/1/1925 at 73/11/10; b. Ossipee; Samuel Nutter and Elizabeth Holmes

John B., d. 7/21/1976 at 84 in Ossipee; b. NH

Louisa, d. 6/17/1899 at 83/9/19 in Ossipee; cardiac dropsy; widow; b. Ossipee; Robert Chick

Margaret K., d. 10/10/1915 at 80; housewife; widow; b. Ossipee; George Nutter (Tuftonboro) and Abigail Twombley

Oliver, d. 12/21/1902 at 76 in Ossipee; hemiplegia left side of body; farmer; widower; b. Wakefield; Alpheus Nutter (Wakefield) and Hannah Smith (Wakefield)

Orrin, d. 1/15/1902 at 69/9/16 in Ossipee; aortic incompetency; farmer; married; b. Ossipee; Thomas Nutter (Ossipee) and Mercy Goldsmith (Ossipee)

O'BRIEN,
Carl Frederick, d. 9/26/1996 at 56 in Ctr. Ossipee; Calvin O. O'Brien and Winnifred P. Smith

O'CLAIR,
Laura, d. 5/6/1973 at 75 in Ossipee; b. NH

O'CONNELL,
Elizabeth Ann, d. 1/23/1975 at 91 in Ossipee; b. NH
John, d. 12/4/1969 at 92 in Ossipee; b. Canada

O'CONNERS,
James M., d. 7/16/1906 at 65/7/4 in Ossipee; accidental drowning; carpenter; widower; b. Montreal, Canada; Michael O'Conner (sic) (NY) and ----- Booth (England)

O'HARA,
Edna Wilson, d. 10/6/1987 at 75 in Wolfeboro; b. Guildhall, VT

O'HARE,
Bertha, d. 10/21/1918 at 37; married; b. Bridgton, ME

O'NEIL,
Thomas Francis, d. 12/28/1995 at 79; William F. O'Neil and Rose Norton

O'SULLIVAN,
Charles H., d. 7/17/2000 in Wolfeboro; John O'Sullivan and Dorothy Ewing

OAKES,
Violet F., d. 1/18/1907 at 73/6 in Ossipee; Bright's disease; housewife; widow; b. Roxbury, ME; Gilbert Hawkes

OCH,
Amelia, d. 9/10/1941 at 70/0/9 in Ossipee; b. Germany

ODELL,
Joseph, d. 1/12/1964 at 76 in Ossipee; b. Madison

OFFUTT,
Jessie, d. 10/3/1900 at 28/4 in Ossipee; gastro enteritis; housegirl; married; b. N. Grant, NS; Colin Chisholm (Scotland) and Jane ----- (NS)

OGBORN,
Alfred L., d. 1/9/1955 at 70 in Wolfeboro; b. PA; William Ogborn and Zoe Herbert
Inez L., d. 6/17/1971 at 84 in Ossipee; b. VT

ORDWAY,
Anna M. C., d. 1/18/1942 at 69/2/21 in Ossipee; b. Merrickville, ON; Theodore Chapman and Mary J. Telford

ORESTEEN,
Dorothy Frances, d. 5/26/1994 at 73; Frances J. Oresteen and Mary White
Frank J., d. 7/17/1958 at 64 in Ossipee; b. E. Boston, MA; Francis Oresteen and Mary Savage
Mary F., d. 7/26/1956 at 61 in Ossipee; b. Chelsea, MA; Robert White and Mary Holland

OSGOOD,
Harriet Alice, d. 1/23/1993 at 94 in Ossipee
Maria Louisa, d. 3/29/1972 at 93 in Ossipee; b. Washington Terr., USA

OTIS,
Mabel L., d. 11/3/1963 at 83 in Ossipee; b. Wakefield

OXNER,
Helen Gertrude, d. 1/27/1998 in Wolfeboro; Carroll Dunbar and Esther Curtis

PACE,
Ruby J., d. 2/3/1997 at 95 in Ossipee; George E. Sadler and Trenetta Corkum

PACKARD,
Elizabeth B., d. 3/13/1986 at 79 in Ossipee; b. Kennebunkport, ME

PAGE,
Benjamin Webster, d. 3/24/1994 at 85; Arthur Page and Mary Remick
Howard F., d. 2/5/1975 at 85 in Ossipee; b. NH

PAIGE,
Calvin E., d. 11/17/1971 at 47 in Lebanon; b. MA

PAINCHAUD,
Janine, d. 3/12/1984

PALMER,
Bertha W., d. 9/11/1979 at 95 in Ossipee; b. NH
Charles William, d. 2/4/1971 at 88 in Ossipee; b. Canada
Frank A., d. 12/27/1921 at 41/10/21 in Ossipee; laborer; single; Joshua Palmer (MA) and Emma Roberts (MA)
Frank E., d. 4/15/1925 at 64/8/28; b. Ossipee; J. F. Palmer and Emily Merrow
Fred L., d. 6/11/1982 at 85 in Ossipee; b. NY
Harlan Clayton, d. 10/2/1991 at 69 in Wolfeboro; b. Ossipee
Harriet, d. 6/22/1937 at 59/0/22 in Wolfeboro; b. Rollinsford; Joseph Tighe and Mary Fogarty

PANNO,
Harry A., d. 10/18/1974 at 73 in Wolfeboro; b. ME

PAQUET,
Evelyn, d. 8/10/1975 at 68 in Rochester; b. NH

PAQUETTE,
Frank, d. 12/8/1940 at 102/6/3 in Ossipee; b. Canada

PARKER,
Boyd Harrison, d. 10/22/1992 at 82 in Wolfeboro; b. Riverside, CA
Elizabeth M., d. 12/23/1991 at 80 in Wolfeboro; b. New Gloucester, ME
George L., d. 9/3/1995 at 82; Lester E. Parker and Irene H. McAllister
Lila, d. 1/18/1977 at 79 in Ossipee; b. Canada
Lola Elisabeth, d. 6/30/1995 at 94; August Schaeffer and Fannie Schmelz
Mabel A., d. 8/1/1985 at 104 in Ossipee; b. Westbrook, ME
Mary Ann, d. 8/6/1995 at 83; Patrick Burke and Sarah Connelly
Muriel Virginia, d. 10/20/1996 at 86 in Ctr. Ossipee; Avard Steele and Emma Rice
Walter, d. 12/31/1956 at 86 in Ossipee; b. Bartlett; Andrew Parker and Mary Emery

PARRIS,
Richard J., d. 12/3/2000 at 41 in Ctr. Ossipee; Edwin Francis Parris and Assunta M. Dioguardi

PARSONS,
Celia A., d. 6/29/1936 at 82/10/5 in Ossipee; b. Madison; Stephen Flanders and Mirinda Ryder
Hortense, d. 3/30/1927 at 77/4/16; b. Freedom; John Parsons and Hanna S. Flanders

John M., d. 4/25/1927 at 74/11/2; b. Freedom; John Parsons and Hanna S. Flanders

PASCOE,
Agnes P., d. 10/24/1981 at 82 in Ossipee; b. Tamworth
Annie A., d. 8/11/1958 at 88 in Wolfeboro; b. Freedom; Leander Laughton and Mary Shaw
Henry J., d. 8/30/1920 at 55/7/9; merchant; married; b. Copperas Hill; Henry Pascoe (England) and P. Dore (Canada)
William H., d. 3/16/1972 at 78 in Ossipee; b. NH

PASSANO,
Emily Evalina, d. 3/7/1997 at 67 in Wolfeboro; Elie St. Jean and Emily Jacques

PATCH,
Agnes, d. 6/20/1998 in Ossipee; Albert Bellavance and Emelda Desbiens
Lucie Maria, d. 6/11/1940 at 83/0/21 in Ossipee; b. Harvard, MA; Andrew Patch and Maria Mead

PATERN,
Robert E., d. 5/28/1974 at 45 in Portsmouth; b. NY

PATRICK,
George H., d. 1/25/1950 at 92 in Wolfeboro; b. Canada; John Patrick and Frances Patrick

PATTEE,
Joseph, d. 3/26/1888 at 79/7/19; farmer; married; b. Fryeburg, MA; David Pattee and Rachel Farington

PATTERSON,
Ernest C., d. 5/6/1981 at 89 in Ossipee; b. Martinsburg, WV
Vera L., d. 8/29/1973 at 84 in Rochester; b. NH
William Tays, d. 10/2/1999 at 56 in Ossipee; Roland Patterson and Margaret Martin

PATTON,
Gertrude L., d. 10/7/1987 at 78 in Ossipee; b. Northampton, MA

PAULSEN,
Richard Anthony, d. 8/3/1989 at 69 in Wolfeboro; b. Lynn, MA

PEARL,
Harry W., d. 5/7/1955 at 71/1/13 in Ossipee; b. ME; Frank Pearl and Caroline Rounds
Sadie E., d. 11/2/1966 at 70 in Ossipee; b. Tamworth

PEARSON,
Albert G., d. 3/10/1984 at 70 in Wolfeboro; b. Sharon, PA
George K., d. 6/25/1952 at 75/9/5 in Ossipee; Kendall Pearson

PEASE,
Bertha E., d. 11/4/1978 at 73 in Wolfeboro; b. ME
Elizabeth A., d. 8/15/1934 at 82/2/26 in Ossipee; b. S. Tamworth; John T. D. Folsom and Asenath Whipple
Thomas C., d. 8/9/1980 at 82 in Wolfeboro; b. ME

PEASLEE,
Dorothy Ellen, d. 7/31/1995 at 90; William Robinson and Nettie Quimby

PEAVEY,
Bernice, d. 2/13/1986 at 97 in Ossipee; b. Wolfeboro
Fanny, d. 3/17/1901 at 46 in Ossipee; laryngeal tuberculosis; single; b. Tuftonboro
Hannah, d. 1/27/1904 at 78 in Ossipee; paralysis; widow; b. Ossipee; Joseph Sias (Ossipee) and Hannah Dodge (Ossipee)
Joshua, d. 12/11/1887 at 75 in Ossipee; single; b. Brookfield
Lydia J., d. 8/10/1891 at 68 in Ossipee; married; Elisha Thorne and Marion Strout
Stephen, d. 5/21/1893 at 82 in Ossipee; farmer; married; b. Tuftonboro

PEAVY,
Carrie F., d. 12/5/1915 at 77; housewife; widow; b. Wolfeboro; Joseph Johnson and Luranna Whittier

PECKHAM,
Margaret L., d. 1/2/1969 at 78 in Ossipee; b. MA
Rosalie Hebert, d. 5/23/1994 at 93; Sylvain Hebert and Virginia Casey

PECUNIES,
Eleanor B., d. 9/16/1988 at 85 in Ossipee; b. Wolfeboro
Russell Q., d. 11/11/1999 at 74 in Ctr. Ossipee; Otto Pecunies and Eleanor Fernald

PELLETIER,
Marion Louise, d. 5/14/2000 at 85 in Ossipee; John D. Blaisdell and Bertha Cate

PENDERGAST,
Michael, d. 3/3/1937 at 83/4/7 in Ossipee; b. Newfoundland; Michael Pendergast and Josephine Menige

PENDEXTER,
Mary, d. 2/27/1973 at 83 in Ossipee; b. NH

PENDLETON,
Lawrence Merriam, d. 10/5/1988 at 77 in Dover; b. Warren, MA
Ruth E., d. 7/22/1980 at 66 in Wolfeboro; b. MA

PENNIMAN,
Clara J., d. 7/4/1923 at 73; b. Moultonboro; John Cook and Eliza Garland

PENNY,
Marion Leola, d. 12/6/1994 at 91; Ernest N. Bean and Minnie E. Brownell
Raymond, d. 6/5/1958 at 62 in Ossipee; b. Wolfeboro; John Penny and Mary Kimball

PERCY,
Margaret C., d. 6/11/1915 at 72/8/8

PERKINS,
Addie West, d. 5/3/1941 at 81/10/21 in Ossipee; b. Marblehead, MA; Mathews C. West and Mary J. Fellows
Blanche C., d. 12/28/1956 at 63 in Concord; b. Ossipee; John W. Thompson and Ida Chadbourne
Blanche Stella, d. 12/13/1943 at 37/5/21 in Farmington; b. Ossipee; John Philbrick and Edith Cook
Charles, d. 9/16/1943 at 76/5/19 in Ossipee; b. Meredith; Forrest Perkins and Abbie Aldrich
Charles E., d. 6/29/1973 at 68 in Rochester; b. NH
Elizabeth, d. 4/24/1887 at 66 in Ossipee; housekeeper; widow; b. Ossipee
Elizabeth R., d. 1/12/1888 at 39; domestic; single; b. Ossipee; Charles L. Perkins
Ella M., d. 7/29/1941 at 67/7 in Ossipee; b. Sandwich; James R. Bryer and Rhoda Bennett
Emma E., d. 12/22/1963 at 95 in Dover; b. Ossipee
Florence E., d. 12/10/1985 at 87 in Ossipee; b. Sanbornville
George, d. 1/8/1923 at 83

Harry, d. 4/5/1948 at 78/2/3 in Ossipee; b. Danvers, MA; George E. Perkins and Sarah Putnam
Harry, d. 11/21/1951 at 72 in Concord; b. Effingham; Harry Perkins and Lizzie Latrone
James, d. 11/27/1891 at 77 in Ossipee; farmer; widower; b. Shapleigh
Jane A., d. 10/15/1981 at 92 in Ossipee; b. Hudson
Joel, d. 6/6/1908 at 85 in Tamworth; valvular disease of heart; b. Jackson
Margaret E., d. 3/17/1993 at 98 in Ossipee
Sidney L., d. 8/30/1951 at 62/3/8 in Wolfeboro; b. Ossipee; Charles Perkins and Emma Eldridge

PERREAULT,
Auguste Joseph, d. 10/24/1973 at 88 in Ossipee; b. Canada

PERRON,
Ada A., d. 10/21/1944 at 68/8/8 in Wolfeboro; b. Ossipee; Hiae Templeton and Effie Williams
Priscilla E., d. 3/13/1985 at 71 in Manchester; b. Swampscott, MA

PERRY,
Agnes V., d. 5/1/1988 at 74 in Ossipee; b. Ossipee
Anne Priscilla, d. 2/–/1937 at 0/2 in Wolfeboro; b. Wolfeboro; Edgar G. Perry and Delphine Ames
Barbara D., d. 9/27/1999 in Wolfeboro; Thornton Gouin and Leona Libby
Donald W., d. 11/22/1988 at 71 in Ossipee; b. Swampscott, MA
Harriet C., d. 1/26/1899 at 75/4 in Ossipee; convulsions; married; b. Monson; David Conant and Harriet Long
Thurley Erentine, d. 3/29/1997 at 79 in Wolfeboro; Ernest Roy McCreary and Lyle Mansfield
William D., d. 9/16/2000 in Wolfeboro; Philip Perry and ----- Douglass

PETERS,
Albert Simon, d. 8/8/1993 at 83 in Ossipee
Georgia E., d. 10/12/1989 at 45 in Dover; b. Dover

PETERSON,
Grace C., d. 7/7/1954 at 67 in Wolfeboro; b. Brooklyn, NY; Charles Peterson

PETTIS,
Charles F., d. 6/28/1991 at 82 in Ossipee; b. Saugus, MA

PHELAN,
Roy G., d. 9/10/1968 at 82 in Ossipee; b. NS

PHILBRICK,
child, d. 2/4/1935 at – in Wolfeboro
Alfred, d. 8/5/1944 at 71/7/3 in Ossipee; b. Bartlett; Hiram Philbrick and Betsy E. Watson
Ann M., d. 11/12/1898 at 88/2/2 in Lynn; paralysis
Ellsworth, Sr., d. 7/20/1948 at 48/7/9 in Exeter; b. N. Waterboro, ME; Alfred Philbrick and Elsie Drowns
Emma A., d. 9/2/1891 at 29/5 in Ossipee; housewife; married; J. Woodman (Wakefield) and Sarah J. Goudy
Florence, d. 6/1/1918 at 8/11/27; scholar; single; b. Tuftonboro; Alfred Philbrick (Bartlett) and Elsa Drowns
Lula M., d. 6/29/1965 at 87 in Ossipee; b. Eaton
Martha, d. 5/18/1898 at 75 in Auburn; gastritis
Millie, d. 1/2/1914 at 46; housewife; b. Wakefield; Simon Philbrick (Wakefield) and Hannah Young (Ossipee)
Nettie B., d. 12/1/1951 at 85 in Ossipee; b. Eaton; John Glines and Mary Sawyer

PHILBROOK,
Edith M., d. 6/2/1934 at 61/7/27 in Farmington; b. Ossipee; James R. B. Cook and Mary A. Bunker

PHILLIPS,
Lydia A., d. 12/24/1904 at 82/1/9 in Ossipee; burned body; housework; widow; b. Wakefield; Mark Wentworth (Wakefield) and Betsy Whitehouse (Brookfield)

PHILPOT,
Agnes E., d. 10/18/1910 at 36/3/14 in Ossipee; cancer rectum; housewife; married; b. Moultonboro; Jeremiah Wiggin (Moultonboro) and Lizzie Welch (Ossipee)

PHINNEY,
John W., d. 1/27/1912 at 12/11/17; b. Wells, ME; Stillman Phinney (Marion, ME) and Sadie V. Emery (ME)
Myron E., d. 4/3/1914 at 17/0/24; farmer; Stillman Phinney (Calais, ME) and Sarah Emery (Parsonsfield, ME)
Rosa A., d. 9/9/1896 at 0/11/9 in Ossipee; cholera infantum; b. Rochester; S. L. Phinney (Marion, ME) and Sadie B. Emery (Parsonsfield, ME)
Sarah B., d. 12/13/1911 at 44/3/21; pulmonary tuberculosis; housewife; married; b. Parsonsfield; Nicholas Emery (Tuftonboro) and Louisa Canney (Ossipee)

PICKERING,
Amanda Belle, d. 9/30/1972 at 81 in Conway; b. NH
Harold M., d. 11/27/1968 at 71 in Conway; b. NH

PICKETT,
Elizabeth Ann, d. 12/15/2001 in Ctr. Ossipee; Clarence McDonald and Mary Coogan

PIDGEON [see Pigeron],
William, Jr., d. 11/9/1929 at 0/1/21 in Ossipee; b. Laconia; William Pidgeon and Gladys Fogg

PIERCE,
William E., d. 9/9/2000 in Wolfeboro; Elmer Pierce and Blanche Dailey

PIGERON [see Pidgeon],
Ruth M., d. 6/16/1935 at 4/3/16 in Ossipee; b. Andover; William Pigeron and Gladys Fogg

PIKE,
Annette, d. 9/8/1937 at 82/2/25 in Granite; b. Effingham; Lawrence Champion and Hannah Meloon
Augusta, d. 5/4/1966 at 102 in Ossipee; b. Limington, ME
Charles, d. 5/6/1892 at 54 in Ossipee; consumption; farmer; married; b. Ossipee; John Pike
Daisy F., d. 10/30/1954 at 71 in Ossipee; b. Ossipee; ----- and Annie Champlin
Edwin, d. 10/3/1939 at 65/2/10 in Wolfeboro; b. Ossipee; Emily F. Wallace
Emily F., d. 4/19/1919 at 67/7/27; housekeeping; married; b. Ossipee; Ambrose Wallace (Ossipee) and Ida White (Ossipee)
Herbert J., d. 2/4/1951 at 64/11/21 in Ossipee; b. Ossipee; John Pike and Emily Wallace
Jane, d. 4/24/1903 at 75/3/21 in Ossipee; chronic bronchitis; housewife; married; b. Ossipee; John Welch (Ossipee) and Jane ----- (Ossipee)
John E., d. 3/21/1988 at 67 in Wolfeboro; b. Ossipee
John I., d. 10/27/1950 at 81/9/3 in Wolfeboro; b. Ossipee; Charles Pike and Annette Champion
John W., d. 3/23/1927 at 76/5/27; b. Tamworth; Joseph H. Pike and Jane Welch
John W., d. 7/22/1937 at 74/3/13 in Wolfeboro; b. W. Ossipee; John W. Pike and Elmira Whitehouse
Joseph H., d. 1/4/1907 at 82 in Ossipee; valvular disease of heart; farmer; widower; b. Tamworth

Ronald Wayne, d. 1/27/1945 at 0/0/0 in Wolfeboro; b. Wolfeboro; Bernard White and Emily F. Pike

Ruth Gladys, d. 1/13/1949 at 0/11/19 in Laconia; b. Wolfeboro; John E. Pike and Alice Woodman

Wallace P., d. 11/1/1920 at 0/0/4; b. Ossipee; Herbert J. Pike (Ossipee) and Alice Dougherty (PEI)

PILLING,
Maude M., d. 7/9/1960 at 84 in Ossipee; b. Ontario, Canada

PINARD,
Eunice M., d. 7/6/1993 at 98 in Ossipee

PINEO,
Charlotte, d. 1/24/1898 at 46 in Ossipee; tuberculosis; housewife; married; b. Ossipee; Upton Hammond (Ossipee)

Ingliss L., d. 8/29/1913 at 57; mail carrier; widower; b. NS; Jonathan Pineo (NS) and Elizabeth Lyons (NS)

Margaret Lapthorn, d. 7/20/1995 at 79; Robert B. Innes and Margaret Lapthorn

PINKHAM,
Charles Robert, d. 10/25/1994 at 73; Charles J. Pinkham and Sara M. Collins

PIPER,
Caroline, d. 4/2/1906 at 69/2/14 in Ossipee; heart disease val.; single; b. Tuftonboro; Samuel T. Piper

Emma, d. 2/3/1970 at 84 in Ossipee; b. NH

Ethel B., d. 8/21/1962 at 56 in Wolfeboro; b. Farmington

Gary S., d. 2/6/1998 in FL; Clinton Piper and Gloria Scott

Helen T., d. 9/23/1988 at 77 in Wolfeboro; b. Tuftonboro

Nathaniel, d. 3/5/1891 at 91 in Ossipee; widower

PIPPIN,
Harold Frank, d. 7/2/1991 at 80 in Ossipee; b. Union

PITMAN,
Ethel E., d. 10/11/1973 at 83 in Ossipee; b. VT

Jacob, d. 6/17/1897 at 57 in Ossipee; gastritis; farmer; widower; b. Ossipee; Asa Pitman (Ossipee) and Ann Stillings (Ossipee)

John T., d. 2/13/1912 at 74/7/3

Leander, d. 4/22/1893 at 48/9 in Ossipee; farmer; married; b. Ossipee; Asa Pitman (Ossipee) and Anna Stillings (Ossipee)

PLACE,
Ivan Fulton, d. 12/1/1977 at 73 in Ossipee; b. NY
Ronald E., d. 3/10/1991 at 63 in Ossipee; b. Gloucester, MA

PLACEY,
Roselthia, d. 7/18/1976 at 79 in Wolfeboro; b. NH

PLANT,
Mary E., d. 9/23/1975 at 82 in Ossipee; b. NH

PLANTE,
Alfred Stephen, Jr., d. 3/16/1999 at 47 in Wolfeboro; Alfred Stephen Plante, Jr. and Mary E. Kelley

PLUMMER,
Frank, d. 12/15/1910 at 57 in Ossipee; paresis; married; b. Laconia; James Plummer

POISSON,
Charles, d. 10/10/1911 at 59; mitral insufficiency; laborer; b. Canada
Elizabeth Maude, d. 12/10/1987 at 86 in Ossipee; b. NS

POLEY,
George, d. 7/17/1924 at 73; b. NB

POLK,
Lavern S., d. 1/10/1973 at 65 in Wolfeboro; b. OH

POLLOCK,
Clayton W., d. 2/2/1974 at 72 in Wolfeboro; b. MA
Frank S., d. 7/5/1964 at 95 in Ossipee; b. Quincy, MA

POOLE,
Hazel, d. 4/7/1996 at 88 in Ossipee; Leslie Poole and Katherine MacKinnon

POPE,
Gordon Arthur, d. 10/21/1992 at 75 in Wolfeboro; b. Medford, MA

POPHAM,
James, d. 12/6/1940 at 84/8/17 in Ossipee; b. St. Andrews, NB; John Popham and Mary A. Baker

PORCELLA,
Vincenzo V., d. 7/18/1992 at 51 in Limington, ME; b. Boston, MA

PORTER,
Burton Vaughn, Jr., d. 9/14/1993 at 77 in Ossipee
Edith L., d. 1/6/1980 at 103 in Ossipee; b. Canada
June Margaret, d. 6/17/1999 at 66 in Wolfeboro; Paul Gillis and Lillian MacEvoy
Lewis H., d. 7/4/1974 at 85 in Ossipee; b. MA

POTTER,
Emma M., d. 8/20/1986 at 78 in Ossipee; b. Brownfield, ME
Mabel Ethel, d. 6/24/1997 at 86 in Ossipee; Wilbur Clarence Dearborn and Mary Susan Avery

POWELL,
Susan N., d. 4/12/1893 at 75/0/18 in Effingham; housewife; widow; b. Wolfeboro; Thomas Young (Rochester) and Mary Nute (Milton)

POWER,
Hannah L., d. 11/15/1913 at 71/11/15

POWERS,
Christine P., d. 2/4/1986 at 50 in Portland, ME; b. Chattanooga, TN, 10/1935
Flora Carr, d. 5/29/1971 at 93 in Ossipee; b. VT
John Harry, d. 6/8/1907 at – in Ossipee; acute indigestion; salesman

PRATT,
Angie B., d. 5/6/1918 at 42; single; b. Salem, MA; John W. Pratt
Ellen P., d. 3/6/1928 at 89/4/27; b. Marblehead, MA; John Jarvis and Mary Dodge
John H., d. 12/23/1957 at 78 in Wolfeboro; b. Salem, MA; John W. Pratt and Ellen P. Jarvis
John W., d. 6/30/1917 at 81/6/19; farmer; married; Samuel Pratt (Salem, MA) and Mary Whitey (Lynn, MA)

PRAY,
Asa, d. 11/25/1924 at 79/10/12; b. Ossipee
Benjamin, d. 12/13/1889 at 42; single; b. Ossipee
Carrie F., d. 9/14/1904 at 71/0/4 in Ossipee; heart disease; housewife; married; b. Effingham; Nicholas Huckins and Nancy Shote
Genevieve H., d. 4/14/1953 at 90/5/16 in Ossipee; b. Orange, MA; J. F. Cooper and Lucinda Howard

Hannah F., d. 10/10/1924 at 87/2/16; b. Stark; Joshua Roberts and Dorothy Hanson

Herbert F., d. 3/1/1948 at 71/2/20 in Ossipee; b. Boston, MA; Charles Pray

Hiram, d. 3/23/1912 at 82/2/25; retired; b. Ossipee; Joseph Pray (Ossipee) and Margaret Hodgkins (Ossipee)

Isaac, d. 6/29/1888 at 87/7; farmer; married; b. Lebanon, ME

Mary A., d. 1/10/1925 at 78/0/24; b. Ossipee; Ambrose Wallace and Lydia White

Mahitable, d. 12/22/1891 at 86 in Ossipee; housewife; single; b. Ossipee

William T., d. 3/19/1904 at 68/8 in Ossipee; carcinoma; farmer; married; b. Ossipee; Isaac Pray (Ossipee) and Sarah Goldsmith (Ossipee)

PREBLE,
Alfred E., d. 7/11/1950 at 69/11 in Ossipee; b. MA; Edward P. Preble and Marcia Alexander

PRENTISS,
Roberta H., d. 4/15/1978 at 50 in Hanover; b. MA

PRESCOTT,
Charles A., d. 10/8/1924 at 68/4; b. Barrington; Nathaniel Prescott

John, d. 12/10/1941 at 69/5/22 in Ossipee; b. San Francisco, CA; John Prescott and Mary Foley

PRESTON,
Emma Elizabeth, d. 8/1/1979 at 88 in Ossipee; b. IN

John Cutler, d. 5/18/1996 at 87 in Laconia; John Howard Preston and Ruth Cutler

Roger E., d. 7/19/1997 at 64 in Manchester; Ralph Preston and Hope Elizabeth Whitney

PRICE,
Annie C., d. 10/14/1952 at 75/1/7 in Ossipee; b. Ossipee; John Price and Lilla C. Merrow

Charles H., d. 8/11/1938 at 50/9/27 in Ossipee; b. Woodstock; John Price and Lilla C. Merrow

Lilla, d. 8/24/1910 at 57/9 in Ossipee; apoplexy; housewife; widow; b. Ossipee; James Merrow (Ossipee) and Caroline Wingate (Wakefield)

PRIDE,
Robert, d. 4/28/1963 at 77 in Ossipee; b. Newfoundland

PRINCE,
Ernest, d. 2/25/1934 at 71/11/14 in Ossipee; b. Canada; Joseph Prince and Mary Gaudebbe

PRINDALL,
Royal D., d. 12/7/1995 at 90; Everett Prindall and Laura Ida -----

PROKEY,
Larrie Pedro, d. 3/1/1939 at 40 in Tuftonboro; b. Russia; Pedro Prokey and Irona Prokey

Violet E., d. 6/2/1940 at 14/3/6 in Wolfeboro; b. Ossipee; Larrie Prokey and Ethel Banfill

PRUDHOMME,
Raymond Roland, Sr., d. 5/24/1993 at 87 in Ossipee

PURRINGTON,
Agustus E., d. 7/5/1955 at 85/1/18 in Ossipee; b. ME; Charles Purrington and Mary -----

Daniel, d. 5/21/1958 at 85 in Ossipee; b. Albany; George Purrington and Susan Moody

PUTNAM,
David, d. 12/31/1936 at 88/3/25 in Ossipee; b. Danvers, MA; Harry Putnam and Mandy Minker

Harold F., d. 11/16/1990 at 93 in Ossipee; b. Worcester, MA

QUARLES,
Samuel D., d. 11/22/1889 at 56/10/6; lawyer; married; b. Ossipee; Samuel J. Quarles and Sarah S. Dalton

QUILL,
John, d. 10/14/1916 at 40; laborer; single; b. Freedom

QUIMBY,
Alice, d. 6/19/1944 at 69 in Ossipee; b. Ossipee; Asa Welch and Serepty Welch

Archie, d. 5/6/1888 at 0/1; George Quimby and Ellen Quimby

Archie, d. 1/14/1897 at 2 in Ossipee; meningitis; b. Ossipee; George Quimby

Ellen, d. 4/8/1900 at 44 in Ossipee; insanity; widow

George W., d. 9/8/1897 at 56 in Ossipee; ulcerative enteritis; married; b. Moultonboro

Stillman, d. 10/17/1936 at 60/10/23 in Wolfeboro; b. Ossipee; Horace B. Quimby and Eva Haddock

QUINLAN,
Martin, d. 9/15/1976 at 88 in Ossipee; b. MA

RAINVILLE,
Leonidas J., d. 1/8/1989 at 76 in Ctr. Ossipee; b. Pembroke

RAMSDELL,
Ethel Pray, d. 4/30/1994 at 101; John E. Pray and Edith Hayford

RANCOURT,
Joseph W., d. 4/21/1972 at 63 in Ossipee; b. NH

RAND,
Eugene N., d. 9/26/1925 at –; b. Ossipee; Nathaniel Rand and Mabel Bean
Roger Wayne, d. 7/2/1991 at 56 in Ossipee; b. Springvale, ME

RANDALL,
Horace Burt, d. 12/23/1977 at 78 in Ossipee; b. MA
Mabel A., d. 12/1/1988 at 87 in Ossipee; b. Milton Mills

RANGER,
John B., d. 3/1/1918 at 58/4/26; farmer; married; b. Thorington; Mark W. Ranger (Hollis, ME) and Hannah L. Church (S. Tamworth)

RAPHAEL,
Blanche, d. 9/9/1958 at 71 in Ossipee; b. Wolfeboro; Charles Leavitt and Alice Tibbetts

RAPP,
Elvira O., d. 10/30/1977 at 79 in Wolfeboro; b. NJ
Frank, d. 6/9/1969 at 74 in Hanover; b. NJ

RAY,
Frank, d. 10/2/1918 at 35/11/18; laborer; single; b. Somerville, MA; E. K. Ray (MA)

READE,
Everett, d. 6/28/1983 at 97 in Ossipee; b. Bangor, ME

REED,
Allen, d. 12/23/1951 at 74 in Concord; b. Roxbury, ME; Stillman Reed and Sarah Judkins
Charles S., Jr., d. 8/17/1992 at 53 in Dover; b. W. Newfield, ME
Elmer, d. 4/27/1947 at 76/7/10 in Wolfeboro; b. E. Wakefield; Henry A. Reed and Hanna E. Moore
George B., d. 9/26/1931 at 56/7/10 in Wolfeboro; b. Roxbury, MA; Stillman Reed and Sarah Judkins
Steven E., d. 12/18/1973 at 14 in Ossipee; b. MA

REGAMEY,
Anthony, d. 5/19/1976 at 77 in Ossipee; b. Switzerland

REGAN,
Mary E., Mrs., d. 11/4/1944 at 49/6 in Ossipee; b. Ireland; Timothy D. Curtin and Cathrine Dennehy

REHAL,
Charles E., d. 5/18/1991 at 70 in Ossipee; b. Salem, MA

REID,
Dorothy M., d. 9/6/1983 at 83 in Ossipee; b. Glen Ridge, NJ

REIS,
Manuel P., d. 9/25/1998 in Wolfeboro; Joseph Reis and Angilina Lopes

REISSFELDER,
William P., d. 10/15/1978 at 39 in Portland; b. NH

REMICK,
Frank, d. 12/11/1935 at 76/6/11 in Ossipee; b. Tamworth; Al D. Remick and A. J. Hurd
Frank P., d. 1/17/1918 at 67/3; farmer; married; b. Sandwich; George W. Remick (Sandwich) and Mary J. Hines (Sandwich)
Hannah, d. 6/30/1896 at 57 in Ossipee; tuberculosis; single
Kate D., d. 12/20/1952 at 82 in Wolfeboro; b. Tuftonboro; George Bean and Sarah Abbott
Lydia, d. 4/15/1904 at 65 in Concord; exhaustion from melancholia; housework; single
Marian E., d. 9/12/1901 at 0/3/13 in Ossipee; marasmus; b. Ossipee; Otis D. Remick (Brookfield) and Cora Tibbetts (Madison)
Mary E., d. 5/12/1915 at 56/11/19; house keeper; single; b. Sandwich; George W. Remick (Tamworth) and Mary J. Hines (Sandwich)
Nelson Atwood, d. 9/13/1985 at 90 in Ossipee; b. Reading, MA

RENNIE,
Wallace, d. 10/25/1985 at 75 in Ossipee; b. Andover, MA

REYNOLDS,
Joseph Patrick, d. 9/19/1995 at 57; Thomas Reynolds and Gladys Kelley

RHINES,
Angie Knox, d. 9/29/1975 at 87 in Ossipee; b. NH
Hannah, d. 1/31/1927 at 83/9/24; b. Cornish, ME; Acel Cole and S. Brown

RHOADS,
Eva N., d. 10/31/1969 at 87 in Ossipee; b. IL

RICE,
James, d. 2/28/1891 at 84 in Ossipee; farmer; widower; b. Wolfeboro

RICH,
Alice V., d. 9/19/1984 at 90 in Ossipee; b. Somerville, MA
Christine Jane, d. 2/13/1996 at 88 in Ossipee; Charles Smith and Cecelia Downing
Gladys W., d. 5/4/2000 in Wolfeboro; Charles Watson and Myra Morrisette
Inez Burnett, d. 12/20/1983 at 92 in Ossipee; b. NS

RICHARD,
Bro. Conrad, d. 6/13/1962 at 62 in Ctr. Ossipee; b. Auburn, ME

RICHARDS,
Edward C., d. 4/8/1930 at – in Ossipee; b. Roxbury, MA

RICHARDSON,
Anna Elizabeth, d. 7/18/1999 at 88 in Ossipee; John H. Richardson and Isabelle Cromwell Davis
Frank H., d. 11/16/1961 at 61 in Ossipee; b. Lawrence, MA
M. D., d. 9/14/1902 at 50/4/14 in Ossipee; bronchial consumption; married; b. Moultonboro; Lucian Richardson (Moultonboro) and Joanna T. Doe (Tuftonboro)
Rose M., d. 8/9/1983 at 77 in Portsmouth; b. Dover
Winifred S., d. 4/23/1941 at 67/0/3 in Wolfeboro; b. Sandwich; Albion Richardson and Elsie A. York

RICKARDS,
Hanford E., d. 3/12/1961 at 56 in Manchester; b. Kingfield, ME

RICKER,
Anna C., d. 6/18/1969 at 84 in Ossipee; b. NH
Bertha H., d. 11/15/1969 at 90 in Wolfeboro; b. NH
Clarena W., d. 12/15/1887 at 20/9 in Ossipee; laborer; single; b. Ossipee; M. V. Ricker (Ossipee) and Lenory Leighton (Ossipee)
Eliza A., d. 12/9/1912 at 74/8; housewife; single; b. Ossipee; Hiram Ricker (Ossipee) and Irene Chick
James E., d. 10/11/1954 at 87/0/7 in Boston, MA; b. Somersworth; William Ricker and Sarah French
Mariah, d. 4/10/1923 at 81/11/11; Daniel Kimball
Marion, d. 11/25/1959 at 95 in Wolfeboro; b. NS; John Fraser
Martha A., d. 5/21/1904 at 57 in Ossipee; cerebral thrombosis; housewife; married
Martin V., d. 6/8/1915 at 76/4/23; farmer; widower; b. Ossipee; Hiram Ricker (Ossipee) and Irine Chick (Ossipee)
Mary, d. 4/9/1904 at 71/1 in Ossipee; cancer; widow; b. Stow, ME
Mary E., d. 5/6/1917 at 46/3/29
Richard Russell, d. 11/26/1973 at 86 in Ossipee; b. NH
William, d. 3/20/1889 at 82; farmer; widower; b. Newfield
William C., d. 3/24/1951 at 86 in Wolfeboro; b. Ossipee; Martin Ricker and Lenora Leighton

RICO,
Frank A., d. 6/19/1953 at 27 in Ossipee; b. Wolfeboro; Peter A. Rico and Helen R. Glidden

RILEY,
Abbie L., d. 2/17/1967 at 77 in Wolfeboro; b. Poland, ME
Daniel Burton, Sr., d. 5/6/1993 at 52 in Wolfeboro
Edith M., d. 10/4/1984 at 74 in Ossipee; b. Hamden, CT
Ernest Grandville, Sr., d. 7/22/1990 at 74 in Wolfeboro; b. Standish, ME
Frederick J., d. 12/9/1961 at 69 in Ossipee; b. Exeter
Henry F., d. 6/11/1946 at 65/8/28 in Ossipee; b. Bridgton, ME; R. Granville Riley and Isabelle York
Herbert F., Sr., d. 9/6/1987 at 64 in Wolfeboro; b. Bridgton, ME
Randy R., d. 9/6/1987 at 23 in Ossipee; b. Wolfeboro

RINES,
Carleton E., d. 2/25/1961 at 58 in Portland, ME; b. Jefferson
Harry H., d. 3/5/1987 at 59 in Wolfeboro; b. Wolfeboro
Irvett L., d. 11/26/1991 at 85 in Wolfeboro; b. Malden, MA
Rebecca L., d. 3/20/1959 at 0/5 in Ossipee; b. Portland, ME; Carl Rines, Jr. and Barbara Virgillio
Stephanie Ann, d. 10/12/1973 at 17 in Conway; b. ME

RINGLAND,
Madeline Lenora, d. 5/31/1976 at 78 in Ossipee; b. ME

RIPLEY,
Lillian G., d. 4/2/1995 at 100; Lemual Rich and Minnie Clark

ROBBINS,
Helen Young, d. 11/20/1993 at 85 in Ossipee
Nettie H., d. 9/1/1887 at 28/10/11 in Ossipee; housewife; married; b. Deblois, ME; Charles Dunton

ROBERGE,
Hazel K., d. 11/19/1969 at 64 in Ossipee; b. ME

ROBERTON,
Gladys Elizabeth, d. 10/22/1988 at 73 in Ossipee; b. N. Conway

ROBERTS,
Aaron P., d. 8/25/1904 at – in Babylon, NY; septicemia; married
Annie, d. 7/22/1945 at 74/10/10 in Concord; b. Ossipee; Potter Roberts and Laura A. Dame
Blanche M., d. 10/5/1999 in Wolfeboro; Frank Sprague and Etta Cummings
Eliza, d. 1/17/1890 at 72 in Ossipee; heart disease; domestic; single; b. Ossipee
Gwendolyn Maude, d. 1/23/1976 at 78 in Ossipee; b. NH
Horace A., d. 11/12/1999 in Wolfeboro; Myron Roberts and Frances Whitman
Laura A., d. 12/2/1913 at 67/9/12
Milton Ogden, d. 1/13/1996 at 74 in Ossipee; Clifford Roberts and Gwendolyn Fernald
Myron, d. 7/12/1959 at 85 in Ossipee; b. Lynn, MA; Horace A. Roberts and Myra Abbott

ROBERTSON,
James W., d. 8/13/1980 at 89 in Ossipee; b. NH
Philip Albert, d. 12/14/1992 at 91 in Ossipee; b. Tamworth
Samuel M., d. 4/20/1943 at 78/2/24 in Ossipee; b. Hyde Park, MA; Charles Robertson and Emma Ells

ROBIN,
Anna E., d. 3/30/1942 at 88/4/14 in ozz; b. Bartlett; Silas M. Pendexter and Lydia D. Hale

ROBINSON,
Alberta Austin, d. 12/12/1996 at 94 in Wolfeboro; William Austin Maddix and Alberta Grimes
George, d. 12/9/1933 at 18/3/9 in Ossipee; b. Wareham, MA; Bertha Wilson
Henry W., d. 3/1/1974 at 81 in Ossipee; b. NH
Mary Ellen, d. 7/26/1971 at 90 in Ossipee; b. Canada
Mary Viola, d. 1/6/1996 at 82 in Wolfeboro; Sam Robinson and Minnie Kennedy
Maybelle, d. 4/18/1959 at 71 in Wolfeboro; b. Wolfeboro; Andrew Whittier and Belle Sargent
Nellie K., d. 1/23/2000 in Rochester; William Karcher and Martha Wilfert
Perley T., d. 12/25/1949 at 72/2/16 in Ossipee; b. Wolfeboro; Franklin Robinson and Emily Thompson

RODRIGUEZ,
Manuel R., d. 1/20/1988 at 84 in Dover; b. Northern Spain

ROGERS,
Bessie E., d. 1/2/1959 at 79 in Ossipee; b. NS; Henry Rogers and Margaret West
Byron L., 3rd, d. 4/15/1953 at 26 in Wolfeboro; b. Ossipee; Byron Rogers and Leona Bean
Clifford L., d. 5/21/1975 at 68 in Ossipee; b. MA
Donald L., d. 11/18/1932 at 7/2/11 in Ossipee; b. Ossipee; Byron L. Rogers and Leona Bean

ROHNSTOCK,
Robert F., d. 9/22/1962 at 47 in Ossipee; b. Somerville, MA

ROKE,
Alice S., d. 8/5/1897 at 18 in Ossipee; pustulent euleritis; b. Boston, MA; Mullbry Roke (Durham, ME) and Julia Sanders (Wakefield)

ROLES,
Alice I., d. 11/17/1897 at 18/6/2 in Ossipee; pulmonary tuberculosis; student; single; b. Ossipee; George A. Roles
Ella, d. 5/2/1900 at 43/10/15 in Somerville, MA; phthisis pulmonalis; married; b. Ossipee
George A., d. 3/27/1910 at 55 in Concord; lumberman; widower; b. Ossipee
John H., d. 12/22/1891 at 52 in Ossipee; farmer; married; b. Ossipee; Samuel I. Roles (Ossipee) and Lucy P. Clark (Wakefield)
Mary E., d. 6/12/1891 at 69 in Boston, MA; widow; William Wood

ROLLINS,
Helen Avery, d. 9/28/1990 at 87 in Ossipee; b. Wolfeboro
Lottie L., d. 9/9/1988 at 96 in Ossipee; b. Wentworth

ROSE,
Elsie Steen, d. 3/22/1988 at 84 in Ossipee; b. Davenport, IA

ROSEEN,
Margaret M., d. 4/21/2001 in Ossipee; Albert Donovan and Mary -----
Paul B., d. 4/28/1990 at 78 in Ossipee; b. Worcester, MA

ROSEWAINE,
Alfred, d. 10/27/1953 at 57 in Plymouth; b. CA; Samuel Rosewaine and Grace Edwards

ROSMARINO,
Deann L., d. 11/27/1990 at 26 in Ossipee; b. Amsterdam, NY

ROSS,
Bernice, d. 7/29/1902 at 34/1/16 in Ossipee; tuberculosis of lungs; housewife; married; b. NS; Israel Poole (NS) and Susan Messenger (England)
Bernice B., d. 1/10/1903 at 0/9/22 in Ossipee; tubercular meningitis; b. Ossipee; Charles I. Ross (Ossipee) and Bernice Poole (NB)
Charles Irving, d. 1/26/1943 at 80/7/23 in Ossipee; b. Ossipee; Robert G. Ross and Lydia Moody
Lucinda D., d. 10/11/1968 at 70 in Ossipee; b. NH
Lydia A., d. 10/19/1916 at 82/9/3; housewife; widow; b. Freedom; Amasa Moody (ME) and Mary A. Cooley (ME)
Robert C., d. 6/14/1907 at 74/9/6 in Ossipee; mitral regurgitation heart; woodturner; married; b. Albany; Robert Ross (Albany) and Lydia Patch (Newfield, ME)
Robert P., d. 2/11/1974 at 76 in Wolfeboro; b. NH
Samuel G., d. 4/10/1905 at 71/8 in Ossipee; bronchitis; shoemaker; married; b. Newfield, ME; Robert Ross (Newfield, ME) and Eliza Drew (Newfield, ME)

ROSSE,
daughter, d. 6/1/1951 at – in Ossipee; b. NH; Arthur Rosse and Marcia Severance

ROTHWELL,
William P., d. 1/28/1988 at 85 in Dover; b. Boston, MA

RUBINO,
Margaret, d. 7/25/2000 in Wolfeboro; Carmine Minchella and Maria Digaetano

RUDD,
Alfred T., d. 1/31/1950 at 69/3/14 in Laconia; b. Canada; William Rudd and Hannah M. Davis

RUMERY,
Aldo M., d. 5/5/1911 at 68/6/25; pneumonia; clerk of court; married; b. Effingham; John Rumery

Howard C., d. 5/9/1945 at 72/1/22 in Ossipee; b. Effingham; Aldo M. Rumery and Sarah M. Quarles

Laura A., d. 5/21/1961 at 87 in Wolfeboro; b. Quincy, IN

Laura Q., d. 12/20/1951 at 77 in Wolfeboro; b. Effingham; Aldo Rumery and Sarah Quarles

Sarah, d. 4/12/1888 at 88; domestic; widow; b. Parsonsfield, ME; Alpheus Nutter and Hannah Smith

Sarah M., d. 5/10/1911 at 74/3/17; pleuro pneumonia; housewife; widow; b. Ossipee; Samuel Quarles (Ossipee) and Sarah Dalton (Parsonsfield)

RUSSELL,
son, d. 4/3/1910 at 0/0/4 in Ossipee; premature birth; b. Ossipee; Jack Russell (Lewiston, ME) and Etta Colby (Ossipee)

Clyde D., d. 12/19/1981 at 70 in Wolfeboro; b. Ossipee

Franklin Gerard, d. 11/30/1978 at 72 in Ossipee; b. NH

Mabel L., d. 9/15/1903 at 32/0/28 in Ossipee; accidental drowning; clerk; single; Elizabeth J. Prouty

Marion Elaine, d. 3/7/1999 at 83 in Ossipee; Daniel B. Craigue and Freda Adel Dore

Mildred Russell, d. 11/29/1992 at 95 in Ossipee; b. Weymouth, MA

RYAN,
Beatrice Mae, d. 1/4/1998 in Wolfeboro; Harry J. Johnson and Alice M. Drake

Ella F., d. 9/19/1915 at 69/6; housewife; married; b. Ossipee; John F. Abbott (Ossipee) and Lucinda Emerson

Jane, d. 3/25/1906 at 44/11/8 in Ossipee; pneumonia; housewife; single; b. NS; Charles T. Ryan (Digby, NS) and Margarett Dowlin (Digby, NS)

RYDER,
Kirk L., d. 11/20/1977 at 17 in Ossipee; b. NH

R. Janet, d. 9/23/1983 at 49 in Wolfeboro; b. Ossipee

RYER,
Alice, Mrs., d. 8/8/1940 at 78/11/12 in Wakefield; b. NS; ----- Goodwin

Chesley R., d. 5/19/1905 at 14/11/25 in Ossipee; accident; single; b. NS; Robert Ryer (NS) and Anna Bean (NS)

Eva L., d. 2/25/1905 at 16/10/10 in Ossipee; pelvic abscess; single; b. NS; Robert Ryer (NS)

Henry W., d. 8/8/1920 at 54; teamster; married; b. Clyde River; ----- (NS)

ST. CLAIR,
Elpha Joseph, d. 10/11/1989 at 77 in Wolfeboro; b. Gorham

Jessie B., d. 7/24/1986 at 75 in Ossipee; b. Bethlehem

ST. LOUIS,
Henry Edward, Sr., d. 9/22/1998 in Ossipee; Edward St. Louis and Eva Becotte

SABA,
Elias, d. 10/14/1972 at 89 in Ossipee; b. Palestine

SABIN,
Charles W., d. 5/10/1970 at 89 in Ossipee; b. ME

SABINE,
son, d. 8/23/1907 at – in Ossipee; stillborn; b. Ossipee; Herbert Sabine (China, ME) and Ida M. Davis (Ossipee)

Herbert L., d. 3/27/1911 at 38/9/7; septicemia; painter; married; b. China, ME; Charles Sabine

Ida, d. 10/7/1918 at 32; nurse; widow; b. Ossipee; Albion E. Davis (Effingham) and Ella F. Thurley (Ossipee)

SACALAS,
Anthony, d. 2/7/1974 at 60 in Manchester; b. CT

SACHE,
daughter, d. 10/1/1922 at 0/0/1 in Ossipee; b. Ossipee; Paul Sache (Lawrence, MA) and Alice Gaukreger (England)

SALLESE,
Gregory Nazareth, d. 8/7/1996 at 90 in Ossipee; Salvatore Sallese and Francesca Villa

SALVADOR,
Eric Jason, d. 9/1/1989 at 20 in Ossipee; b. Hyannis, MA

SANBORN,
Carlton Wilbur, d. 3/17/1988 at 52 in Ossipee; b. Limerick, ME
Frank M., d. 3/3/1925 at 71/6/1; b. Ossipee; Abram Sanborn and Mary Harriman
Lula E., d. 1/12/1942 at 77/3/6 in Ossipee; b. Boscawen; Mark G. Duston and Eliza Sanborn
Luther M., d. 9/11/1926 at 77/9/12; b. Wakefield; Calvin Sanborn and Annie Hodsdon
Mary D., d. 6/22/1948 at 70/6/7 in Ossipee; b. Waterboro, ME; David Fry
Orin, d. 1/16/1967 at 90 in Ossipee; b. Conway
Rebecca Josephine, d. 11/29/1998 in Ossipee; Albert G. Pitman and Nellie Clough
Roland Earl, d. 7/16/1994 at 84; Arthur Sanborn and Mary Chase
Wilbur F., d. 4/15/1942 at 68/1/1 in Ossipee; b. Stoneham; Luther Sanborn and Nellie C. Blake

SANDERS,
Clara W., d. 12/22/1912 at 52/4; b. Tamworth; Benjamin Wentworth (Wakefield) and Mary A. Roberts
Daniel J., d. 9/22/1902 at 76/4/19 in Ossipee; bronchitis; farmer; married; b. Ossipee; Robert Sanders and Comfort Philbrick
Eliza, d. 11/1/1902 at 74/11 in Ossipee; pleurisy; housewife; widow
Elizabeth L., d. 7/7/1909 at 91/11/4 in Ossipee; fracture neck femur; housekeeper; b. Ossipee; Jacob Leighton (Farmington) and Sarah Wentworth (Dover)
Ernest L., d. 11/14/1945 at 71/11/23 in Tewksbury, MA; b. E. Boston, MA; Andrew J. Sanders and Abbie Norton
Isiah H., d. 3/2/1908 at 87/8/28 in Ossipee; old age; farmer; b. Ossipee; John Sanders (Epsom) and Betsey Buzzell
Maria, d. 1/28/1888 at 70; housekeeper; married; b. Ossipee
Mattie, d. 8/–/1895 at 49 in Ossipee; phleg's gastritis; single; b. Ossipee; Israel L. Sanders (Ossipee) and Elizabeth Leighton (Ossipee)
Melvinia, d. 1/8/1896 at 65/3/10 in Ossipee; bronchitis; single; b. Ossipee; Robert Sanders (Rye) and Comfort Philbrick (Epsom)
Obed, d. 6/17/1905 at 88/9 in Ossipee; old age; farmer; married; b. Strafford; William Sanders (Rye) and M. Roberts (Strafford)
Robert, d. 11/30/1892 at 80/4/1 in Ossipee; heart disease; shoemaker; widower; b. Ossipee; William Sanders
Vila, d. 6/1/1924 at 75/9/12; b. Ossipee; Israel Sanders and Elizabeth Leighton

SANFORD,
Cynthia M., d. 10/18/1945 at 3/8/23 in Ossipee; b. York, ME; Thomas J. Sanford and Cynthia W. Wilbur

SARGENT,
Charity, d. 7/9/1897 at 77 in Ossipee; gastritis; housewife; widow; b. Ossipee; Jane Bean (Sanford, ME) and Eunice Murray (Lebanon)
Edna S., d. 8/25/1979 at 71 in N. Conway; b. NH
Eldora F., d. 11/29/1954 at 81 in Ctr. Ossipee; b. Porter, ME; Samuel French and Lucie Danforth
Erwin N., d. 8/23/1975 at 75 in Wolfeboro; b. ME
Everett F., d. 10/27/1936 at 73/8/27 in Conway
Gerald W., Sr., d. 8/2/1986 at 58 in Wolfeboro; b. Ossipee
Hazel, d. 2/27/1958 at 63 in Wolfeboro; b. Ossipee; Warren Sargent and Julia Welch
Jeffrey Everett, d. 7/31/1971 at 6 hrs., 59 min. in Wolfeboro; b. NH
Lewis A., d. 2/12/1942 at 93/0/28 in Ossipee; b. Boston, MA; John A. Sargent and Mary A. Higgins
Mary Ann, d. 10/22/1891 at 76 in Ossipee; domestic; widow
Samuel, d. 3/12/1904 at 87 in Ossipee; old age; b. Fryeburg
Warren, d. 3/5/1902 at 1/4/22 in Ossipee; pneumonia; Warren Sargent (Ossipee) and Julia Welch (Ossipee)
Warren, d. 5/9/1918 at 52/10; laborer; married; b. Chichester; Daniel Sargent

SAULNIER,
Addie May, d. 8/23/1970 at 96 in Ossipee; b. NH

SAUNDERS,
George H., d. 4/20/1968 at 88 in Ossipee; b. MA
Lillian, d. 5/5/1963 at 66 in Ossipee; b. N. Conway

SAWYER,
son, d. 11/28/1958 at – in Wolfeboro; b. Wolfeboro; Hayes Sawyer, Jr. and Ann J. McHugh
Ann J., d. 6/9/2001 in Dover; Thomas McHugh and Margaret McHugh
Daniel F., d. 2/26/1924 at 78; Daniel Sawyer and Hulda Sawyer
Hayes W., d. 3/13/1964 at 63 in Ossipee; b. Ossipee
Louise D., d. 4/20/1967 at 75 in Wolfeboro; b. N. Conway
Luther E., d. 3/9/1972 at 93 in Wolfeboro; b. NH
Milton A., d. 12/9/1933 at 22/1/7 in Ossipee; b. Taunton, MA; Dorothy Sawyer
Phyllis Hodgdon, d. 5/25/1975 at 76 in MA; b. NH
Robert Cushman, d. 9/30/1974 at 75 in Ossipee; b. NH
Robert F., d. 3/29/1991 at 84 in Wolfeboro; b. Concord

Violet B., d. 11/16/1983 at 85 in Wolfeboro; b. Ossipee
William L., d. 4/16/1953 at 77/0/4 in Ossipee; b. Tuftonboro; George Sawyer and Christie Cate

SAYRE,
Allen G., d. 3/24/1961 at 74 in Wolfeboro; b. St. John, NB
Olga, d. 1/26/1975 at 89 in Ossipee; b. Norway

SCANNELL,
Francis Fidelis, d. 12/30/1997 at 80 in Wolfeboro; David Anthony Scannell and Edna McNeill

SCATES,
Clark S., d. 1/16/1904 at 76/4 in Ossipee; cancer of neck; farmer; widower; b. Ossipee; Oliver Scates
Harriet O., d. 8/26/1900 at 72/5/6 in Ossipee; cerebral softening; housewife; married; b. Effingham; Oliver Chadborne (Effingham) and Mary Hill (Madbury)
Ida F., d. 1/30/1981 at 84 in Ossipee; b. Crofton, KY

SCEGGEL[L],
son, d. 8/4/1913 at 0/0/1; b. Ossipee; Benjamin Sceggel (Ossipee) and Edna Demerritt (Conway)
Benjamin, d. 7/28/1889 at 58; farmer; married; b. Ossipee; Moses Sceggell and Abigail Wentworth
Charles, d. 1/7/1938 at 79/0/6 in Ossipee; b. Ossipee; Woodbury Sceggel and Maria Page
Charles B., d. 5/5/1917 at 53; painter; widower; b. Ossipee; Roswell Sceggell (England) and Hannah Worthing (England)
George O., d. 1/16/1917 at 77/10/8; farmer; widower; b. Ossipee; Moses Sceggell (Ossipee) and Abigail Wentworth (Ossipee)
Hannah B., d. 11/20/1912 at 98/4; widow; b. Ossipee; M. F. Sceggell (Ossipee) and Abbie Wentworth (Ossipee)
J. A., d. 3/17/1891 at 66/0/4 in Ossipee; domestic; single; b. Ossipee; Jeremiah Sciggell (sic) (Ossipee) and Fanny Quarles (Ossipee)
Martha J., d. 12/12/1914 at 70/0/15; housewife; b. Effingham; Joseph Sias (Portsmouth) and Sarah Hammond (Ossipee)
Moses, d. 12/29/1912 at 85; farmer; single; b. Ossipee; Moses Sceggell (Ossipee) and Abigail Wentworth (Ossipee)
W. B., d. 11/2/1919 at 82/5/8; farmer; widower; b. Ossipee; Zachriah Sceggell (Ossipee) and Lydia Brackett (Effingham)

SCHANSCHIEFF [see Schonschieff],
Kristine, d. 5/28/1948 at 74/7/19 in Concord; b. NY; ----- Fister and Christine Fister

Marion K., d. 11/4/1983 at 75 in Wolfeboro; b. Portsmouth
Peter, d. 3/1/1992 at 86 in Ossipee; b. Amityville, NY

SCHENKER,
Hanssen, d. 9/2/1996 at 77 in Ossipee; Frank P. Schencker and Elizabeth Hanssen

SCHICKS,
Charles George, d. 12/30/1943 at 63/3/17 in Ossipee; b. Somers, CT; George C. Schicks and Emma Smith

SCHILLARE,
Jean L., d. 3/12/1984 at 88 in Ossipee; b. Northampton, MA

SCHMIDT,
Edwin Allen, d. 2/8/1999 at 76 in Ossipee; Edwin Adolf Schmidt and Hilda Arlene Briggs

SCHMOTTLACH,
George R., d. 4/1/1980 at 64 in Wolfeboro; b. MA

SCHONSCHIEFF [see Schanschieff],
Nicholas A., d. 11/21/1949 at 82 in Wolfeboro; b. Russia; Alexandra Schonschieff

SCHOOLCRAFT,
Herman, d. 11/17/1915 at 76; b. Canada

SCHOONMAKER,
Evelyn Horne, d. 12/29/1990 at 74 in Ossipee; b. N. Shapleigh, ME
Weld Day, d. 12/7/1992 at 81 in Ossipee; b. Ware, MA

SCHULTZ,
Joseph H., d. 11/22/1912 at 63/9; farmer; married; A. Schultz and Jane Blackman
Peter B., d. 7/2/1987 at 90 in Ossipee; b. Amsterdam, Holland
Sarah A., d. 1/18/1942 at 94/0/3 in Ossipee; b. St. George, NB; David Bonney and Cynthia Bonney

SCOLARO,
Frank Anthony, d. 2/3/1999 at 75 in Ossipee; Bartolo Scolaro and Thersa Miore

SCOTT,
Clarence N., d. 11/17/1974 at 87 in Wolfeboro; b. MA
Helen Folsom Smart Avery, d. 12/11/1996 at 90 in Wolfeboro; Harry Preston Smart and Harriett Colomy
James, d. 6/16/1911 at 73/11/26; paralytic shock; RR foreman; married; b. NB; William Scott (Scotland) and Mary A. Smith (Scotland)
Leslie James, d. 12/16/1998 in Ossipee; John Jacob Scott and Margaret Hibbs
Louise B., d. 12/22/1982 at 85 in Ossipee; b. Buffalo, NY

SCRUTON,
Elizabeth, d. 7/7/1961 at 83 in Norway, ME; b. Fox River, Canada

SEABURY,
Ralph H., d. 5/30/2001 in Wolfeboro; Ralph Seabury and Leona Bowler

SEAVEY,
Ithma, d. 4/8/1929 at 84/7/11 in Ossipee; b. Conway; Tufton Seavey and Ruth Carleton
Louise, d. 3/16/1926 at 72; b. Boston, MA

SEAVY,
Frank, d. 6/12/1940 at 81/4/3 in Ossipee; b. Conway; Richard Seavy and Elizabeth Charles
Herbert T., d. 1/26/1965 at 68 in Wolfeboro; b. Stoughton, MA

SEGUIN,
Arthur, d. 12/3/1973 at 88 in Laconia; b. ME
Bruce Elwin, Sr., d. 5/9/1989 at 54 in Wolfeboro; b. Alexandria
Colby A., d. 12/17 or 18/1986 at 0/1/2 in Wolfeboro; b. N. Conway
Donna-Lee A., d. 2/3/1984
Joan M., d. 9/18/1946 at 0/5/23 in Ossipee; b. Kezar Falls, ME; Roger K. Seguin and Mary E. Eldridge
John, d. 3/13/1954 at 55/7/11 in Ossipee; b. Lewiston, ME; Lewis Seguin and May Laford
Roger Kenneth, d. 12/13/1987 at 64 in Wolfeboro; b. Alexandria

SELLS,
Janet Regua, d. 1/5/1991 at 67 in Ossipee; b. Terrytown, NY

SEVERANCE,
Hollace E., d. 1/3/1892 at 47/6 in Ossipee; la grippe; farmer; single

SEWARD,
Turner N., d. 8/4/1912 at 78/7/4

SEWELL,
Helen Theresa, d. 1/24/1986 at 92 in Wolfeboro; b. Salem, MA

SHACKFORD,
Charlotte, d. 12/29/1962 at 80 in Wolfeboro; b. Fitchburg, MA
Eugene D., d. 1/21/1952 at 76 in Wolfeboro; b. Eaton; Frank S. Shackford and Ada L. Smith

SHAFER,
Katherine J., d. 1/29/2000 in Wolfeboro; Kent Smith and Erma Goldman

SHANNON,
Allen W., d. 11/20/1977 at 22 in Ossipee; b. NH

SHAPLEIGH,
Bradford Goodwin, d. 2/23/1997 at 79 in Ossipee; Sydney Shapleigh and Charlotte Goodwin
Elizabeth A., d. 12/20/1965 at 89 in Ossipee; b. Brookline, MA

SHARMAN,
Fred H., d. 3/24/1933 at 65/6/7 in Ossipee; b. E. Machias, ME; Dean R. Sharman and Elmira Huntley

SHATTUCK,
Madeliene A., d. 2/12/1999 at 80 in Wolfeboro; Jeremiah L. Watson and Florence M. MacKay

SHAW,
child, d. 8/11/1888 at 0/2/21; b. Wolfeboro; Henry Shaw
Alfred R., d. 7/20/1936 at 61/7/28 in Ossipee; b. NS; Charles Shaw and Isabel Tyder
Caroline, d. 9/14/1993 at 91 in Ossipee
Ira, d. 5/3/1947 at 74/8/13 in Hebron, ME; b. S. Paris, ME; William C. Shaw and Achsa Durrell
Julia, d. 9/17/1897 at 71/7/19 in Ossipee; cardiac dropsy; housewife; widow; b. Union, ME; Charles Titus (ME) and Pamelia Butters (ME)
Margaret Ann, d. 3/22/1941 at 72/9/7 in Wolfeboro; b. Lakeport; Hiram Philbrick and Betsy Cook
Pearl Elizabeth, d. 11/16/1994 at 78; Edgar Shaw and Lizzie Lowd
Sarah F., d. 3/21/1913 at 76; housework; single; b. MA

SHEA,
Ruth E., d. 4/6/1974 at 43 in Wolfeboro; b. NH

SHEAFF,
Arthur R., d. 10/4/1981 at 66 in Ossipee; b. Guilford, ME

SHEAN,
Thomas, d. 2/16/1927 at 73; b. Ireland

SHECK,
Olive Estelle, d. 12/19/1989 at 96 in Ossipee; b. Ithaca, NY

SHEERIN,
Lucy E., d. 9/18/1978 at 64 in Hanover; b. MA

SHEPHERD,
Belinda, d. 1/26/1907 at 89/8/7 in Ossipee; cancer of uterus; housewife; widow; b. Ossipee; Silas White (Ossipee) and Deborah Plummer (Ossipee)

SHEPPARD,
Maisie, Rev., d. 2/21/1999 at 87 in Ossipee

SHEPPERSON,
Herbert, d. 2/25/1986 at 97 in Ossipee; b. Ipswich, MA

SHERBERTES,
Margaret, d. 2/7/1994 at 69; John N. Reilly and Lymena T. Baxter

SHIFFER,
Leigh B., d. 7/16/1980 at 90 in Ossipee; b. PA

SHOEMAKER,
Martha B., d. 11/2/1985 at 81 in Ossipee; b. Cincinnati, OH

SHOREY,
Amos J., d. 5/25/1964 at 88 in Ossipee; b. Bay City, MI
Earl, d. 4/28/1966 at 70 in Ossipee; b. Oakfield, ME
Ruth L., d. 5/4/1962 at 69 in Wolfeboro; b. Winchester, MA

SHORTRIDGE,
Everett D., d. 4/14/1914 at 48/7/30; lumberman; b. Wolfeboro; James H. Shortridge and Mary J. Twombly (Wolfeboro)

SIAS,
Alice, d. 12/4/1899 at 9 in Ossipee; acute articular rheumatism; b. Ossipee; Newell P. Sias (Ossipee) and Etta Bertwell (Ossipee)
Annie G., d. 3/20/1895 at 0/5/2 in Ossipee; cardiac paralysis; b. Ossipee; Newell P. Sias (Ossipee) and Etta Bertwell (Ossipee)
Edith, d. 8/28/1893 at 15/3/14 in Ossipee; scholar; b. Ossipee; John F. Sias (Ossipee) and Josie Abbott (Ossipee)
Eliza B., d. 4/11/1919 at 96/7/10; housekeeping; widow; b. Richmond, ME; J. Coleman (Richmond, ME) and Abigail Sedgley (Bowdoinham)
Ellen E., d. 6/15/1932 at 85/0/0 in Somersworth; b. Ossipee
Emanuel, d. 1/18/1899 at 49 in Ossipee; influenza; single; Henry Sias
Etta, d. 4/30/1913 at 46; housewife; married; b. Ossipee; Robinson Bertwell
Frances, d. 3/30/1952 at 68/9/17 in Tamworth; b. NH
George, d. 7/16/1939 at 73/3/24 in Wolfeboro; b. Ossipee; George B. Sias and Martha H. Fogg
George B., d. 4/13/1898 at 70/1/29 in Ossipee; suicide; speculator; married; b. Ossipee; Joseph Sias (Ossipee) and Hannah Dodge (Ossipee)
Gladys, d. 9/11/1896 at 4 in Ossipee; dysentery; b. Ossipee; Newell P. Sias (Ossipee) and Etta Bertwell (Ossipee)
Henry E., d. 1/12/1894 at 50/4 in Ossipee; interstrubel nepotelis; mechanic; married; b. Ossipee; Joseph Sias (Ossipee) and Abbie Sias (Ossipee)
James B., d. 5/13/1902 at 26/2/29 in Medford, MA; consumption; married; George B. Sias
Jennie, d. 3/30/1903 at 31/9 in Ossipee; carcinoma; housewife; married
John C., d. 11/19/1916 at 66; none [occupation]; b. Tuftonboro; Jonathan Sias (Ossipee) and Eliza B. Calman (Richmond, ME)
Joseph F., d. 10/21/1917 at 64/0/2; married; b. Ossipee; Jonathan Sias (Ossipee) and Eliza A. Codman (Richmond, ME)
Louie T., d. 5/3/1894 at 0/9/27 in Ossipee; acute pneumonia; b. Ossipee; Newell P. Sias (Ossipee) and Etta Bertwell (Ossipee)
Marian, d. 8/31/1896 at 0/6/19 in Ossipee; dysentery; b. Ossipee; Newell P. Sias (Ossipee) and Etta Bertwell (Ossipee)
Newell P., d. 8/9/1948 at 85/0/5 in Ossipee; b. Ossipee; Jonathan Sias and Liza Colbroth

SIDELINGER,
Eleanor Stover, d. 8/14/1995 at 81; Arthur Aaron Black and Ruby Stover

SIDMORE,
Alada W., d. 1/6/2001 in Ossipee; William H. Walker and Nella Swett

SIMMONDS,
Caroline S., d. 4/27/1914 at 70/2/13; housewife; b. Charleston, ME; Asa Carpenter and Susan Young

SIMMONS,
Charles L., d. 8/19/1905 at 62 in Ossipee; general paresis; married; b. Charlestown, ME; Jehiar Simmons (ME) and Sarah Garland (ME)
Emma, d. 4/19/1945 at 75/7/4 in Concord; b. Ossipee; John Geralds and Mary Moody

SIMPSON,
Harry Austin, Jr., d. 8/28/1998 in Ctr. Ossipee; Harry Austin Simpson, Sr. and Mary Cullen
Mildred A., d. 4/5/1966 at 62 in Ossipee; b. Portland, ME

SINCLAIR,
Abbie, d. 1/17/1908 at 69 in Ossipee; valvular disease of heart
Achsa, d. 3/4/1907 at 66/10 in Ossipee; pneumonia; housewife; widow; b. Ossipee; Daniel Wentworth and ----- Scates
Alfreda C., d. 12/19/2001 in Wolfeboro; Theodore Champagne and Albena Valley
Carlton V., d. 9/23/1973 at 74 in Concord; b. NH
Jeremiah G., d. 6/9/1888 at 54; postal clerk; widow; b. Ossipee; Leander D. Sinclair and Olive Sinclair
John K., d. 9/22/1903 at 57 in Ossipee; paralysis of heart; janitor; widower; b. Ossipee; Leander D. Sinclair (Essex, VT) and Olive W. Kimball (Kennebunk, ME)
Leander D., d. 10/28/1889 at 85/0/7; station agent; married; b. Essex, VT; Jeremiah Sinclair and Abigail Glines
Lucy E., d. 1/15/1908 at 43 in Ossipee; pneumonia; housewife; b. Exeter; George W. Drew and Lydia -----
Moses C., d. 5/24/1904 at 62/5/27 in Ossipee; cerebral hemorrhage; farmer; married; b. Ossipee; Leander Sinclair and Olive Kimball
William C., d. 3/21/1924 at 69/1/18; b. Ossipee; Leander D. Sinclair and Olive W. Kimball

SISLANE,
Jean Muriel, d. 2/22/1991 at 82 in Ossipee; b. Canada

SKILLIN,
Ray, d. 1/17/1921 at 41/4/25 in Ossipee; teamster; divorced; E. J. Skillin (Garland, ME) and Harriet Foss

SKILTON,
Raymond N., d. 7/29/1961 at 71 in Ossipee; b. Cambridge, MA

SKINNER,
Albert Brown, d. 6/6/1994 at 84; Edward E. Skinner and Minnie B. Brown
Clara, d. 8/15/1900 at 45 in Ossipee; insanity; married
Olga B., d. 5/21/1991 at 82 in Ossipee; b. Wakefield

SLACK,
Leroy, d. 6/19/1943 at 48/11/20 in Ossipee; b. Needham, MA; Edward Slack and Frances McMasters

SLADE,
Beatrice V., d. 8/22/1975 at 70 in Ossipee; b. MA

SMALL,
Agnes H., d. 11/24/1990 at 92 in Ossipee; b. Boston, MA
Arleen C., d. 5/–/1917 at 38; housework; married; John Curry (NB) and Elizabeth Curry (NB)
Jennie H., d. 3/29/1916 at 42/0/9; preacher; married; b. Hampden, ME; John M. Hamlin (Hampden, ME) and Jane M. Foster (Hampden, ME)

SMART,
child, d. 3/14/1933 at – in Ossipee; b. Ossipee; Edward C. Smart and Beatrice Giles
Adeline J., d. 11/4/1958 at 76 in Wolfeboro; b. Grand Isle, VT; Jackson Eddy
Beatrice Giles, d. 12/23/1989 at 83 in Ossipee; b. Freedom
Charles E., d. 12/19/1960 at 80 in Ossipee; b. Ossipee
Charles H., d. 3/2/1917 at 71/8/22; manufacturer; married; b. Campton; Luther T. Smart (Campton) and Mary Dore (Wakefield)
Edward C., d. 3/7/1988 at 84 in Wolfeboro; b. Ossipee
Harriet Colomy, d. 3/11/1981 at 97 in Ossipee; b. Farmington
Harry, d. 11/7/1982 at 100 in Wolfeboro; b. Ossipee
Helen Asenath, d. 5/31/1940 at 85/9/16 in Ossipee; b. Tamworth; John T. D. Folsom and Asenath Whipple
Luther T., d. 8/6/1890 at 76 in Ossipee; peritonitis; cabinet maker; married; b. Ossipee
Mary D., d. 5/23/1891 at 78/4/21 in Ossipee; widow; b. Newfield, ME; James Doane
Mildred B., d. 6/14/1923 at 45/9/24; b. Parsonsfield, ME; Daniel O. Blazo and Emily Perkins
Preston B., d. 3/26/1969 at 66 in Wolfeboro; b. ME

Susie E., d. 1/5/1952 at 67/2/25 in Rochester; b. Wolfeville, NS; Willard N. Dodge and Jane Singer

SMITH,
Ann Looram, d. 10/27/1993 at 77 in Ossipee
Carol M., d. 5/29/1987 at 73 in Wolfeboro; b. Brookline, MA
Charles Crosby, d. 9/27/1943 at 87/8/28 in Tamworth; b. Ossipee; Allen L. Smith and Betsy Jane Moody
Cora E., d. 1/13/1958 at 84 in Ossipee; b. Beverly, MA; Weldon Smith and Ella Foster
Daniel, d. 4/23/1904 at 79/9/22 in Parsonsfield; progressive apoplexy; farmer; single; b. Ossipee; John Smith (Ossipee) and Sally Ambrose (Ossipee)
Doris C., d. 3/4/1989 at 81 in Ossipee; b. St. Steven, NB
Elizabeth J., d. 3/25/1914 at 86; housekeeper; Peter Smith
Florence T., d. 4/4/1977 at 70 in Hanover; b. MA
Fred W., d. 7/9/1949 at 79/1 in Ossipee; b. Newfield, ME; Abraham Smith and Ellen Patch
George L., d. 4/14/1917 at 48/0/18; U.S. inspector; married; Charles A. Smith (Limington, ME) and Caroline Brooks (Freedom)
Gladys Gertrude, d. 12/16/1974 at 86 in Ossipee; b. MA
Hannah C., d. 12/26/1918 at 85/8/20; housewife; widow; Elijah Kenny and Hannah Cook
Harriet M., d. 1/31/1915 at 78; housewife; widow; b. Danbury; John Templeton and Jerusha Eldridge (Ossipee)
Hattie, d. 1/5/1944 at 88/6/3 in Ossipee; b. Conway; Daniel Smith and Emma Doloff
Henry, d. 2/6/1973 at 76 in Ossipee; b. NH
Herman, d. 10/27/1917 at 51/7; lumberman; widower; b. Lakeport; George H. Smith (Lakeport) and Mary Bunker (Gilmanton)
Isiah, d. 3/27/1900 at 93/10/1 in Ossipee; senile gangrene; farmer; married; b. Lebanon, ME; Tobias Smith (Lebanon) and Julia Clark (Lebanon)
Jennie, d. 12/9/1930 at 76/6/22 in Ossipee; b. Cornish, ME; Elisha Brown and Mary Irish
Joseph F., d. 2/15/1963 at 81 in Ossipee; b. Newark, NJ
Laura E., d. 4/5/1928 at 63; b. Ossipee; J. C. Welch and Ellen Welch
Lloyd Clifford, d. 12/13/1993 at 84 in Ctr. Ossipee
Margaret C., d. 3/26/1959 at 71 in Ossipee; b. Dover; James Campbell and Elizabeth McNiece
Marguerite Lillian, d. 3/16/1998 in Ctr. Ossipee; John Albert Eastman Smith and Florence Bertha Dearborn
Mary A., d. 5/31/1896 at 63 in Ossipee; insanity; housekeeper; b. Ossipee; William B. Smith and Polly Brown
Norman Lee, d. 9/18/1987 at 81 in Ossipee; b. Fryeburg, ME

Peter E., d. 6/27/1971 at 17 in Ossipee; b. MA
Ray Gates, d. 5/31/1977 at 79 in Wolfeboro; b. NH
Robert J., d. 9/22/1931 at 25/2/20 in Ossipee; b. Dover; Perley A. Smith and Marguerite Campbell
William G., d. 7/20/1982 at 31 in Hanover; b. Patterson, NJ
William N., d. 5/10/1958 at 75 in Water Village; b. Roxbury, MA; Frank Smith and Emily Nason

SNIDER,
Thomas E., Jr., d. 8/10/1993 at 68 in Wolfeboro

SNOW,
Boaz, d. 9/9/1897 at 1/3/2 in Ossipee; bronchitis; b. Moultonboro; Elbridge Snow (Wilton, ME) and Jesse McPiper (PEI)
Elbridge, d. 12/27/1918 at 67; laborer; married; b. Milton, MA; Elbridge Snow (Milton, MA) and Olive J. Day (Brownfield, ME)
Jessie A., d. 11/14/1929 at 75/5/8 in Ossipee; b. PEI; Donald McPhee and Margaret Nicholson
Karl Russell, Jr., d. 9/23/1971 at 27 in Ossipee; b. MA
Olive J., d. 11/5/1916 at 83/9/5; housewife; widow; b. Ossipee; Alvah Day (Alfred, ME) and Eliza Wentworth (Alfred, ME)
Pauline, d. 5/3/1909 at 0/2 in Ossipee; catarrhal bronchitis; b. Ossipee; Elbridge E. Snow (Milton, MA) and Eva Williams (Ossipee)

SNYDER,
Elsa, d. 10/10/1976 at 85 in Ossipee; b. CT

SOANES,
Albert Joseph, d. 4/30/1998 in Ossipee; George Soanes and Catherine Murray

SOUCY,
Alphonse, d. 9/12/1957 at 83 in Ossipee; b. Canada; Prospere Soucy and Mary Massie
Omer J., d. 8/10/1966 at 81 in Ossipee; b. Canada
Rosanna Mary, d. 4/29/1980 at 79 in Ossipee; b. NH

SOUZA,
Leona May, d. 11/11/1992 at 86 in Ctr. Ossipee; b. Winthrop, MA

SPARKS,
Bernie G., d. 11/9/1968 at 80 in Wolfeboro; b. VT

SPAULDING,
Marion Ida, d. 5/25/1994 at 85; Robert C. Spaulding and Eunice Hoag

SPEAR,
Alphonso A., d. 1/29/1912 at 69/10/14; farmer; married; Eli O. Spear (Standish, ME) and Mary A. Hamlin (Gorham, ME)
Sarah E., d. 7/18/1924 at 80/7/11; b. Ossipee; Ebenezar Hodsdon and Catherine Tuttle

SPEIGHT,
Martha, d. 4/1/1941 at 75/1/19 in Ossipee; b. Kendol, England; James Parker and Alice M. Hargrave

SPENCE,
Robert E., d. 7/15/1990 at 77 in Wolfeboro; b. Peabody, MA
Virginia Edith, d. 9/29/1995 at 77; Philip Davis and Edith -----

SPINELLI,
Jennifer Marie, d. 4/24/1994 at 17; Ralph F. Spinelli and Anna Loretta Amato

SPRAGUE,
Alice P., d. 12/2/1986 at 89 in Wolfeboro; b. Tuftonboro
Garland Elbert, d. 6/17/1989 at 61 in Wolfeboro; b. Stratton, ME
Russell, d. 9/23/1916 at 0/1/18; b. Effingham; Ernest Sprague (Effingham) and Allace Hoyt (Tuftonboro)

STACKPOLE,
Charles E., d. 11/20/1904 at 76 in Ossipee; heart disease; shoemaker; widower

STAFFORD,
Clifton C., d. 6/2/1962 at 58 in Ossipee; b. Stowe, VT

STANDARD,
Robert L., d. 4/3/1990 at 79 in Wolfeboro; b. NY

STANLEY,
Harold L., d. 11/24/1984 at 66 in Manchester; b. Farmington

STANTON,
Florence Marie, d. 1/4/2001 in Ctr. Ossipee; Homer Ash and Florence Dunkinson
Nancy C., d. 1/25/1900 at 70 in Concord; brain disease

STAPLES,
Ada, d. 5/16/1977 at 73 in Wolfeboro; b. NH
Alice J., d. 5/15/1959 at 85 in Ossipee; b. Ossipee; Thatcher Thompson and Fannie Tibbetts
Charlotte W., d. 11/21/1988 at 94 in Ossipee; b. Ossipee
Edith M., d. 6/6/1981 at 93 in Ossipee; b. Farmington, ME
Ervin E., d. 7/6/1968 at 76 in Wolfeboro; b. NH
Lizzie, d. 8/20/1910 at 37/2 in Ossipee; bronchitis; housewife; married; b. Ossipee; Frank A. Nichols (Ossipee) and Lizzie Nichols (Ossipee)
Marion A., d. 8/14/1976 at 76 in Wolfeboro; b. MA
Myric, d. 11/17/1927 at –; b. Ossipee; Irving Staples and Lottie White
Sara H., d. 11/10/1942 at 57 in Wolfeboro; b. Ireland; Michael Hughes and Sara Kelley
Willard J., d. 12/19/2000 in N. Conway; Ervin Staples and Sara Hughes

STEAD,
Charles Edward, d. 6/16/1994 at 53; Herold L. Stead and Helen A. Richardson

STEEVES,
Linda Maureen, d. 9/16/1997 at 29 in Ctr. Ossipee; James Bower and Thelma Robinson

STEPHENS,
Nanna, d. 9/7/1948 at 87/10/12 in Ossipee; b. Beaver Falls, PA; Jefferson Wilson

STEPHENSON,
Ella, d. 5/17/1957 at 90 in Gorham, ME; b. England; John Stephenson and Anne Devon
Joseph Newell, d. 11/11/1975 at 92 in Ossipee; b. NY

STERLING,
Beatrice M., d. 4/30/1989 at 88 in Ossipee; b. Milton

STERN,
Adam Dearsmith, d. 10/15/1995 at 30; Morton Stern and Susan Clark
Hattie Corfield, d. 8/2/1940 at 71/7/7 in Ossipee; b. E. Boston, MA; Thomas Corfield and Elizabeth Pineo

STEVENS,
Agnes Gallant, d. 1/21/1997 at 93 in Ossipee; Clarence Edgar Stevens and Nellie Gallant
Alfred S., d. 6/5/1961 at 93 in Ossipee; b. Greene, ME

Bruce Ellsworth, d. 9/3/1993 at 86 in Ossipee
Henry E., d. 9/15/1947 at 84/6/4 in Ossipee; b. Clompton, Canada
James L., d. 2/10/1915 at 89; carpenter; widower; Joseph Stevens
Lawrence, d. 10/19/1996 at 68 in Wolfeboro; ----- Stevens and Agnes -----
Lester W., d. 11/25/1887 at 0/9/15 in Ossipee; b. Ossipee; Edwin A. Stevens (Ossipee) and Lucy B. (Hamilton, MA)
Lucy B., d. 4/22/1927 at 75/11/20; b. Hamilton, MA; William M. Smith and Lucy Brown
MariJane, d. 7/26/1987 at 31 in Laconia; b. N. Conway
Mary E., d. 6/6/1925 at 92/10/17; b. Alton; Dana Kimball and Mary Evans
Oren J., d. 3/30/1976 at 83 in Wolfeboro; b. MA
Robert, d. 6/16/1977 at 37 in Wolfeboro; b. MA

STEWART,

Edmund Ladner, d. 3/21/1978 at 96 in Ossipee; b. Canada
Lucinda, d. 12/30/1931 at – in Ossipee; b. Cornish, ME; Joseph Cole and Lorriean Sargent

STIFF,

Bernard George Edmund, d. 9/8/2001 in Ossipee; Charles J. Stiff and Winnifred Carpenter

STILES,

Earle G., d. 10/24/1926 at 34/7/9; b. Sanbornville; Harry G. Stiles and Christine S. Howard
Frederick H., d. 3/13/1968 at 85 in Ossipee; b. MA
Mary E., d. 6/4/1911 at 62; pneumonia; teacher; single; b. Dover; Samuel Stiles (Rollinsford) and Zelpha Leavitt (Effingham)

STILLINGS,

Addie E., d. 4/7/1887 at 1/10/27 in Ossipee; b. Ossipee; Charles Stillings
Agnes M., d. 7/1/1954 at 45/8/3 in Ossipee; b. Wolfeboro; David Whitton and Nellie Hoyt
Albert D., d. 4/7/1914 at 81/5/28
Alonzo, d. 3/3/1909 at 75/3/12 in Ossipee; catarrhal pneumonia; clergyman; b. Ossipee; Isaac Stillings (Ossipee) and Mary Colby (Ossipee)
Charles, d. 8/18/1935 at 81/11/9 in Tuftonboro; b. Ossipee; Ivory Stillings and Lydia Wentworth
Cora E., d. 6/26/1902 at 40/4 in Ossipee; pulmonary tuberculosis; housewife; married; b. Tuftonboro; Nemiah Bean
Edith Lewis, d. 1/2/1974 at 93 in Ossipee; b. NH
Edwin L., d. 4/5/1960 at 65 in Wolfeboro; b. Ossipee
Ivory, d. 11/13/1894 at 75/1/13 in Ossipee; apoplexy; farmer; widower; James Stillings and Mehitable Gilman

Kate M., d. 11/3/1953 at 79 in Wolfeboro; b. Ossipee; George Sawyer and Christie Cate
Lydia P., d. 12/29/1892 at 76/4 in Ossipee; cerebral hemorrhage; married
Mary J., d. 7/11/1907 at 71/5/4 in Ossipee; cerebral thrombosis; housewife; married; b. Tamworth; William Hyde (Ossipee) and Jennie Mason (Tamworth)
Roscoe, d. 7/7/1982 at 74 in Ossipee; b. Tuftonboro
Susan, d. 9/18/1892 at 56/8/15 in Ossipee; anaemia; housewife; married; b. Ossipee; Richard Beacham (Ossipee) and Mary Hersey (Tuftonboro)

STINCHFIELD,
Ralph S., d. 11/16/1992 at 81 in Ossipee; b. Wolfeboro

STIRRUP,
Michael Pye, d. 4/19/1949 at 0/0/1 in Wolfeboro; b. Wolfeboro; Joseph B. Stirrup and Claire Cohen

STOCKBRIDGE,
Lavinia Affie, d. 8/21/1998 in Ctr. Ossipee; Earl T. Merrow, Sr. and Flora Templeton
Melisse C., d. 12/10/1968 at 89 in Ossipee; b. NH

STODDARD,
Donald T., d. 6/2/1953 at 18 in Wolfeboro; b. Melrose, MA; Russell Stoddard and Grace Thurston
Russell A., d. 4/6/1947 at 44/8/2 in Ossipee; b. Melrose, MA; Clark M. Stoddard and Clara Melven

STOKES,
Arline L., d. 6/3/1964 at 79 in Ossipee; b. Hamden, CT
Arthur P., d. 9/8/1954 at 61/2/14 in Ossipee; b. Harrison, ME; ----- Stokes and Annie -----
Catherine B., d. 3/12/1982 at 91 in Ossipee; b. Milton, MA
Edward Jacob, d. 10/29/1972 at 63 in Ossipee; b. NH

STONE,
George, d. 2/15/1968 at 86 in Ossipee; b. VT
John Paul, d. 8/11/1994 at 69; Joseph Stone and Caroline Willow

STORER,
Ida M., d. 7/4/1893 at 57 in Ossipee; housewife; married; b. Wakefield; William Copp (Wakefield) and Mary Remick

John, d. 8/19/1892 at 59 in Ossipee; acute gastritis; farmer; married; b. Wakefield

STORRS,
Ethel A., d. 11/20/1981 at 88 in Ossipee; b. Brooklyn, NY

STOWE,
Gail, d. 7/5/1944 at 0/11/10 in Wolfeboro; b. Bridgton, ME; Philip Stowe and Irene Leso
William J., d. 5/26/1944 at 67/4/4 in Ossipee; b. Strafford

STRAIN,
David F., d. 7/13/1988 at 55 in Wolfeboro; b. S. Gate, CA

STREETER,
Joseph, d. 11/17/1930 at 90 in Ossipee; William Streeter and Phebe Lolladay
William H., d. 2/18/1960 at 72 in Ossipee; b. Sanbornville

STRICKLAND,
Geraldine A., d. 5/6/1989 at 75 in Ossipee; b. Westfield, MA

STUART,
Evelyn L., d. 3/11/1969 at 55 in Conway; b. MA
Joseph A., d. 3/14/1899 at 35 in Ossipee; dropsy; fireman; married; b. NS
Robert R., d. 8/20/1966 at 67 in Conway; b. Marlboro, MA

STURDIVANT,
Leon H., d. 2/9/1942 at 74/10/4 in Tamworth; b. Hardwick, MA; Charles R. Sturdivant and Mary J. Bond

STURGIS,
Mina D., d. 1/12/1898 at 29/8/12 in Ossipee; pneumonia; housewife; single; b. Ossipee; John Douglass (Bridgton, ME) and Hannah Jewell (Cornish, ME)
Theodore J., d. 12/29/1969 at 78 in Ossipee; b. MA

STURTEVANT,
Leroy E., d. 12/5/1992 at 77 in Ossipee; b. Haverhill, MA

SULLIVAN,
Andrew, d. 2/25/1911 at 22; old age (sic - probably should be pneumonia); farmer; married; b. Tuftonboro
Elsie A., d. 5/7/1986 at 79 in Wolfeboro; b. Leominster, MA

Margaret C., d. 9/28/1995 at 89; Frank Regine and Theresa Despino

SURRETTE,
Luis D., d. 1/7/1914 at 57; salesman; b. Concord, MA; Luis A. Surrette

SWANSBURG,
Nancy Brugman, d. 10/25/2001 in Ctr. Ossipee; Francis Brugman and Mary Grace
Stephen, d. 9/26/2001 in Ctr. Ossipee; George F. Swansburg and Nancy Brugman

SWASEY,
Betsy, d. 10/6/1894 at 82 in Ossipee; marasmus senilis; single; b. Wolfeboro

SWEAT,
daughter, d. 3/13/1910 at 0/8 in Ossipee; pharyngitis; b. Ossipee; Bessie Sweat (Wolfeboro)

SWEDLOVE,
Arthur, d. 7/11/1934 at 19/7/7 in Ossipee Lake; b. Roxbury, MA; Lewis Swedlove and Dora Kerrol

SWEENEY,
Dorothy E., d. 4/7/2000 at 87 in Ossipee; Samuel Sampson and Elizabeth Digue
Lillian Weiss, d. 1/21/2000 at 87 in Ossipee; Josef Weiss and Emma Zollier

SWEET,
Clyde A., d. 4/15/1955 at 74/4/21 in Ossipee; b. NH; Edgar Sweet and Ellen Schackett

SWEETLAND,
Gerald Esty, d. 4/28/1991 at 54 in Ossipee; b. Melrose, MA

SWEETZER,
son, d. 8/15/1904 at 0/0/2 in Ossipee; cyanosis neotonium; b. Ossipee; George Sweetzer and Bessie Ainsworth (Stowe, ME)

SWINERTON,
Anna M., d. 6/8/1990 at 79 in Wolfeboro; b. Wolfeboro

TALBOTT,
Cecil A., d. 12/3/1981 at 72 in Ossipee; b. Des Moines, IA

TALLMAN,
Ethel May, d. 6/4/1940 at 0/0/9 in Wolfeboro; b. Wolfeboro; Harry Tallman and Doris M. Brooks
Harry T., Jr., d. 3/15/1977 at 65 in Ossipee; b. ME

TANGLEY,
Ella M., d. 2/12/1983 at 95 in Ossipee; b. Lynn, MA

TAPPAN,
Harriett M., d. 10/2/1940 at 80 in Wolfeboro; b. Moultonboro; John B. Knowles and Betty J. Morrill
Sarah M., d. 11/24/1948 at 80/3/12 in Ossipee; b. Sandwich; Amos W. Bennett and Sarah Sanborn

TASKER,
Dana J., d. 5/2/1960 at 85 in Laconia; b. Milton
George F., d. 1/8/1925 at 58/1; b. Ossipee; Moses Tasker and Saloma Nichols
Julia A., d. 4/26/1960 at 81 in Ossipee; b. Ossipee
Lena S., d. 4/13/1971 at 94 in Laconia; b. NH
Moses, d. 1/24/1893 at 78 in Ossipee; farmer (see following entry)
Moses S., d. 1/24/1894 at 78 in Ossipee; pneumonia; farmer; married; b. Strafford; Joseph Tasker (see preceding entry)
Salome, d. 6/25/1901 at 79/7/28 in Ossipee; apoplexy; housewife; widow; b. Ossipee; James Nichols (Ossipee) and Lydia White (Ossipee)

TATE,
Eva M., d. 10/31/1962 at 61 in Ossipee; b. Laconia

TAYLOR,
Janice Appler, d. 4/1/1995 at 85; Charles Ross Apler and Ida Streeper Trayer
Marie K., d. 10/12/1992 at 78 in Ossipee; b. Hollis, ME
Nellie B., d. 7/1/1972 at 88 in Ossipee; b. NH
Winfield, d. 1/21/1911 at 47; septicemia; farmer; married; b. Milan; Jonathan Tyler (sic)

TEAL,
Frank H., d. 9/10/1913 at 52/3; salesman; married; b. Peabody, MA; George M. Teal and Abbie Swan

TEARE,
Helen M., d. 7/16/1972 at 89 in Ossipee; b. NY

TEBBETTS [see Tibbetts],
Dora A., d. 1/14/1989 at 64 in Wolfeboro; b. Nashua
Herbert W., d. 8/19/1987 at 67 in Wolfeboro; b. Foxboro, MA
Ida E., d. 8/21/1887 at 34/10/3 in Ossipee; housekeeper; married; b. Ossipee; Peter Welch (Ossipee)
Louise, d. 3/22/1890 at 70 in Ossipee; consumption of bowels; domestic; single; b. Ossipee
Marta, d. 2/29/1976 at 86 in Ossipee; b. NJ
Martha A., d. 4/18/1892 at 65 in Ossipee; erysipelas; housekeeper; married; b. Gorham; S. Manson and Eliza Sawyer
Maurice, d. 11/26/1945 at 55/1/8 in Ossipee; b. Ossipee; Charles Tebbetts and Lucy A. Hoyt
Moses P., d. 8/2/1888 at 63/3/17; farmer; widower; b. Ossipee; Edward Tebbetts and Sarah Colorn

TEELE,
Harold Leonard, d. 1/17/1979 at 76 in Ossipee; b. BWI

TEMPLETON,
child, d. 10/2/1927 at –; b. Ossipee; John Templeton and Louise Abbott
Afia, d. 10/29/1913 at 54/3/1; housework; single; b. Ossipee; Samuel Williams (Ossipee) and Esther Welch (Ossipee)
Ahial, d. 9/5/1909 at 78/6/8 in Ossipee; gastritis acute; farmer; b. Ossipee; John Templeton
Ahiel, d. 11/17/1925 at 28; b. Ossipee; Ahiel Templeton and Affie Williams
Annie, d. 1/20/1969 at 84 in N. Conway; b. NH
Arthena T., d. 10/1/1983 at 83 in Hanover; b. Ossipee
Arthur W., d. 10/15/1986 at 64 in N. Conway; b. Ossipee
C. A., d. 7/20/1919 at 59/9/23; laborer; single; b. Ossipee; Aheil Templeton (Washington) and Elmira Nichols (Ossipee)
Charles M., d. 11/30/1906 at 84 in Ossipee; paralysis heart; farmer; widower; b. Ossipee; John Templeton (Ossipee) and Judith Eldridge (Ossipee)
Fannie, d. 5/9/1890 at 1/11/1 in Ossipee; convulsions; b. Ossipee; Charles Templeton and Robine Templeton
Gertrude M., d. 6/23/1980 at 86 in Ossipee; b. ME
Harold, d. 9/25/1979 at 73 in Ossipee; b. NH
Ira, d. 7/31/1967 at 79 in Ossipee; b. Ossipee
John, d. 10/28/1927 at 26/11/28; b. Ossipee; Ahial Templeton and Effie Williams
Roberline, d. 5/31/1933 at 89/3/18 in Ossipee; b. Wolfeboro; Stephen Johnson and Sarah Jenness

Ruth D., d. 2/2/1986 at 68 in Wolfeboro; b. Ossipee

TENY,
son, d. 1/10/1915 at –; b. Ossipee; Frank Teney (NS) and Susan Rogers (Lowell, MA)

TER WEELE,
Margery Catherine, d. 4/12/2000 at 87 in Ossipee; Joshua Crane and Ethel M. Hill

TERGESSON,
Harry, d. 12/19/1953 at 55/1/1 in Ossipee; b. Norway; August Tergesson and Carolyn Hanson

TEWKSBURY,
Charles H., d. 3/24/1933 at 63/4/20 in Ossipee; b. Winthrop, MA; Charles H. Tewksbury and Francina Pendleton
Joseph, d. 2/21/1889 at 76; farmer; widower; b. Sandwich; T. Tewksbury and Mary Tewksbury
Nina S., d. 7/1/1947 at 66/2/7 in Wolfeboro; b. Effingham; Orrin Stillings and Augusta Chick

THAYER,
Russell J., d. 5/5/1961 at 65 in Beverly, MA; b. Grafton, OH

THEURER,
Harold Craig, d. 6/8/1994 at 68; Albert Theurer and Ema Rosenthal

THIBADEAU,
Peter, d. 5/23/1931 at 63 in Ossipee

THIBODEAU,
Ovila, d. 10/5/1968 at 70 in Ossipee; b. MA

THISSELL,
Anna, d. 3/7/1923 at 62; b. Ossipee; Jonathan Sias
Susie M., d. 11/9/1933 at 59/1/20 in Ossipee; b. Union; James Applebee and Hannah Bertwell
Theodore D., d. 11/15/1942 at 83/2/22 in Ossipee; b. Beverly, MA; Nichnolic Thissell and Mary A. Dodge

THISTLE,
Lillian, d. 7/25/1972 at 87 in Ossipee; b. MA

THOMAS,
Elfreda Jennie, d. 1/8/1996 at 91 in Ossipee; Frank J. Eldridge and Abbie Hodgdon
Frank Foster, d. 3/24/1996 at 85 in Ossipee; Wingate Thomas and Mabel R. Owen

THOMPKINS,
James F., d. 6/21/1956 at 90 in Ossipee; b. Presque Isle, ME; Humphrey Thompkins and Amelia Waters

THOMPSON,
Algernon, d. 3/4/1942 at 74/6/23 in Nashua; b. Effingham; Joseph Thompson and Ebbie Merrill
Alice Terrell, d. 8/9/1988 at 100 in Ossipee; b. Milton, MA
Carrie, d. 2/27/1958 at 93 in Amherst; b. Ossipee; James Bodge and Betsy Goodwin
Charles A., d. 10/2/1943 at 49/1/5 in Ossipee; b. Conway; Alvin Thompson and Ruth A. Davis
Charles Alman, d. 10/27/1940 at 72/6/17 in Ossipee; b. Ossipee; Allan Swasey and Sarah Thomson
Charlotte A., d. 6/12/1978 at 98 in Ossipee; b. NH
Cora, d. 5/11/1931 at 58 in Ossipee; b. Eaton; Daniel Thurston and Mary Littlefield
Dorothy M., d. 5/17/1987 at 87 in Ossipee; b. W. Newfield, ME
Eleazer, d. 1/17/1907 at 90 in Ossipee; old age; brick maker; single; b. Bartlett
Emeline, d. 8/20/1908 at 79/0/9 in Ossipee; cholera morbus; housewife; b. Ossipee; Joshua Canney (Dover) and Mary Davis (Madbury)
Emma W., d. 5/15/1952 at 70/2/17 in Ossipee; b. Ossipee; John P. Walker and Aurille Palmer
Frances M., d. 5/23/1925 at 0/0/2; b. Mountainview; Roy O. Thompson and Una G. Hutt
Frank F., d. 1/26/1944 at 71/0/21 in Ossipee; b. Cambridge, MA; Freeman F. Thompson and Sarah Bacon
Freeman, d. 5/15/1911 at 71; paralysis of heart
Ida E., d. 8/18/1946 at 86/2/1 in Ossipee; b. Ossipee; Issac Chadbourn and Emily Leighton
Jennie P., d. 3/22/1921 at 73/1/22 in Ossipee; housewife; widow; Albert W. Godfrey (Hampton) and Sarah Lamprey (Hampton)
John, d. 12/31/1931 at 80/7/15 in Ossipee; b. Tuftonboro; Theodore Thompson and Hannah Beacham
John G., d. 5/22/1962 at 74 in Wolfeboro; b. Effingham
LeRoy Oscar, d. 3/29/1949 at 58/3/3 in Ossipee; b. Cornish, ME; Thatcher Thompson and Mary Hodgdon

Mary E., d. 1/5/1945 at 72/3/15 in Wolfeboro; b. Cornish, ME; Francis Hodgdon and Lizzie Storer
Mildred Louise, d. 3/27/1993 at 82 in Ossipee
Nancy, d. 5/24/1939 at 72/4/7 in Ossipee; b. N. Conway; Lorensa Lamb and Susan Ann Eastman
Ruth Adams, d. 11/23/1977 at 84 in Ossipee; b. NY
Samuel J., d. 9/5/1914 at 81/6/17; millman; b. Ossipee; Samuel Thompson (Ossipee) and Betsy Canney (Ossipee)
Sarah F., d. 7/27/1956 at 80 in Wolfeboro; b. Ossipee; Jacob Abbott and Harriett Fernald

THORNDIKE,
George R., d. 2/4/1976 at 94 in Ossipee; b. MA

THURLEY,
Augusta, d. 5/19/1910 at 42 in Ossipee; marasmus; single; b. Ossipee
George H., d. 3/14/1897 at 53/8/24 in Ossipee; lobar pneumonia; farmer; married; B. T. Thurley
George H., Jr., d. 3/11/1897 at 25/4/2 in Ossipee; pneumonia; farmer; married; b. Ossipee; George H. Thurley (Ossipee) and Annie P. Hanson (Ossipee)
Helen G., d. 6/11/1976 at 101 in Center Harbor; b. NH
William, d. 3/16/1895 at 78/7/22 in Ossipee; enlargement heart

THURSTON,
daughter, d. 8/16/1938 at – in Wolfeboro; b. Wolfeboro; Parker Thurston and Madeline Eldridge
Ada E., d. 4/24/1924 at 71/3/1; b. Freedom; Simon Huckins and Cordelia Noble
Charles, d. 12/2/1932 at 72/2/12 in Ossipee; b. Wolfeboro; Isaac Thurston and Susan Avery
Clarence G., d. 2/8/1970 at 76 in Wolfeboro; b. NH
Clayton, d. 9/7/1917 at 22; farmer; single; b. Brownfield, ME; Martin V. Thurston (ME) and Addie Adams (NS)
Daniel, d. 5/3/1903 at 56 in Ossipee; carcinoma; farmer
Daniel C., d. 8/2/1976 at 44 in Hartford; b. NH
Danny O., d. 2/19/1956 at .55 days in Wolfeboro; b. Wolfeboro; Alfred J. Thurston and Jean M. Chase
Edith G., d. 4/8/1963 at 89 in Ossipee; b. Effingham
Hosmer C., d. 1/25/1946 at 64/6/20 in Ossipee; b. Charlestown, MA; Edwin E. Thurston and Ada Huckins
John E., d. 9/26/1972 at 79 in Rochester; b. NH
Lenora M., d. 2/1/1990 at 57 in Wolfeboro; b. Ossipee
Lois Eaton, d. 3/21/1995 at 86; Edwin Eaton and Grace Philbrick

Parker, d. 1/23/1996 at 81 in Ossipee; John Edwin Thurston and Sarah Stokes

Ruth Barbara, d. 8/29/1974 at 56 in Ossipee; b. MA

TIBBETTS [see Tebbetts],

Ada E., d. 9/14/1895 at 1/5/16 in Ossipee; cholera infantum; b. Ossipee; Charles Tibbetts (Portsmouth) and Lucy Hoyt

Adah, d. 1/16/1906 at 50 in Ossipee; tuberculosis; single; b. Tamworth

Arthur D., d. 10/15/1959 at 89 in Ossipee; b. Wolfeboro; Jeremiah Tibbetts and Jennie Gale

Charles Edwin, d. 1/7/1995 at 80; Archie H. Tibbetts and Abbey Wiggin

Charles W., d. 5/24/1912 at 63/0/16; farmer; married; b. Ossipee; Moses Tibbetts (Ossipee) and Clara Buswell

Charlotte, d. 7/14/1937 at 63/10/28 in W. Long Branch, NJ; b. England; William Young

Harriett Milliken, d. 5/22/1988 at 84 in Ossipee; b. Baldwin, ME

Ina M., d. 9/7/1889 at 1/9/14; b. Ossipee; John E. Tebbetts (sic) and Annie M. Tebbetts (sic)

Jessie M., d. 11/11/1979 at 96 in Ossipee; b. Canada

John G., d. 3/12/1903 at 86 in Boston; la grippe; widower

John H., d. 8/14/1920 at 72/7/24; laborer; widower; b. Wolfeboro; Moses Tibbetts (Wolfeboro) and Sarah York (Sandwich)

Lila Reed, d. 9/29/1987 at 91 in Ossipee; b. Columbia

Louis C., d. 10/7/1983 at 84 in Ossipee; b. Denmark, ME

Louis Everett, d. 11/9/1991 at 88 in Ossipee; b. Brookfield

Lucinda, d. 3/28/1903 at 90/0/28 in Ossipee; la grippe; housewife; widow; b. Ossipee; Timothy White

Martha, d. 5/20/1910 at 71/1 in Ossipee; anemia; widow; b. Kingston

Stephen R., d. 2/9/1902 at 79/9 in Ossipee; valvular disease of heart; farmer; widower; b. Eaton; Samuel Tibbetts and Betsey Hodsdon

Vesta, d. 2/24/1967 at 83 in Ossipee; b. Tilton

TIBBITTS [see Tibbetts],

Mary A., d. 4/27/1924 at 74/2/10; b. Ossipee; Henry C. Nichols and Lydia Nichols

TIGHE,

Helen B., d. 8/8/1928 at 44/10/21; b. Rollinsford; Joseph Tighe and Mary Fogarty

TILLINGHAST,

Louis C., d. 8/14/1975 at 67 in Ossipee; b. MA

TILTON,

Herman F., d. 8/15/1970 at 71 in Concord; b. NH

TIMMINS,
John A., d. 2/23/1963 at 64 in Ossipee; b. Newton, MA

TISDALE,
Jacqueline Ann, d. 12/3/1991 at 52 in Wolfeboro; b. Union, NY

TOAT,
Mary A., d. 3/3/1891 at 77 in Ossipee; domestic; widow; b. Gilmanton; John Dame (Wakefield)

TOBIN,
Perley A., d. 9/11/1958 at 76 in Ossipee; b. Waterville, VT; Christopher Tobin and Jennie Mann

TOLAR,
Rachel S., d. 8/22/1985 at 92 in Ossipee; b. Dover

TORREY,
Roswell, d. 10/22/1923 at 88; b. Limerick; Roawell Torry and Sarah Hardy

TOWLE,
Elizabeth M., d. 4/25/1908 at 83/2/25 in Ossipee; weak heart and asthma; b. Ossipee; Daniel Goldsmith (Ossipee) and Mary Sias (Ossipee)

TRACY,
Reynold L., d. 3/4/1990 at 82 in Ossipee; b. Bartlett

TRASK,
Alfred, d. 9/25/1939 at 63/8 in Concord; b. Sandwich; Charles Trask and Arbella -----

TRAVERSY,
Philip A., d. 5/12/1969 at 80 in Ossipee; b. MA

TRAVIS,
Maude S., d. 4/28/1982 at 74 in Ossipee; b. Brooklyn, NY

TREAMER,
Percy Vincent James Valentine, d. 8/9/1998 in W. Ossipee; Matthew George Treamer and Susannah Isabella Matthews

TRECARTEN,
Henrietta Linnea, d. 9/13/1972 at 80 in Ossipee; b. ME
Walter Neal, d. 4/11/1974 at 83 in Nashua; b. NH

TREFREY,
Edna Alice, d. 6/29/1999 at 71 in N. Conway; Walter C. Hutchins and Grace E. Robarge

TREMBLAY,
Alice T., d. 10/2/1972 at 89 in Wolfeboro; b. Canada
Eugene F., d. 2/12/1992 at 42 in Ossipee; b. Dover

TRIPP,
John W., d. 6/22/1967 at 60 in Ossipee; b. N. Conway

TRIPPLE,
Inez E., d. 4/19/1910 at 19/3/26 in Ossipee; acute tuberculosis of lungs; clerk; married; b. Topsfield, MA; Henry Jones (Rochester) and Nellie D. Jones

TROTMAN,
Scott Garrison, d. 7/24/1995 at 26; John F. Trotman and Ruth Crowell

TROTT,
Ica E., d. 6/16/1927 at 72/0/18; b. Wakefield; John Mathews and Elizabeth Emerson
Thayer S., d. 2/4/1922 at 72/8 in Ossipee; farmer; married; b. Portland, ME; Thomas B. Trott (Peaks Island, ME) and Deborah Lincoln
Winifred L., d. 4/21/1966 at 84 in Ossipee; b. Portland, ME

TROY,
John J., d. 5/28/1935 at 46/11/21 in Ossipee; b. Portsmouth; Robert Troy and Johanna Fitzpatrick

TRUE,
Cathrine, d. 11/3/1946 at 74/1/6 in Wolfeboro; b. Canada
Wilbur, d. 8/18/1943 at 70/2/18 in Wolfeboro; b. Salisbury, MA; Charles True

TUBMAN,
Daniel Colesworthy, d. 10/2/1993 at 68 in Madison
Lois Wright, d. 3/23/1995 at 67; J. Fred Wright and Martha Allard

TUCKER,
daughter, d. 9/18/1899 at 0/0/19 in Ossipee; bronchitis; b. Ossipee; Wilber Tucker (Ossipee) and Addie Templeton (Ossipee)
Madeleine Coolidge, d. 11/7/1993 at 88 in Ossipee
Morris A., d. 11/10/1976 at 79 in Ossipee; b. NH

Ralph M., d. 9/17/1996 at 92 in Ossipee; Wallace M. Tucker and Lettie E. -
----

Wallace M., d. 2/26/1936 at 78/11 in Ossipee; b. Kingston; Jacob P. Tucker and Mehitable Bean

TUCKERMAN,
Alice D., d. 5/3/1947 at 93 in Ossipee

TUFF,
Lillian, d. 1/9/1992 at 94 in Wolfeboro; b. Newfoundland

TULLEY,
James, d. 7/9/1912 at 72; laborer; b. ME
Leon, d. 12/27/1896 at 0/6 in Ossipee; bronchitis; b. Wolfeboro; James Tulley and Fanny Geralds

TURSCHMANN,
E. Blanche, d. 3/21/1988 at 90 in Ossipee; b. Middleton

TUTTLE,
Abbie F., d. 12/31/1984 at 90 in Ossipee; b. Wakefield
Marion T., d. 6/15/2000 in Exeter; Samuel Taylor and Nora Nichols
Rena M., d. 7/24/1970 at 41 in Ossipee; b. ME

TWOMBLY,
Edith L., d. 8/1/1979 at 94 in Ossipee; b. NH
Mary F., d. 2/6/1913 at 66; none [occupation]

TYLER,
Estella M., d. 11/27/1969 at 85 in Ossipee; b. NH
Leon, d. 10/26/1950 at 69 in Ossipee; b. Benton; Fred Tyler and Mary Keezar
Leslie H., d. 12/25/1991 at 86 in Ossipee; b. W. Milan
Raymond E., d. 7/8/1983 at 76 in Laconia; b. Albany, NY
Wayne P., d. 7/25/1999 in Wolfeboro; Norman Tyler and Una Elliott

USHER,
Bertha D., d. 2/14/1980 at 94 in Ossipee; b. MA

UTLEY,
Henry Lester, d. 4/5/1977 at 91 in Ossipee; b. MA

VALDMAA,
Pauline K., d. 7/6/1981 at 63 in Ossipee; b. Estonia

VALENTINE,
Donald C., d. 6/7/1975 at 24 in MA; b. MA

VALLEE,
Mandy, d. 8/20/1946 at 81/7/0 in Ossipee; b. Canada

VALLEY,
Lois A., d. 12/17/1987 at 53 in Wolfeboro; b. Ossipee

VALLIERE,
Lucy L., d. 12/10/2001 in Ossipee; Joseph Deschaies and Alvina Theberge

VAN BLARCOM,
Florence E., d. 8/9/1999 in Wolfeboro; Lincoln Robinson and Jeanette McPherson

VAN DYKE,
James P., d. 12/1/1980 at 57 in Wolfeboro; b. Dumont, NJ

VANDERPOOL,
John, d. 7/3/1957 at 98 in Ossipee; b. Worcester, NY; Henry Vanderpool and Elizabeth Hannis

VARNEY,
Ernest Raymond, d. 10/5/1995 at 83; George E. Varney and Emma Demeritt
Forrest Beecher, d. 1/14/1982 at 80 in Ossipee; b. Alton
Harold M., d. 6/19/1969 at 55 in Wolfeboro; b. NH
Ida B., d. 6/14/1965 at 93 in Ossipee; b. Wolfeboro
Sadie, d. 2/12/1941 at 60/11/3 in Ossipee; b. Moultonboro; John Knowles and Betsy Moulton
Sidney J., d. 3/16/1911 at 52; la grippe; caterer; b. Dover
Viola A., d. 6/24/1970 at 46 in Wolfeboro; b. NH

VEASEY,
Lavinia, d. 12/21/1903 at 73/10/8 in Ossipee; valvular disease of heart; housewife; single; b. Ossipee; Nathaniel Veasey (Brentwood) and Sarah Twombly (Dover)

VENDRILLO,
Margaret E., d. 9/5/1995 at 91; John Murray and Katherine Stapelton

VENOE,
son, d. 1/28/1891 at –; b. Ossipee; Joseph Venoe (Canada) and Rose Inarchand

VENTOLA,
Mary Ann Florence, d. 1/12/1997 at 93 in Ossipee; Henry Fisher and May Jenkins Merritt

VIENT,
Harold E., Sr., d. 9/6/1961 at 50 in Ossipee; b. Lynn, MA

VIGNEAULT,
William J., d. 7/13/1971 at 50 in Ossipee; b. MA

VINCENT,
Laura Josephine, d. 2/1/1993 at 82 in Wolfeboro

VINNICOMBE,
Blanche, d. 12/7/1968 at 85 in Ossipee; b. MA

VINTON,
daughter, d. 8/30/1960 at 0/0/1 in N. Conway; b. N. Conway
Elizabeth A., d. 12/21/1960 at 45 in Ossipee; b. Bridgeport, CT
Robert W., d. 1/5/1983 at 87 in Conway; b. Stoneham, MA
Roberta E., d. 5/13/1955 at 0/7/25 in Wolfeboro; b. NH; Robert Vinton and Elizabeth Allen

VISNEY,
John Victor, d. 5/2/1995 at 89; John Visney and Susanna -----

VITTUM,
Merton Clark, d. 11/29/1998 in Wolfeboro; Herbert Vittum and Alice Clark
Norman E., II, d. 7/30/1971 at 13 in Ossipee; b. NH
Rachel Merrow, d. 11/30/1989 at 79 in Ossipee; b. Ossipee

VOELKER,
Rauha Agnes, d. 9/24/2001 in Ossipee; Tuomas V. Wegelius and Sanna Lahtinen

VOSE,
Madeline Dyer, d. 11/7/1995 at 98; Edwin Haines Vose and Isadore Birsten

VOUSDEN,
Ellen B., d. 10/24/1956 at 83/2/4 in Ossipee; b. Kent, England; David Benge and Elizabeth Benge
William R., d. 1/18/1966 at 86 in Ossipee; b. England

WADE,
Bert C., d. 7/14/1937 at 71/11/11 in Wolfeboro; b. E. Bridgewater; Calvin Wade and Myra Anidon

WAKEFIELD,
Arthur Albert, d. 1/3/2001 in Ossipee; Clarence H. Wakefield and Clara M. Messer
Fred E., d. 2/21/1918 at 46/11/24; sawyer; married; b. Newton; Benjamin F. Wakefield (Brownfield, ME) and Mary A. Chapman (Tamworth)

WALDIE,
Dorothy Potts, d. 12/13/2000 at 84 in Ossipee; John Potts and Isabella ----
George Scott, d. 1/29/1997 at 83 in Ossipee; Alexander Waldie and Elin Larson

WALDRON,
Cora Emily, d. 3/4/1944 at 77/6/5 in Wolfeboro; b. Charlestown, MA; George H. Seman and Cordelia Rikeman
Llewellyn G., d. 5/4/1945 at 82/4/22 in Wolfeboro; b. Wakefield; John C. Waldron and Lydia Sevard

WALKDEN,
Alfred Thomas, d. 10/4/1991 at 66 in Wolfeboro; b. Fall River, MA

WALKER,
Aida, d. 3/3/1958 at 71 in Wolfeboro; b. Malden, MA; Franklin Miner and Emma Townsend
Adelaide, d. 1/4/1900 at 53 in Ossipee; acute gastritis; widow
Aurilla, d. 6/19/1917 at 68/10/18; divorced; b. Plymouth; Daniel Palmer (America) and Hannah Boyden
Bernice Irene, d. 12/19/1990 at 70 in Ossipee; b. Baldwin, ME
Betsey, d. 11/16/1888 at 95; domestic; widow
Charles, d. 9/5/1934 at 80/3/10 in Ossipee; b. Conway; Robert Walker and Lucinda Harriveau
James L. T., d. 3/23/1900 at 13/1/9 in Ossipee; fatty degeneration of heart; b. Ossipee; John C. Walker (Thorndike) and Marilla Palmer (Plymouth)
John P., d. 7/10/1891 at 52 in Effingham; married

Virginia Louise, d. 3/13/1939 at 0/0/27 in Milford; b. Nashua; E. Guy Walker and Hattie Parks

Warren F., d. 8/18/1963 at 77 in Wolfeboro; b. Malden, MA

William, d. 5/23/1906 at 0/0/5 in Ossipee; bronchitis; b. Kennebunkport; Benjamin Walker (Troy, ME) and Clara Ames (Ossipee)

WALLACE,

Bertha I., d. 9/10/1938 at 70/11/23 in Ossipee; b. Ossipee; Arthur Clay and Olive Tibbetts

Berthana, d. 8/14/1910 at 70 in Ossipee; ch. gastric catarrh; widow

Charles, d. 1/14/1918 at 40/11; minister; married; b. NB; William Wallace (NB) and Frances A. Fraser (NB)

David H., d. 6/15/1955 at 66/8/23 in Ossipee; b. NY; Rev. S. R. Wallace and Josephine Williamson

Donald Wilson, d. 2/14/1993 at 84 in Ossipee

Drusilla, d. 6/7/1906 at 75/0/22 in Ossipee; old age; widow

Emily, d. 10/7/1894 at 65/9/29 in Ossipee; telid rhinitis; housewife; married; b. Ossipee; Robert Merrow

Frank W., d. 1/12/1950 at 83/5/15 in Wolfeboro; b. Ossipee; Samuel Wallace and Bethany -----

Harry A., d. 6/9/1943 at 72/11/26 in Ossipee; b. Ossipee; Simeon P. Wallace and Emily Merrow

John, d. 10/4/1901 at 82 in Ossipee; senile gangrene; laborer; widower; --- Wiggin

Josephine L. H., d. 1/8/1914 at 75

Mary, d. 5/8/1900 at 80/9/12 in Ossipee; apoplexy; married

Simeon P., d. 11/30/1905 at 74/9/16 in Ossipee; paralysis agitans; farmer; married; Samuel Wallace

Susan B., d. 10/12/1939 at 73/9/28 in Ossipee; b. Freedom; Silas W. Brooks and Hannah Gentleman

WALLER,

Elmar, d. 1/6/1996 at 84 in Laconia; Fernand Waller and Elisa Glastberg

WALSH,

Arthur John, Sr., d. 1/31/1997 at 82 in Ossipee; William Walsh and Mary Igo

WANZER,

Jessie Houston, d. 1/31/2000 at 106 in Ossipee; William Spratt and Lillian Coates

WARD,

Anna Edna, d. 6/1/1982 at 96 in Ossipee; b. Newark, NJ

Anne L., d. 2/10/1966 at 63 in Wolfeboro; b. Harrington, ME

Daniel C., d. 4/4/1930 at 71/2/12 in Ossipee; b. Eaton; Daniel Ward and Mehitable Thompson
Emily A., d. 1/23/1894 at 68 in Ossipee; pneumonia; housewife; single; b. Freedom; H. Watson (Lee) and Patty Thurston (Lee)
Emma J., d. 4/19/1965 at 86 in Ossipee; b. Tuftonboro Ctr.
Ralph Asa, d. 2/25/1977 at 48 in Ossipee; b. NH
Susan, d. 7/30/1935 at 89/0/23 in Ossipee; Emily Watson

WARNER,
Charlotte Wheeler, d. 8/24/1996 at 92 in Wolfeboro; Martin Douglas and Charlotte Eleanor Mitchell

WARREN,
Charles, d. 7/27/1971 at 89 in Ossipee; b. ME
Earl Ray, d. 10/19/1974 at 84 in Wolfeboro; b. ME
Harry, d. 1/6/1941 at 65/0/27 in Ossipee; b. Madison; Henry G. Warren and Abbie E. Thompson

WASSON,
Annie L., d. 5/6/1910 at 4/9/29 in Ossipee; peritonitis; b. Ossipee; Joseph S. Wasson (NB) and Josie Colby (Ossipee)
Clarence W., d. 1/8/1996 at 94 in Ossipee; Joseph Wasson and Josephine Colby
Hazel M., d. 11/24/1986 at 89 in Wolfeboro; b. Dover, ME
Joseph, d. 5/18/1958 at 88 in Wolfeboro; b. Canada; Joseph Wasson and Nora Hurheleigh
Lena May, d. 11/24/1939 at 64/9/5 in Ossipee; b. Otis, ME; Benjamin J. Jordon and Alice E. Stanley
Leslie, d. 5/7/1991 at 79 in Wolfeboro; b. Ossipee
Perley J., d. 1/27/1986 at 89 in Ossipee; b. Ossipee

WATERHOUSE,
Leland L., d. 7/3/1997 at 73 in Wolfeboro; Lester Waterhouse and Irene Parshley

WATERS,
Marion, d. 6/9/1986 at 88 in Ossipee; b. Hyde Park, MA

WATSON,
Darlene J., d. 12/31/1980 at 35 in Ctr. Ossipee; b. Sanford, ME
Harriet S., d. 7/7/1955 at 81 in Rochester; b. NH; Jackson Shaw and Eliza Stevens
Melvin L., d. 6/9/1967 at 90 in Ossipee; b. Freedom
William Kirkman, d. 5/8/1994 at 83; William Watson and Bertha -----

William W., d. 12/17/1949 at 88/5/14 in Ossipee; b. Freedom; ----- and Mary A. Bean

WEBB,
Kenneth W., d. 12/27/1986 at 71 in Ossipee; b. Boston, MA

WEBBER,
Relief, d. 12/27/1889 at 85; domestic; widow
Susan R., d. 1/27/1894 at 59 in Ossipee; acute pasen'tous nep's; clothier; single; Horace Webber and Relief Tyler

WEBSTER,
Carroll, d. 8/31/1899 at 1/4/31 in Ossipee; killed by train; b. Ossipee
Florence B., d. 6/11/1962 at 78 in Ossipee; b. Ossipee
Georgia I., d. 10/21/1968 at 89 in Ossipee; b. NH
Locero, d. 3/13/1992 at 83 in Manchester; b. Hampstead
Minnie F., d. 11/28/1990 at 89 in Ossipee; b. Ossipee
Nelson, d. 5/31/1891 at 70 in Ossipee; farmer; widower; b. Sandwich; Josiah Webster (Sandwich) and Ruth Atwood (Sandwich)
Parker, d. 2/3/1924 at 64; b. Dover; Charles Webster and Sarah Hayes
Wilbur F., d. 4/3/1944 at 64/9/22 in Wolfeboro; b. Tamworth; Horace Webster and Ada S. Hobbs

WEED,
Ada C., d. 10/16/1928 at 43/11/19; b. Waterbury, CT; William C. Nicholson and Helen Beere
Rosemond S., d. 12/24/1927 at 82/10/4

WEEKS,
Albert, d. 6/5/1901 at 68 in Ossipee; emphysema; farmer; single
Calvin, d. 12/31/1904 at 75 in Ossipee; paralysis of heart; single; b. Ossipee; John Weeks (Ossipee) and Polly -----
Eliza, d. 10/31/1903 at 78 in Ossipee; cerebral hemorrhage; housewife; married
Eliza, d. 12/18/1904 at 79/5 in Ossipee; heart failure; domestic; single; John Webb (sic) (Ossipee) and Polly Nason (Ossipee)
Hephzibah, d. 12/28/1896 at 80/11/11 in Ossipee; old age; widow; b. Springvale, ME; Elisha Goodwin (Springvale, ME) and Mary Hooper (Springvale, ME)
Isabel M., d. 9/27/1918 at 68/10/5; housewife; married; b. Ossipee; Joseph Q. Rolss (Ossipee) and Mary E. Wood (Dover)
Levi B., d. 12/12/1916 at 66/10/10; farmer; single; b. Ossipee; Levi Weeks (Wakefield) and Hephz'h Goodwin (Shapley)
Polly, d. 8/15/1889 at 89; widow

Rhoda, d. 8/17/1894 at 53/6/10 in Ossipee; gastro enteritis; housewife; single; b. Ossipee; John Welch and Polly Mason (Ossipee)
Rubin Wyman, d. 1/9/1947 at 94/7/1 in Ossipee; b. Bartlett; Josiah Weeks and Mary Eastman
Sarah J., d. 9/27/1935 at 93/10/10 in Ossipee; b. Ossipee; Levi Weeks and Hepzebar Goodwin
William, d. 9/30/1959 at 82 in Wolfeboro; b. Wakefield; Brackett Weeks and Matilda Allen

WELCH,
daughter, d. 2/16/1888 at 0/0/12; b. Ossipee; Lyford Welch and Elizabeth Eldridge
son, d. 1/2/1889 at 1/7; b. Ossipee; John B. Welch and Carrie Templeton
daughter, d. 3/29/1890 at – in Ossipee; deformed and premature; b. Ossipee; John S. Welch (Ossipee) and Almira Knox (Ossipee)
son, d. 2/26/1894 at 0/0/16 in Ossipee; bronchitis; b. Ossipee; Silas Welch (Ossipee)
son, d. 10/22/1900 at 1/4 in Ossipee; acute tuberculosis; b. Ossipee; James Welch (Ossipee) and Mabel Shultz (Charlestown)
daughter, d. 1/12/1905 at – in Ossipee; stillborn; b. Ossipee; Silas Welch (Ossipee) and E. Templeton (Ossipee)
child, d. 4/1/1942 at 0/0/12 in Wolfeboro; b. Wolfeboro; Kenneth Welch and Elizabeth Pearson
Agnes B., d. 9/22/1906 at 3/7/3 in Ossipee; acute nephritis; b. Ossipee; Silas Welch (Ossipee) and Emma Templeton (Ossipee)
Allie, d. 3/30/1968 at 74 in Ossipee; b. NH
Alston B., d. 10/17/1953 at 75 in Wolfeboro; b. Ossipee; Jeremiah Welch and Ellen Welch
Bertha, d. 9/12/1942 at 59/10/23 in Wolfeboro; b. Ossipee; Fonila Merrow and Barbara E. Silsby
Blanche E., d. 8/2/1959 at 60 in Ossipee; b. Tuftonboro; Howard Emery and Emma Swasey
Carrie M., d. 7/18/1971 at 79 in Wolfeboro; b. NH
Charles, d. 11/16/1918 at 31/5/20; laborer; single; John S. Welch (Ossipee) and Elmira Knox (Ossipee)
Charles P., d. 4/7/1900 at 39/5/2 in Ossipee; pulmonary tuberculosis; teamster; single; b. Ossipee; Peter Welch (Ossipee) and Abbie Blaisdell (Lebanon)
Chester R., d. 12/26/1985 at 72 in Ossipee; b. Ossipee
Cora B., d. 2/19/1953 at 72/10/2 in Ossipee; b. Ossipee; Valentine Davis and Abbie Davis
Cyrus, d. 11/26/1905 at 4/5 in Ossipee; meningitis; b. Ossipee; Walter S. Welch (Ossipee) and Dora Davis (Ossipee)
Deborah P., d. –/–/1897 at 83/6 in Ossipee; weak heart; single; b. Ossipee; Paul Welch (Ossipee) and Hannah Williams (Ossipee)

Dorothy Louise, d. 8/10/2001 in Ossipee; Benjamin French and Lillian M. Roy

Edville O., d. 11/1/1941 at 74/2/21 in Ossipee; b. Ossipee; William H. Welch and Eliza J. Tibbetts

Elizabeth, d. 7/11/1940 at 77/8/14 in Ossipee; b. Meredith; Alpheus Eldridge and Dorothy Jenness

Ellen J., d. 11/15/1915 at 69/3; housewife; widow; b. Ossipee; Brasilla Welch (Ossipee) and Julia Templeton

Elmira, d. 6/15/1948 at 90/11/14 in Ossipee; b. Ossipee; Thomas Y. Knox and Hannah Welch

Emma, d. 7/20/1910 at – in Ossipee; mitral regurgitation; housewife; widow; b. Ossipee; Ahial Templeton

Emma F., d. 9/16/1936 at 44/10/10 in Ossipee; Andrew Demerritt and Kate E. Brown

Ernest L., d. 6/28/1888 at 0/10; b. Ossipee; Orin E. Welch and Mary White

Ervin W., d. 11/8/1918 at 22/8/11; laborer; single; b. Ossipee; John S. Welch (Ossipee) and Elmira Knox (Ossipee)

Fannie, d. 4/14/1898 at 7/5/15 in Ossipee; pneumonia; b. Ossipee; John Welch (Ossipee) and Carrie Templeton (Ossipee)

Fanny, d. 10/3/1948 at 67/2/4 in Wolfeboro; b. Porter, ME; Warren Merrifield and Eliza Jose

Fred J., d. 6/28/1969 at 77 in Wolfeboro; b. NH

George, d. 8/31/1964 at 81 in Wolfeboro; b. Ossipee

George H., d. 6/1/1900 at – in Ossipee; tuberculosis; laborer; single; b. Ossipee; Peter Welch and Abbie Blaisdell (Lebanon)

George W., d. 5/10/1887 at 64/9/18 in Ossipee; farmer; widower; b. Ossipee; James Welch

Harry D., d. 6/2/1966 at 76 in Ossipee; b. Ossipee

Helen B., d. 11/27/1990 at 93 in Ossipee; b. Farmington

Henry, d. 3/20/1908 at 68/11/12 in Ossipee; cancer of neck; farmer; b. Ossipee; Silas Welch (Ossipee) and Aphia Nichols (Ossipee)

Idella M., d. 6/2/1974 at 77 in Wolfeboro; b. NH

Jennie E., d. 1/17/1951 at 81 in Moultonboro; b. Ossipee

Jeremiah P., d. 9/16/1914 at 73; farmer; b. Ossipee; Paul Welch (Ossipee) and Lucy Varney (Ossipee)

John, 3rd, d. 5/2/1910 at 75/1/22 in Ossipee; cancer of bladder; farmer; married; b. Ossipee; Silas Welch (Ossipee) and Aphia Welch (Ossipee)

John B., d. 12/17/1893 at 43 in Ossipee; farmer; married; b. Ossipee; B. Welch (Ossipee) and J. A. Templeton (Ossipee)

John H., d. 3/30/1900 at 81 in Ossipee; carcinoma; married; b. Ossipee

John S., d. 3/13/1920 at 72; laborer; married; b. Ossipee; John Welch (Ossipee) and Susan Welch (Ossipee)

Laford, d. 12/7/1893 at 36/11 in Ossipee; farmer; married; b. Ossipee; B. Welch (Ossipee) and J. A. Templeton (Winsor)

Laura B., d. 5/21/1975 at 70 in Wolfeboro; b. Canada
Lawrence E., d. 4/16/1988 at 77 in Ossipee; b. Ossipee
Leon J., d. 1/31/1963 at 69 in Manchester; b. Ossipee
Lewis, d. 9/27/1913 at 0/4/19; b. Ossipee; Harry S. Welch (Ossipee) and Carrie M. Emery (Ossipee)
Lydia E., d. 8/17/1963 at 66 in Meredith; b. Canada
Lydia M., d. 11/23/1929 at 84/7 in Ossipee; b. Cornish, ME; Acel Cook and Desire Brown
Mary, d. 9/28/1903 at 76/5 in Ossipee; chronic bronchitis; housewife; widow; b. Ossipee; John Welch (Ossipee) and Jane Welch (Ossipee)
Moses, d. 4/24/1957 at 78/9/2 in Ossipee; b. Ossipee; Moses B. Welch and Sarah Welch
Moses P., d. 9/22/1919 at 73/2; farmer; married; b. Ossipee; Paul Welch (Ossipee) and Lucy Varney (Ossipee)
Orrin E., d. 6/30/1940 at 78/0/2 in Wolfeboro; b. Ossipee; John Welch and Lydia Elliott
Paul Joseph, d. 10/3/1995 at 69; Benjamin Welch and Estella -----
Peter, d. 8/23/1898 at 73/8 in Ossipee; hepaticus; farmer; married; b. Ossipee
Peter P., d. 10/27/1954 at 65 in Rochester; b. Ossipee; Lyford Welch and Lizzie Eldridge
Philip W., d. 5/26/1956 at 22/9/13 in Ossipee; b. W. Ossipee; Laurence Welch and Dorothy Brown
Preston E., d. 2/26/1976 at 64 in Wolfeboro; b. NH
Ruth Elizabeth, d. 4/12/1991 at 72 in Wolfeboro; b. Ossipee
Sara J., d. 11/25/1926 at 79/5/13; b. Ossipee; John Welch and Susie Welch
Sesipta, d. 1/4/1912 at 71; widow
Silas, d. 12/31/1906 at 47/3 in Ossipee; carcinoma of stomach; farmer; married; b. Ossipee; John Welch (Ossipee) and Susan Welch (Ossipee)
Silas, Jr., d. 1/18/1898 at 0/1/7 in Ossipee; tonsillitis; b. Ossipee; Silas Welch (Ossipee) and Emma Templeton (Ossipee)
Theiza, d. 11/16/1889 at 0/4; b. Ossipee; John B. Welch and Carrie Templeton
Vera I., d. 10/10/1948 at 36/9/6 in Ossipee; b. Tuftonboro; Warren C. Bodge and Maude F. Hanson
Walter S., d. 4/12/1948 at 71/9/27 in Laconia; b. Ossipee; Jeremiah Welch and Ellen Welch
Wilber S., d. 3/24/1892 at 27 in Ossipee

WELLMAN,
Delia, d. 9/10/1914 at 60; housewife; b. Effingham; Asa Clark (Effingham)

WELSH,
Anice C., d. 2/25/1960 at 97 in Ossipee; b. Moultonboro

WENTWORTH,
Amanda, d. 12/8/1887 at 51 in Ossipee; single; b. Ossipee
Andrew, d. 3/4/1904 at 74 in Ossipee; nephritis acute; fireman
Bertha May, d. 11/28/1887 at 8 in Ossipee; b. Ossipee; George E. Wentworth (Lowell, MA) and Susan F. (Falmouth)
Betsy, d. 2/20/1899 at 85 in Ossipee; paralysis of heart; housekeeper; widow
D. W. C., d. 5/6/1901 at 85 in Ossipee; ch. bronchitis; farmer; married; b. Wakefield; Elias Wentworth and Lydia Chadwick
Daniel, d. 5/8/1904 at 71/0/14 in Ossipee; cerebral embolism; farmer; married; b. Ossipee; Daniel Wentworth and Mariah Scates (Ossipee)
Frank, d. 3/1/1928 at 65
Fred S., d. 1/10/1943 at 75/5/12 in Ossipee; b. Acton, ME; James Wentworth and Elizabeth Gilman
Gordon C., d. 2/17/1981 at 76 in Ossipee; b. Somersworth
Ida M., d. 12/31/1894 at 2/6 in Conway; meningitis
Ira, d. 11/17/1905 at 68 in Ossipee; valvular disease of heart; driver; single; b. Jackson
Irving, d. 8/31/1948 at 77/8/29 in Ossipee; b. Wolfeboro; Mark Wentworth and Harriet Gerry
Jeanne Annette, d. 7/6/2000 at 72 in W. Ossipee; David Stocks and Frances Smith
M. J., d. 8/11/1918 at 82/10/20; housewife; widow; b. Effingham; Oliver Chadbourne (Berwick, ME) and Mary Fan (Madbury)
Martha, d. 6/19/1890 at 47/11/7 in Ossipee; cancer; housekeeper; married; b. Ossipee; Caleb Hodgdon and Mrs. Champion
Mary, d. 6/4/1899 at 78/1/18 in Ossipee; apoplexy; housekeeper; widow; b. Milton; Samuel Wallingford (Milton) and Sally Worcester (Berwick)
Mary D., d. 11/4/1906 at 84/8 in Ossipee; old age; housewife; widow; b. Salem; Eliphalet Page and Hannah Dinsmore
Susan, d. 4/3/1901 at 93/4/24 in Ossipee; influenza; widow; b. Tamworth; Samuel Ames (Newmarket) and Susie Glidden (Durham)
Walter E., d. 3/27/1996 at 95 in Ossipee; Henry E. Wentworth and Mabel Heath

WEST,
Alice A., d. 9/8/1985 at 89 in Ossipee; b. Brentwood
Lillian, d. 4/15/1979 at 92 in Ossipee; b. NH
Nancy B., d. 12/14/1994 at 63; John C. Hutton and Emma F. Clark

WESTCOTT,
Dorothea Frances, d. 10/28/1988 at 83 in Ossipee; b. Rochester

WESTON,
Alfred, d. 9/13/1923 at 79/3/10; b. Wolfeboro; William Weston
Edward Everett, d. 6/6/1995 at 87; Edward Weston and Edith Coleman
John, d. 3/27/1906 at 72/2/7 in Ossipee; gastritis; farmer; widower; b. Fryeburg, ME; Edward Weston (Lincoln, MA) and Rachel Lord (Fryeburg, ME)
Priscilla, d. 10/4/1986 at 75 in Wolfeboro; b. Montreal, Canada

WEYMOUTH,
child, d. 4/25/1912 at 0/0/1; b. Ossipee; G. F. Weymouth (Wakefield) and Ethel Eldridge (Ossipee)
John H., d. 9/18/1912 at 28/10/7; married

WHALEY,
Kenneth A., d. 3/5/1990 at 82 in Ossipee; b. Providence, RI

WHEATON,
Lutena, d. 2/2/1889 at 27/8/24; housekeeper; married; James Milliken

WHEELER,
F. Robert, d. 2/6/1999 at 92 in Ossipee; Frederick Wheeler and Nora Sullivan
Leon C., d. 11/5/1958 at 78 in Ossipee; b. Rockland, MA; Charles Wheeler and Beulah Monk
Philip J., d. 1/13/1936 at 0/0/3 in Wolfeboro; b. Wolfeboro; Fred K. Wheeler and Ruth Olgen Pike

WHIPPLE,
Blanche, d. 12/1/1973 at 91 in Ossipee; b. NH

WHITCROFT,
Russell, d. 4/7/1896 at 23 in Ossipee; valvular disease of the heart; clerk; single; G. H. Whitcroft

WHITE,
son, d. 9/21/1959 at – in Wolfeboro; b. Wolfeboro; Harold White and Frances Dow
Ada, d. 11/6/1936 at 36 in Pembroke; b. Ossipee; Calbert Williams and Helen Nichols
Agnes May, d. 11/21/1973 at 55 in Wolfeboro; b. NH
Allen A., d. 12/5/1940 at 80/1/14 in Ossipee; b. Ossipee; Daniel White and Myrah J. Gannett

Allen H., d. 3/8/1903 at 27/11/22 in Ossipee; gunshot wound of abdomen; blacksmith; single; b. Ossipee; W. H. White (Ossipee) and Mary Williams (Moultonboro)

Anita Elizabeth, d. 1/2/1944 at 0/3/25 in Ossipee; b. Wolfeboro; Harold E. White and Frances A. Dow

Augusta M., d. 12/1/1931 at 71/9/9 in Ossipee; b. Effingham; Lorenzo Champion and Sarrina Day

Belmont A., d. 7/15/1958 at 58 in Ossipee; b. Ossipee; Scott White and Reusina Welch

Bernard Lee, d. 7/28/2000 at 74 in Ossipee; Belmont White and Grace Eldridge

Catherine E., d. 2/28/1987 at 89 in Wolfeboro; b. Melrose, MA

Charles A., d. 2/15/1932 at 77/5/15 in Ossipee; b. Ossipee; Allen White and Elizabeth Lougee

Charles W., d. 12/13/1921 at 66/4/13 in Ossipee; retired; married; Josiah G. White (Ossipee) and Hannah M. Devnell (Haverhill, MA)

Chester A., d. 10/18/1971 at 68 in Ossipee; b. NH

Cythera A., d. 7/3/1946 at 83/7/19 in Ossipee; b. Tamworth; Alonzo Nickerson and Melissa Ham

Daniel A., d. 5/22/1931 at 66/11/16 in Ossipee; b. Ossipee; Mayhew White and Jane Wallace

David N., d. 1/15/1922 at 77/6/15 in Ossipee; farmer; widower; b. Ossipee; Nat White (Ossipee)

Elizabeth A., d. 6/29/1965 at 88 in Wolfeboro; b. Freedom

Ella M., d. 10/5/1961 at 88 in N. Conway; b. Ossipee

Elmer Clifford, d. 5/30/1995 at 71; James R. White and Jennie Rowe

Emma J., d. 2/18/1937 at 79/0/2 in Ctr. Ossipee; b. Ossipee; John F. Palmer and Emily H. Merrow

Estella May, d. 10/11/1993 at 94 in Wolfeboro

Eunice A., d. 7/30/1916 at 71/10; none [occupation]; married; b. Ossipee; Moses C. Nutter (Ossipee) and Loisa Chick (Ossipee)

Frances A., d. 2/3/1999 in Laconia; Ellis Dow and Agnes Phinny

George B., d. 3/9/1900 at 39/11/23 in Ossipee; chronic gastritis; merchant; widower; b. Ossipee; Allen White (Ossipee) and Elizabeth Lougee (Parsonsfield)

George O., d. 11/2/1902 at 53/10/9 in Ossipee; heart failure; watchmaker; married; b. Ossipee; Josiah G. White (Ossipee) and Miranda Page

Golden M., d. 7/20/2001 in N. Conway; William May and Nellie Potter

Grace Bertha, d. 3/29/1988 at 81 in Ossipee; b. Ossipee

Hannah M., d. 9/22/1899 at 66/10/15 in Ossipee; senile gangrene; widow; b. Strafford; Jomes Dennell (England) and Elizabeth Tucker (Strafford)

Jane, d. 8/21/1910 at 84/3/27 in Ossipee; cholera morbus; housewife; widow; b. Ossipee; Samuel White (Effingham) and Dolly French (Effingham)

John W., d. 8/6/1888 at 41/11/23; laborer; single; b. Tuftonboro; Mayhew C. White and Jane Wallace

Josiah G., d. 3/22/1895 at 77/5/26 in Ossipee; enlargement heart and gangrene; farmer; b. Tamworth; Timothy White and Esther Ross (Kennebunk)

Kate E., d. 4/3/1892 at – in Ossipee; pl. phthisis

Kenwood Charles, d. 2/29/1983 at 81 in Wolfeboro; b. Ossipee

Lowenstein L., d. 1/5/1929 at 56/8/8 in W. Ossipee; b. Haverhill, MA; George O. White and Elizabeth A. Felker

Lyman C., d. 12/19/1914 at 82/0/4; millman; b. Canton, NY; ----- (NY) and Perline Abernethy (NY)

Maria Conry, d. 7/27/1939 at 64/9/16 in Ossipee; b. Sligo, Ireland; James Conry and Beatrice Lang

Mayhew C., d. 6/20/1888 at 66/4; farmer; married; b. Tuftonboro; John White and Jane Wallace

Mayhew O., d. 3/16/1917 at 57; farmer; married; b. Ossipee; Mayhew O. White (Ossipee) and Jane Wallace (Ossipee)

Minnie C., d. 3/9/1926 at 44/5/9; b. Ossipee; David N. White and Eunice A. Nutter

Nathaniel, d. 1/2/1912 at 93/3/3; farmer; widower; b. Ossipee; Silas White (Ossipee) and D. Plummer (Ossipee)

Orlando L., d. 11/21/1888 at 39/4/9; merchant; single; b. Ossipee; Allen White and Elizabeth B. Lougee

Reufina Beatrice, d. 3/30/1939 at 68/11/10 in Ctr. Ossipee; b. Ossipee; William Henry Welch and Eliza Jane Tibbetts

Rodney Allen, Sr., d. 12/17/1997 at 69 in Wolfeboro; Belmont Asa White and Grace Eldridge

Sarah, d. 1/30/1891 at 55 in Ossipee; housekeeper; married; b. Ossipee

Scott Lougee, d. 8/20/1941 at 74/8/8 in Ossipee; b. Ossipee; Allen White and Elizabeth Lougee

Violet R., d. 8/30/1914 at 0/10/25; b. Revere, MA; Joseph W. White (Hyde Park, MA) and Rena Bovering (Newfoundland)

Virgil D., d. 6/15/1964 at 75 in Wolfeboro; b. Ossipee

Walter Gordon, d. 4/9/1996 at 96 in Wolfeboro; Lowenstein L. White and Elizabeth A. Pascoe

Willie E., d. 11/17/1893 at 16/0/22 in Ossipee; single; b. Ossipee; Henry White (Ossipee) and Mary Williams (Effingham)

WHITEHOUSE,

Asa, d. 2/23/1900 at 84/11 in Ossipee; pneumonia; married; b. Brookfield

Caroline S., d. 7/30/1926 at 81; b. Ossipee; Thomas Peavey and Deborah Sherburne

Charles, d. 2/13/1900 at 45 in Ossipee; acute nephritis; laborer

Charles C., d. 11/28/1914 at 55/9/19; farmer; b. Ossipee; Ezra D. Whitehouse (Tuftonboro) and Sara P. Hilton (Ossipee)

Cora B., d. 3/31/1946 at 83/9/19 in Laconia; b. Ossipee; Henry Kenney and Sarah Weed

Dana, d. 4/8/1932 at 79/6/17 in Ossipee; b. Tuftonboro; Wesley Whitehouse and Matilda Thompson

Ezra D., d. 12/28/1905 at 75/11/28 in Ossipee; heart disease; farmer; married; b. Ossipee

Gladys, d. 10/28/1987 at 69 in Ossipee; b. Moultonboro

James, d. 8/29/1894 at 6/6/21 in Ossipee; accidental; b. Charlestown, MA; E. E. Whitehouse (Ossipee)

John, d. 1/24/1958 at 97 in Concord; b. NH; Wesley Whitehouse and Matilda Thompson

Laura Ellis, d. 1/4/1971 at 72 in Ossipee; b. NY

Sarah P., d. 6/23/1908 at 75/11/3; cerebral embolism; housewife; b. Ossipee; Richard Hilton (Ossipee) and Nancy Dore (Ossipee)

William, d. 9/5/1891 at 28 in Ossipee; blacksmith; single; b. Ossipee; W. Whitehouse (Tuftonboro) and Phebe F. Hanson (Ossipee)

WHITING,

Addie P., d. 1/2/1975 at 59 in Ossipee; b. NH

Clifford C., d. 1/22/1977 at 65 in Ossipee; b. NH

Clyde, d. 12/5/1913 at 0/3/19; b. Ossipee; Leon Whiting (Ossipee) and Mollie Francis

Cora, d. 3/4/1952 at 89 in Rochester; b. Ossipee; George H. Smith and Mary Bunker

Duane M., d. 1/16/1949 at 0/3/18 in Ossipee; b. Wolfeboro; Russell F. Whiting and Helen Eldridge

Leon L., d. 11/29/1938 at 62/6/21 in Ossipee; b. Tamworth; George Whiting and Nettie Swain

Mary F., d. 1/13/1953 at 65 in Tuftonboro; b. Cambridge, MA; Joseph Francis and Rose Gomey

Russell F., Sr., d. 3/12/1990 at 62 in Wolfeboro; b. Ossipee

WHITTEMORE,

son, d. 3/8/1947 at – in Wolfeboro; b. Wolfeboro; James F. Whittemore and Florence E. Foster

Susan, d. 3/19/1889 at 72; domestic; widow; b. Wolfeboro

WHITTEN,

Samuel, d. 2/14/1953 at 93 in Ossipee; b. Moultonboro; Joseph Whitten and Sarah Wallace

WHITTIER,

Everett M., d. 8/5/1968 at 70 in Wolfeboro; b. NH

Sarah, d. 11/7/1898 at – in Ossipee; caravona

WHITTUM,
Viola Vada, d. 3/28/1972 at 71 in Ossipee; b. MA

WHYNOTT,
T. Raymond, d. 7/21/1972 at 50 in Ossipee; b. MA

WICKER,
Minion E., d. 6/9/1947 at 68/4/2 in Wolfeboro; b. Sandwich; Wesson Pettingill and ----- Bennett

WIDERSTROM,
Wilbert Frederick, d. 5/16/1993 at 79 in Ossipee

WIDMAN,
Edna C., d. 4/9/1975 at 79 in Wolfeboro; b. WI

WIGGIN,
child, d. 9/5/1893 at 0/8 in Ossipee; William Wiggin
Alice, d. 8/16/1982 at 99 in Ossipee; b. Malden, MA
Charles A., d. 3/4/1943 at 78/3/12 in Ossipee; b. Ossipee; George P. Wiggin and Eliza Allen
Charles G., d. 3/17/1962 at 82 in Concord; b. Ossipee
Edwin, d. 11/7/1952 at 69 in Dover; b. Ossipee; William Wiggin and Sophie -----
Edwin D., d. 3/3/1893 at 47 iun Ossipee; married; R. L. Wiggin (Tuftonboro) and M. J. Demerritt (Thornton)
Effie May, d. 1/15/1950 at 83/2/5 in Ossipee; b. Middleton, MA; Elden Bennett and Ella Tewksbury
Elizabeth, d. 3/13/1926 at 89/6/27
Ella M., d. 12/2/1899 at 59 in Ossipee; carcinoma; rubber mfg.; single; b. Tuftonboro
Esther, d. 12/31/1901 at 6 in Ossipee; meningitis; b. Ossipee; Arthur Wiggin (Ossipee)
Ethel, d. 1/21/1903 at 11/10/13 in Ossipee; pernicious anemia; b. Ossipee; William H. Wiggin (Moultonboro) and Sophronia Eldridge (Ossipee)
George P., d. 10/30/1916 at 80/6/4; farmer; widower; b. Ossipee; Frederick Wiggin and Hannah Gilman
Grover C., d. 4/22/1960 at 75 in Ossipee; b. Ossipee
Hazell, d. 12/6/1897 at 3/4/29 in Ossipee; congestion lungs; b. Ossipee; Charles Wiggin (Ossipee) and Effie Bennett
Jeremiah, d. 8/2/1914 at 72/1/29; stonemason; b. Moultonboro; Jeremiah Wiggin (Wakefield) and Lizzie Williams (Ossipee)
Jerry, d. 6/22/1942 at 59/5/21 in Ossipee; b. Ossipee; Jeremiah Wiggin and Elizabeth M. Welch

John C. F., d. 5/8/1888 at 27/6/10; merchant; single; b. Ossipee; John G. Wiggin and Lovina Wiggin

Laura, d. 9/12/1969 at 84 in Benton; b. MA

Lavinia E., d. 12/27/1914 at –; housework; b. Ossipee; Daniel Merrow (Wakefield) and Sarah Garland (Ossipee)

Linda L., d. 3/36/1988 at 40 in Wolfeboro; b. Wolfeboro

M. E., Mrs., d. 8/20/1934 at 49/11/28 in Ossipee; b. Ossipee; John F. Horne and Jennie Smith

Margaret, d. 3/27/1982 at 86 in Salem; b. Yarmouth, NS

Mary A., d. 2/28/1907 at 67/4/24 in Ossipee; cerebral embolism; housewife; married; b. Ossipee; Edward White (Ossipee) and Delenia Brown (Dover)

Pierce C., d. 4/5/1938 at 47/79 in Ossipee; b. Wolfeboro; Pierce C. Wiggin and Hattie Leavitt

Shirley W., d. 7/13/1980 at 70 in Wolfeboro; b. NH

Sophia, d. 10/26/1931 at 72 in Ossipee; b. Ossipee; Daniel Eldridge and Susan Eldridge

Thelma H., d. 10/29/1981 at 75 in Wolfeboro; b. Dover

Velma Meloon, d. 11/18/1973 at 86 in Ossipee; b. NH

William H., d. 4/8/1910 at 67/2/1 in Ossipee; pneumonia; millman; married; b. Moultonboro; Jeremiah Wiggin (NY) and Lizzie Williams (Effingham)

WIGNOT,

Richard Gordon, d. 6/28/1999 at 94 in Ossipee; Jacob Ernest Wignot and Mary Alena Carmichael

WILCOX,

Lillian M., d. 2/11/1974 at 85 in Ossipee; b. ME

WILDER,

George F., d. 3/27/1892 at 35 in Ossipee; heart failure; sta. agent; married; C. W. Wilder

WILDES,

Ellen A., d. 2/26/1988 at 102 in Ossipee; b. Lawrence, MA

WILES,

May Valdine, d. 8/5/1997 at 94 in Ossipee; William M. Damlin and Mathilda Lund

WILEY,

Beverly Sherwood, d. 1/11/1998 in Ossipee; Walter Sherwood and Florence Moorhouse

WILFRET,
Sarah C., d. 12/11/1942 at 72/6/23 in Ossipee; b. NY

WILKINS,
Abbie J., d. 12/23/1922 at 77/10/23 in Ossipee; housewife; widow; b. Chatham; Newell Cook (Fryeburg, ME)
Agnes J., d. 1/1/1965 at 65 in Ossipee; b. Boston, MA
Cary, d. 3/16/1916 at 71/2/17; farmer; married; b. Norfolk, VA; Jacob Wilkins and Vena ----
Dora S., d. 8/29/1953 at 72 in Laconia; b. ME; Frank Sawyer and Elura Shaw
Elmer L., d. 1/4/1972 at 65 in Ossipee; b. NH
Erlin L., d. 5/11/1976 at 93 in Wolfeboro; b. NH
Geraldine A., d. 7/9/1984 at 81 in Wolfeboro; b. Ossipee
Leslie O., d. 12/4/1949 at 55 in VT; b. Wolfeboro; William C. Wilkins and Marion A. Allen
Leslie W., d. 11/5/1969 at 40 in Wolfeboro; b. NH
Lloyd William, d. 5/10/1989 at 20 in Ossipee; b. Wolfeboro
Verna, d. 12/1/1984

WILKINSON,
Blanche, d. 3/6/1965 at 62 in Ossipee; b. Shapleigh, ME
Dana, d. 4/27/1903 at 74/10 in Wolfeboro; senility; farmer; married; b. Alton
Ellen K., d. 8/17/1974 at 39 in Ossipee; b. MA
Emily, d. 12/4/1913 at 74; housekeeping; widow; b. Wolfeboro; Simon F. Beacham and Loiza Young
Forrest Leslie, d. 2/10/1978 at 72 in Manchester; b. NH
Frank, d. 7/18/1907 at 65 in Ossipee; grummata of brain; farmer; single; b. Effingham
Lester G., d. 11/30/1950 at 66/6/7 in Wolfeboro; b. ME; Plummer Wilkinson
Lida K., d. 6/26/1987 at 77 in Ossipee; b. Effingham
Marion Louise, d. 3/9/1993 at 82 in Ossipee
Maurice F., Jr., d. 8/17/1974 at 48 in Ossipee; b. MA
Walter, d. 6/25/1974 at 85 in Ossipee; b. NH
Winnie, d. 3/17/1898 at 36 in Ossipee; tuberculosis; widow

WILL,
James A., d. 1/23/1977 at 90 in Ossipee; b. MA

WILLAND,
Emma J., d. 1/15/1937 at 81/1/15 in Water Village; b. Ossipee; Elisha Hanson and Doris Hanson

Eugene, d. 5/30/1900 at 40 in Ossipee; injury, epilepsy; single; b. Tuftonboro; John F. Willand (Ossipee) and Mary ——

Howard A., d. 3/18/1979 at 84 in Concord; b. NH

Karen Earlene, d. 5/22/2001 in Ctr. Ossipee; Earl F. Willand, Jr. and Eleanor Corson

Leander S., d. 9/25/1927 at 84/6/7; b. Ossipee; Edward Willand and Martha J. Brown

Mabel E., d. 11/10/1974 at 96 in Wolfeboro; b. NH

WILLARD,

Betsey J., d. 5/25/1905 at 84/7/26 in Ossipee; old age; widow; b. Wolfeboro; Moses Brown and Mary Lampson (Wolfeboro)

Shawn Edward, d. 5/15/1998 in Ossipee; Edward Willard and Rose Hamel

WILLEY,

Clinton, d. 5/17/1924 at 75; b. Gorham; Curtis Willey and Abigail Emery

Earl B., d. 1/11/1961 at 63 in Wolfeboro; b. New Durham

Francis, d. 3/20/1893 at 90 in Ossipee; blacksmith; widower

Henry, d. 5/3/1926 at 71; b. Bartlett; Thomas J. Willey and Jane Weeks

John N., d. 8/30/1925 at 63; b. Bartlett

Mary J., d. 7/17/1985 at 93 in Ossipee; b. Conway

WILLIAMS,

Abbie, d. 2/5/1897 at 7/6/19 in Ossipee; scarlet fever; b. Freedom; L. Williams (Effingham) and Annie Andrews (Freedom)

Blanche E., d. 11/22/1961 at 70 in Wolfeboro; b. Old Orchard, ME

Calbert, d. 5/20/1918 at 67; farmer; married; b. Ossipee; Samuel Williams (Ossipee) and Esther Welch (Ossipee)

Charles, d. 10/10/1918 at 13; laborer; single; b. Ossipee; Etta Wiggin

Charles H., d. 10/3/1967 at 80 in Laconia; b. Ossipee

Charles J., d. 12/31/1970 at 75 in Ossipee; b. MA

Dorothy M., d. 7/10/2001 in Wolfeboro; Perley Williams and Margaret Custer

Evelyn L., d. 6/29/1988 at 62 in Wolfeboro; b. Milton

Harriet Susan, d. 1/27/1939 at 91/9/24 in Ossipee; b. Tuftonboro; Albert Peavey and Sarah Bryant

Harry, d. 1/25/1899 at 1/4/15 in Ossipee; mitral regurgitation; b. Ossipee; Ren Williams (Effingham) and Abbie Nichols (Ossipee)

Hazel Kennedy, d. 11/6/1990 at 90 in Ossipee; b. Richford, VT

Ira S., d. 7/5/1990 at 93 in Ossipee; b. Ossipee

John, d. 1/4/1892 at 60 in Ossipee; diabetes; inmate; single; b. Effingham

John, d. 3/2/1958 at 57/9/26 in Ossipee; b. Ossipee; Samuel Williams and Nellie Eldridge

John T., d. 7/26/1902 at 58/0/5 in Ossipee; pneumonia; farmer; married; b. Ossipee; William Williams

Juanita M., d. 7/11/1952 at 42/3/19 in Effingham; b. W. Rye; Manville Knox and Mabel Thompson
Lewis C., d. 11/30/1965 at 72 in Ossipee; b. Ossipee
Lizzie, d. 1/25/1915 at 26; b. Ossipee; Calbert Williams (Ossipee) and Eileen Nichols
Lorenzo, d. 3/21/1911 at 53; arterio sclerosis; laborer; married; b. Effingham; James Williams
Louise Gladys, d. 2/3/1985 at 102 in Ossipee; b. Pentre, Wales
Marion Irma, d. 12/7/1993 at 93 in Ossipee
Marjorie, d. 10/27/1925 at 77/9/19; b. Ireland; Thomas Custer and Mary —
Nellie, d. 12/11/1932 at 68/0/2 in Ossipee; b. Ossipee; Wentworth Nichols
Nellie, d. 7/4/1968 at 91 in Laconia; b. NH
Pearl J., d. 1/26/1910 at 18/7/26 in Ossipee; pneumonia; laborer; single; b. Ossipee; Frank Williams (Ossipee) and Jennie Eldridge (Ossipee)
Perley J., d. 12/15/1984
Perley N., d. 6/17/1961 at 69 in Wolfeboro; b. Tuftonboro
Samual, d. 4/16/1941 at 73/6/12 in Ossipee; b. Ossipee; Samual Williams and Esther Welch
Samuel, d. 5/16/1898 at 77 in Ossipee; apoplexy; farmer; married; b. Ossipee; Samuel Williams
Samuel, d. 7/18/1969 at 78 in Concord; b. NH
Shaber, d. 3/23/1894 at 75 in Ossipee; fatty deg. of heart; widower; b. Ossipee
Willis, d. 10/21/1958 at 44 in Wolfeboro; b. Ossipee; Perley Williams and Margie Custor

WILLIS,
Annie, d. 10/15/1920 at 61/6/8; housewife; married; b. Freedom; John R. Stacy (Freedom) and Olive Shaw (Freedom)

WILMER,
Amy H., d. 10/24/1946 at 84/1/17 in Ossipee; b. New Bedford, MA; Stephen Hatch and Eleanor Stearns

WILSON,
Albert W., d. 10/14/1919 at 37; laborer; married; b. Boston, MA; Albert Wilson (Boston, MA) and Mary Doyle (Boston, MA)
Bertha, d. 1/6/1944 at 75/3/8 in Ossipee; b. Reading, MA
Edith, d. 3/1/1970 at 96 in Ossipee; b. NH

WILTKINS,
James H., d. 12/17/1923 at 52/3/1; b. Groveton

WINKLEY,
Bessie M., d. 10/18/1957 at 64 in Ossipee; b. Ossipee; George Abbott and Jennie Champion
Ervin M., d. 5/4/1970 at 84 in Ossipee; b. NH
Florence Ella, d. 10/1/1938 at 77/8/16 in Ossipee; b. Eliot, ME; Ephraim Trefethen and Pamelia Langley
Mark Henry, d. 4/21/1938 at 76/10/28 in Ossipee; b. Strafford; Mark H. Winkley and Sally Foss Leighton

WINSOR,
Richard H., d. 5/12/1983 at 69 in Wolfeboro; b. E. Boston, MA

WITHERAL,
William, d. 2/7/1907 at 75 in Ossipee; paralysis; b. Effingham

WITHERELL,
Warren F., d. 7/30/1999 in Franklin; Percy Witherell and Alice Grover

WITTERWELL,
Edmund A., d. 12/16/1963 at 91 in Ossipee; b. New York, NY

WLINICH,
Kenneth P., d. 2/15/2001 in Ctr. Ossipee; Peter Wlinich and Edna Chase

WOOD,
son, d. 1/13/1899 at 0/0/2 in Ossipee; intestinal disease of heart; b. Ossipee; Frank Wood (Ossipee) and Eliza Speedy (NB)
daughter, d. 6/18/1903 at – in Ossipee; stillborn; b. Ossipee; Frank Wood (Ossipee) and Eliza Speedy (NB)
Amalia, d. 2/21/1997 at 77 in Wolfeboro; Epamindias Demosthenes and Katherine Zerbinopoulos
Eliza, d. 10/25/1918 at 47/7/4; cook; married; b. St. John, NB; James Speedy (Ireland) and Margaret Speedy (PEI)
Erbon Wirt, d. 1/30/1943 at 63/2/11 in Wolfeboro; b. Waterville, ME; Charles Wood and Christine Reynolds
Inez Patterson, d. 2/25/1988 at 101 in Ossipee; b. Boston, MA
John M., d. 2/12/1973 at 81 in Wolfeboro; b. RI
Lawrence J., d. 5/6/1990 at 74 in Wolfeboro; b. Dover
Marion L., d. 2/7/1952 at 58 in Wolfeboro; b. RI; Frank Sinclair and Bea ---
Rose, d. 1/31/1958 at 72/8/13 in Ossipee; b. Newmarket; Frank Gay and Octovia Cote

WOODARD,
Edith M., d. 1/17/1970 at 70 in Tamworth; b. MA

WOODBURY,
Carleton J., d. 7/20/1975 at 55 in Ossipee; b. NH

WOODHOUSE,
Nancy, d. 10/1/1895 at 67 in Ossipee; general debility; pauper; single

WOODMAN,
Herman J., d. 7/6/1900 at 26/2/12 in Ossipee; suicide; farmer; single; b. Newfield; John Woodman (Effingham) and Sarah J. Goudy (Great Falls)
Jno., d. 8/22/1902 at 73 in Ossipee; mitral regurgitation; farmer; married; b. Wakefield
Marilyn M., d. 12/3/1984 at 32 in Concord; b. Lowell, MA
William O., d. 1/12/1936 at 65/6/4 in Newfield, ME; b. Newfield, ME; J. Woodman and Sarah J. Goudy

WOODS,
Exelia, d. 6/21/1988 at 87 in Ossipee; b. Magog, Canada
Jerry, d. 9/22/1985 at 91 in Ossipee; b. Newburyport, MA

WOODWARD,
Harry S., d. 3/27/1990 at 74 in Wolfeboro; b. Swampscott, MA

WOOSTER,
George, d. 11/19/1919 at 65; millman; b. W. Lebanon; Benjamin Wooster (Derby Line, VT) and ----- (Bradford, VT)

WOOTTON,
Violet Bell, d. 10/24/1970 at 88 in Ossipee; b. Scotland

WORMHOOD,
Hulda, d. 3/10/1890 at 57/7/18 in Ossipee; apithelsoma; housewife; married; b. Ossipee

WORMSTEAD,
Bessie J., d. 2/7/1991 at 76 in Wolfeboro; b. Lynn, MA
George E., Sr., d. 11/3/1993 at 71 in Wolfeboro

WORMWOOD,
Charles, d. 9/22/1899 at 71/4/13 in Ossipee; acute meningitis; painter; widower; b. Kennebunk
Nellie F., d. 4/4/1887 at 21 in Ossipee; housekeeper; married; b. Kennebunk, ME; John B. Gouch (Kennebunk, ME) and Precilla Ellis (Kennebunk, ME)

WORTHEN,
Sarah, d. 3/29/1897 at 75 in Ossipee; anemia; single

WRIGHT,
Arthur Edward, d. 10/16/1995 at 81; Elwin Wright and Lena Grace Farr
William L., d. 10/6/1990 at 63 in Rochester; b. Lincoln, NB

WYMAN,
Albert, d. 7/9/1947 at 79/7/20 in Ossipee; b. Andover, ME
George F., d. 2/7/1897 at 42/10/20 in Ossipee; pulmonary tuberculosis; farmer; married; b. Ossipee; John Wyman (Kennebunk) and Nancy Nichols (Ossipee)
Gertrude Louise, d. 2/27/1977 at 88 in Ossipee; b. Washington, DC
Nancy, d. 9/15/1890 at 60 in Ossipee; cancer; widow; Moses Nichols
Ruth Patricia, d. 1/19/1991 at 62 in Wolfeboro; b. Everett, MA

WYSE,
Arthur Russell, d. 1/18/1996 at 85 in Ossipee; George Wyse and Eva Rudy

YEATON,
Merton L., d. 11/13/1984 at 88 in Ossipee; b. Conway

YELLE,
Ernest N., d. 5/19/1996 at 58 in Wolfeboro; Francis Yelle and Marie Fraughton

YORK,
Hannah, d. 2/19/1905 at 72 in Ossipee; ilio colitis
William, d. 3/8/1976 at 88 in Ossipee; b. NH

YOUNG,
Abigail, d. 10/15/1896 at 81/8/14 in Ossipee; broncho pneumonia; single; Isaac Wiggin
Alonzo, d. 1/7/1911 at 87/5; valvular dis. of heart; farmer; single; b. Wolfeboro; Samuel Young (Wolfeboro) and Sallie Burleigh (Ossipee)
Angie B., d. 9/26/1973 at 89 in Rochester; b. NH
Anna P., d. 9/23/1891 at 0/2/11 in Ossipee; b. Whitefield; Charles B. Young (Wolfeboro) and Addie Stevens (Brookfield)
Celia L., d. 3/29/1963 at 86 in Wolfeboro; b. Stoneham, MA
Emma F., d. 6/13/1931 at 79/1/13 in Granite; b. Granite; Solomon Kennison and Hannah Cooley

Hannah, d. 1/28/1895 at 73/6 in Ossipee; pleuro pneumonia; housewife; married; b. Waterboro, ME; Noah Chick (Waterboro) and Mary Hanson (Dover)
Howard E., d. 4/7/1955 at 82 in Wolfeboro; b. NH; Arthur Young and Emma Kenniston
Jefferson, d. 8/8/1937 at 75/1/7 in Wolfeboro; b. Hyde Park, VT; Alishia D. Young and Sophie Jones
John, d. 8/7/1890 at 68 in Ossipee; farmer; married; b. Wolfeboro; Samuel B. Young and Nancy Burleigh
John, d. 8/17/1891 at 68 in Ossipee; married
John L., d. 11/12/1956 at 73 in Rochester; b. Ossipee; Arthur Young and Emma Kennison
Martha, d. 2/4/1889 at 35; domestic; single; b. Ossipee; Thomas E. Young and Abigail Young
Mary A., d. 3/19/1896 at 22/11/12 in Ossipee; tubercular consumption; housekeeper; married; b. Wakefield; John Doyle and M. Wentworth (Milton)
Minnie A., d. 12/12/1950 at 81/5 in Wolfeboro; b. Canada; Cyrus Andrews and Sarah Bonney
Nathaniel, d. 2/5/1896 at 85/3/9 in Ossipee; old age; farmer; married; b. Wolfeboro; Samuel Young and Nancy Burleigh
Susan, d. 11/8/1898 at 90/8 in Ossipee; old age; widow; b. Tuftonboro; Gideon Wiggin (Exeter) and Dolly Lyford (Exeter)
Thomas, d. 5/9/1890 at 78 in Ossipee; spinal sclerosis; farmer; single; b. Ossipee
Thomas C., d. 8/31/1887 at 72/3 in Ossipee; farmer; married; b. Ossipee
Walter H., d. 12/8/1946 at 78 in Ossipee; b. Ossipee; Joseph Young and Hannah Chick

YOUNGSTRAND,
Edward, d. 7/2/1934 at 66/3 in Ossipee; b. Northern Sweden

ZERVAS,
Arthur, d. 1/7/2000 in Manchester; Emmanuel Zervas and Ella Galvin

ZINSER,
Mabel R., d. 8/10/1984 at 85 in Ossipee; b. Union City, NJ

UNKNOWN,
person, d. 11/–/1907 in Wolfeboro at –

Visit
HERITAGE BOOKS, INC.
online at
www.heritagebooks.com

EXTENSIVE SELECTION OF
BOOKS & CD-ROMS
• • •
HISTORY • GENEALOGY • AMERICANA